Informatik aktuell

Herausgeber: W. Brauer
im Auftrag der Gesellschaft für Informatik (GI)

W. Stucky A. Oberweis (Hrsg.)

Datenbanksysteme in Büro, Technik und Wissenschaft

GI-Fachtagung
Braunschweig, 3.–5. März 1993

Springer-Verlag Berlin Heidelberg GmbH

Herausgeber

Wolffried Stucky
Andreas Oberweis
Universität Karlsruhe, Institut für Angewandte Informatik
und Formale Beschreibungsverfahren
Kaiserstraße 12, W-7500 Karlsruhe

CR Subject Classification (1992): A.0, C.2.4, E.2, H.2, H.3, H.4, H.5

ISBN 978-3-540-56487-4 ISBN 978-3-642-86096-6 (eBook)
DOI 10.1007/978-3-642-86096-6

Ursprünglich erschienen bei Springer-Verlag Berlin Heidelberg New York 1993

Satz: Reproduktionsfertige Vorlage vom Autor/Herausgeber
33/3140-543210 – Gedruckt auf säurefreiem Papier

Vorwort der Herausgeber

Die GI-Fachtagung "Datenbanksysteme in Büro, Technik und Wissenschaft" (BTW) wird 1993 zum fünften Mal durchgeführt, diesmal an der Technischen Universität Braunschweig. Die Vorgänger-Tagungen fanden

1985 in Karlsruhe,

1987 in Darmstadt,

1989 in Zürich und

1991 in Kaiserslautern

statt. Veranstalter der Tagungsreihe ist der Fachausschuß 2.5 "Rechnergestützte Informationssysteme" der Gesellschaft für Informatik - teilweise in Zusammenarbeit mit anderen deutschsprachigen Informatik-Gesellschaften. Zum Fachausschuß 2.5 gehören die Fachgruppen

2.5.1 Datenbanksysteme,

2.5.2 Entwicklungsmethoden für Informationssysteme und deren Anwendung,

2.5.3 Verläßliche Informationssysteme,

2.5.4 Information Retrieval

und der Arbeitskreis "Grundlagen von Informationssystemen".
Erstmals haben sich an der diesjährigen BTW die Fachgruppen 2.5.3 und 2.5.4 sowie der Arbeitskreis aktiv beteiligt.

Die Tagung soll ein Forum für Datenbank-Forscher und -Praktiker darstellen, um aktuelle Fragen des Datenbankeinsatzes in den Gebieten Büro, Technik und Wissenschaft zu diskutieren und Lösungskonzepte vorzustellen. Es werden Fragestellungen bezüglich Entwurfsmethoden- und werkzeugen, Modellierung und Darstellung von Daten oder Wissen sowie Systemarchitekturen und Realisierungskonzepten erörtert.

Zur Tagung wurden 45 Langbeiträge (d.h. Umfang ca. 20 Seiten) und 13 Kurzbeiträge (Umfang ≤ 10 Seiten) eingereicht. Dabei lag der Anteil von Beiträgen aus der industriellen Praxis bei etwa 15 Prozent. Die eingereichten Beiträge wurden jeweils von 3 Gutachtern bewertet. Das Programmkomitee hat 13 Langbeiträge sowie 3 Kurzbeiträge ausgewählt. Außerdem wurden 9 weitere Langbeiträge in gekürzter Form als Kurzbeiträge angenommen. Während in Langbeiträgen insbesondere über abgeschlossene Arbeiten mit wissenschaftlich gesicherten Ergebnissen berichtet wird, soll in Kurzbeiträgen auch ermöglicht werden, laufende Projekte, Erfahrungen aus Anwendungen oder noch unfertige - aber originelle - Forschungsarbeiten vorzustellen. Bei den akzeptierten Beiträgen beträgt der Anteil aus der industriellen Praxis wiederum ca. 15 Prozent.

Die Beiträge wurden fünf verschiedenen Themengebieten zugeordnet:

- aktive Datenbanken (3),
- Nicht-Standard-Anwendungen (11),
- Implementationsaspekte (4),
- Objektorientierung (4) sowie
- deduktive Datenbanksysteme (3).

Zusätzlich konnten drei renommierte Referenten für eingeladene Vorträge gewonnen werden: Professor Dennis McLeod von der USC Los Angeles mit dem Thema "Beyond Object Databases", Professor Catriel Beeri von der Hebrew University of Jerusalem mit dem Thema "Some Thoughts on the Future Evolution of Object-Oriented Database Concepts" und schließlich Privatdozent Dr.-Ing. Reiner Anderl von der Universität Karlsruhe mit dem Thema "STEP: Grundlage der Produktmodelltechnologie".

Danken möchten wir an dieser Stelle zunächst allen Autoren, die einen Beitrag zur Tagung eingereicht haben, auch wenn dieser nicht in das Tagungsprogramm aufgenommen werden konnte. Wir danken den Mitgliedern des Programmkomitees sowie den zusätzlichen Gutachtern für die sorgfältige Beurteilung der Beiträge und die Unterstützung bei der Zusammenstellung des Programms. Unser besonderer Dank für die gute Zusammenarbeit gilt Professor Ehrich von der Technischen Universität Braunschweig als Tagungsleiter und Leiter des Organisationskomitees sowie seiner gesamten Gruppe (S. Conrad, G. Denker, M. Gogolla, T. Hartmann, R. Herzig, K. Hülsmann, R. Jungclaus, P. Löhr-Richter, C. Müller, K. Neumann, G. Saake und N. Vlachantonis) für ihr Engagement bei der Vorbereitung und Durchführung der Tagung.

Karlsruhe, im Dezember 1992

Wolffried Stucky　　　　　　　　Andreas Oberweis

Veranstalter:

Fachausschuß 2.5 der Gesellschaft für Informatik

Tagungsleitung:

H.-D. Ehrich, TU Braunschweig

Programmkomitee:

W. Stucky, Uni Karlsruhe (Vorsitz)

H.-J. Appelrath, Uni Oldenburg
H. Biller, Siemens-Nixdorf, München
P. Dadam, Uni Ulm
K. Dittrich, Uni Zürich
H.-D. Ehrich, TU Braunschweig
N. Fuhr, Uni Dortmund
W. Gerhardt, TU Delft
G. Gottlob, TU Wien
T. Härder, Uni Kaiserslautern
A. Heuer, TU Clausthal
W. Kießling, TU München
K. Küspert, IBM WZ Heidelberg
W. Lamersdorf, Uni Hamburg
G. Lausen, Uni Mannheim
R. Manthey, Uni Bonn
A. Oberweis, Uni Karlsruhe
H.-J. Schek, ETH Zürich
D. Schubert, TU Dresden
H. Schweppe, FU Berlin
R. Studer, Uni Karlsruhe
B. Thalheim, Uni Rostock
H. Thoma, Ciba-Geigy AG, Basel
R.R. Wagner, Uni Linz
B. Walter, Uni Trier

Organisationskomitee:

H.-D. Ehrich (Vorsitz)

S. Conrad
G. Denker
M. Gogolla
T. Hartmann
R. Herzig
K. Hülsmann
R. Jungclaus
P. Löhr-Richter
C. Müller
K. Neumann
G. Saake
N. Vlachantonis

(alle TU Braunschweig)

Sponsoren:

Die Tagung wurde in großzügiger Weise unterstützt von
IBM Deutschland GmbH, Stuttgart.

Zusätzliche Gutachter:

Margita Altus
Jürgen Angele
Helge Behrends
Franz Burger
Helmut Eirund
Thomas Eiter
Rolf Erbe
Andrew Frank
Gerhard Friedrich
Stella Gatziu
Vera Goebel
Martin Gogolla
Wilfried Grafik
Martin Härtig
Thorsten Hartmann
Axel Herbst
Ulrike Jaeger
Heinrich Jasper
Dirk Jonscher
Ralf Jungclaus
Christian Kalus
Gerti Kappel
Dimitris Karagiannis
Gerhard Köstler
Angelika Kotz-Dittrich
Wolfgang Kowarschick
Josef Küng
Dieter Landes
Burkhard Lau
Perdita Löhr-Richter
Barbara Messing
Susanne Neubert
Karl Neumann
Peter Pistor
Siegfried Reich
Angelika Reiser
Reinhard Schauer
Siegfried Schönberger
Markus Stumptner
Norbert Südkamp
Stefan Vieweg
Pavel Vogel

Inhaltsverzeichnis

Eingeladene Beiträge

Sitzungen

Aktive Datenbanken

Nicht-Standard-Anwendungen 1

Nicht-Standard-Anwendungen 2

Implementationsaspekte

Objektorientierung

Deduktive Datenbanksysteme

Nicht-Standard-Anwendungen 3

Beyond Object Databases

Dennis McLeod[1]

Computer Science Department
University of Southern California
Los Angeles, CA 90089-0781
U.S.A.[2]

Abstract

Object database systems, those based on semantic and object-oriented data models, have emerged as the practical database management technology for the 1990s. A viewpoint on the principal characteristics of object databases is presented, as well as the evolution of data modeling leading to the current state-of-the-art. Some thoughts on the future of data models and systems, beyond object databases, are examined. Database system interoperation is identified as a major focus for database research in the next decade. The importance of object database concepts, as well as those beyond, are examined as key to addressing the problem of interoperability. The Remote-Exchange research project at USC is reviewed to illustrate an approach to information sharing and exchange among autonomous, heterogeneous database systems.

1. Introduction

Computerized databases are essential and inseparable components of the vast majority of today's information systems. Database systems are utilized at all levels of management, research and development, and production to provide uniform access to and control of consistent information. Applications in which the use of database systems are critical include large "commercial" applications such as banking, reservations, personnel, and inventory systems. Further, other database-intensive applications are becoming more-and-more important, including those to support computer-supported cooperative work, computer-aided design, computer assisted manufacturing, personal databases, and scientific information management.

The 1980s witnessed the predominance of general-purpose relational database management systems (DBMSs) and accompanying fourth generation database manipulation languages as viable and practical tools. This generation of database technology represents significant

[1] This research was supported, in part, by the National Science Foundation under grant IRI-9021028.

[2] The author may be contacted via internet electronic mail as mcleod@pollux.usc.edu, and via telephone at (213) 740-4504.

breakthroughs in the generality, flexibility, evolvability, user friendliness, and mathematical foundations of such systems over their historical predecessors. Relational, and pseudo-relational database management systems are now widely utilized in a wide variety of application environments, and on computers ranging from large-scale mainframes to personal machines.

In the 1990s, object-based database systems are emerging as the next generation of practical database management system technology. Research on "semantic" and "object-oriented" data models and systems during the 1980s [5, 21] has laid the foundation for a generation of commercial object database management systems. These systems provide additional capabilities above and beyond those of relational technology, and address many of the limitations thereof. The tools and systems of this new generation of database systems supply additional modeling and abstraction power, explicitly support semantic integrity constraint specification and enforcement, more substantively facilitate graceful database evolution, support a wider diversity of modalities of database objects, and provide for higher level user and program interfaces.

One might quite reasonably ask at this point: "so what lies beyond object databases?". The very idea that "yet another" data model may be useful in database management elicits a yawn from many of those who have worked in this area for years. We can observe that after a great deal of activity in the data modeling area from 1970-1990, we now see a bit of a quiet on the data modeling front. Why is this? Is it clearly not because we have produced a model that satisfies all the needs of users. It is probably to an extent a consequence of the fact that database researchers and practitioners are tired of the proliferation of models. In part it may also be because researchers have run out of new fundamental modeling concepts. In point of fact, it appears that the class of object-based data models, including the basic features of semantic (structurally object-oriented) and behaviorally object-oriented data models, represent a stable point for practical data modeling in the 1990s. This is very much as was the case for relational data modeling in the 1980s.

Perhaps one of the key open problems for database technology in the next decade is effectively addressing the problem of the sharing and exchange of information among database and data-intensive systems, sometimes termed "database system interoperability". Techniques of object data modeling, and those beyond, are key to addressing this important area. In fact, current trends in research are leading to a common "core object model" for databases, which is a prime candidate as an inter-database communications and sharing forum (viz., the foundation for a "database network").

Figure 1 informally illustrates some of the main trends in emphasis of database research and development over the past twnety years, leading to the current focus on object database systems and database system interoperation.

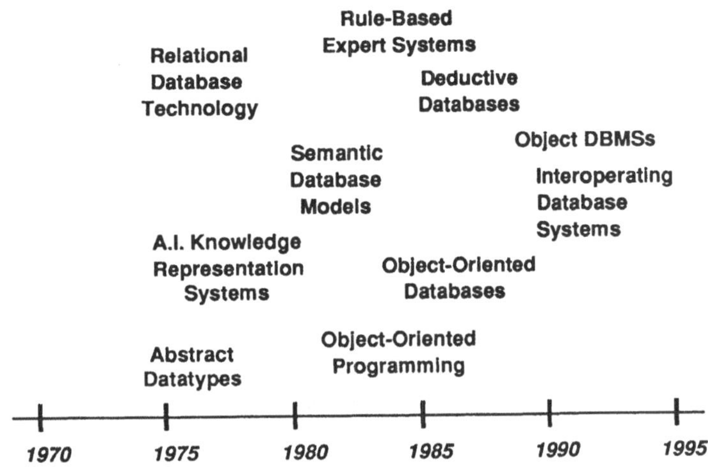

Figure 1. Data Modeling Technology Trends

In what follows, we first provide a review of the main characteristics of object database systems, from a modeling point of view. A historical perspective of the research and development leading to the current state-of-the-art is then presented. We next examine the problem of database system interoperation, and illustrate with a review of the Remote-Exchange project at USC, which is developing an approach to information sharing and exchange among autonomous, heterogeneous database systems [8, 9, 10, 11].

2. A Viewpoint on Object Data Models and Systems

At the core of any database system is a data model, which is a mechanism for specifying the structure of a database and operations that can be performed on the data in that database. As such, a data model should: allow databases to be viewed in a manner that is based upon the meaning of data as seen by its users; accommodate various levels of abstraction detail; support both anticipated and unanticipated database uses; accommodate multiple viewpoints; and be free of implementation and physical optimization detail (physical data independence).

Abstractly speaking, a data model is a collection of generic structures, (semantic integrity) constraints, and primitive operations. The structures of a data model must support the specification of information units (which we may term "objects"), object classifications, and inter-object relationships. The semantic integrity constraints of the data model specify restrictions on states of a database or transitions between such states, in order that the database accurately reflect its application environment. Some constraints are embedded within the structural component of a data model, while others may be expressed separately and enforced externally to the DBMS. We traditionally refer to the specification of a particular database constructed using these general-purpose structures and constraints as a (conceptual) schema. The operational component of a data model consists of a general-purpose collection of primitives that support the query and modification of a database; viz., given a database with an associated conceptual schema, the operations facilitate the manipulation of that database in terms of the schema. Such primitives may be embodied in a stand-alone end-user interface or a specialized language, or embedded within a general-purpose programming language. Database-specific operations can be constructed utilizing the primitives of the data model as building blocks. Database-specific units of manipulation (operations, methods) may also be placed in the database itself.

We shall specifically use the term "object database systems" to refer to a class of systems with the following characteristics, with specific respect to the data model they embody:

Individual object identity:
Objects in a database can include not only primitive (atomic) data values, such as strings and numbers, but also abstract objects representing entities in the real world and intangible concepts. Relationships among and classifications of such objects can themselves be considered as abstract objects in the database. Graphical, image, and voice objects can also be accommodated. Such abstract objects can be directly represented and manipulated.

Explicit semantic primitives:
Primitives are provided to support object classification, structuring, semantic integrity constraints, and derived data. These primitive abstraction mechanisms support such features as aggregation, classification, instantiation, and inheritance. The roots of these semantic primitives are in the "semantic" data models [1, 15], and in artificial intelligence knowledge representation techniques [3, 4].

Active objects:
Database objects can be active as well as passive, in the sense that they can exhibit behavior. Various specific approaches to the modeling of object behavior can be adopted, such as an inter-object message passing paradigm, or abstract data type encapsulation. The important point is that behavioral abstraction is supported, and procedures to manipulate data are represented in the database.

Object uniformity:
All information (or nearly all) in a database is described using the same object model. Thus, descriptive information about objects, referred to here as meta-data, is conceptually represented in the same way as specific "fact" objects. Meta-data is considered dynamic, and can be modified in a manner analogous to that utilized to alter fact objects.

In the above, the concepts and techniques underlying "semantic" and "object-oriented" databases have been aggregated to accentuate the main thrust of the object-based approach. It is however important to note that the first two characteristics, object identity and explicit semantic primitives, can be more directly ascribed to "semantic data models" and DBMSs based upon them; such systems are sometimes termed structurally object-oriented [7]. The last characteristic, object uniformity, is also addressed to an extent by semantic data models and systems. In addition to object identity, explicit semantic primitives, and object uniformity, behaviorally object-oriented systems (sometimes termed just "object-oriented") also address the issue of active objects, viz., accommodating application-specific methods or procedures on objects in the database itself. It is of further note that some significant differences exist between the way semantic primitives are handled in structurally and behaviorally object-oriented systems (e.g., inheritance).

2.1. A Historical Perspective

To provide a historical perspective on state-of-the-art of object data models and systems, figure 2 shows a twenty year time line with descriptive terms highlighting some of the most significant developments and the major conceptual trends underlying them. We note in the top left of this figure the introduction and subsequent development of the relational data model. Work on normalization focused on the design of "good" relational conceptual schemas, while work on constraints for the relational model addressed the problem of adding additional semantics to the simple relational structures. Following to the right, we see RM/T, the structural model, SAM/OSAM*, and GEM, which are extensions of the relational model to capture more meaning.

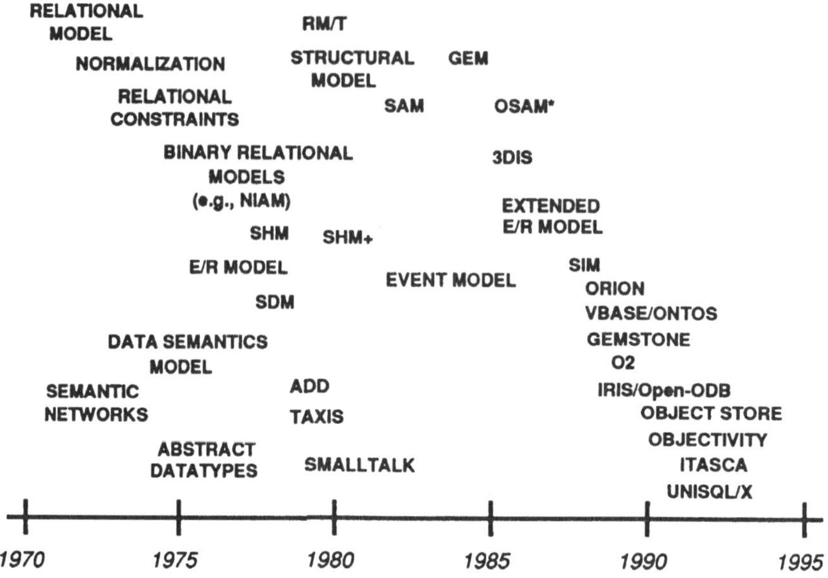

Figure 2. Some Key Data Modeling Developments

Functional models explored the use of mappings from one data set to another, and are related to the binary relational models (including, e.g., NIAM). The data semantics model was an early binary semantic model. The entity-relationship model was originally introduced as a design tool for record-based databases (as were many of the semantic data models), and the SHM (semantic hierarchy model) focused on the importance of aggregation and generalization primitives. SDM was a complex semantic data model, containing a rich collection of modeling primitives, and supporting a variety of semantic integrity constraints and derived data specifications.

On the bottom left of figure 2, we see work on semantic networks which represented a significant step in the structuring of knowledge for artificial intelligence applications; subsequent work on the ADD and Taxis systems explored more directly the applicability of fundamental semantic model primitives (such as "is-a" or generalization) to database systems. Work on abstract data types and Smalltalk in the programming language arena developed the importance of behavioral abstraction. SHM+ and the event model incorporated behavior modeling notions into the semantic data model framework. The 3DIS incorporated ideas of merging schema and data into a uniform framework (as did work on Smalltalk and early work on Orion).

Significantly, we note that commercial implementations of object-based database systems, and well as many research prototypes, have now appeared. In the bottom right of figure 2, we see several examples of such systems listed. While the specifics of these different systems obviously vary, it is clear that a common core "object data model" is beginning to emerge. The many standardization efforts currently focusing on this are evidence of the convergence, as well as the importance of object database systems.

3. On Database System Interoperation

Let us now turn our attention to a key problem for research and development in the next decade, the interoperation database systems, and examine the importance of data modeling in this regard. Consider an environment consisting of a collection of data/knowledge bases and their supporting systems, and in which it is desired to accommodate the controlled sharing and exchange of information among the collection. The individual (autonomous) data/knowledge base systems in such an environment will be termed "components", and the collection of components will be termed a "federation". The components may be heterogeneous, and to a large degree independent (autonomous). Such environments are very common in various application domains, including computer-supported cooperative work, computer-aided design, computer assisted manufacturing, personal databases, and scientific information management. The trend towards the decentralization of computing that has occurred over the past decade has accentuated the need for effective principles, techniques, and mechanisms to support the sharing and exchange among the component data/knowledge base systems in such a federated database environment (see, e.g., [14, 19, 22, 24]).

Traditional research on "distributed databases", assumed a common, integrated database specification (conceptual database schema). While some of the research results obtained in this general area of endeavor are applicable in the federated database environment, such approaches generally assume a single conceptual database which is physically distributed. Work on "multi-databases", "super-views", and "virtual databases" has stressed the need to provide a unified, perhaps partial, global view of a collection of existing databases. Techniques for database integration [2], which are often primarily considered for the design of a single database system based upon a number of application subsystems, can be brought to bear on the problem of partially integrating existing heterogeneous databases as well. It is certainly clear that many open and essential problems remain to provide the basis for practical federated database systems (see, e.g., [6, 8, 12, 13, 18, 23, 25]).

3.1. Heterogeneity in a Federation

A key aspect of federated database systems is accommodating diversity among the components of a federation. Note that this heterogeneity may be at various levels of abstraction:

Meta-data language (conceptual database model):
The components may use different collections of and techniques for combining the structures, constraints, and operations used to describe data.

Meta-data specification (conceptual schema):
While the components share a common meta-data language (conceptual database model), they may have independent specifications of their data (varied conceptual schemas).

Object comparability (database):
The components may agree upon a conceptual schema, or more generally, agree upon common subparts of their schemas; however, there may be differences in the manner in which information facts are represented (see, e.g., [17]). This variety of heterogeneity also relates how information objects are identified, and to the interpretation of atomic data values as denotations of information modeled in a database (naming).

Low-level data form format:
While the components agree at the model, schema, and object comparability levels, they may utilize different low-level representation techniques for atomic data values (e.g., units of measure or description).

Tool (database management system):
The components may utilize different tools to manage and provide an interface to their data. This kind of heterogeneity may exist with or without the varieties described immediately above.

In the ongoing Remote-Exchange project [8, 9, 10, 11], we specifically address the middle three kinds of heterogeneity above, which we term *semantic heterogeneity*. We can observe that semantic heterogeneity involves variations among component databases in the structure, organization, and conceptual description of information units (objects) and units of behavior (functions or methods) for manipulating those objects. We specifically consider semantic heterogeneity at both the conceptual schema and database levels, but assume that the federated system supports a common object data model as an inter-component communications forum.

Remote-Exchange considers three aspects of sharing and interconnection in the federated database environment. These key aspects center around the handling of semantic heterogeneity in a federation. These may be viewed in the context of a given component database system (C), which intends to import and/or export information of other ("non-local") components:

Discovery and identification by component C of relevant non-local information;

Resolution of the similarities and differences between C's information and relevant non-local information;

Efficient realization and implementation of actual *sharing and transmission* of information to and from C and other components.

3.2. The Architecture of Remote-Exchange

Figure 3 illustrates the top level architecture of Remote-Exchange. Here, a number of component database systems (DBSs) share information via a sharing mechanism that supports our candidate "kernel object data model" (KODM). A DBS may be based upon KODM, or may support another model via a tailored translator; the requirement is that the DBS "speak" KODM at its federation interface. Note that this provides a framework in which to address database system heterogeneity (the fifth kind of semantic diversity above), but that this approach provides no specific support for it. An interesting special case is the one in which each DBS supports KODM as a kernel, with some higher level model built on top of it. In this case, the heterogeneity supported involves the meta-data and object levels.

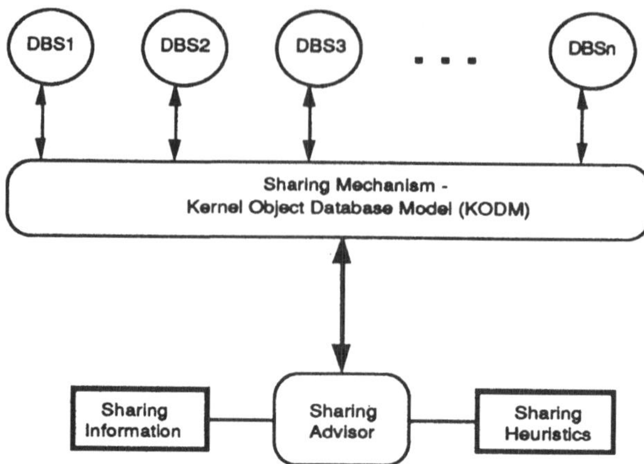

Figure 3. The Architecture of Remote-Exchange

KODM can be best viewed as a minimal object data model, including the following main features:

Objects at various levels of abstraction and granularity are accommodated, including atomic data values, abstract objects, objects from various media, and types (classifications of objects).

Inter-object relationships are supported, which represent associations among all varieties of objects, including meta-objects (such as object types).

A pre-defined set of abstractions is provided, including subtyping (specialization) and inheritance of relationships. The set of abstractions is extensible, allowing new ones to be defined.

Constraints (semantic integrity rules) and derived data are supported. A pre-defined set of primitives is provided, which is extensible.

Operations which support the behavioral manipulation of objects (methods) or provide "services" can be defined.

We can observe that the top level architecture of Remote-Exchange offers the flexibility to accommodate a number of detailed architectural and implementation alternatives. In particular, each component database system (DBS) may see its local database plus several remote databases, or it may see a single unified remote database. Further, we may choose to make the remote database(s) transparent to the component or not. In the initial Remote-Exchange experimental prototype, each component interacts with a logically centralized advisor (as described immediately below), and establishes and evolves sharing patterns with other components via this advisor. For performance reasons, the sharing mechanism facilitates the direct communication of information among components.

The Remote-Exchange sharing advisor serves as an "intelligent" aid to the users of component DBSs. This advisor collects information on various components, and dynamically supports the establishment of new sharing patterns. Associated with the advisor is a collection of information which describes the inter-component sharing connections that have been established, and includes a level of meta-data description to describe relationships among information units in various components; this is a data/knowledge base in its own right. To support sharing at the meta-data, object, and data form levels, we note that the notion of equivalence of information, at some level of abstraction, is central; in particular, we focus on the notions of object relative equivalence and behavioral relative equivalence. As a simple example of object relative equivalence at the meta-data level, note that one component may express a relationship between two objects by means of an inter-object mapping (attribute), while another component may express the same or closely related information by encapsulating the inter-object relationship in a third object. An example of behavioral relative equivalence is a situation in which one component has an operation which is semantically identical (or similar at some level of abstraction) to an operation of another component.

Also associated with the Remote-Exchange advisor is a collection of heuristics which are used to attempt to "intelligently" assist users in locating and establishing access to remote data. As a starting point for our approach here, we note that an analogy can be made between the existence of related but not necessarily identical information in several databases, and the evolution of the content of a single database with time. In consequence, our initial attempt at representing the inter-component sharing data/knowledge base draws upon techniques we have developed to support database evolution using cooperation between user and system utilizing a collection of simple learning heuristics.

The sharing advisor and its associated data/knowledge base can be centralized, or can be logically decentralized. In the latter case, each component has an advisor with an associated data/knowledge base tailored to it. As noted above, our initial experimental system employs a logically centralized advisor. The alternative of a decentralized advisor has the advantage of providing additional autonomy for the component DBSs, and avoiding a potential problem of over-integration; this of course comes at the possible price of more chaos. In the Remote-Exchange experimental environment, we are exploring both the centralized and decentralized advisor approaches, and are analyzing their relative merits and utility.

3.3. Research Focus

As noted above, we are focusing on three key aspects of sharing and interconnection in the federated database environment: discovery and identification, resolution, and sharing and transmission. We now review these in the context of the Remote-Exchange experimental system, and indicate the main thrusts of our ongoing research.

Discovery and Identification:

Our approach to the discovery and identification of relevant non-local information focuses on the perspective of a given component in a federation. In particular, we concentrate without loss of generality upon techniques for determining which non-local objects are "relevant" to a given local object. Since all information is modeled as objects, such analysis can accommodate the relevance of simple or complex objects, collections (types/classes), and units of behavior (operations/methods). We utilize the notion of relative equivalence, at some level of abstraction, as a basis for comparison. Probabilistic techniques exported from the domain of document retrieval are combined with techniques of applied machine learning to this end.

Resolution:

As noted above, Remote-Exchange specifically provides a common inter-component communication and sharing model (KODM). This model provides a framework in which to address the resolution of similarities and differences among component databases in a federation. A semantic heterogeneity resolution methodology is employed by the Remote-Exchange advisor to support this process.

Sharing and Transmission:

Clearly, a critical aspect of the effectiveness of a federated system is the efficient realization and implementation of the sharing and transmission of information across component boundaries. Given the goal of maximizing component autonomy, a major goal of Remote-Exchange is to make remote information as seamlessly integrated into a local component's database as possible. In order to maintain this transparency, efficient access to non-local information is essential; otherwise, remote information will not appear even close to transparent. We also stress seamless integration in order to allow components to utilize their local database management tools. The interconnection and exchange of objects, collections of objects (types/classes), and units of behavior (operations/methods) is specifically addressed. In the context of our experimental system, we have devised an approach to interconnection and sharing, and are exploring the use of various performance enhancement techniques, including object caching, the utilization of specific transport protocols, etc. Our performance studies to date have been couched in the context of an experimental prototype implementation based upon the IRIS object database management system developed by Hewlett-Packard, and the Omega system under development at USC [11].

4. Some Thoughts on a Next Generation Data Model

We have asserted that object database models are the key modeling development of the past decade, and that object database systems represent the next generation of practical database technology. We can however safely say that object database systems do not solve all of the information management problems of current and future data-intensive systems, e.g., those for computer-supported cooperative work. We have further identified the significance of an object-based model as a basis for database system interoperation. One of the key additional observations we can make from our work on Remote-Exchange is that a richer specification of the meaning of a database is important and necessary in identifying and resolving semantic heterogeneity in federated database systems. The above observations lead us to ask the natural question: is it appropriate to consider a new generation of data models beyond those of object databases?

For the sake of discussion here, let us assert that the answer to the above question is "yes". Such a next generation data model would not be record based, not object based, not logic based, but something different. The reason for this is that we are reaching the limits of what we can usefully do with models of these kinds. Let us consider a spectrum of data/knowledge models with natural language on one extreme, and say the relational data model on the other. In between are object database models, much closer to the relational model than to natural language. General purpose knowledge representation techniques (e.g., KL-ONE [3]) and general-purpose common sense knowledge representation schemes built using them, are clearly closer to natural language than to the relational and object models. Given the limitations of the relational and object data models, and the difficulty in managing rich, natural language type knowledge representations in computer systems, we can consider the possibility of a model somewhere between object models on the one hand and general, all-encompassing knowledge representations on the other. We have come to the conclusion that it is a model such as this that is appropriate for dealing with semantic heterogeneity in federated databases. Such a model would also be quite useful for a single database system, since it is more expressive of the meaning of data than existing models. Such a new model must of course be simple and manageable, for it to be practically useful.

Let us briefly consider a kind of data model which attempts to model "memory" in the sense of memory in human beings. This model, if supported by a database system, would allow a database to function in a meaningful way as an extension of its user's memory. Of course, A.I. researchers and to some extent database researchers have been working on information representation for a long time. Various theories of human information modeling and processing have been proposed. But we are suggesting something here that is limited: it works in a way similar to human memory - just the memory and that's it. This may still be difficult, for science has failed to model human memory very well. Let us assert that a reasonable hypothesis here might be that human memory is based on a simple mechanism at the top level, perhaps complex in its detail, but simple in concept and architecture. There is evidence that such simplicity at the top level exists throughout biological organisms. Take for example, the handling of genetic information. A simple, uniform mechanism is used to code genetic information, although the details are complex and rich. We might conjecture that something similar is the case for human memory. One thing is certain: human memory is not based on records, SQL, multiple inheritance, formal logic, etc. The concepts underlying these kinds of data modeling techniques may come into play in human memory, but none of them is the key to the unifying top level memory framework.

These final comments on future data models are admittedly quite "flaky". The purpose here is more to stimulate thought and discussion, rather than to propose a specific new approach to data modeling. We shall see what the next decade brings!

Acknowledgments

The author would like to acknowledge the fruitful discussions of the topic of this paper with a number of colleagues, including Michael Brodie, K. J. Byeon, Doug Fang, Shahram Ghandeharizadeh, Joachim Hammer, Richard Hull, Bill Kent, Roger King, Erich Neuhold, and Antonio Si.

References

1. Afsarmanesh, H. and McLeod, D., "The 3DIS: An Extensible, Object-Oriented Information Management Environment", *ACM Transactions on Information Systems*, 7(4): 339-377, October 1989.

2. Batini, C., Lenzerini, M. and Navathe, S., "A Comparative Analysis of Methodologies for Database Schema Integration", *ACM Computing Surveys*, 18(4): 323-364, December 1986.

3. Brachman, R. and Schmolze, J., "An Overview of the KL-ONE Knowledge Representation System", *Cognitive Science*, 9: 171-216, 1985.

4. Brodie, M., Mylopoulos, J. and Schmidt, J. (editors), *On Conceptual Modeling - Perspectives from Artificial Intelligence, Databases, and Programming Languages*, Springer-Verlag, 1984.

5. Cardenas, A. and McLeod, D. (editors), *Research Foundations in Object-Oriented and Semantic Database Systems*, Prentice Hall, 1990.

6. Chomicki, J. and Litwin, W., "Declarative Definition of Object-Oriented Multidatabase Mappings", in *Distributed Object Management* (editors Ozsu, T., Dayal, U., and Valduriez, P.), Morgan Kaufman, 1993.

7. Dittrich, K., "Object-Oriented Database Systems: The Notions and the Issues", *Proceedings of International Workshop on Object-Oriented Database Systems*, IEEE, 1986.

8. Fang, D., Hammer, J., McLeod, D., and Si, A., "Remote-Exchange: An Approach to Controlled Sharing among Autonomous, Heterogeneous Database Systems", *Proceedings of Compcon Conference*, IEEE, February 1991.

9. Fang, D., Hammer, J., and McLeod, D., "An Approach to Behavior Sharing in Federated Database Systems", in *Distributed Object Management* (editors Ozsu, T., Dayal, U., and Valduriez, P.), Morgan Kaufman, 1993.

10. Fang, D., and McLeod, D., "Seamless Interconnection in Federated Database Systems", in *Database Systems for Next-Generation Applications: Principles and Practice* (editor Kambayashi, Y.), World Scientific, 1993.

11. Fang, D., Ghandeharizadeh, S., McLeod, D., and Si, A., "The Design, Implementation, and Evaluation of an Object-Based Sharing Mechanism for Federated Database Systems", *Proceedings of International Conference on Data Engineering,* April 1993 (to appear).

12. Fankhauser, P. and Neuhold, E., "Knowledge Based Integration of Heterogeneous Databases", *Proceedings of IFIP DS-5 Working Conference on the Semantics on Interoperable Database Systems*, Elsevier, 1993.

13. Hartig, M. and Dittrich, K., "An Object-Oriented Integration Framework for Building Heterogeneous Database Systems", *Proceedings of IFIP DS-5 Working Conference on the Semantics on Interoperable Database Systems,* Elsevier, 1993.

14. Heimbigner, D. and McLeod, D., "A Federated Architecture for Information Systems", *ACM Transactions on Office Information Systems,* 3(3): 253-278, July 1985.

15. Hull, R. and King, R., "Semantic Data modeling: Survey, Applications, and Research Issues", *ACM Computing Surveys,* 19(3): 201-260, September 1987.

16. Karl, S. and Lockemann, P., "Design of Engineering Databases: A Case for More Varied Semantic Modeling Concepts", *Information Systems,* 13(4): 335-357, 1988.

17. Kent, W., "The Many Forms of a Single Fact", *Proceedings of Compcon Conference,* IEEE, February 1989.

18. Kent, W., "Object Identification in Multidatabase Systems", *Proceedings of IFIP DS-5 Working Conference on the Semantics on Interoperable Database Systems,* Elsevier, 1993.

19. Litwin, W., Mark, L., and Roussopoulos, N., "Interoperability of Multiple Autonomous Databases", *ACM Computing Surveys,* 22(3): 267-296, September 1990.

20. Lyngbaek, P. and McLeod, D., "Object Management in Distributed Information Systems", *ACM Transactions on Office Information Systems,* 2(2): 96-122, April 1984.

21. Maier, D. and Zdonik, S. (editors), *Readings in Object-Oriented Databases,* Morgan Kaufman, 1990.

22. Malone, T., Grant, K., Turbak, F., Brobst, S. and Cohen, M., "Intelligent Information-Sharing Systems", *Communications of the ACM,* 30(5): 390-402, May 1987.

23. Schek, H. and Wolf, A., "Cooperation Between Autonomous Operation Services and Object Database Systems in a Heterogeneous Environment", *Proceedings of IFIP DS-5 Working Conference on the Semantics on Interoperable Database Systems,* Elsevier, 1993.

24. Sheth, A. and Larson, J., "Federated Database Systems for Managing Distributed, Heterogeneous, and Autonomous Databases", *ACM Computing Surveys,* 22(3): 183-236, September 1990.

25. Sheth, A., "Schemata of Interoperable Databases Systems: Beyond Data Modeling", *Proceedings of IFIP DS-5 Working Conference on the Semantics on Interoperable Database Systems,* Elsevier, 1993.

Some thoughts on the future evolution of object-oriented database concepts *

Catriel Beeri
Institute of Computer Science
and
The Leibniz Center for Research in Computer Science
The Hebrew University of Jerusalem

Abstract

In the last decade, the emphasis in database research has shifted from the relational to semantic and object-oriented models. The latter are supposed to enable us to construct application domain descriptions that are more faithful to how humans conceive reality than what was previously possible. Although current OODB's are superior to value-based models, nevertheless they are still restricted in their modeling power. To understand how to use them properly, and more importantly to know what to ask for in the next generation of systems, requires that we consider not only purely technical implementation-related issues, but also more abstract problems, such as: What are the distinctions, if any, between objects and values? What are the mechanisms for identification of objects? How are abstractions related to, and represented by objects? Answers to these and similar problems are important for the development of computational object-oriented models, hence dealing with them is in the realm of Computer Science, although they are also of general philosophical interest and have been considered in previous centuries by philosophers, such as Leibniz. These questions, with examples and motivation, are discussed in the paper.

Introduction

During the last decade, the emphasis in database research has shifted from the relational to semantic and object-oriented models. This is quite natural — familiarity with the relational model has revealed not only its advantages, but also its shortcomings. The semantically richer models enable us to construct application domain descriptions that are more faithful to how humans conceive reality than what was previously possible; and the new programming paradigm promises to provide better support for the efficient development of application software. As object-oriented database systems (OODB's) enter the market, we actually see a graduate, albeit slow,

*Research partially supported by a grant from GIF — The German Israeli Foundation.

shift even in the commercial world towards an object-oriented approach to the design and implementation of applications.

So far, researchers have been busy understanding the basic concepts of the new paradigm, developers have been mainly occupied with getting the first generation of object-oriented database systems on the market, and the market is still hesitating about what to do with these systems. But, we have now understood the principles, and are gaining some experience in using the new systems. It is time for analysis, to find out the weaknesses of the new approach (it must have some), and prepare our shopping list for the next generation of systems. This paper is a modest contribution in this endeavor.

This paper discusses a few subjects relevant to OODB's. We assume familiarity with the basic concepts. These have been discussed extensively in the literature. Some papers on the subject are [1, 2, 3, 4, 6, 15]. Our goal is the presentation of a complete 'shopping list', nor do we reach concrete and complete conclusions. We simply take a critical look at, and draw attention to issues that we feel are important and interesting. Three main topics are discussed, in the next three sections: Object identification, abstractions and their representations, and meta-level concepts and their use.

We note that these, or at least the first two, are not purely technical issues. Although they certainly belong now to the realm of Computer Science, they are also of general philosophical interest, and have been considered in depth by philosophers. Somewhat to our surprise, we find ourselves dealing with issues considered previously mostly by philosophers. We should be careful to keep our more narrow goals in mind — for this is a deep and wide sea. We touch on this briefly in the conclusions.

ON IDENTITY

It is a central tenet of object-oriented models that they support the notion of an *object with identity*. The intuitive idea is that in the real world, the entities we perceive have an immutable identity; that is, the identity does not change even when the properties of the entity change. We meet a classmate from highschool after twenty years, and it is the same person, although he may have lost most of his hair; we see the changes in our car after an accident, but we know it is the same car — our beloved car. Identity exists not only in the physical reality, but also in the reality of our mind — our abstractions also are entities endowed with identity. The notion of identity in OODB's captures some of this intuition, and is commonly considered an important and very useful feature. Let us consider carefully what it really is and just how useful it is.

Values and Objects

OODB's, like all database systems, store and manipulate values such as numbers, characters, text, bit strings. Additionally, they have a notion of *object*, used to *represent* other entities that are not values. (As a rule, an OODB does not really contain the entities of the application[1]. People, cars, projects, are not in there — only their representations are.) This dichotomy is mirrored in the classification of the relational model, and some of its extensions, as *value-based*, as opposed to *object-based* systems, and in particular *object-oriented* databases. To understand identity, we need to understand these notions, value and object.

I have discussed the distinction between values and objects at length in [4]. Briefly, it is the following. Values, such as integers, are abstractions invented by the human mind. They and their meanings are generally known, although names and representations differ among culture and systems. The universally known meaning of a value is the information it carries — a value is in *itself* the information. Given the number 7, we know what it is, and we do not ask the system to provide us with additional properties of it.

On the other hand, the objects in a OODB are used to represent those entities that do not necessarily have universally, or at least system-wide, known and used meanings, and most importantly that require additional descriptions. Examples of the latter kind are: Physical entities, like people and employees; abstractions like marriages, projects, work assignments, CAD/CAM designs. We want to store information about them — their components, properties, relationships, and so on. The fact that a certain object represents an employee carries some information, but by itself is of very little use; we need to know, hence store, his name, address, salary, and many other relevant fields. Objects stand for these entities in OODB's. These objects are supposed to have an identity, and separately from it, various properties. The latter are the means by which we collect in the system the knowledge about those entities that is relevant to our application.[2]

Identification Mechanisms

In a relational database, all the information about entities is stored as collections of values — sets of tuples. However, there is still the need to identify the entities described by these tuples. This is accomplished by the notion of *key*. A key attribute in a relation has a different value for each tuple, thus serving as a *unique identifier* for the relation. A key value from a relation can appear in a tuple of another relation, where it is called a foreign key, and then it serves as a reference to the entity it identifies.

In an OODB, we represent entities by objects with identity. The common way of realizing the notion of identity is to associate each object with a system-maintained *object identifier*, or o-id. This o-id has properties that are quite similar to those of keys. It is guaranteed to be unique for each object; it can be used wherever we need a reference to the object it identifies. Thus, a spouse of a person can be stored as the o-id of the spouse object. Since the o-id can appear in many places, we achieve *sharing*, and we can also have *cycles* as in the relationships of a person to its spouse, and of

[1] If the application's entities are computerized records, or designs, then perhaps it does.

[2] Note that if, for example, a company decides not to store information about its CEO in the database, and its uses 'CEO' to represent it, then this can be considered as a value, just like 7. Indeed, it is not universally known, but in the given system, 'CEO' carries its own meaning, which is known to all the users.

the spouse to its spouse which is that person. Now, all that can also be accomplished by using keys. The important idea is that in an OODB it is all transparent to the user — it is in the realm of the system's responsibility. O-id's are invisible; there are no operations to manipulate them or display them. A user can only ask whether two objects are identical or not.

There have been proposals to the effect that not every object's identity should be implemented by an o-id. For the cases where natural keys exist, why not use them? Such proposals and others are feasible because of the principle that we just described: In the user model, objects in the system have unique, immutable, identities. The interface does not reflect the internal mechanism used to implement this notion, and the implementation is irrelevant for conceptual model

Who Shall I Kill?

Consider the following scenario: A spy is sent to Hamburg, his mission to to be given to him in the usual manner. He gets the note, opens it in his hotel, and reads: "Go the delicatessen shop in Damtor station, on Tuesday, 21:47; you will see a man, around forty, medium height, smoking a cigar; follow and kill him." He goes to the shop, where he sees two persons fitting the description. Now, who should he kill? The problem arises since he was given an identification of an unknown person by properties of the person, and the properties do not form a unique identification.

This problem has an analog in the OODB world. As we just saw, object identities exist, but their 'actual value' is transparent at the user interface. Now, suppose that our OODB contains two distinct objects, that is objects with different identities, but all their property values, and all the relationships in which they participate are the same. Can we delete one without deleting the other? or do any other operation on just one? Obviosuly not.[3] With the exception of asking if two given objects are identical or not, the model allows us only to use values in our language. In particular, once two objects in the system reach a state where they cannot be distinguished by values, they will never be separated again. So why keep two of them?

Let us diverge for a minute, and ask: Is the idea that two objects cannot be distinguished in a given system well-defined? What are the mechanisms that can be used for distinguishing between two objects? Answers to these questions have been formalized for a simple model in [5]. We can model an OODB (an instance database) as a labeled graph. The nodes are the entities — values and objects, and their labels provide information about them. For example, a node representing an atomic value is labeled by that value; a node representing a set is labeled by 'set'; a node representing an object is labeled by 'object'; and a node representing a class is labeled by 'class' and additionally by the class name. The edges and their labels describe relationships: the relationship between a set and its members, or a class and its member objects, is represented by edges labeled with $\in$; that between a tuple and its attribute values by edges labeled with the attribute names. This simple representation is sufficient to capture many features of OODB's.

[3] Unless we go below the conceptual interface, down to the implementation level, where sets are actually stored as lists, and use a 'get-next' primitive.

Now, the idea of objects that are indistinguishable can be captured by considering certain homomorphic mappings between such graphs, that preserve both structure and labels. (The precise definition is given in [5].) Given a database, represented as a graph, and two nodes in it, we ask: is there another graph, and such a mapping from our graph to that graph, such that these two nodes are mapped to the same node?

Example 1: Consider the graph

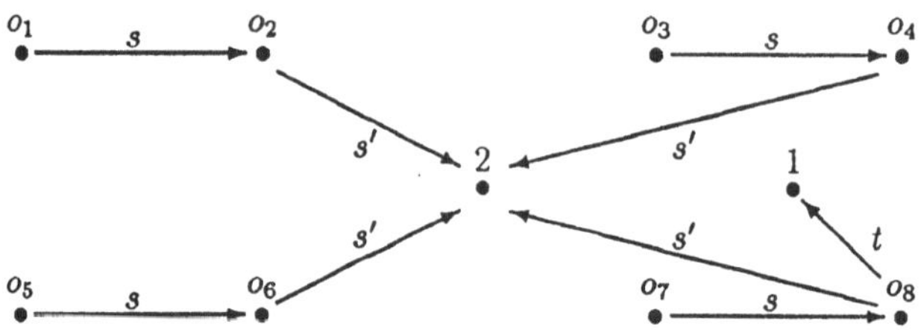

The numbers 1, 2 are atomic, i.e., self-identifying, hence they are distinguishable from each other, and from the eight objects. Each odd-numbered object can be distinguished from each even-number object, since odd- (even-) numbered objects have no (one) incoming edge. The object o_8 is the only one that has two differently labeled outgoing edges, to two distinct values, so it is distinct from all the others. Since o_7 is the only object with an s-edge to o_8, it is also distinguishable from all the others. However, there does not seem to be any feature that will allow us to separate the objects in $\{o_1, o_3, o_5\}$ from each other, and similarly for $\{o_2, o_4, o_6\}$. In a sense, if we identify the three objects in each of these two sets, we obtain a graph that carries the same information. Thus, we can define a homomorphism that takes each of $1, 2, o_7, o_8$ to itself, and takes each of o_1, o_3, o_5 to o_1, and each of o_2, o_4, o_6 to o_2.
Note that if we add edges, we may expect to be able to distinguish more objects from each other. For example, if we add an edge labeled t' from o_8 to o_2, then o_1 and o_2 can be distinguished from the others as well. □

It turns out that this notion of indistinguishabilty of objects is well-behaved: If one pair of objects can be identified using one mapping, and another pair can be identified using a second mapping, there is a mapping that both identifies the first pair, and identifies the second pair. More than that, there is a *strongest* mapping that identifies each pair that can be identified by some mapping. Thus, the relationship 'the objects can be identified by some mapping' is an equivalence relation on the nodes of the graph, and the strongest mapping collapses each equivalence class into a single node. We can now say that an object is *uniquely identifiable* in a given OODB, if there is no mapping that identifies [4] it with any other object.

The example illustrates an alternative, more positive definition: An object is uniquely identifiable if there is a query that retrieves it, and no other object. This definition assumes a query language, but it is easy to associate a simple query language with such labeled graphs. For example, each of the following two queries retrieves

[4]Beware of the two meanings of 'identify' here.

precisely o_8 in the example:

select o *from* object *where* $t(o, 1)$

select o *from* object *where* $t(o, x) \wedge s'(o, y)$

It turns out that the two alternative definitions are equivalent. That is, given a graph and the associated query language, two objects can be identified by a mapping iff every query returns a set that contains either both or neither.

These results show that the notion of uniquely identifiable object is well-defined, for quite a general model. But the discussion also reveals that objects are not really *identified* by the internal mechanism, but rather by what is known about them at the conceptual level. That includes relationships in which they participate, and the other entities that participate in those relationships. The ultimate means of identification is association with values; in this context, relationship names can be considered as a kind of value as well.[5] These are basically the same mechanisms used in value-based (e.g, relational) systems. To guarantee unique identification, we need to impose constraints in the schema, generalizations of the key constraints of relational databases. An analysis of this issue, with some solutions, appear in in [14, 13]. Such constraints of course will prohibit unrestricted use of the *new* primitive; each new object will need to be identified by the predefined mechanisms. The discussion above strongly suggests that any more general solutions will still have the same flavor. And in summary, note that once we understand such mechanisms, if we have a value-based model that supports the same type system as a given OODB, but does not support objects with identity, we can use the same mechanism in the value-based model.

If, even in OODB's, object identification is value-based, and the internal identity plays no role in it, then what are the system maintained o-id's good for? The answer is that they serve as a reference mechanism. The use of an object in the *spouse* position of a person is a reference to that object. References supports sharing and cycles. In relational systems, the same can be achieved by using keys as foreign keys. Now, if we have a complex type system, and the identification mechanism is also complex, then an object may be identified by a collection of paths and the values at their endpoints. To use such a collection as a foreign key is complicated, probably infeasible. To alleviate this, in a value-based model, one would need to invent an artificial key — a roundabout method, that does not correspond to reality. *This* is where the identity mechanism supported by an OODB is useful, by supporting references in a simple and easy to understand manner.

Summary

We have assumed, so far, that any two objects should be distinguishable from each other. This follows Leibniz's Principle of the Identity of Indiscernibles:

> If two things were distinct individuals, there had to be something that was true of the one, but not of the other (thereby making them different species) [10].

[5] Of course, once an object is identified by association with a value, another object can be identified by association with that object.

But, whereas Leibniz was referring to reality, as he believed it to be, our systems only reflect restricted views. We mention briefly two cases where unique identification is difficult, or a priori unattainable. The first is *views*. Although OODB's currently do not support sophisticated view mechanisms, I believe that these will emerge, and will play a significant role in future systems. But, in contrast to the full conceptual model, a view is almost always restricted in some way. It hides some classes, it may not allow update capabilities for other classes, and it hides some of the attributes and methods. It follows that in many views, the attributes and relationships need for unique identification will not be included. This, of course, is the case also in value-based systems. It is, I believe, a goal for object-oriented design methods to consider carefully the interactions between the (lack of) unique identification and the operations allowed in a view.

A second case in point is heterogeneous systems, consisting of collections of databases defined, constructed and maintained by different organizations. There the problem is really, in a sense, a human interaction problem. Even if the same class and attribute names are used in the different systems, and two objects in the 'same' classes have the same values for the 'same' attributes, are we certain that they are the same object? Do the names really have the same meaning in the two systems? So far, only values enjoy the status of universal meanings. As long as we do not find a way to extend this agreement to some of the names used in systems, identification will remain a thorny issue.

ABSTRACTIONS

We have mentioned people and cars as entities represented by objects, but objects are often used for representing abstractions. The structure and relationships of abstractions are potentially more flexible and complex than that of physical entities. We consider here how they are represented in today's models and systems, and whether this leaves something to be desired.

Built-in Abstractions

There are certain kinds of abstractions that are built into todays models: types and classes. In addition to dealing with individual objects, we record some information about collections of objects, in particular the following: the syntactic structure of the objects' interface, the semantics of the interface, i.e., the behavior of the objects — their responses to messages, and grouping of objects into collections.[6] The first kind is often associated with types, and the other two with classes, although different approaches may be found in systems. Current systems place severe restrictions on the membership of objects in classes — typically an object cannot belong to two classes unless they are related in a certain way by the inheritance hierarchy. This is because otherwise we may not know how to interpret a message sent to an object — it may have different meanings in different classes.

[6]The last is unique to databases. In programming systems, it is often a by-product of the other two.

However, it seems we may need a more flexible approach to the representation of abstractions. Let us consider a few examples.

Abstractions: Collections or Objects?

The profession of an employee may be recorded as 'mechanical engineer', and that of another as 'electrical engineer'. These can be considered as values. However, since we often also want to record some information about these professions, let us make them objects, and replace the text strings values by references to these objects. But, if the company is large, it has employees of many many professions and it may be necessary to record relationships, such as "mechanical engineers, electrical engineers, ... are engineers", or "plumbers, electricians, ... are maintenance workers". We may also want to query about all engineers with a salary above a certain threshold, or about electrical engineers satisfying this condition. These are the kind of relationships we have and queries we ask about classes. Thus, we make *engineer, electrical engineer*, ..., into classes, where *electrical engineer* is a subclass of *engineer*.

But, this solution is hardly satisfactory. In current models, membership in a class is not an attribute value — it is a basic property of an object. As mentioned above, current systems restrict membership in classes; one class is recorded for an object, and it belongs to it and its superclasses. Hence if *employee* and *engineer* are not related by a subclass relationship, an object cannot belong to both. Should we make *employee* a subclass of all the profession classes or, vice versa, should we make all the latter subclasses of *employee*. Neither solution seems natural and generally acceptable. Another objection is that we may actually record a lot of data about professions, and then we naturally want to query and update this data. Quite probably we may want to associate professions with types and classes that describe their common structure and behavior. Thus, objects again?

One may raise the issue that all these viewpoints are not likely to exist about the same entity, at least not in the same database. Obviously they do exist in different databases: A small company may represent professions as values. The Arbeitsamt certainly needs to record a lot of information about professions, as well as about their relationships; it probably also records information about jobseekers, including their profession. A large company may need to merge these viewpoints and actually be in the situation described above. But there is a stronger statement to be made: A company will not keep its own database of professions it is can freely and cheaply access a public database on the subject. As communications and remote accesses to data repositories become increasingly common, the boundaries between databases will disappear. While today most applications normally work within one database, and the prevailing approach is "the company database is the world", we see more and more applications that routinely access many databases, both local and remote. For such applications, a database name is just like a class name, it is used to define a scope for a subprogram or a subquery. There are many difficult problems to be solved in this area, because of the great variety of models, languages, transaction management protocols, and other components that exist in current database systems, but they are mostly outside the scope of this paper. But even if we make the extremely simplifying assumption that all the databases *we* access are implemented on the same system, hence the same object-oriented model, we still need to answer the question: What are the facilities or concepts of the *global model* that allow us to simultaneously have different viewpoints of entities, as described above?

Let us mention one more application where similar problems occur. Consider engineering databases, and to be concrete, imagine a technician doing field service for electronic equipment, say for computers. He has a small bag with a personal computer, that has stored in it information about all the possible components, their properties, the potential malfunctions and their symptoms, and so on. There is also an expert system that guides the technician in the diagnosis process, but let us concentrate on the database. Typical data might be: All x disk drives have the three components *bli, bla, blu*; the x-13 drives have in addition *glo* and *gle* components. A *bli* typically has ..., but in an x-13-a drives it has an additional subassembly, a *bli-wrench*, that may *screech* if you open it the wrong way. (A customer may take this to be a malfunction.) And so on, usually for several hundred pages worth of data.

Now, what are the classes and the objects here? One possible viewpoint is that the x, x-13, x-13-a, *bli* ... are classes. The objects are the individual disk drives and their subassemblies that are installed at the customers' locations — it is these that the technician has to diagnose and fix. The information described above, indeed looks very much like a class hierarchy, where subclasses have more detailed information than their superclasses. But alas, this viewpoint fails to explain the fact that the database contains no information at all about these individual objects. It does not contain even on bit on the model x, serial number 987654321, installed at a client company, that has two hours ago stopped functioning.[7] The entities of interest, about which information is recorded, are the *generic* components. In the traditional database viewpoint, these are therefore the objects of this database. But, then, how do we account for the class-like relationships between them? And note that it is crucial in this kind of database to rely heavily on such 'inheritance' relations, for otherwise the data will contain too many redundancies, and potential incompatibilities.

Designs

The discussion above illustrates a need to consider abstractions both as entities with properties and relationships, and as templates that have (a collection of) instances. Plans and designs are another common example. Consider a travel agency [16]. Certainly, one of the kinds of data that is important to its business is travel plans. A plan normally has many options or choices, related to various stages of a trip — choices of flights, hotels, attractions and so on. Since there are many plans, it makes sense to have a class of travel plans, and in reality we may have subclasses such as Aegean-tours, Across-USA, ...But there are also clients, and they work with an agent on their own travel plan, which at the end of the process is going to be a specific plan with no choices at all. During the process, certain choices have been made, some are still open, and some are in the middle (waiting for a confirmation). As a matter of fact, some choices may have to be undone, becuase of negative replies to requests, or simply because the client changed his or her mind.

[7] As these systems develop, this may change, and the database may actually store interesting past cases, as well as information about the current case and the actual components involved.

Finally, note that the system can be so much more useful if the two subsystems, of travel plan templates, and of clients, are connected, and the system knows that a client's plan is an ***instance*** of a certain generic plan. For there may be various restrictions and constraints that apply to a generic plan, and there may be a certain predefined ***plan development scenario*** associated with it, and using those the system can assist the agent in plan development. It is also useful to know how many people are registered in instances of certain plan, possibly qualified by conditions, or what are their addresses, and so on.

There actually has been some work done on the subject, motivated by engineering design problems [8, 9]. They describe in length engineering applications where for designing a required product, there are guidelines and established company procedures. These involve choices to be made from given options at various stages and for various subcomponents, and constraints to be satisfied that include both price and performance characteristics (that vary from order to the next) and the available inventory (that also varies with time). They also identify kinds of queries of interest in such a scenario. These include queries about the sets of options of designs (such as "do the sets of options for components A and B intersect?"), and queries about completed designs such as "is there a design ...?", "is it true that for all designs ...?". Thus, one can pose hypothetical queries. Queries can also be posed on partially completed designs.

Now, they represent the information using an almost standard OODB, except that sets may be designated as "*or*-objects", to signal the fact that a set is actually a set of options to be chosen from. Thus, there is no object, ar any database entity, that stands for a design template. Similarly, there is no object that represents a given completed design. These are captured in the query language, where one can mark a query as *structural*, meaning that it refers to the data as it explicitly appears, i.e., as sets of options, or mark it as *interpretational*, i.e., referring to (partial or full) designs.

In summary, we would like to have the option to represent directly both a design template and partial or full instantiations thereof in a database. More generally, as seen in the previous discussion, we would like to be able to treat abstractions both on the data level, as objects, and on the schema level, as templates, with associated collections. The standard dichotomy of types, classes, and objects does not seem sufficient for that. It is only fair to observe that this is not a trivial task. To deal with engineering design templates (or any other notion of plan), we have to consider difficult issues, some of which are:

- Having tree or graph structures as values of objects, including such that may not have a predefined rigid structure.
- Efficiently representing and manipulating the 'instance-of' relationship.
- Many of the queries that can be posed are actually combinatorial optimization problems, and their inherent complexity may be high, so one has to find reasonable classes of practically interesting queries that can be answered efficiently.
- The interaction with the notion of object identity may pose problems. Is an instance of a design template a value or an object? In the latter case, if we ask

a query about hypothetical designs, we clatter our system with a large amount of quite useless objects with identity. (A similar observation is made in [15].)

META-LEVEL CONCEPTS

Tuples and objects belong to the data-level of a system, whereas relation schemes, types, and class definitions are meta-data, as they serve to describe the data. We consider here some recent ideas concerning the representation and use of meta-data, and of mixing data and meta-data in various ways. These ideas originate because of considerations similar to those of the last section.

Representing and Using Meta-Data

It is traditional in relational systems to store schema information in the same format as the data itself, that is in relations. A major reason for that is to be able to use the access and manipulation languages developed for data users also for the meta-data users. Thus, even users that need access to the meta-data, need to learn only one interface rather than two. Moreover, assuming that we have done our best in developing the languages for the regular users, why not use these also for meta-data. These considerations apply also to OODB's, but there is one more. We have learned by now that relations are not suitable for representing all kinds of data. A major motivation for introducing OODB's is that they support expressive and flexible type systems, that can adequately represent many different kinds of data. A prime test for this claim is the system's data; if the OODB cannot represent and store its own schemas, then it may fail on other applications as well.

It is important to note that even when meta-data is represented as regular data, and accessed by using the same language, there still is, usually, a clear separation between the two levels, as they have different roles, and their uses are not mixed. because of the special role of meta-data, while it can in principle be queried freely, update is severely restricted, and is allowed only as an effect of executing schema DDL statements. Some of the ideas to be considered below relax those restrictions.

A recent proposal for representing and using meta-data in an OODB as objects is presented in [7]. They provide several reasons, one of which is the one just described. Another motivation they present is the following: They consider a graphics application. In such a system, one wants to define various kinds of graphic objects, and also define graphics objects that are instances of them. Although some basic kinds may be supplied with a system, it it reasonable to expect that applications will have specific kinds. Furthermore, it seems that common activities in such applications demand the ability to mix in one query subqueries on both object kinds, and objects. In other words, both the objects and the object kinds defined for an application are application data. It is reasonable to represent the object kinds as classes. In addition to capturing the abstraction-instance relationship, it allows one also to easily capture relationships between abstractions by subclassing. This is essentially idea of having an abstraction represented both as a data object, and as an abstraction that has a collection of instance objects, considered in the previous section (but the notion of *partial instances is not considered here).*

Roles

There have been several recent proposals that have the flavor of decreasing the significance of classes, and suggesting other concepts to partially or totally replace them. One of those is the Melampus project [11, 12]. They propose the notion of *aspect*, which is similar to a type or a class. An object can be accessed through an aspect, and then its structure and behavior are determined by the aspect. However, there is no fixed relationship between an object and an aspect, like that between an object and its class. Rather, an aspect is used at run-time according to need. Also, there is no restriction on the association of objects with aspects, and the same object may be accessed through many aspects, and exhibit a different behavior for each of them. For example, a person may be accessed as an employee and then have a salary, or as a student, in which case he or she has a study plan, or as a car owner, in which case ...Note that, as we have already mentioned, many of today's system will not permit an object to belong to multiple classes that are not related by a subclass relationship. This proposal directly addresses this issue. Aspects have the property of meta-data in that they describe data, but in this proposal they are much closer to being stored and manipulated as regular data.

Ullman's proposal [15] of *classless databases* is a suggestion, rather than a project, and is simpler in that it proposes to do away with classes, but proposes no alternative. Ullman's motivation, as presented, is that as databases grow, and the number of classifications grow, it is going to be increasingly difficult to remember them and use them properly. In his example 6, he assumes all people in the world are represented. There is a huge number of properties, each combination of which may end up as a class, and a huge number of attributes, or methods, distributed among these classes. Class names will be very long and difficult to remember, and since almost every person will have a combination of properties not shared by other persons (recall Leibniz's principle), class extensions will be small.

What is common to both proposals, it seems, is a dissatisfaction with the inflexibility of the representation and use of abstractions in today's systems. A person may be a student, an employee, a car owner, a president of an organization, and many such roles are valid simultaneously. Forcing each such role to be a class causes problems due to the restrictions on class membership, and the proliferation of classes. Current systems also hardly allow an object to present different interfaces when playing different roles (except as permitted by subclass relationships). Finally, one has the infamous class migration problem. Thus, it seems desirable to do away with classes.

My own favorite proposal (at the time of writing) mixes the two and adds some ingredients (all found in the literature). In principle, class membership can be thought of as a binary attribute. An object has one such "belongs to" attribute for each class (they need not be stored physically), and may belong to many classes. A class has an associated interface for its objects, as usual. An object may have many attribute values stored for it, and many methods to which it can respond. To send a message to an object, the class has to be known, for it determines what method is to be invoked.

So far, this is very much a classless world (and the classes should better be called aspects). But, the fact is that our mental models of the world are not classless. We do use classifications to understand the world and interact with it. One way to capture this is to distinguish between *base classes* and *role classes*. For example, for people *person* may be taken as a base class, whereas *employee, student, red cross volunteer* are role classes. The intuition is simple: Once a person - always a person, but one can become a student, then stop being a student. We can either enforce that an object belongs to one base class only, or to compatible base classes, or allow an object to belong to a number of base classes, assuming that since there is a small number of base classes, name clashes between them are easier to check. In either case, no restriction of compatibility applies to role classes. Of course, as with all proposals with this flavor, there is a price to pay: as an object has many applicable methods, accesses have to specify a class. But a base class can serve as a default, and alleviate this need in many cases.

The proposal can be extended in various ways. We can use a *generalization* concept to form new kinds of classes: A legal entity is either a company or a person. We can use the notion of a view to have different structures of base and role classes imposed on the same collection of objects. A role does not have to be a class, in the sense of having many instances. The president of the USA is a role for the base class person, and it does not have many instances. Finally, we could have the notion of an *abstraction*, as discussed in the previous section, as another kind of role, since it also imposes some behavior on its instances.

Let us conclude with some observations. First, this section deals not only with better representations of abstractions and meta-data. It is important to realize that meta-data can be manipulated like data. In the concept of aspect (or role) this is evident in that an aspect is associated with an object dynamically. But we should look further. As we now ask for all the objects in a class, we should be able to ask for all the objects that can play a given role, and even more, all the roles that an object can currently play. We should be able to construct roles on the fly as part of a query, and to define new roles dynamically. Second, there is a close relationship between roles and identity. A well-known example is that of the morning star and the evening star. (This example was pointed out to me when I gave a talk on the subject at Hamburg University.) Astronomers know they are the same star, but some people don't. But when we ask if it is the same object, what should the answer be? It is not clear that an astronomer should answer positively, for does the question refer to being the physical entity, the star, or to playing the same role?

CONCLUSIONS

This paper has discussed ideas and issues, but no complete fully-baked solutions were presented, nor was this the intention. Hopefully, these ideas, with ideas proposed by others, will promote more research on OODB models.

The connection to philosophical investigations was briefly mentioned. Let us note that work on such issues in philosophy was concerned to a large extent with the nature of reality. Philosophers (and others) also considered how humans conceive reality, and there are good reasons to believe that even our conception of reality is a complex and ever evolving set of abstractions. In Computer Science, and in the database area in particular, we are only interested in practically useful approaches to modeling pieces and aspects of reality or, as is often the case, pieces and aspects of our conception of reality or, sometimes, a piece of something that is only in our imagination, although it may become a reality (such as designs). In any case, we accept a priori that our approaches be restricted, since they need to be implementable, and efficient in use. Although it is very useful to have an active imagination (at least, it seems in this area), the criteria of implementability and efficiency should always guide us, and prevent us from forever sailing the sea of our imagination.

This remark in particular applies to the more narrow framework of object-oriented systems. A large number of OO programming languages and systems was developed in the last decade, and many of them are very flexible, so that ideas as those described in this paper can be (or actually have been) implemented in them. But, relational systems were successful, first since they offered a very simple (that is restricted) model, and second because many people worked hard for years to make their implementations deal efficiently with large amounts of data. A lot of work was also invested in relational design theory, so that we know how to use the restricted model to the best results. To implement an idea in a modern flexible programming language is often easy. The real challenges in the OODB area are: (i) To find the right collection of concepts that can be of most use in the development of flexible and easy-to-use applications; (ii) to understand what is and what is not provided by various concepts, so that we know how to fit the pieces of our ever-changing reality into the mold provided by a given fixed model.

Acknowldgements: I would like to thank the many people with whom I have had the occasion to discuss ideas on this subject, and in particular Joachim Schmidt and Ingrid Wetzel from Hamburg University, and Eran Palmon from the Hebrew University.

References

[1] S. Abiteboul and P.C. Kanellakis, Object identity as a query language primitive. Proc. ACM SIGMOD Int. Conf., Portland, Oregon, 1989, 1159–173.

[2] M. Atkinson et al. The object-oriented database system manifesto, in *1st Int'l Conf. on Deductive and Object Oriented Databases.* W. Kim, J-M. Nicolas, S. Nishio (eds), 1989, 370-395

[3] F. Bancilhon Object-oriented database systems, *Proc. 7th PODS*, 1988, pp. 152-162.

[4] C. Beeri. A Formal approach to object-oriented databases. *Data and Knowledge Engineering* 5,(1990), 353–382. A preliminary version in *1st Int'l Conf. on Deductive and Object Oriented Databases.* W. Kim, J-M. Nicolas, S. Nishio (eds), 1989, 370-395

[5] C. Beeri and B. Thalheim, Can I see your identification, please? — Identification is well-founded in object-oriented databases, manuscript, Dec. 1992.

[6] H.-D. Ehrich, G. Saake, and A. Sernadas, Concepts of object-orientation. Proc. 2nd Information System and KI Workshop, Ulm 1992.

[7] J. Göers, and A, Heuer, Definition and application of metaclasses in an object-oriented database model, to appear *Proc. DE conf.* Vienna, April 1993.

[8] T. Imilienski, S. Naqvi, and K.Vadaparty. Non-determinism in object-oriented databases for design and planning applications, *Proc. ACM SIGMOD Conf.* 1991.

[9] T. Imilienski, S. Naqvi, and K.Vadaparty. Querying design and planning applications, *Proc. 2nd DOOD Conf.* Munchen, Dec. 1991, Springer LNCS, 525–543.

[10] G. MacDonald Ross. *Leibniz.* Past Masters - Oxford, Univ. Press, 1984.

[11] J. Richardson, and p. Schwarz. Aspects: extending objects to support multiple, independent roles, *Proc. ACM SIGMOD Conf.* 1991.

[12] J. Richardson, and p. Schwarz. MDM: An object-oriented data model, *Proc. 3rd DBPL Workshop*, Greece, Aug. 1991, Morgan-Kaufmann, 86–95 .

[13] K.-D. Schewe, J.W. Schmidt, B. Thalheim, and I. Wetzel. Extensible safe object-oriented design of database applications. Preprint Computer Science Dept. 09 - 91, University Rostock, 1991.

[14] K.-D. Schewe, J.W. Schmidt, and I. Wetzel, Identification, genericity and consistency in object-oriented databases. *Proc. ICDT92*, Berlin, Germany, Oct. 1992, Springer LNCS, pp. 341–356.

[15] J. D. Ullman, A comparison between deductive and object-oriented database systems, *Proc. 2nd DOOD Conf.*, Munchen, Dec. 1991, Springer LNCS, pp. 263–278.

[16] I. Wetzel, Hamburg Univ., private communication, 1992.

STEP - Grundlagen der Produktmodelltechnologie

Reiner Anderl

Institut für Rechneranwendung in Planung und Konstruktion
Universität Karlsruhe (TH)

Postfach 69 80
Kaiserstr. 12
W - 7500 Karlsruhe 1
Deutschland

Tel.: (+ 49) 721/608-33 74
Fax: (+ 49) 721/66 11 38

Kurzfassung

Die Verarbeitung von Produktdaten, die während des gesamten produktlebenszyklus entstehen, gewinnt zunehmend an Bedeutung. siw wird zu einer wesentlichen Augabe um die Datenverarbeitung in den technischen Unternehmensbereichen zu verbessern. Die Wettbewerbssituation erfordert von allen Unternehmen höhere Flexibilität, kürzere Entwicklungszeiten und höhere Produkt- und Prozeßqualität. Weitere Anforderungen an die Produktdatenverarbeitung resultieren aus der zunehmenden Verringerung der Fertigungsreife und den Änderungen im Produkthaftungsgesetz. Dabei muß ein einfacher und dennoch zuverlässiger Austausch von Produktdaten zwischen Kooperierenden Unternehmen gewährleistet werden, sowie die Speicherung und Archivierung der Produktdaten auf eine neue Basis gestellt werden. Die Schnittstelle STEP (Standard for the Exchange of Product Model Data) bietet hierfür eine Grundlage. Die Entwicklung der STEP-Schnittstelle, die zugrundeliegenden Konzepte, sowie die Überführung in die industrielle Praxis werden im folgenden Beitrag erläutert.

1. Einleitung

Die Nutzung von Datenverarbeitungssystemen (DV-Systemen) in der industriellen Anwendung hat be-reits einen hohen Druchdringungsgrad erreicht. Effiziente Anwendungen sind dabei immer dann zu erreichen, wenn einmal erstellte Pro-duktdaten immer wieder verwendet werden können. Die DV-Systeme werden darüber hinaus ständig weiterentwickelt. So sind heute z. B. CAD-Systeme verfügbar, die eine vollständige geometrische Modellierung von Bauteilen erlauben und, ergänzt um Fähigkeiten zur parametrischen Modellierung und zur Form Feature (Formelemente) Modellierung, Auf-fabenfelder des Entwurfes und Detaillierens im Konstruktionsprozeß ab-decken. Mit der Steigerung der Leistungsfähigkeit von CAD-Systemen sind auch weitere Potentiale der Wieder- und Weiterverwendung von Produktdaten erschließbar geworden (z. B. Prozeßkette CAD/NC, CAD/PPS etc.). Daraus ergibt sich die Forderung nach einem Austausch von Produktdaten zwischen CAD-Systemen, wie auch zwischen CAD-Systemen und anderen Datenverarbeitungssys-temen (wie z. B. zwischen CAD- und NC Programmiersystemen). Der Datenauschtausch muß dabei sowohl unternehmensintern (z. B. zwischen Abteilungen) wie auch unternehmensextern (zwischen kooperierenden Unternehmen) eingerichtet werden. Durch den Datenaustausch werden dabei hauptsächlich die folgenden Ziele verfolgt:

- Vermeidung des erneuten Eingabeaufwandes,
- Vermeidung von Fehlerquellen (bei erneuter Beschreibung),
- Verkürzung der Durchlaufzeiten,
- Erhöhung der Flexibilität in der Produktion und
- Erhöhung der Qualität (Vollständigkeit, Genauigkeit und Konsistenz der Produktdaten).

Neben dem Produktdatenaustausch ist die Produktdatenspeicherung und -archivierung von wesentlicher Bedeutung. Dies geht aus Untersuchungen hervor, die eine Zunahme des Produktdatenaustausches einerseits und diese erhebliche Zunahme der Produktdatenmenge andererseits ausweist (Bild 1 und Bild 2).

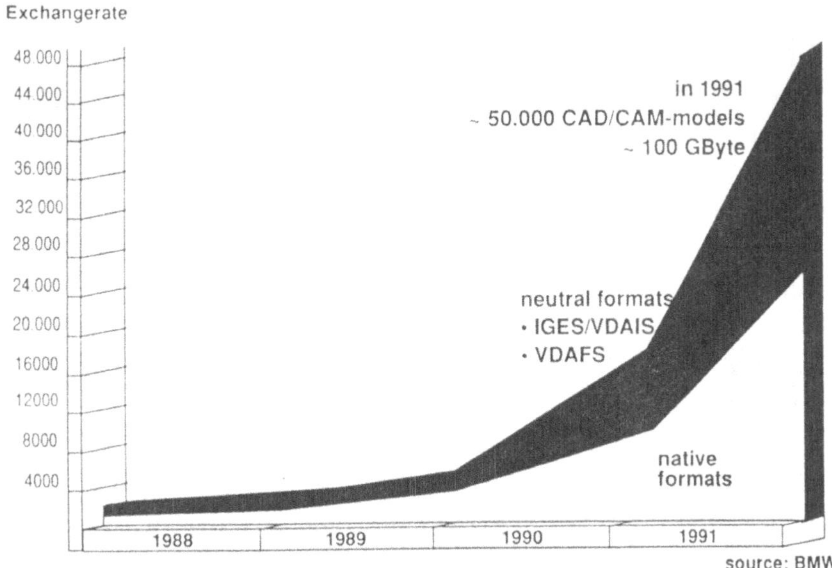

Bild 1: Entwicklung der Produktdatenaustauschmenge

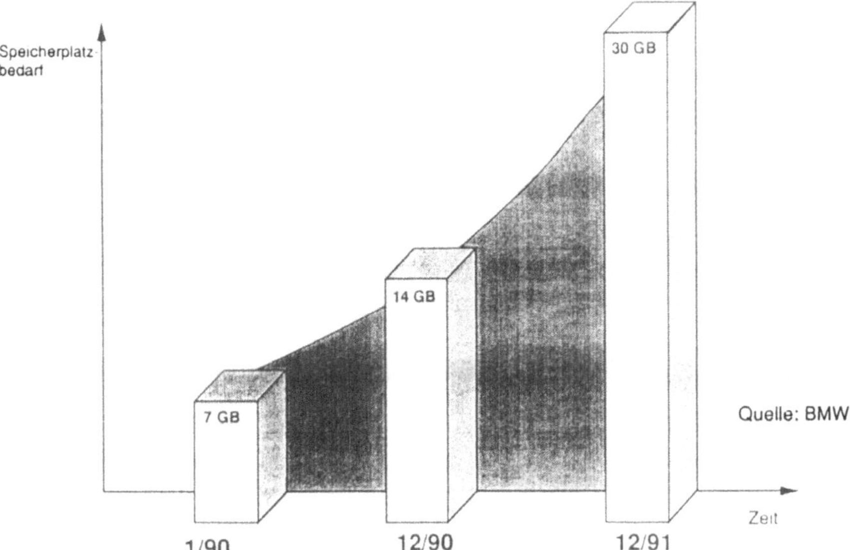

Bild 2: Zunahme des Speicherplatzbedards für Produktdaten

Während der CAD-Datenaustausch heute mit Schnittstellen wie IGES (Initial Graphics Exchange Specification), SET (Standard d«Echange et de Transfert), VDAFS (Flächenschnittstelle des Verbandes der deutschen Automobilindustrie) oder DXF (Data Exchange File Specification) praktiziert wird, zeichnet sich ab, daß eine gleiche Konzeptionelle Datenmodelle für den Datenaustausch und die Datenspeicherung / archivierung erforderlich sind, um Informationsverluste zu vermeiden. Diese Anforderung wird durch STEP (Standard for the Exchange of Product Model Data) erfüllt. STEP unterscheidet sich ge-genüber den vorangenannten Schnittstellen hauptsächlich durch die nachfolgenden Merkmale:

1. STEP definiert nicht nur Geometrie- und Zeichnungsdaten in neutraler Form, sondern spezifiziert ein Produktdatenmodell, das alle Produktdaten im gesamten Produktlebenszyklus umfaßt.

2. STEP zielt nicht nur auf den Datenaustausch, sondern ist so angezeigt, daß alle Funktionen der Produktdatenverarbeitung (also auch die Datenspeicherung in Datenbanken, die Datenarchivierung, die Daten-verarbeitung in interaktiven Systemen) bedient werden können.

Die Entwicklung und Normung von STEP wird im Rahmen der ISO (International Standardization Organization), dort in TC 184/SC4, durchgeführt.

2. Entwicklungs- und Spezifikationsmethodik

Die Entwicklung von STEP basiert auf einer methodischen Vorgehensweise die Anforderungen zur modernen Entwicklung von STEP Software und zur Anwendung der STEP Software berücksichtigt. Softwareentwickler wie auch Anwender haben die Entwick-lung von STEP gemeinsam gestaltet. Zur Spezifikation von STEP wurden Methoden und Werkzeuge so ausgelegt, daß dabei die folgenden Zielsetzungen berücksichtigt worden sind:

o Spezifikation eines Produktdatenmodells, das alle Produktmerkmale im Verlauf des Produktlebenszyklus abbildet,

- o Spezifikation des Produktdatenmodells unabhängig von seiner Implementierung,
- o Herleitung des Produktdatenmodells aus der Anwendung, daher 3-Schichtenkonzept zur Beschreibung des Produktdatenmodells mit Anwendungsschicht, logischer Schicht und physikalischer Schicht,
- o Objektorientierter Entwurf des Produktdatenmodells,
- o Spezifikation eines objektorientierten Datenmodells und
- o Konsequente Herleitung der auf die Schichten bezogenen Spezifikationen über Abbildungsregeln (sogenannten Mapping Rules).

Der methodischen Vorgehensweise zur Spezifikation des Produktdatenmodells können im wesentlichen vier Phasen zugrunde gelegt werden /ANDE-89/. Es sind dies die Konzeptphase, die Spezifikationsphase, die Validierungsphase und die Implementierungsphase (Bild 3).

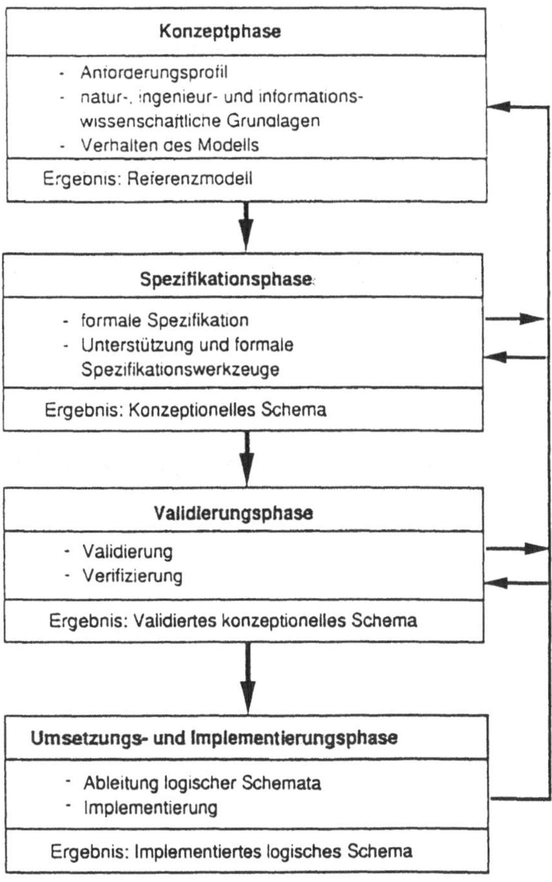

Bild 3: Methodische Vorgehensweise zur Entwicklung des STEP-Produktdatenmodells

In der Konzeptphase wird das Anforderungsprofil einer Anwendung festgelegt und daraus der Entwurf des Produktdatenmodells entwickelt. Zunächst wird eine Analyse der Funktionen zur Erstellung und Verarbeitung der Produktdaten durchgeführt. Mit Hilfe der Methode IDEF0 (ICAM Definition Method No. 0) werden so Aktivitäten untersucht und definiertdie Produktdaten erstellen oder weiterverarbeiten. Diese Methode ist auch unter dem Namen SADT (Structured Analysis Design Technique) /ROSS-77/ bekannt geworden. Als Ergebnis der Funktionsanalyse wird so ein Aktivitätenmodell (engl. Activity Model) aufgebaut. Dieses Aktivitätenmodell dient dann als Grundlage zum Entwurf des Datenmodells. Der Entwurf des Datenmodells erfolgt mit Hilfe graphischer Entwurfsmethoden. Dies sind entweder IDEF 1x (I-CAM Definition Method No. 1 Extended), NIAM (Nijssen Analysis Method /NIHA-89/) oder EXPRESS-G (Graphische Darstellungsmethode zu EXPRESS /EXPR-91/). Bild 4 zeigt ein Beispiel eines Datenmodellentwurfs mit Hilfe von EXPRESS-G. Diese graphischen Entwurfsmethoden erlauben die objektorientierte Beschreibung von Datenmodellen wobei die Sachverhalte über eine vordefinierte Symbolik und über Begriffe ausgedrückt werden können. Dies dient dazu, nicht nur die Daten selbst festzulegen, sondern auch die Bedeutung (Semantik) der Daten bezüglich ihrer Anwendung. Es wird daher auch von dem Entwurf eines semantischen Datenmodells gesprochen. Das Ergebnis des Entwurfs wird auch als Referenzmodell (engl. Reference Model) bezeichnet.

In der Spezifikationsphase wird, das Referenzmodell (also der graphische Entwurf des Datenmodells einschließlich der verwendeten Begriffe) in eine formale Spezifikation abgebildet. Hierzu wird die Spezifikationssprache EXPRESS verwendet. EXPRESS ist eine Spezifikationssprache zur formalen, objektorientierten Beschreibung von Datenmodellen. Die formale Spezifikation ist erforderlich, um eine konsistente, widerspruchsfreie und eindeutige Beschreibung des Produktdatenmodells zu erhalten. Bild 4 zeigt ein Beispiel einer formalen Spezifikation mit EXPRESS. Das in EXPRESS ausgedrückte Datenmodell ist noch unabhängig von einer Implementierung, es liegt jedoch in rechnerverarbeitbarer Form vor. Damit kann das formal spezifizierte Datenmodell mit Hilfe von Softwarewerkzeugen in verschiedene Zielimplementierungen abgebildet werden. Das Ergebnis der formalen Spezifikation wird auch als interpretiertes Modell (engl.: Interpreted Model) bezeichnet.

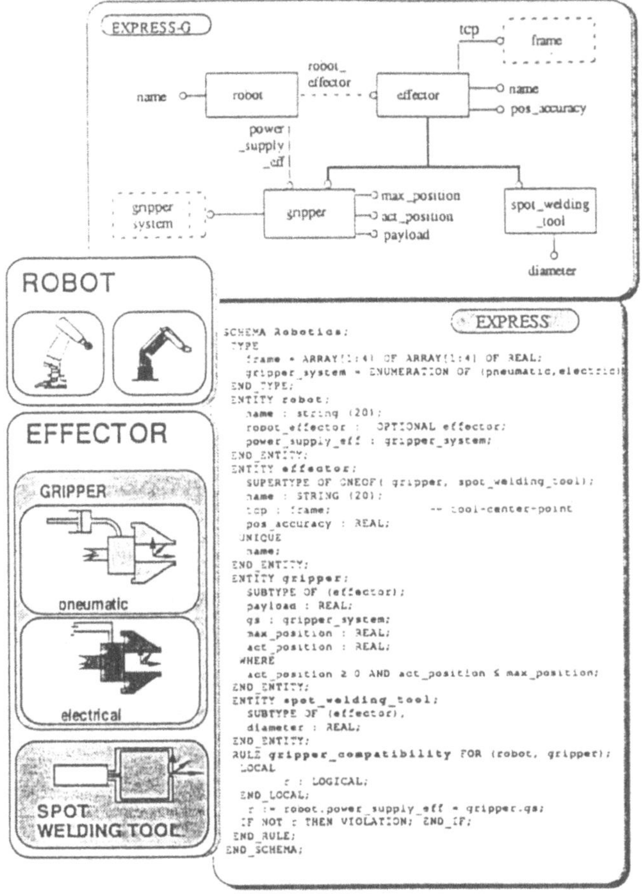

Bild 4: Abbildung eines Systems in EXPRESS und EXPRESS-G

In der Validierungsphase wird die Gültigkeit der formalen Spezifikation gegenüber dem Anforderungsprofil der Anwendung überprüft. Hierzu werden manuelle Prüfverfahren eingesetzt und Testbed - Implementierungen durchgeführt.

Die Darstellung des Produktdatenmodells in einem Implementierungsformat wird in der Implementierungsphase festgelegt. Darüber hinaus werden anwendungsbezogene Vorschriften zur Implementierung definiert. Es liegen beispielsweise Implementierungsregeln zur Abbildung der formalen Spezifikation in

- o eine physikalische, sequentielle Datei,
- o ein Arbeitsformat und
- o Datenbanken

vor.

3. Aufbau und Struktur von STEP

Die STEP Spezifikation zielt auf die Beschreibung eines Datenmodells, in dem sämtliche Merkmale eines Produktes abgebildet werden. Dieses STEP-Produktdatenmodell basiert hauptsächlich auf den folgenden Anforderungen:

1. das STEP-Produktdatenmodell soll alle Produktmerkmale beinhalten, die während des gesamten Produktlebenszyklusses entstehen und zu verarbeiten sind.

2. dem STEP-Produktdatenmodell soll ein kohärentes Datenmodell zugrunde liegen,

3. die Entwicklung des Produktdatenmodells muß unter Berücksichtigung der Funktionen zur Erstellung und zur Verarbeitung der Produktdatenmodelle erfolgen.

Daneben liegen der Entwicklung des STEP-Produktdatenmodells Anforderungen zugrunde, die sich auf seine Bedeutung als Schnittstellennorm beziehen. Diese Anforderungen umfassen Vollständigkeit, Archivierungsfähigkeit,Erweiterbarkeit, Effizienz, Kompatibilität mit anderen Normen (z. B. denen der Computer Graphik), Minimum an Informationseinheiten, Unabhängigkeit von der Hard- und Softwareumgebung, Fähigkeit zur Bildung von anwendungsspezifischen Implementierungsvorgaben, Dokumentation, Validierung und Zertifizierung von STEP Software. Um diesen umfassenden Anforderungen gerecht zu werden, baut das STEP-Produktdatenmodell und seine Entwicklung auf den Grundlagen einer Methodik zur Produktdatenspezifikation, der Nutzung von Entwicklungsmethoden und -werkzeugen und auf einem bestimmten Ablauf der Modellsspezifikation auf. Merkmale von STEP sind einerseits ihr Aufbau und andererseits die Inhalte des Produktdatenmodells. Wegen seines Umfangs wurde STEP strukturiert und in verschiedene sogenannte Serien gegliedert (Bild 5).

ISO 10303 - STEP

1 Overview & Fundamental Principles

Description Methods

11 The EXPRESS Language Reference Manual
12 EXPRESS-Instantiation

Implementation Methods

21 Clear Text Encoding of the Exchange Structure
22 STEP Data Access Interface Specification (SDAI)

Conformance Testing Methodology & Framework

31 General Concepts
32 Requirements on Testing Laboratories and Clients
33 Structure & Development of Abstract Test Suits
34 Abstract Test Methods

Integrated Resources

41 Fundamentals of Product Description & Support
42 Geometric & Topological Representation
43 Representation Structures
44 Product Structure Configuration
45 Materials
46 Visual Presentation
47 Shape Tolerances
48 Form Features
49 Product Life Cycle Support

Application Resources

101 Draughting
102 Ship Structures
103 Electrical Functional
104 Finite Element Analysis
105 Kinematics

Application Protocol

201 Explicit Draughting
202 Associative Draughting
203 Configuration Controlled Design
204 Mechanical Design Using Boundary Representation
205 Mechanical Design UsingSurfaces
206 Mechanical Design using Wireframe
207 Sheet Metal Part Processing & Design
208 Product Change Process
209 Design through Analysis of Composite & Metallic Structures
210 Electronic Printed Curcuit Assemly, Design & Manufacture
211 Electronics Test, Diagnostics & Remanufacture
212 Electronical Plant
213 Numerical Control Process Plans for Machined Parts
214 Core Data for Automotive Mechanical Design Processes

Bild 5: Aufbau von STEP

o ISO 10303 Serie 1 - 10 "Grundlagen"
In dieser Serie werden Grundlagen zu STEP und der generelle Aufbau der Spezifikation beschrieben. Hierbei werden insbesondere auch die Begriffe eingeführt und erklärt, die dann in den nachfolgenden Serien verwendet werden.

o ISO 10303 Serie 11 - 20 "Spezifikationsmethoden"
In dieser Serie werden Beschreibungs- und Spezifikationsmethoden für STEP festgelegt. So beschreibt ISO 10303 - 11 beispielsweise die Spezifikationssprache EXPRESS. EXPRESS-G, die graphische Notation für EXPRESS ist in Anhang dieses Teils definiert.

o ISO 10303 Serie 21 - 30
Diese Serie enthält die Spezifikation von STEP-Implementierungszielen. So umfaßt ISO 10303 - 21 z.B. das sequentielle Dateiformat und ISO 10303 - 22 die Datenbankzugriffschnittstelle (SDAI, STEP Data Access Interface) für STEP.

o ISO 10303 Serie 31 - 40

Anwendungsprotokolle legen damit auch den Umfang für eine Implementierung von STEP fest. Dies bedeutet, daß STEP-Software immer auf einem Anwendungsprotokoll basieren muß. Folgende Anwendungsprotokolle liegen bereits vor; für Zeichnungsdaten mit expliziter und mit assoziativer Darstellung, für Produktstrukturdaten in Verbindung mit 3-D-Liniengeometrie, für Volumenmodelldaten und für Flächenmodelldaten.

Während die ersten 4 Serien grundlegende Konzepte für die Spezifikation des STEP-Produktdatenmodells beschreiben, wird die eigentliche formale Spezifikation der STEP-Partialmodelle in den Serien 41 - 200 festgelegt. Die Serie 201 - 300 schließlich enthält Implementierungsvorgaben in Form der Anwendungsprotokolle.

Ein Anwendungsprotokoll beschreibt einen Ausschnitt aus einem oder mehreren Partialmodellen und gibt vor, wie dieser Abschnitt von STEP abhängig von einer speziellen Anwendung zu verwenden ist.

Der Aufbau eines Anwendungsprotokolls umfaßt die folgenden Inhalte:

- o Scope and Requirements
  enhält die Festlegung, welche Funktionen der Produktdatenverarbeitung im Rahmen des Anwendungsprotokolls berücksichtigt werden. Das heißt, es werden Anforderungen beschrieben sowie Gültigkeitsbereich und Abgrenzung des Anwendungsprotokolls festgelegt.

- o Application Reference Model
  umfaßt die Beschreibung eines Referenzmodells aufbauend auf Begriffen der Anwendung. Das Referenzmodell ist ein semantisches Datenmodell, in dem die für die Datenverarbeitungsfunktionen benötigten Daten strukturiert beschrieben werden.

- o Application Interpreted Model
  das "Application Interpreted Model" repräsentiert die formale Spezifikaiton des Anwendungsprotokolls. Das Referenzmodell wird auf Konstrukte der formalen Spezifikationssprache EXPRESS umgesetzt und um Rand- und Zwangsbedingungen ergänzt.

In dieser Serie werden die Grundlagen und Methoden zum Konformitätsnachweis festgelegt. Es werden dabei allgemeine Konformitätskriterien, Testverfahren und Vorgehensweisen zur Testdurchführung beschrieben.

- ISO 10303 Serie 41 - 100
  Mit dieser Serie beginnt die Spezifikation des Produktdatenmodells. Sie beschreibt den Kern des Produktdatenmodells und die anwendungsunabhängigen Basismodelle (sogenannte "General Resources"). Dies sind Partialmodelle, die nicht für ein bestimmtes Anwendungsgebiet entwickelt wurden. Kennzeichnend ist dabei, daß ISO 10303 - 41 den Kern des Produktdatenmodells ("Fundamentals of Product Description and Support") beschreibt, in dem Struktur und Zusammenhänge der Partialmodelle, Daten zur Handhabung und Kontrolle der Produktdaten und allgemeine organisatorische Daten festgelegt wurden. Weitere Partialmodelle dieser Serie umfassen die Geometrie und Topologie, die geometrische Repräsentation, die Produktstruktur und -konfiguration, die Materialeigenschaften, die Abbildung in eine graphische Darstellung, die Toleranzen, die Formelemente und die Produktdatenzuordnung zu Phasen des Produktlebenszyklusses.

- ISO 10303 Serie 101 - 200
  In dieser Serie werden Basismodelle beschrieben, die auf einen bestimmten Anwendungszweck bezogen sind (die sogenannten "Application Resources"). Zu diesen anwendungsbezogenen Basismodellen zählen z.B. das Basismodell für technische Zeichnungen (Draughting), zur Abbildung von Schiffsstrukturen (Ship Structures), zur Abbildung von elektrischen Funktionen (Electrical Funktions) und zur Abbildung von Finiten Elementen (Finite Element Analysise) wie auch von kinematischen Strukturen (Kinematics).

- ISO 10303 Serie 201 - 300
  Die Serie 201 - 300 enthält die Spezifikation von sogenannten Anwendungsprotokollen (Application Protocols). Anwendungsprotokolle sind notwendig, um einen Ausschnitt auf dem gesamten STEP-Produktdatenmodell zu beschreiben. Dieser Ausschnitt wird unter der Zielsetzung gewählt, eine bestimmte Anwendung zu unterstützen.

- o Protocol Usage Guide
  enthält die Vorgaben zur Benutzung des Anwendungsprotokolls.

- o Conformance Requirements and Test Purpose
  stellt Testkriterien für Implementierungen des Application Protocols zusammen.

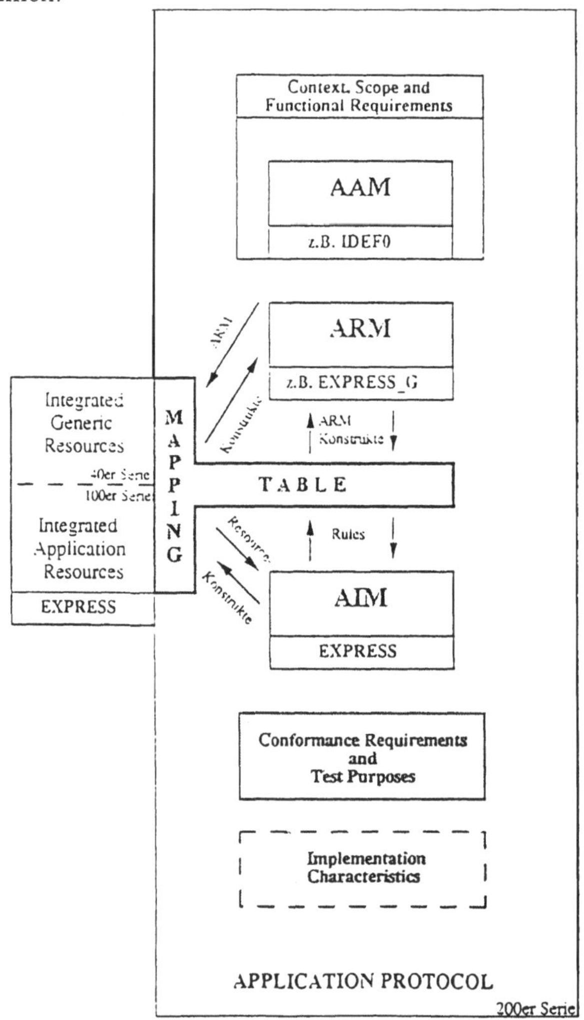

Bild 6: Inhalt eines Application Protocols

Anwendungsprotokolle sind die Teile der STEP-Spezifikation, die für eine Implementierung relevant sind. Sie stellt Implementierungsvorschriften dar, auf denen die eigentliche STEP-Software (z. B. Pre- und Postprozessoren für den Produktdatenaustausch) aufsetzt.

4. Softwareentwicklung für STEP

Der Umfang des durch STEP spezifizierten Produktmodelles hat dazu geführt, daß die Entwicklung der Prozessoren verstärkt durch moderne Softwaretools unterstützt wird. Dazu gehören bei der Programmierung von Scanner und Parser die Werkzeuge LEX und YACC. Auch bei der Umwandlung des EXPRESS-Schemas, das das Produktmodell beschreibt, in eine C- oder Pascal-Datenstruktur werden Tools eingesetzt, die diesen Vorgang weitgehend automatisch und fehlerfrei durchführen.

Es werden außerdem Tools eingesetzt, um die gerade entstandenen oder von anderen Benutzern erhaltenen Dateien auf inhaltliche oder semantische Korrektheit zu überprüfen. Andere Werkzeuge stellen den Inhalt einer STEP-Datei auf dem Bildschirm dar, ohne sie bereits für ein spezifisches CAx-System zu konvertieren.

Für eine gezielte und sichere Einführung einer neuen Schnittstelle wie STEP in ein Unternehmen ist für eine gewisse Übergangszeit auch Konvertierungssoftware nötig, die andere neutrale Formate, wie z. B. IGES oder VDAFS nach STEP umwandelt. Diese Konvertierungsprogramme werden daher auch dann benötigt, wenn sich die rechnerinternen Modelle der Systeme, zwischen denen Daten ausgetauscht werden sollen, grundlegend unterscheiden. Ein Beispiel für eine solche Konvertierung wäre hierbei die Umwandlung eines CSG-Modells in ein BREP-Modell.

Durch den Einsatz dieser Tools werden Routineaufgaben gelöst und die Entwickler können sich weitestgehend auf die Umwandlung des systemspezifischen in das neutrale Schema konzentrieren.

Der Austausch von Daten mit Hilfe von Dateien in einem neutralen und genormten Format ist zur Zeit Stand der Technik in vielen Unternehmen. Er ist gekennzeichnet durch die Beibehaltung der lokalen Datenhaltung in systemspezifischen Formaten. Daten eines CAx-Systems werden nur dann in das neutrale Format umgewandelt, wenn sie mit einem anderen CAx-System ausgetauscht werden sollen.

Eine andere Form des Datenaustausches wird den Austausch von Dateien in einem neutralen Format in Zukunft aber ersetzen: Die Integration verschiedener Anwendungen über eine gemeinsame Datenbank. Dies führt zu einer Systemintegration über Datenbanken (PBD), in der die Daten STEP-konform abgespeichert werden.

Ein wichtiger Grundsatz dieser Systemintegration ist dabei, daß nur noch die in der Datenbank gespeicherten Daten verbindlich für die Anwender sind.

Der Aufbau von STEP Softwarewerkzeugen (Toolkits) sieht so aus, daß mittels EXPRESS ein Datenmodell spezifiziert würde und aus dieser Spezifikation automatisch ein STEP Datenspeicher generiert wird. Der STEP Datenspeicher ist z. B. eine C++ Datenstruktur, die einfache Schreib- und Lesemethoden für die einzelnen Objektattribute besitzt.

Durch den Aufbau des Datenspeichers ist eine objektorientierte Programmierschnittstelle definiert. Um diesen Datenspeicher lassen sich eine Menge von Anwendungsmodulen gruppieren (Bild 7), die Daten im Datenspeicher generieren, löschen oder verändern.

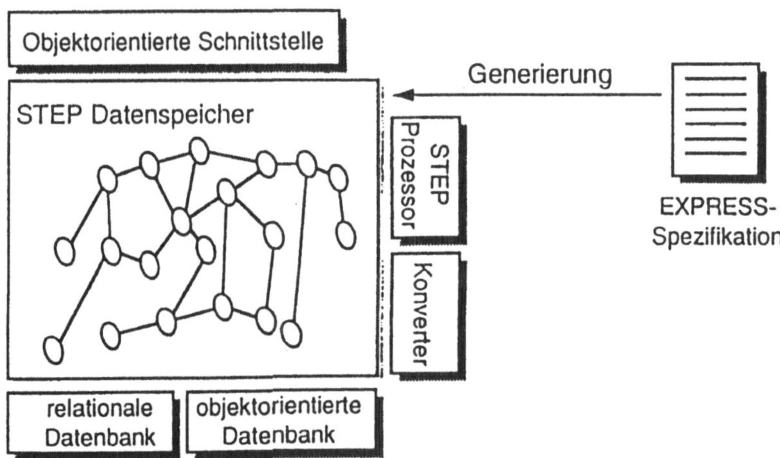

Bild 7: STEP Datenspeicherkonzept

Durch die C++ Programmierschnittstelle lassen sich beliebige weitere Module für den STEP Datenspeicher entwickeln. Je nach Aufbau des Moduls lassen sich nur feste STEP Datenspeicher (in Verbindung mit einem vorgegebenen Schema) oder frei spezifizierbare STEP Datenspeicher einsetzen. So ist z.B. die Ankopplung einer objektorientierten Datenbank nicht mit einem festen Schema verbunden.

STEP Toolkits basieren im wesentlichen auf der Umsetzung einer in EXPRESS spezifizierten Datenstruktur in eine C++ Datenstruktur, die um einfache Methoden zum Lesen und Schreiben von Attributen angereichert wird. Der STEP Datenspeicher ist so aufgebaut, daß beliebige Module zur Datenverarbeitung in dem Speicher angeschlossen werden können (Prozessoren, Konverter, usw.).

Der Datenspeicher könnte auch unmittelbar oder über eine Prozeßkopplung in ein CAx-System integriert werden (Bild 8). Mittels eines Abbildungsalgorithmuses könnte das Datenmodell des CAx-Systems auf den STEP Datenspeicher abgebildet werden. Dort würden dann alle bekannten Module zur Verfügung stehen. Der Abbildungsalgorithmus ist wesentlich einfacher als die Realisierung eines vollständigen Prozessors. Außerdem können natürlich zusätzlich eine Menge vorgefertigter Module eingesetzt werden.

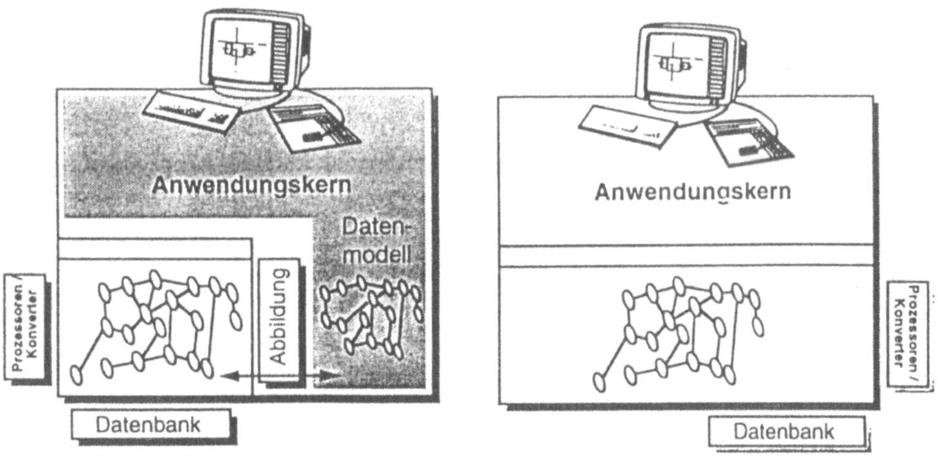

Bild 8: Verschiedene Anwendungsmöglichkeiten der STEP Tools

Um so ähnlicher das Datenmodell der Anwendung dem Modell des Datenspeichers ist, um so einfacher ist der Abbildungsalgorithmus.

Die Datenbanktechnik zielt darauf ab Objekte einheitlich zu verwalten und verschiedenen Anwendungen zur Verfügung zu stellen. Es können vier verschiedene Datenbanktypen [KoSi-91] unterschieden werden:

- o Hierarchische Datenbanksysteme,
- o Netzwerkdatenbanksysteme,
- o Relationale Datenbanksysteme und
- o Objektorientierte Datenbanksysteme.

Objektorientierte Datenbanken haben zum Ziel komplexe Datenstrukturen verwalten und komplexe Objekte im Zugriff halten.

Objektorientierte Datenbanksysteme können nach Dittrich [Ditt-89, AWMB-91] in

- o strukturell objektorientiert,
- o verhaltensmäßig objektorientiert und
- o voll objektorientierte

Systeme klassifiziert werden. Struturell objektorientiert bedeutet, daß komplexe Objekte in einer Datenbank gespeichert werden können. Eine ODMS ist verhaltensmäßig objektorientiert, wenn Funktionen gespeichert werden können. Voll objektorientierte Systeme können sowohl komplexe Daten als auch die zugehörigen Funktionen speichern. Die zur Zeit kommerziell verfügbaren Systeme sind den strukturell objektorientierten Systemen zuzuordnen.

Traditionelle DBMS sind satzorientierte Systeme und besitzen alle ein einfaches Grundmodell, wie z.B. die Objekte Tabellen, Zeilen und Spalten bei relationalen DBMS. Komplexe Objekte müssen auf dieses Modell abgebildet werden. Objektorientierte DBMS besitzen im Grund kein Modell zur Speicherung der Objekte. Sie übernehmen das Modell der Anwendung. ODBMS besitzen jedoch weitere Funktionen, bei denen ein gewisses Modell zu Grunde gelegt wird. Dies sind z.B. die Handhabung von Schemaänderungen und die Clusterung von Objekten. Hier sind z.B. Techniken der Objektversionierung zu nennen.

Im ersten Ansatz können ODBM Systeme für einen C++ Entwickler als eine natürliche Erweiterung der Funktionalität seiner Programmiersprache verstanden werden, d.h. er muß keine neue Programmierschnittstelle erlernen. Mußten bisher explizite Prozeduren geschrieben werden um Daten aus dem Hauptspeicher in den persistenten Speicher zu verlagern übernimmt dies nun das Datenbanksystem.

Dadurch fallen die aufwendigen Algorithmen zum Speichern und laden weg. Das wirkt sich so aus, daß alle Anwendungsdaten zu jeder Zeit persistent auf Platte verfügbar sind.

5. Umsetzung von STEP in die industrielle Anwendung

Im Rahmen des Verbundforschungsprojektes KCIM wurden Grundlagen zu STEP erarbeitet /KCIM-90/.

In einer Reihe von Forschungsprojekten, die Umsetzung der STEP Technologie in Softwaresysteme nachgewiesen. Dies wurde in den folgenden Projekten geleistet:

- o STEP Pre- und Postprozessoren für den Datenaustausch, (wie z. B. in den ESPRIT-Projekten CAD*1 /CAD-89/, CADEX /CADEX-91/, NIRO /NIRO-90/,

- o Datenbankfunktionen zur Abbildung des STEP-Produktdatenmodells auf Datenbanken (wie z. B. in den ESPRIT Projekte IMPPACT /IMPP-91/, NEUTRABAS /NEUT-91/ und

- o Integrationskonzepten zur Einbettung des STEP Produktdatenmodells in interaktiv arbeitende DV-Systeme (wie im ESPRIT-Project VIMP /VIM-91/.

Neben diesen Grundlagen und Forschungsprojekten zu STEP wurde in

Deutschland wurde das ProSTEP-Projekt gegründet, das als STEP Zentrum fungiert. ProSTEP hat zum Ziel STEP Software für die industrielle Praxis zu entwickeln und verfolgt die folgende Schwerpunkte (Bild 9).

- o Entwicklung eines Softwarebaukastens,
- o Entwicklung von STEP Pre- und Postprozessoren,
- o Entwicklung einer Produkt- und Betriebsmitteldatenbank,
- o Entwicklung von Konvertierungssoftware zur Umsetzung von z. B. VDAFS-, VDAIS- und VNS-Daten in STEP und umgekehrt,
- o Entwicklung eines Konzeptes zur Langzeitarchivierung auf der Basis von STEP und die
- o Entwicklung von STEP-Anwendungsprotokollen.

❒ Softwarebaukasten

- EXPRESS-Sprachverarbeitung
- File-Analyse/-Formatierung
- Validierung/Fehlererkennung
- Modelltransformation
- Datenverwaltung

❒ Prozessorentwicklung

Entwicklung von STEP-Prozessoren in Zusammenarbeit mit Systemanbietern

❒ Produkt- und Betriebsmittel-datenbank

- Analyse
- Entwurf
- Implementierung eines Prototyps

❒ Konverter

- VDAFS 2.0
- VDAIS komplett
- VNS

❒ Langzeitarchivierung

- Erarbeitung eines Konzeptes

❒ AP-Entwicklung

- Automotive Design
- Electrical Fundamentals

Bild 9: ProSTEP Arbeitspakete

ProSTEP beabsichtigt damit zu Projektende ein Szenario für die

Produktdatenverarbeitung exemplarisch zu realisieren. Dieses Szenario wird in Bild 10 vorgestellt und ermöglicht die Realisierung der Funktionen:

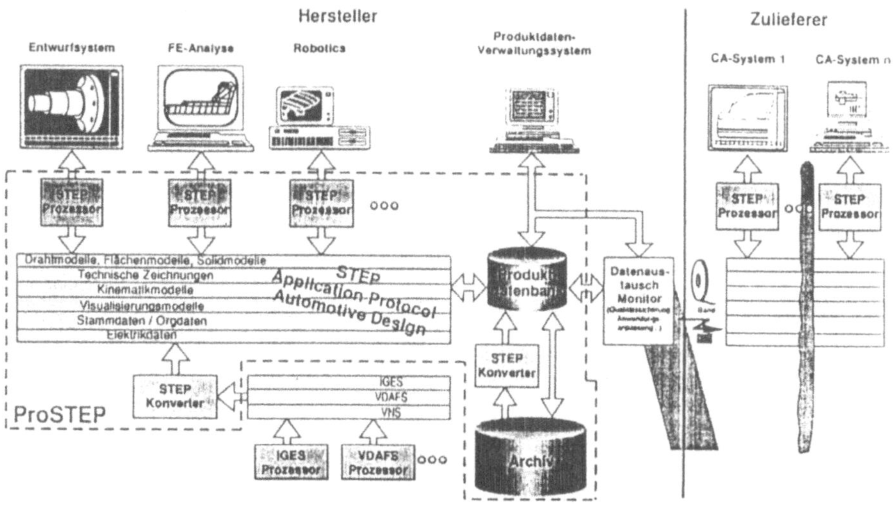

Bild 10: ProSTEP Anwendungsszenarium

- o Produktdateaustausch,
- o Produktdatenspeicherung,
- o Produktdatenarchivierung,
- o Produktdatenkovertierung sowie
- o Monitoring und Managementfunktionen zur Kontrolle von Produktdatenflüssen.

Weitere Aufgaben von ProSTEP liegen im Zusammentragen des vorhandenen Know-How's über STEP um seine Eisetzbarkeit in der industriellen Anwendung nachzuweisen.

6. Zusammenfassung und Ausblick

Die Entwicklung von STEP ist weit fortgeschritten. STEP spezifiziert jedoch nicht nur eine Schnittstelle, vielmehr bietet STEP eine technologische

Grundlage um die Produktdatenverarbeitung unternehmensintern, wie auch unternehmensübergreifend zu gestalten. Die künftige Herausforderung wird sein Systeme zur Produktdatenverarbeitung basierend auf STEP zu entwickeln, Softwarewerkzeuge zum Einsatz von STEP in die industrielle Praxis einzuführen.

Literaturverzeichnis

/ANDE-89/ Anderl, R.: Integriertes Produktmodell
ZwF Jahrg. 84 (1989), Heft 11

/GASS-89/ Grabowski, H.; Anderl, R.; Schilli, B.; Schmitt, STEP-Entwicklung einer Schnittstelle zum Produktdatenaustausch
VDI-Z 131, Nr. 9, 1989

/GRAS-89/ Grabowski, H.; Anderl, R.; Schmidt, M.:
Das Produktmodellkonzept von STEP
VDI-Z 131, Nr. 12, 1989

/HOLL-91/ Holland, M.:
Das STEP-Toleranzenmodell
VDI-Z 133, Nr. 10, 1991

/IMPP-91/ N.N.:
Proceedings zum IMPPACT Workshop
Berlin 1991

/KCIM-90/ N.N.:
Jahresbericht der CIM-AG CAD
DIN Berlin 1990

/NIHA-89/ Nijssen; G.M.; Halpin, T.A.:
Conceptual Schema and Relational Database Design
(A Fact Oriented Approach)
Prentice Hall 1989, ISBN 0-7248-0151-0

/CADEX-91/ Heinrichs, H.; Helpenstein, H.:
CADEX-Ways to STEP Data Exchange Processors
Proceedings zum IMPPACT Workshop, Berlin 1991

/NEUT-91/ Nowacki, H.:
NEUTRABAS-A Neutral Product Definition Database for Large Multifunctional Systems;
Proceedings zum IMPPACT Workshop, Berlin 1991

/NIRO-90/ N.N.:
NIRO Project Description and Overview
Kernforschungszentrum Karlsruhe 1990

/CADI-89/ Schlechtendahl, E.G.:
CAD Data Transfer for Solid Models
Springer Verlag, 1989

/VIMP-91/ Anderl, R.; Geiger, K.; Schmitt, M.:
VIMP: Vision Inspection Project
Product Data International, Nov. 1991

/PROS-92/ N.N.:
Dokumentation zum ProSTEP-Forum
Stuttgart 1992

/ROSS-77/ Ross, D.T.:
Structured Analysis (SA):
A Language for Communicating Ideas;
IEEE Transactions of Software Engineering
Vol. 3, No. 1, 1977

Adding Active Functionality to an Object-Oriented Database System - a Layered Approach

Angelika Kotz Dittrich

Union Bank of Switzerland
UBILAB (UBS Informatics Laboratory)
Universitätsstrasse 84, 8033 Zurich
eMail: dittrich@zh010.ubs.ubs.arcom.ch

Abstract

This paper describes how active functionality was integrated into an existing commercial object-oriented database system. We describe the layered architecture approach taken and the components of the various system layers. It will be shown which advantages and problems arise when adding triggers and operational rules to an ooDBMS which has to be treated as a black box.

1. Introduction

Active DBMS provide common, application-independent functionality for complex dynamic control structures. Beside managing merely the "passive" data structures (or data types with fixed operations), an active DBMS handles an event-driven flow of activities. Instead of having each application survey events and conditions individually and schedule the appropriate reactions (like consistency checks, notification procedures, automatic materialization of derived data etc.), the scheduling is incorporated into the DBMS.

The concepts of object-oriented and active DBMS do not necessarily belong together - active features can also be found in relational DBMS - but they obviously complement each other well. Complex data structures plus operations plus event-driven control flow are very powerful instruments for realizing advanced DBS applications as may be found in the CA* world, but also in non-technical fields like financial modeling and analysis.

The situation today for a database user is that object-oriented DBMS products come without active features. However, as the object-oriented data model (or models, to be more precise) is a very powerful mechanism for "programming in the database", it is possible to make an existing ooDBMS active by adding certain classes and attaching some special mechanisms (concerning process communication and the like). All elements of the active DBMS can be modeled in the object-oriented paradigm and may be accessed exactly as other data.

In the following, we describe how the integration of an existing ooDBMS and active DB functionality was accomplished at UBILAB. The idea was to design a system with the ooDBMS as the basis and several "active layers" of growing complexity on top. As a first platform, a Smalltalk-based ooDBMS - GemStone [Serv91] - was chosen, which proved very useful for prototyping purposes (as had been expected because of the Smalltalk-like approach). In our system, we had to treat the ooDBMS as a black box, i.e. all additional features had to be implemented on top of the officially accessible interfaces of the DBMS. This is a realistic scenario for other systems as well because the internal interfaces are usually not disclosed to users and the basic DBMS software is not open to modifications. Of course, these are rather limiting conditions which make an optimal solution - as to efficiency and even full functionality - impossible, but on the other hand, the approach is easily portable and product-independent.

We will first give a short survey of the state of the art in active DBMS (section 2). Subsequently in section 3, the activity model used in our system will be described. In section 4, the layered approach of the system architecture and the various components of the layers will be presented. Some examples and experiences made during the realization will close the paper (section 5 and 6 respectively).

2. State of the Art

Early forms of trigger concepts may already be found more than a decade ago in the CODASYL data model (in the very rudimentary concept of ON-procedures) and in System R, the relational DBMS prototype of IBM. The first commercial relational DBMS to offer a trigger mechanism has been Sybase. Ingres followed some time later with its rules and alerters similar to the rule system of Postgres ([SHP88], [SJGP90]).

Trigger mechanisms available in commercial DBMSs are comparatively simple in that actions can only be triggered by database operations (like Update, Delete) and that the form of actions is limited. More powerful active rule concepts for a relational DBMS are currently under development at IBM Almaden Research Center in the Starburst project [WCL91]. In Starburst, the stress is on the optimized set-oriented execution of operational rules.

The combination of object-oriented and active database features is a promising field of research, as both concepts complement each other very well. Unfortunately, commercially available ooDBMS do not yet offer triggers or rules (though some of them announce it for future versions). Several research projects have addressed the subject, the most well-known being the HIPAC project (CCA/Xerox AIT, [DBM88], [Daya89], [Chak90]). Part of the terminology and basic ideas of active DBMS have been coined in this project (like ECA-rules, various execution modes of actions etc.). The work on HIPAC has definitely influenced our project. Another ooDBMS integrating rules (though only in the research version of the system) is O2 formerly developed at Altaïr [MP91].

The project SAMOS at the University of Zurich [GGD91], carried out in cooperation with Ubilab, currently also deals with the problem of an active object-oriented DBMS. The effort of SAMOS and our work complement each other in that SAMOS deals with the higher modeling and interface concepts, while we concentrate more on the basic layers on top of the ooDBMS.

There can also be found a certain relationship between active DBMS and deductive DBMS [Mink88]. An active DBMS deals with operational rules triggering operations by certain events which may be raised within or outside the DBS. In contrast to that, a deductive DBMS supports production rules which are used to derive data in case of queries. The deduction process is carried out completely within the DBS. Both kinds of rules are complementary and may even partly use similar techniques.

3. The activity model

We define an active DBMS to be a system that - beside the usual features common to DBMSs - is able to automatically react to specific situations by executing or initiating given actions. Situations that cause the DBMS to react may be of various kinds:

- states or state transitions of the database
- execution of certain operations on the database
- time-related events
- arbitrary events arriving from outside the DBMS

Actions executed in response to these conditions must be able to

- operate on the database
- change the state of the DBMS
- operate outside the DBMS (including communication with applications, operating system commands, display of information etc.)

For modeling the control flow on situations and actions, we use the concept of event-condition-action rules (ECA rules). This term - coined in the HIPAC project at CCA/Xerox AIT - denotes operational rules (in contrast to deductive rules) with three components: an event, a condition and an action. The semantics can be described in short as

on event **if** condition **do** action

An ECA rule may be degenerated to the special cases
- EA rule (there is no condition to check) or
- CA rule (the rule is fired whenever the condition becomes true)

Remark: Evidently, CA rules represent the most complicated case to manage and, for this reason, are often excluded from active DBMS. We do not want to exclude this class as it provides a very comfortable, declarative way of specification, relieving the user from the need to identify each single event relevant to a condition (comparable to the advantages of a declarative language as opposed to explicit control structures). We are aware that the analysis of arbitrary CA rules may not be feasible (i.e. rule detection may become very inefficient), but at least a restricted set of conditions can be handled.

Events signal situations inside or outside the DBS. Each event is defined with a name and an optional list of formal parameters which during rule execution may be passed on to the condition and the action.

Example:

Create the event "accountOpen" with parameters customer and city
```
Event create: 'accountOpen' with: ('customer', 'city')
```
Raise this event with a concrete customer and city object
```
(Event named: 'accountOpen' ) raise: (<aCustomerObject>, <aCityObject>)
```

Within the object-oriented data model, we distinguish between *external events* not related to any object or class and *internal events* signaling changes and method execution on specific objects. External events may signal quite general situations - like the end of a transaction, the start of an application or some special status of the DBMS. A special case of external events are the *time-related events* that signal absolute or relative points in time. Internal events are raised by operations executed on objects or classes.

Furthermore, we distinguish between *simple events* and *complex events*, the latter being defined by means of an event algebra. The event algebra allows to connect simple events and complex events recursively by the operators **and, or, not** and **;** (sequence). A complex event is raised as soon as the corresponding simple events have been raised according to the algebraic expression. The event algebra is can be described in BNF as follows:

```
simple_event_expr     ::= <event identifier> | event_negation | '(' event_expression ')'
event_negation        ::= 'not' simple_event_expr
event_conjunction     ::= simple_event_expr | event_conjunction 'and' simple_event_expr
bool_event_expr       ::= event_conjunction | bool_event_expr 'or' event_conjunction
event_expression      ::= bool_event_expr | event_expression ';' bool_event_expr
```

Example:

(E1 and E2); E3 or E4; not E5; E6

This defines the complex event: E1 and E2 are raised in arbitrary order. Then E3 or E4 (or both) are raised. Finally E6 is raised without E5 being raised before it.

In the current implementation, we make the simple assumption that each complex event has to occur totally within the scope of one transaction (i.e. the state nets described below cannot be shared across transaction boundaries). In the future, this has to be extended in two ways:

- by additional options as to the scope of a complex event, i.e. the scope in which all its simple events have to occur (this might be within one transaction, within one session, within all sessions of the same user or within the global scope of all sessions.).
- by extending the event algebra with time boundaries to specify a time limit for event sequences to occur or - in case of negation - not to occur (see also end of section 4.2).

Internally, complex events are represented by state nets. The nodes of the nets represent states during the complex event, the complex event being raised when the final state is reached. Similar to a Petri net, several states may be fulfilled (or marked) at the same time. At any time, the set of actual (marked) states consists of all states that have been reached by *at least one* incoming edge and have not yet been left by *all* outgoing edges. There are two types of edges connecting nodes. Edges labeled by the name of a simple event mean that a state transition occurs when the simple event is raised. Unlabeled edges model the **and** operation, i.e. the new node is reached when the predecessor nodes of all unlabeled edges leading into it have been marked.

Example:

Figure 1 shows the state net for the above expression (1 is the start state, 6 the final state).

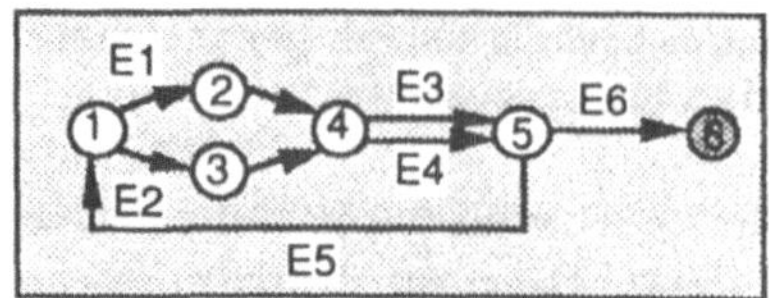

Fig.1: Example of a state net for a complex event

In each scope, there is only one active state net per complex event, i.e. a complex event cannot be raised several times in parallel. (In the current implementation, this means that a complex event has one active state net per transaction.)

Example:

E1 or E2; E3

E1 raise - E2 raise - E3 raise
The complex event will be raised only once
E1 raise - E1 raise - E3 raise - E3 raise
The complex event will be raised only once, namely on the first "E3 raise".

Within the event algebra, there is a need to express that two subsequent events belong to each other (like the start and end event of a transaction or method). For this purpose, the special concept of *grouped events* is introduced. A grouped event is either a start event or a following event. When raising a start event, a unique event occurrence object is generated which has to be referred to when raising the following event. In the event algebra, grouped events are indexed to define which occurrences belong together.

Example:

OP_A_begin [1]; OP_A_begin [2]; OP_A_end [2]; OP_A_end[1]

The complex event will be raised if during the execution of OP_A the same operation is once more executed completely.

Conditions are boolean expressions that are checked as preconditions of actions. Each condition is described by a name, an optional list of formal parameters and the boolean expression to be evaluated. In an ECA rule, the condition is checked whenever the event occurs. In a CA rule, the situation is far more complicated as we have to find out when to check the condition and whether to check only part of it incrementally. The condition has to be analyzed to find out the events which may make the condition come true (like inserting or deleting objects, modifying attributes etc.). The condition (or an appropriate part of it) is checked whenever these events occur. (In our implementation, we have not yet realized condition analysis and we consider to restrict the expressiveness of conditions in CA-rules to make analysis feasible.)

Actions are executable routines within or outside the DBMS. We distinguish between internal actions written in the DML (in the case of GemStone this is called OPAL) and external actions written as operating system commands (in our case UNIX shell scripts). Each action definition consists of the action's name, its formal parameters and the code to be executed.

An action can be executed in different modes with respect to the transaction in which the rule was fired. For this we define the execution mode and coupling mode of an action within a rule. The execution mode indicates whether the action is executed immediately after the event has been raised (exec mode = immediate) or is deferred to the end of the transaction (exec mode = deferred). The coupling mode defines whether the action is executed synchronously as part of the transaction in which the event occurred (coupling mode = coupled) or asynchronously in a separate transaction (coupling mode = decoupled).

By definition of various rules, the same event may fire different actions. Therefore, the order of action execution has to be decided on. We provide the user with the option to define the sequence of actions triggered by the same event. Without user defined priorities, action execution is random.

4. The layered architecture

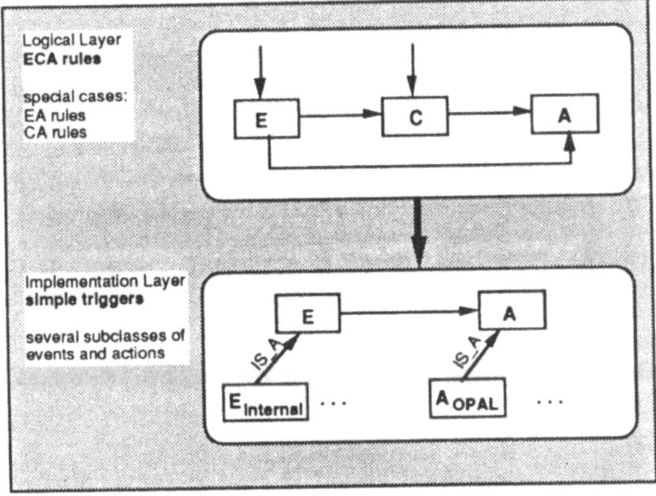

Fig.2: The two layer approach to active DBMS functionality

The first step to structure the system was to split up the active functionality in two layers that separate the analysis and execution of rules from the control flow between events and actions (see fig.2). On the lower level, a simple **trigger mechanism** (similar to [Kotz89]) is realized, a trigger being just a pair of event and action without the notion of condition. The mechanism for raising events and firing actions, the different kinds of events and actions (internal events, complex events etc.) and the different modes of action execution are implemented on this layer. In the upper layer, **ECA rules** (including the special cases EA and CA rules) are implemented and mapped onto the trigger system. Figure 2 shows the two conceptual layers.

In the design of the final system architecture, the 2 conceptual layers were further split up resulting in 4 levels built upon the ooDBMS. As shown in figure 3, we distinguish:

1. Basic mechanisms
2. The trigger mechanism
3. The ECA rule system
4. The level of high-level interfaces and tools

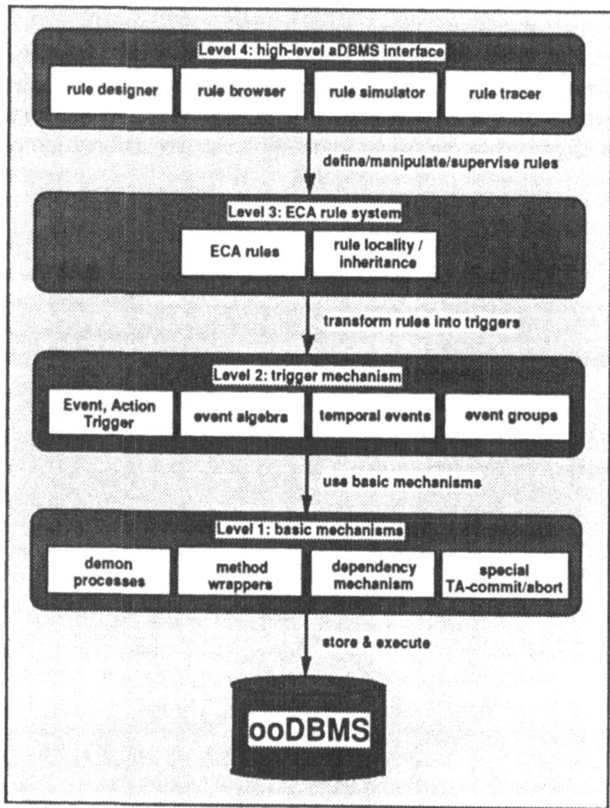

Fig.3: The 4 level system architecture

In the following, we will give details about the different layers and their components.

4.1 Basic mechanisms

On this level, some fundamental services are provided like

- demon processes for the asynchronous execution of actions
- a mechanism to wrap methods in order to raise the corresponding events

- a dependency mechanism to notify objects about the changes in other objects
- a special transaction commit/abort

Demon processes

While synchronous execution of action is done within the DBMS process, asynchronous action execution is done in separate processes. As it is too expensive to start a new process for every action, we use the concept of demon processes that are waiting for actions to be carried out. Each demon process is able to carry out actions of a specific type, one at a time. Orders to carry out actions are passed from DBMS process to demon processes via a queuing mechanism. Depending on system load, the process configuration can be tuned by assigning several demons for the same action type. We distinguish demons for various action types like DML actions (these actions require the demon to login to the database system), general UNIX actions and notification actions operating on the window system. Other types, like e.g. SQL actions accessing a relational DBMS, can be added easily.

Method wrappers

The begin and end of a method can be signaled by internal events. By that it is e.g. possible to have a method trigger an access control check at the beginning and a consistency check at the end. Instead of programming these checks into the method code, they can be added flexibly and explicitly by the definition of ECA rules. To raise the internal events, the original method is replaced by a wrapper method that contains the event operations and a call to the original method (see figure 4). The ability to generate wrappers for its own methods is implemented in a class *activeObject*, which also implements the notion of objects with internal events. Every class raising internal events in its methods has to be a direct or indirect subclass of *activeObject*. Method wrappers are created dynamically as soon as rules refer to a method.

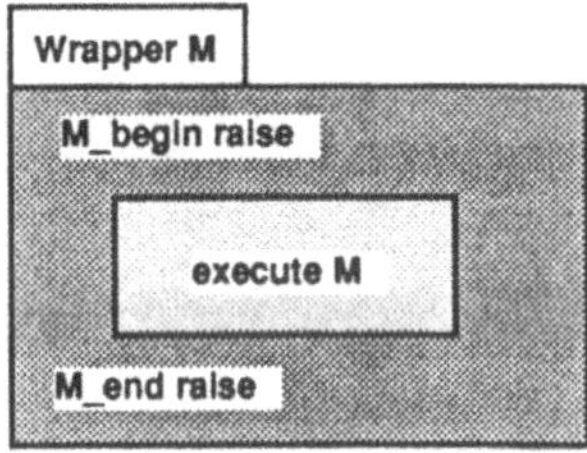

Fig.4: Method wrapper in the active DBMS

Extended dependency mechanism

The dependency mechanism known from Smalltalk allows for objects to signal their changes to other "dependent" objects that may react to the changes. We considered this mechanism useful for active database behavior and therefore implemented it on top of the ooDBMS (which did not provide any kind of notification concept itself). The dependency mechanism was implemented as a feature of the class *activeObject*. Compared to the Smalltalk dependency concept, we introduced two extensions:

1. The notification is not via an unspecific broadcast to all dependent objects, but more selective in that different kinds of events are signaled to different sets of dependents. Objects are notified only if they are registered as dependent on a specific change aspect.
2. We distinguish between dependents on objects and on classes. Changes to the class will only notify the class dependents, while changes to a specific object will notify the dependents of that object as well as those of the class.

The principle of the dependency mechanism is shown in figure 5.

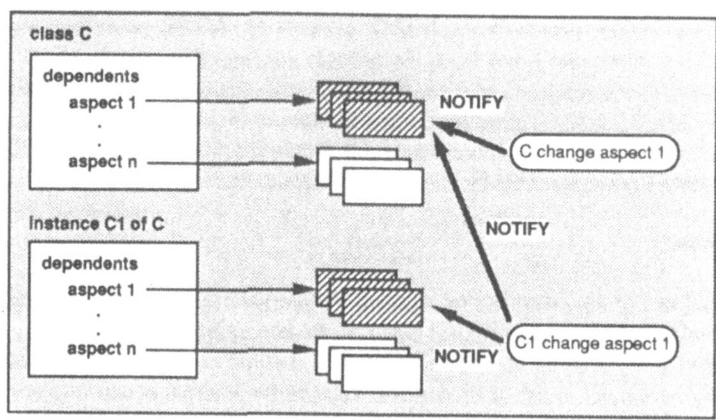

Fig.5: The extended dependency mechanism

Special transaction commit/abort

The system-defined commit and abort operations were overwritten to fulfill two additional tasks:

- Raise the events 'TA_commit' or 'TA_abort' respectively so that triggers may be defined on these situations.
- Execute all actions triggered in deferred execution mode on commit (or discard these actions on abort).

4.2 The trigger mechanism

On this level, the concept of simple triggers is implemented by mapping its elements to the object-oriented data model and by using the basic mechanisms. All the functionality of raising various kinds of events and triggering actions in different modes is incorporated in classes and their methods. Each event, action or trigger is represented as an object that may be queried and manipulated by means of the DBMS. Specializations like composite events, internal events, Opal and Unix actions etc. are modeled by the subclass mechanism. The event algebra, grouped events and time-related events are also located on this level.

Mapping events, actions and triggers to classes

The three basic concepts of the trigger mechanism are mapped to classes *Event*, *Action* and *Trigger*. To capture the notion of the same action being triggered with different parameters, modes and execution order, we further introduced the class *ActionCall*. Figure 6 shows how these classes are interrelated.

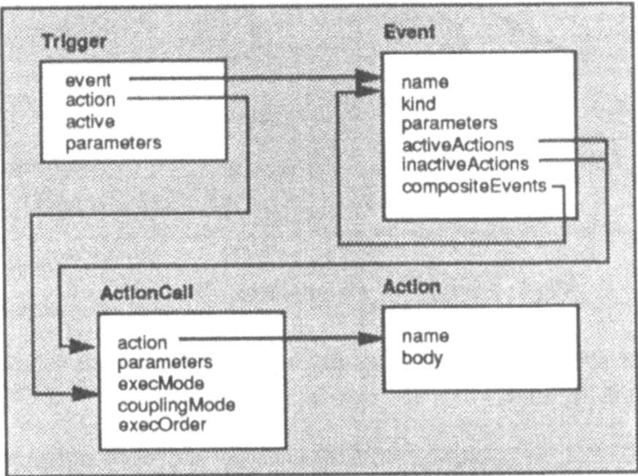

Fig.6: The central classes of the trigger mechanism

Each object of class *Trigger* references its corresponding event and action call. A trigger may be activated or deactivated, indicated by a boolean attribute *active*. Furthermore, the trigger contains a parameter list, specifying for each action parameter how it is to be computed when the trigger fires (action parameters may be calculated from event parameters, constants and arbitrary database values). Objects of class *Event* have attributes specifying the name, kind of event and formal parameter list. Furthermore, each event references all - active and inactive - action calls which are triggered by this event (these redundant references are kept for efficiency reasons). Finally, a simple event references all composite events which are currently "waiting" for it to be raised. Class *Action* provides only attributes name and body, leaving the decision whether to have parameters to its subclasses. Each *ActionCall* object references an action and contains information on how the action is to be executed, i.e. computation of parameters (if any), execution and coupling mode and execution priority.

The above classes (apart from actionCall) were not derived directly from the system class *Object*, but from our own specialization *ObjectWithHierarchExt* (object with hierarchical extension). This class - not specific for the active DBMS, but of general usefulness - supports the notion of classes whose extension (i.e. the collection of all instances of the class) is managed as a tree of sets. By the hierarchical structure of the extension, we can differentiate which instances are visible to which users. Querying the extension, each user will get only those instances that are available to him. Figure 7 shows an example of a such a class extension (user 1 will see objects {O1, O2, O3, O4, O5, O9, O10}, user n objects {O1, O2, O3, O6, O7, O8, O11}). By deriving from this superclass, we can separate events relevant for one user only from events for a user group or central events visible to everybody (the same is true for actions and triggers).

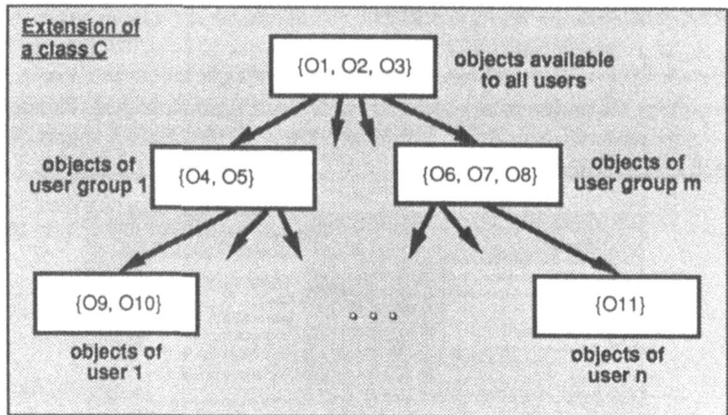

Fig.7: Example of a hierarchical class extension

To model the various special cases of events and actions, appropriate subclasses have been derived as can be seen in figure 8.

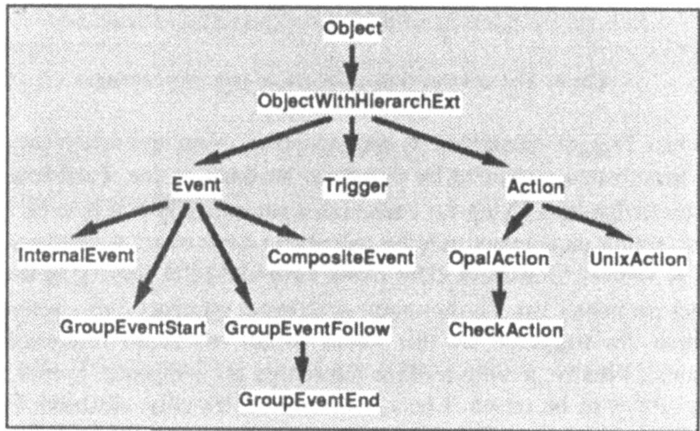

Fig.8: Class hierarchy implementing the trigger mechanism

Class event has been specialized to provide for internal, composite and grouped events (see section 4.). As illustrated in figure 9, each of these subclasses comes with its own additional structure. An *InternalEvent* references the active object to which it is local, the object containing an inverse reference to all its internal events. Each *CompositeEvent* references its state diagram which contains the structure of the event network as well a special data structure for grouped event occurrences. Each composite event also records its actual states. *GroupedEvents* that are start events have a list of all occurrences for which no corresponding end event has yet occurred. Each following event (including the end event) references its start event partner.

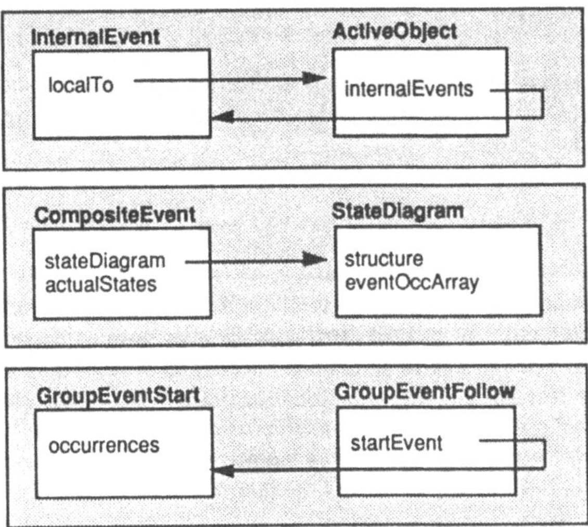

Fig.9: Structure of event subclasses

There are currently two direct and one indirect subclasses of *Action*. Objects of class UnixAction have a UNIX shell script as their body. Parameters can be specified in the usual $-notation. By the different coupling modes, the UNIX commands can be executed synchronously or asynchronously with respect to the DBMS process. *OpalActions* have (GemStone-)DML code as their body. Each such action may be defined with an arbitrary number of parameters. *CheckActions* are a special case of DML actions that return a boolean result and raise a true- or false-event at their end (for the rule layer, check actions evidently serve to check conditions).

Time-related events

An important subclass of events are the time-related events. They indicate situations like

- an absolute point in time (e.g. "on 1.1.1992 at 12:00")
- a relative point in time (e.g. "two hours from now", "10 minutes after program A has terminated")
- periodical events (e.g. "daily at 12:00", "every 10 minutes from now")

The event algebra may also be extended to take into account the time aspect. You can define time limits for sequential or conjunctive events like

- E1 and E2 [within 1 minute]
- E1; E2 [at least/at most 10 seconds later]

In our current implementation, we did not yet further work out the details of time-related events.

4.3 The ECA rule system

The elements of this level - mainly conditions and ECA rules - are also modeled as objects of the ooDBMS. Methods of these classes provide the mapping of rules to simple triggers and the analysis of conditions.

ECA rules

Rules are modeled by a class *EcaRule* (see figure 10). Each rule object references an event, a condition and an action object. (references to either the event or the condition may be undefined). A rule is either active or inactive, indicated by a boolean attribute. Furthermore, each rule references the options for condition and action execution as well as the parameters to be passed in each case (for EA and CA rules the condition options and parameters are undefined!). The class *EcaOptions* contains information on execution and coupling mode as well as the order of triggered actions. Class *condition* simply contains the name, parameters and text of the condition. From each condition text a method (global to class *condition*) is compiled that will do the checking.

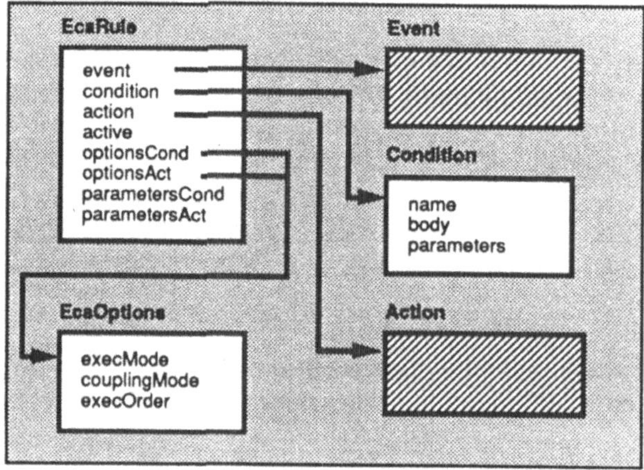

Fig.10: The central classes of the rule system

Rule locality/inheritance

According to our general concept, rules may be either global to the database or local to a single class or object. Global rules may reference any classes or objects, though only via their public interface. The events triggering global rules can be of arbitrary kind, especially external events. If a rule is local to a class, it is inherited along the subclass hierarchy. Rules that are local to a class may refer to private attributes of that class just as methods may access these private components. Local rules will only be triggered by internal events of the class.

As our black box approach did not allow us to change the class definition mechanism of the underlying ooDBMS, there was no way to implement local rules in a well encapsulated and easily usable way. So until now, we restrained ourselves to global rules only, not allowing for any kind of rule inheritance. Until now, we did not come upon an urgent need for local rules, so the restriction seems to work rather well.

4.4 The level of high-level interfaces and tools

The upper level of the hierarchy allows for comfortable design and control of the rule system. Though there is not yet a detailed concept for this level, we consider it indispensable for the efficient and secure use of a rule base. The components of this level as described below must not be seen as standalone tools, but form a closely interacting system.

Rule designer

The rule designer is a (partly graphical) tools for rule definition, allowing to specify events, conditions and actions and to correlate them in a set of rules. Errors like incompatibility with class definitions or inconsistent formulas of the event algebra have to be discovered automatically.

Rule browser

The user must be able to browse through the set of rules interactively with graphical support. The browser should allow for various criteria to restrict or structure the rule set (to retrieve the rule objects, the query capabilities of the ooDBMS can be exploited). Examples are:

- all rules triggered by the same event and/or condition
- all rules local to a class
- all rules raised by time-related events in a certain interval (in time order)
- all rules that may be triggered recursively by another rule (as far as decidable by static analysis)

Rule simulator

As actions may be arbitrary programs, static analysis is not always sufficient to decide which rules will be executed when and in which order. Therefore, the user should be given a simulation tool to try out various rule scenarios without really changing the database. Thus the user may try out which consequences an update on the database will have taking into account all the rules currently defined. The simulator will show the rules fired as well as the potential changes to the database and the external effects brought about by these rules.

Rule tracer

In contrast to the rule simulator that does not modify the database, the rule tracer logs all rule executions during real database operation. By analyzing the rule log, the sequence of rule applications can be analyzed for purposes of error detection, rule set optimization etc. As a basis for the rule tracer, we implemented a logging mechanism on the trigger level which (recursively) records all triggers (i.e. events and actions) that have fired.

5. Examples

We will give three examples, two for the use of the trigger mechanism and one for the use of the ECA rule system.

Example 1:

This example shows the definition of a simple trigger. First the event 'myEvent' is created with a parameter called text. Then a UNIX action 'myAction' is defined that writes its parameter to a file 'myFile'. 'myEvent' is to trigger 'myAction' passing over its text parameter. The trigger is active, the action will be executed synchronously (coupled) at the end of the transaction (deferred). When 'myEvent' is raised with a string, this string will be written to 'myFile' on the next commitTransaction.

```
Event create: 'myEvent' with: #(#text)

UnixAction create: 'myAction' withBody: 'echo $1 >> myFile'

Trigger  on: (Event named: 'myEvent')
         do: (Action named: 'myAction')
         with: #(#text)
         active: true
         execMode: #deferred
         couplingMode: #coupled.

(Event named: 'myEvent') raise: #('This text will be written to the file.')
MySystem commitTransaction
```

Example 2:

In this example the rating of shares is supervised to notify the user in case certain limits are exceeded. First, two actions are defined that check for a rating interval of 50 to 500 and for the relationship with the average rating. The two OPAL actions created next open a window each (by calling the notify demon process) and display a notification text in it. The notifications are triggered by the true events raised at the end of the check actions. In class *share*, the modification of the rating attribute will be signaled by internal events (a method wrapper is created internally). When the rating has been changed (i.e. on the internal event rating_e), the two check actions will be triggered. ratingLimit will be triggered on any share, ratingGTAvg only for the share object identified by 'IBM'.

```
" Check whether a new value is within the interval [50..500]. A check action raises a true event if
its result is true. The method createStandard generates a check action with 4 parameters:
theObject, theOp, oldValue und newValue (these are exactly the parameters transfered by the
internal events in an update operation."

CheckAction createStandard: #ratingLimit
    withBody:
    '( newValue >= 50 ) | ( newValue <= 500 )'.
```

```
" Check whether a new value is greater than twice the average rating of the set containing all
shares"

CheckAction createStandard: #ratingGTAvg
     withBody:
     'newValue > ( (share avgRating: setOfAllShares) * 2) '.

" Notify the user with the following text:
  The rating of share <shareId>  is out of limits [50..500].
  New rating is <new rating> "

OpalAction create: #notifyRatingLimit
     withParam: #(#shareId #newRating)
     withBody:
     '(DemonType of: "NOTICE demon")
     send: (   string new +
               "The rating of share " + shareId
               + " is out of limits [50..500].' New rating is: " + newRating asString)
     resultTo: R1.'.

" Notify the user with the following text:
  The rating of share <shareId>  is <new rating>.
  This is greater than twice the average rating: 2 * <average rating>. "

OpalAction create: #notifyRatingGTAvg
     withParam: #( #shareId #newRating )
     withBody:
     ' (DemonType of: "NOTICE demon")
      send: (   string new +
                "The rating of share " + shareId + " is "
                + newRating asString
                +  "This is greater than twice the average rating: 2 * "
                + ( share avgRating: setOfAllShares ) asString )
      resultTo: R1.'.

" If ratingLimit is true, trigger notification "

Trigger   on: ((CheckAction named: #ratingLimit) trueEvent)
          do: (Action named: #notifyRatingLimit)
          with: #[ #[ #theObject, [ :o | o name ] ], #newValue].

" If ratingGTAvg is true, trigger notification "

Trigger   on: ( ( CheckAction named: #ratingGTAvg ) trueEvent )
          do: ( Action named: #notifyRatingGTAvg )
          with: #[ #[ #theObject, [ :o | o name ] ], #newValue ].
```

```
" Generate the internal events and the method wrapper for the update method on the rating
attribute in class share"

share makeInstUpdateEventsFor: #(#rating)

" On modification of attribute rating trigger the limit check. Do this for all shares. "

Trigger  on: (share InternalEventNamed: #rating:_e)
         do: (CheckAction named: #ratingLimit)
         with: #[ #theObject, #theOp, #oldValue, #newValue ].

" On modification of attribute rating trigger the average check. Do this only for the share object
with id 'IBM'"

Trigger  on: ((share id: 'IBM') internalEventNamed: #rating:_e)
         do: (CheckAction named: #ratingGTAvg)
         with: #[ #theObject, #theOp, #oldValue, #newValue ].
```

Example 3:

This examples shows an ECA rule that is fired by an event El with a parameter 'name'. After El is raised, a condition Cl is checked to find out whether 'name' is an element of a 'testSet'. If this is true, a corresponding message is printed via the notification demon.

```
Event create: #E1 with: #(#name).

Condition createF: #C1
      withParam: #(#testString)
      withBody: ' testSet includesValue: testString '.

OpalAction create: #A1
      withParam: #(#foundString)
      withBody:
      ' (DemonType of: "NOTICE demon")
      send: (string new add: ( "testSet contains the string:" + foundString ))
      resultTo: R1'.

EcaRule  on: (Event named: #E1)
         if: #[(Condition named: #C1), #[#name] ]
         do: #[(Action named: #A1), #[#testString] ].

"Raise E1: If the string 'Hello World' is an element of testSet, the user will be notified."

(Event named: #E1) raise: #('Hello world')
```

6. Experiences

The integration of active functionality into the object-oriented DBMS proved to be very well feasible. The main advantages were that

- all components of the active DBMS (like events, rules etc.) can be modeled by classes and stored as objects, taking advantage of mechanisms like inheritance, encapsulation etc. As rules are objects, the same query and manipulation facilities can be applied as to any other data in the ooDBMS. Recovery, multi-user synchronization, access control etc. are available as well.

- much of the active functionality can be encapsulated in methods of the ooDBMS. Thus the DBMS has full control of the consistent use of rules for all applications. To exploit the active functionality, the user has just to login to the DBMS (and open a database that contains the appropriate classes!). There is no need to link the application with any additional code. (Note: There are ooDBMS that do not manage methods as first class database objects; for these systems, this advantage does not apply to full extent).

The fact that we used a Smalltalk-based ooDBMS proved to be valuable in two respects:

- The system was very comfortable for rapid prototyping of the active DBMS. Using an interpretative approach, various concepts could easily be modified and tested.

- The dynamic nature of the DML allows for the definition and modification of methods at runtime. Thus it is easy to map actions and conditions into methods at any appropriate time. Wrappers for methods raising internal events can be created dynamically, just when these wrappers are actually needed for some defined rule, reducing the overhead of event raising to a minimum. (We did not make use of the possibility to define whole classes at runtime.)

The experiences with the black box approach using a commercial ooDBMS product without any support for active functionality can be summarized as: It is feasible (and much better than no active functionality at all), but it is not completely satisfying. Without the appropriate mechanisms of the ooDBMS, some active features cannot be implemented efficiently or even cannot be implemented at all.

- Much of the active functionality could be implemented much more efficiently if it was incorporated into the lower levels of the DBMS not accessible to us.

- The locality and inheritance of rules cannot be made part of the class definition mechanism without changing this mechanism within the DBMS.

- The simple transaction mechanism offered in the ooDBMS used is not well suited to action execution from within transactions. Nested transactions (present in some other ooDBMS) would help a lot. Furthermore, a concept of shared or cooperative transactions would be useful to share data between a transaction and separate actions carried out on behalf of this transaction. With the help of shared transactions, the DBMS process could exchange data with the demon processes via the database instead of additional process communication channels. The strict separation of transactions without the possibility of prereleasing selected data, is too restrictive for our purposes. E.g. composite events across transaction boundaries (i.e. with simple events arriving from various parallel transactions) cannot be handled with the strict isolation of simple transactions.

- Basic functionality like the dependency mechanism or the method wrapping facility should be provided by the basic classes of the DBMS (like class Object or Collection). We were not able to change these classes (it was not absolutely impossible, but the problems as to error support from the vendor, release changes etc. would have been tremendous). So we put this functionality in a derived class *activeObject* from which all classes with active features must be derived. Unfortunately, the ooDBMS did not provide for multiple inheritance, so it was impossible to have a class inherit from *activeObject* as well as from some system-defined class like *Array, Collection, Dictionary* etc. Therefore, an active version must to be provided for any single system class (there are over 30 such classes). In our current implementation, we only provide an active version of Object, not allowing for sets, arrays etc. with active behavior (these would have to be "packaged" as attribute of an object).

- In the ooDBMS we used, it is not possible to trigger actions implicitly by the assignment to attributes, but only explicitly by the methods that operate on these attributes. Thus all internal events of a class or object have to be tied to methods. In a C++ based ooDBMS a different solution would be possible by overwriting the assignment operator. On the other hand, the present solution is not necessarily a disadvantage as it keeps the active DBMS from violating the encapsulation of the ooDBMS (it is an open question in active DBMS whether rules should break encapsulation or not).

7. Outlook

Taking everything into account, the extension of an ooDBMS by active functionality (as long as the ooDBMS does not come with a rule mechanism itself) has proven a realistic and useful procedure. We have built a prototype system that is based on the GemStone ooDBMS, Version 2.5, and runs on Sun SPARCstations under SunOS 4.1 and OpenWindows. Until now, this prototype includes the complete functionality of level 1 (basic mechanisms), level 2 (trigger mechanism) without time- and scope-related aspects, and level 3 (ECA rule system) without rule locality/ inheritance and without analysis of CA rules.

Work to be addressed in the future includes:

- Going into more detail about the system components that are not yet implemented, especially level 4 of the architecture (high-level interface).

- Further work on communication and distribution aspects (How can communication between the DBMS and other processes be improved? What about rules pertaining to more than one database? etc.)

- Better integration of transaction management and active DBMS (postponed to later versions of the ooDBMS for which extended transaction concepts have been announced).

- Reimplementation of the active functionality on top of another ooDBMS, namely one of the C++ based kind. Because of the more static nature of the C++ based model, the implementation will require several modifications and less functionality can be fully integrated into the DBMS. We have recently started an implementation on ObjectStore

- Application of the active DBMS prototype to a concrete application. We are planning to apply it in the framework of a system for time series management. In this area, triggers can be useful to automatically compute aggregated data, notifying users about unusual data constellations etc.

References

[Atki89] Atkinson, M., et al (1989). The Object-Oriented Database System Manifesto. Proc. DOOD 89, Kyoto, Japan.

[Catt91] Cattell, R. (1991). Object Data Management. Addison Wesley 1991.

[Chak90] Chakravarthy, S., Nesson, S. (1990). Making an Object-Oriented DBMS Active: Design, Implementation, and Evaluation of a Prototype. In Proceedings Extending Database Technology (EDBT) 1990, Lecture Notes in Computer Science 416, Springer Verlag.

[Daya89] Dayal, U. (1989). Active Database Management Systems. SIGMOD RECORD, 18(3), 150 - 169.

[DBM88] Dayal, U., Buchmann, A., McCarthy, D. (1988). Rules are Objects too: A Knowledge Model for an Active, Object-Oriented Database System. In Advances in Object-Oriented Database Systems, (pp. 129-143).

[GGD91] Gatziu, S., Geppert, A., Dittrich, K.R. (1991). Integrating Active Concepts into an Object-Oriented Database System. In Proceedings of the 3rd Int. Workshop on Database Programming Languages, 1991.

[Kotz89] Kotz, A. (1989). Triggermechanismen in Datenbanksystemen. Springer Verlag.

[Mink88] Minker, J. (ed.) (1988). Foundations of Deductive Databases and Logic Programming. Morgan Kaufmann Publishers.

[MP91] Medeiros, C., Pfeffer, P. (1991). A Mechanism for Managing Rules in an Object-Oriented Database. Techn. Report, Altaïr.

[Serv91] Servio Corp. (1991). GemStone Version 2.5 for UNIX Workstations, Systemdokumentation.

[SHP88] Stonebraker, M., Hanson, E.,Potamianos, S. (1988). The POSTGRES Rule Manager. IEEE Trans. on Software Engineering, 14(7).

[SJGP90] Stonebraker, M., Jhingram, A., Goh, J., Potamianos, S. (1990). On Rules, Procedures, Caching and Views in Database Systems. In Proc. ACM SIGMOD, pp. 281 - 290.

[WCL91] Widom, J., Cochrane, J.R., Lindsay, B.G. (1991). Implementing Set-Oriented Rules as an Extension to Starburst. In Proceedings of the 17th Int. Conf. on Very Large Data Bases, 1991, (pp. 275 - 286).

Die Entwicklung aktiver Datenbanken am Beispiel der Krebsforschung

H.-J. Appelrath, H. Behrends, H. Jasper, H. Ortleb
Universität Oldenburg
Fachbereich Informatik
Postfach 2503
2900 Oldenburg

Zusammenfassung

Diese Arbeit beschreibt erste Schritte bei der Entwicklung eines Werkzeugkastens für die Realisierung aktiver Datenbanken. Schwerpunkte sind dabei die Definition einer Sprache zur Beschreibung von komplexen Ereignissen, die insbesondere auch zeit- und raumbezogener Natur sein dürfen und bei ihrem Auftreten differenzierte Aktionen anstoßen, sowie die Realisierung eines entsprechenden Laufzeitsystems, das auf relationalen DB-Systemen aufsetzt. Weiterhin wird die Entwicklung von Entwurfshilfsmitteln für aktive Informationssysteme und - in einem Parallelprojekt ohne unsere direkte Beteiligung - die Realisierung einer Erklärungskomponente für die Systemaktionen verfolgt.

Das erste mit diesem Werkzeugkasten entwickelte Anwendungssystem ist Active_INEKS, eine aktive Datenbank zur Krebsforschung. Motiviert ist diese Arbeit durch Erfahrungen aus dem Projekt INEKS, in dem ein ORACLE-basiertes Krebsregister aufgebaut wurde. Da trotz kontinuierlicher Dokumentation gemeldeter Krebserkrankungen und -todesfälle die Datenbank signifikante Häufungen natürlich (!?) nicht "von sich aus" meldet, wird eine "Aktivierung" des Krebsregisters angestrebt.

Die Arbeit beschreibt zunächst anwendungsbezogen Anforderungen an eine epidemiologische Krebsforschung, dann einen weitgehend konventionellen DB-Ansatz zur Lösung einiger Teilaspekte des Problems, das Konzept für eine forschungsrelevante Systemverbesserung und dann schließlich die dabei intendierte, applikationsunabhängige Werkzeugentwicklung im Bereich aktiver Datenbanken.

Die konkrete Gliederung: In Kapitel 1 wird das Problem der rechnergestützten Krebsforschung betrachtet. Kapitel 2 stellt INEKS, ein auf einer relationalen DB beruhendes Informationssystem zur Krebsforschung, vor. Auf dieser Basis wird dann in Kapitel 3 die Weiterentwicklung von INEKS zu einem aktiven Informationssystem skizziert, das Hypothesen in Form von berechneten Raten, Quoten oder Risiken, die Hinweise auf vermutete Krebsnester geben, generiert. Kapitel 4 stellt die für eine solche Realisierung notwendige Entwicklungsumgebung vor: ein AIS genannter Werkzeugkasten, der u.a. die Spezifikation von Ereignis-Aktions-Regeln und die Integration von Raum-Zeit-Modellen erlaubt. Kapitel 5 schließt mit einem kurzen Ausblick.

1. Rechnergestützte Krebsforschung

Das Problem

Abb. 1.1 zeigt ein typisches Beispiel für eine Zeitungsmeldung zum Thema Krebsgefährdung. Charakteristisch sind folgende Merkmale in der Reihenfolge des Auftretens in der Meldung:

- "... *Industriestandorte* ...": es spielen Geo-Objekte eine Rolle, die gelegentlich mit metrischen (z.B. Distanz zu Emissionsquellen) oder topologischen (z.B. entlang der überregionalen Hochspannungsleitungen) Beziehungsangaben ergänzt werden
- "... *Krebs-Sterblichkeit von Männern im Arbeitsalter* ...": es werden Angaben zu Krebssterblichkeit und/ oder -erkrankungen gemacht, die i.a. alters- und geschlechtsspezifisch sind
- "... *um 18% über dem Landesdurchschnitt* ...": um das Bemerkenswerte der Meldung zu begründen, sind Angaben zur Signifikanz notwendig, bei denen aber die methodische Untermauerung ausbleibt
- "... *mögliche Ursachen nach Mutmaßungen* ...": es folgen in der Regel Hypothesen oder Erklärungsversuche für die tatsächliche oder auch nur vermeintliche Häufung von krebsbedingten Todesfällen oder Erkrankungen
- "... *Aufbau eines regionalen Krebsregisters* ...": zum Abschluß finden sich dann häufig Forderungen nach anschließenden Studien, politischen Konsequenzen und DV-technischer, i.a. DB-basierter Unterstützung durch ein Krebsregister.

Hohe Krebs-Sterberate in Industrienähe

Auffällig viele Männer - Hiller kündigt Landesregister an

rev Hannover. Neben auffällig vielen Leukämiefällen in der Elbmarsch (Kreis Harburg) und Sittensen (Kreis Harburg) häufen sich in den Regionen Salzgitter, Emden und Wilhelmshaven Fälle von Krebserkrankungen.

"In diesen drei Industriestandorten liegt die Sterblichkeit von Männern im Arbeitsalter aufgrund von Krebs um 18 Prozent über dem Landesdurchschnitt", erklärte Thomas Steg, Sprecher des Sozialministeriums, am Donnerstag.

Während im Landesdurchschnitt jedes Jahr 270 von 100 000 Menschen in Niedersachsen den Krebstod sterben, sind es in Emden 313. Mehr als 300 werden in Wilhelmshaven und Salzgitter registriert. Die niedrigste Krebs-Sterberate hat der Landkreis Gifhorn mit 240 von 100 000 Einwohner.

Nach Angaben von Steg ist dabei auffällig, daß in Emden, Wilhelmshaven und Salzgitter nur Männer im arbeitsfähigen Alter von der hohen Sterblichkeitsrate befallen sind Eine mögliche Ursache könne nach Mutmaßungen von Medizinern in den Industriebetrieben (Werften an der Küste und Stahlverarbeitung in Salzgitter) liegen, sagte Steg.

Mit diesen Zahlen, die sich auf Nachsorge-Daten der Kassenärztlichen Vereinigung beziehen, untermauerte das Ministerium den gestern von Sozialminister Walter Hiller angekündigten Aufbau eines regionalen Krebsregisters für Niedersachsen.

Abb. 1.1 Zeitungsausschnitt zum Thema "Erhöhte Krebs-Sterberate"

Wenn man der durch eine solche Meldung aufgeworfenen Frage nach der Existenz sogenannter Krebsnester, das sind Gebiete mit einer signifikanten Häufung von Krebsfällen, systematisch nachgehen will, sind Methoden der Epidemiologie (siehe nächsten Abschnitt) gefragt, die häufig rechnergestützt angewandt werden und idealerweise - aber noch selten - durch große, konsistente Datenbasen untermauert sind.

Epidemiologie und Krebsregister

Die Epidemiologie [Wahrendorf'91] insgesamt befaßt sich mit dem Studium des Auftretens von Krankheiten und ihren verursachenden Faktoren in menschlichen Populationen. Die deskriptive Epidemiologie hat zur Aufgabe, die Häufigkeit sowie zeitliche und geographische Variation chronischer Krankheiten, insbesondere auch Krebs, in der Bevölkerung zu untersuchen. Aus den in über 30 Ländern teilweise seit über 40 Jahren geführten bevölkerungsbezogenen Krebsregistern (in der Bundesrepublik Deutschland z.B. [Becker et al. '84], [Saarland '91]) werden dazu alters-, geschlechts- und ursachenspezifische Inzidenz- (im Beobachtungszeitraum neu Erkrankte), Prävalenz- (insgesamt Erkrankte) und Mortalitätsraten (im Beobachtungszeitraum Verstorbene) berechnet [Muir et al.'87]. Um diese Raten untereinander vergleichen zu können, wird eine Altersstandardisierung anhand künstlicher, normierter Standardpopulationen vorgenommen. Durch regionale Krebsregister wird versucht, Hypothesen über geographische Besonderheiten, zeitliche Trends bei den Neuerkrankungen oder auch gefährdete Personengruppen zu gewinnen und in Studien zu verifizieren.
Die unterschiedlichen Vorkommen von Krebserkrankungen bezüglich Ort und Zeit - so sie überhaupt erkannt werden - dienen als Arbeitshypothesen für eine ganze Reihe der deskriptiven Epidemiologie methodisch nachgeschalteten Studien, z.B. Korrelations-, Kohorten-, Fall-Kontroll- und Interventionsstudien. Diese Studien bedienen sich, falls vorhanden, meist auch der Krebsregister, d.h. rechnergestützter Datensammlungen mit patientenspezifischen Angaben über Krebserkrankungen und -todesfälle. Die Hypothesen stammen aber jeweils aus den Köpfen von Epidemiologen oder Medizinern.
Nicht - oder zumindest nicht durch rechnergestützte Werkzeuge begleitet - untersucht wurde bisher die automatische Generierung möglicher Hypothesen aus vorhandenen Krebsregistern.

Medizinische Anforderungen an eine Krebsregistrierung

Die Ursachenforschung für Krebserkrankungen besitzt trotz isoliert erfolgreicher Erkenntnisse immer noch weitgehend spekulativen Charakter. Es ist deshalb dringend erforderlich, umfassende Daten zu Krebserkrankungen sowie -todesfällen zu erhalten und zur Auswertung in Krebsregistern zu speichern. In den neuen Bundesländern ist dies vergleichbar vollständig geschehen, das Saarland und Hamburg sind etablierte Beispiele in den alten Bundesländern. In Niedersachsen wird dies u.a. durch den angekündigten Aufbau eines regionalen Krebsregisters forciert.
Die rechnergestützte deskriptive Krebsepidemiologie eröffnet nicht nur die Möglichkeit der Generierung von Hypothesen für Häufungen von Krebsinzidenz und -mortalität, sondern bietet auch neue Perspektiven für die anschließenden, differenzierten epidemiologischen Studien und somit schließlich eine gesichertere Basis für die aus medizinischer Sicht entscheidende Krebsbekämpfung.
Immer wieder diskutierte Faktoren wie unterschiedliche Ernährungsweise, Alkoholkonsum, Nikotinabusus, Einflüsse von Industriestandorten usw. können nur fixiert werden, wenn exakte Daten über die Krankheits- und Todesfälle einer Region erfaßt und zuzüglich zu vermutender pathogenetischer Faktoren ausgewertet werden. Dabei sind Korrelationen zu klinischen Daten (primäres Krankheitsstadium, Therapie-Maßnahmen, Langzeitverlauf) wünschenswert, um präventive und therapeutische Möglichkeiten intensivieren bzw. verbessern zu können.

2. INEKS- ein Informationssystem zur epidemiologischen Krebsforschung

Randbedingungen

Seit 1990 entwickeln die Städtischen Kliniken Oldenburg, Klinik für Innere Medizin, Prof. Dr. med. H. J. Illiger, und die Universität Oldenburg, Fachbereich Informatik bzw. OFFIS, das Oldenburger Forschungs- und Entwicklungsinstitut für Informatik-Systeme und -Werkzeuge gemeinsam mit finanzieller Unterstützung durch das Land Niedersachsen ein Informationssystem zur rechnergestützten Analyse von Krebsregistern für die epidemiologische Krebsforschung.
Das im Rahmen des Projektes INEKS (Informationssystem zur epidemiologischen Krebsforschung) schon realisierte Informationssystem gleichen Namens ergänzt eine ältere Datenbank für Tumordaten, mit der in einer Nachsorgeleitstelle für Krebspatienten als Serviceleistung für nachsorgende Ärzte sowie zur Erfüllung der Aufgaben einer Basisdokumentation für das Bundesgesundheitsamt in Berlin onkologische Daten verwaltet werden.

Datenbasis und Funktionalität

Die patientenspezifische Dokumentation von Tumordaten mit INEKS bietet u.a. folgende Datensätze:

- Patientenidentifikation
  Hier werden Patientenstammdaten (Name, Geschlecht, Geburtsdatum, Adresse, Krankenversicherung etc.) abgelegt.
- Tumor/ Diagnose
  Informationen bezüglich eines Primärtumors und dessen Diagnose (ICD-O-Schlüssel) können hier zusammengefaßt werden, z.B. Diagnosedatum, Lokalisation, Histologie des Tumors etc.
- Sekundärmanifestation
  Dieser Datensatz enthält Daten über weitere, d.h. zusätzlich zum Primärtumor diagnostizierte Tumore, u.a. das Datum und die Art der Sekundärmanifestation.
- Behandlung
  Informationen über die Behandlung (Operation, Bestrahlung oder systemische Therapie) werden in diesem Datensatz festgehalten, z.B. Art, Ziel, Beginn/ Ende, Ergebnis der Therapie. Des weiteren können zusätzliche Untertypen zu verschiedenen Therapiearten spezifiziert werden, wie z.B.
  - Strahlentherapie: u.a. Dosis, Zielgebiet, Applikationsart/-technik, Strahlenart, computergestützte Planung.
  - Chemotherapie: u.a. Wirkstoffkombination, Anzahl der Zyklen und Nebenwirkungen.
  - Hormon-/ Immuntherapie: u.a. Therapieart und Wirkstoffe.
- Nachsorge
  Hier werden Daten zu Nachsorgeterminen und -untersuchungen des Patienten, wie z.B. Beginn/ Ende der Nachsorge, gespeichert.
- Abschluß
  Dieser Datensatz gibt Auskunft darüber, wann und warum die Registrierung eines Patienten abgeschlossen wurde.

Grundlage für die Entwicklung und den Einsatz von INEKS bildet das relationale Datenbanksystem ORACLE mit den Werkzeugen CASE, SQL*Forms, SQL*ReportWriter, SQL*Graphics und Pro*C.

INEKS unterstützt über eine grafische Benutzungsoberfläche die dialogorientierte, menügesteuerte Dokumentation und Auswertung klinischer Daten zu Krebspatienten. Zur Beantwortung differenzierter medizinischer, klinisch relevanter oder administrativer Fragestellungen können die jeweiligen Ergebnisse grafisch dargestellt werden, um die Aussagekraft der Daten zu erhöhen.

INEKS-Basissystem

Bis zum Jahre 1991 wurde ein einsatzfähiges INEKS-Basissystem zur Tumordokumentation geschaffen, das die im letzten Abschnitt beschriebene Datenbasis und Funktionalität umfaßt. Das Basissystem wurde 1991/ 92 um zwei wesentliche Komponenten ergänzt und bietet derzeit zwei entsprechende Erweiterungen, die erst die Anforderungen einer - wenn auch noch nicht aktiven - DB-gestützten epidemiologischen Krebsforschung erfüllen:

- eine Komponente, mit der an die INEKS-DB temporär zusätzliche Daten angebunden werden, die zur Stützung einer epidemiologischen Hypothese gebraucht werden, wobei die SQL-Oberfläche für den Benutzer unverändert bleiben soll (Beschreibung im nächsten Abschnitt), und

- eine Komponente, mit der man die INEKS-DB mit raumbezogenen Daten von Geo-Objekten (aus der Klasse Punkt, Strecke, Polygon) wie Industriestandorte etc. in Beziehung setzen und zu epidemiologischen Hypothesen über regionale Einflußgrößen für Krebsfälle nutzen kann (Beschreibung im übernächsten Abschnitt).

Integration von DB-externen Daten und INEKS-DB

Bei der Verfolgung epidemiologischer Hypothesen besteht i.a. ein erhöhter Bedarf an Auswertungen, die ihre Daten zwar größtenteils aus einer zugrundeliegenden DB - in diesem Falle INEKS - beziehen, zusätzlich aber auch DB-externe Daten verwenden möchten, die z.B. aus Files oder hauptspeicherresidenten Datenstrukturen wie records und arrays stammen oder nur zu Testzwecken über Tastatur eingegeben werden sollen. Diese DB-externen Daten werden oft nicht in die DB integriert, weil sie z.B. nur von temporärem Interesse sind (und eine aufwendige Reorganisation des DB-Schemas nicht rechtfertigen) oder nur einen Teil der DB um zusätzliche Attribute erweitern und damit für den restlichen DB-Ausschnitt Konsistenzprobleme (Nullwerte!) aufwerfen würden.
Eine epidemiologische Krebsforschung erreicht aber erst dann die gewünschte neue Qualität, wenn die permanent in der INEKS-Datenbank gespeicherten Daten temporär mit Werten in Beziehung gebracht werden können, die aufgrund von Hypothesen über z.B. Ernährungsweise, Arbeitsplatzbedingungen usw. gezielt gesammelt werden. "Vermutungen" der Mediziner können so auf der Basis des umfangreichen gespeicherten Datenmaterials verifiziert werden und eventuell eine solche Relevanz erlangen, daß eine Erweiterung der Datenbank gerechtfertigt erscheint.

Bei der Integration von relationalen Datenbanken und DB-externen Datenstrukturen lassen sich drei Sprachschichten identifizieren:

- die "normale" relationale Datendefinition und -manipulation (hier SQL-DDL bzw. -DML)
- die Definition geeigneter Datenstrukturen und darauf anwendbarer Operationen zur Verwaltung der nur DB-externen Daten
- eine integrierte Gesamtschicht für die Abfrage und Änderung von Daten, die aus der DB stammen und/oder DB-extern sind, d.h. die ESQL (Erweitertes SQL) genannte Sprachschale kapselt die Information über Ort und Zugriffsmechanismus aller Daten.

Die entstandenen Module wurden mit Hilfe konkreter Krebsdaten und temporärer Daten von Hypothesen aus dem Weser-Ems-Bereich getestet und evaluiert. Der Prototyp bietet die Möglichkeit, weitere Erfahrungen mit der INEKS-Datenbank zu sammeln und bisher "von Hand" durchzuführende epidemiologische Arbeitshypothesen DB-gestützt prüfen zu lassen.

Raumbezogene Auswertungen

Ein weiterer wichtiger Bestandteil der epidemiologischen Krebsforschung ist die Korrelationen der Daten der INEKS-Datenbank zu geographischen Besonderheiten einer Region. Dabei soll es u.a. möglich sein, sogenannte Krebsnester zu entdecken, epidemiologische Auffälligkeiten um ein Krebsnest anzuzeigen sowie die Änderung der Häufigkeit von Krebsfällen unter Einbeziehung raumbezogener Objekte (z.B. Fluß, Hochspannungsleitung, Industrie mit Emissionen u.ä.) zu ermitteln. Dafür wurde SQL um epidemiologisch relevante, topologische und metrische Operatoren zur Sprache GSQL (Geo-SQL) erweitert.

Solche Operatoren in GSQL sind u.a.

- "along_of": Bestimmung der Häufigkeit von Krebsfällen entlang eines "Weges" wie z.B. eines Flusses
- "point_of": Bestimmung eines signifikanten Punktes, z.B. des Zentrums eines Krebsnestes, innerhalb eines Gebietes
- "near_by": Betrachtung der Krebsfälle innerhalb eines Gebietes um einen signifikanten Punkt, z.B. um ein Krebsnest herum (siehe Abb. 2.1).

Die Abbildung geo-relationaler Operatoren auf eine relationale DML wie QUEL oder SQL ist - wie schon vergleichbare Versuche gezeigt haben - i.a. sehr laufzeitintensiv, aber in der hier betrachteten Anwendungsklasse mit Einbenutzer-Arbeitsplätzen und keiner Erwartung bezüglich unmittelbarer Antworten des Systems zeitunkritisch.

Die konkrete Realisierung der Zuordnung der Wohnadresse von Krebspatienten zu Geo-Koordinaten (wie z.B. Gauß-Krüger-Koordinaten im Raster von 100 m x 100 m im Hamburger Krebsregister) ist bei einem Flächenland wie Niedersachsen - insbesondere in der ländlichen Weser-Ems-Region - problematisch. Die bisherige Zuordnung der Adresse zu den Koordinaten eines virtuellen Mittelpunktes der Gemeinde, zu der die Wohnadresse gehört, ist eine gute Lösung, weil die Fallzahlen sehr gering sind. Eine Präzisierung bezüglich unterschiedlicher Gemeindegrößen und eine DV-technische Unterstützung durch geeignete Schlüsseltabellen wird im Rahmen der Etablierung des niedersächsischen Krebsregisters notwendig sein.

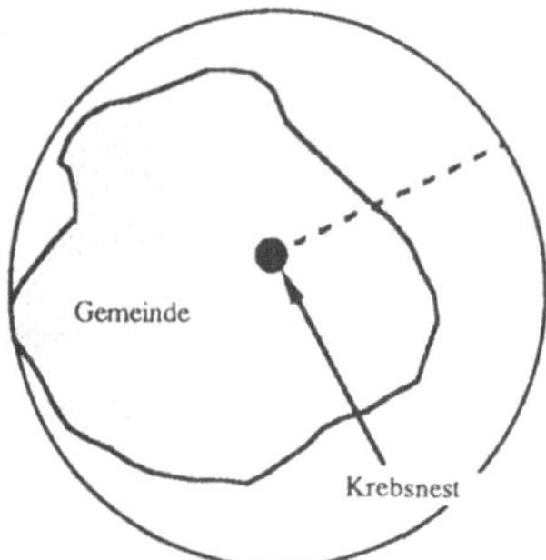

Abb. 2.1 Betrachtung der Erkrankungshäufigkeit um ein Krebsnest

GSQL wurde wie ESQL als anwendungsneutrale Sprache entwickelt, und kann damit in anderen Applikationen mit ähnlichen Anforderungen bezüglich einer Integration DB-externer Daten und des Raumbezugs zugrundeliegender Daten der INEKS-DB verwendet werden.

Das bisherige INEKS ist mit diesen beiden Erweiterungen (ESQL und GSQL) ein Informationsystem, das Elemente moderner Nichtstandard-Datenbanken bietet wie

- eine gewisse Flexibilität des zugrundeliegenden Schemas, da temporär zusätzliche Attribute integriert und bei Bedarf ins Schema übernommen werden können, und
- eine auf Raumdaten bezogene Abfragesprache.

3. Active_INEKS - eine aktive Krebs-Datenbank

Vision einer "aktiven Epidemiologie"

Die Arbeit mit INEKS und vergeichbaren DB-gestützten Krebsregistern hat aus epidemiologischer Sicht (und nicht nur aus dieser!) ein entscheidendes methodisches Defizit, das in folgender These plakativ und überspitzt formuliert ist.

These: *Man findet Krebsnester bisher nicht in Krebsregistern, selbst wenn sie DB-gestützt praktisch vollständige Angaben über Krebsinzidenz und -mortalität einer Region enthalten, sondern nur zufällig aufgrund von unmittelbaren, Register-unabhängigen Beobachtungen aufmerksamer Mediziner oder Epidemiologen.*

Dies ist unmittelbar einsichtig, da die Krebsregister ihr mögliches Wissen über signifikante Krebshäufungen ja nicht von sich aus preisgeben, sondern erst auf eine darauf gezielte, konkrete Abfrage eines Benutzers. Aber dann liegt diese Hypothese über eine Signifikanz schon vorher vor und soll "nur" noch verifiziert werden .... Nur die "Negativmeldung", daß die gestellte Hypothese durch das Register nicht zu untermauern ist, kommt vom System. Diese Systemleistung wird nicht publik, während die "Positivmeldung" der menschliche Hypothesenfinder für sich reklamieren wird.

Hier setzt die Vision einer aktiven Datenbank ein: sie enthält im "normalen" DB-Teil personenbezogene Krebsdaten, Informationen zu Bevölkerung und Struktur der Region, aus der die gemeldeten Krebsfälle stammen, sowie standardisierte Raten etwa zu alters,- ursachen- und geschlechtsspezifischer Krebsinzidenz und -mortalität. Eine solche passive DB ist nun um ein Laufzeitsystem zu ergänzen, das bei Eintritt von Ereignissen die Relevanz von Regeln prüft und ggfls. deren Aktionen ausführt. In die Regeln wird epidemiologisches Wissen codiert, indem auf Raum und Zeit bezogene Auffälligkeiten als globale Hypothesen geeignet repräsentiert werden. Deren Variablen werden dann kontinuierlich mit konkreten Geo-Objekten und Zeitmarken instantiiert und im Erfolgsfall als konkrete Hypothesen automatisch vom System generiert. Das System (re)agiert mit dieser konkreten Hypothese dann vermeintlich selbständig, obwohl ja nur eine passende Belegung einer globalen Hypothese gefunden wurde.

Abb. 3.1 zeigt die mögliche Entwicklung von einer "normalen", passiven, nur auf gezielte Abfragen hin reagierenden DB (links in der Abb.) zu einer aktiven, auch auf DB-Änderungen oder auch nur durch das Verstreichen von Zeit hin mit "Antworten" und Hinweisen "von sich aus" reagierenden DB (rechts in der Abb.).

Konzept einer aktiven Datenbank

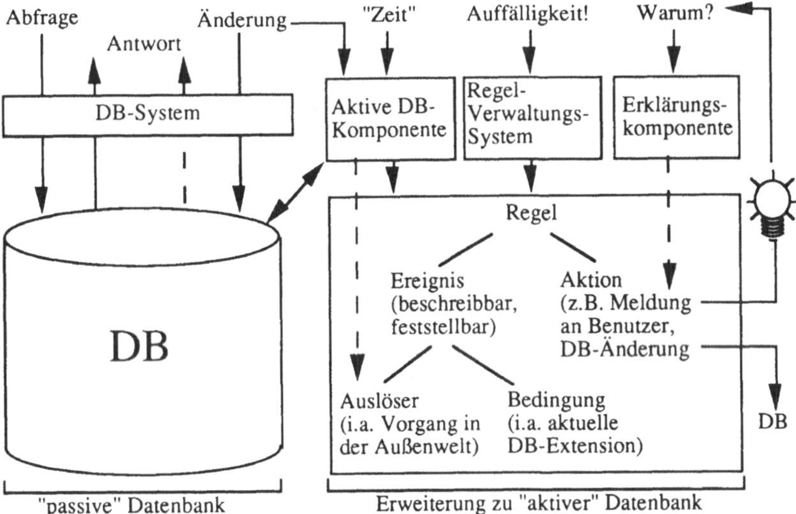

Abb. 3.1 Von der passiven zu einer aktiven Datenbank

Die *passive Datenbank* gibt ihr Wissen grundsätzlich nur auf genau darauf zielende Abfragen durch Antworten preis. Auch Änderungen können zu einer sichtbaren Reaktion führen, aber nur dann, wenn etwa Konsistenzbedingungen durch ein Update verletzt werden.

Ein *aktives DB-System* erfordert mindestens drei, im folgenden weiter beschriebene Komponenten: ein Regel-Verwaltungssystem, eine aktive DB-Komponente (in engem Zusammenspiel mit der passiven DB und einem Ausführungsmodell für die Regeln) und schließlich eine Erklärungskomponente.

Das *Regel-Verwaltungssystem* bereitet den Einsatz einer aktiven Datenbank vor. Hier sind Auffälligkeiten (und die nach ihrer Feststellung gewünschte Behandlung) zu definieren, die konkret in Form von Regeln als Ereignis-Aktions-Paare spezifiziert werden:

- ein Ereignis muß beschreib- und feststellbar sein und setzt sich i.a. aus zwei Bestandteilen zusammen: der Spezifikation möglicherweise eintretender und zum Ereignis führender, von "außen" kommender Auslöser und einer zusätzlich vorliegenden, i.a. auf die DB-bezogenen, "inneren" Bedingung
- eine Aktion, die dann auszuführen ist, wenn das Ereignis eintritt, d.h. die Prämissen zum "Feuern" der Regel vorliegen.

Die *aktive DB-Komponente*

- erhält Änderungen der Außenwelt in Form von DB-Updates und Informationen über die "Zeit" (Erreichen von Zeitpunkten, Verstreichen von Zeitintervallen usw.)
- prüft, ob damit Ereignisse eingetreten sind, die aufgrund der Regelspezifikation zu Aktionen führen müssen
- führt ggfls. entsprechende Aktionen durch und hält Abhängigkeiten in Form dadurch eintretender neuer Auslöser, die wiederum zu relevanten Ereignissen führen können, nach
- greift bei Bedarf auf die passive DB zu, um Informationen über die aktuelle DB-Extension zu erhalten
- hinterlegt evtl. auch Ergebnisse, die bei einer möglicherweise notwendigen Erklärung an den Benutzer verwendet werden können.

Die *Erklärungskomponente* liefert - im besten Fall nach Benutzerprofil und -wünschen differenziert - Erläuterungen zu Systemreaktionen. Im Vergleich zu passiven Datenbanken, wo Reaktionen des DB-Systems immer direkten Bezug zu unmittelbar vorhergehenden Eingaben des Benutzers haben, wird bei einer aktiven DB mit Systemreaktionen ohne vorhergehende Benutzeranforderung ein erhöhter Erklärungsbedarf bestehen.

Der Einsatz einer aktiven DB sollte in der Regel zeitunkritisch sein, da der Benutzer nicht auf eine Antwort wartet, da er ja auch gar nichts gefragt hat (keine Erwartungshaltung). Die Idee ist, daß aktive Datenbanken evtl. zeitverzögert zum eingetretenen Ereignis bzw. Auslöser Phasen nutzen, in denen der Rechner nicht so ausgelastet ist. Anschaulich gesprochen reicht es in vielen Anwendungen, wenn Aktionen mit Verzögerung zum Auslösereintritt eingeleitet werden (Beispiel: "Der Hinweis auf ein Krebsnest kann auch Montagmorgen erst vorliegen, selbst wenn die letzte auslösende Erkrankungsmeldung am Freitag eingegangen ist").

Entwicklung von INEKS zu einer aktiven Datenbank

Das in Kapitel 2 vorgestellte INEKS ist in dem Sinne eine passive DB, als Antworten zum Krebsregister nur direkt auf Abfragen des Benutzers erfolgen. Vielfach ist es jedoch wünschenswert, daß auch Ereignisse wie Änderungen des Datenbestandes durch Krebsmeldungen Aktionen auslösen. So sollte für die epidemiologische Krebsforschung das Auftreten von Krebsfällen zur Generierung entsprechender Hypothesen führen, die anschließend geprüft werden müssen. Durch die Weiterentwicklung von INEKS zu Active_INEKS, einem aktiven Informationssystem zur Krebsepidemiologie, soll die Suche nach Korrelationen zwischen vorhandenen Daten bzw. nach regional begrenzten Häufungen spezieller Krebsarten, den sogenannten Krebsnestern, automatisiert werden.

Ein Ereignis kann von zeitlicher Natur sein, wie etwa die Änderung eines Wertes um mindestens 20% in höchstens 30 Tagen, auf das mit einer Aktion automatisch reagiert wird, z.B. durch die Benachrichtigung einer zuständigen Person. Ein Ereignis kann sich auch auszeichnen durch eine überdurchschnittliche Häufung von Einträgen zu geographisch eingegrenzten Objekten, die topologisch (z.B. als Nachbarschaftsbeziehung) oder metrisch (z.B. durch Abstandsangabe) spezifiziert sind. Die ausgelösten Aktionen müssen dem Benutzer angemessen präsentiert und geeignet erklärt werden können.

Beispiel für eine Hypothese: `Schilddrüsenkrebs ist in Küstennähe weniger häufig als im Durchschnitt der Weser-Ems-Region.`

Anmerkung: Um eine derartige Hypothese "seriös" testen zu können, muß sie methodisch abgesichert statistisch aufbereitet werden. Dazu wird mittels einer "Schätzer"-Funktion ein Erwartungswert - in diesem Fall für Schilddrüsenkrebs in Küstennähe - berechnet. Dieser Wert hängt von der Alterstruktur der Bewohner in Küstennähe und in der Weser-Ems-Region, von der Bevölkerungsdichte in den beiden Gebieten, von den Fallzahlen in den betrachteten Gebieten, dem Meldeverhalten der Ärzte usw. ab.
Durch ein geeignetes Testverfahren wird nun zu einem festgelegten Signifikanzniveau geprüft, ob Unterschiede in den Fallzahlen von Schilddrüsenkrebs in der Küsten- bzw. Weser-Ems-Region Zufall sind oder nicht.

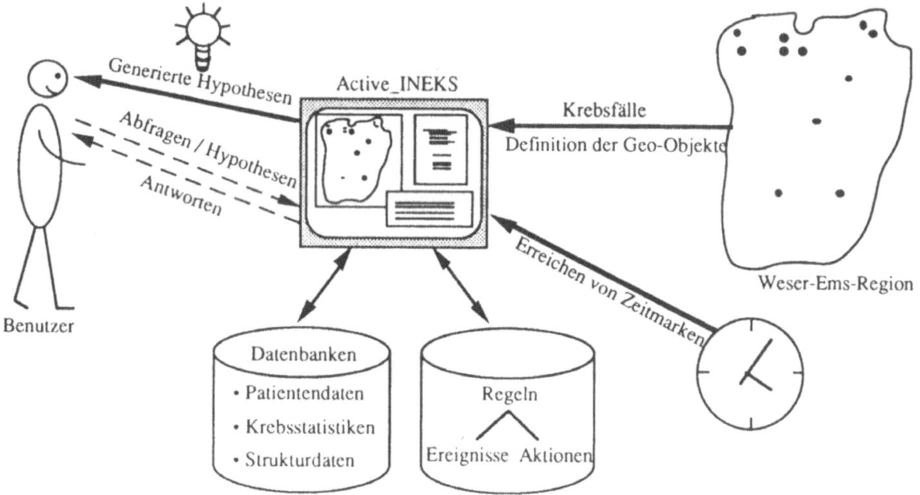

Abb. 3.2 Anwendungs-Szenario von Active_INEKS

In der Abb. 3.2 ist in Anlehnung an Abb. 3.1 das Szenario von Active_INEKS skizziert. Neben der üblichen Frage-Antwort-Interaktion wird beim Auftreten signifikanter Ereignisse, wie Eintragen neuer Patienten, Definition neuer Erfassungsregionen oder Erreichen von Zeitmarken, eine entsprechende Aktion, z.B. Überprüfung auf Häufungspunkte und evtl. anschließende Meldung an den Epidemiologen, automatisch durchgeführt. Dazu benutzt Active_INEKS Patienten- und Strukturdaten sowie Krebsstatistiken in Form geschlechts- und altersstandardisierter Raten. Das Wissen über die automatisch durchzuführenden Aktivitäten wird mit Hilfe der Ereignis-Aktions-Regeln beschrieben, die Ereignisse definieren, auf die das System mit spezifizierten Aktionen "aktiv" reagiert.

Active_INEKS überprüft Hypothesen selbständig, indem es beim Auftreten relevanter Ereignisse die notwendigen Aktionen durchführt. Relevante Ereignisse für Active_INEKS sind

- DB-Ereignisse: z.B. das Einfügen der Daten eines neuen Krebspatienten,
- Geo-Ereignisse: z.B. Ändern von Flächen innerhalb eines beobachteten Gebiets,
- Zeit-Ereignisse: z.B. das Erreichen eines Überprüfungszeitpunktes.

Beispiel für ein relevantes DB-Ereignis: `5 Schilddrüsenkrebsfälle in einem Jahr in Küstennähe.`

Solche Ereignisse können Aktionen auslösen. Aktionen sind einzeln ausführbare Programmfragmente, die aus Befehlen bestehen. Einzelne Befehle sind z.B. DB-Abfragen oder Datenmanipulationen, aber auch Berechnungen und Ausgaben an der Benutzungsoberfläche oder das Erzeugen "neuer" Ereignisse. Befehle können zu zusammengesetzten Aktionen verknüpft werden.

Beispiel für eine zusammengesetzte Aktion:

```
Suche alle Fälle von Schilddrüsenkrebs in Küstennähe: N_K
Bestimme die zugehörige Bevölkerung in Küstennähe: B_K
Bilde die Rate E_K = N_K/B_K * 100.000
Suche alle nicht zu N_K gehörenden Fälle von Schilddrüsenkrebs: N_R
Bestimme die nicht zu B_K gehörende Bevölkerung: B_R
Bilde die Rate E_R = N_R/B_R * 100.000
Falls E_K<2/3E_R melde "Schilddrüsenkrebs in Küstennähe signifikant weniger häufig"
```

Diese vereinfacht dargestellte Aktion überprüft die o.a. Hypothese zum Schilddrüsenkrebs, wobei Signifikanz angenommen wird, sobald die Standardrate in Küstennähe kleiner als 2/3 der Standardrate in der übrigen Region ist. Diese Aktion kann der Epidemiologe auch als "normale" Abfrage vom System evaluieren lassen. Ist die Hypothese aufgrund des vorhandenen Datenmaterials nicht verifizierbar, so wird in herkömmlichen Systemen eine solche Abfrage nach einiger Zeit oder nach Einfügen weiterer Daten vom Benutzer wiederholt. In Active_INEKS besteht demgegenüber die Möglichkeit, diese Aktion abhängig von Zeit- oder Update-Ereignissen zu spezifizieren. Dadurch wird die Hypothese beim Auftreten der definierten Ereignisse überprüft und das jeweilige Ergebnis dem Epidemiologen automatisch vom System mitgeteilt. Dieses selbstständige Vorgehen des Systems wird als ereignisgesteuertes aktives Verhalten bezeichnet.

4. Eine integrierte Entwicklungsumgebung für Active_INEKS

Für die Realisierung von Active_INEKS muß die Funktionalität herkömmlicher DB-Entwicklungsumgebungen insbesondere um die Möglichkeit zur Beschreibung von ereignisgesteuertem aktiven Verhalten erweitert werden. Die sogenannten aktiven Datenbanken (siehe z.B. [Dayal et al.'88], [Gatzia et al.'91]) unterstützen ein derartiges automatisches Ausführen von Aktionen beim Auftreten auslösender Ereignisse. Sie bieten dazu regelorientierte Spracherweiterungen, wie u.a. in [Beeri/ Milo'91], [Chakaravarthy'90], [Hanson'92], [Hull/Jacobs'91], [McCarthy/ Dayal'89], [Rosenthal et al.'89], [Schreier et al'91], [Stonebraker et al.'90] und [Widom et al'91] beschrieben. Eine Regel besteht in den dort beschriebenen Ansätzen aus jeweils einem Ereignis-, Bedingungs- und Aktionsteil. Das Erkennen eines in einer Regel spezifizierten Ereignisses löst die Überprüfung der zugehörigen Bedingung und bei positivem Ergebnis die Ausführung der Operationen der entsprechenden Aktion aus. Diese sogenannten Event-Condition-Action-(ECA-)Regeln berücksichtigen üblicherweise nur DB- und Zeitereignisse, die durch boolesche Operatoren miteinander verknüpft werden.

Für Active-INEKS wird eine AIS genannte DB-Entwicklungsumgebung realisiert, die eine derartige Regelsprache in der L-AIS-Schicht (Languages for Active Information Systems, siehe Abb. 4.1) zur Beschreibung von ereignisgesteuertem aktiven Verhalten beinhaltet. Die Regeln bestehen aus einem evtl. sehr komplexen Ereignis- und einem Aktionsteil. Aus den bereits in Kapitel 1 beschriebenen Anforderungen wird ersichtlich, daß Ereignisse aus so unterschiedlichen Bereichen wie "DB, Geo oder Zeit" beschreibbar und erkennbar sein müssen. Für diese unterschiedlichen Bereiche werden jeweils abstrakte Datentypen bereitgestellt, die sogenannte Primärereignisse und atomare Aktionen mit entsprechenden Parametern anbieten und Schnittstellen zu existierenden Systemen sind. Eine solche Schnittstelle mit ihren Typen, Primärereignissen und atomaren Aktionen wird im folgenden Modell genannt. Im einzelnen sind für Active_INEKS ein Datenmodell, ein Zeitmodell, ein Geo-Modell, ein Statistik-Modell und das Modell einer Benutzungsschnittstelle (UIMS: User Interface Manangement System) vorgesehen, siehe die I-AIS-Schicht (Interfaces for Active Information Systems) in Abb. 4.1. Bei der Realisierung stützen sich diese Modelle auf die in Kapitel 2 beschriebene Funktionalität des erweiterten INEKS-Basissystems (für DB und Geo), auf ein Zeitnetzverwaltungssystem (siehe [Ossowski'92]) und auf ein existierendes UIMS (X-Fantasy, siehe [Götze'92]) ab.

In Abb. 4.1 wird auch der Werkzeugkasten T-AIS (Tools for Active Information Systems) zur Realisierung von AIS-Anwendungen wie Active_INEKS angedeutet. Im wesentlichen baut dieser auf der Sprache L-AIS auf, die Schnittstellen zur Datenbank, zum Geo-, zum Statistik- und zum Zeitmodell sowie zum Modell der Benutzungsoberfläche nutzt. Dem Anwendungsentwickler sollen Werkzeuge wie Texteditoren zur Erstellung von Programmen, Browser zur Visualisierung von Schemata, Daten und Regeln sowie grafische Modellierer zur Verfügung stehen. Letztere bieten grafische Sprachen für die Spezifikation von Konzepten und Beziehungen; dies sind sowohl Objekte und deren Attribute als auch Ereignisse und zugehörige Aktionen. Zur Reduktion der Komplexität werden die Grafiken thematisch (z.B. nach Geo-Attributen oder zeitabhängigen Beziehungen) geschichtet (siehe [Jasper'92]). Die Ergebnisse einer solchen grafischen Modellierung werden unter Mitwirkung des Anwendungsentwicklers in L-AIS-Programme überführt.

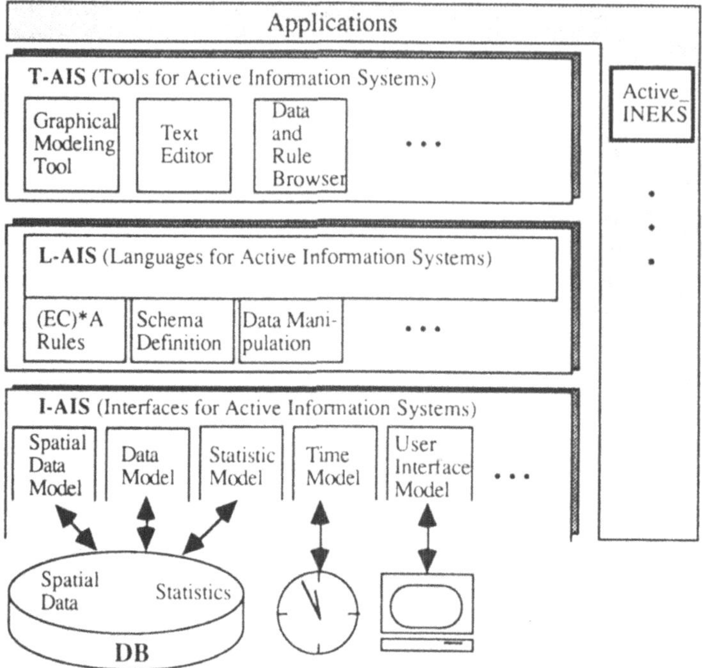

Abb. 4.1 AIS-Entwicklungsumgebung

Im folgenden werden die I-AIS- und L-AIS-Schicht der Entwicklungsumgebung genauer betrachtet.

I-AIS: Modelle für existierende Systeme

Die für Active_INEKS vorgesehenen Modelle in der I-AIS-Schicht sind

- Das DB-Datenmodell: Es bietet die Operatoren INSERT, DELETE, UPDATE und READ zur Datenmanipulation. Das Ausführen eines solchen Operators löst ein DB-Ereignis aus. Ebenso werden Transaktionsereignisse wie TRANS_BEGIN, TRANS_COMMIT und TRANS_ABORT unterstützt.

- Das Geo-Modell: Es bietet die Datentypen POINT, LINE, POLYGON und REGION sowie die Operatoren DISTANCE, INTERSECTION und INSIDE, ALONG_OF, POINT_OF und NEAR_BY mit denen im Zusammenhang mit DB-Ereignissen komplexe Geo-Ereignisse wie das Definieren oder Ändern einer Region beschrieben werden können.

- Das Statistikmodell: Aufbauend auf den üblichen Zahlentypen bietet das Statistikmodell vordefinierte Verfahren für statistische Tests, z.B. den χ^2-Test (siehe [Hartung/Klösener'91]), sowie Ereignisse in Form von erkannten signifikanten Fallzahlen, Quoten oder Risiken. In dem Statistikmodell wird ein neues, sequentielles Testverfahren realisiert, das gegenüber klassischen Statistiktests "Ausreißer" in den Fallzahlen, Quoten oder Risiken findet, sobald diese erkennbar sind.

Dem gegenüber muß bei den klassischen Statistiktests immer eine bestimmte Menge an Stichproben vorhanden sein, bevor eine Hypothese verworfen wird oder feststeht, daß keine Aussage gemacht werden kann (in der Statistik werden typischerweise nur negative Aussagen geprüft). Damit nicht erst nach mehreren Jahren (wie aufgrund der geringen Fallzahlen zu erwarten ist) statistisch signifikante Aussagen über Krebsursachen möglich sind, prüft das hier betrachtete sequentielle Verfahren zu genau festgesetzten Zeitpunkten, ob die Fallzahlen, Quoten oder Risiken zu einer Hypothese ein vorgegebenes Signifikanzniveau überschreiten, wie in der folgenden Abb. 4.2 dargestellt. Sobald ein solcher Fall eintritt, bricht das Verfahren die weitere Analyse ab und liefert als Ereignis z.B. eine signifikante Quote.

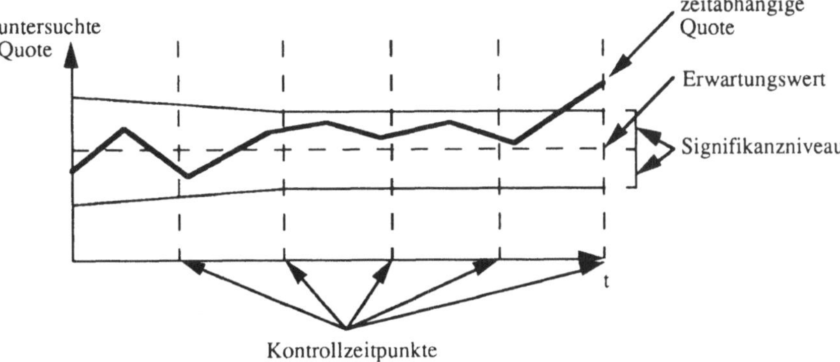

Abb. 4.2 Sequentielles statistisches Testverfahren

- Das Zeitmodell: Es kennt die Typen T_POINT und T_INTERVALL sowie die Operatoren BEFORE, AFTER und DURING. Als Ereignisse werden das Erreichen einer Zeitmarke, das Verstreichen eines Zeitintervalls etc. erkannt, die im wesentlichen von einer Systemuhr überwacht werden.
- Das Benutzungsmodell: Es stellt Operationen eines User Interface Management Sytems zur Verfügung. Es liefert auch anwendungsspezifische Ereignisse, etwa erzeugt durch Menüauswahl oder Selektion von Objekten.

L-AIS: Die Programmiersprache für aktives Verhalten

Die von den Modellen der I-AIS-Schicht bereitgestellten Primärereignisse und primitiven Aktionen werden als Sprachelemente in den Ereignis-Aktions-Regeln genutzt. Letztere werden hier (EC)*A-Regeln genannt und sind neben den Elementen zur Datendefinition und -manipulation die zentralen Konstrukte der Sprache L-AIS, die den Sprachkern der Entwicklungsumgebung darstellt. In den (EC)*A-Regeln können Primärereignisse zu komplexen Ereignissen kombiniert werden, damit Ereignisse wie

"das Auftreten von 5 Schilddrüsenkrebsfällen in einem Jahr in Küstennähe" (e_{SK})

in Active_INEKS modelliert werden können. Abb. 4.3 zeigt einen Auszug aus der (EC)*A-Regel-Syntax.

```
(EC)*A_Rule                   ::= Composed_Event_Type "->" Action_Specification

Basic_Event_Type              ::= <modellspezifischer Ereignistyp>

Condition                     ::= <boolesche Funktion>

Composed_Event_Type           ::=   Basic_Event_Type
                                  | Composed_Event_Type "AND" Condition
                                  | Composed_Event_Type "AND" Composed_Event_Type
                                  | Composed_Event_Type "OR" Composed_Event_Type
                                  | "COUNT(" Composed_Event_Type ")) Op Expression
                                  | Ext_Composite_Event_Type

Ext_Composite_Event_Type      ::=  <modellspezifischer Ereignistyp-Konstruktor>

Action_Specification          ::=   Basic_Action_Specification
                                  | Action_Specification ";" Action_Specification
                                  | Condition "->" Action_Specification

Basic_Action_Specification ::=      "CreateEvent("Basic_Event_Type")"
                                  | <modellspezifische Aktion>
:  .  .
```

Abb. 4.3 Auszüge aus der (EC)*A-Regel-Syntax

Anmerkung: *Zur Zeit diskutieren wir einen weiteren Sprachansatz, bei dem Regeln in der Form "Ereignis - Bedingung - Folgeereignis(se)" betrachtet werden. Das führt zu einfacheren Ereignisbeschreibungen mit der Folge, daß evtl. mehr Regeln als bei der (EC)*A-Syntax zur Spezifaktion von gewünschtem aktiven Verhalten notwendig sind.*

Bei der Spezifikation von komplexen Ereignissen können in den (EC)*A-Regeln Primärereignisse sowohl modellinhärent (z.B. zwei DB-Ereignisse) als auch modellübergreifend (z.B. ein Zeitereignis mit einem DB-Ereignis) zusammengesetzt werden. Um jedoch die "Schilddrüsenkrebsfälle" im obigen Ereignis (e_{SK}) modellieren zu können, ist eine weitere Steigerung der Ausdrucksmächtigkeit für die Spezifikation von komplexen Ereignissen notwendig. Dieses wird durch Bedingungen erreicht, die über Systemkomponenten, insbesondere über den Zustand der Datenbank und den Werten der Ereignisparameter Aussagen machen. Hierzu werden von den oben beschriebenen Modellen boolesche Funktionen angeboten, die mit den üblichen Junktoren (AND, OR, NOT) verknüpfbar sind. Im Ereignisteil von (EC)*A-Regeln können Ereignisse und Bedingungen zu sogenannten logischen Ereignissen kombiniert werden.

Ein logisches Ereignis ist ein Primär- oder komplexes Ereignis, an das eine Bedingung geknüpft ist, geschrieben E' = E AND B (E ist ein Ereignis, B eine Bedingung). E' tritt dann ein, wenn beim Eintreten von E die Bedingung B gilt. Somit können Primärereignisse und Bedingungen in beliebiger Reihenfolge mit Junktoren aus der (EC)*A-Syntax (z.B. dem Zählkonstruktor COUNT) oder mit modellspezifischen Konstruktoren (wie AFTER(E1, E2) aus dem Zeitmodell) zu komplexen Ereignissen kombiniert werden. Eine geschachtelte Kombination von Ereignissen und Bedingungen wird in der Literatur nur bei [Gehani et al.'92] beschrieben, wobei aber lediglich DB- und Zeitereignisse diskutiert werden. Dieser Ansatz unterscheidet sich von SAMOS ([Gatziu/Dittrich'93]) durch die explizite Integration anwendungsspezifischer Ereignistypen aus den Bereichen Geo und Statistik.

Die Spezifikation des komplexen Ereignisses e_{SK} kann in (EC)*A wie folgt aussehen:

```
E1   =  INSERT(Patient)
B1   =  Patient.Wohnort INSIDE Küstenregion
        AND Patient.Befund = Schilddrüsenkrebs
E2   =  E1 AND B1
eSK  =  (COUNT(E2) DURING 1 YEAR) ≥ 5
```

Abarbeitung von (EC)*A-Regeln

Die Überprüfung des (EC)*-Teils einer Regel geschieht mit Hilfe eines Automaten (für jede Regel ist ein solcher Automat definiert). Dieser erkennt die durch den (EC)*-Ausdruck spezifizierten Ereignisse. Damit nicht alle Automaten bei jedem eintretenden Primärereignis überprüft werden müssen, wird zu jedem Automaten eine Menge sogenannter Initialisierungsereignisse spezifiziert, die ihn in einen Anfangszustand versetzen, sobald eines der in dieser Menge spezifizierten Ereignisse eintritt. Der Automat führt bei darauf folgenden, relevanten Ereignissen Zustandsübergänge aus, bis er in einen das Ereignis erkennenden Endzustand gelangt. Der Algorithmus in PASCAL-ähnlichem Pseudo-Code für den Automaten, der das obige komplexe Ereignis e_{SK} erkennt, sieht wie folgt aus:

```
Automat für eSK
  Initialisierungsereignisse = {INSERT(Patient) und keine Kopie
                                dieses Automaten existiert};
  LOOP
     IF INSERT(Patient) AND
        Patient.Wohnort INSIDE Küstenregion AND
        Patient.Befund = Schilddrüsenkrebs
     THEN Speichere <Patient, Aktuelles_Datum, Speicher>
     END
     IF Anzahl_Tupel(Speicher) ≥ 5
     THEN IF DISTANCE(Aktuelles_Datum, Erstes_Tupel(Speicher).Datum) ≤ 1 YEAR
          THEN Ereignis erkannt
          ELSE Lösche(Erstes Tupel im Speicher)
          END
     END
  END LOOP
```

Abb. 4.4 Algorithmus zur Erkennung von e_{SK}

Der AIS-Regel-Interpreter realisiert die ereignisgesteuerte Regelauswahl und Aktionsausführung mit Hilfe einer Blackboard-Architektur. Es wird angenommen, daß Primärereignisse in einer definierten Reihenfolge ankommen und in einer Ereignisschlange (Eventqueue) gespeichert werden. Der Interpreter entnimmt ihr das jeweils nächste Primärereignis, initialisiert - wenn notwendig - entsprechende Kopien von Automaten auf dem Blackboard und versucht dann, bei allen auf dem Blackboard existierenden Automaten Zustandsübergänge durchzuführen. Für alle Automaten, die in einen Endzustand gelangen, wird dann die zugehörige Aktion ausgeführt, wobei auch neue Ereignisse erzeugt und an die Ereignisschlange angefügt werden können. Danach werden die Automaten, die in einem Endzustand gelangt waren, vom Blackboard gelöscht. In dem vorgestellten Modell können sich mehrere Kopien für den Automaten einer Regel gleichzeitig auf dem Blackboard befinden, die aber jeweils in einem anderen aktuellen Zustand sind. Abb. 4.5 skizziert die Kontroll-Schleife des AIS-Regel-Interpreters.

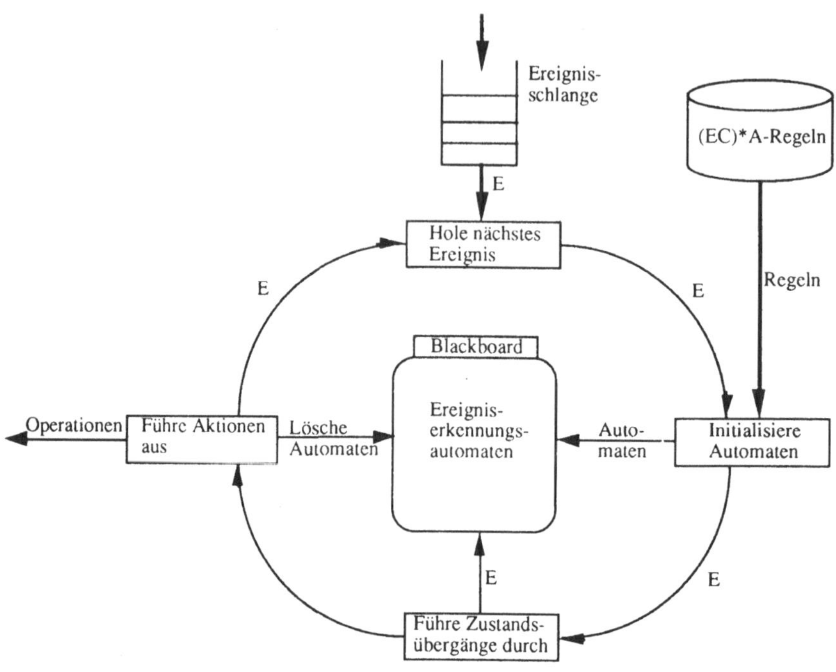

Abb. 4.5 Kontroll-Schleife des AIS-Regel-Interpreters

Für den hier vorgestellten Interpreter existieren noch einige offene Fragen.

- Die Semantik des umgangssprachlichen Ausdrucks "das Auftreten von 5 Schilddrüsenkrebsfällen in einem Jahr in Küstennähe" ist nicht eindeutig, denn während im Beispiel beim erstmaligen Auftreten der spezifizierten 5 Schilddrüsenkrebsfälle eine entsprechende Meldung wohl stets als richtig empfunden wird, bleibt unklar, ob überhaupt und in welcher Art "Folgemeldungen" erwartet werden. Treten etwa 20 Fälle von Schilddrüsenkrebs in einem Jahr in der Küstenregion auf, so werden bei dem hier vorgestellten Interpreter-Modell 4 Ereignisse erkannt und entsprechend viermal die zugehörige Aktion ausgeführt. Denkbar aber wäre auch eine einmalige Meldung oder als anderes Extrem weitere 15 Ausgaben, nämlich jeweils eine pro Überschreitung des Schwellwertes
- Bisher ist die Komplexitätsklasse der Automaten für die Erkennung von Ereignissen noch offen, jedoch werden bei den hier vorgesehenen (EC)*-Ausdrücken (im Gegensatz zu [Gehani et al.'92]) endliche Automaten nicht ausreichen, wie aus folgendem Beispiel "COUNT(E_1) = COUNT(E_2)" für beliebige Ereignisse E_1 und E_2, das der Sprachklasse $\{A^nB^n | n \in \mathbb{N}\}$ entspricht, ersichtlich ist.
- Die Problematik der Integration des DB-Transaktionsmanagers in die Regelausführung wurde hier nicht behandelt. Im Gegensatz zu den meisten Arbeiten zu aktiven Datenbanken ist für die hier betrachtete Anwendung Active_INEKS eine zeitliche Entkopplung von Updates der DB und davon ausgelösten Hypothesenüberprüfungen durchaus sinnvoll, wie schon in Kapitel 3 dargestellt. Daher ist zu

prüfen, ob die aus der Literatur bekannten unterschiedlichen Kopplungsmodi für DB-Transaktionen und Regelausführung bei der Realisierung des AIS-Laufzeitsystems unberücksichtigt bleiben können.

5. Ausblick

Eine Arbeitsgruppe "Aktive Informationssysteme", bestehend aus drei wissenschaftlichen Mitarbeitern und unterstützt durch eine studentische Projektgruppe (zweisemestrige Lehrveranstaltung zur arbeitsteiligen Erstellung eines komplexen Softwaresystems) mit 12 Mitgliedern, implementiert bis Herbst 1993 eine prototypische AIS-Entwicklungsumgebung.

Als erste Anwendung wird mit dieser Entwicklungsumgebung Active_INEKS realisiert, mit dem auch ein Beitrag für das im Aufbau befindliche Niedersächsische Krebsregister geleistet werden soll. Abb. 5.1 zeigt den Entwurf einer im Original farbigen Benutzungsoberfläche für einen Active_INEKS-Prototypen mit folgenden Fenstern (von oben nach unten und von links nach rechts):

- *Weser-Ems-Region*: Hier soll die für die Anwendung relevante Region grafisch veranschaulicht werden, indem alle Gemeinden (Städte und Landkreise) der Weser-Ems-Region in ihrer räumlichen Ausdehnung repräsentiert werden. Die Gebiete sind maussensitiv aktivierbar und deaktivierbar sowie je nach Auswertungsergebnis gestellter Abfragen farbig darstellbar (z.B. von dunkelrot für signifikante Häufung von Krebsfällen bis dunkelgrün für "normale" Gebiete, wie es bei Krebsatlanten üblich ist).

- *Regional-Informationen*: Zu den aktivierten Gebieten sollen Regional-Informationen verfügbar sein, die in dem Regional-Informations-System RIS der Arbeitsstelle DIALOG der Universität Oldenburg für die gesamte Region verfügbar sind (z.Zt. sechs Datenbanken mit beispielsweise Daten zu Struktur und Konjunktur, Unternehmen, Gewerbeflächen usw. aus 13 Städten und Landkreisen der Weser-Ems-Region, die kontinuierlich von diesen aktualisiert und von ihnen sowie anderen Interessenten "on line" genutzt werden).

- *Regel-Editor*: In diesem, nur für den Systemadministrator oder für den zur Regel-Manipulation und damit zur Änderung des Signifikanzmodells (!) berechtigten Benutzer verfügbaren Fenster sollen durch einen syntax-gesteuerten Editor die Regeln eingegeben, gelöscht und geändert sowie einige Tests bzw. Plausibilitätsprüfungen durchgeführt werden können.

- *INEKS-Patientendaten*: Hier wird ein kleiner Ausschnitt der patientenbezogenen Daten aus dem INEKS-Basissystem vorgehalten, da dies dem Epidemiologen den oft gewünschten Zugriff auf die zur Signifikanz beitragenden Einzelfälle gestatten. Auch benutzerdefinierte SQL-, GSQL- oder ESQL-Abfragen sollen hier absetzbar sein.

- *Krebs-Statistik*: Dieses Fenster ist das für den epidemiologischen Benutzer wohl entscheidende, da es in komprimierter Form die wichtigsten Informationen zur Krebsmortalität, -inzidenz und -prävalenz in Form von Balkendiagrammen vergleichend zu Standardraten präsentiert. Die Informationswünsche sollen sich mindestens durch Angabe von Betrachtungszeitraum, Geschlecht, Krebsart (nach ICD-O) und/ oder Altersintervall (mit üblichen 5-Jahresintervallen) spezifizieren lassen.

- *Erklärung*: Hier erfolgt die Ausgabe von erklärenden Texten zu systemseitigen Reaktionen, die insbesondere bei überraschenden Aktionen des Sytems unverzichtbar sind.

- *Dialog*: In diesem Standardfenster erfolgen sonstige, nicht in anderen Fenstern auftretende systemseitige Meldungen und ggfls. Benutzereingaben über Tastatur sowie die Auswahl von Dialogmodi.

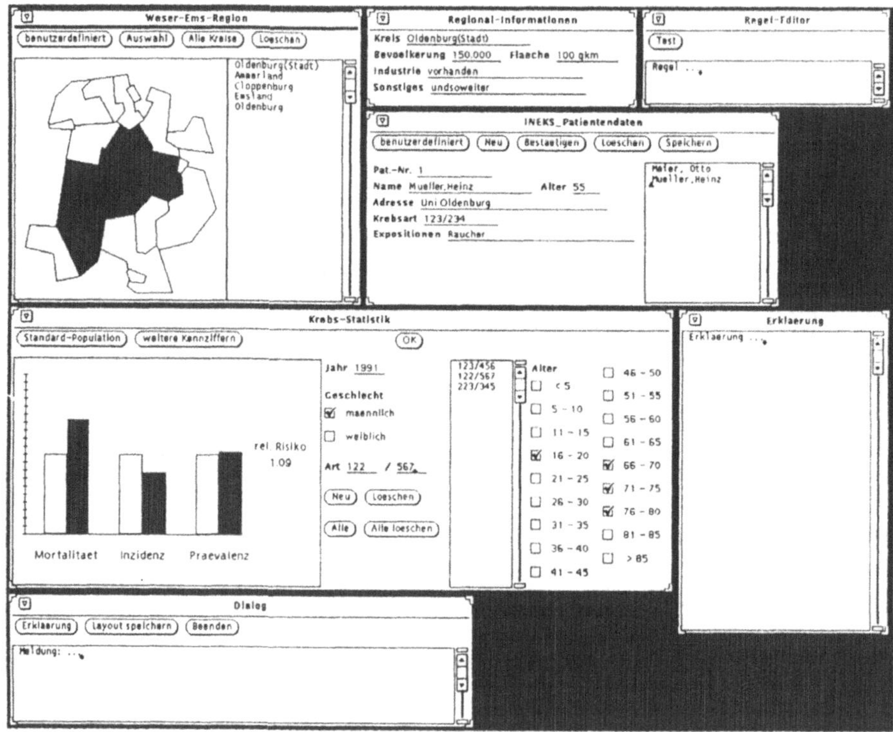

Abb. 5.1 Entwurf einer Benutzungsoberfläche für Active_INEKS

Literatur

Appelrath et al.'91	H.-J. Appelrath, H. Volbers, R. Zimmerling: "INEKS - Ein Informationssystem zur epidemiologischen Krebsforschung", Interner Bericht, Uni Oldenburg, 1991.
Becker et al.'84	N. Becker, R. Frentzel-Beyme, G. Wagner: "Krebsatlas der Bundesrepublik Deutschland", Springer-Verlag, 1984.
Beeri/Milo'91	C. Beeri, T. Milo: "A Model for Active Object Oriented Database", Proc. of the 17th International Conference on Very Large Data Bases, Barcelona, 1991.
Chakaravarthy'90	S. Chakravarthy: "Making an Object-Oriented DBMS Active: Design, Implementation, and Evaluation of a Prototyp", EDBT'90 Int. Conf. on Extending Database Technologie, 1990.
Dayal et al.'88	U. Dayal, B. Blaustein, A. Buchmann, U. Chakaravarthy, M. Hsu, R. Ledin, D.R. McCarthy, A. Rosenthal, S. Sarin: "The HiPAC Project: Combining Active Databases and Timing Constaints", SIGMOD RECORD Vol. 17, March, 1988.
Gatziu/Dittrich'93	S. Gatziu, K.R. Dittrich: "Eine Ereignissprache für das aktive, objektorientierte Datenbanksystem SAMOS", in diesem Band.
Gatziu et al.'91	S. Gatziu, A. Geppert, K.R. Dittrich: "Integrating Active Concepts into an Object-Oriented Database System", Proc. 3rd. Int. Workshop on Database Programming Languages (DBPL), Nafplion, 1991.
Gehani et al.'92	N. Gehani, H. V. Jagadish, O. Shmueli: "Event Specification in an Active Object-Oriented Database", Proc. of the ACM SIGMOD International Conference on Management of Data, 1992.
Götze'92	R. Götze: "Object-Oriented Specification of Complex Dialogues", Proc. Eurographics Workshop on Object-Oriented Graphics, Champery, 1992.
Hanson'92	E.N. Hanson: "Rule Condition Testing and Action Execution in Ariel", Proc. of the ACM SIGMOD International Conference on Management of Data, 1992.
Hartung/Klösener'91	J. Hartung, K.-H. Klösener: "Statistik", Oldenbourg Verlag, München, 1991.
Hull/Jacobs'91	R. Hull, D. Jacobs: "Language Constructs for Programming Active Databases", Proc. of the 17th International Conference on Very Large Data Bases, Barcelona, 1991.
Jasper'92	H. Jasper: "Aktive Informationssysteme und ihr Entwurf", 4. GI-Workshop "Grundlagen von Datenbanken", TR ECRC-92-13.
McCarthy/Dayal'89	D.R. McCarthy, U. Dayal: "The Architecture Of An Active Data Base Management System", Proc. of the ACM SIGMOD International Conference on Management of Data, 1989.
Muir et al.'87	C. Muir, J. Waterhouse, T. Mack, J. Powell, S. Whelan: "Cancer Incidence in Five Continents", International Agency for Research of Cancer, Lyon, 1987.
Ossowski'92	S. Ossowski: "Systeme für Zeitliches Schließen", Diplomarbeit, Uni Oldenburg, 1992.
Rosenthal et al.'89	Arnon Rosenthal, Sharam Charavarthy, Barbara Blaustein: "Situation Monitoring for Active Databases", Proc. of the 17th International Conference on Very Large Data Bases, Barcelona, 1991.
Saarland'91	Statistisches Landesamt Saarland: "Morbidität und Mortalität an bösartigen Neubildungen im Saarland 1988 - Jahresbericht des Saarländischen Krebsregisters", Sonderheft 157/1991.
Schreier et al'91	U. Schreier, H. Pirahesh, R. Agrawal, C. Mohan: "Alert: An Architecture for Transforming a Passiv DBMS into an Active DBMS", Proc. of the 17th International Conference on Very Large Data Bases, Barcelona, 1991.
Stonebraker et al.'90	M. Stonebraker, A. Jhingran, J. Goh, S. Potamianos: "On Rules, Procedures, Caching and Views in Data Base Systems", Proc. of the ACM SIGMOD International Conference on Management of Data, 1990.
Wahrendorf'91	J. Wahrendorf: "Grundbegriffe der Epidemiologie", in K.-O. Gundermann, H. Rüden, H.-G. Sonntag (Hrsg.): "Lehrbuch der Hygiene", Gustav Fischer Verlag, 1991.
Widom et al.'91	J. Widom, R. J. Cochrane, B. G. Lindsay: "Implementing Set-Oriented Production Rules as an Extension to Starburst," Proc. of the 17th International Conference on Very Large Data Bases, Barcelona, 1991.

Eine Ereignissprache für das aktive, objektorientierte Datenbanksystem SAMOS

Stella Gatziu, Klaus R. Dittrich
Forschungsbereich Datenbanktechnologie
Institut für Informatik, Universität Zürich
Email: {gatziu|dittrich}@ifi.unizh.ch

Kurzfassung

Aktive Datenbanksysteme (aDBS) basieren auf Ereignis/Bedingung/Aktions-Regeln (ECA-Regeln), mit deren Hilfe dem System mitgeteilt wird, wie es bei Eintreten bestimmter modellierter Situationen reagieren soll. Besonders den für die Formulierung von Ereignissen angebotenen Konzepten kommt dabei hohe Bedeutung für die Leistungsfähigkeit des Systems zu. In diesem Papier wird die Ereignissprache von SAMOS, einem aktiven, objektorientierten Datenbanksystem, präsentiert, welche die Modellierung mehrerer Arten komplexer Umweltsituationen als Ereignisse ermöglicht.

1 Motivation & Randbedingungen

Neue Entwicklungen der Datenbanktechnologie haben häufig zum Ziel, mehr Umweltsemantik in der Datenbank selbst modellieren zu können. Damit können Anwendungen von Informationsverwaltungsaufgaben entlastet werden, und mehr Information ist explizit und anwendungsunabhängig zugänglich. Objektorientierte Datenbanksysteme sind Repräsentanten für dieses Bestreben; sie unterstützen beispielsweise Mechanismen für die Definition neuer Objekttypen (Klassen), für Typhierarchien und für die Modellierung komplexer Objektstrukturen. Aktive Datenbanksysteme (aDBS) sind in der Lage, zusätzlich zu den bekannten Fähigkeiten eines "passiven" Datenbanksystems definierbare Situationen in der Datenbank (und wenn möglich darüber hinaus) zu erkennen und als Folge davon bestimmte (ebenfalls definierbare) Reaktionen auszulösen. Als *passiv* bezeichnen wir alle Datenbanksysteme (inklusive relationaler und objektorientierter), welche Operationen ausschliesslich unmittelbar nach expliziter Anforderung eines Benutzers oder einer Applikation ausführen.

In einem aDBS können einerseits relevante *Situationen* (absolute oder relative Zeitpunkte, das Eintreten bestimmter DB-Zustände etc.) sowie *Aktionen* (ausführbare Programme, die ihrerseits selbst Operationen auf der Datenbank enthalten können) registriert werden; andererseits wird die Definition sog. *Situation/Reaktions-Regeln* (eine spezielle Art von Produktionsregeln) ermöglicht, die den Zusammenhang zwischen Situationen und gewünschten Reaktionen herstellen. Die Beschreibung einer Situation kann in die eines *Ereignisses* (event) und einer *Bedingung* (condition) aufgespalten werden. Wir sprechen dann von *ECA-Regeln* (*E*vent-*C*ondition-*A*ction) [DBB 88]. Das Eintreten des Ereignisses muss vom aDBS erkannt werden, worauf die entsprechende Regel *ausgelöst* wird. Die *Regelausführung* besteht dann aus der Bedingungsevaluation und der Aktionsausführung.

Ein Ereignis ist der Indikator für das eigentliche *Eintreten* einer bestimmten Situation. Eine Bedingung hingegen beschreibt den Datenbankzustand, welcher beim Eintreten eines Ereignisses erfüllt sein soll. Sie ist also ein Prädikat über dem Datenbankzustand, welches als eine Abfrage an die Datenbank formuliert werden kann. Ein Ereignis ist immer ein bestimmter Zeitpunkt. Die Art, wie ein solcher Zeitpunkt bestimmt wird, beispielweise durch eine explizite Zeitangabe ("um 18:00 Uhr") oder durch den Beginn oder das Ende einer Datenbankoperation, ermöglicht verschiedene Varianten für die Definition von Ereignissen. Ein aDBS stellt daher dem Benutzer eine *Ereignissprache* zur Verfügung, welche Konstrukte zur Formulierung von Ereignissen anbietet. Die meisten existierenden Ansätze aktiver Datenbanksysteme beschränken sich hierbei auf einfache Möglichkeiten. Aktuelle Arbeiten [CM 91], [GJS 92a] versuchen, die Definition von mächtigeren Ereignissprachen. Ein aDBS soll in verschiedensten Anwendungen einsetzbar sein; dies ist nur dann möglich, wenn eine Ereignissprache zur Modellierung einer grossen Vielfalt von Umweltsituationen angeboten wird.

In diesem Papier wird die Ereignissprache von SAMOS (*S*wiss *A*ctive *M*echanism-Based *O*bject-Oriented Database *S*ystem) präsentiert. SAMOS integriert aktive Mechanismen in eine objektorientierte Datenbankumgebung. Einer der Schwerpunkte ist die Entwicklung ausdrucksstarker Konzepte zur Modellierung komplexer Situationen im allgemeinen und damit Ereignissen im besonderen, wie etwa "10 Minuten nach dem Eintreten eines Ereignisses X, aber nur nachmittags".

In einem aktiven, objektorientierten Datenbanksystem spielt der Einfluss objektorientierter Eigenschaften (wie Klassen, Einkapselung oder Vererbung) auf die aktiven Mechanismen eine wichtige Rolle [GGD 91]. Im Rahmen der Ereignissprache sind hiervon in erster Linie die Ereignisarten für die Modellierung des Eintretens von Datenbankoperationen betroffen. Ausserdem werden in SAMOS objektorientierte Konzepte bestmöglich für die sachgerechte Verwaltung der Regeln und Regelkomponenten eingesetzt; zum Beispiel sind Ereignisse im System als Objekte dargestellt.

Ein weiterer Schwerpunkt von SAMOS ist die effiziente Regelbearbeitung. So werden zum Beispiel Strategien für die effiziente Entdeckung komplexer Situationen oder für Gruppierungen von Regeln (um die ausgelösten Regeln schnell zu ermitteln) in der speziellen Umgebung eines objektorientierten Datenbanksystems unterstützt.

Gegenstand dieses Papieres sind jedoch nur diejenige Aspekte von SAMOS, die in Beziehung zu Ereignissen stehen. Kapitel 2 erläutert die Ereignisse und deren Spezifikationsmöglichkeiten genauer. Kapitel 3 geht kurz auf einen Teil der Implementierung von Ereignissen ein. In Kapitel 4 wird ein Vergleich zu existierenden Ereignissprachen gegeben.

2 Ereignisse und ihre Spezifikation

Die breite Einsetzbarkeit eines aDBS hängt sehr von der Vielfalt der Möglichkeiten zur Modellierung von Umweltsituationen ab. Falls die Ereignissprache unterschiedliche Konstrukte zur Definition von Ereignissen anbietet, kann der Benutzer jeweils die passenden auswählen. Ein Ereignis ist grundsätzlich ein Zeitpunkt. Da jedoch nur manche Zeitpunkte von Interesse sind (nämlich diejenigen, für die Regeln formuliert werden sollen), müssen diese auf irgendeine Weise spezifiziert werden. Hierzu kommt die Angabe von Uhrzeiten in Frage, es können aber auch Beginn und Ende von Datenbank(system)operationen dazu dienen. Wir sprechen in diesem Fall von *primitiven* Ereignissen[1]. SAMOS kennt jedoch auch *zusammengesetzte* Ereignisse; ein solches wird mit Hilfe einer Reihe von Ereigniskonstruktoren spezifiziert und beschreibt denjenigen Zeitpunkt, zu dem das letzte einer bestimmten Kombination von (letztlich primitiven) Ereignissen eingetreten ist.

Das eigentliche Eintreten eines Ereignisses wird erst bekannt, wenn das System das Ereignis entdeckt und eine Meldung an die für die weitere Bearbeitung zuständige Systemkomponente schickt ("das Ereignis wird *signalisiert*"). Eine effiziente Realisierung hat dafür zu sorgen, dass zwischen Eintreten und Entdecken nur eine tolerierbare Zeitspanne vergeht.

Gelegentlich soll das Eintreten eines Ereignisses in Beziehung zu einem Zeit<u>raum</u> betrachtet werden. Beispielsweise mag ein Ereignis nur dann interessieren, wenn es an einem Samstag oder Sonntag eintritt. Wir sprechen dann vom *Überwachungsintervall* eines Ereignisses, welches denjenigen Zeitraum bezeichnet, in welchem das Ereignis eintreten muss, damit es signalisiert wird (also für eine Regel von Interesse ist).

Man beachte, dass prinzipiell zwischen *Ereignisklasse* und *Ereignisinstanz* unterschieden werden muss. In Regeln werden stets Ereignisklassen spezifiziert. Unter einer Ereignisinstanz verstehen wir das aktuelle Eintreten eines Ereignisses einer Ereignisklasse. Üblicherweise (nämlich immer dann, wenn nicht ein einmaliger Zeitpunkt, wie etwa "`92.12.30, 12:53 Uhr`", spezifiziert wird) werden im Laufe des Systembetriebs zahlreiche Einzelereignisse (Instanzen) einer Ereignisklasse auftreten. Im folgenden werden wir trotzdem allgemein über Ereignisse sprechen. Welcher der beiden Aspekte gemeint ist, geht jeweils aus dem Kontext hervor. Die *Parametrisierung* von Ereignisklassen ermöglicht die Weitergabe von Informationen, welche beim Eintreten des Ereignisses zur Verfügung stehen (beispielsweise den Zeitpunkt der Entdeckung eines Ereignisses), an die Bedingung und/oder die Aktion einer Regel. Zusätzlich werden Parameter bei der Modellierung zusammengesetzter Ereignisse berücksichtigt.

Ein Ereignis kann in mehreren Regeldefinitionen vorkommen, was der Auslösung von mehreren Regeln beim Eintreten dieses Ereignisses entspricht. Um eine wiederholte Definition dieses Ereignisses in jeder

---

1. Genauer müsste es heissen: "die primitive Spezifikation von Ereignissen"; da nur spezifizierte Ereignisse interessieren, werden wir vereinfachend im weiteren meistens nur diese als "Ereignisse" bezeichnen.

Regel zu vermeiden, wird die Definition von Ereignissen (genauer von Ereignisklassen) auch ausserhalb von Regeldefinitionen ermöglicht. Hierzu können Ereignisse mit einem eindeutigen Namen versehen werden, welcher in Regeldefinitionen verwendet werden kann. Dies ist besonders dann von Bedeutung, wenn Ereignisse recht komplex sind und in weiteren zusammensgesetzten Ereignisse eingehen. Eine getrennte Definition von Ereignissen bringt auch den Vorteil mit sich, dass man zuerst Ereignisse und erst später (wenn die gewünschten Reaktionen bekannt sind) Regeln definieren kann.

All diese Aspekte manifestieren sich in der Ereignissprache von SAMOS und werden in diesem Kapitel ausführlich betrachtet.

2.1 Primitive Ereignisse

Primitive Ereignisse beschreiben Zeitpunkte, welche aufgrund von Zuständen, die in der Datenbank (*Methoden-* und *Wertereignisse*), im DBMS (*Transaktionsereignisse*) oder im Umfeld der Datenbank (*Zeitereignisse, abstrakte Ereignisse*) entstehen, spezifiziert sind.

2.1.1 Zeitereignisse

Als erstes kommt für die Spezifikation von Ereignissen die explizite Angabe von Uhrzeiten in Frage. Solche Ereignisse werden *Zeitereignisse* genannt. Sie werden in Form absoluter, periodisch wiederkehrender, impliziter oder relativer Zeitpunkte spezifiziert. *Absolute Zeitpunkte* werden durch Angabe von Jahr, Monat, Tag, Stunde und Minute bestimmt (auf die Angabe von Sekunden wird verzichtet), beispielsweise `93.01.30,16:15`. Bei der Bestimmung absoluter Zeitpunkte können beliebige Teile weggelassen werden; SAMOS sieht in diesem Fall eine Reihe von Standardwerten vor, zum Beispiel das aktuelle Jahr beim Fehlen der Jahresangabe.

Periodisch wiederkehrende Zeitpunkte können auf der Basis von Jahr, Monat, Woche, Tag, Stunde und Minute gemäss folgender Syntax definiert werden:

```
EVERY [frequency] (YEAR|MONTH|WEEK|DAY|HOUR|MINUTE) <time> [interval]
```

Die Angabe des Wiederholungsfaktors `frequency` in Form einer ganzen Zahl beispielsweise `EVERY 10. DAY 20:00` bewirkt, dass das Zeitereignis nicht jeden Tag sondern jeden 10. Tag um 20:00 signalisiert wird. Bei fehlender Angabe von `frequency` wird der Wert 1 angenommen, beim vorherigen Beispiel würde also das Zeitereignis jeden Tag um 20:00 signalisiert. Das Zeitintervall `interval` bestimmt den Zeitraum, in welchem das periodische Ereignis auftreten soll. Zum Beispiel wird das Zeitereignis `EVERY DAY 20:00 [05.01-05.31]` nur im Monat Mai jeden Tag um 20:00 signalisiert. Ohne Angabe eines Zeitintervalls, wird das periodische Ereignis ab dem Zeitpunkt seiner Definition fortwährend bzw. bis zum Löschen der entsprechenden Regel an den definierten wiederkehrenden Zeitpunkten signalisiert.

Oft kann ein Zeitpunkt bei seiner Definition nicht explizit durch die Angabe einer Uhrzeit, sondern nur bezüglich des Stattfindens einer Systemaktivität, wie etwa dem Eintreten eines anderen Ereignisses, spezifiziert werden; ein solcher Zeitpunkt wird als *impliziter Zeitpunkt* bezeichnet. Die in SAMOS vorgesehenen Möglichkeiten für die Definition impliziter Zeitpunkte werden in Kapitel 2.6 ausführlich diskutiert. *Relative Zeitpunkte (t+x)* setzen sich aus einer angegebenen *relativen Zeit x* und einem bekannten Zeitpunkt *t*, welcher normalerweise implizit ist, zusammen.

2.1.2 Methodenereignisse

In einer objektorientierten Umgebung kommunizieren Objekte durch das Senden von Nachrichten miteinander. Ein Objekt reagiert auf den Empfang einer Nachricht mit der Ausführung der entsprechenden Methode. Das Senden einer Nachricht und demzufolge der Aufruf einer solchen Methode kann als Ereignis, als sog. *Methodenereignis*, angesehen werden. Da ein Ereignis immer ein Zeitpunkt ist, die Ausführung einer Methode aber eine Zeitdauer in Anspruch nimmt, muss man genauer zwischen den Ereignissen *Beginn* (Anforderung trifft beim Objekt ein) und *Ende* (Methode ist vollständig ausgeführt) eines Methodenaufrufs unterscheiden. Der jeweils gewünschte Zeitpunkt wird mittels der Schlüsselwörter *BEFORE* oder *AFTER* bei der Definition eines Methodenereignisses festgelegt.

Methodenereignisse beziehen sich auf eine oder mehrere Klassen oder auf einzelne Objekte. Anhand eines Beispiels sollen die verschiedenen Varianten für die Definition eines Methodenereignisses präsentiert werden. Gegeben sei eine Klasse `Stadt` mit einer Methode `Nicht_belegte_Zimmer(kategorie:integer):integer`. Diese Methode gibt die Anzahl der freien Zimmer aller Hotels einer bestimmten Kategorie für eine bestimmte Stadt an. `Zürich` sei ein Objekt der Klasse `Stadt`.

a) Ereignisse auf Objektebene:

- `BEFORE.Zürich.Nicht_belegte_Zimmer` wird nach dem Senden der Nachricht `Nicht_belegte_-Zimmer` an das Objekt `Zürich` unmittelbar vor der Methodenausführung signalisiert.
- `BEFORE.Zürich` wird nach dem Senden einer beliebigen (für die Klasse `Stadt` definierten) Nachricht an das Objekt `Zürich` signalisiert.

b) Ereignisse auf Klassenebene:

- `BEFORE.Stadt.Nicht_belegte_Zimmer` wird nach dem Senden der Nachricht `Nicht_belegte_-Zimmer` an irgendein Objekt der Klasse `Stadt` signalisiert.
- `BEFORE.Stadt` wird nach dem Senden einer beliebigen (für die Klasse `Stadt` definierten) Nachricht an irgendein Objekt der Klasse `Stadt` signalisiert.
- `BEFORE.-.Nicht_belegte_Zimmer` wird nach dem Senden der Nachricht `Nicht_belegte_Zimmer` an irgendein Objekt beliebiger Klasse, welche eine Methode mit diesem Namen hat, signalisiert.

Auch Umweltsituationen, welche dem Erstellen und Löschen eines Objektes entsprechen, können mit Hilfe von Methodenereignissen (nämlich bezüglich den vorgesehenen Konstruktor- bzw. Destruktormethoden) modelliert werden.

2.1.3 Wertereignisse

Ereignisse sollen auch die Zeitpunkte bezeichnen können, an denen Datenmanipulationsoperationen beginnen oder enden. In einer relationalen Umgebung beispielsweise handelt es sich um die bekannten Operationen auf einer Relation. In einer objektorientierten Umgebung sind es Operationen auf dem Wert eines Objektes (Wertoperationen), die immer Teile von Methoden sind (strenge Einkapselung vorausgesetzt). Da Wertoperationen in verschiedenen Methoden vorkommen können, müsste für jede dieser (vorhandenen und auch später neu hinzukommenden) Methoden ein Ereignis definiert werden. Um all diesen Ereignisdefinitionen zu entgehen, stellt der Zugriff auf den Wert eines Objektes eine weitere Ereignisart dar, das sog. *Wertereignis*. Da das "Aussehen" der Datenmanipulationsoperationen zwischen den verschiedenen objektorientierten Datenbanksystemen sehr stark variiert, verzichten wir an dieser Stelle auf die Angabe einer konkreten Syntax für Wertereignisse. Die Definition von Wertereignissen durch Benutzer oder Anwendungsprogramme würde das Konzept der Einkapselung verletzen. Um dies zu verhindern, legen wir fest, dass nur der Klassenimplementierer Regeln mit Wertereignissen[2] definieren und bearbeiten darf.

2.1.4 Transaktionsereignisse

Der Anfang (*BOT*), das (erfolgreiche) Ende (*EOT*) oder der Abbruch einer Transaktion (*abort*) stellen ebenfalls oft interessierende Ereignisse dar. Ein *Transaktionsereignis* bezieht sich auf jede gestartete Transaktion. Unter der Voraussetzung, dass das explizite Benennen von Transaktionsprogrammen ein Teil der Funktionalität des Transaktionsmodells ist, kann der Einsatz eines Transaktionsereignisses auf genau einen Transaktionstyp beschränkt werden. Unter Transaktionstyp verstehen wir ein (benanntes) Transaktionsprogramm.

2.1.5 Abstrakte Ereignisse

Die Semantik der bisher besprochenen Ereignisarten ist SAMOS bekannt; das System ist somit selbst in der Lage, deren Eintreten zu erkennen. Darüberhinaus gibt es viele datenbankexterne Situationen, deren Darstellung als Ereignisse zwar erwünscht ist, die aber durch das System nicht automatisch erkannt werden können. Zu diesem Zweck können *abstrakte Ereignisse* definiert werden. Ein abstraktes Ereignis spezifiziert (wie andere Ereignisse) auch einen Zeitpunkt, welcher aber bei der Definition des Ereignisses unbekannt ist. Somit wird bei der Definition des abstrakten Ereignisses nur ein Name für die interessierende Situation angegeben, zum Beispiel `DEFINE EVENT Programmtest`. Ein Aufruf der Operation *RAISE* <name> (wie zum Beispiel `RAISE Programmtest`), welche das abstrakte Ereignis signalisiert, liefert dann quasi den vorher unbekannten Zeitpunkt ("jetzt").

2.2 Zusammengesetzte Ereignisse

Bei komplexen Anwendungen genügt es nicht, den Zeitpunkt des Eintretens einer Umweltsituation nur durch das Eintreten eines primitiven Ereignisses zu bestimmen. Von Interesse ist hier das Eintreten von

---

2. Mit diesen sog. klasseninternen Regeln lassen sich insbesondere auch viele Aufgaben lokal in einem Objekt erledigen, wodurch ein hoher Grad an "Objekt-autonomie" verwirklicht werden kann. Eine ausführliche Diskussion dieses Aspektes findet sich in [GGD 91].

kombinierten Ereignissen. In SAMOS besteht daher die Möglichkeit, neben primitiven auch *zusammengesetzte* Ereignisse zu definieren. Diese werden mit einer *Ereignisalgebra* beschrieben. In einem Ausdruck der Ereignisalgebra können einfache oder zusammengesetzte Ereignisse mittels von sechs *Ereigniskonstruktoren* verknüpft werden.

Das Eintreten einer *Disjunktion* (*E1 | E2*) zweier Ereignisse *E1* und *E2* wird signalisiert, wenn eines der beiden Ereignisse eingetroffen ist. Mit diesem Ereigniskonstruktor erreicht man eine Reduktion der Regelmenge, da auf die Definition mehrerer Regeln mit gleichem Bedingungs- und Aktionsteil verzichtet werden kann. Das Eintreten einer *Sequenz* (*E1 ; E2*) von Ereignissen *E1* und *E2* wird signalisiert, wenn die Teilereignisse *E1* und *E2* in der angegebenen Reihenfolge eingetreten sind. Zwischen dem Eintreten von *E1* und demjenigen von *E2* können durchaus weitere Ereignisse eintreten. Das Eintreten einer *Konjunktion (E1 , E2*) von Ereignissen *E1* und *E2* wird signalisiert, wenn beide Teilereignisse eingetreten sind, wobei die Reihenfolge unbedeutend ist.

Die folgenden drei Ereigniskonstruktoren ermöglichen die Überwachung des Eintretens von Ereignisinstanzen einer bestimmten Ereignisklasse innerhalb eines Zeitintervalls[3]. Ein *negatives Ereignis NOT E* erlaubt die Überwachung des *Nicht*-Eintretens von *E* innerhalb eines vordefinierten Zeitraums. *NOT E* wird erst dann signalisiert, wenn dieser Zeitraum abgelaufen ist und *E* nicht eingetreten ist. Das Einsetzen des Schlüsselworts *any* anstelle eines konkreten Ereignisses, ermöglicht durch die Definition *NOT any* die Überwachung des Nicht-Eintretens aller definierter Ereignisse innerhalb des vorgegebenen Zeitraums. Der *Stern-Operator*, dargestellt durch *, ermöglicht es, das wiederholte Eintreten eines (primitiven oder zusammengesetzten) Ereignisses (einer bestimmten Ereignisklasse) innerhalb eines vorgegebenen Zeitintervalls nur einmal zu signalisieren. Das Eintreten des Ereignisses **E* wird signalisiert, sobald das Ereignis *E* das erste Mal innerhalb des Zeitintervalls eingetreten ist.

Bei manchen Anwendungen ist gerade die Anzahl des (wiederholten) Eintretens eines Ereignisses von Bedeutung. So sollen zum Beispiel Aktien einer Firma verkauft werden, sobald deren Kurs zehnmal innerhalb eines Tages gestiegen ist. Dies führt zum Begriff des *historischen Ereignisses*, dargestellt durch *TIMES(n, E*), wobei *TIMES* der sogenannte *Geschichte-Operator* ist und *n* die gewünschte Häufigkeit des Eintretens von (Ereignisinstanzen der Ereignisklasse) *E* innerhalb eines vordefinierten Zeitraums angibt. Die Anzahl der Wiederholungen wird entweder exakt durch eine Zahl *n* oder in Form eines Intervalls *[n1-n2]* angegeben. Im ersten Fall gilt *TIMES(n, E*) als eingetreten, sobald *E* innerhalb des Zeitintervalls *n*-mal eingetreten ist. Im zweiten Fall wird das historische Ereignis *TIMES([n1-n2], E)* am Ende des Zeitintervalls signalisiert, wenn das Ereignis *E* mindestens *n1*-mal, aber höchstens *n2*-mal eingetreten ist.

2.3 Parametrisierung von Ereignissen

Die Parametrisierung von Ereignisklassen ermöglicht die Weitergabe von Informationen, welche beim Eintreten des Ereignisses zur Verfügung stehen (beispielsweise der Zeitpunkt der Entdeckung eines Ereignisses), an die Bedingung und/oder an die Aktion. Die aktuellen Parameter werden bei der Instanzierung an die formalen Parameter der Ereignisklassen gebunden. Formale Parameter sind in SAMOS vorgegeben, d.h. der Benutzer kann bei der Ereignisdefinition in der Regel keine selbstgewählten Parameter angeben. Einzige Ausnahme bilden hier die abstrakten Ereignisse, für die der Benutzer die formalen Parameter bei der Ereignisdefinition festlegen kann. Die aktuellen Parameter werden beim Aufruf von *raise* angegeben.

Es wird zwischen Parametern für Umgebungsinformationen (*Umgebungsparameter*), die für alle Ereignisarten von Bedeutung sind, und *Ereignisartparametern*, die von der Ereignisart abhängig sind, unterschieden. Umgebungsparameter sind:

- der Zeitpunkt der Entdeckung eines Ereignisses (als absoluter Zeitpunkt zu betrachten), bezeichnet durch *occ_point;*
- der Identifikator der Transaktion, in welcher das Ereignis eingetreten ist (die sog. *Auslöser-Transaktion*), bezeichnet durch *occ_tid*;
- der Identifikator des Benutzers, welcher die Auslöser-Transaktion gestartet hat, bezeichnet durch *user_id.*

3. Auf die genaue Definition des Zeitraums werden wir später bei der Einführung von Überwachungsintervallen eingehen.

Die Umgebungsparameter zusammengesetzter Ereignisse beschränken sich auf den *occ_point*, weil die Teilereignisse in mehreren Transaktionen, die von verschiedenen Benutzern gestartet worden sind, eintreten können.

Wir werden nun die Ereignisartparameter betrachten. Methodenereignisse weisen als Ereignisartparameter die Parameter der Methode und den Identifikator des Objekts auf, für das die Methode ausgeführt werden soll bzw. wurde. So werden etwa (im oben eingeführten Beispiel) beim Methodenereignis `BEFORE.Stadt.Nicht_belegte_Zimmer` nach dem Senden der Nachricht `[Zürich Nicht_belegte_Zimmer(5)]` den Parameter `stadt` und `kategorie` die Werte `Zürich` und `5` zugewiesen. Wertereignisse haben als Parameter den Identifikator und den Wert des Objektes, auf welches die entsprechenden Wertoperationen zugreifen. Transaktionsereignisse weisen als Parameter den Identifikator der entsprechenden Transaktion auf, bezeichnet durch *tid*, welcher identisch zum Umgebungsparameter *occ_tid* ist. Zeitereignisse haben keine Parameter.

Die Ereignisartparameter einer Disjunktion sind diejenigen des eingetretenen Teilereignisses. Sequenzen und Konjunktionen haben als Parameter die Parameter der zwei Teilereignisse. Die Parameter eines negativen Ereignisses sind die Parameter des Ereignisses, dessen Nicht-Eintreten überwacht wird. Beim Stern- oder Geschichte-Operator wird bekanntlich das Eintreten mehrerer Instanzen einer bestimmten Ereignisklasse innerhalb eines bestimmten Zeitintervalls überwacht. Daher ergeben sich die Parameter beispielsweise einer Instanz der Ereignisklasse *TIMES(n, E)* durch die Vereinigung der Parameter der in diesem Zeitintervall *n* eingetretenen Ereignisinstanzen von *E*.

2.4 Einfluss der Parameter von Teilereignissen auf die Definition zusammengesetzter Ereignisse

In die Definition der verschiedenen Ereigniskonstruktoren ist bislang nicht eingegangen, ob die Instanziierungen der Teilereignisse über die gleichen aktuellen Parameter (Umgebungs- oder Ereignisartparameter) verfügen müssen oder nicht. In manchen Fällen möchte man aber beispielsweise formulieren können, dass die Teilereignisse einer Konjunktion in derselben Auslöser-Transaktion eintreten, d.h. die gleichen Parameterwerte für *occ_tid* aufweisen müssen. Die Erweiterung der einzelnen Ereigniskonstruktoren um diesen Aspekt holen wir in diesem Abschnitt nach. Hierzu muss die Definition der Zusammensetzung um das Konstrukt *same(x)* erweitert werden, wobei *x* festlegt, welche Parameter gleiche Werte haben sollen.

Die Unterscheidung, ob die Teilereignisse eines zusammengesetzten Ereignisses die gleichen oder verschiedene Parameterwerte haben, muss nur gemacht werden, wenn mehrere (Teil-)Ereignisse tatsächlich eintreten können. Die Parameter spielen daher bei der Disjunktion (immer nur ein Teilereignis tritt ein) und bei der Negation (das Ereignis tritt nicht ein) keine Rolle. Im folgenden wird auf diese beiden Ereignisarten nicht näher eingegangen.

Bei einer Konjunktion oder einer Sequenz sollen in manchen Fällen die Teilereignisse die gleichen Parameterwerte für die Umgebungsparameter *occ_tid* und *user_id* aufweisen. Damit wird eine Überprüfung dieser Umgebungsparameter nötig, d.h. das zusammengesetzte Ereignis soll nur dann signalisiert werden, wenn die Teilereignisse in derselben Auslöser-Transaktion eingetreten sind, bzw. die Auslöser-Transaktionen von demselben Benutzer gestartet wurden. Dies wird ausgedrückt durch: *same(transaction)* oder *same(user)*, zum Beispiel

```
(E1,E2):same(user)
```

Für den Stern- und Geschichte-Operator muss unterscheidbar sein, ob sie das Eintreten mehrerer Ereignisinstanzen mit den gleichen oder mit verschiedenen aktuellen Parametern überwachen. Der in Abschnitt 2.2 eingeführte Stern-Operator bewirkt beispielsweise, dass das mehrfache Eintreten des Ereignisses nur einmal signalisiert wird, wobei jede Ereignisinstanziierung andere Parameterwerte aufweisen kann. Analog zu einer Konjunktion oder einer Sequenz können auch hier die Ereignisinstanzen denselben *occ_tid* oder *user_id* haben. Von Interesse sind zusätzlich die Ereignisartparameter. So bedeutetet *same(parameter)* (beispielsweise in **E:same(parameter)*), dass die Ereignisinstanzen dieselben Parameterwerte aufweisen müssen.

Bei Methoden- und Wertereignissen (in jeder Zusammensetzung) kann zusätzlich auch die Bedingung aufgestellt werden, dass die entsprechenden Methoden oder Wertoperationen auf dem selben Objekt ausgeführt werden müssen. Die Ereignisdefinition wird dann um *same(object)* erweitert. Nehmen wir zum Beispiel das Ereignis `*BEFORE.Stadt.Nicht_belegte_Zimmer:same(object)` mit den Parametern `stadt` und `kategorie`. Das Senden der Nachrichten `[Zürich Nicht_belegte_Zimmer(5)]` und `[Bern Nicht_belegte_Zimmer(3)]` wird jetzt zweimal signalisiert.

2.5 Überwachungsintervalle

Überwachungsintervalle sind erforderlich, wenn das Eintreten eines (primitiven oder zusammengesetzten) Ereignisses nur während eines bestimmten Zeitintervalls vom System signalisiert werden soll. Dies wurde beispielsweise bereits bei der Einführung der Ereigniskonstruktoren, wie etwa der Negation, erwähnt. Da für die Definition von Überwachungsintervallen die allgemeinen Richtlinien, die zur Bestimmung von Zeitintervallen in SAMOS aufgestellt wurden, von Bedeutung sind, soll zuerst darauf näher eingegangen werden.

2.5.1 Zeitintervalle in SAMOS

Ein Zeitintervall ist eine abgeschlossene Menge von Zeitpunkten. Es wird von einem *start_point* und einem *end_point* begrenzt und als *[start_point - end_point]* dargestellt. *Start_point* und *end_point* sind entweder (jeweils) absolute, implizite oder relative Zeitpunkte. Neben der Bestimmung von konkreten Intervallen wie `[92.06.01 - 92.07.01]` werden auch periodisch wiederkehrende Zeitintervalle unterstützt. Periodische Zeitintervalle werden analog zu den periodischen Zeitpunkten definiert, zum Beispiel wird "`jeden Monat vom 15. um 18:00 bis 16. um 18:00`" durch `EVERY MONTH [15,18:00 - 16,18:00]` beschrieben.

Für Zeitintervalle stehen eine Reihe von Intervalloperatoren zur Verfügung, wie zum Beispiel die Operatoren *overlap*(interval, interval) und *extend*(interval, interval). Bei beiden Operatoren resultiert aus der Verknüpfung der beiden Intervalle ein neues *zusammengesetztes* Intervall. Im ersten Fall ist dies die überlappende Zeitdauer ("Durchschnitt") und im zweiten Fall die zeitliche "Vereinigung" der beiden Intervalle. Bei der Vereinigung zweier aneinander angrenzender Intervalle I1 und I2 weist das neue Intervall, als *start_point* den *start_point* von I1 und als *end_point* den *end_point* von I2 auf, sofern I1 das frühere und I2 das spätere Intervall ist; ansonsten besteht die Vereinigung der zwei Intervalle aus genau diesen beiden Intervallen.

2.5.2 Definition von Überwachungsintervallen

Überwachungsintervalle können einerseits während der Ereignisdefinition bestimmt werden:

```
DEFINE EVENT E1 Programmtest FOR [92.05.01 - 92.08.30]
DEFINE RULE R1
     ON E1
     ...
```

Andererseits können Überwachungsintervalle während der Regeldefinition, d.h. nach der Definition des Ereignisses innerhalb der Regel, angegeben werden:

```
DEFINE RULE R2
     ON BOT(UpdateGehalt) FOR EVERY WEEK [Sa - So]
     ...
```

Im ersten Fall ist die Angabe des Überwachungsintervalls ein Teil der Ereignisdefinition; sobald dieses Ereignis in einer Regeldefinition verwendet wird, ist auch das entsprechende Überwachungsintervall zu berücksichtigen. Wird das Ereignis also in mehreren Regeln verwendet, braucht das Überwachungsintervall nur einmal bestimmt zu werden. Im Gegensatz dazu ist im zweiten Fall das Überwachungsintervall nur für die entsprechende Regel (d.h. für keine andere Regel, welche das gleiche Ereignis hat) von Bedeutung.

2.5.3 Überwachungsintervalle bei zusammengesetzten Ereignissen

Manche Ereigniskonstruktoren, beispielsweise der Stern-Operator, erfordern in der Regel die Angabe eines Zeitintervalls, in welchem das mehrfache Eintreten eines Ereignisses nur einmal signalisiert wird. Dieses Zeitintervall ist das *Überwachungsintervall* für das Ereignis mit dem Stern-Operator. Wir werden jetzt die verschiedenen Möglichkeiten zur Definition von Überwachungsintervallen bei zusammengesetzten Ereignissen betrachten.

Bei einer Sequenz *E3 = (E1 ; E2)* soll *E2* in den meisten Fällen *innerhalb eines bestimmten Zeitintervalls* nach dem Eintreten von *E1* eintreten, was die Notwendigkeit eines Überwachungsintervalls für *E2* zeigt und eine Definition der Art *(E1 ; E2 [s2 - e2])* enstpricht. Weitere Möglichkeiten für die Angabe des Überwachungsintervalls sind: *(E1 [s1 - e1] ; E2 [s2 - e2])* oder *(E1 ; E2) [s3 - e3]* oder *(E1 [s1 - e1] ; E2 [s2 - e3]) [s3 - e3]*.

Wie bei der Sequenz ist es auch bei einer Konjunktion in manchen Fällen erwünscht, die Zeitspanne, in welcher die Einzelereignisse eintreten müssen, zu bestimmen. Negative Ereignisse und Ereignisse mit dem Stern- oder Geschichte-Operator benötigen in der Regel ein Überwachungsintervall. Die einzige

Ausnahme von dieser Regel bilden diejenigen Ereignisse, die Teilereignisse einer Konjunktion oder einer Sequenz sind. Zum Beispiel hat das negative Ereignis `NOT E1` in einer Sequenz `(NOT E1;E2)[s3-e3]` das Überwachungsintervall `[s3-occ_point(E2)]`.

Der Einsatz des Stern-Operators in einer Sequenz oder Konjunktion und das Zusammenspiel mit den entsprechenden Überwachungsintervallen wird mit Hilfe einer möglichen Eintretensreihenfolge von Ereignissen gezeigt. Nehmen wir an, dass es innerhalb des Zeitintervalls `[s-e]` zu folgenden Ereigniseintritten kommt:

```
E1 E2 E1 E1 E2 E2 E2 E1
```

Eine Sequenz `(E1;E2)` wird dann dreimal signalisiert. Eine Konjunktion `(E1,E2)` wird viermal signalisiert, das Ereignis `*(E1,E2)[s-e]` jedoch nur einmal. Das Ereignis `(*E1;E2)[s-e]` entspricht der Definition `(*E1[s-occ_point(E2)];E2(occ_point(E1)-e])` und wird zweimal signalisiert. Das Ereignis `(E1;*E2[s-e])` entspricht der Definition `(E1;*E2[max(occ_point(E1),s)-e])` und wird nur einmal signalisiert. Das Ereignis `*(E1;E2)[s-e]` wird nur einmal signalisiert.

2.6 Implizite Zeitpunktbestimmung

Die Definition von Überwachungsintervallen soll nicht nur durch absolute Zeitpunkte (d.h. explizit), sondern auch durch Zeitpunkte erfolgen können, welche aufgrund des Eintretens anderer Ereignisse oder aufgrund des Endes der Ausführung von Regeln spezifiziert werden. Dies entspricht einer impliziten Definition von *start_point* und *end_point*. Implizite Zeitpunktbestimmung kann natürlich nicht nur bei der Definition von Überwachungsintervallen, sondern auch in anderem Zusammenhang verwendet werden.

Als erstes kommt der Zeitpunkt des Eintretens eines Ereignisses (*occ_point*(event_name)) als Anknüpfungspunkt zur impliziten Zeitpunktbestimmung in Frage. Ein Beispiel ist das Überwachungsintervall `overlap([92.08.01 - 92.08.31],[occ_point(E2) - 2DAYS])` für das Ereignis `NOT E2`, welches die Überwachung des Nicht-Eintretens von `E2` im August für 2 Tage nach dem erstmaligen Eintreten von `E2` im August ermöglicht. Ausserdem kann ein Zeitpunkt auch in Abhängigkeit vom Ende der Ausführung einer Regel (*end_execution*(rule_name)), d.h. vom Ende der Ausführung der Aktion, definiert werden. Das Überwachungsintervall `[end_execution(R1)-7DAYS]` eines negatives Ereignisses `NOT E1` bestimmt, dass das Nicht-Eintreten von `E1` eine Woche lang nach der Ausführung von `R1` überwacht werden muss.

Implizite Zeitpunkte werden häufig auch bei der Definition relativer Zeitpunkte verwendet (wie bei den Zeitereignissen erwähnt wurde). Zum Beispiel wird das Zeitereignis `occ_point(E1)+00:10` 10 Minuten nach dem Eintreten von `E1` signalisiert.

2.7 Wertung der Ereignissprache

Die Ereignissprache von SAMOS ermöglicht es mit Hilfe der in den vorherigen Abschnitten eingeführten Konstrukte, ein breites Spektrum von Umweltsituationen als Ereignisse zu modellieren. Beim Entwurf der Sprache wurde versucht, mit wenigen, aber orthogonal anwendbaren Konzepten auszukommen und ähnliche Aspekte in einheitlicher Weise darzustellen (zum Beispiel Zeitereignisse und Überwachungsintervalle).

Trotzdem bringt die leistungsfähige Ereignissprache von SAMOS (wie aktive Mechanismen generell) einen hohen Grad an Komplexität mit sich. Dies kann dazu führen, dass der Benutzer eine im konkreten Anwendungsfall "ungünstige" Ereignismodellierung wählt, weil ihm hierfür viele verschiedene Alternativen zur Verfügung stehen und ihm die Auswahl der passenden Konstrukte Schwierigkeiten macht. Deshalb ist es sinnvoll, für spezifische Anwendungsbereiche jeweils nur einen Teil der Ereignissprache von SAMOS zur Verfügung zu stellen. Anwendungen im Bankbereich etwa (zum Beispiel Börsenapplikationen) sind häufig von statistischer Natur und benötigen daher zum grössten Teil zusammengesetzte Ereignisse mit dem Stern- und Geschichte-Operator sowie implizite Zeitpunktbestimmung.

Zur Bewältigung der Komplexität der Ereignissprache müssen dem Benutzer noch Werkzeuge zur Entwurfsunterstützung angeboten werden, zum Beispiel graphische, interaktive Werkzeuge für die Ereignisdefinition, wobei auch Inkonsistenzen automatisch festgestellt werden sollen. Solche Werkzeuge sind unerlässlich zum effizienten und sicheren Handhaben der Ereignissprache.

3 Implementierungsaspekte

SAMOS als aDBS muss im Vergleich zu einem passiven DBS eine Reihe von zusätzlichen Aufgaben erledigen, wie zum Beispiel das Entdecken von Ereignissen oder das Bestimmen der auszuführenden Regeln. Demzufolge muss die Architektur eines passiven DBS um neue Komponenten erweitert werden. Die prototypische Implementierung von SAMOS basiert auf dem objektorientierten Datenbanksystem ObjectStore. Da in den Quellcode dieses DBSs nicht eingegriffen werden kann, müssen die verschiedenen Komponenten aufgesetzt werden. Zuerst müssen Regel- und Ereignisdefinitionen verstanden und überprüft werden. Dafür ist der *Analysator* zuständig, welcher korrekte Definitionen dem *Regel-* oder dem *Ereignismanager* übergibt. Im Ereignismanager wird das Wissen über die Definition der Ereignisse abgelegt. Der Ereignismanager veranlasst dann den *Ereignisdetektor*, zu jedem Ereignis die notwendigen Datenstrukturen etc. für die Entdeckung der aktuell interessierenden Ereignisse anzulegen.

Wenn ein Ereignis vom Ereignisdetektor entdeckt ist, wird dieses im *Ereignisregister* eingetragen, welches eine Liste mit allen eingetretenen Ereignissen führt. Das Ereignisregister meldet nun den neuen Eintrag dem Regelmanager, wodurch die auszuführende Regel ausfindig gemacht wird. Der Regelmanager benachrichtigt seinerseits die *Regelausführungskomponente*, die für die Bedingungsevaluation und die Aktionsausführung zuständig ist.

Die Implementierung des Ereignisdetektors ist besonders massgebend für die Effizienz des aDBS. Die Vielfalt der Ereigniskonstruktoren macht besonders die Entdeckung der zusammengesetzten Ereignisse komplex. In SAMOS verwenden wir Petri-Netze für die Modellierung und die Entdeckung zusammengesetzter Ereignisse. Ein Petri-Netz besteht aus Stellen (Eingabe und Audgabe), die Ereignisklassen modellieren, und aus Transitionen. Sobald ein primitives Ereignis vom enstprechenden Ereignisdetektor entdeckt wird, wird die entsprechende Eingabestelle markiert. Entsprechend zu den "Schaltregeln" eines Petri-Netzes werden ein oder mehrere Ausgabestellen markiert, was die Signalisierung des ensprechenden zusammengesetztes Ereignisses bewirkt. Für jeden Ereigniskonstruktor wurde ein entsprechendes Petri-Netz "Muster" definiert. Das System verwaltet ein Kombinations-Petri-Netz, welches die Petri-Netze für alle definierten zusammengesetzten Ereignisse enthält. Ein Ereignis kann in mehreren Zusammensetzungen teilnehmen, im Kombinations-Petri-Netz existiert hierfür stattdessen nur eine Stelle. Ein Vorteil der Verwendung von Petri-Netzen ist, dass zusammengesetzte Ereignisse schrittweise, nach jedem Eintreten eines primitiven Ereignisses, entdeckt werden können. Andererseits wäre jeweils eine Inspektion der ganzen Menge der im Ereignisregister gespeicherten (primitiven) Ereignisse erforderlich.

4 Vergleich mit vorhandenen Arbeiten

Einige der klassischen Arbeiten im Gebiet von aDBS sind die Arbeiten von [DBB 88], [KDM 88] und [Stone 89], welche die bei uns auch verwendeten Prinzipien von aDBS, wie etwa die ECA-Regeln eingeführt haben. Aktuelle Arbeiten beschäftigen sich mit der Erweiterung relationaler ([WCL 91]) oder objektorientierter ([DBM 88], [GJ 91], [DPG 91], [MP 90] und [GGD 91]) Datenbanksysteme um ECA-Regeln. Die Wichtigkeit von Ereignissprachen wurde in letzter Zeit immer deutlicher, wie die Arbeiten in *Snoop* [CM 91] und die Arbeiten in *ODE* [GJS 92a], [GJS 92b] zeigen. Zusammengesetzte Ereignisse werden sowohl in Snoop als auch in ODE unterstützt.

Der Vergleich zwischen der Ereignissprache von SAMOS und der Ereignissprache von Snoop und ODE zeigt, dass die beiden letzteren Systeme, besonders ODE, eine Reihe von Ereigniskostruktoren anbieten, um die Sprache ausdruckstärker zu machen. In SAMOS hingegen wurde die Anzahl der Ereigniskonstruktoren gering gehalten, um die gesamte Komplexität des aktiven Mechanismus nicht über Gebühr ansteigen zu lassen. Zudem werden in SAMOS verschiedene orthogonale Konzepte wie Überwachungsintervalle, implizite Zeitpunktbestimmung und Ereignisparameter angeboten. Die Konzepte sind für sich genommen einfach, aber ihre Kombination ermöglicht vielfältige Ereignisdefinitionen. Als Beispiel nehmen wir einen Ereigniskonstruktor von Snoop, welcher extra eingeführt wurde, um ein Ereignis `E` nur dann zu signalisieren, wenn dieses innerhalb des Zeitraums, welcher vom Eintreten zwei anderer Ereignisse `E1` und `E2` bestimmt wird, eingetreten ist. In SAMOS kann `E` das Überwachungsintervall `[occ_point(E1)-occ_point(E2)]` zugeordnet werden, womit derselbe Effekt erreicht wird.

5 Zusammenfassung

SAMOS integriert aktive Mechanismen in eine objektorientierte Datenbankumgebung. Einer der Schwerpunkte ist die Entwicklung einer ausdrucksstarken Ereignissprache, welche aufgrund von Überwachungsintervallen, impliziter Zeitpunktbestimmung, verschiedener Ereigniskonstruktoren und Ereignisparametern die Modellierung von komplexen Umweltsituationen ermöglicht. Die Ereignissprache und ein auf Petri-Netzen basierender Mechanismus zur Entdeckung des Eintretens komplexer Ereignisse wurden in diesem Papier präsentiert. Andere Arbeiten im SAMOS-Projekt betrachten u.a. die Regelausführung. Die Ausführung von Regeln wird untereinander und mit anderen gleichzeitig ausgeführten Transaktionen synchronisiert und in das Modell geschachtelter Transaktionen integriert. Mehrfache Regelauslösung basiert auf Prioritäten; auch für die geschachtelte Regelauslösung stehen entsprechende Konzepte zur Verfügung [GGD 91].

Momentan wird an der Implementierung von SAMOS gearbeitet. Die verschiedenen Komponenten werden auf das objektorientierte Datenbanksystem ObjectStore (unter Inkaufnahme von Leistungseinbussen) aufgesetzt, da in den Quellcode dieses DBS nicht eingegriffen werden kann. Dies ist jedoch insofern erträglich, als es um die Demonstration aktiver Datenbankmechanismen geht, ohne den DBMS-spezifischen Teil von SAMOS neu implementieren zu müssen. Die Konzeptarbeit in SAMOS verfolgt das Ziel, zumindest den Grobansatz, zu welchem auch die Ereignissprache gehört, möglichst unabhängig von einem konkreten objektorientierten Datenbanksystem zu halten.

6 Danksagung

An dieser Stelle möchten wir uns bei der Schweizerischen Bankgesellschaft für die Finanzierung dieses Projektes bedanken. Für Korrekturen des Textes möchten wir uns bei Barbara Rieche und Martin Härtig bedanken.

7 Literatur

[CM 91] Chakravarthy S., Mishra D.; An Event Specification Language (Snoop) For Active Databases and its Detection; Technical Report September 91.

[DBB 88] Dayal U., Blaustein B., Buchmann A., Chakravarthy U., Hsu M., Ladin R., McCarthy D., Rosenthal A., Sarin S., Carey M.J., Livny M., Jauhari R.; The HiPAC Project: Combining Active Databases and Timing Constraints; ACM Sigmod Record, 17(1), March 88.

[DBM 88] Dayal U., Buchmann A. P., McCarthy D.R.; Rules Are Objects Too: A Knowledge Model For An Active, Object-Oriented Database System; Dittrich K. R.(ed.); Proc. 2nd Intl. Workshop on Object-Oriented Database Systems, LNCS 334, Springer 88.

[DPG 91] Diaz O., Patom N., Gray P.; Rule Management in Object-Oriented Databases: A Uniform Approach; Proc. 17th Intl. Conf. on Very Large Data Bases, Barcelona, September 91.

[GGD 91] Gatziu S., Geppert A., Dittrich K.R.; Integrating Active Concepts into an Object-Oriented Database System. Proc. of the 3. Intl. Workshop on Database Programming Languages, August 91.

[GJ 91] Gehami N.H., Jagadish H.V.; Ode as an Active Database: Constraints and Triggers; Proc. 17th Intl. Conf. on Very Large Data Bases, Barcelona, September 91.

[GJS 92a] Gehami N.H., Jagadisch H.V., Schmuelli O.; Event Specification in an Active Object-Oriented Database; Proc. ACM SIGMOD, June 92.

[GJS 92b] Gehami N.H., Jagadisch H.V., Schmueli O.; Composite Event Specification in Active Databases: Model & Implementation; Proc. 18th Intl. Conf. on Very Large Data Bases, Vancouver, August 92.

[KDM 88] Kotz A.M., Dittrich K.R., Mülle J.A.; Supporting Semantic Rules by a Generalized Event/Trigger Mechanism; Proc. Intl. Conf. on Extending Database Technology, Lectures Notes in Computer Science 303, Springer 88.

[MP 90] Medeiros C., Pfeffer P.; A Mechanism for Managing Rules in an Object-Oriented Database; Internal Report ALTAIR, 90.

[Stone 89] Stonebraker M. L.; A Commentary to the Postgres Rule System; SIGMOD Record, 18 (3), September 89.

[WCL 91] Widom J., Cochrane R.J., Lindsay B.G.; Implementing Set-Oriented Production Rules as an Extension to Starburst; Proc. 17th Intl. Conf. on Very Large Data Bases, Barcelona, September 91.

Transaktionskonzepte in der Fertigung

Ursula Schmidt
Universität Stuttgart
IPVR
Breitwiesenstr.20-22
7000 Stuttgart 80
email:ursula.schmidt@informatik.uni-stuttgart.de

Abstract: In diesem Artikel wird im Rahmen einer regulären Architektur zur Transaktionsverarbeitung ein erweiterter Typ von Resource Manager vorgestellt, ein Physical Resource Manager, der Fertigungsoperationen unter Transaktionsschutz anbietet. Dabei bildet eine Transaktion einen Bearbeitungsschritt, z.B. Bohren oder Fräsen, eines Arbeitsplans ab und enthält maximal eine physische Operation. Bei der Spezifikation eines dazu befähigten Physical Resource Managers (PRM) muß besonders berücksichtigt werden, daß dessen Operationen oft nicht rücksetzbar sind. Ein solcher PRM kann maximal nur ein *Reset* im Gegensatz zu einem regulären Rollback ausführen. Dies schließt den klassischen Ansatz der Backward Recovery zur Fehlerbehandlung aus und erfordert eine zusätzliche Komponente zur Fehlerbehandlung, den Physical Recovery Manager. Insgesamt wird eine Neufassung des Begriffes des Ununterbrechbarkeit notwendig.

1 Einleitung

In diesem Kapitel soll der Einsatz von Transaktionen in der Fertigung motiviert werden und eine Abgrenzung zu bisherigen Arbeiten der Fehlertoleranz in Informatik und Fertigung gezogen werden.

1.1 Einführung

Die Bearbeitung von Werkstücken und der Einsatz von automatisch gesteuerten Maschinen blikken auf eine lange Tradition zurück. Schon im Jahre 1808 wurden gelochte Blechkarten zur automatischen Steuerung von Webmaschinen benutzt. Der Sprung zur Technik der numerischen Steuerung erfolgte 1952, als am M.I.T. erstmalig binär kodierte Lochstreifen verwendet wurden, um eine Werkzeugmaschine mit Daten zu versorgen. Die Entwicklung und der technologische Fortschritt nahmen jedoch von Anfang an ihren Ausgangspunkt an der jeweiligen Maschine - Aspekte einer maschinenübergreifenden und systemeinheitlichen Steuerung wurden erst in den letzten Jahren mit dem Aufkommen flexibler Fertigungssysteme Gegenstand wissenschaftlicher Untersuchungen. Vor allem die Forderung nach einer "Just-in-time" Produktion macht jetzt eine Integration der betrieblichen Abläufe in ein allgemeines Systemkonzept notwendig. Während sich für die Kommunikation in der Fertigung inzwischen erste Standards durchsetzen konnten ([MAP, MMS]), fehlen allgemeine Mechanismen zur Steuerung und zur Fehlerbehandlung.

In der Informatik hingegen existieren vor allem im Bereich der verteilten Systeme, der Fehlertoleranz und der transaktionsverarbeitenden Systeme eine Vielfalt von Konzepten und Erfahrungen. Um damit ein Konzept zur einfachen und effektiven Fehlerbehandlung in einer Fertigungsumgebung definieren zu können, wollen wir ein definiertes failfast Verhalten der beteiligten Komponenten zugrundelegen. Dies heißt, wenn eine Komponente von einem Fehler betroffen ist, hält sie an, und zwar in einem wohldefinierten Zustand. Um dieses Verhalten zu gewährleisten, wollen wir Transaktionen verwenden, die ihre Vorteile und Nützlichkeit in transaktionsverarbeitenden Systemen und allgemein in verteilten Systemen zur Genüge unter Beweis gestellt haben.

Der Vorteil des klassischen "ACID"-Transaktionskonzeptes (siehe z.B. [Gr81]) liegt darin, daß zusammen mit einer sicheren, konsistenten Ausführung im logischen Einbenutzerbetrieb eine atomare Ausführung der Gesamtheit der zu einer Transaktion gehörenden Operationen garantiert wird. Daraus entwickelten sich Konzepte zur Behandlung langdauernder, komplexer Transaktionen. Hier ist zum Beispiel das Konzept der Sagas zu nennen [GS87], bei dem Einzeltransaktionen verkettet und explizite Kompensationstransaktionen für den Fehlerfall angegeben werden können. Daraus entstand das ConTract-Modell [WR91], das klassische Transaktionen als Einheiten für Bearbeitung und Kontrollfluß verwendet. Es ist keine Erweiterung des klassischen Transaktionskonzepts, sondern entspricht durch expliziten Kontrollfluß und die sichere Weitergabe von Information (Kontext) über Transaktionsgrenzen hinweg eher einem allgemeinen Programmiermodell.

Alle diese Ansätze legen klassische ACID-Transaktionen als Einheiten der Recovery zugrunde, und insbesondere das Prinzip der Ununterbrechbarkeit. Implizit wird dabei auch immer eine einheitliche Art der Recovery angenommen, nämlich Backward Recovery durch Zurücksetzen der betroffenen Daten auf ihren Ausgangszustand. Dies ist möglich, da die von einer Transaktion ausgeführten Operationen erst zum Zeitpunkt der Transaktion externalisiert werden und da die Operationen immer rücksetzbar und wiederholbar sind.

Erst in letzter Zeit gibt es Versuche, die Vorteile von Transaktionen in weitergehenden Anwendungsgebieten wie der Fertigung einzusetzen. Probleme ergeben sich durch die Andersartigkeit der zu schützenden Operationen, da die bisherigen Annahmen nicht mehr greifen. Die grundlegende Problematik bei der Einbindung von *real actions*, d.h. Operationen, die Auswirkungen auf die reale Welt haben, liegt einerseits darin, daß diese Auswirkungen unmittelbar externalisiert werden und andererseits, daß sie oft nicht rückgängig gemacht werden können. Selbst wenn man sich auf Operationen aus dem Fertigungsbereich beschränkt, findet man Operationen mit den verschiedensten Eigenschaften vor, die einer einheitlichen Recovery im Wege stehen. Dies erfordert eine Erweiterung der bisherigen Konzepte.

1.2 Abgrenzung zu bisherigen Arbeiten

Überlegungen zur Integration von real actions in Transaktionen reichen weit zurück. So wird in [Gr81] vorgeschlagen, real actions erst zum Zeitpunkt des Commit der umgebenden Transaktion durchzuführen. Dies setzt implizit voraus, daß real actions immer gelingen oder daß sie zumindest die Transaktion nicht entscheidend beeinflussen. In unserer Arbeit gehen wir jedoch davon aus, daß real actions fehlschlagen können und daß sich die umgebende Transaktion möglichst nach dem Ergebnis dieser real action auszurichten hat. In [Pa88] werden real actions in verschiedene semantische Klassen unterteilt, um davon ausgehend eine Fehlerbehandlung durchführen zu können[1]. Exemplarisch wurde ein System erstellt, das Eingaben und Ausgaben auf einem Bildschirm unter Transaktionsschutz stellt.

Zwei weitere Arbeiten untersuchen den Einsatz von Transaktionen im Bereich der Fertigungssysteme. In [WZ 87] werden in Anlehnung an den hierarchischen Aufbau eines Fertigungssystems Abstraktionsebenen einer Steuerungshierarchie eingeführt, darunter auch die Ebene der Fertigungstransaktionen. Hier wird die Eigenschaft, daß Transaktionen von einem definierten Zustand in einen anderen definierten Zustand überführen, benutzt, um bestimmte Eigenschaften eines Werkstücks zu beschreiben: eine Fertigungstransaktion überführt ein Teil mit genau festgelegten Eigenschaften in ein neues Teil mit genau festgelegten Eigenschaften. Transaktionen werden zur Modellierung von Vorgängen verwendet; auf Fehlerbehandlung wird nicht eingegangen. [JWZ88] beschreiben das Problem der Nichtrücksetzbarkeit physischer Operationen und motiviert die Notwendigkeit von Forward Recovery. Unter Einführung des Begriffs "point of no return" werden die Unterschiede zwischen Transaktionen in kaufmännischen und technischen Anwendungen herausgehoben.

Im Bereich der flexiblen Fertigungssysteme existieren zahlreiche Arbeiten zum Thema Fehlerdiagnose, jedoch kaum Arbeiten im Hinblick auf die Fehlerbehebung. Falls in Leitsystemen Fehlerbehandlung durchgeführt wird, liegt die Verantwortung für das Ergreifen korrekter Maßnahmen beim Maschinen- und Leitsystembediener. Nach [DIN] ist Qualitätssicherung die "Gesamtheit der Tätigkeiten des Qualitätsmanagements, der Qualitätsplanung, der Qualitätslenkung und der Qualitätsprüfungen". Die Qualitätssicherung in Leitsystemen befaßt sich damit, Fehler im Vorfeld oder während der Produktion zu vermeiden oder fehlerhafte Teile zu erkennen und auszusortieren. Hier haben sich folgende Vorgehensweisen und Begriffe etabliert: Bei der Fehlermöglichkeits- und Einflußanalyse (FMEA) wird versucht, schon vor der Produktion nach möglichen Fehlerquellen zu suchen und diese zu eliminieren. Dies ist sowohl für das Produkt als auch für den Prozeß möglich. Ein ähnlicher Ansatz findet sich beim Quality Function Deployment (QFD oder auch "House of Quality"): Ausgehend von Kundenanforderungen wird das Produkt auf Schwachstellen analysiert. Dagegen soll Statistical Process Control (SPC) im laufenden Produktionsbetrieb systematische Abweichungen von Prozeßsollwerten feststellen und diesen gegensteuern. Dieses Prinzip schließt auch die Überwachung der Werkzeugabnutzung und das rechtzeitige Ersetzen verbrauchter Werkzeuge ein. Total Quality Management (TQM) schließlich hat zum Ziel, die Gesamtheit aller unternehmerischen Aktivitäten unter Qualitätsgesichtspunkten zu optimieren. Unser Ansatz hingegen geht von einem schon eingetretenen und erkannten Fehler aus; im Verlauf dieses Artikels wird beschrieben, wie unter Verwendung des Transaktionskonzeptes die Auswirkungen des Fehlers transparent für die Anwendung umgangen werden und wie weitergearbeitet werden kann.

---

[1] Wir haben diesen Ansatz um eine generische Klasse und orthogonale Unterscheidungskriterien erweitert; dieses dient als logisches Grundgerüst für den in diesem Artikel nicht näher beschriebenen Physical Recovery Manager.

Auf dem Gebiet der Roboteranwendungen existieren zahlreiche Arbeiten zum Thema Fehlererkennung, -diagnose und -behebung. Es wird von autonomen Robotern ausgegangen und es werden hauptsächlich Methoden der Künstlichen Intelligenz eingesetzt. [Do87] untersucht, wie mit Fehlern im Weltmodell eines Roboters, d.h. mit Planungsfehlern, verfahren werden kann. Andere Arbeiten befassen sich mit der Ausnahmebehandlung für Roboter, wobei fest vorgegebene Ersatzpläne vorgesehen sind: In [MH88] werden Roboterausfälle entweder durch Neuplanung für die verbleibenden Aufträge abgefangen oder durch das (dort nicht näher spezifizierte) Anbieten von Ersatzoperationen. Die Probleme der nicht unmittelbar entdeckbaren Fehler und der unvorhergesehenen Ereignisse werden ausführlich in [Gi90] behandelt. Alle diese Arbeiten definieren und benutzen ihre eigene Entwicklungsumgebung. Unser Ansatz konzentriert sich auf Vorgänge in allgemeinen Fertigungssystemen, speziell auf Werkzeugmaschinen. Dort wird eine flexible, dynamische Fehlerbehandlung eigesetzt und gleichzeitig eine automatisch gesicherte Datenkonsistenz geboten.

Dieser Artikel ist wie folgt aufgebaut: Kapitel 2 beschäftigt sich mit den Schnittstellen, die ein Physical Resource Manager (PRM) dem transaktionsverarbeitenden System anbieten muß, ebenso wie mit den relevanten Eigenschaften der Anwendung und deren Auswirkungen auf die Operationen, die eine Transaktion umfassen kann. Im dritten Kapitel wird die Frage behandelt, ob ein PRM Dienste oder reale Maschinen repräsentiert. Daraus werden erste Folgerungen für die Recovery und die Architektur eines PRM vorgestellt. Im vierten Kapitel wird dessen Recovery ausgehend vom physischen Aufbau beschrieben. Kapitel 5 schließt mit einigen zusammenfassenden Bemerkungen und einem Ausblick auf mögliche, folgende Forschungsaktivitäten.

2 Einbettung des PRM in eine transaktionsverarbeitende Architektur

Ein PRM als Teil eines transaktionsverarbeitenden Systems (TPS) muß sowohl die definierten Schnittstellen anderer Komponenten nutzen als auch eigene, definierte Schnittstellen nach außen anbieten. Als Teilnehmer einer globalen Transaktion muß er sowohl mit dem Transaction Manager, der die Koordination aller an einer Transaktion beteiligten Komponenten übernimmt, kooperieren als auch Anwendungen transaktionsgeschützte Dienste anbieten. Hier soll auf die wichtigsten dieser Aspekte eingegangen werden.

2.1 Eigenschaften eines PRM

Zunächst muß geklärt werden, worin sich ein PRM, der Fertigungsoperationen auf einem Werkstück unter Transaktionsschutz anbietet, von einem regulären Resource Manager unterscheidet. Real Actions im allgemeinen, und Fertigungsoperationen im speziellen, besitzen im Vergleich zu Datenbankoperationen die Eigenschaft, daß ihre Auswirkungen sofort sichtbar werden und daß diese Auswirkungen oft nicht rücksetzbar sind. Es kann also nicht vorausgesetzt werden, daß ein Zurücksetzen oder ein Kompensieren möglich sind. Um dennoch Transaktionsschutz zu erreichen, wird im Fehlerfall für eine Transaktion mit Fertigungsoperationen nicht der letzte konsistente Zustand, der Zustand vor Beginn der Transaktion, sondern der nächste konsistente Zustand angestrebt. Mit Hilfe von Forward Recovery wird versucht, die unterbrochene Transaktion erfolgreic zu Ende zu bringen. Es wird semantische Information über die physische Operation ausgewertet, um geeignete Fehlerbehebungsmaßnahmen zu bestimmen. Es muß aber klargestellt werden, daß es Fälle gibt, in denen auch Forward Recovery nicht hilft. Dann muß die Transaktion geregelt zurückgesetzt werden.

2.2 Schnittstellen zum Transaction Manager

Hier stellt sich als erstes die Frage, ob ein PRM seine im Vergleich zu regulären Resource Managern unterschiedliche Recovery externalisiert oder ob er dem (globalen) Transaction Manager eine Schnittstelle bietet wie jeder normale Resource Manager auch. Beim *externalisierten Recoveryverhalten* könnte ein PRM nach einem nicht behebbaren Fehler z.B. ein "physical abort" anstelle eines einfachen "abort" zurückgeben. Hier muß das TPS darauf eingerichtet sein, PRMs mit unterschiedlichen Verhalten zu koordinieren. Die Anwendung hingegen, d.h. der Anwendungsprogrammierer, muß nicht mit diesen Aspekten belastet werden. Die zweite Möglichkeit ist, daß der PRM zum TPS hin ein *reguläres Verhalten* wie ein klassischer RM an den Tag legt. Es ist dann Sache allein des PRMs, Befehle vom Transaction Manager intern in die entsprechenden, semantisch korrekten Aufrufe umzusetzen. Hier muß der Benutzer des TPS wissen, daß er auf Resource Managern arbeitet, die physische Operationen durchführen und ein anderes Verhalten beim Rücksetzen besitzen.

Im Endeffekt läuft dies darauf hinaus, daß entweder das TPS oder der Benutzer des TPS die Unterschiede in den Resource Managern kennen muß. Wir haben uns aus folgenden Gründen für die zweite Möglichkeit entschieden:

- Ein Benutzer einer Fertigungsumgebung weiß ohnehin, wie seine Umgebung beschaffen ist. Er geht nicht davon aus, daß nach dem Fehlschlagen eines Bearbeitungsvorgangs das Werkstück sich wieder im unbearbeiteten Zustand befindet. Er weiß, daß im Fehlerfall Fertigungsoperationen nicht einfach zurückgesetzt werden, da dies nicht generell möglich und oft auch nicht sinnvoll ist. Ist zum Beispiel das aktuelle Werkstück bei einem Transportvorgang beschädigt worden, macht es wenig Sinn, es zunächst zurückzutransportieren, um es dann erst wegzuwerfen.

- Ist jeder Resource Manager (regulärer RM und PRM) für die korrekte Ausführung der empfangenen Aufrufe eigenverantwortlich, können einheitliche Schnittstellen geboten werden, und damit können die unterschiedlichsten Resource Manager in ein (existierendes) TPS eingebunden werden. Andernfalls könnten schon geringfügige Änderungen in einem Resource Manager oder das Einbinden neuer Resource Manager einen Neuentwurf des gesamten Systems notwendig machen.

Ein PRM muß also am Zwei-Phasen-Commit-Protokoll für verteilte Transaktionen teilnehmen können.

2.3 Schnittstellen zur Anwendung

Die Schnittstellen zur Anwendung werden von der Wahl des TPS entscheidend beeinflußt. Wir wollen eine Architektur zur verteilten Transaktionsverarbeitung auf ihre Unterstützung für den Einsatz von PRMs untersuchen und davon ausgehend Anforderungen an geeignete Anwendungsschnittstellen formulieren. Die Anwendung ist dabei jene nicht näher spezifizierte Instanz, die Befehle an RMs ausschickt.

Mit dem Distributed Transaction Processing Model (DTP-Modell) [X/O91] wurde vom X/Open Ausschuß eine allgemeine Systemarchitektur zur verteilten Transaktionsverarbeitung entwickelt (Abb. 1). Es beschreibt, wie verschiedene Resource Manager zu einer Anwendung dazugebunden werden können:

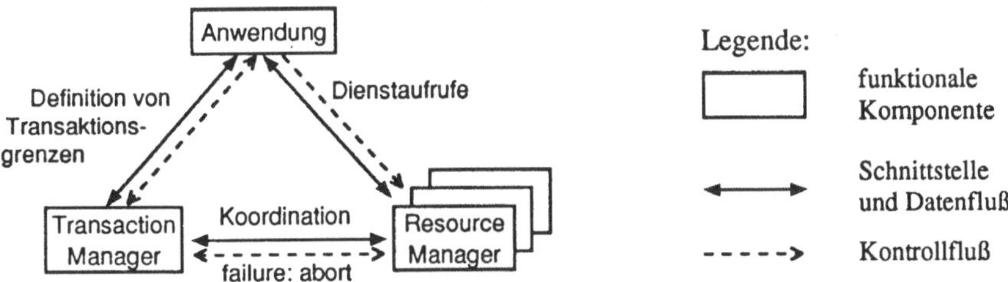

Abb. 1 Architektur nach X/Open

Hier werden autonome Resource Manager vorausgesetzt; der Transaction Manager (TM) übergibt lediglich zu Beginn einer Transaktion einen Transaktionsbezeichner an die beteiligten Resource Manager und koordiniert deren Abschluß. Die Anwendung übergibt beim Aufruf eines Resource Managers keinen Transaktionsbezeichner. Vielmehr muß der Resource Manager die Transaktion anhand des *threads*[1] erkennen, von dem aus er sowohl vom Transaction Manager als auch von der Anwendung aufgerufen wird. Wird z.B. der thread anhand seiner Prozeßkennung identifiziert, so muß diese auf den Transaktionsbezeichner abgebildet werden, um die durch den Prozeß geleistete Arbeit der richtigen Transaktion zuzuordnen. Dadurch läßt sich die natürliche Anwendungsschnittstelle eines Resource Managers ohne Modifikation nutzen.

Zentralisierte Recovery: Es gibt ein ähnliches Modell zur Beschreibung einer Systemarchitektur, das in [GR92] ausführlich beschrieben ist. Hier wird von einem zentralen Transaction Manager ausgegangen, und es wird auch ein zentraler Log für alle Resource Manager angenommen, mit Hilfe dessen der Transaction Manager Recovery für die Resource Manager durchführt. Durch die Zentralisierung der Recovery können fortgeschrittene Recoverytechniken realisiert werden.

[1] Ein thread ist hier ein Betriebssystemprozeß.

Unser Ansatz nimmt unabhängige Resource Manager mit eigenem Log und selbständiger Recovery an. Bei Aufrufen eines RM wird immer der dazugehörige Transaktionsbezeichner mit übergeben. Dies ist uns vor allem bei der Fehlerbehandlung wichtig. Für die Recovery werden die Grundtechniken des Modells des zentralen Logs übernommen, speziell die im folgenden verwendete Undo- und Redo-Logik.

2.4 Die Anwendung - Integration des PRM in ein Fertigungssystem

Die Frage, wie ein TPS mit PRMs in der Fertigung eingesetzt werden kann, wirft die Frage nach der Art der Anwendung, die die PRMs aufruft, auf.

Nach dem allgemeinen Modell zur verteilten Transaktionsverarbeitung ist die Anwendung die Instanz, die Dienstaufrufe an die RMs sendet. Unsere Betrachtungen beziehen sich auf die Fertigung, genauer auf die Möglichkeiten der automatischen Fehlerbehebung in Fertigungs- oder CAM (Computer Aided Manufacturing) - Systemen, und als Anwendung kommt hier nur ein Leitsystem in Betracht. Von den vielfältigen Funktionen innerhalb eines Leitsystems wie Auftragseinplanung, Werkzeugüberwachung oder Betriebsdatenüberwachung interessiert uns besonders die sogenannte Auftragsdurchsetzung. Sie ist dafür zuständig, die für die Bearbeitung von Werkstücken notwendigen Operationen zu initiieren und durchführen zu lassen und dabei einen von anderen Funktionen erstellten Zeitplan einzuhalten. Die Aufrufe für die Durchführung der Operationen sollen jetzt nicht mehr direkt an die jeweiligen Maschinen gesendet werden, sondern an die Physical Resource Manager gehen, die die jeweilige Maschine oder Zelle repräsentieren. Erst nach dem Ausführen der notwendigen Maßnahmen, um die Operation unter Transaktionsschutz zu stellen, werden die einzelnen PRM-Aufrufe an die zugrundeliegenden Maschinen weitergeleitet.

Hier stellt sich die Frage, wie und von wem die Transaktionsgrenzen gesetzt werden. Hierzu ist es nötig, sich die Abläufe im Leitsystem von der Auftragserteilung bis zur Auftragsdurchsetzung anzusehen (es soll hier aber nicht auf den prinzipiellen Aufbau von Leitsystemen eingegangen werden). Nach der Auftragserteilung wird für das Werkstück[1] der Arbeitsplan[2] abgearbeitet, und alle Operationen werden zur Bearbeitung an verschiedenen Maschinenklassen eingeplant. Die nötigen Transportvorgänge zwischen den Bearbeitungsmaschinen werden erst bei Bedarf bestimmt, da die Instanzen des geforderten Maschinentyps und damit deren Positionen nicht von vornherein feststehen.

Hier bietet es sich geradezu an, jeden Schritt des Arbeitsplans durch eine Transaktion als Einheit der Recovery zu modellieren; in diesem Fall können die Transaktionsgrenzen automatisch beim Umsetzen des Arbeitplans in Operationen auf Maschinen gesetzt werden. Aus der sequentiellen Struktur eines Arbeitsplans für einen Werkstücktyp ergibt sich eine sequentielle Folge der einzel-

[1] Der Einfachheit halber wird von Losgröße eins ausgegangen.

[2] Ein Arbeitsplan ist eine Sequenz von Operationen (ohne Transportvorgänge), die an einem Werkstück durchgeführt werden sollen, unter Angabe von Parametern wie Maschinentyp oder Bearbeitungsdauer.

nen Transaktionen, Transaktionskette genannt. Jedes zu bearbeitende Werkstück wird durch eine Instanz seines Transaktionskettentyps beschrieben; diese Instanz wird dann abhängig von der tatsächlichen Ausführungsfolge modifiziert.

2.5 Annahmen über Transaktionen

Transaktionen auf PRMs enthalten physische und nichtphysische Operationen. Physische Operationen sind Operationen, die das Werkstück in seiner Form verändern, beispielsweise Fräsen, Bohren oder Drehen, und Transportoperationen, die das Werkstück bewegen. Als nichtphysische Operationen bieten PRMs typischerweise Operationen der Programmverwaltung (z.B. Laden, Binden oder Starten) oder auch das Lesen und Schreiben von Statusvariablen an[1].

Physische Operationen haben keine "prepare"-Phase. Entweder schlagen sie fehl oder sie gelingen - ihr Ergebnis wird aber in jedem Fall sofort sichtbar. Nichtphysische Operationen in einer Transaktionen sind oft vom Ergebnis der physischen Operation semantisch abhängig, und daher muß man versuchen, das Ergebnis der Gesamttransaktion vom Ergebnis der physischen Operationen abhängig zu machen. Beim parallelen Ablauf zweier physischer Operationen in einer Transaktion jedoch gibt es, wenn die Operationen nicht entweder beide erfolgreich beendet werden oder beide scheitern, kein gemeinsames Ergebnis, nach dem sich der Ausgang der Gesamttrans-aktion richten kann. Wr können zwar für die fehlgeschlagene Operation Forward Recovery veranlassen, aber es gibt Fälle, in denen diese nicht gelingt. Um die Konsistenz der Daten zu erhalten, müßten dann die semantischen Abhängigkeiten der nichtphysischen von den physischen Operationen bekannt sein, was wir nicht voraussetzen können. Der Fall zweier paralleler physischer Operationen, und damit der mehrerer paralleller physischer Operationen, innerhalb einer Transaktion muß daher ausgeschlossen werden. Die parallele Ausführung mehrerer Operationen, z.B. Doppellochbohren, kann jedoch als eine einzige Operation aufgefaßt werden, solange sie von einem einzigen Dienstaufruf verursacht wird und somit auch nur ein Ergebnis liefert.

Es werden also nur Transaktionen betrachtet, die genau eine physische und beliebig viele nichtphysische Operationen umfassen. Prinzipiell ist es zwar möglich, Transaktionen mit mehreren, sequentiellen physischen Operationen zu behandeln; dies bedingt jedoch eine höhere Komplexität der Recoverymechanismen. Um die grundlegenden Mechanismen zu erklären, beschränken wir uns auf den einfacheren Fall einer physischen Operation je Transaktion.

Des weiteren nehmen wir an, daß die Aufrufe einer noch nicht abgeschlossenen Transaktion über jede Art von Fehler hinaus erhalten bleiben. Dies könnte durch eine stabile Warteschlange für Aufrufe realisiert werden, aus der diese Aufrufe nur entfernt werden, wenn sie erfolgreich bearbeitet worden sind (siehe dazu [BHM90]). Damit wird das Fortsetzen einer Transaktion nach erfolgreicher Fehlerbehandlung ermöglicht.

---

[1] Typische Dienste eines Fertigungsgerätes sind z.B. im Kommunikationsprotokoll Manufacturing Message Specification (MMS) beschrieben [MMS].

2.6 Einhalten der ACID - Eigenschaften

Insgesamt stellt sich die Frage, inwieweit die von uns auf RMs und PRMs definierten Transaktionen noch die Eigenschaften klassischer Transaktionen bewahren.

Nichtphysische Operationen auf PRMs sollen genauso geschützt werden wie nichtphysische Operationen auf regulären RMs[1]. (Diese Thematik allerdings war und ist Gegenstand zahlreicher Untersuchungen, und es soll in diesem Artikel nicht weiter darauf eingegangen werden).

Es wurde schon erklärt, daß Ununterbrechbarkeit nur noch für die PRMs, nicht mehr aber für das Werkstück garantiert werden kann. Konsistenz ist ebenfalls gewährleistet, zumindest nach unseren Anforderungen: im Falle eines Fehlers werden alle Daten zurückgesetzt und mit Abbruch der Transaktion verschwindet auch das Werkstück, logisch gesehen, aus dem System[2]. Wir können diese Eigenschaften garantieren, da wir nur (P)RMs betrachten, die reguläre Resource Manager und Fertigungsgeräte im weiteren Sinne darstellen. Für das Werkstück selbst steht aber im TPS kein Repräsentant zur Verfügung, außer der Instanz der Transaktionskette und den das Werkstück beschreibenden Variablen, für die jedoch wieder die klassischen Transaktionseigenschaften geboten werden. Isolation und Dauerhaftigkeit gelten unverändert.

3 Resource Manager und Transaktionen

Vor der eigentlichen Beschreibung der Recovery für einen Physical Resource Manager müssen noch zwei grundlegende Aspekte der Modellierung geklärt werden: Zum einen stellt sich die Frage, welche Objekte oder Dienste ein PRM denn nun darstellen soll - eine Maschine, eine Fertigungszelle[3] oder eine Klasse von Operationen, und es muß festgelegt werden, welcher Mechanismus bei Abbruch einer Transaktion an die Stelle des Rollbacks tritt. Zum anderen muß geklärt werden, wie ein PRM aufgebaut ist.

3.1 Abbildung von Werkzeugmaschinen auf Resource Manager

Es gilt also zu klären, wie Dienste auf einen Physical Resource Manager abgebildet werden können und um welche Dienste es sich dabei handelt. In einer Fertigungsumgebung konkretisiert sich dieses Problem zu der Frage, ob ein PRM Klassen von Diensten oder Klassen von Maschinen zum TPS hin vertritt. Davon hängt ab, ob sich Konzepte klassischer Resource Manager auch auf PRMs übertragen lassen.

---

[1] Siehe dazu jede relationale Datenbank oder transaktionsgeschützte Dateisystems wie in [SW91] oder [EMS89].

[2] Die Daten über das Werkstück können natürlich weiterverwendet werden, z.B. bei einer manuellen Weiterbearbeitung außerhalb von Transaktionen.

[3] Eine Fertigungszelle ist eine Gruppe gleichartiger Werkzeugmaschinen, die nach außen, d.h. zum Leitsystem wie eine einzige Maschine wirkt und auch als eine einzige Maschine angesprochen wird.

Repräsentation von Werkzeugmaschinen: Viele Werkzeugmaschinen bieten verschiedene Klassen von Operationen an - auf manchen Bearbeitungszentren kann sowohl gebohrt als auch gefräst werden, Drehmaschinen erlauben oft auch Fräsarbeiten. Durch das direkte Aufeinanderfolgen der Operationen lassen sich Be- und Entladezeiten ebenso einsparen wie die Zeit, die möglicherweise für eine neue Einspannung gebraucht wird. Andererseits können in einem Fertigungssystem verschiedene Maschinen auch den gleichen Typ von Operation, zum Beispiel Fräsen, anbieten. Wir bevorzugen die direkte Abbildung einer Werkzeugmaschine auf einen PRM aus zwei Gründen:

- Jede Werkzeugmaschine verhält sich anders, wenn sie eine Operation durchführt. Sie kann z.B. unterschiedliche Genauigkeitsklassen anbieten oder nach bestimmten Fehlern die Fortsetzung der unterbrochenen Operation (d.h. des Bearbeitungsprogramms) unterstützen. Es erscheint nicht angebracht, Operationen mit derart verschiedenem Verhalten von einer einzigen Instanz anbieten zu lassen.

- Bei der direkten Abbildung wird die Integration eines Resource Managers in ein Leitsystem vereinfacht. Anstelle einer realen Werkzeugmaschine wird der stellvertretende PRM beauftragt; Planungs und Scheduling müssen nicht von der Leitsystemebene in die der Resource Manager verlagert werden.

Konzept der Serverprozesse: In der klassischen Transaktionsverarbeitung existiert das Konzept, identische Serverprozesse einer Serverklasse und damit einem Resource Manager zuzuordnen und bei Bedarf neue Serverprozesse erzeugen zu lassen. Man könnte nun versucht sein, in der Fertigungsumgebung das Analogon in einem PRM, der eine Fertigungszelle darstellt, zu sehen. Prozesse jedoch sind billig, schnell und leicht zu replizieren - was auf Fertigungsmaschinen nicht zutrifft und auch nicht auf die von ihnen angebotenen Dienste. Die Beziehungen zwischen diesen Elementen werden in Abb.2 mit Hilfe eines Entity-Relationship-Diagramms dargestellt:

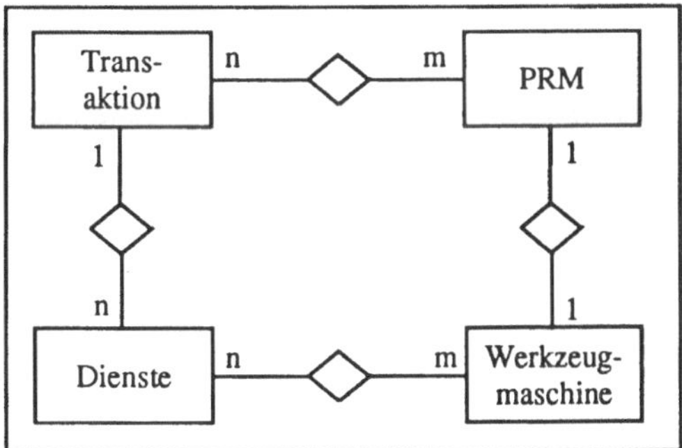

Jede Transaktion kann verschiedene PRMs aufrufen; dabei ist jedoch zu beachten, daß nur einer dieser PRMs eine physische Operation ausführen darf. Jeder PRM kann von verschiedenen Transaktionen aufgerufen werden.

Jeder Dienst wird zu einem bestimmten Zeitpunkt für genau eine Transaktion ausgeführt; eine Transaktion kann beliebig viele Dienste aufrufen, aber nur einer davon darf eine physische Operation sein.

Abb. 2 Beziehungen zwischen Transaktionen, Resource Managern, Maschinen und Diensten

Dennoch ist es möglich, eine Fertigungszelle von einem einzigen PRM darstellen zu lassen. Die Fehlerbehandlung innerhalb einer solchen Fertigungszelle, beispielsweise das Wiederholen eines durch Maschinenausfall unterbrochenen Bearbeitungsvorganges auf einer funktionsfähigen Maschine, wird nach außen hin nicht sichtbar und ist dann auch nicht Sache des PRM's. Die Vorgehensweise enspricht derjenigen auf Inter-PRM-Ebene[1], und es wird an dieser Stelle nicht weiter darauf eingegangen.

Prozeßmigration: Ähnliches trifft auch für die Prozeßmigration zu. In der regulären Transaktionsverarbeitung kann ein Prozeß auf einen anderen Knoten migrieren, indem dessen Daten und Kontext übertragen werden. Dort kann er fortgesetzt werden, als ob er sich auf dem ursprünglichen Knoten befände und nicht unterbrochen worden wäre. Wie jedoch ist der Kontext der Bearbeitung eines Werkstücks auf einer Werkzeugmaschine zu sehen? Wir beschränken uns vereinfachend auf die Achspositionen der Maschine, die mit Sicherheit zum Kontext zählen. Nun könnte eine identische Werkzeugmaschine, falls verfügbar, die gleichen Achspositionen einnehmen, was durch ein Wiederholen das Programms bis zum Unterbrechungszeitpunkt erfolgen kann. Zudem muß das Werkstück geladen werden, unserem Gegenstück zu den Daten, und genau hier treten die Probleme auf. Das Werkstück muß geladen werden, bevor die Achsen die "Kontext"-positionen einnehmen, da diese sich beim Ladevorgang in sicheren Positionen befinden müssen, d.h. in Positionen, in denen keine Möglichkeit einer Kollision mit dem Werkstück besteht. Üblicherweise müssen dazu die Achsen sogenannte Referenzpunkte anfahren. Erst nach dem Laden des Werkstücks kann der Kontext geladen, d.h. das Programm neu begonnen werden. Selbst wenn wir annehmen, daß das Werkstück die Programmunterbrechung unbeschadet überstanden hat, können wir doch nicht annehmen, daß die Operation wiederholbar ist, d.h. daß das Werkstück eine Wiederholung des Programmes bis zur Einnahme der Achspositionen zum Unterbrechungszeitpunkt im Sinne der Anwendung unbeschadet übersteht.

Eine Migration im Sinne eines physischen Ortswechsels des Werkstücks und Neustart des Programmes kann, wenn überhaupt, nur vom Physical Recovery Manager veranlaßt werden, der explizit den Transport eines Werkstückes und die folgende Zwischen- und Weiterbearbeitung auf einer anderen Maschine veranlaßt. Zur Unterstützung einer solchen Migration sollte die Maschinenadressierung nicht direkt, sondern relativ über einen Zeiger auf die aktuelle Maschine erfolgen. Beispielsweise führt ein maschinenbezogener Befehl der Art "Schreibe Ergebnis der vorigen Operation auf PRM A" nach einer Migration von Maschine A auf Maschine B zu einer Inkonsistenz, der Befehl "Schreibe Ergebnis auf aktuelle Maschine" liefert jedoch das gewünschte Resultat.

3.2 Reset, Rollback und Abort

In herkömmlichen TPS wird ein Abort einer Transaktion mit Hilfe eines Rollback, also des Zurücksetzens der Effekte der bisher durchgeführten Operationen, auf den beteiligten Resource Managern durchgeführt.

---

[1] Hier zeigt sich, wie sich analog zum hierarchischen Aufbau eines Fertigungssystems eine ebenfalls hierarchische Fehlerbehandlung entwickelt.

Ein Physical Resource Manager kann kein Rollback durchführen, wenn er schon eine physische Operation ausgeführt hatte. Ihm bleibt nur ein *Reset*: Ein *Reset* ist das Gegenstück eines PRMs zum Rollback eines regulären RMs. Es setzt alle Operationen einer Transaktion zurück, wobei die Rücksetzoperationen für nichtphysische Operationen aus dem Log bestimmt werden. Physische Operationen werden insofern zurückgesetzt, als die Maschine in ihre Referenzposition gefahren und das Werkstück herausgeladen wird. Aus Sicht der Werkzeugmaschine ist damit der Zustand, der vor Beginn der Transaktion herrschte, wiederhergestellt worden und somit wird auch eine eingeschränkte Art von Ununterbrechbarkeit erreicht. Die Sicht, genauer: der Zustand, des Werkstücks kann beim Reset nicht berücksichtigt werden.

3.3 Laden und Entladen eines Werkstückes

Allgemein ist eine generelle Strategie notwendig, die das Laden und Entladen von Werkstücken im Rahmen der Fehlerbehandlung abdeckt. Ein Reset eines PRM wird dann, und nur dann, durchgeführt, wenn die Transaktion zumindest auf diesem PRM nicht mehr aus- oder fortgeführt werden kann. Wir fordern, daß beim Auftreten eines Resets die Maschine in einem Zustand hinterlassen wird, in dem prinzipiell noch andere Transaktionen darauf ablaufen können. Dies bedeutet auch, daß das aktuelle Werkstück entladen werden muß. Dabei kann vorausgesetzt werden, daß das Entladen eines Werkstückes immer mit dem Einnehmen der Referenzpositionen durch die Werkzeugmaschine (Referenzfahrt) gekoppelt ist. Diese Aktion kann nur vom Physical Recovery Manager durch den Aufruf des Reset initiiert werden[1]. Damit wird auch das zu Beginn erwähnte failfast-Verhalten erreicht - nach erfolgloser Recovery befindet sich der PRM in einem wohldefinierten Ausgangszustand.

3.4 Komponenten eines Physical Resource Managers

Nach den bisherigen Ausführungen hat ein PRM die Aufgabe, eine Werkzeugmaschine zum transaktionsverarbeitenden System hin zu vertreten. Nun muß der realen Aufbau eines solchen PRMs beschrieben werden. Prinzipiell besteht ein PRM aus zwei Teilen, der eigentlichen NC-Maschine und dem PRM-Kern mit dem Log, der die NC-Maschine nach außen mit Transaktionssemantik anbietet. Die Maschine selbst wird über eine numerische Steuerung (NC) mit Daten und Programmen versorgt (Abb. 3). Jede dieser drei Komponenten kann sich auf einem separatem Knoten befinden. Es gibt sogar Implementierungen, bei denen die Steuerung auf mehrere Knoten verteilt ist. Vom funktionalen Gesichtspunkt jedoch kann und muß die Steuerung als eine Komponente betrachtet werden. Es ist deren Aufgabe, nach außen ein korrektes Verhalten zu zeigen.

---

[1] Der Physical Recovery Manager hat eine Zwischenstellung zwischen Anwendung und Transaktionsmanager.

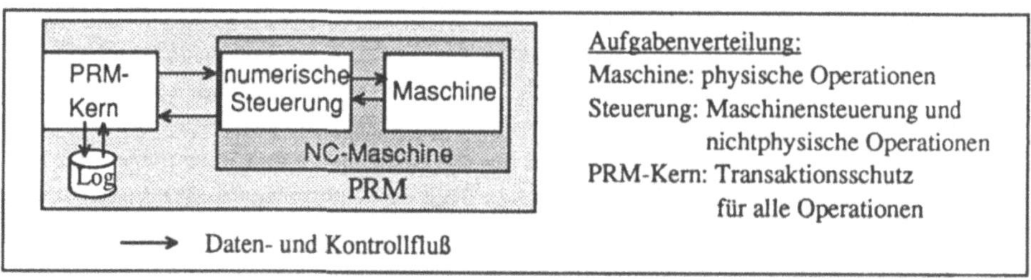

Abb. 3 Komponenten eines Physical Resource Managers

PRM-Kern: Der PRM-Kern ist die Schnittstelle des PRM zum TPS und dafür verantwortlich, eintreffende Dienstaufrufe unter Transaktionsschutz durchzuführen. Im Normalbetrieb beschränken sich seine Aktivitäten darauf, diese Dienstaufrufe in einen Log zu schreiben (dazu mehr in den folgenden Abschnitten) und die gewünschten Operationen durchzuführen bzw. von der NC-Maschine durchführen zu lassen. Der PRM-Kern nutzt die NC-Maschine als Server, um deren Dienste der Außenwelt anzubieten.
Der PRM-Kern und die NC-Maschine müssen möglicherweise über ein Netzwerk miteinander kommunizieren - dies wird bei der Erweiterung existierender NC-Maschinen zu PRMs oft unumgänglich. Im Vergleich zu regulären RMs vergrößert dies die Verantwortung des PRM-Kerns, doch nur auf diese Weise lassen sich existierende Maschinen in ein TPS integrieren[1].

Nichtphysische Operationen auf einer Werkzeugmaschine: Die Verwaltung von Programmen und Daten einer Werkzeugmaschine zählt zu den Aufgaben einer NC. Wir nehmen daher an, daß der Datenserver für die nichtphysischen Operationen sich auf dem gleichen Knoten wie die NC befindet. Bei sehr intensivem Datenzugriff mag eine separate Komponente, die auch dem PRM-Kern zugeordnet sein kann, notwendig werden. Da jedoch physische Operationen die typischen und auch langwierigsten Operationen in der Fertigung sind und Operationen auf Daten normalerweise nicht der Engpaß sind, gehen wir auf diesen Fall nicht weiter ein.

Der Log: Der Log dient dem sicheren und dauerhaften Speichern von Einträgen zur Unterstützung der Recovery. Der PRM benutzt ihn, um für jeden empfangenen Aufruf einen Logeintrag, bestehend aus dem Dienstaufruf mit seinen Parametern und dem Transaktionsbezeichner sowie den dazugehörigen Redo- und Undo-Einträgen, sicher zu speichern. Dieser Eintrag wird vom PRM vor der eigentlichen Ausführung des Dienstes gemacht. Dann ist es für die Recovery unwesentlich, ob der Fehler vor oder nach der Ausführung des Dienstes geschehen ist: Da wir Idempotenz für nichtphysische Operationen annehmen, hinterlassen sowohl das Undo einer noch nicht ausgeführten Operation als auch das Redo einer schon ausgeführten Operation keine unerwünschten Effekte. Physische Operationen werden gesondert vom Physical Recovery Manager behandelt, da sie im allgemeinen nicht einfach zurückgesetzt werden können.

---

[1] Bei der Entwicklung neuer Maschinen könnten PRM-Kern und NC-Steuerung integriert werden, und beim Entwurf der NC - Steuerung sollte auch auf die Belange des PRM-Kerns eingegangen werden.

Bestimmung der Log-Einträge: Um die Undo- und Redo-Einträge zu einer Operation bestimmen zu können, muß ein PRM zu jeder Operation (außer einer physischen) die entsprechenden Undo- und Redo-Operationen kennen. Für Leseoperationen beispielsweise ist die Undo-Operation die leere Operation, für Schreiboperationen ist es die Wiederherstellung des ursprünglichen Werts. Geladene Segmente oder Dateien werden durch Löschen zurückgesetzt. Nimmt man als Anwendungsschnittstelle MMS[1] an, so kann man von ungefähr achtzig Diensten ausgehen, von denen eine reale Werkzeugmaschine in der Regel nur eine Untermenge realisiert. Die Zuordnung von Aufruf zu Undo-Aufruf kann daher mit Hilfe einer einfachen Tabelle im PRM erfolgen. Der Redo-Aufruf ist aufgrund der Idempotenz im allgemeinen der Aufruf selbst.

Implementierung des Log: Wir nehmen für PRMs einen Log an, der direkt auf stabilen Speicher zugreift. Im Vergleich zu Höchstleistungsdatenbanksystemen tritt bei der Kommunikation mit Fertigungsgeräten nur ein geringer Datenverkehr auf. Da zudem jeder PRM einen eigenen Log besitzt, sollte dieser nicht die Ursache für Durchsatzminderungen sein. In hochentwickelten Transaktionsverarbeitungs-systemen hingegen kann ein Log, der direkt auf stabilen Speicher zugreift, leicht zum Engpaß werden. Dort ist man zum Teil dazu übergegangen, zur Durchsatzerhöhung Einträge im flüchtigen Hauptspeicher zwischenzuspeichern. Dies führt zu einer erhöhten Komplexität der Recoveryalgorithmen.

4 Recovery

In diesem Kapitel wird beschrieben, wie ein PRM Fehler behandelt. Unter Fehlern verstehen wir hier nicht konzeptuelle Fehler oder Programmfehler, sondern ausschließlich Fehler, die durch Ausfälle einzelner Komponenten bedingt sind. Weiter wird angenommen, daß Fehler immer entdeckt oder mitgeteilt werden. Als erstes werden die Maßnahmen bei isolierten Fehlern der beteiligten Komponenten beschrieben. Daraus lassen sich die Recoveryalgorithmen bei Fehlern mehrerer Komponenten ableiten. In diesem Zusammenhang wird auch auf die Reaktion auf einen Rücksetz-Befehl des Transaktionsmanagers eingegangen.

Das Vorgehen besteht darin, bei Auftreten eines Fehlers die Transaktion wieder in den Zustand zum Fehlerzeitpunkt zu bringen und danach weiterzuarbeiten. Mit dem erneuten Versuch der Durchführung soll ein Abbruch der Transaktion möglichst verhindert werden. Prinzipiell kan dies durch Abarbeiten der Undo- und Redo- Einträge aus dem Log erreicht werden: müssen Op erationen rückgängig gemacht werden, wird der Log sequentiell abgearbeitet, beginnend mit der Undo-Operation des letzten Aufrufes und endend mit der der ersten Aufrufes. Beim Wiederholen schon durchgeführter Operationen hingegen wird mit der als erstes ausgeführten Operation begonnen. Eine effektive Implementierung eines Logs zur Unterstützung dieses Vorgehens ist in [GR92] ausführlich beschrieben. Die Sonderstellung der physischen Operationen wird im folgenden noch besprochen.

---

[1] MMS (Manufacturing Message Specification) ist ein Anwendungsprotokoll des auf dem ISO/OSI - Referenzmodell basierenden Profil MAP (Manufacturing Automation Protocol) und ist für die offene Kommunikation in Fertigungsumgebungen entwickelt worden.

Motiviert wird diese Art der Forward Recovery durch den Unterschied zu regulären Resource Managern. Bei ihnen führt ein Fehler unter Einsatz von Backward Recovery zum Rücksetzen der globalen Transaktion. Dort ist im Normalfall ein Wiederholen der Transaktion möglich, in der Fertigung jedoch nicht. Ein PRM versucht zunächst auf lokaler Ebene, d.h. auf dem betroffenen PRM, den Fehler zu beheben und die Transaktion fortzuführen. Schlägt die lokale Recovery fehl, wird versucht, die Transaktion auch unter Einbezug anderer PRMs zu Ende zu bringen. Nur wenn keine Möglichkeit zur Weiterführung mehr besteht, darf zurückgesetzt werden.

Wir wollen vergleichend das Recoveryprotokoll eines PRMs dem für einen regulären RM gegenüberstellen. Abb. 4 zeigt, wie prinzipiell mit einer Transaktion verfahren wird, in deren Verlauf ein Fehler auftritt.

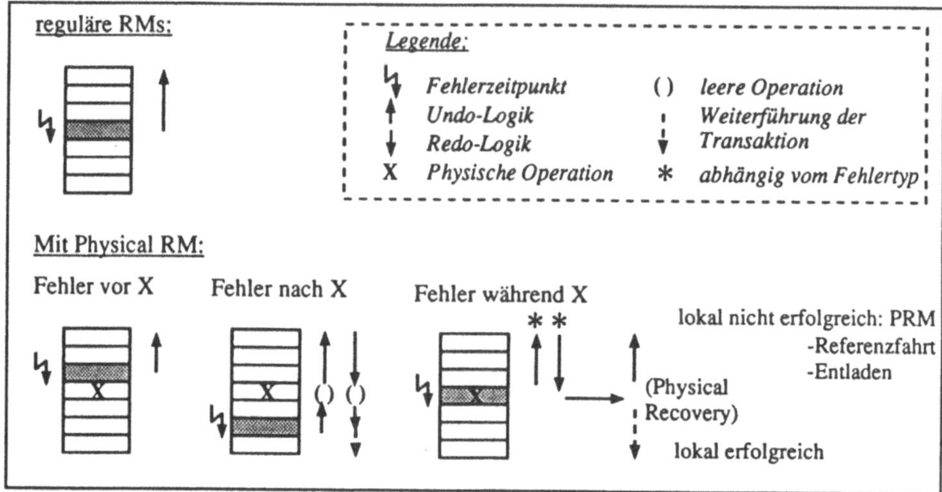

Abb. 4 Recovery für einen PRM

Die folgenden Abschnitten gehen auf die verschiedenen Fehler- und Rücksetzursachen und ihre Auswirkungen auf diese Vorgehensweise ein.

4.1 Rücksetzen

Ein PRM kann von seinem Transaction Manager aus Gründen, die außerhalb seiner Kontrolle liegen, eine Aufforderung zum Rücksetzen erhalten. Hier bleibt nichts anderes übrig, als ein "Reset" durchzuführen. Die Maschine wird also in die Grundposition gebracht, das Werkstück gegebenenfalls entladen und für die nichtphysischen Befehle die Undo-Logik angewendet.

4.2 Isolierter Fehler der Maschine

Die Recoverymaßnahmen für physische Operationen hängen von zahlreichen Faktoren ab, die oft erst zum Fehlerzeitpunkt bestimmt werden können. Da eine Einplanung aller Fehlerfälle, Faktoren und Recoverymöglichkeiten in den Arbeitsplan diesen soweit aufblähen würde, daß eine effektive Bearbeitung nicht mehr gesichert scheint, wird eine eigene Komponente, der Physical Recovery Manager, zur Verfügung gestellt. Er bestimmt bei Bedarf, und nur dann, die angemessenen Recoverymaßnahmen. Hier fließen Faktoren wie Art der Operation, Art des Fehlers, Zustand des Werkstückes, Zustand der Maschine oder auch allgemeine Strategien ein. Wir unterscheiden zwei Arten von Operationen: unterbrechbare, die weiter in wiederholbar, weiterführbar oder kompensierbar eingeteilt werden, und nicht unterbrechbare. Der Physical Recovery Manager bestimmt as all diesen Faktoren die jeweiligen Maßnahmen und fügt sie in den Arbeitsplan ein, der von der Anwendung, die nichts von dem Fehler bemerkt, abgearbeitet wird (siehe auch Abb. 5). Eine ausführlichere Beschreibung der Arbeitsweise des Physical Recovery Managers findet sich in [Sc92].

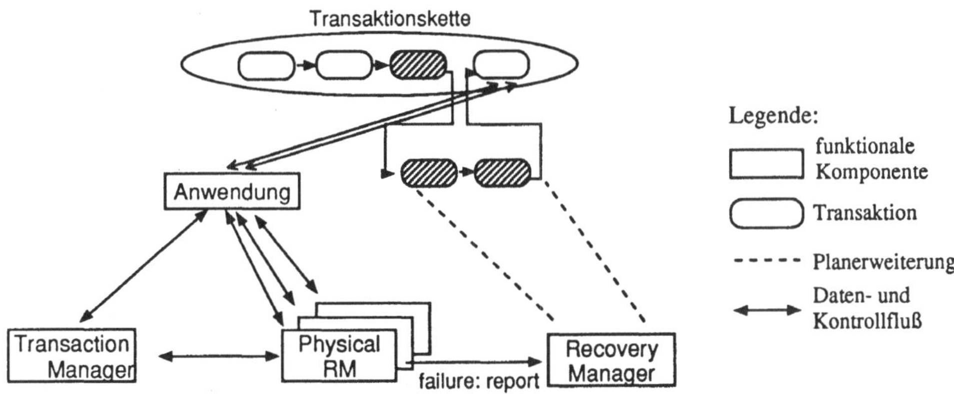

Abb. 5 Fehlerbehandlung bei physischen Operationen

Wichtig hierbei ist, daß die Recovery innerhalb der gleichen Transaktion stattfindet. Dies wird bewerkstelligt, indem der Transaktionsbezeichner der aktuellen Transaktion allen zur Recovery gehörenden Aufrufen mitgegeben wird. Bei lokaler Recovery, d.h. bei einer Fehlerbehebung ohne Einbezug anderer PRMs, werden die aktuellen Sperren der Transaktion gehalten und die Transaktion wird auf diesem PRM nach erfolgreicher Recovery weitergeführt. Im Prinzip geschieht hier nichts anderes, als daß die Transaktion durch Einfügen von Reparaturschritten erweitert wird. Sind Schritte auf anderern PRMs notwendig, wird auf dem aktuellen PRM ein Reset durchgeführt, damit dort zumindest noch andere Transaktionen ausgeführt werden können. Nun kann es durchaus geschehen, daß mehrere physische Reparaturschritte im Rahmen einer Fehlerbehandlung durchgeführt werden. Im Falle des endgültigen Scheiterns müssen dann alle beteiligten PRMs einen Reset durchführen. Falls ein PRM mehrere physische Operationen durchgeführt hatte, wird nur eine Referenzfahrt der Maschine durchgeführt.

4.3 Isolierter Fehler der NC-Steuerung

Aus Sicherheitsgründen führt dieser Fehler unmittelbar zu einem Nothalt der angesteuerten Maschine. Da in der Steuerung aufgrund des Fehlers mit großer Wahrscheinlichkeit Information über den realen Zustand der Maschine verlorengegangen sein kann, müssen das Bild, das die Steuerung von der Maschine besitzt, und der reale Zustand der Maschine wieder konsistent gemacht werden. Andernfalls entstünde ein beträchtliches Gefahrenpotential, das unter allen Umständen verhindert werden muß. Die einzige Möglichkeit, wieder Übereinstimmung zu erreichen, ist, sowohl die Maschine als auch die Steuerung zurückzusetzen, z.B. durch eine Referenzfahrt und einen Warmstart.

Da wir vorausgesetzt hatten, daß die Verwaltung von nichtphysischen Operationen einer Transaktion der Steuerung zugeordnet sind, entspricht der Warmstart der Steuerung dem Rücksetzen des nichtphysischen Teils der Transaktion. Zusammen mit der Referenzfahrt der Werkzeugmaschine erhalten wir also einen Zustand ähnlich dem nach einem Reset, mit dem Unterschied, daß das Werkstück nicht ausgeladen wurde.

Als nächstes wird die Transaktion wiederholt. Dazu holt der PRM-Kern die bisher ausgeführten Aufrufe, genauer gesagt: die Redo-Einträge, aus dem Log und führt diese aus, bis die physische Operation erreicht wird oder bis keine Redo-Einträge mehr im Log vorhanden sind. Falls jetzt keine Redo-Operationen mehr im Log vorhanden sind, wird mit der Transaktion an der unterbrochenen Stelle fortgefahren. Falls sich noch Redo-Einträge im Log befinden, gibt es zwei Möglichkeiten:

1.) Im einfachen Fall erfolgte der Nothalt, nachdem die physische Operation schon beendet war (in diesem Fall hatte er keine unmittelbaren Auswirkungen auf das Werkstück). Der Log-Eintrag für die physische Operation wird dann einfach übersprungen und die Redo-Einträge werden weiter abgearbeitet. Vor der Abarbeitung des letzten Log-Eintrages besteht eine gewisse Unsicherheit, ob diese Operation schon begonnen oder beendet wurde. Hier kann der Zustand der Transaktionswarteschlange weiterhelfen. Da wir idempotente nichtphysische Operationen annehmen, richtet es aber ohnehin keinen Schaden an, die Operation möglicherweise zu wiederholen.

2.) Im komplexeren Fall war die unterbrochene Operation eine physische. Hier muß der Physical Recovery Manager zu Rate gezogen werden, wie weiter verfahren werden soll. Nach erfolgreicher Recovery wird dann mit dem ursprünglichen Arbeitsplan fortgefahren[1].

Dieser Ansatz berücksichtigt noch nicht, daß eine Steuerung endgültig ausfallen kann, z.B. durch elektromechanische Fehler oder durch Fehler im Programmspeicher. Der Physical Recovery Manager kann damit zwar umgehen, für die interne Fehlerbehandlung des PRM ist dann aber, anstelle eines Wiederholens der Transaktion auf dem betroffenen PRM, folgendes Vorgehen nötig:

---

[1] Es gibt Maschinen, die parallel zur Bearbeitung von Werkstücken noch Dienste der Programm- oder Variablenverwaltung ausführen können. Da wir innerhalb einer Transaktion sequentielle, synchrone Aufrufe voraussetzen, müssen beide Operationen verschiedenen Transaktionen angehören, und in diesem Fall muß für beide beteiligten Transaktionen Recovery durchgeführt werden.

Fällt die Steuerung aus, bevor die physische Operation initiiert wurde, wird die gesamte Transaktion wiederholt, wobei der PRM durch eine funktionsfähigen, gleichartigen PRM ersetzt wird. Ist ein solcher nicht verfügbar, muß für die Gesamttransaktion ein Abort durchgeführt werden.

Bei einem Fehler nach Abschluß der physischen Operation ist ein Wiederholen der Transaktion auf einem anderen PRM nicht mehr möglich: Da wir keine Informationen über den Datenfluß innerhalb einer Transaktion besitzen, müssen wir die Möglichkeit berücksichtigen, daß orts- oder zeitabhängige Daten der physischen Operation gespeichert werden sollen. Diese dann auf einem anderen PRM abzubilden, kann die semantische Konsistenz verletzen. Auch hier ist ein Rücksetzen unumgänglich.

4.4 Isolierter Fehler des PRM-Kerns

Aufgabe des PRM-Kerns ist es, für eintreffende Aufrufe die für eine Fehlerbehandlung notwendige Information sicher zu speichern, die Ausführung der gewünschten Dienste zu initiieren und gegebenenfalls Recovery durchzuführen. Die Initiierung von Diensten bedeutet, den Aufruf in geeigneter Form an die NC-Maschine weiterzuleiten. Fällt der PRM-Kern aus, kann die NC-Maschine mit der Bearbeitung des momentanen Dienstes fortfahren, da sie unabhängig vom PRM-Kern arbeitet. Auch hier gibt es wieder zwei Varianten:

1.) Nach dem Restart könnte der PRM-Kern mit dem nächsten Request der Transaktion fortfahren - dies wird neben dem Vorhandensein einer stabilen Warteschlange auch durch einen Network Recovery Manager [Sc92] unterstützt, der die sichere Übertragung von Nachrichten, und daher auch der Antwort der Maschine, garantiert. Diese Methode kann angewendet werden, wenn zur Fortsetzung der Transaktion keine Information aus dem flüchtigen Speicher des PRM-Kerns benötigt wird. Sie ist insofern effektiv, als daß keine Operation zweimal ausgeführt wird. Der Nachteil ist aber, daß sie nicht in jeder Umgebung realisiert werden kann. Wir ziehen daher einen anderen Ansatz vor:

2.) Die Transaktion wird, wieder mit Ausnahme der physischen Operation, wiederholt. Die physische Operation war nicht vom Fehler des Kerns betroffen und darf nicht wiederholt werden, da Idempotenz nicht vorausgesetzt werden kann. Auch hier müssen die undo-Operationen nicht ausgeführt werden.

4.5 Kombinierte Fehler

Fehler der einzelnen Komponenten können unabhängig voneinander auftreten, aber sie müssen es nicht. Besonders, wenn sich die Komponenten eines PRMs auf dem gleichen Knoten befinden oder bei einem Stromausfall, können sie in jeder beliebigen Kombination auftreten.

- Falls alle Komponenten ausfallen, muß die Transaktion erst zurückgesetzt und dann wiederholt werden. Physische Operationen werden, wie oben beschrieben, gesondert behandelt.

- Fällt die gesamte NC-Maschine aus, d.h. sind sowohl die Steuerung als auch die eigentliche Maschine betroffen, der PRM-Kern arbeitet jedoch weiter, so kann nicht mehr von einem konsistenten Maschinenabbild in der Steuerung ausgegangen werden. In diesem Fall muß die gleiche Undo-Redo-Logik wie bei einem isolierten Fehler der Steuerung angewendet werden.

- Der Fall, daß Kern und Steuerung ausgefallen sind, die Maschine an sich jedoch noch operabel ist, tritt nicht auf. Bei einem Fehler der Steuerung wird automatisch der Nothalt ausgelöst und die Maschine muß zurückgesetzt werden; dies entspricht einem totalen Stromausfall.

- Im letzten verbleibenden Fall - der Kern und die Maschine sind ausgefallen, die Steuerung jedoch noch operabel - müssen analog zu einem totalen Stromausfall alle beteiligten Komponenten zurückgesetzt werden, um wieder Konsistenz zu erreichen.

5 Zusammenfassung und Ausblick

Ein PRM verwendet Transaktionstechnologie sowohl für physische als auch für nichtphysische Operationen. Für nichtphysische Operationen kann weiterhin Backward Recovery eingesetzt werden, Fehler bei physischen Operationen werden mit Hilfe von Forward Recovery behoben. Zum Transaktionsmanager und zur Anwendung hin verhält sich ein Physical Resource Manager wie ein regulärer Resource Manager und dies erlaubt ein einfaches Einbinden eines PRMs in ein bestehendes TPS.

Durch den Neubeginn oder die Erweiterung von Transaktionen im Fehlerfall wird versucht, den Abbruch von Transaktionen, und somit der gesamten Bearbeitung, zu vermeiden. Nach einem Ausfall von Einzelmaschinen oder des Gesamtsystems werden wohldefinierte Zustände erreicht, was die Wiederanlaufzeiten erheblich verkürzt. Die im Physical Recovery Manager komprimierte Fehlerbehandlung für Bearbeitungsoperationen erlaubt ein übersichtliches und effizientes Programmieren von Arbeitsplänen und steigert die Systemzuverlässigkeit.

Zur Zeit wird eine Simulationsumgebung für fertigungstechnische Abläufe erstellt, die zeigen wird, daß automatische Fehlerbehandlung durch Einsatz des Transaktionskonzepts auch für real actions möglich ist. Eine Erprobung mit echten Geräten muß zeigen, ob und inwieweit durch Anpassung an existierende, nichtideale Geräte Einschränkungen der Funktionalität eines PRMs auftreten und in welchem Umfang diese einer sinnvollen Integration eines PRM in ein TPS entgegenstehen. Mit dem hier vorgestellten Konzept ist jedoch der erste Schritt in Richtung einer Integration fertigungstechnischer Abläufe in transaktionsverarbeitende Systeme getan.

6 Literatur

[BHM90] Bernstein, Phil & Hsu, Meichun & Mann, Bruce: Implementing Recoverable Requests Using Queues. In: Proc. ACM SIGMOD, 1990.

[DIN] DIN 55350, Teil 11. Begriffe der Qualitätssicherung und Statistik. Grundbegriffe der Qualitätssicherung. Beuth Verlag, 1987.

[Do87] Donald, Bruce R.: Error Detection and Recovery in Robotics. Lecture Notes in Computer Science, 336, Springer, 1987.

[EMS91] Eppinger, J.L. & Mummert, L.B. & Spector, A.Z.: Camelot and Avalon: A Distributed Transaction Facility. San Mateo, CA, Morgan Kaufmann.

[Gi90] Gini, Maria: Automatic Error Detection and Recovery. In: Rembold, Ulrich (Ed.): Robot Technology and Applications, Marcel Dekker, 1990, pp. 445-483.

[GS87] Garcia-Molina, Hector & Salem, Kenneth: Sagas.
In: Proc. ACM SIGMOD, San Francisco, 1987,

[Gr81] Gray, Jim: The Transaction Concept: Virtues and Limitations.
In: Proc. 7th Int. Conf. on VLDB, Cannes, 1981.

[GR92] Gray, Jim & Reuter, Andreas: Transaction Processing - Concepts and Techniques.
Morgan Kauffman Publishers, 1992.

[JWZ88] Jablonski, S. & Wedekind, H. & Zörntlein, G.: Fehlerbehandlung in Flexiblen Fertigungssystemen (FFS). In: Informatik Forsch. Entw. (1988) 3:53-63.

[MAP] Manufacturing Automation Protocol Specification Version 3.0, 1988.

[MH88] Meijer, G.R. & Hertzberger, L.O.: Exception handling for robot manufacturing process control. In: Proc. 4th CIM Europe Conf., 18-20 May 1988, pp. 213-222.

[MMS] ISO 9506: Manufacturing Message Specification. Part I: Service Definition.

[Pa88] Pausch, Randy: Adding Input and Output to the Transactional Model.
CMU, Ph.D.Thesis, 1988.

[Sc92] Schmidt, Ursula: A Framework for Automated Error Recovery in FMS.
In: Proceedings of the 2nd Int. Conf. on Automation, Robotics and Computer Vision, Sept. 16 - 18, 1992; Singapore.

[SW91] Schmuck, Frank & Wyllie, Jim: Experience with Transactions in Quicksilver.
In: Proc. 13th ACM Symp. on Operation System Principles, Oct.13-16,1991, Pacific Grove, Ca.

[X/O91] X/Open: Distributed Transaction Processing: the XA-Specification.
Reading: X/Open Company, 1991.

[WR91] Wächter, Helmut & Reuter, Andreas: "The ConTract Model".
In: A.K. Elmagarmid (Ed.): Transaction Models for Advanced Database Applications.
Morgan Kauffmann Publishers, 1991.

[WZ87] Wedekind, H. & Zörntlein, G.: Eine konzeptuelle Basis für den Einsatz von Datenbanken in Flexiblen Fertigungssystemen.
In: Informatik Forsch. Entw. (1987) 2:83-96.

The KRISYS Project: a Summary of What We Have Learned so far

S. Deßloch, F.-J. Leick, N.M. Mattos[1], J. Thomas
University of Kaiserslautern, CS Department
P.O.Box 3049, 6750 Kaiserslautern, Germany
e-mail: {dessloch,leick,thomas}@informatik.uni-kl.de

Abstract

KRISYS is a prototype of a Knowledge Base Management System whose first implementation was completed at the University of Kaiserslautern in 1989. Since then, the system has been used for the development of various applications which allowed us to perform a well-founded evaluation of the system. In this paper, we summarize our evaluation by describing the major lessons we have learned from the design and implementation of KRISYS and, above all, from its use in the development of these applications. We address issues related with the concepts available for application modeling and processing, the support of designing an application, as well as the overall means for efficient processing in a workstation/server environment. Additionally, we point out in how far these experiences validate our approach or stimulate improvements and future research.

1. Introduction

In the last years, substantial research efforts in the area of Database Management Systems (DBMS) have been conducted to support advanced or so-called non-standard database applications [HR85]. This research was, among other things, sparked by the lack of semantic expressiveness in current DBMS [HK87, KDE90]. They do not support the following modeling concepts, which are indispensable in obtaining a more accurate model of complex application domains:

- Abstraction concepts [BMW84,Br81,Ma88a,SS77] are primarily important for the support of a semantically enriched object description. Additionally, they define means for object organization [MM89] which, in turn, can be used to describe distinct application aspects [MDL91].
- There is a need for the integration of behavior into the application model in the form of procedural attributes, user-defined functions, or methods [At89,MMM92]. Such procedures can be used to describe actions in which application objects are involved, thereby permitting the integration of application-oriented operations into the system [DHMM89].
- Reasoning facilities [DK76,Fr86] are necessary to exploit intensional information, to deal with incomplete specifications as well as to control the overall application process, thereby also supporting an active system behavior [DHMM89].

Besides the drawbacks of their modeling concepts, current DBMS also fail to support the process of developing a complex application. This deficiency is becoming even more apparent due to the increasing costs that originate from the use of different models and tools in the development phase (e.g., ER model) and the operation phase (e.g., relational model), which is required when current DBMS are applied as the underlying management system. The need for a single, uniform tool for modeling support has a significant impact on the functionality of future DBMS: they have to be able to act not only as management systems, but also as modeling tools for developing complex applications!

Finally, the processing needs of the applications have to be fulfilled in an efficient and reliable manner, requiring also the consideration of an appropriate runtime environment for non-standard applications [HM90,Ma91]. While 'classical' DBMS technology was largely based on a centralized system architecture, workstation/server environments have emerged as typical for advanced application systems. Therefore, the overall architecture of future DBMS should be suitable for such a hardware environment [DFMV90, HHMM88, KDG87, Ma91]. In this setting, locality of reference should be exploited as far as possible; buffering objects close to

1. The address of Mr. Mattos is: IBM, Database Technology Institute, 555 Bailey Av., San Jose - CA - 95150, USA, e-mail: mattos@stlvm14.vnet.ibm.com.

the application seems to be the only means to achieve efficient object references. Also, coupling some kind of 'DBMS' and 'XPS' components in existing architectures is responsible for cumbersome handling and for quite poor performance in most cases [Ma90]. For this reason, the integration of knowledge-based and DBMS techniques in an effective way is one of the main issues to be addressed.

The enhancement of DBMS according to the above mentioned requirements resulted in so-called Knowledge Base Management Systems (KBMS) [BM86,Ma89,ST89]. In such systems, pieces of applications in form of user-defined functions, methods on abstract data types, abstraction relationships, and inference rules are moved inside the KBMS for better performance and higher flexibility.

Along these lines, the KBMS KRISYS (Knowledge Representation and Inference System) was developed at the University of Kaiserslautern [Ma89]. More than thirty diploma and project thesis works were involved in the overall project. The system became completely operational in 1989 [Kr89], when we started to develop several applications from different areas with it. Since 1991, KRISYS is also successfully used in a practical semester course on KBMS and object-orientation at our university.

The experiences gained with the development of these applications as well as the feedback received by using KRISYS in this practical course served as a broad and solid basis for evaluating the system from various points of view. While some of the results consolidated our approach towards KBMS, others helped to reveal some deficiencies. The goal of this paper is to summarize the results of this evaluation and present the 'concrete lessons learned' in the KRISYS project so far. After this introduction, Section 2 gives a brief overview of the architecture of KRISYS and of its main components. In Section 3, the main part of the paper, we present the results of our evaluation followed by some conclusions and an outlook which are given in Section 4.

2. A Brief Overview of KRISYS

2.1 Overall System Architecture of KRISYS

From a conceptual point of view, there are three orthogonal ways of looking at KBMS [BL86,Ma88b], corresponding to the different kinds of requirements that should be supported by these systems: the needs of the applications (i.e., knowledge manipulation means for solving problems), knowledge engineering support (i.e., modeling concepts for KB construction), and suitable resources and implementation aspects (i.e., mechanisms for efficiently coping with knowledge storage and retrieval). The support of these three classes of requirements leads to a natural division of the KBMS architecture in three layers, which were denoted in the KRISYS project as application, engineering, and implementation layer [Ma89] (Figure 1a).

KRISYS follows this conceptual architecture of KBMS, refining it in order to become suitable for a workstation/server environment: The implementation layer is divided into the working-memory system residing at the workstation (together with the application and engineering layer components) and the DBMS kernel managing the KB on the server side (Figure 1b) [Ma88b, Ma91]. Considering the overall system architecture, KRI-

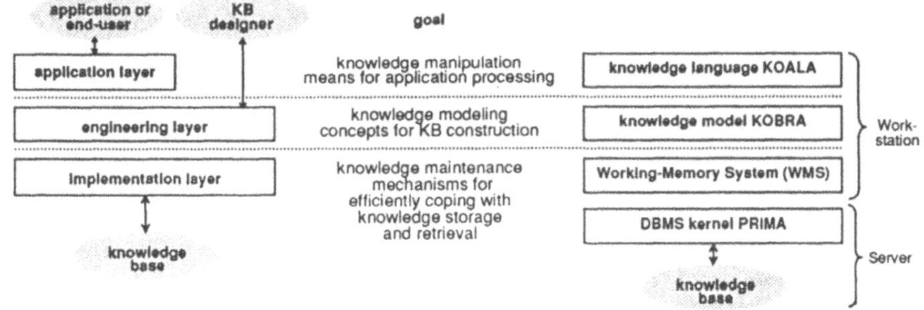

a) conceptual KBMS architecture b) overall system architecture of KRISYS

Figure 1: The KRISYS approach towards KBMS

SYS can therefore be seen as an 'incarnation' of the DBMS-kernel architecture for non-standard DBS proposed in [HR85]. In the following, we give a short description of the different system components.

2.2 KOBRA

The KOBRA knowledge model [Ma89], corresponding to the engineering layer, provides an object-centered representation of the application world for the KB designer. It supports the specification of descriptive, organizational, and operational knowledge in an integrated manner. That is, all these kinds of knowledge are incorporated in one basic concept, called **schema** (not to be confused with a DB schema), which is used to represent the entities of the world being modeled. A schema (others call it object) is uniquely identified by a name (or object identifier), and contains a set of attributes to describe its characteristics. Attributes are used for the representation of descriptive knowledge, i.e., properties of a schema and its relationships to other schemas (in this case, they are called slots), as well as for the specification of operational knowledge, i.e., behavioral aspects of an entity (in this case, they are called methods). In order to characterize a schema in more detail, attributes can be further described by aspects (possible-values, cardinality, etc.). For example, the object 'mercedes-500' shown in Figure 2 has slots such as 'price' or 'has-motor', and methods such as 'order'. The slot 'price' is further described by a 'possible-values' aspect and 'unit' as a user-defined aspect.

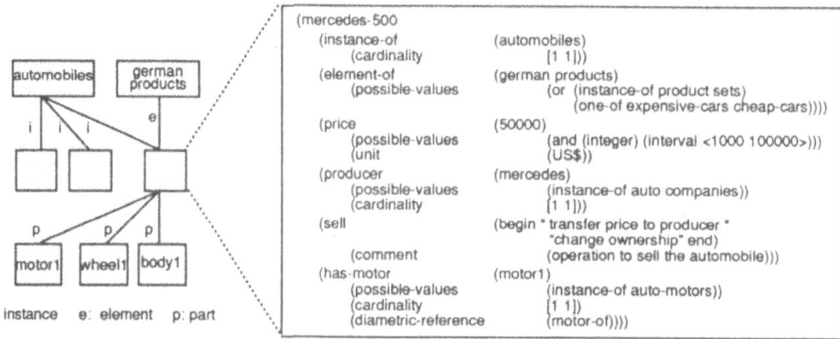

Figure 2: Example description of the schema 'mercedes-500'

For representing organizational knowledge, KOBRA supports the abstraction concepts of classification, generalization, association, and aggregation [Ma88a] which are incorporated into the model by means of special, system-controlled attributes. That is, these concepts are seen as special, predefined relationships between objects, defining the overall organization of a KB as a kind of complex network of objects. Hence, each schema can be related to other schemas by means of any abstraction concept. Classification/generalization as well as association and aggregation each form a directed acyclic graph rooted in a system-defined schema. Since each schema can be a node in each of these graphs, the KB can be seen as the superposition of three graphs. The same object can, for example, represent a class with respect to one object and a set or even an instance with respect to another. In other words, KOBRA supports an *integrated view of KB objects*, i.e., there are no separate representations for sets, classes, instances, or complex objects. For example, 'mercedes500' in Figure 2 is at the same time an instance of 'automobiles', an element of 'german products' and an aggregate consisting of 'motor1', 'body1', and 'wheel1'. Therefore, the separation of data and meta-data, which is a characteristic of existing data models, is eliminated in KOBRA so that meta-information is integrated into the KB [MM89]. A similar approach can for example be found in the language F-Logic [KL89]. The semantics provided by the abstraction concepts [Ma88a,RHMD87] are guaranteed by the system by means of *built-in reasoning facilities* which also enforce the *integrity constraints inherent in the abstraction concepts* [De90]. The best known of these reasoning facilities, *inheritance*, is built into the classification and generalization concepts, and allows the system to derive the structure of classes and instances based on the definition of their (super-) classes and to control model-inherent integrity by refusing attempts to delete inherited attributes (for a description of other built-in reasoning facilities see [Ma88a, MM89, De90]).

Besides the support of methods, KOBRA provides the concepts of demons and rules for the specification of operational knowledge [Ma89, De90]. This allows the KB designer to utilize *different programming paradigms* (object-oriented, data-oriented, and rule-based) when implementing applications. Demons allow for the attachment of procedures to attributes, which are (similar to triggers in DBMS) automatically activated when the attributes are accessed. General reasoning facilities are supported by rules defined in terms of conditions (if-part) and actions (then-part), which are specified by means of KOALA (see Sect. 2.3). Rules can be flexibly grouped together into rule sets according to reasoning tasks. KOBRA provides methods for forward and backward reasoning which are activated with respect to such rule sets. In order to influence the course of inference processes, the user can specify flexible control parameters, like conflict resolvers, search strategies, termination conditions. Demons as well as rules and rule sets are themselves *represented as objects of the KB* and are organized by means of the abstraction concepts.

Finally, the KOBRA model provides means for maintaining the semantic integrity of a KB [De91]. In order to specify constraints for *attribute value consistency*, the possible values and cardinality aspects can be used to restrict the value domain and number of values allowed for an attribute. More complex constraints can be realized by employing the concepts of rules and demons, which also allows to incorporate reactions on constraint violations. Additionally, the KOBRA model regards *methods as units of integrity*, similar to (nested) transactions in DBMS. If an integrity violation occurring during the execution of a method cannot be resolved, a roll-back operation is initiated for the method. Roll-back continues in a cascading manner up to the top level of the (arbitrarily nested) method invocation, unless some method within the hierarchy requests to handle integrity violations internally. If so, the roll-back operation is terminated at this point, and control is returned to the requesting method.

In order to support not only the description of an application model using the above mentioned concepts, but also the process of application development, KRISYS allows the *interactive construction of a KB in a stepwise fashion* [MM89]. After each design operation (e.g., the definition of a class, the reorganization of a class hierarchy, the creation of an attribute, etc.) immediate feedback is provided in the sense that the consequences of a design decision (as, e.g., the inheritance of attributes to existing classes or instances) are directly reflected in the KB state. At any point during the design process, the KB designer may validate the application model by performing operations on the knowledge base (e.g., by activating methods or starting a reasoning process). A *design environment* [Kr89] offers the possibility to save design states and restore them later in case some design decisions turn out to be wrong, and allows the user to test operational knowledge (as for example methods or demons) without having to fear an erroneous behavior of them.

2.3 KOALA

KRISYS provides as its user and application interface KOALA, a high-level, descriptive language for retrieving and manipulating KB contents. (A detailed description of this language is given in [DLM90].) Information is retrieved from a KB using the ASK statement. For example, the statement

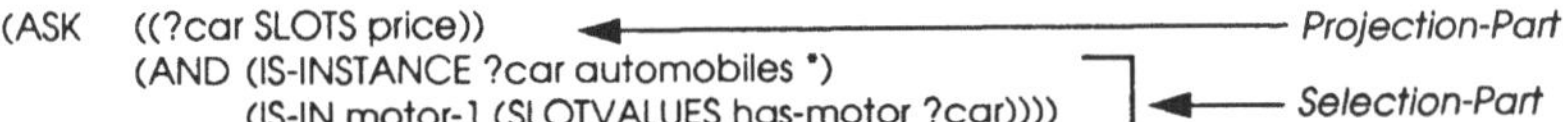

retrieves the names and prices of all instances of 'automobiles', which have 'motor1' as motor. The selection part of the ASK statement is expressed as a formula using logical connectives and predefined predicates (e.g., IS-INSTANCE) and functions (e.g., SLOTVALUES) that embody the semantics of the KOBRA model. *Set-oriented queries* are specified by using so-called query variables (e.g., ?car) in the selection formula, which are then instantiated during query evaluation. The variables may be used in the projection clause in order to precisely describe the desired information.

It is also possible to specify *implicit and explicit joins* in a selection by nesting SLOTVALUE-functions and using more than one query variable. Furthermore, queries may involve additional logical connectives (disjunction, conjunction), negation, quantifiers, as well as special predicates and functions for expressing *(generalized) transitive closure* queries, making the language in some aspects more powerful than SQL [DLM90].

The TELL statement is used to manipulate KB contents. For example, the statement

```
(TELL  (IS-ELEMENT ?car expensive-cars 1)         <-------------- Assertion-Part
       WHERE
       (AND (IS-INSTANCE ?car automobiles *)
            (> (SLOTVALUE price ?car) 20000)))    <-------------- Selection-Part
```

will make sure that all cars costing more than 20.000 dollars are direct elements of the set 'expensive-cars'. Again, *set-oriented changes* are easily achieved using corresponding query variables in the selection and the assertion part. Note that changes are not specified in terms of insert, update, and delete operations, but in a *state-oriented* manner by describing the goal state of the KB in the assertion part [Ma89, DLM90]. It is the task of the system to figure out how to achieve this goal. For example, the above statement may involve the insertion of objects into a set, as well as the creation of the object 'expensive-cars' if it does not exist already. Moreover, (parts of) the goal state may already be contained in the current state (before the execution), so that there might be no changes necessary at all. Thus, state-oriented changes free the user or application from knowing the exact state of the KB, when specifying updates. However, only a subset of KOALA can be used to describe the goal state in the TELL statement so that ambiguities can not arise. TELL statements may also contain *multiple assertions* within the same statement. Additionally, it is possible to *access meta-information* within both ASK and TELL statements through special predicates and functions. (These two latter issues also make KOALA go beyond SQL [DLM90].)

In KRISYS, *rules are defined by a TELL statement*, meaning that the rule condition part (the if-part) corresponds to a TELL selection, and the conclusions (the then-part) to the TELL assertions. KOALA is therefore the language used to write queries as well as to specify rules.

2.4 The DBMS Kernel PRIMA

The DBMS kernel chosen for KRISYS, named PRIMA (PRototype Implementation of the MAD model), concentrates on efficient and reliable KB management on secondary storage at the server side and provides application independent data management functions at its interface. PRIMA was developed for supporting applications that require a suitable representation of complex objects, i.e., those whose inner structures (the components) are also objects of the DB [Hä88, HMMS87].

The basic modeling constructs of the MAD (Molecule Atom Data) model [Mi89a] are called atoms, which, in analogy to tuples in the relational model, are composed of attributes and have their structure determined by an atom type. Atoms possess an identifier which is used for a *direct and symmetric representation of relationships* (1:1, 1:n, n:m) by means of links, providing a view of the DB as a *complex network of atoms*. For each specified link, there is always a corresponding back-reference in the related atom, whose mutual referential integrity is automatically maintained by the system. *Complex objects* are dynamically defined by the specification of so-called molecules as a graph having atoms as nodes and relationships (i.e., links) as edges. Thus, molecules are *dynamically derived views* of the atom network.

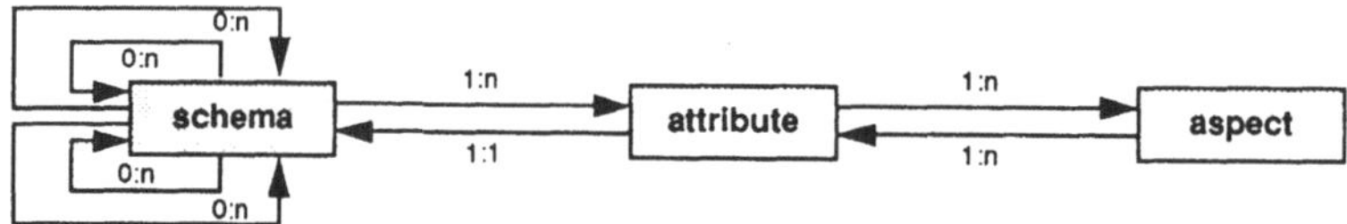

Figure 3: MAD-schema diagram

KOBRA knowledge structures (i.e., schemas representing real world objects, attributes expressing their properties and relationships, and aspects describing the attributes) are mapped to MAD in a straightforward manner [Mi88,Ma90a]. The MAD schema contains three atom types ('Schema', 'Attribute', and 'Aspects') connected via the references (i.e., relationships) has_attributes and has_aspects[2]. The abstraction relationships are represented as recursive MAD references involving the atom type 'schema' (see Figure 3).

2. The MAD schema can be seen as a kind of meta-schema, reflecting the basic modelling concepts of KOBRA, and not the application domain (i.e., specific classes, sets, etc.)

2.5 The Working-Memory System (WMS)

The task of the WMS [LM89] is the support of a processing model based on the 'nearby application locality' concept. The WMS provides two mechanisms in order to fulfil this task.

First, it maintains an application buffer called Working Memory (WM), which temporarily holds the objects being used by the application in order to avoid long execution paths of KB accesses (involving workstation/ server communications) as well as time-consuming requests to secondary storage. The WM represents KOBRA objects in a format similar to the MAD structures described above (i.e., separated in 'schema', 'attribute', and 'aspect' parts) and offers access to the stored objects via hash tables.

Second, the WMS provides the concept of processing contexts representing the knowledge needed by an application during a specific processing phase. In principle, contexts are composed of several KB objects (in general of different types) and objects may be elements of several contexts. They have to be defined by the KB designer and are represented explicitly as KOBRA schemas and specified by means of KOALA. During application processing, the WMS exploits the specification of a context to generate a complex set-oriented access to the kernel in order to prefetch required objects and store them in the WM as a new application processing phase is entered. Thereafter, most or perhaps all objects referenced during the processing phase are found in the WM, so that only a few or no further calls to the kernel are necessary. At the end of the processing phase, the corresponding context is then discarded from the WM and the context requested by the following phase is loaded.

3. What have we learned?

The KRISYS system became fully operational in 1989, when a number of applications from different areas began to be developed (see Table 1 for examples).

Title	Application Area / Problem Class	References
MED2 XPS-shell [Pu86]	Diagnosis	Mi89b
XPS for Trip Planning	Classification	Rh89
Real-Estate Valuation Support	Decision Support in Finance	Mö91
'Intelligent' CAD	Architectural Design	DHMM89, MDL91, Th90
TechMo	Mechanical Design	DHMS90, DHMS91, Du91
Mapping Generator	Physical DB Design	Sch91, Su91, Kn92
3D Objects	Spatial Reasoning and Integrity	Sch89, Mö90
Restaurant	(sample KB for practical course and demos)	DD91
Dialogue Component Tool	XPS	DK91
Integrated Product Model Environment	Design	Re90
Publication Management	Information Retrieval	Kr90
Multi-Media Application	Multi-Media	Zi91

Table 1: Applications of the KBMS KRISYS

While some applications were restricted in functionality, size, and depth and were developed either for demonstration purposes or to evaluate specific modeling concepts, others (esp. the first six applications in Table 1) can be more or less seen as 'realistic' in the sense that they cover a 'real-world' problem in sufficient depth and generality. The variety of realized applications mentioned above on one hand allowed to validate in how far the modeling and processing requirements of the applications were met by KRISYS, and on the other hand permitted to evaluate the techniques for supporting an efficient overall processing within a workstation/server environment. Since these aspects do not primarily depend on an increased KB size, we usually refrained from populating the KBs with a large amount of data, but concentrated on the realization of the overall application functionality. A fairly large amount of data/knowledge was only collected once for a KB for car repair diagnosis [Bo83] with the MED2 XPS-shell [Pu88], which contained over 2500 deductive rules, besides a larger number of other objects, representing symptoms, diagnoses, technical analyses, etc.

In the following, we will present our evaluation by stating the concrete 'lessons' we have experienced. The lessons are grouped into subsections according to the main topics of our evaluation. While the first group covers representation and application processing aspects, the second is mainly concerned with our experiences in providing a modeling tool functionality in addition to the support of knowledge management tasks. The third group contains the lessons about the overall concepts for knowledge processing in KRISYS w.r.t. a workstation/server environment.

3.1 Application Modeling and Processing

Modeling Concepts

Lesson 1: The support of modeling constructs for representing descriptive, operational, and structural knowledge is essential [DHMM89].

Besides the concepts for representing descriptive aspects of the application domain (i.e., schemas and slots), constructs for specifying structural and operational information (i.e., the abstraction concepts as well as methods, demons, and rules) were widely used in all KRISYS applications[3]. This observation, which comes to no surprise, again emphasizes the need for advanced data and knowledge modeling facilities in order to support the construction of more precise and complete application models.

Lesson 2: The four abstraction concepts (classification, generalization, association, and aggregation) are at the heart of knowledge modeling [MM89].

The complete support and the clear distinction of the abstraction concepts has turned out to be the fundamental concept for modeling our application KBs. Especially the distinction between the notion of a class (generalization) and a set (association), and the support of an integrated view on the abstraction concepts, i.e., the possibility to model an object as playing different roles (e.g., a class, a set, or even an instance) at the same time, have helped to improve the clarity of the application domain description[4]. Without an integrated view, redundancy would have to be introduced into the KB (e.g., different schemas for representing the object as a class, set, and instance) and would have to be handled by the application.

Operational Concepts

Lesson 3: The (sum of) constructs for operational knowledge should be computationally complete.

When looking at the 'amount' of application processing realized within the representational framework of KRISYS, compared to the processing performed in an application program outside the KB, significant differences between the applications became apparent. While in some applications only basic processing tasks were performed in the KB, others were realized completely with the modeling constructs of KRISYS. The question 'Where does the KB end and where does the application program begin?' can only be answered by the KB designer. Therefore, a KBMS must not anticipate the answer by limiting the expressive power of its operational concepts (e.g., to sequences of DML statements), thereby restricting the amount of application processing that can be integrated into the KB.

Lesson 4: A KBMS should support different programming paradigms.

We had chosen to support in KRISYS several concepts for representing operational information (methods, demons, and rules), which allow the application designer to use different programming paradigms (object-oriented, data-oriented, and rule-based) when realizing the application. In our evaluation we found out that a 'typical' application (w.r.t. the paradigm(s) used) does not exist. Methods were used in many applications, but were usually combined with either demons or rules, or both. As certain paradigms may be more suitable for certain problem classes than others, a KBMS should allow the application designer to flexibly choose the paradigms that fit best.

3. Note, that this is not necessarily the case for the operational aspects, since an application designer might choose to dispense some of the operational constructs of KRISYS completely, and realize application processing outside the KB by embedding KRISYS statements for interacting with the KB in application programs written in a general programming language (CommonLisp).

4. Note, an integrated view does not contradict the clear separation of distinct abstraction concepts [Ma88a, MM89]!

Integrity Constraints

Lesson 5: A uniform, powerful and flexible concept for modeling integrity constraints must be provided [De90].

Our applications, especially the ones from the area of design such as the intelligent CAD system and TechMo, posed ambitious requirements w.r.t. constraint modeling. In these systems, various kinds of application constraints ranging from physical laws to legal regulations and (user-defined) design restrictions (i.e., goals) had to be represented, requiring an increased flexibility, concerning

- the constrained objects, i.e., if a constraint should be valid for all objects of a certain class, or only for specific instances (like a design goal),
- reactions on constraint violations, which have to include corrective actions, user interaction, or even tolerating/recording the inconsistencies, besides the (usual) roll-back operation,
- the specification of checking operations and reactions, which can sometimes become very complex, making procedural specifications necessary,
- the time of activation, which must not be restricted to the immediate/deferred activation scheme, but should be relatable to arbitrary units or levels of integrity, as well as
- the 'usage' of a constraint: While in some cases a constraint has to be used to check consistency (e.g., of a design object), the same constraint is used in a different situation in a rule-like fashion to derive or compute new information (e.g., if a design object is not completely specified by the user)[5].

In all, the KRISYS concepts used for constraint modeling (i.e., special aspects, demons, rules) left a lot to be desired w.r.t. the above requirements. Additionally, the fact that several modeling concepts can (and sometimes have to) be used for representing constraints, which sometimes have different notions of activation, possible reactions, etc., rendered the modeling of an application more difficult (from an integrity point of view).

Lesson 6: Low-level concepts (e.g., triggers, demons) do not offer a satisfactory modeling of constraints.

Although event-based or trigger-like concepts usually provide the flexibility required to fulfil several of the above mentioned points, they are not suitable as modeling concepts for constraints, but should only be seen as an internal basis for their implementation. As the number of constraints of an application exceeded a certain limit, the semantics of the set of demons used for their realization was hard to capture. Several demons were necessary to realize a single constraint, and the overall effect of their activation was hard to foresee.

Lesson 7: An object-centered framework offers various opportunities for the integration of concepts for integrity constraints into the knowledge model [De91].

The decision to represent constraints uniformly as special (first-class) objects of the KB turned out to be especially good. This approach offered the advantage that constraints were represented explicitly and could be organized in the KB according to various criteria, using the abstraction concepts. In KRISYS, we have represented demons as well as rules in this way. In our applications, we could therefore easily locate certain constraints, and modify or extend them. Also, the ability to introduce new attributes for the constraints as an additional description turned out to be a useful selection criterion for querying the KB w.r.t. its constraints, which contributed to increase the modifiability of the constraint set.

Another opportunity was given by the possibility to associate the activation of integrity constraints with the execution of methods, allowing a flexible specification of activation time. In this context, the methods could be seen as (arbitrarily nested) units of integrity, allowing the realization of various integrity levels (for a detailed description of how methods and demons can be used to model different levels of integrity, see [De91]). Moreover, update operations in object-oriented systems usually involve only single attributes (and not complete tuples or records as in relational systems). This granularity of updates, which is consequently reflected in the definition of update events, is more suitable for initiating integrity checks than in conventional DBS, because most constraints are specified for (combinations of) attribute values.

5. This requirement questions to some extent the difference between rules and integrity constraints, which is usually made in KBMS!

Query Language

Lesson 8: Access to KB contents should rely on a declarative, set-oriented query language.

KRISYS provides two separate external interfaces[6]: KOALA, a declarative query language, and a functional interface embedded in LISP[7], which offers a predefined set of functions for basic interactions (e.g., accessing slotvalues, creating and deleting objects, calling methods, etc.) based on object identifiers (i.e., schema names). While KOALA can be used for ad-hoc queries and for KB interaction within methods or application programs in a declarative fashion, the functional interface is more suitable for programming in a more object-oriented, navigational style.

Our experiences concerning the usage of these interfaces were the following:

- The 'navigational' interface proved to be appropriate and sufficient for some, but not all types of application methods. Obviously, associative access could be addressed only inadequately, therefore requiring a declarative language.
- Even in cases where the navigational language was sufficient to implement some tasks, it required quite complex programming efforts that could be expressed in KOALA without any difficulties, leading to simpler and more readable method definitions. We observed that specially for this purpose the features of KOALA that go beyond SQL [DLM90] (e.g., multiple updates on multiple classes within one single TELL statement) were very useful.
- In spite of the 'superiority' of KOALA when compared to the navigational interface, KB designers started realizing methods using only the navigational language and often stayed with this interface as long as possible (some applications were even realized without using KOALA at all [Th90]). Basically, the following two reasons were given by the KB designers to justify this. First, getting familiar with a new language based on a different semantics or paradigm than the procedural one requires efforts that should not be underestimated. However, in cases in which the KB designers became familiar with KOALA, they appreciated its advantages and found the use of KOALA in methods more appropriate then using the navigational interface. Second, KOALA was conceived primarily as an ad-hoc query language, and little effort was put into the development of a satisfactory coupling or integration with the host language (i.e., CommonLisp). Therefore, the well-known problems of impedance mismatch between query and host language occurred, and additional programming efforts were necessary to interpret the results of an ASK statement within the Lisp program or to pass parameters into a TELL statement, thereby discouraging the use of KOALA in methods.

All in all, our experience proved that the support of a declarative, set-oriented query language in a KBMS environment, even in combination with an object-oriented representation, is necessary and useful[8]. However, significant efforts have to be put into an appropriate integration of declarative and object-oriented programming languages in order to harmonize these two paradigms as far as possible.

Lesson 9: For using a query language as a basis for rule definition, a state-oriented language semantics is desirable.

Another argument for supporting a query language is that a declarative query language can resemble an adequate basis for the definition of deduction rules in a KBMS environment. In contrast to deductive DBS where rules can only be used to derive intensional information, rules in KRISYS can also be used to modify the extension of the KB upon their activation. For this purpose, the notion of state-oriented changes as supported by KOALA, which was briefly introduced in Section 2, has shown to simplify the specification of rule-based systems significantly [DLM90, Rh89]. Without state-orientation, one would have to clearly identify in the conclusion-part of the rules the exact operation that has to be performed on the KB upon rule activation (e.g.,

6. The reason for providing two alternative interfaces is mainly a historical one: The implementation of KOALA was completed after the 'object-oriented' interface had already been realized. Nevertheless, this double effort of implementation gave us the opportunity to provide completely different interfaces for the KB designer, and the chance to find out which one is more suitable for his/her purposes.
7. This interface is also provided as part of a graphical environment running on X-Windows.
8. Note, that these observations have only considered the needs of the users and KB designers. Efficiency considerations will be discussed in subsequent parts of this section.

insertion of a new object or modification of an existing one)[9]. Because this operation is dependent on the KB state at the time of activation and is not necessarily known when the rule is being specified, it leads to the multiplication of the number of rules: Predicates for determining the actual state of the KB (e.g., existence or inexistence of an object) would have to be included into the condition part in order to apply the correct operation, causing additional rule definitions for each distinguished state.

3.2 Knowledge Modeling vs. Knowledge Management

Support of modeling activities

Lesson 10: Support of application development and processing within the same framework is necessary.

KRISYS was constructed to appropriately support both the design and the operation of applications within the same representational and operational framework. The possibility to develop the application in a stepwise fashion and to immediately validate design decisions was greatly appreciated by all application designers. Moreover, we learned during several practical courses based on KRISYS that the possibility to interactively develop and run applications facilitated getting acquainted with the system and sped up the development of these applications. Instead of being forced to define the structure of a knowledge base before actually working with the system, users could immediately try out the features of KRISYS without any previous specification.

Lesson 11: The KB design process has to be supported by an appropriate system environment that enables (re-)designs, taking back design decisions, saving and restoring design states.

Throughout the application developments, we made the experience that the user should not be forced to definitively integrate his design decisions or even whole design steps into the KB because in a lot of cases he/she is not yet sure about the correctness of his/her decisions. KBMS should allow an easy reverting of such activities whenever necessary.

To this end, KRISYS offers the design environment [Kr89], which proved to be essential in the design of our applications. When design decisions turned out to be wrong, a consistent, earlier design state could be restored by simply going back to the corresponding KB state. Moreover, this feature allowed the user to validate operational knowledge, as for example methods or demons, without having to fear an erroneous behavior of them. By allowing the user to save the state of the KB prior to execution, the design environment relieved the user from the gravity of decisions and allowed him or her to use KRISYS more freely as a modeling tool. Without such kind of support, the designers would have been forced to either keep copies of the complete KB or issue complex compensating actions to restore a consistent KB state in case of an erroneous action.

Lesson 12: The dynamic behavior of the abstraction concepts, providing built-in reasoning and consistency, proved to be the basis for stepwise, interactive KB design [MM89].

The abstraction concepts are the means to organize a KB, i.e., to define its structure. As already pointed out in Section 2, built-in reasoning facilities (e.g., inheritance) and consistency conditions are associated with these concepts, describing their semantics. In KRISYS, the semantics of the abstraction concepts is guaranteed dynamically after each operation, which turned out to be very effective for supporting an easy modeling of a KB. As the designers changed abstraction relationships, defined new attributes, and created or specialized aspect definitions, the built-in reasoning facilities were automatically activated to reflect the consequences of such operations (e.g., changes in the object structure through inherited attributes) or detect and prevent inconsistencies, such as cyclic abstraction relationships or inheritance conflicts. This behavior proved to be essential for an immediate validation of design decisions.

Lesson 13: Eliminating the difference between regular and meta-information is advantageous for supporting modeling activities.

In KRISYS, this elimination, which is reflected in the knowledge model as well as in the query language, has shown to be an important support for KB design in several ways. First of all, the integration of meta-information and 'regular' information provides the KB designer with a uniform operational and representational plat-

9. This type of definition is comparable to the specification of the action-part in ECA rules or triggers.

form for defining the structure of a KB as well as for effectively validating and testing applications. In KOBRA, the schema is the representational basis for structural information (e.g., a schema as a class) as well as for regular knowledge (e.g., a schema as the instance of a class), and all operations are carried out on schemas of the KB. Second, the integrated access to meta-information within the query language KOALA provides a useful means for retrieving meta-information and reorganizing KB contents during KB design. KOALA turned out to be a good support for the designer when he/she needed to keep track of the current KB structure or to perform restructuring measures.

Additionally, the implementation of the design environment was greatly facilitated by the fact that meta information is stored in the KB and can be treated just like regular knowledge. We could easily use the mechanisms already implemented for effective data management (like transactions and savepoints) in order to keep track of design decisions and to make them revertible.

Relationship between Design and Operation Phase

Lesson 14: Design phase and operation phase can be distinguished [Ma91].

XPS tools (e.g.,KEE [FK85,Fi88], Knowledge Craft [FWA85]), which support applications comparable to those of KBMS, assume that an application is subject to design changes continuously throughout its life time. For this reason, these systems do not distinguish between the design phase and the operation phase of an application. Contrary to this assumption, we have found that for the applications we have developed with KRISYS, it was reasonable to distinguish between the two phases since there was a dramatic shift of interest when moving from one phase to the other. In the design phase the KB designer(s) were interested in flexibly structuring the application. When processing (parts of) the application in this phase, he/she was interested in the validation of the KB, aiming at the redesign of the KB if the application did not exhibit a desired behavior. In the operation phase, the user of the application (who was in most cases not the KB designer) was interested in an efficient processing of the application. Therefore, in each application we developed, we observed a certain point at which the design phase ended and the operation phase started because the KB designer became satisfied with the behavior of the application. At this point, efficiency, and not flexibility, became the major issue (see also lesson 16).

Lesson 15: A strict separation of the design phase from the operation phase without the possibility to perform redesigns is however undesirable.

During the complete life-cycle of our applications, we have observed points, where even in the operation phase a reconsideration of the KB structure was necessary (e.g., new requirements became apparent or structural changes in the KB became necessary). In such situations, a return to the design phase was then needed. However, these situations were not frequent (compared with the iterations in the initial design phase) and usually had only limited effects on the running application, leaving large parts of the structure of the KB untouched. Nevertheless, they were enough to show another argument for integrating the functionality of both a knowledge modeling tool and a knowledge management system within the same environment. A strict separation, as prescribed in DBMS by the need to define and maintain DB schema and actual database in different locations or even in different representational frameworks, is a severe obstacle in the fulfillment of the above stated requirement.

Lesson 16: Design and operation phase differ fundamentally in the kinds of operations applied [Ma91].

We have performed an in-depth analysis of the different phases of the applications' life cycle w.r.t. to the operations performed during each phase. Thereby, we observed that during the design phase operations provoking changes in the KB structure were prevailing, as for example the generation of classes, the creation of attributes, the restructuring of sets or the definition of aggregation hierarchies. Also, the operational knowledge represented in the KB (i.e., methods, rules, demons) was frequently changed until it was free of errors and exhibited the desired behavior. On the other hand, during application processing (i.e., in the operation phase) these kinds of operations occurred only very rarely (or not at all). In this phase, objects were selected by conditions based on the value of certain attributes or on their relationships to other objects. Attribute values were manipulated by the system, instances and elements were created and/or deleted [Sch91]. Also, operational constructs (e.g., methods) were activated, but only rarely modified. Therefore, the flexibility needed during the design phase was no longer required in the operation phase. This observation to some extent contradicted the assumption made by XPS tools, as stated in lesson 14.

Lesson 17: After the design phase is finished, optimizations have to be performed.

As demonstrated above, the operational phase does not require the functional flexibility of the design phase because the operations performed in these two phases differ. Therefore, we learned that switching from the design phase to the operational phase also allows changing the emphasis of system support to improve performance. To reach this goal, an additional phase, the so-called optimization phase, has to be introduced between design and operational phase, which can be initiated explicitly by the KB designer at the end of the design phase. A prime candidate for an optimization to be performed in this phase is the optimization of the mapping scheme used to map KOBRA to MAD because it greatly influences the performance of the operations of the application. We observed that the mapping described in Section 2.4 (Figure 3) was ideal for the design phase, since any design operation, even structural changes, did not provoke any changes in the MAD schema, but only the insertion, deletion or modification of tuples (instances) in one (or several) atom types. However, this kind of mapping caused a significant overhead for select operations (which were prevailing in the operation phase) since each object had to be constructed from its components (attributes and their aspects), leading to a rather complex query even if the object was selected by means of its object identifier. In the optimization phase, the system should therefore be switched to a more specific mapping, which reflects the application domain and does not exhibit the above described drawbacks.

However, changes on the mapping between KOBRA and MAD are not the only optimization actions that can take place after finishing the design phase. We also concluded that it was then possible and necessary (for performance reasons) to compile and therefore optimize all operational concepts used in the application, thereby going out of an interpretative mode into a compiled and consequently more efficient mode. For example, queries contained within methods should be optimized and compiled. Integrity constraints should be transformed into an internal format and necessary integrity checks for update operations should be generated and placed into the code of methods which perform the corresponding updates. Rule processing should be supported by means of building dependency graphs for each ruleset as well as improved by compiling and optimizing the rules themselves.

KRISYS clearly failed to fulfil the requirements formulated in this lesson because none of the above described means for optimizations were supported.

Lesson 18: The structure of the KB and the processing characteristics of each application are application dependent and determine an optimal mapping scheme between KOBRA and MAD [Ma91].

A thorough analysis of our applications has shown that the structure of their KBs differed very much. They differed for example in the number of hierarchies, in the kind of abstraction hierarchies (generalization, association, aggregation), their height, their shape (only trees or even graphs), in the distribution of the instances in the hierarchy, etc. [Sch91, Ma91]. Furthermore, we observed that the processing characteristics of the applications were also very different. They showed differences in the programming paradigm they were using (object-oriented, data-driven, rule-based, hybrid), in the exploitation of context definitions, in the kinds of queries, frequency of updates, existence of schema evolution, etc. We finally observed that all the characteristics strongly influenced the shape of an optimal mapping scheme between KOBRA and MAD.

Lesson 19: KBMS cannot be based on a fixed mapping scheme, but have to be able to handle distinct, application-dependent mappings [Ma91].

Based on the above lessons, we could then conclude that the mapping between KOBRA and MAD should be adapted to the requirements of each specific application after the completion of the design phase, when such requirements are well defined because the KB structure as well as the processing characteristics of an application are application dependent. Naturally, in order to exploit specific mapping schemes, the MAD schema and the corresponding transformation process of KOBRA objects to MAD atoms must not be fixed to a certain mapping scheme, but have to be adaptable to distinct, application-dependent mappings. Therefore, the optimization phase has to support the generation of an application-specific mapping and allow the transformation of the KB into the new format.

Lesson 20: Most of the work done during in the generation of an appropriate mapping can be done by the system during the optimization phase.

The main goal of the optimization phase is the generation of an application-oriented and consequently efficient mapping scheme for a certain application. Once an appropriate mapping has been found the transformation of the KB into the derived MAD schema can be performed automatically by the system. We had experienced in our attempts to find optimal mappings for our applications that this task involves the consideration of a lot of information and requires complex decisions to be made. However, most of the information needed for this task can be derived by the system because it is already somehow stored in or can be inferred from the KB, mainly from information about the KB structure (e.g., the number of hierarchies, their height, their shape, etc.). Also, some information concerning the processing characteristics of the application can be derived by the system from the rules in rulesets, from the kinds of demons, their activation time, etc. Only information not represented in the KB like the number of expected instances per class, elements per set, the relevance of membership stipulations for access purposes, etc., has to be specified by the knowledge engineer. Therefore, the system is able to perform most of the work necessary to generate an optimal mapping. However, because of the large amount of relevant information and the enormous number of potential mappings that can be generated, one cannot expect that a fixed procedure can be followed by the system in order to derive the appropriate mapping for an application. The system has to make use of a number of existing heuristics to automatically derive an adjusted MAD schema for each application.

3.3 Overall Processing Support of KRISYS

General Architectural Considerations

Lesson 21: A layered system architecture with well-defined interfaces is useful and facilitates physical distribution of system components.

Considering the functionality provided by KRISYS, the system consists of several hierarchically ordered layers, thereby following general design rules known from existing DBMS [HR85]. The advantages of this architectural approach (ease of implementation, maintenance, and extension) became apparent during the implementation of KRISYS, especially because the system was continuously under extension and improvement . In the special case of KRISYS, the approach also enabled us to design the system in such a form that the layers of the system naturally reflected the three major classes of requirements of KBMS. All in all, it permitted us to realize well-defined interfaces providing modularity, data independence and extensibility in the various layers. It also facilitated the assignment of system components to workstation and server.

Lesson 22: 'Loose coupling' of workstation and server components with the support of locality of reference is necessary to reduce communication and transfer overhead.

As mentioned in Section 2, the KRISYS architecture was designed to fit into a workstation/server environment with decentralized and autonomous processors. In such an environment, the kind of interaction between the server and the client is a very important design issue [Hä89, Ma90a]. Regarding this issue, we learned that a close 'coupling' between server and workstation results in a huge amount of communication between the server and the workstation component combined with high transfer cost, since every user action can provoke 'thousands' of accesses to the KB. Furthermore, this kind of coupling results in a failure dependence, which is a very critical design issue, because the users may be affected by any kind of failure throughout their typically long-term activities. Therefore, we strongly believe that the only reasonable approach for a system like KRISYS is to rely on loosely coupled system components with interfaces that minimize communication traffic and KB accesses. We learned that this approach can only be successful if accompanied by the support of a high degree of locality of reference on the workstation side for performance reasons calling for an application buffer in the workstation, as will be discussed in lesson 25.

Lesson 23: In order to exploit the advantages of a workstation/server environment, knowledge model semantics and application-oriented processing should be shifted towards the workstation [De91, Ma91].

Considering the constructs underlying KOBRA at the workstation and the MAD model at the server, it should become clear that KOBRA is located at a higher semantic level than MAD. Upon realizing the existence of this gap in the KRISYS architecture, one would directly conclude that this was a problem and try to come up with the idea of enhancing MAD with KOBRA semantics to equal both models. However, we have learned that efforts to equal MAD and KOBRA do not promise to offer solutions (see [De91, Ma91] for a detailed discussion on this topic). By placing the 'borderline' between workstation and server on the enhanced MAD interface, all the functionality of KOBRA would be completely delegated to the server, otherwise KOBRA semantics would have to be duplicated at the workstation (implying that the MAD enhancement is meaningless). Such a complete delegation would hopelessly overload the server component of KRISYS with additional processing since the maintenance of abstraction concepts, the execution of their built-in reasonings, the evaluation of methods, demons, and rules are now completely undertaken by the server. Processing at the workstation would be limited to a minimum, leading to a more or less centralized system architecture that neglects the advantages provided by workstation/server environments. Consequently, only basic, application independent tasks should be delegated to the server component. The server has to treat knowledge structures simply as a kind of network of complex objects to be consistently, reliably, and efficiently managed. It has to provide flexible means to select sets of objects and transfer them to the workstation or to write them back into the KB. In summary, the division of the system architecture of KRISYS with KOBRA and KOALA at the workstation side and the DBMS kernel at the server side proved to be correct.

Lesson 24: The NDBS-kernel approach is the appropriate architectural environment for KBMS.

The architecture of KRISYS follows the principles of the NDBS-kernel approach that has been proposed in [HR85]. The proposal claimed that NDBS should be constructed by a loose coupling of workstation and server, implementing the functionality required by a specific application class on the workstation and using the NDBS kernel for general data-management tasks. Although KRISYS is not restricted to an application class but rather offers a general platform for developing applications, it was yet another example of the advantages of the approach mentioned above, as can also be seen from lessons 21, 22, and 23. Thus, we can conclude that the affirmations in [HR85] could be demonstrated in practice by the KRISYS implementation.

Application Buffer

Lesson 25: An application buffer to support locality of reference is a key concept for efficient workstation/server processing.

In all applications developed we have observed locality of reference, i.e., there are many timely related accesses to the same object and even to the same attribute of an object [Ma90b]. This observation, which was not surprising during the operation phase, was also valid during the modeling phase of an application (subsequent modeling activities often involved the same hierarchy and even the same object) and the optimization phase. As already argued in lesson 21, this locality of reference must be supported to improve the performance of the application. For this reason, the integration of the working memory into the KRISYS architecture has proven to be the right decision. We performed several measurements with each of the developed applications and we observed that the use of the WM led to a significant reduction in application run-time by a factor 10 - 30 (i.e., from hours to some minutes). Therefore, it is absolutely necessary to support application processing in workstation/server environments efficiently.

Lesson 26: Pure hashing is inappropriate for accessing objects in the application buffer.

In our applications, parts of an object's structure (e.g., attributes or aspects) were usually accessed several times in the WM within a certain phase [Ma90b]. However, we observed that a pure hashing method for organizing the application buffer did not support these repeated references in a satisfactory way. Instead of being able to exploit the current position of an object for a faster relative access, KRISYS always had to compute the absolute position of the next relevant part of that object from scratch. Moreover, a hash method could neither support navigation through hierarchies nor set-oriented access of related objects. Because we also observed that these two kinds of operations were performed intensively in each application 'phase' (e.g., navigational access to support the inheritance of a new defined attribute to all subclasses and instances and set-oriented access to perform selections on instances of a class and its subclasses), we concluded that hash methods are not sufficient to appropriately support the kinds of accesses performed in the WM.

Lesson 27: An object representation in the buffer closer to the knowledge model and the support of navigational as well as set-oriented processing of buffer objects are essential for efficient processing.

In a first version of the application buffer, we had chosen an internal representation similar to the one used inside the DBMS kernel to speed up the load and unload tasks. No transformation was necessary when objects were brought into the WM or written back. However, since the knowledge model needed a different representation of the objects (both to support modeling activities and query processing [TMMD92]), the objects had to be converted each time they were accessed by a KOBRA or KOALA operation. Measurements showed that this conversion had consumed a lot of time (up to 30% of the workstation processing time). Thus, we concluded that objects should be represented in the application buffer in a form close to the knowledge model of KRISYS, resembling a direct representation of the hierarchies formed by the abstraction concepts (e.g., by means of main-memory links). The kind of representation of the objects stored in the application buffer is very important for the efficiency of the operations of the knowledge model and the processing of queries. Pursuing this observation and the observations of the previous lesson, we can then summarize our conclusions by saying that an application buffer should provide an internal representation of objects that is as close as possible to the knowledge model and that efficiently supports both navigational and set-oriented processing [La91].

Lesson 28: Query processing must fully exploit the application buffer.

We learned from the query processing in KOALA that in order to adequately support the processing of queries in the workstation, the application buffer has to provide means for the explicit representation of results of subqueries delegated to the DBMS kernel as well as intermediate results of the query evaluation (i.e., sets of objects or parts of them). Otherwise, the query processor has to maintain structures containing copies of the qualified objects or object parts leading to a redundant representation of objects in the workstation. Based on these access structures, the application buffer should provide (in addition of both kinds of accesses given in the previous lesson) a powerful, explicit cursor concept to scan over the objects, allowing value-based selections of objects as well as operations concerning an object set as a whole (e.g., sorting objects by some criteria or merging two object sets).

Lesson 29: Support of main-memory indices on the application buffer is needed to increase efficiency.

In our investigations, we also observed (even in the smallest applications) that the 'amount' of data that had to be processed and consequently had to be passed to the workstation during the operation phase was growing rapidly. Supported by modern workstations, which are equipped with several MB of main memory with strong growing tendency, this will cause the size of the application buffer, the number of objects stored within it, and the size of the intermediate results to grow rapidly as well. Thus, the application buffer has to provide a number of different main-memory indices [La91] to accelerate the processing of these large sets of objects by the query processor [Hä91, TMMD92] (e.g., a value-based scan over the objects) similar to main-memory DBMS.

Processing Contexts

Lesson 30: Processing contexts are a useful means for further reduction of server calls through prefetching.

Our measurements have shown that the definition of processing contexts and their exploitation to generate a set-oriented access to the server in order to prefetch the corresponding objects and store them within the application buffer was an adequate means for further improving the efficiency of application processing. The number of server calls could be reduced by a factor of 2-5 and the time consumed by the server component decreased by 15-30% resulting in a 10-20% acceleration of application processing [Ma90b].

Lesson 31: The system should support the KB designer in the definition of such processing contexts by analyzing the queries, operational concepts, and constraints.

The development of our applications also revealed insights regarding the practical handling of processing contexts. We observed that the concept was rarely used by the KB designers although they were the persons who knew best about the details of an application. Even for those experts, it was hard to 'locate' contexts within the application, i.e, objects required in certain phases of the application, as they were often hidden in the specification of queries, methods, problem solving strategies, integrity constraints, etc. For this reason, even when the KB designers specified such contexts, they proved to be inexact, i.e., did not contain all objects really needed in the corresponding phase of the application. A factor that contributed to this problem was that the choice of the most appropriate 'point in time' for the specification of contexts proved to be rather difficult. When defining the contexts during the modeling of the application, they had to be adapted each time the algorithm was changed because of necessary reformulations and redesigns. When defining the contexts after finishing the modeling phase, an additional deep analysis of all parts of the applications was required which was then hard to perform and also very time consuming. However, we realized that most of these contexts could be extracted from queries, rules, and demons, a task of which the system could easily take care. It became then clear that it is possible to support the KB designer in his/her task of defining contexts by providing the functionality to automatically analyze the specification of rules, demons, and queries in methods in order to be able to find out which objects are needed in each phase of an application.

Lesson 32: Internal contexts should be exploited automatically by the system.

Independent of processing contexts that can be derived from the phases of an application, the internal processing of KRISYS also revealed the existence of sets of objects which are needed for processing system operations. During the inheritance of a newly defined attribute, for example, all objects in the generalization hierarchy below the corresponding class were accessed by the system. Also each query and subquery implicitly defined a context, containing the query results. Another example was the evaluation of rules in which every ruleset (the set of corresponding rules) together with the rules themselves (which can be seen as a query) defined a context. The system should, of course, make use of this to automatically define processing contexts in order to prefetch the required objects and to reduce the number of server calls.

Query Processing

Lesson 33: Query processing should rely on an algebraic framework, allowing the exploitation of optimization techniques known from (relational) DBS.

In the first version of KRISYS, KOALA was implemented with the primary goal of making it available for use. The internal representation of KOALA queries permitted only local optimizations and did not allow the use of any standard optimization techniques known from the field of databases. However, a detailed study of these techniques revealed that they are very useful in the KRISYS architecture, if adapted to the issues of a server/workstation environment [Hä91, Ro92, TMMD92]. This made us conclude that KOALA should be reimplemented based on an algebraic approach and oriented at the framework of general query processing [JK84] that permits to apply some of the existing (especially relational) optimization techniques [TMMD92].

Lesson 34: For query processing, a set-oriented, declarative server interface is required, otherwise a preselection of transferred objects is not possible.

KOALA is a set-oriented query language relying on a declarative description of its referenced objects. Due to the expressive power of KOBRA, large 'pieces' of a KOALA query have to be executed in the workstation requiring a large number of relevant objects to be installed in working memory [De91]. Instead of requesting single objects upon reference to the server, a better and far more efficient approach is to load the objects into the WM prior to executing the corresponding parts of the query. For this purpose, a set-oriented, declarative interface to the server DBMS is essential. Only then, it is possible to preselect the objects requested by (some part of) a query giving way to the exploitation of a very efficient two-staged query evaluation (as outlined in [TMMD92]): parts of the query evaluation are performed in the workstation and parts in the server.

Lesson 35: A declarative description of the buffer contents is a prerequisite for optimizing queries in this framework.

Due to the application's locality of reference, some or even all objects needed to process a query in the workstation may already reside in the WM because they were previously referenced by another query. Those objects can directly be used for query processing and need not be loaded from the server. Therefore, the consideration of the contents of the application buffer is an important measure to increase the efficiency of query evaluation. To reach this end, KRISYS should maintain a declarative description of the objects currently being installed in the WM in groups corresponding to the way such groups are referenced by KOALA. Thus, the KOALA processing system could make full use of the contents of the WM. As a simple example consider a KOALA query where all schemas that are elements of a certain set are referenced via the IS-ELEMENT predicate, and the same set has been referenced in a previous query, so that the required schemas are already in the WM. If the WM contents were only described by a list of identifiers of the contained schemas, the query processing component would still have to evaluate the KOALA predicate (requiring access to the server) in order to determine the names of the requested schemas, before being able to decide whether they are already in the WM. However, if the WM contents were described by the IS-ELEMENT predicate (meaning that the elements are completely contained in the WM), this decision could be made by comparing the query predicate with the WM description, requiring no additional server access.

4. Conclusions and Outlook

The KBMS KRISYS - developed at the University of Kaiserslautern - has been operational since 1989. Since then a lot of applications coming from different application classes were modeled with KRISYS to evaluate its adequacy for application design and operation. The experiences we drew from these works were presented in this paper.

We have shown that many concepts offered by KRISYS proved to be well-suited to support the requirements of both the design phase and the operational phase of the applications.

- First of all, this is true for the knowledge representation framework offered by KRISYS. The KOBRA knowledge model, characterized by object-centered approach, allows a uniform representation of descriptive, procedural, and structural facets of an application domain by attributes. Especially, the abstraction concepts of classification, generalization, association, and aggregation are major features for organizing the knowledge base.
- The integration of regular and meta information into the knowledge base made up the second positive experience we had. The difference between structuring and use of a KB on a physical level and on an operational level is eliminated respectively because all information about the knowledge base including schema information is stored there and because the same set of operations applies for manipulating the knowledge base and the meta-information. We observed that this is a major prerequisite to support an incremental development process which is typical for all application classes. Therefore, KRISYS proved to offer integral system support throughout an application's life cycle.
- KOALA, the query language of KRISYS, supports KB access in a set-oriented and declarative fashion and was used in many applications because of its expressive power and its easy use. The latter is due to the fact that KOALA is a state-oriented language that enables the user to manipulate the knowledge base (either by ad-hoc queries or by rules) by only describing the state expected from the result of the operation. Thus, the specification of queries and rules can be done independently from the current state of the knowledge base, resulting in an easier modeling and in a reduction of the number of rules.
- Moreover, the system architecture showed a good support for the applications running on workstation/server environments. The appropriate distribution of tasks between workstation and server and the integration of an application buffer into the workstation enabled most of the semantics offered by KRISYS to be realized in the workstation. The server, hosting the DBMS, is only responsible for providing general management of the data that make up the KB. By integrating an application buffer (the working memory) into the workstation, the applications' locality of reference could be exploited, thus minimizing the commu-

nication between workstation and server. In addition, this architecture makes possible a two-staged processing scheme characterized by first loading the relevant knowledge into the working memory and subsequently processing it there.

We have also demonstrated that our evaluation revealed that some of the features offered by KRISYS are not yet sufficient to support the applications in an optimal way. This especially applies for the optimization of KOALA queries, its embedding into a programming language, for integrity management, for the internal structure of the working memory, and for the mapping scheme used by KRISYS. While we were aware of some of these shortcomings from the start (e.g., those related to the implementation of KOALA), there were several observations that became apparent only over time. For this reason, these experiences turned out to be the most important for us.

- KOALA must be integrated into an algebraic framework that provides the basis for applying query processing techniques from the field of (relational) databases, after adapting them to the 'problems' of a workstation/server environment.
- A new mechanism for supporting integrity constraints that is more flexible concerning the definition of constraints, their scope, and their activation is required to better fullfil the needs of applications.
- The working memory must provide a representation closer to the knowledge model, navigational as well as set-oriented accesses to its contents. All these measures aim at an efficient mapping of higher-level operations (e.g., KOBRA and KOALA operations) on the working memory without the need to perform any transformations on the knowledge residing there or to maintain copies of the objects or intermediate results.
- It is also worth increasing the functionality of the working memory to make its contents available for query processing through declarative descriptions that can directly be exploited by the query optimizer. By doing so, the transfer of information between workstation and server can be deduced by testing whether the knowledge already residing in the application buffer subsumes parts of the knowledge required by a query.
- For the different phases of an application, appropriate mapping schemes from the knowledge model of KRISYS to the data model of the database system must be supplied. These schemes must be based on a detailed analysis of the knowledge base underlying an application. A change in the mapping occurs each time a new design cycle has been concluded and the application is going into its operational phase.

Based on the experiences described in this paper, a new KRISYS architecture has been designed and is currently being implemented. In this new design, we tried to take into consideration all the lessons we learned from the old system. The current state of the implementation is such that the tasks relating to the working memory - except the maintenance of a declarative description of its contents - and the realization of the component responsible for providing and generating appropriate mappings between knowledge model and data model have been completed. The implementation of the algebraic framework for KOALA is currently being undertaken, as well as that of the new component for integrity control. We have also extended KRISYS to support advanced transaction facilities for cooperative design applications [IRLM92]. In addition, we are considering the exploitation of parallelism in the scope of query processing, since the workstation/server environment of KRISYS and the distribution of tasks between those components offer a good framework for this [Th92, TMMD92].

We believe that we have accumulated enough experiences and knowledge from the first version of KRISYS, that it is now time to 'start all over again' to build an even 'better' system that will hopefully show the benefits but not the problems described in this paper. These issues will however be the subject of forthcoming papers.

Acknowledgements

We would like to acknowledge the support of Prof. Theo Härder in giving us the opportunity and necessary support to carry out this research project. Additionally, we would like to thank in particular all the students that have participated in the KRISYS project, whose combined efforts resulted in the KRISYS implementation and in most of the results described in this paper: Ch. Altenhofen, S. Bauer, S. Damaschke, Ch. Differding, K. Duchow, R. Durben, A. Grasnickel, E.Hänsel, M. Höhfeld, S. Hörth, M. Keil, Ch. Knecht, S. Kraft, D. Langkafel, S. Lind, L. Mangels, M. Michels, H. Möllenkamp, F. Mohr, J. Reinert, F. Rezende, B. Rheinberger, N. Ritter, R. da Rocha, P. Schneider, D. Schulte, R. Stauffer, M. Strobel, B. Surjanto, Ch. Thomczyk, and R. Zimmer.

References

At89 Atkinson, M., et.al.: The Object-Oriented Database Manifesto, in Proc. First Int. Conf. on Deductive and Object-Oriented Databases, 1989, Kyoto, Japan, pp.40-57.

BL86 Brachman, R., Levesque, H.: The Knowledge Level of KBMS, in: [BM86], pp. 9-12.

BM86 Brodie, M.L., Mylopoulos, J. (eds.): On Knowledge Base Management Systems (Integrating Artificial Intelligence and Database Technologies), Topics in Information Systems, Springer-Verlag, New York, 1986.

BMW84 Borgida, A., Mylopoulos, J., Wong, H.K.T.: Generalization/Specialization as a Basis for Software Specification, in: On Conceptual Modelling (Perspectives from Artificial Intelligence, Databases, and Programming Languages), Topics in Information Systems, (eds.: Brodie, M.L., Mylopoulos, J., Schmidt, J.W.), Springer-Verlag, New York, 1984, pp. 87-114.

Bo83 Borrmann, H.P.: MODIS - An Expert System for Supplying Repair Diagnosis of the Otto-Motor and its Aggregates (in german), Research Report No. 72/83, University of Kaiserslautern, Computer Science Department, Kaiserslautern, 1983.

Br81 Brodie, M.L.: Association: A Database Abstraction for Semantic Modelling, in: Proc. 2nd Int. Entity-Relationship Conference, Washington, D.C., Oct. 1981.

DD91 Damaschke, S., Differding, Ch.: Validating the Modeling Concepts of the KBMS KRISYS using a Sample Application (in German), University of Kaiserslautern, Kaiserslautern - Germany, September 1991.

De90 Deßloch S.: Enforcing Integrity in the KBMS KRISYS, in: Proc. of the 2nd Workshop on Foundations of Models and Languages for Data and Objects, Aigen (Austria), September 1990, pp.123-138.

De91 Deßloch, S.: Handling Integrity in a KBMS Architecture for Workstation/Server Environments, in: Proc. GI-Fachtagung "Datenbanksysteme in Büro, Technik und Wissenschaft", Kaiserslautern, März 1991, Hrsg. H.-J. Appelrath, Informatik-Fachberichte 270, Springer-Verlag, S.89-108.

DFMV90 DeWitt, D.J., Futtersack, P., Maier, D., Velez, F.: A Study of Three Alternative Workstation Server Architectures for Object-Oriented Database Systems, in Proc. 16th VLDB Conf., Brisbane, Australia 1990.

DHMM89 Deßloch, S., Härder, T., Mattos, N., Mitschang, B.: KRISYS: KBMS Support for Better CAD Systems, in: Proc. 2nd Int. Conf. on Data and Knowledge Systems for Manufacturing and Engineering, Gaithersburg - Maryland, Oct. 1989, pp.172-182.

DHMS90 Deßloch, S., Hübel, C., Mattos, N., Sutter, B.: KBMS Support for Technical Modeling in Engineering Systems, in: Proc. 3rd International Conference of Industrial and Engineering Applications of Artificial Intelligence and Expert Systems, Charleston - South Carolina, July 1990, pp. 790-799.

DHMS91 Deßloch, S., Hübel, C., Mattos, N., Sutter, B.: Handling Functional Constraints of Technical Modeling Systems in a KBMS Environment, in: International Journal of Systems Automation: Research and Applications (SARA), 1, 1991,pp. 347-367.

DK76 Davis, R., King, J.: An overview of production systems, in Elcock, E., Michie, D. (eds.): Machine Intelligence, Wiley, New York, pp. 300-332, 1976.

DK91 Duchow, K. & Keil, M.: A General Tool for the Development of Dialog Components for Knowledge-based Systems (in German), University of Kaiserslautern, Kaiserslautern - Germany, January 1991.

DLM90 Deßloch, S., Leick, F.J., Mattos, N.M.: A State-oriented Approach to the Specification of Rules and Queries in KBMS, ZRI-Report 4/90, University of Kaiserslautern, 1990.

Du91 Durben, R.: Modeling Technical Functional Constraints with KRISYS (in German), University of Kaiserslautern, Kaiserslautern - Germany, September 1991.

Fi88 Filman, R.E.: Reasoning with Worlds and Truth Maintenance in a Knowledge-based Programming Environment, in: Communications of the ACM, Vol. 31, No. 4, April 1988, pp. 382-401.

FK85 Fikes, R., Kehler, T.: The Role of Frame-based Representation in Reasoning, in: Communications of the ACM, Vol. 28, No. 9, Sept. 1985, pp. 904-920.

FWA85 Fox, M., Wright, J., Adam, D.: Experience with SRL: an Analysis of a Frame-based Knowledge Representation, Technical Report CMU-CS-81-135, Carnegie-Mellon University, Pittsburgh 1985.

Fr86 Frost, R. A.: Introduction to Knowledge Base Systems, Collins, London, 1986.

Hä88 Härder, T. (ed.): The PRIMA Project : Design and Implementation of a Non-Standard Database System, SFB 124 Research Report No. 26/88, University of Kaiserslautern, Kaiserslautern, 1988.

Hä89 Härder, T.: Engineering Applications - a Challenge for the Next Generation of DBMS, invited talk at the 2nd German INGRES user conference, 1989.

Hä91 Hänsel, E.: Query Processing in the Knowledge Base Management System KRISYS (in German), Diploma Thesis Work, University of Kaiserslautern, Kaiserslautern - Germany, July 1991.

HM90 Härder, T., Mattos, N.: An Enhanced DBMS Architecture Supporting Intelligent CAD (invited lecture), in: Engineering Information in Data Bases and Knowledge Based Systems - TECHNO-DATA'90, (eds. Richter, D. Grabowski, H.), Akademie-Verlag, Berlin -Germany, 1990, pp. 28-50.

HHMM88 Härder, T., Hübel, C., Meyer-Wegener, K., Mitschang, B.: Processing and Transaction Concepts for Cooperation of Engineering Workstations and a Database Server, in: Data and Knowledge Engineering, Vol. 3, 1988, pp. 87-107.

HK87 Hull, R., King, R.: Semantic Database Modeling: Survey, Applications, and Research Issues, in ACM Computing Surveys, vol.19, no.3, September 1987, pp. 201-260.

HMMS87 Härder, T., Meyer-Wegener, K., Mitschang, B., Sikeler, A.: PRIMA - A DBMS Prototype Supporting Engineering Applications, in: Proc. 13th VLDB Conf., Brighton, UK, 1987, pp. 433-442.

HR85 Härder, T., Reuter, A.: Architektur von Datenbanksystemen für Non-Standard-Anwendungen, in: Proc. GI-Proc. GI Conf. on Database Systems for Office, Engineering and Scientific Applications, p.253-286, Karlsruhe, Germany, März85, IFB 94, Springer Verlag,Heidelberg.

IRLM92 Iochpe, C., Rezende, F. F., Livi, M.A.C, Mattos, N.M.: Implementing a Design Management and Cooperation Model on the Basis of KRISYS, September 1992, submitted for publication.

JK84 Jarke, M., Koch, J.: Query Optimization in Database Systems, in: ACM Computing Surveys, vol.16, no.2, 1984, pp.111-151.

KDE90 IEEE Transactions on Knowledge & Data Engineering, special issue on database prototype systems, March 1990, vol.2, no 1.

KDG87 Küspert, K., Dadam, P., Günauer, J.: Cooperative Object Buffer Management in the Advanced Information Management Prototype, Proc. 13th VLDB Conf., Brighton, England, Sept. 1987, pp. 483-492.

KL89 Kifer, M., Lausen, G.: F-Logic, a Higher-Order Language for Reasoning about Objects, Inheritance and Schema, Proc. of the ACM SIGMOD Int. Conf. on Management of Data, 1989, pp. 134-146.

Kn92 Knapmeyer, Ch.: Optimization of the Database Mapping in the KBMS KRISYS Using Load Information (in German), Diploma Thesis Work, University of Kaiserslautern, Kaiserslautern - Germany, June 1992.

Kr89 The KBMS Prototype KRISYS - User Manual, Version 2.3, Kaiserslautern, West Germany, 1989.

Kr90 Kraft, S.: An Analysis of Existing Systems for Knowledge Modeling (in German), Diploma Thesis Work, University of Kaiserslautern, Kaiserslautern - Germany, February 1990.

La91 Langkafel, D.: A Component for Graph-oriented Management of Knowledge Base Contents (in German), Diploma Thesis Work, University of Kaiserslautern, Kaiserslautern - Germany, June 1991.

LM89 Leick, F.J., Mattos, N.M.: A Framework for an Efficient Processing of Knowledge Bases on Secondary Storage, in: Proc. of the 4th Brazilian Symposium on Data Bases, Campinas-Brazil, April 1989.

Ma88a Mattos, N.M.: Abstraction Concepts: the Basis for Data and Knowledge Modeling, in: 7th Int. Conf. on Entity-Relationship Approach, Rom, Italy, Nov. 1988, pp. 331-350.

Ma88b Mattos, N.M.: KRISYS - A Multi-Layered Prototype KBMS Supporting Knowledge Independence, in: Proc. Int. Computer Science Conference - Artificial Intelligence: Theory and Application, Hong Kong, Dec. 1988, pp. 31-38.

Ma89 Mattos, N.M.: An Approach to Knowledge Base Management - Requirements, Knowledge Representation, and Design Issues -, Doctoral Thesis, University of Kaiserslautern, Computer Science Department, Kaiserslautern,1989, also appeared as: Lecture Notes in Artificial Intelligence, Vol. 513 , Springer, 1991.

Ma90a Mattos, N.: An Approach to DBS-based Knowledge Management (invited talk), in: Proc. 1st Workshop "Information Systems and Artificial Intelligence", Ulm - West Germany, March 1990.

Ma90b Mattos, N.: Performance Measurements and Analyses of Coupling Approaches of Database and Expert Systems and Consequences to their Integration, in: Proc. 1st Workshop 'Information Systems and Artificial Intelligence', Ulm - Germany, March 1990.

Ma91 Mattos, N.M.: KRISYS - a KBMS Supporting Development and Processing of Knowledge-based Applications in Workstation/Server Environments, ZRI-Bericht 5/91, Universität Kaiserslautern, submitted for publication.

MDL91 Mattos, N.M., Deßloch, S., Leick, F.-J.: A Knowledge-based Approach to Intelligent CAD for Architectural Design, in: Proc. IEA/AIE'91 - 4th International Conference on Industrial and Engineering Applications of Artificial Intelligence and Expert Systems, Kauai, Hawaii, June 1991, S. 409-418.

Mi88 Mitschang, B.: Towards a Unified View of Design Data and Knowledge Representation, in: Proc. of the 2nd Int. Conf. on Expert Database Systems, Tysons Corner, Virginia, April 1988, pp. 33-49.

Mi89a Mitschang, B.: Extending the Relational Algebra to Capture Complex Objects, in: Proc. of the 15th VLDB Conf., Amsterdam, 1989, pp. 297-306.

Mi89b Michels, M.: The KBMS KRISYS from the Viewpoint of Expert Systems for Diagnosis (in German), University of Kaiserslautern, Kaiserslautern - Germany, March 1989.

MM89 Mattos, N.M., Michels, M.: Modeling with KRISYS: the Design Process of DB Applications Reviewed, in: Proc. the 8th Int. Conf. on Entity-Relationship Approach, Toronto - Canada, Oct. 1989, pp. 159-173.

MMM92 Mattos, N.M., Meyer-Wegener, K., Mitschang, B.: Grand Tour of Concepts for Object-Orientation from a Database Point of View, to appear in: Data and Knowledge Engineering.

Mö90 Möllenkamp, H. T.: Ensuring Spatial Semantics of 3D Objects with Semantic Integrity Constraints (in German), University of Kaiserslautern, Kaiserslautern - Germany, August 1990.

Mö91 Möllenkamp, H.: Knowledge based Support for Real-Estate Valuation - Application Analysis, Conception and Prototypical Implementation (in German), Diploma Thesis Work, University of Kaiserslautern, Kaiserslautern - Germany, December 1991.

Pu86 Puppe, F.: Diagnostic Problem Solving with Expert Systems (in german), Doctoral Thesis, University of Kaiserslautern, Computer Science Department, Kaiserslautern 1986.

Pu88 Puppe, F.: Introduction to Expert Systems (in german), Springer, Berlin, 1988.

Re90 Reinert, J.: A Model for Representing Satic and Dynamic Aspects in Design (in German), Diploma Thesis Work, University of Kaiserslautern, Kaiserslautern - Germany, February 1990

Rh89 Rheinberger, B.: A XPS for trip planning as application of the KBMS KRISYS (in German), Diploma Thesis Work, University of Kaiserslautern, Kaiserslautern - Germany, March 1989.

RHMD87 Rosenthal, A., Heiler, S., Manola, F., Dayal, U.: Query Facilities for Part Hierarchies: Graph Traversal, Spatial Data, and Knowledge-Based Detail Supression, Research Report, CCA, Cambridge, MA, 1987.

Ro92 Rocha, R. P. da: Transformation and Rewrite in the Query-Processing System of the KBMS KRISYS (in Portuguese), Master Thesis, CPGCC, UFRGS, Porto Alegre, Brasil, May 1992.

Sch89 Schulte, D.: Conception and Implementation of a Knowledge Base for the Representation of three-dimensional objects with the KBMS KRISYS (in German), University of Kaiserslautern, Kaiserslautern - Germany, October 1989.

Sch91 Schulte, D.: An Approach to Flexible Mapping of Knowledge Models to Data Models (in German), Diploma Thesis Work, University of Kaiserslautern, Kaiserslautern - Germany, June 1991.

SS77 Smith, J.M., Smith, D.C.P.: Database Abstractions: Aggregation and Generalization, in: ACM Transactions on Database Systems, Vol. 2, No. 2, June 1977, pp. 105-133.

ST89 Schmidt, J.W., Thanos, C. (ed.): Foundations of Knowledge Base Management, TOIS, Springer-Verlag, 1989.

St92 Strobel, M.: Conception of a Component for Context Management in the KBMS KRISYS (in German), Diploma Thesis Work, University of Kaiserslautern, Kaiserslautern - Germany, June 1992.

Su91 Surjanto, B.: Conception and Implementation of a knowledge based system for the generation of an application oriented DB schema for a KRISYS KB (in German), Diploma Thesis Work, University of Kaiserslautern, Kaiserslautern - Germany, October 1991.

Th90 Thomczyk, Ch.: An Expert System for Design as Application of the Knowledge Base Management System KRISYS (in German), Diploma Thesis Work, University of Kaiserslautern, Kaiserslautern - Germany, January 1990.

Th92 Thomas, J.: An Approach to Parallelism in KRISYS, ZRI-Report 1/92, University of Kaiserslautern, Computer Science Department, March 1992.

TMMD92 Thomas, J., Mitschang, B.,Mattos, N., Deßloch, S.: Knowledge Processing in Workstation/Server Environments - the KRISYS Approach, September 1992 (submitted for publication).

Zi91 Zimmer, R.: Modeling a Multi-Media Application with the KBMS KRISYS (in German), University of Kaiserslautern, Kaiserslautern - Germany, July 1991.

Flexible Entwurfsdatenverwaltung für CAD-Frameworks: Konzept, Realisierung und Bewertung

W. Käfer*, B. Mitschang
Fachbereich Informatik, Universität Kaiserslautern
Postfach 3049, 6750 Kaiserslautern
e-mail: {kaefer | mitsch}@informatik.uni-kl.de

Kurzfassung:

Eine der Hauptzielrichtungen von CAD-Frameworks ist die Integration von einzelnen, eigenständigen CAD-Werkzeugen mittels einer zentralen Datenverwaltung. Wesentliche Aufgaben hierbei sind die Verwaltung aller entwurfsrelevanten Daten sowie die effiziente Bereitstellung werkzeugrelevanter Daten für den werkzeugspezifischen Entwurfsschritt. Hierzu sind die vom jeweiligen Werkzeug zu bearbeitenden Entwurfsdaten bzw. Entwurfsobjekte zu selektieren und in der jeweils benötigten Form bereitzustellen. Nach Beendigung des Entwufsschrittes sind die geänderten Daten in den aktuellen Datenbestand zu integrieren. Um diese schwierige Aufgabe meistern zu können, ist es nötig, die vorherrschenden Objekt- und Entwurfsstrukturen entsprechend zu berücksichtigen.

Das hier vorgestellte Objekt-Versions-Modell OVM soll diesen hohen Anforderungen entsprechen. Mit OVM werden (versionierte) Objekte aus Elementarobjekten zusammengesetzt; zwischen diesen Objekten können Objekt-, Versions-, und Konfigurationsbeziehungen in flexibler Art und Weise aufgebaut werden. Die zugehörige Manipulationssprache OML erlaubt ein adäquates Arbeiten mit den so strukturierten Objekten. OVM bietet eine hohe Abstraktion von der zugrundeliegenden Datenrepräsentation, so daß eine OVM-Realisierung im Prinzip mit unterschiedlichen DBS durchgeführt werden kann. Unsere OVM-Realisierung mittels des PRIMA-Systems wird vorgestellt, die gewonnenen Erfahrungen berichtet und eine vergleichende Bewertung zu Realisierungsalternativen gegeben.

1. Motivation

Ein wesentlicher Schritt zur Beherrschung der Komplexität des Entwurfs (etwa VLSI-Entwurf oder CAD im Maschinenbau, in der Architektur, im Bau- und Raumwesen), stellt der Einsatz Integrierter Rechnergestützter Entwurfsumgebungen (engl. "integrated computer-aided design environment" oder einfach "CAD Frameworks") dar [RS92, HNST90]. Diese Umgebungen bieten eine Sammlung rechnergestützter Dienste in Form von einzelnen Werkzeugen an, die jeweils miteinander gekoppelt und fein aufeinander abgestimmt sind und alle (wesentlichen) Phasen des Entwurfsprozesses in kontinuierlicher Weise unterstützen. Hierbei stellt die integrierte Datenhaltung eine wesentliche Voraussetzung zur gewünschten Werkzeugintegration dar.

Eine wichtige Aufgabe von CAD-Frameworks ist somit die zentrale Verwaltung aller ***entwurfsrelevanten Daten*** sowie die Bereitstellung der ***werkzeugrelevanten Daten*** für den werkzeugspezifischen Entwurf. Die Anwendung eines CAD-Werkzeuges bedeutet das Ausführen eines sog. *Entwurfsschrittes*, der in mehrere Phasen unterteilt werden kann. Das hier zugrundeliegende *kontext-basierte Verarbeitungskonzept* unterscheidet im wesentlichen drei Phasen. Mittels einer Checkout-Operation werden die werkzeugrelevanten Daten bei der Datenhaltungskomponente angefordert. Nach deren Bereitstellung in einem lokalen Verarbeitungsbereich wird der eigentliche Entwurfsschritt durchgeführt. Dabei wird häufig auf die Daten im Verarbeitungsbereich zugegriffen und diese auch i. allg. geändert bzw. neue Entwurfsdaten erzeugt. Vor Beendi-

*) Zur Zeit als Gastwissenschaftler bei IBM, Almaden Research Center, San Jose, Kalifornien.

gung der Werkzeugausführung werden diese Änderungen mittels einer Checkin-Operation wieder der zentralen Datenhaltung zurückgegeben.

In vielen Fällen dienen Versionierungs- und Konfigurationsstrukturen zur Organisation der Entwurfsdaten [DL88, Ka90, Kä91] entsprechend den Anforderungen des werkzeugspezifischen Entwurfs. Beispielsweise können diese Strukturen den Entwurfsprozeß bzw. dessen Entwurfsschritte reflektieren und erlauben somit insbesondere eine Zuordnung von Werkzeugläufen und Entwurfsobjekten bzw. Entwurfsobjektversionen. Weiterhin dienen sie der Übergabe von aktuellen Entwurfsdaten von einem Werkzeug zum nächsten und erlauben ein kontrolliertes Weiterschreiben von Entwurfsobjektversionen.

Die werkzeugrelevanten Daten stellen den für ein konkretes Werkzeug und einen konkreten Entwurfsschritt relevanten Ausschnitt der Entwurfsdaten dar. Dieser sog. ***Verarbeitungskontext*** setzt sich i. allg. aus verschiedenen Elementarteilen zusammen, die über (sog. strukturelle) Beziehungen miteinander verbunden sind. Dabei sind die Beziehungen dem Werkzeug bekannt und werden auch für die werkzeugbezogene Verarbeitung benutzt, was im wesentlichen ein Entlanglaufen dieser Beziehungen bedeutet. Aus Leistungsgründen ist es daher erforderlich die Navigation entlang der strukturellen Beziehungen durch entsprechend geeignete Repräsentation des Verarbeitungskontextes im Verarbeitungsbereich des Werkzeugs zu unterstützen.

Aus dem Blickpunkt der Datenhaltung entspricht ein Verarbeitungskontext einer *Sicht* (engl. view) auf den Datenbestand, die durch eine (Anfrage-)Sprache spezifiziert ist. Evaluieren der Sicht (bei der Checkout-Operation) bedeutet entsprechend das Extrahieren des spezifizierten Kontextes und dessen Bereitstellung im werkzeuglokalen Verarbeitungsbereich. Um die Komplexität der Datenhaltungsaufgaben eines Werkzeuges weiter zu verringern, wird dem Werkzeug während seiner Verarbeitung eine versionsfreie Sicht auf die Entwurfsdaten geboten. Die Checkout- bzw. die Checkin-Operationen müssen jedoch vorhandene Versionierungs- und Konfigurationsstrukturen berücksichtigen. Schon allein dieser komplexe Extraktionsprozeß legt die Verwendung von Sichten nahe. Durch die Trennung von Spezifikation des Verarbeitungskontextes, eigentlicher Extraktion aus dem Entwurfsdatenbestand und anschließender Bereitstellung erhält die Datenhaltungskomponente die freie Wahl von Datenhaltungsmethoden und Datenrepräsentation sowie von Datenbereitstellungskonzepten im Verarbeitungsbereich. Weiterhin ist zu bemerken, daß verschiedene Werkzeuge i. allg. auf unterschiedlichen Verarbeitungskontexten basieren, die sich häufig auf den zugrundeliegenden Entwurfsdaten überlappen.

All diese Überlegungen ergeben, daß ein Modell und eine zugehörige Sprache erforderlich sind, welche zusammen eine flexible und abstrakte Spezifikation von Verarbeitungskontexten erlauben. Das hier vorgestellte Objekt-Versions-Modell OVM entspricht diesen Anforderungen. Mit OVM werden (versionierte) Objekte aus Elementarobjekten zusammengesetzt. Zwischen diesen Objekten können Objekt-, Versions-, und Konfigurationsbeziehungen in flexibler Art und Weise aufgebaut werden. Die zugehörige Manipulationssprache OML erlaubt ein adäquates Arbeiten mit den so strukturierten Objekten. Die Spezifikation von Verarbeitungskontexten entspricht in OVM der Definition von Sichten, die OVM-Objekte ansprechen bzw. bearbeiten. OVM bietet dabei eine hohe Beschreibungsebene, die insbesondere von der zugrundeliegenden Repräsentation der Elementarobjekte abstrahiert. Dies wiederum bedeutet, daß eine OVM-Realisierung im Prinzip mit unterschiedlichen Datenhaltungssystemen bzw. Datenbanksystemen (DBS) durchgeführt werden kann. Für alle nachfolgenden Diskussionen wird angenommen, daß die Entwurfsdaten durch ein DBS verwaltet werden, dessen Eigenschaften dann ggf. konkretisiert werden.

Bevor allerdings OVM erklärt und an einem Beispiel aus dem VLSI-Entwurf vorgestellt wird (Kapitel 3), sollen in Kapitel 2 grundlegende Eigenschaften und Anforderungen an Objektmodelle für den Entwurf diskutiert werden. In Kapitel 4 wird eine mögliche OVM-Realisierung mittels unseres Non-Standard-DBS PRIMA [HMMS87, GG92] vorgestellt und die dabei gewonnenen Erfahrungen berichtet. Eine vergleichende

Bewertung von alternativen Realisieungsmöglichkeiten und ein kurzes Resümee (in Kapitel 5) schließen die Diskussion ab.

2. Objektmodelle für den Entwurf

Im folgenden werden die Charakteristika der werkzeugbasierten Verarbeitung diskutiert. Dabei ergeben sich zwei unterschiedliche Abstraktionsebenen. Die Berücksichtigung dieser Aspekte in einem Objektmodell wird dann anschließend betrachtet.

2.1 Charakteristika eines werkzeugbasierten Entwurfsschrittes

In Entwurfsanwendungen müssen zwei Arten der Verarbeitung unterschieden werden [GHM92, Kä91]. Auf der Ebene der Entwurfssteuerung, also des Einsatzes bestimmter Entwurfsmethoden zur *Ablaufsteuerung des Entwurfsprozesses*, sind Entwurfsobjekte bzw. mehr noch Entwurfsobjektversionen Gegenstand des Interesses. Hier ist eine abstrakte Sicht auf die Entwurfsdaten vorteilhaft, da lediglich die Abhängigkeiten zwischen Entwurfsobjektversionen bzw. die Zusammenhänge zwischen Entwurfsobjektversionen und einzelnen Werkzeugläufen, also Entwurfsschritten, berücksichtigt werden müssen.

Die zweite Art der Verarbeitung erfolgt durch die *spezialisierten Entwurfswerkzeuge*, die die Entwurfsdaten im Sinne des Entwurfsziels transformieren. Die Art der Datenverarbeitung basiert auf dem 'inneren' Aufbau der Entwurfsobjektversionen. Den Werkzeugen wird daher eine versionsfreie Sicht auf die zu bearbeitenden Objekte geboten. Die Auswahl der zu lesenden Versionen bzw. die Integration der erzeugten Versionen erfolgt somit strikt getrennt von der eigentlichen Verarbeitung der Entwurfsdaten. Diese Trennung in *versionsfreie Werkzeugsicht* und *versionsbehaftete Entwurfssteuerungsebene* ist ein wesentlicher Beitrag zur Beherrschung des Entwurfsprozesses und zur Reduktion der Komplexität der werkzeugbasierten Verarbeitung. Diese beiden Abstraktionsebenen werden auch von CAD-Frameworks forciert und drücken sich in den folgenden sechs Phasen der werkzeugbasierten Verarbeitung aus:

1. Die *Daten- bzw. Versionsauswahl* für den aktuellen Verarbeitungsschritt wird aufgrund entwurfsspezifischer bzw. entwurfsmethodenspezifischer Überlegungen zumeist von einem Entwerfer bzw. durch die Entwurfssteuerung getroffen. Hierzu müssen die betreffenden Ausschnitte (Entwurfsobjektversionen) aus den Entwurfsdaten einfach und kompakt bezeichnet bzw. beschrieben werden können.

2. Der Werkzeuglauf beginnt mit der *Extraktion der Eingabedaten* aus der Datenbank durch eine sog. *Checkout*-Operation. Dies muß einfach und effizient anhand einer deskriptiven Beschreibung erfolgen können. Der ausgewählte Kontext liefert eine versionsfreie Sicht auf die werkzeugrelevanten Daten.

3. Nach der Bereitstellung der werkzeugrelevanten Daten in einem werkzeuglokalen Verarbeitungsbereich wird der eigentliche Entwurfsschritt durchgeführt. Die *Verarbeitung* der Daten im Werkzeug erfolgt i. allg. traversierend und entlang der strukturellen Beziehungen, die die Elementarobjekte miteinander verbinden. Dabei werden Daten im Verarbeitungsbereich geändert bzw. neue Entwurfsdaten erzeugt. Effizienter Datenzugriff und Navigationsunterstützung (etwa durch entsprechende Hauptspeicher-Datenstrukturen) bestimmen die Leistungsfähigkeit der Verarbeitung.

4. Vor Beendigung der Werkzeugausführung werden die durchgeführten Änderungen mittels einer *Checkin*-Operation wieder dem DBS zurückgegeben.

5. Die *Integration der erzeugten Entwurfsversionen* erfolgt nach den für den aktuellen Verarbeitungsschritt geltenden Kriterien. Diese Kriterien sind von der verwendeten Entwurfsmethodik festgelegt und regeln i. allg. Abhängigkeiten zwischen den Entwurfsdaten, wie etwa die Ableitung von neuen Entwurfsversionen aus vorherigen Entwurfsversionen.
6. In einem letzten, *bewertenden Schritt* müssen die favorisierten Lösungen ausgewählt und zusammen mit den Ergebnissen anderer Entwurfsschritte im Hinblick auf das gesteckte Entwurfsziel beurteilt werden. Dies wird häufig unter dem Begriff *Konfigurierung* subsumiert.

Durch diese Phaseneinteilung werden die Trennung von *werkzeugspezifischen und entwurfsspezifischen Aspekten* und damit auch gleichzeitig die zwei unterschiedlichen Abstraktionsebenen verdeutlicht. Die Schritte 2, 3, und 4 bilden das kontext-basierte Verarbeitungskonzept und basieren auf einer versionsfreien Datensicht, wie sie von Entwurfswerkzeugen benötigt wird. Hingegen sind alle entwurfsspezifischen und damit zumeist auch die Versionierung betreffende Aspekte in den Schritten 1, 5 und 6 zusammengefaßt. Im nächsten Abschnitt wollen wir die Organisation der Entwurfsdaten eingehender untersuchen und zu einer klareren Begriffsbildung kommen. Die werkzeugbasierte Verarbeitung wird später (in Kapitel 4) nochmals aufgegriffen und in einem Architekturansatz für CAD-Frameworks aufgezeigt.

2.2 Organisation der Entwurfsdaten

2.2.1 Entwurfsobjekte und Entwurfsobjektversionen

Wir führen den Begriff des Entwurfsobjekts bzw. kurz des ***Objekts** als eindeutig benennbare und leicht zu handhabende, strukturierte Ansammlung von elementaren Daten* ein (vgl. Bild 1), der als Grundlage der werkzeugbasierten Verarbeitung dienen soll. Objekte können durch eine Reihe von sog. ***Objektattributen*** in ihrer Gesamtheit beschrieben werden. Die im Objekt zusammengefaßten *elementaren Objekte*, die sog. ***Elementarobjekte***, beschreiben die für die Werkzeugausführung notwendigen Daten und können durch ***Elementarobjektattribute*** vollständig beschrieben werden; sie entsprechen damit in ihrer Ausdrucksmächtigkeit etwa den Tupeln im Relationenmodell. Die Elementarobjekte sind gemäß den sog. ***Strukturbeziehungen*** (die auch als *Elementarobjektbeziehungen* bezeichnet werden) organisiert. Ein Objekt beschreibt somit alle (oder zumindest einen signifikanten Teil) der für ein konkretes Werkzeug relevanten Daten. *Unterschiedliche Zustände der im Objekt zusammengefaßten Daten werden als Objektversionen* oder kurz als ***Versionen*** *bezeichnet.* Analog den Objekten können die in Versionen zusammengefaßten Daten in ihrer Gesamtheit durch sog. ***Versionsattribute***[*] charakterisiert werden.

Die Ableitung einer neuen Objektversionen erfolgt i. allg. innerhalb eines Entwurfsschrittes durch die Anwendung eines Entwurfswerkzeugs auf eine (oder auch mehrere) bereits bestehende Entwurfsversionen. Die Abhängigkeiten zwischen (Ausgangs-)Versionen und den daraus entwickelten (neuen) Versionen, die die Fortentwicklung der beteiligten Objekte beschreiben, werden in Form sog. ***Abstammungsgraphen*** repräsentiert. Der Abstammungsgraph kann sich als gerichteter, linearer, baumartiger oder allgemein als azyklischer Graph entwickeln.

Neben der beschriebenen Fortentwicklung initialer Versionen ist aber auch die Erzeugung mehrerer initialer Versionen eines Entwurfsobjekts durch ein Werkzeug zu berücksichtigen. Jede dieser Versionen kann dann unabhängig voneinander weiterentwickelt werden. Hierdurch entstehen Gruppen von jeweils abhängigen Objektversionen eines Objekts, dessen Abstammungsgraph sich dann als *unzusammenhängender* Graph aus-

*) In allen nachfolgenden Bildern sind Objekt- und Versionsattribute nicht gezeigt.

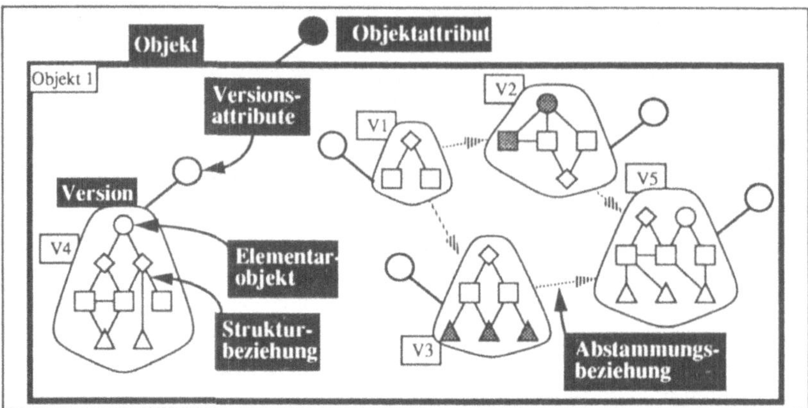

Bild 1:Objekt mit Versionen und Abstammungsgraph

bildet. Versionen, die zu unterschiedlichen Zusammenhangskomponenten des Abstammungsgraphen gehören, also nicht direkt voneinander abhängig sind, bezeichnen wir als ***alternative*** Objektversionen (Versionen 1, 2, 3 und 5 sind "alternativ" zu Version 4), da sie i. allg. durch *alternativ* ausgeführte Verarbeitungsschritte entstanden sind. Ein gutes Beispiel hierfür ist die Anwendung eines Entwurfswerkzeugs auf die gleichen Entwurfsdaten mit unterschiedlichen Steuerungsparametern.

2.2.2 Beziehungen zwischen Entwurfsobjekten bzw. Entwurfsobjektversionen

Die Beziehungen zwischen Objekten, Objektversionen oder auch alternativen Objektversionen sind sehr vielfältig. Zum einen werden sie *explizit* in Form von Objekt- und/oder Versionsbeziehungen definiert, zum anderen ergeben sie sich *implizit* durch objekt- bzw. versionsüberlappende Daten - sind also eine Folge von überlappenden Objektdefinitionen. Bild 2 illustriert die unterschiedlichen Beziehungsbegriffe, die wir im folgenden kurz charakterisieren wollen.

Objektbeziehungen repräsentieren zwischen Objekten bestehende Relationen [DL88, Wi87]. Obwohl Objektbeziehungen auch für sich alleine existieren können, ist es häufig sinnvoll, sie auf Versionen zu verfeinern. Sie werden dann als ***Versionsbeziehungen*** bezeichnet. In diesem Fall können die zugehörigen Objektbeziehungen als *Abstraktion* ihrer Versionsbeziehungen verstanden werden. Auf der anderen Seite, können Versionsbeziehungen nur in Verbindung mit einer zugehörigen Objektbeziehung existieren. Das explizite Nachführen von Versionsbeziehungen bei der Ableitung bzw. Entstehung neuer Versionen kann durch sog. ***generische*** Versionsbeziehungen [BM88, DL88, Sc91] vermieden werden. Hierbei werden an der Beziehung teilnehmende Versionen nicht fest durch ihren Identifikator, sondern dynamisch bei der Evaluierung der Beziehung beispw. mit Hilfe eines Suchausdrucks bestimmt [BM88, Sc91]; so kann etwa die jeweils zuletzt erzeugte Version als Beziehungspartner ermittelt werden.

Zusätzlich zu den beschriebenen expliziten Verknüpfungen zwischen Versionen können weitere implizite Beziehungen vorhanden sein (vgl. Bild 2). Sie ergeben sich durch Datenüberlappungen als Folge von überlappenden Objekttypdefinitionen. Die Datenüberlappungen können dabei über Elementarobjekte selbst oder über Strukturbeziehungen entstehen. Im ersten Fall werden Elementarobjekte mehreren Versionen *unterschiedlicher Objektausprägungen* zugeordnet; wir sprechen demgemäß von ***überlappenden Objektversionen*** bzw. kurz von ***überlappenden Objekten***. Ein Beispiel hierfür ist die Objektüberlappung zwischen Objekt 1 Version 4 und Objekt 3 Version 2 dargestellt in Bild 2. Grundlage des zweiten Falls sind definierte

Strukturbeziehungen. ***Intra-Strukturbeziehungen*** sind auf die aktuelle Objektversion beschränkt. Hingegen überschreiten ***Inter-Strukturbeziehungen*** die Objektversionsgrenzen. Da letztere nur im Kontext der beteiligten Objektversionen vollständig interpretiert werden können, wird durch sie auch eine Art Objektüberlappung definiert. Dieser, zur Interpretation notwendige Kontext, führt direkt zum Begriff der ***Konfiguration*** [BM88, DL88, Ka90].

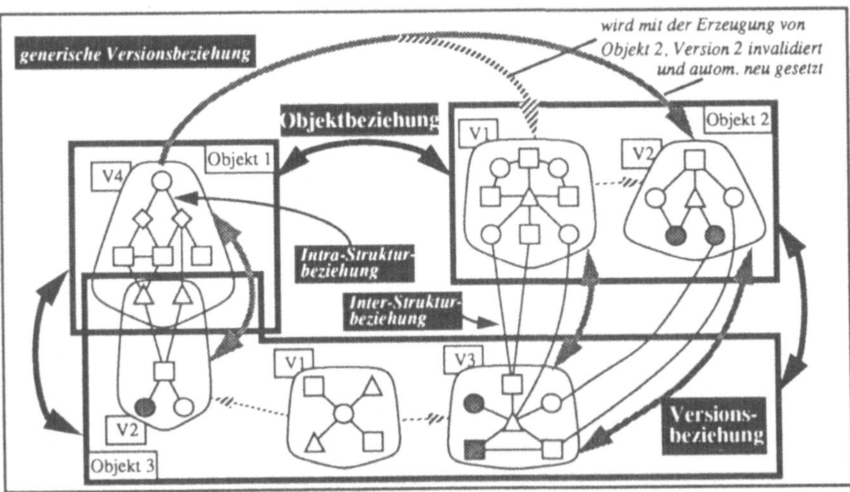

Bild 2: Objekt-, Versions- und Strukturbeziehungen

Beziehen wir uns auf Bild 2 und vergegenwärtigen wir uns, daß jede Objektversion das Objekt vollständig beschreibt; dies bedeutet, daß Version 3 von Objekt 3 entweder nur mit Version 1 oder nur mit Version 2 von Objekt 2 in Beziehung stehen darf. Um eine saubere Trennung der Inter-Strukturbeziehungen zu erreichen, müßte somit eine neue Version von Objekt 3 erzeugt werden. Dies löst jedoch einen Schneeballeffekt aus, falls weitere Inter-Strukturbeziehungen betroffen sind. Um dies zu vermeiden, setzt man zur Trennung der Inter-Strukturbeziehungen Konfigurationen ein, d.h. *Inter-Strukturbeziehungen dürfen nur innerhalb einer Konfiguration interpretiert werden.* In unserem Fall müßten also zwei Konfigurationen (Objekt 2, Version 1 mit Objekt 3, Version 3 und Objekt 2, Version 2 mit Objekt 3, Version 3) gebildet werden.

2.3 Zusammenfassung

Damit haben wir alle wesentlichen Begriffe eingeführt, die zur Strukturierung der Entwurfsdaten notwendig sind. Elementarobjekte und Elementarobjektbeziehungen erlauben die Beschreibung und Handhabung der werkzeugrelevanten Daten und ermöglichen somit eine werkzeugbasierte Verarbeitung gemäß dem in Abschnitt 2.1 vorgestellten kontext-basierten Verarbeitungskonzept. Diese sog. ***Elementarobjektebene*** realisiert die werkzeugspezifischen Aspekte und stellt eine erste Abstraktion von der eigentlichen Repräsentation der Entwurfsdaten dar. Objekte, Objektversionen und die zwischen ihnen definierten Objekt- und Versionsbeziehungen erlauben eine nochmals abstraktere Sichtweise auf die Entwurfsdaten. Diese Abstraktionsebene nennen wir auch ***Objektversionsebene***. Sie unterstützt die entwurfsspezifischen Aspekte und damit die Entwurfssteuerungsebene.

Eine wesentliche Aufgabe bei der Entwurfsdatenmodellierung besteht in der Konsistenzsicherung der Daten. Wir haben hierzu Konfigurationen eingeführt, die eine konsistente, versionsfreie Sicht auf die Entwurfsdaten garantieren. Zusätzlich müssen jedoch auch Abhängigkeiten zwischen den beiden Datenabstraktionsebenen berücksichtigt werden. Liegt eine Objektüberlappung bzw. eine Objektversionsüberlappung auf Elementarobjektebene vor, so muß diese Abhängigkeit auch auf der höheren Abstraktionsebene, also auf der Objektversionsebene sichtbar sein. Aus diesem Grund, ist eine Objektüberlappung nur dann erlaubt, wenn zwischen den beteiligten Objekten bzw. Objektversionen eine Objekt- bzw. Versionsbeziehung existiert. Damit ist auf semantisch höherer Ebene, also auf der Objektversionsebene, die Objektüberlappung auf Elementarobjektebene manifestiert und kann somit auch entsprechend interpretiert werden.

3. Das Objekt-Versions-Modell OVM

Nachdem wir die grundlegenden Strukturen von Entwurfsdaten identifiziert haben, wollen wir nun das Objekt- und Versionsmodell OVM vorstellen, das entsprechend den zuvor erarbeiteten Vorgaben konzipiert wurde.

3.1 Beispielanwendung VLSI-Entwurf

Zur Illustration und gleichzeitig auch zur Evaluierung der Adäquatheit des Objekt-Versions-Modells (OVM) wollen wir eine (vereinfachte) VLSI-Entwurfsumgebung verwenden, die wir im folgenden kurz einführen wollen. Eine ausführlichere Beschreibung dieser Entwurfsumgebung sowie des OVM findet sich in [Kä92]. Ziel des Kapitels ist es, ein vereinfachtes Informationsmodell für einige wichtige Bereiche des VLSI-Entwurfs zu entwickeln, die anschließend durch die Sprachmittel von OVM beschrieben werden sollen.

Die in [Zim86] eingeführte Entwurfsmethodik unterscheidet verschiedene Entwurfsbereiche, die jeweils durch hierarchisch angeordnete Beschreibungsebenen schrittweise verfeinert werden. Der Bereich "Verhalten" spezifiziert die Funktion (Operation, Algorithmus, Prozeß) des betreffenden Entwurfsobjekts möglichst genau. Im Bereich "Struktur" wird das Objekt in seiner realisierungsunabhängigen Zusammensetzung beschrieben; dieser umfaßt u.a. Schaltplan und Komponentenliste. Letztere besteht aus einer Modulliste und einer Netzliste. In der Modulliste werden die Module (Zellen) beschrieben, die innerhalb der aktuell zu entwerfenden Zelle als Subzellen zu plazieren sind. Die Modulbeschreibung enthält neben dem Namen weitere Parameter wie u.a. die voraussichtliche Modulfläche und die Außen-/Innenanschlüsse. In der Netzliste wird die Struktur der Zelle, d.h. die Verbindungen der Subzellen untereinander beschrieben. Weitere Bereiche machen Aussagen über den konkreten Aufbau des Entwurfsobjekts. Dazu gehört ein Floorplan (Bereich "Topographie"), der als Grobstruktur anschließend schrittweise bis zum Masken-Layout (Bereich "physikalische Realisierung") konkretisiert wird.

Da typischerweise die Anzahl der Standardzellen für eine zu entwerfende Zelle sehr groß ist (~ 10^6 Standardzellen), wird der Entwurf *hierarchisch* durchgeführt, d.h., man entwirft hierarchisch aufgebaute Zellen, die jeweils aus ca. 50 bis 100 Subzellen bestehen. Weiterhin wird ausgenutzt, daß häufig Subzellen mit gleicher Funktionalität mehrfach in einer Zelle verwendet werden. Diese Subzellen unterscheiden sich jedoch beispw. durch ihre geometrische Position innerhalb der Zelle bzw. durch ihre geometrische Form. Zur Modellierung dieser Aspekte verwendet man eine spezielle Art von Typisierung, auf die wir später nochmals eingehen werden.

Im Rahmen des sog. Chip Planning [ASZ92] wird eine Modul aus dem Bereich Struktur in den Bereich Topographie überführt. Diese Aufgabe wird i. allg. durch eine Gruppe von Entwurfswerkzeugen ausgeführt. In einem ersten Schritt wird zunächst eine Floorplan-Topologie generiert, die lediglich die relative Lage der Subzellen zueinander festlegt. Die dazu benötigten Algorithmen versuchen Kostenfunktionen zu minimieren, deren Parameter aus Modulfläche und Netzlängen bestehen. Hierauf aufbauend wird nun eine globale Verdrahtung der Subzellen gemäß der vorgegebenen Netzliste durchgeführt. In einem abschließenden Schritt kann dann die Floorplan-Topographie bestimmt werden.

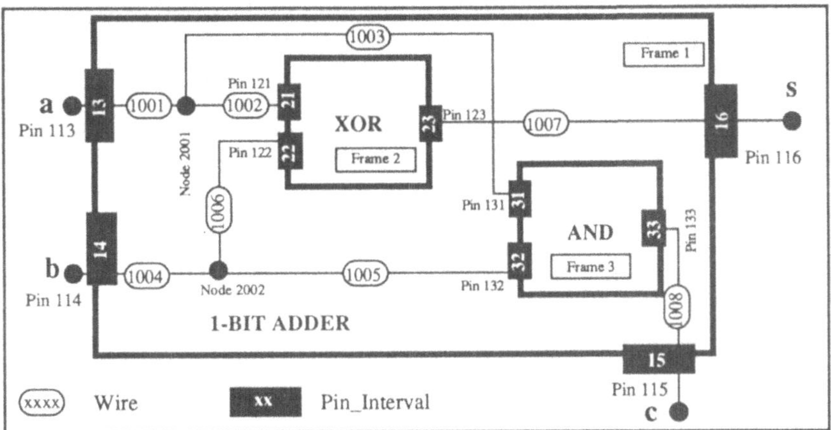

Bild 3: (Vereinfachte) graphische Darstellung des 1-Bit-Addierers

Bild 3 illustriert die vorgestellten Informationsstrukturen anhand einer vereinfachten Darstellung eines 1-Bit-Addierers. Zunächst läßt sich die ***Hierarchisierung*** innerhalb der Entwurfsdaten gut erkennen: Die Beschreibung der Zelle des 1-Bit-Addierers setzt sich direkt in der Beschreibung der Subzellen (XOR- und AND-Zelle) fort. Aus der gewählten Darstellung sind direkt ersichtlich die Modulliste (der 1-Bit-Addierer besteht aus einem AND- und einem XOR-Modul) sowie die Netzliste (also die Verbindungen zwischen den Modulen). Damit wird dann auch die topographische Anordnung der Subzellen und der Verbindungsleitungen suggeriert. Weiterhin ist das Prinzip der ***Typisierung***, also der Aufspaltung der Zellbeschreibung in ihre Schnittstellen-, ihre Implementierungs- und ihre Verwendungsinformation gut erkennbar. Die *Schnittstellen* der Zellen sind dabei jeweils durch einen Rahmen und Anschlußbereiche für Leitungen gegeben. Die *Implementierung* plaziert die Subzellen (*Instanzen*) in die aktuell zu entwerfende Zelle und verdrahtet die einzelnen Anschlußbereiche mittels durch Polygonzüge dargestellter Verdrahtungsstrecken. Die Verdrahtungsstrecken können über Kontaktstellen miteinander verknüpft werden.

3.2 Objektdefinition in OVM

Ausgehend von Bild 3 lassen sich die wesentlichen Beschreibungselemente leicht identifizieren. Zur Beschreibung der Zellen benötigen wir ihren Rahmen, sowie die darauf befindlichen Anschlußintervalle. Zur Beschreibung der Leitungen ist zum einen der Leitungsverlauf und zum anderen die Beschreibung der Kontaktstellen notwendig. Diese Elementarobjekte, werden im folgenden Kapitel mittels OVM beschrieben.

3.2.1 Elementarobjekt- und Beziehungstypen im OVM

Elementarobjekttypen werden durch Attribute unterschiedlichen Typs beschrieben und enthalten jeweils ein Attribut, das einen systemvergebenen Identifikator aufnehmen kann. Sie *können nicht versioniert werden* und entsprechen somit in ihrer Beschreibungsmächtigkeit etwa den Relationen des Relationenmodells.

Strukturbeziehungen zwischen Elementarobjekten werden durch ***Strukturbeziehungstypen*** definiert; sie können vom Typ 1:1, 1:n oder n:m sein, dürfen keine Attribute enthalten, sind jeweils auf maximal zwei Elementarobjekttypen beschränkt und können durch Kardinalitätsrestriktionen eingeschränkt werden*. Zur Beschreibung einer Zelle, wie sie beispw. in Bild 3 graphisch dargestellt ist, benötigen wir die in Bild 4 gezeigten Elementarobjekt- und Beziehungstypen. Der Rahmen einer Zelle wird durch den Elementarobjekttyp 'Frame' beschrieben. Auf dem Rahmen können in den durch 'Pin_Interval' beschriebenen Bereichen Anschlüsse erfolgen. Jeder konkrete Anschluß und dessen Position wird im Elementarobjekttyp 'Pin' vermerkt. Die Anschlüsse werden durch Leitungsbahnen ('Wire') in Form von Polygonzügen oder über Kontakte ('Node') miteinander verbunden. Die Leitungen einer Zelle werden zu Netzlisten ('Netlist') zusammengefaßt. Neben diesen sechs Elementarobjekttypen werden sechs Strukturbeziehungstypen benötigt: Zu jedem Rahmen ('Frame') müssen die zugeordneten Instanzen von 'Pin_Interval' und 'Pin' gebunden werden. Weitere zwei Beziehungstypen werden benötigt, um die Leitungsbahnen alternativ mit 'Pin'-Instanzen oder 'Node'-Instanzen verbinden zu können. Der letzte Beziehungstyp erlaubt die Zusammenfassung aller Leitungsbahnen zu einem Netz.

```
DEFINE ELEMENTARY_TYPE Frame          DEFINE ELEMENTARY_TYPE Pin_Interval
   (f_id:      IDENTIFIER,               (pt_id:     IDENTIFIER,
    width:     REAL,                      name:      LIST_OF (BYTE),
    height:    REAL);                     position:  HULL(2));

DEFINE ELEMENTARY_TYPE Pin            DEFINE ELEMENTARY_TYPE Netlist
   (p_id:      IDENTIFIER,               (n_id:      IDENTIFIER);
    position:  HULL (2));

DEFINE ELEMENTARY_TYPE Node           DEFINE ELEMENTARY_TYPE Wire
   (n_id:      IDENTIFIER,               (w_id:      IDENTIFIER
    position:  HULL (2));                 polygon:   LIST_OF (HULL (2)));

DEFINE ELEMENTARY_LINK_TYPE Frame.to_Pin_Interval (1,32), Pin_Interval.to_Frame (1,1);
DEFINE ELEMENTARY_LINK_TYPE Pin_Interval.to_Pin (0, *), Pin.to_Pin_Interval (1,1);
DEFINE ELEMENTARY_LINK_TYPE Frame.to_Pin (1,32), Pin.to_Frame (1,1);
DEFINE ELEMENTARY_LINK_TYPE Wire.to_Pin (0,2), Pin.to_Wire (0,1);
DEFINE ELEMENTARY_LINK_TYPE Wire.to_Node (0,2), Node.to_Wire (3,*);
DEFINE ELEMENTARY_LINK_TYPE Netlist.to_Wire (1,1), Wire.to_Netlist (1,*);
```

Bild 4: Elementarschema des VLSI-Entwurfsbeispiels

Das in Bild 4 gezeigte ***Elementarschema*** modelliert nicht die Sicht eines bestimmten Werkzeugs, sondern beschreibt alle werkzeugrelevanten Entwurfsdaten für den gesamten Entwurfsbereich "Struktur". Der nächste Abschnitt beschäftigt sich mit der für den Entwurfsablauf relevanten abstrakteren Ebene der Entwurfsobjekte bzw. der Entwurfsobjektversionen.

3.2.2 Objekte, Versionen und Beziehungen im OVM

Zur Steuerung des Entwurfsablaufs, also insbesondere zur Koordinierung von Werkzeugläufen wird eine abstraktere Sicht auf die Entwurfsdaten benötigt. Hierdurch angesprochen ist die Objektversionsebene, auf der die entwurfsspezifischen Aspekte modelliert werden. Wir realisieren diese abstraktere Ebene durch die Definition ***komplexer Objekttypen***. Hierbei stehen zwei Aspekte im Vordergrund: welche entwurfsrelevanten

*) Diese Form von Beziehungen ist in Entwurfsanwendungen dominant; eine Erweiterung auf n-äre, attributierte Beziehungen ist im Rahmen des vorgestellten Modells jedoch durchaus möglich.

Daten sind für den Entwurfsablauf von Interesse und welche werkzeugrelevanten Daten sind ihnen zuzuordnen? Bild 5 zeigt das auf dem Elementarschema basierende, abstraktere ***Objektschema***. Es werden drei komplexe Objekttypen definiert:

- 'Interface' zur Beschreibung der Schnittstelle, bestehend aus den Elementarobjekttypen 'Frame' und 'Pin_Interval',
- 'Instance' zur Beschreibung der Verwendung einer Schnittstelle, bestehend aus 'Frame' und 'Pin' sowie
- 'Contents' zur Beschreibung der Implementierung, also im wesentlichen der Verdrahtung einer Zelle bestehend aus 'Netlist', 'Wire' und 'Node'.

```
DEFINE OBJECT_TYPE Interface AS Frame, Pin_Interval VERSIONED
      (OBJECT_ATTRIBUTES:     if_id:                IDENTIFIER,
                              if_v_no:              VERSION_NO,
                              name:                 LIST_OF (BYTE),
                              function:             LIST_OF (BYTE),
                              no_of_pins:           INTEGER,
       VERSION_ATTRIBUTES:    if_v_id:              IDENTIFIER,
                              scale_factor:         REAL,
                              no_of_feedthroughs:   INTEGER)
       VERSION DERIVATION GRAPH IS LIST;
DEFINE OBJECT_TYPE Instance AS Frame, Pin NOT_VERSIONED
      (OBJECT_ATTRIBUTES:     ist_id:               IDENTIFIER,
                              position:             HULL(2));
DEFINE OBJECT_TYPE Contents AS Netlist, Wire, Node VERSIONED
      (OBJECT_ATTRIBUTES:     c_id:                 IDENTIFIER,
                              name:                 LIST_OF (BYTE),
       VERSION_ATTRIBUTES:    ct_v_id:              IDENTIFIER,
                              ct_v_no:              VERSION_NO,
                              no_of_wires:          INTEGER,
                              length_of_wires:      REAL,
                              no_of_feedthroughs:   INTEGER)
       VERSION DERIVATION GRAPH IS TREE;
```

Bild 5: Objektschema des VLSI-Entwurfsbeispiels

Jeder dieser komplexen Objekttypen besteht i. allg. aus einer Reihe von Elementarobjekttypen* und wird durch Attribute in seiner Gesamtheit beschrieben (s. Klausel OBJECT_ATTRIBUTES). Jeder Objekttyp muß ein Attribut zur Aufnahme des systemvergebenen eindeutigen Objektidentifikators enthalten. Die Strukturbeziehungen zwischen den Elementarobjekttypen eines Objekttyps sind bzgl. der gewünschten Abstraktion nicht von Bedeutung und demzufolge auch nicht Teil der Objekttypdefinition. Falls Elementarobjekttypen zur Beschreibung mehrerer Objekttypen benötigt werden und entsprechend in deren Definitionen verwendet werden, so sprechen wir von überlappenden Objekttypen. In unserem Beispiel wird der Elementarobjekttyp 'Frame' sowohl zur Beschreibung der Schnittstelle einer Zelle ('Interface') als auch zur Beschreibung einer Zellinstanz ('Instance') benötigt. Diese typmäßige Objektüberlappung führt zu überlappenden Objekten†, da die Positionsangaben in den Elementarobjekten 'Pin_Interval' und 'Pin' nur bzgl. des konkreten Zellrahmens ('Frame') von Bedeutung sind. Dies bedeutet, daß alle Werkzeuge, die mit diesen Positionsangaben arbeiten, auch die entsprechenden Rahmendaten benötigen. Da Objekte Einheiten der Verarbeitung darstellen, müssen somit sowohl die 'Interface'- als auch die 'Instance'-Objekte die entsprechen-

*) Die Angabe von Elementarobjekttypen zur Definition eines Objekttyps ist optional.

†) Nicht jede typmäßige Überlappung muß zu überlappenden Objekten (also Objekte, die die gleichen Elementarobjekte benutzen) führen, noch kann von nicht-überlappenden Objekttypen auf nicht-überlappende Objekte geschlossen werden.

den Informationen enthalten. Die durch die Objektüberlappung implizit gebildete Beziehung zwischen den Objekten muß durch eine entsprechend gebildete explizite Beziehung (s.u.) legitimiert werden.

Objekte können im Gegensatz zu Elementarobjekten versioniert werden, d.h., es können sowohl versionierte als auch nicht-versionierte Objekttypen definiert werden. Bei versionierten Objekten (Schlüsselwort VERSIONED) kann der Inhalt des Objekts (also nicht die Objektattribute) in mehreren unterschiedlichen Zuständen, die wir als Objektversionen bezeichnen, vorliegen. Nicht-versionierte Objekte können somit als versionierte Objekte mit genau einer Objektversion verstanden werden. Die einzelnen Objektversionen eines Objekts können analog dem Objekt selbst durch eine Reihe von Attributen beschrieben werden, die wir als Versionsattribute bezeichnen (s. Klausel VERSION_ATTRIBUTES). Eines der Versionsattribute wird wiederum zur Aufnahme eines systemvergebenen eindeutigen Identifikators benötigt. Zusätzlich ist die Definition eines zweiten Attributs zur Aufnahme einer systemvergebenen Versionsnummer notwendig, die alle Versionen *eines Objekts* aufsteigend (mit 1 beginnend) durchnumeriert*. Es kann zusätzlich ein Attribut des Typs TIMESTAMP zur Abspeicherung des Entstehungszeitpunktes der Version angegeben werden, das dann systemseitig gesetzt wird.

3.2.3 Objekt- und Versionsbeziehungen im OVM

Die ***Objektbeziehungstypen*** besitzen zunächst die gleichen Eigenschaften wie die schon vorgestellten Elementarbeziehungstypen zwischen Elementarobjekttypen, d.h., sie sind symmetrisch, attributfrei und binär. Es können Beziehungstypen des Typs 1:1, 1:n und n:m direkt modelliert werden. Im Gegensatz zu den Elementarbeziehungstypen können Objektbeziehungstypen jedoch von der Versionierung der Beziehungspartner betroffen sein. Da Objektversionen einem bestimmten Zustand des Objekts entsprechen, ist es zumeist notwendig, auch die Verknüpfung des Objekts in diesem Zustand zu anderen Objektversionen zu beschreiben. Dies bedeutet, daß Objektbeziehungen i. allg. zu Beziehungen zwischen Objektversionen, den sog. ***Versionsbeziehungen*** verfeinert werden. Dies bedeutet, daß *Versionsbeziehungen nur in Verbindung mit einer Objektbeziehung existieren können.* Entsprechend können Versionsbeziehungstypen nur im Zusammenhang mit Objektbeziehungstypen definiert werden. Die Handhabung von Versionsbeziehungen verlangt nach speziellen Mechanismen, da die unabhängige Versionierung der verschiedenen Objekte auf Ebene der Versionsbeziehungen zu besonderen Problemen führt, die wir im folgenden untersuchen wollen. Betrachten wir hierzu in Bild 6 die Definition der Beziehungstypen für unser Entwurfsbeispiel.

```
DEFINE LINK_TYPE  Instantiation BETWEEN Interface, Instance
     CARDINALITY  FROM Interface TO Instance IS (0, *), FOR VERSIONS (0, *),
                  FROM Instance TO Interface IS (1, 1), FOR VERSIONS (1, 1);
DEFINE LINK_TYPE  Aggregation BETWEEN Contents, Instance
     CARDINALITY  FROM Contents TO Instance IS (1, 1000), FOR VERSIONS (1, 1000
                  FROM Instance TO Contents IS (1, 1), FOR VERSIONS (1, *);
DEFINE LINK_TYPE  Implementation BETWEEN Interface, Contents
     CARDINALITY  FROM Interface TO Contents IS (0, 1), FOR VERSIONS (0, *),
                  FROM Contents TO Interface IS (1, 1), FOR VERSIONS (1, *);
```

Bild 6: Objekt- und Versionsbeziehungen des VLSI-Entwurfsbeispiels

Zunächst wird der Objektbeziehungstyp 'Instantiation' zwischen dem versionierten Objekttyp 'Interface' und dem nicht-versionierten Objekttyp 'Instance' definiert. Durch die Klausel FOR VERSIONS wird die Verfeinerung des Beziehungstyps auf Versionsebene erreicht. Aus diesem Grund müssen neben den Kardi-

*) Die Versionsnummer TOPICAL ist die höchste vergebene und erlaubt zusammen mit dem Objektidentifikator die Adressierung der neusten Version eines Objekts.

nalitätsrestriktionen auf Objektebene auch die Restriktionen auf Versionsebene angegeben werden. Wie die Definition des Beziehungstyps 'Implementation' zeigt, können hierbei unterschiedliche Angaben* sinnvoll sein. Beispielsweise soll ein 'Instance'-Objekt in genau einem 'Contents'-Objekt verwendet werden. Liegen aber unterschiedliche Versionen des 'Contents'-Objekts vor, so sollen hierfür nicht immer wieder neue 'Instance'-Objekte erzeugt werden müssen, da anzunehmen ist, daß viele Instanzen beim Versionsübergang überhaupt nicht verändert werden. Auf Versionsebene kann deshalb ein 'Instance'-Objekt mehreren 'Contents'-Versionen zugeordnet werden. Die gleichen Überlegungen gelten für die Beziehung zwischen 'Interface' und 'Contents': Jede Schnittstelle wird durch genau eine Implementierung realisiert. Es dürfen jedoch mehrere (alternative) Versionen der Implementierung existieren. Im Gegensatz zu bisher, werden bei ***generischen Versionsbeziehungen*** die an der Beziehung teilnehmenden Versionen dynamisch, nach einem vorgegebenen Verfahren (Auswahlbedingung), bestimmt. Beispielsweise kann damit ein bequemer Zugriff von der Schnittstelle auf die jeweils neuste Version der Implementierung ermöglicht werden. Eine ausführlichere Diskussion dieses Konzeptes kann in [Kä92] nachgelesen werden.

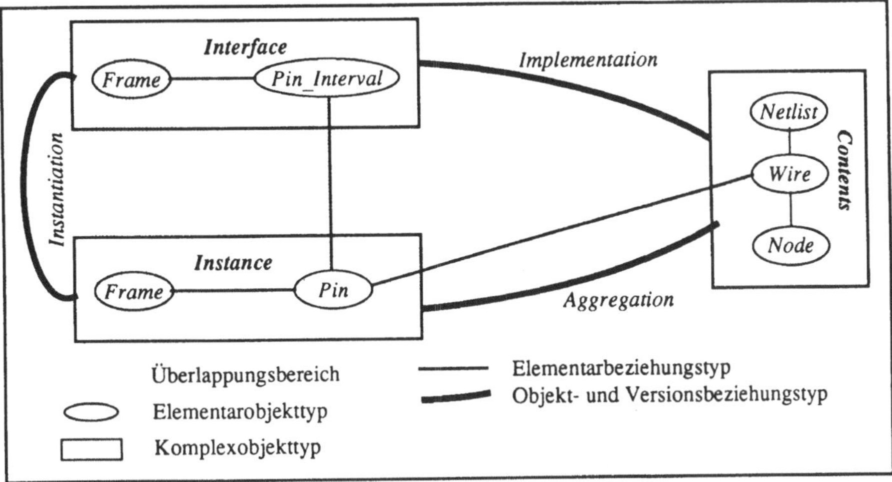

Bild 7: Graphische Darstellung des Gesamtschemas

Bild 7 zeigt eine graphische Gesamtdarstellung des entwickelten OVM-Schemas: die Elementarobjektebene abstrahiert von der eigentlichen Repräsentation der Entwurfsdaten und berücksichtigt die werkzeugspezifischen Aspekte; die Objektversionsebene unterstützt die entwurfsspezifischen Aspekte und damit die Entwurfssteuerungsebene. Die grauen Hinterlegungen heben Objekt- und Versionsüberlappungen hervor. Die in Kapitel 3.1 beschriebenen *Entwurfsbereiche* werden reflektiert durch mehr oder minder vollständige Objektversionen. Das dort ebenfalls angesprochene Prinzip der *Hierarchisierung* wird mittels der drei in Bild 7 aufgezeigten Objekt- bzw. Versionsbeziehungen realisiert: Ausgehend von einer Zelle ('Interface') wird über ihre Implementierung ('Contents') die darin enthaltenen Subzellen ('Instance') bzw. deren Schnittstellen ('Interface') erreicht. Ein solches Objektversions-Ensemble stellt einen typischen Verarbeitungskontext (in diesem Fall für das "Chip Planning"-Werkzeug) dar. Eine Sprache zur Bereitstellung solcher Verarbeitungskontexte wird im nächsten Abschnitt vorgestellt.

---

*) Wegen der Existenzbindung der Versionsbeziehung an die Objektbeziehung müssen die Kardinalitätsrestriktionen der Versionsbeziehung immer die Kardinalitätsrestriktionen der Objektbeziehung einschließen.

3.3 Objektmanipulation mit OML

In diesem Kapitel werden die wesentlichen Konzepte der Sprache OML (Object Manipulation Language) beschrieben. OML ermöglicht die Manipulation der Objekte, Versionen und Beziehungen in OVM. OML ist eine deskriptive, mengenorientierte Sprache. Die Form der Anweisungen sind an SQL angelehnt, d.h., für jede Operation werden in der FROM-Klausel die betroffenen Objekt- oder Beziehungstypen spezifiziert, deren Ausprägungen dann von der Operation betroffen sind. Diese können zusätzlich durch die Angabe einer WHERE-Klausel eingeschränkt werden. Bild 8 zeigt die Datenmanipulationsoperationen von OML im Überblick, von denen wir einige im folgenden näher besprechen wollen.

Operation	Beschreibung
CREATE OBJECT	Erzeugen eines Objekts, das durch seine Objektattribute beschrieben wird. Diese Operation erlaubt gleichzeitig die erste Version dieses Objekts, die durch ihre Versionsattribute und die Elementarobjekte beschrieben ist, zu erzeugen.
CREATE VERSION	Erzeugen einer Objektversion. Sie wird durch die Angabe der Versionsattribute und der Elementarobjekte beschrieben. Die Angabe der zugehörigen Objektausprägung bzw. der Vorgängerversion(en) im Abstammungsgraphen ist notwendig.
DELETE OBJECT	Löschen eines Objekts (inklusive seiner Versionen).
DELETE VERSION	Löscht eine einzelne Version eines Objekts mit allen Elementarobjekten.
UPDATE OBJECT	Ändern der Objektattribute (die "alten" Werte werden überschrieben).
UPDATE VERSION	Ändern der Versionsattribute (die "alten" Werte werden überschrieben).
CONFIGURE	Konfigurieren von Versionen.
CREATE LINK	Setzen von Objekt- und Versionsbeziehungen.
DELETE LINK	Auflösen von Objekt- und Versionsbeziehungen.

Bild 8: Die Datenmanipulationsanweisungen von OML

In der ersten Anweisung von Bild 9 wird ein Schnittstellenobjekt erzeugt, das keine Version enthält. Einige der Objektattribute werden mit Werten belegt. Die zweite Anweisung erzeugt eine Schnittstellenversion, die mittels der Angabe in der WHERE-Klausel explizit zu dem zuvor kreierten Schnittstellenobjekt gebunden

```
CREATE Interface  (OBJECT:   name := "1-Bit Adder",                    ⇒ if_id = 4711
                             function := "s, c := a + b",
                             no_of_pins := 4)
FROM Interface;

⇒ das Schnittstellenobjekt erhält den Identifikator 4711 (if_id).

CREATE Interface  (VERSION:  scale_factor := 1.0,                      ⇒ if_v_no = 1
                             no_of_feedthroughs := 0)
                   Frame         (width := 2.1,                        ⇒ f_id = 1
                                  height := 5.8)
                   Pin_Interval  (name := "x",                         ⇒ pt_id = 13
                                  position := [(0,1.4),(0,1.7)])
                   :
                   Pin_Interval  (name := "s",                         ⇒ pt_id = 16
                                  position := [(5.8, 1.2),(5.8,1.6)]);
FROM Interface
WHERE if_id = 4711;
```

Bild 9: Erzeugen eines Schnittstellenobjekts und seiner ersten Version

wird. Neben der Angabe der Versionsattribute müssen auch alle Elementarobjekte mit Werten belegt und abgespeichert werden; dies umfaßt auch die zwischen den Elementarobjekten bestehenden Strukturbeziehungen. Da die Version nur ein Elementarobjekt des Typs Frame umfaßt und nur ein Beziehungstyp zwischen 'Frame' und 'Pin_Interval' definiert ist, werden alle Elementarobjekte des Typs 'Pin_Interval' automatisch mit diesem verbunden.

Zur Datenwiedergewinnung stehen in OML die Operationen SELECT OBJECT und SELECT VERSION zur Verfügung, die auf der Objekt- bzw. auf der Objektversionsebene arbeiten und entsprechend Daten auf Objekt- oder Versionsebene aus der Datenbank extrahieren. Bild 10 zeigt zwei unterschiedliche Selektionsanweisungen, von denen die erste Anweisung bewußt die Tatsache der Versionierung zur Gewinnung einer abstrakteren Sicht auf die Daten unterbindet. Die zweite Anweisung operiert hingegen explizit auf der Versionsebene.

```
(1) SELECT OBJECT Interface (function, no_of_pins), Contents (ALL)
    FROM   Interface - <Implementation> Contents
    WHERE  Interface.name = "1-Bit Adder";

(2) SELECT VERSION Interface (ALL),
           Contents (name, length_of_wires, Wire (ALL), Node (position) ), Instance (ALL)
    FROM   Interface - (<Implementation> Contents, <Instantiation> Instance)
    WHERE  (Interface.name = "1-Bit Adder") AND (Contents.ct_v_no = 3);
```

Bild 10: Selektion eines (versionierten) Objekts

In der Projektionsliste werden analog SQL die Attribute von Elementarobjekten, Versionen und Objekten aufgelistet, die im Ergebnis enthalten sein sollen. Hierbei ist es möglich, auch Objekte und Versionen auszublenden, falls diese nicht den Zusammenhang der in der FROM-Klausel spezifizierten Objekttypstruktur zerstören. Die FROM-Klausel beschreibt einen gerichteten Teilgraphen des OVM-Schemas. Hierzu werden abwechselnd die benutzten Objekt- und Beziehungstypen aufgezählt*. Natürlich können hierbei gerichtete Versionsbeziehung nur gemäß ihrer Definition in einer Richtung verwendet werden, während die symmetrischen Elementarbeziehungstypen in jeder der beiden Richtungen benutzbar sind. Anweisung 1) aus Bild 10 zeigt eine Selektionsanweisung, die keine Versionierung beachtet und sich auf eine einfache Objekthierarchie bezieht. Es werden ausschließlich Objekte und Objektattribute von der Schnittstelle und zugehöriger Implementierung des 1-Bit-Addierers selektiert. Die zweite Anweisung selektiert zu allen Schnittstellenversionen des 1-Bit-Addierers die zugehörige dritte Implementierungsversion (bzw. die davon in der Projektionsklausel angeforderten Daten) und Instanzierungen. Die hierzu notwendige Verzweigung des Objektypgraphen wird mit Hilfe der angegeben Klammerung '(... , ...)' spezifiziert.

3.4 Zusammenfassung und verwandte Arbeiten

OVM bietet adäquate Konzepte zur Modellierung von werkzeugrelevanten Daten (Elementarobjektebene) als auch zur Modellierung entwurfsspezifischer Aspekte (Objektversionsebene) der Entwurfsdaten an. Die Sprache OML erlaubt darüberhinaus eine angepaßte Verarbeitung der so beschriebenen Objektnetze. So können etwa die Anweisungen aus Bild 10 als Spezifikationen für verschiedene Verarbeitungskontexte interpretiert werden. Die dort benutzten Versionsstrukturen werden ausgewertet und liefern als Ergebnis eine vesionsfreie Sicht auf die spezifizierten Werkzeugdaten, die anschließend im werkzeuglokalen Verabeitungsbereich bereitgestellt werden.

*) Beziehungstypen müssen dabei in spitze Klammern ("<...>") eingeschlossen werden.

Unser Modell- und Sprachansatz unterscheidet sich von anderen [BB84, BK85, BM88, DL88, Ka90, Sc91, Wi87] im wesentlichen durch die gleichrangige Unterstützung von Elementarobjekt- und Objektebene sowie in der flexiblen und deskriptiven Handhabung der Objektstrukturen. Die explizite Trennung der beiden angesprochenen Ebenen ist in keinem der zitierten Ansätze enthalten. .[Ka90] konzentriert sich auf die Unterstützung der Objektebene. Zusätzlich zum vorgestellten Ansatz werden 'Repräsentationen' von Objekten unterschieden, die durch sog. 'Äquivalenzrelationen' verbunden werden. Auf der anderen Seite wird nur eine starre Realisierung des Abstammungsgraphen (ein Abstammungsbaum) angeboten. [DL88] definieren ein allgemeines Basisversionsmodell, das jedoch ein starres Konzept für die Organisation der Versionen bzw. der versionierten Daten festlegt. Weiterhin werden benutzerspezifische Konfigurationen unterstützt. Eine deskriptive Auswahl von Versionsnetzen bzw. der zugehörigen Daten ist nicht vorgesehen. [BB84, BK85] stellen ein speziell auf den VLSI-Entwurf zugeschnittenes Versionsmodell vor; so ist die Trennung von 'Schnittstelle' und 'Implementierung' systeminhärent. Dies erlaubt natürlich eine starke Anwendungsunterstützung schränkt aber gleichzeitig den Anwendungsraum des Modells ein. Es wird, wie bei den vorigen Modellen, keine spezielle Unterstützung zur Verarbeitung von Elementarobjektnetzen angeboten. [Wi87] beschreibt ein allgemeines Versionsmodell, das mittels 'Objekt-Generalisierung' und 'Objekt-Assoziation' eine relativ flexible Beschreibung von Objekt- und Versionstrukturen erlaubt. Insbesondere die Verwendung von 'Partitionen' und 'Graphen' zur Beschreibung der Assoziation ermöglichen die Nachbildung der meisten vorgestellten Modelle. Die vorgestellte Sprache vHDBL erlaubt darüberhinaus sowohl den Zugriff auf versionierte komplexe Objekte als auch auf nicht versionierte Objekte. Aspekte der Konfigurierung bzw. von Objekt- und Versionsbeziehungen auf der einen Seite sowie eine spezielle Unterstützung der Elementarobjektverabeitung auf der anderen Seite werden nicht adäquat behandelt.

Insegesamt gesehen zeichnet sich der hier vorgestellte Ansatz OVM durch eine adäquate Behandlung von Objektnetzen und einer hohen deskriptiven Auswahlmächtigkeit sowie durch eine explizite Trennung zwischen Elementarobjekt- und Objektversionsebene aus. Letzteres ermöglicht, daß Versions- und Konfigurationsaspekte unabhängig von Datenbereitstellungsaspekten (etwa zur effizienten Navigation entlang von Strukturbeziehungen) betrachtet werden können. Wir werden auf diesen Aspekt nochmals in Kapitel 4 zurück kommen.

4. Realisierung von OVM/OML

Die Realisierung unseres durch OVM und OML gegebenen Objektmodells kann auf recht vielfältige Art und Weise erfolgen. In diesem Kapitel beschreiben wir eine Realisierung, die an der Universität Kaiserslautern durchgeführt wurde und detailliert in [Kä92, KS92] beschrieben ist. Als Basissystem wurde das ebenfalls an der Universität Kaiserslautern entwickelte Non-Standard-DBS (NDBS) PRIMA [HMMS87, GG92] gewählt. Momentan wird die hier vorgestellte Implementierung von OVM/OML in der DB-basierten Entwurfsumgebung PRIMA-Framework [GHM92] getestet.

4.1 Architektur

Die DB-basierte Entwurfsumgebung PRIMA-Framework [GHM92, Su92], skizziert in Bild 11, besteht im wesentlichen aus zwei Komponenten: der Objekt- und Versionsverwaltung (OVV) und der Entwurfsablaufssteuerung (EAS). Beide zusammen ermöglichen ein einfaches ein- und aushängen von CAD-Werkzeugen. Die Komponente OVV implementiert das Objektmodell OVM und stellt an ihrer Schnittstelle die Sprache OML zur Verfügung. Die Komponente EAS regelt den werkzeugbasierten Entwurfsprozeß. Ausgehend von einem festgelegten Ablaufplan steuert sie die Aktivierung einzelner Werkzeuge sowie die, für die Werkzeuge notwendige Ver- und Entsorgung von werkzeugrelevanten Entwurfsdaten. Diese werden mittels OML-Anweisungen bei der OVV angefordert (vgl. Schritt (1) in Bild 11), aus dem Entwurfsdatenbestand extrahiert (Schritt (2)) und in den Objektpuffer eingelagert (Schritt (3)). Der Objektpuffer dient als werkzeuglokaler Arbeitsbereich auf den das Werkzeug effizient zugreifen und auch Datenänderungen durchführen kann (Schritt (4)).

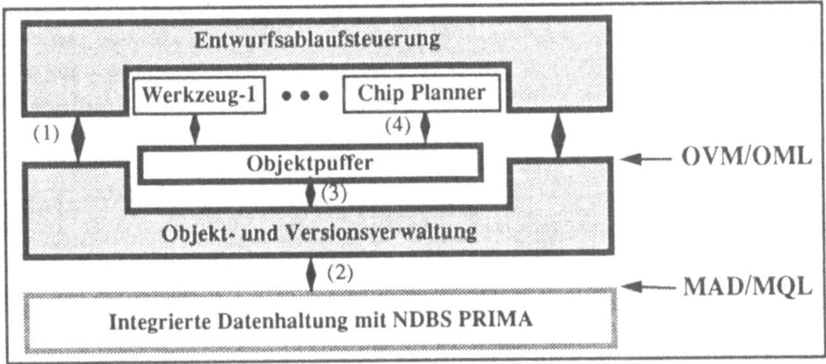

Bild 11: Grobarchitektur von PRIMA-Framework

Die Zuordnung der einzelnen Schritte zu den 6 Phasen eines werkzeugspezifischen Entwurfsschritts (s. Abschnitt 2.1) ist offensichtlich und kann leicht nachvollzogen werden. Es sei hier nur erwähnt, daß die Schnittstelle von der OVV zum Objektpuffer (in Bild 11 mit (3) markiert) eine versionsfreie Werkzeugsicht unterstützt. Im Gegensatz dazu ist die Schnittstelle von der OVV zur EAS (mit (3) markiert) versionsbehaftet und realisiert entwurfsspezifische Aspekte. An der Objektpufferschnittstelle ist die Semantik des Elementarschemas bekannt und es werden daher nur diesbezüglich konsistente Strukturen aufgebaut, die dann an die OVV übertragen und hinsichtlich der Entwurfssemantik geprüft werden, bevor sie dann der Datenhaltung übergeben werden. Dazu hat die OVV-Komponente eine Abbildung von der OVM-Ebene auf die Ebene des Datenmodells der Datenhaltungskomponente zu leisten.

4.2 Abbildung von OVM/OML auf MAD/MQL

Das NDBS PRIMA [GG92] ist eine Erweiterung des Relationenmodells um ein flexibles Komplexobjekt-Konzept. PRIMA implementiert das Molekül-Atom-Datenmodell (kurz MAD) und die mengenorientierte Anfragesprache MQL. MAD/MQL erlaubt die Verarbeitung von Komplexobjekten (Moleküle), die aus Elementarobjekten (Atomen) aufgebaut und über definierte Strukturbeziehungen zusammengesetzt sind. Es wird keine Versionierung dieser Daten unterstützt. Die Strukturbeziehungen werden in MAD/MQL über Referenzattribute gebildet, die die Identifikatoren der zu referenzierenden Atome enthalten. Um symmetrische Beziehungen zu garantieren, werden immer Paare von (zueinander entgegengesetzt gerichteten) Referenzattributen verlangt. Details über die PRIMA-Implementierung und MAD/MQL sind u.a. [GG92, Mi88] zu entnehmen.

Zur Abbildung von OVM/OML auf MAD/MQL muß die OVV-Komponente zum einen ein OVM-Schema als MAD-Schema realisieren und zum anderen die OML-Operationen auf entsprechende MQL-Operationen abbilden. Details können in [Kä92, KS92] nachgelesen werden. Hier beschränken wir uns auf die prinzipielle Vorgehensweise.

Die Konzeption der Elementarobjekttypen ist stark durch die Ideen von MAD beeinflußt, so daß deren Abbildung im wesentlichen syntaktischer Art ist. Die Definition eines Elementarobjekttyps wird durch eine entsprechende Atomtypdefinition und die Definition eines Strukturbeziehungstyps entsprechend durch ein Paar von Referenzattributen realisiert. Diese Vorgehensweise liegt darin begründet, daß die Verarbeitung der Elementarobjekte i. allg. durch Entwurfswerkzeuge erfolgt, die komplexe Algorithmen auf den Daten ausführen. Die Unterstützung solcher Verarbeitungsstrategien (in einem Objektpuffer) ist eine wesentliche Eigenschaft von MAD, so daß hier sinnvollerweise die Konzepte und Methoden von MAD eingesetzt werden. Die Abbildung der Objekt- und Versionstypen erfolgt mit Hilfe weiterer Atomtypdefinitionen sowie der Definition weiterer Referenzattribute. Die Abbildung von Objekt- und Versionsbeziehungen ergibt sich in natürlicher Weise aus der Objekttypabbildung: sie werden jeweils durch Referenzattributpaare in den Objektrepräsentanten und in den Versionsrepräsentanten realisiert.

```
                                                                              MQL
(1) SELECT Interface (function, no_of_pins), Contents
    FROM   Interface.Implementation - Contents
    WHERE  Interface.name = "1-Bit Adder" ;

(2) SELECT Interface, Interface_Version, Contents(name),
           Contents_Version(length_of_wires), Wire, Node (position), Instance, Instance_Version
    FROM   Interface_Version - ( .object - Interface,
                         .Implementaion - Contents_Version - ( .object - Contents,
                                                               .ref_Wire - Wire,
                                                               .ref_Node - Node )
                         .Instantiation - Instance_Version - (  .object - Instance,
                                                               .ref_Frame - Frame,
                                                               .ref_Pin - Pin ) )
    WHERE (Interface.name ="1-Bit Adder") AND (Contents_Version.ct_v_no = 3);
```

Bild 12: Beispiel zur Abbildung der Objekt- und Versionsselektion auf MQL

Zur Beschreibung der Abbildung von OML-Anweisungen auf MQL-Anweisungen sei wiederum auf [Kä92, KS92] verwiesen. An dieser Stelle soll ein einfaches Beispiel genügen. Die zu den beiden in Bild 10 dargestellten OML-Anweisungen zugehörigen äquivalenten MQL-Anweisungen sind in Bild 12 gezeigt. Dabei wird deutlich, daß im wesentlichen jede Klausel einzeln abgebildet wird. Die FROM-Klausel in OML wird modifiziert entsprechend der Schemaabbildung für die Objekt-und Versionsstrukturen (s.o.) und die Projektionsklausel der MQL-Anweisung übernimmt die Angaben aus der OML-Anweisung, wobei allerdings eine Aufteilung der Objekt- und Versionsattribute auf die entsprechenden Repräsentanten erfolgt. Die WHERE-Klausel ist, wie am Beispiel verdeutlicht, nach dem gleichen Prinzip auf die entsprechenden Repräsentanten anzupassen.

4.3 Einsatzerfahrung, Bewertung und Weiterentwicklung

Mit dem praktischen Einsatz unseres PRIMA-Frameworks wird auch gleichzeitig die OVV-Implementierung von OVM/OML getestet. Unser aktueller Einsatzbereich ist der Chip-Entwurf. Dafür haben wir einen Chip-Planner [ASZ92] implementiert und als Werkzeug in den PRIMA-Framework integriert, d.h., die Datenversorgung für eine versionsfreie Werkzeugsicht läuft über die OVV. Weiterhin existiert eine (noch primitive) Entwurfsablaufsteuerung. Sie stellt auch Kooperationskonzepte [HKS92] für den werkzeugbasierten Entwurf bereitstellt, die im wesentlichen auf den vorhandenen Objekt- und Versionskonzepten basieren und daher die Objektversionsebene von OVM/OML benutzen. Die gewonnenen Erfahrungen zeigen, daß die von der OVV bereitgestellte Schnittstelle sich sowohl funktional als auch bzgl. der Abstraktionsebene als geeignet erwiesen hat. MAD/MQL kennt kein Versionenkonzept, bietet dafür aber mit seiner dynamischen Molekülbildung (entlang vordefinierter Strukturbeziehungen) ein mächtiges Werkzeug zur Handhabung von Versionsstrukturen (etwa des Abstammungsgraphen) [KS92]. Werkzeugbasierter Entwurf, Entwurfssteuerung, Kooperation, Verarbeitungskontexte sind nur einige der Konzepte, die wichtig sind für CAD-Frameworks und basierend auf OVM/OML realisiert werden konnten. Trotz dieser erfreulichen ersten Akzeptanz, ist die OVV-Implementierung noch nicht abgeschlossen. Eine wichtige Weiterentwicklung betrifft die Optimierung der generierten MQL-Anfragen. Hierzu wurden schon Konzepte (Algebraische Optimierung, Parallele Anfrageverarbeitung) erarbeitet und z.T. auch schon realisiert [HMS92, Schö90].

4.4 Alternative Realisierungen

Aufgrund des gewählten Architekturkonzeptes werden auch andere Realisieungsmöglichkeiten für OVM/OML ermöglicht. Im folgenden wollen wir einige dieser Alternativen etwas näher beleuchten und bewerten. NF2-artige DBS [DK86, SPSW90] scheinen aufgrund der stark vernetzten Entwurfsdaten (s. Bild 2) weniger gut geeignet zu sein. Objektorientierte DBS (OODBS) hingegen unterstützen netzwerkartige Datenstrukturen, besitzen aber auf der anderen Seite oft nur eingeschränkte Anfragesprachen, da sie (zumindest ursprünglich) nur für eine direkte Objektpuffer-Verarbeitung vorgesehen waren. Diese Verarbeitungsweise zielt darauf ab, Objekte mehr oder weniger direkt (und ohne Umformungen) im Objektpuffer bereitzustellen. Dabei werden Objekte meistens über Fehlerbedingungen (etwa: "Referenziertes Objekt ist nicht im Puffer") angefordert. Diese Arbeitsweise steht in direktem Widerspruch zur werkzeugbasierten Verarbeitung, welche durch das Anfordern eines ganzen Verarbeitungskontextes charakterisisert ist. Hier werden Fehlerbedingungen im vorhinein ausgeschlossen und zudem dem DBS vielfältige Möglichkeiten zur Anfrageoptimierung eröffnet. Auch die mangelnde Sichtenunterstützung in OODBS ist ein wichtiges Bewertungskriterium, da die werkzeugspezifischen Daten (als Verarbeitungskontext via OML-Anweisung angefordert) im wesentlichen Sichten über dem OVM-Schema darstellen. Natürlich sind die Systemerfahrungen, die mit OO-Pufferverarbeitung gemacht wurden, nützlich und ergänzen die Objektpufferkonzepte für Komplexobjekt-DBS. Überraschenderweise finden die Abstraktionskonzepte (Generalisierung, Klassenhierarchie, Vererbung) und auch das Methodenkonzept keine direkte Anwendung. Ein anderer DBS-Ansatz ist XNF [MPP93], eine Erweiterung von SQL. Dort werden Komplexobjekte mittels entsprechenden Anfragekonstrukten über relationalen Datenbanken aufgebaut. Damit können ähnliche Objektstrukturen wie in MAD/MQL aufgebaut und verarbeitet werden. Eine OVV-Realisierung unter Verwendung von XNF kann daher ähnlich bewertet werden wie unsere PRIMA-Realisierung.

5. Resümee

Mit diesem Aufsatz hoffen wir, trotz der Kürze der Darstellung, gezeigt zu haben, daß ein Objektmodell, welches ein Versionskonzept, unterschiedliche Datenabstraktionsebenen (Elementarobjektebene und Objektversionsebene) und eine zugehörige Manipulationssprache (mit Sichtenbildung) unterstützt, gewinnbringend als flexible Entwurfsdatenverwaltung in CAD-Frameworks eingesetzt werden kann. Aufgrund der vorhandenen Abstraktionsebenen, kann Unabhängigkeit von der konkreten Realisierung erreicht werden. Damit besteht die Möglichkeit neue Realisierungskonzepte (etwa aus dem Bereich von OODBS oder Komplexobjekt-DBS) in einfacher Weise zugänglich zu machen. Nach aktuellem Wissensstand läßt sich sagen, daß Komplexobjekt-DBS, die Netzwerkstrukturen aufbauen und verarbeiten können, als Realisierungsbasis prinzipiell in Frage kommen. Über die Verwendbarkeit von OODBS kann momentan noch nicht endgültig entschieden werden. Einige der hier erwähnten Unzulänglichkeiten von OODBS bilden aktuelle Forschungsthemen und lassen für die nahe Zukunft auf deutliche Verbesserungen hoffen.

6. Literatur

ASZ92 Altmeyer, J., Schürmann, B., Zimmerman, G.: Three-Phase Chip Planning - An Improved Top-Down Chip Planning Strategy, to appear in: Proc. of the Int. Conf. on CAD (ICCAD), Santa Clara, Calif., 1992.

BB84 Batory, D.S., Buchman, A.P.: Molecular Objects, Abstract Data Types and Data Models: A Framework, in: Proceedings of the 10th VLDB, Singapore, 1984, S. 172-184.

BK85 Batory, D., Kim, W.: Modeling Concepts for VLSI CAD objects, ACM TODS, Vol. 10, No. 3, S. 322-346.

BM88 Beech, D., Mahbod, B.: Generalized Version Control in an Object-Oriented Database, in: Proc. of the 4th Int. Conf. on Data Engineering, 1988, S. 14-22.

DK86 Dadam, P., Küspert, K. et al.: A DBMS Prototype to Support Extended NF2 Relations: An Integrated View on Flat Tables and Hierarchies, in: Proc. of the ACM SIGMOD Conf., Washington D.C., 1986, S. 356-367.

DL88 Dittrich, K.R., Lorie, R.A.: Version Support for Engineering Database Systems, IEEE TOSE, Vol. 14, No. 4, 1988, S. 429-437.

GG92 Gesmann, M., Grasnickel, A., et al.: Eine Einführung in PRIMA, Forschungsbericht Nr. 20/92, SFB 124, Universität Kaiserslautern, 1992.

GHM92 Gesmann, M., Härder, T., Mitschang, B., et al.: Supporting Cooperative Design in a DBMS-based Design Environment, Forschungsbericht Nr. 29/92, SFB 124, Universität Kaiserslautern, 1992.

HKS92 Hübel, C., Käfer, W., Sutter, B.: Controlling Cooperation Through Design-Object Specification - a Database-oriented Approach, in: Proc. of the European Design Automation Conference, Brussels, Belgium, 1992, S. 30-35.

HMMS87 Härder, T., Meyer-Wegener, K., Mitschang, B., Sikeler, A.: PRIMA - A DBMS Prototype Supporting Engineering Applications, in: Proc. of the 13th VLDB, Brighton, 1987, S. 433-442.

HMS92 Härder, T., Mitschang, B., Schöning, H.: Query Processing for Complex Objects, in: Data and Knowledge Engineering 7, 1992, S. 181-200.

HNST90 Harrison, D., Newton, R., Spickelmier, R., Barnes, T.: Electronic CAD Framework, in: Proc. of the IEEE, Vol. 78, No. 2, 1990, S. 393-417.

Ka90 Katz, R.: Toward a Unified Framework for Version Modeling in Engineering Databases, ACM Computing Surveys, Vol. 22, No. 4, 1990, S. 375-408.

Kä91 Käfer, W.: A Framework for Version-based Cooperation Control, Proc. of the 2nd Symposium on Database Systems for Advanced Applications, Tokyo, Japan, 1991, S. 527-536.

Kä92 Käfer, W.: Geschichts- und Versionsmodellierung komplexer Objekte - Anforderungen und Realisierungsmöglichkeiten am Beispiel des NDBS PRIMA, Dissertation am Fachbereich Informatik der Universität Kaiserslautern, 1992.

KS92 Käfer, W., Schöning, H.: Mapping a Version Model to a Complex Object Data Model, Proc. of the 8th Int. Conf. on Data Engineering, Tempe, Arizona, 1992.

Mi88 Mitschang, B.: Ein Molekül-Atom-Datenmodell für Non-Standard-Anwendungen - Anwendungsanalyse, Datenmodellentwurf und Implementierungskonzepte, Dissertation, Universität Kaiserslautern, IFB 185, Springer Verlag, 1988.

MPP93 Mitschang, B., Pirahesh, H., Pistor, P., Lindsay, B., Südkamp, N.: SQL/XNF - Processing Composite Objects as Abstractions over Relational Data, in: Proc. of Ninth Int. Conf. on Data Engineering, Wien, April 1993.

RS92 Rammig, F.J., Steinmüller, B.: Frameworks und Entwurfsumgebungen, in: Informatik Spektrum, Springer-Verlag, Band 15, Heft 1, Februar 1992, S. 33-43.

Sc91 Sciore, E.: Multidimensional Versioning for Object-Oriented Databases, in: Proc. of the 2nd Conf. on Deductive and Object-Oriented Databases, München, 1991, S. 355-370.

Schö90 Schöning, H.: Realisierungskonzepte für die parallele Bearbeitung von Anfragen auf komplexen Objekten, in: Härder, T., Wedekind, H., Zimmermann, G.(Hrsg.): Entwurf und Betrieb verteilter Systeme, IFB 264, Springer Verlag, 1990, S. 204-220.

SPSW90 Schek, H.-J., Paul, H.-B., Scholl, M.H., Weikum, G.: The DASDBS Project: Objectives, Experiences, and Future Prospects, in: IEEE Transactions on Knowledge and Data Engineering, Vol. 2, No. 1, 1990, S. 25-43.

Su92 Sutter, B.: Ansätze zur Integration in technischen Entwurfsanwendungen - angepaßte Modellierungswerkzeuge, durchgängige Entwurfsunterstützung, datenorientierte Integration, Dissertation am Fachbereich Informatik der Universität Kaiserslautern, 1992.

Wi87 Wilkes, W.: Der Versionsbegriff und seine Modellierung in CAD/CAM-Datenbanken, Dissertation, Fern Universität / Gesamthochschule Hagen, 1987.

Zi86 Zimmermann, G.: Top-Down Design of Digital Systems, in: Logic Design and Simulation, E. Hörbst (Hrsg.), Elsevier Science Publ., B. V., 1986.

Eine vergleichende Untersuchung der Speicherungsformen für multimediale Datenobjekte

Rolf Käckenhoff, Detlef Merten und Klaus Meyer-Wegener

Lehrstuhl für Datenbanksysteme
Friedrich-Alexander-Universität Erlangen-Nürnberg
Martensstraße 3, 8520 Erlangen
{kaeckenhoff, merten, kmw}@informatik.uni-erlangen.de

Kurzfassung

In diesem Beitrag werden die verschiedenen Typen von Datenhaltungssystemen hinsichtlich ihrer Eignung für die Speicherung von multimedialen Datenobjekten betrachtet. Die Untersuchung umfaßt Dateisysteme, relationale Datenbanksysteme mit langen Feldern sowie erweiterbare und objektorientierte Datenbanksysteme. Ausgehend von Objekten eines Medientyps, die sich intern in Roh-, Registrierungs- und Beschreibungsdaten gliedern lassen, werden u.a. das Konzept der Abstrakten Datentypen, die Spezifikation von Beziehungen zwischen den Datenobjekten und die Unterstützung der Suche als wesentliche Kriterien bei der funktionalen Beurteilung identifiziert. Aber auch die Verfügbarkeit der Systeme und der mit ihrem Einsatz verbundene Aufwand werden in die Betrachtung mit einbezogen. Die Untersuchung schließt mit einer Aufstellung der von allen Systemen noch ungenügend berücksichtigten Anforderungen, die Ausgangspunkt für die Konzeption von MOM, einem spezifischen Verwaltungssystem für multimediale Datenobjekte, ist.

1 Einleitung

Es gibt bereits zahlreiche, auch kommerziell verfügbare, multimediale Anwendungen, so z.B. in den Bereichen Ausbildung (Computer-Based Training, CBT), Publikation (Desktop Publishing, DTP), Medizin und Geographie. Diese Anwendungen haben bisher jedoch eher Beispielcharakter. Sie zeichnen sich durch relativ kleine Datenbestände aus, die in einem speziellen Format abgelegt werden und bei denen die Einbringung in andere Anwendungen noch keine große Rolle spielt. Es ist aber bereits abzusehen, daß diese Datenbestände wachsen werden, und damit werden sich Probleme der Archivierung und der Weitergabe ergeben. Die anwendungsneutrale Verwaltung großer Bestände von multimedialen Datenobjekten (MMOs) sollte deshalb systematischer untersucht und frühzeitig in Systemkonzepte umgesetzt werden.

Hier bietet sich der Einsatz bewährter Datenbanktechniken an, und in der Tat gibt es schon eine Reihe von Untersuchungen und Vorschlägen zu *Multimedia-Datenbanken* [Meye91, Woel87, Masu87]. Die Systeme befinden sich jedoch noch in der Entwicklung, weshalb in diesem Aufsatz das ganze Spektrum der Datenhaltung für MMOs untersucht wird. Aufwand und Verfügbarkeit stellen dabei ebenso wichtige Kriterien dar wie die systemtechnischen Aspekte.

Der Beitrag gliedert sich wie folgt: Im nächsten Kapitel werden MMOs kurz charakterisiert, um deutlich zu machen, *was* zu verwalten ist. Im dritten Kapitel wird erörtert, welche Leistungen ein Speicherungssystem für diese Datenobjekte erbringen sollte. Das vierte Kapitel stellt diesen Anforderungen die Charakteristika verfügbarer und vorgeschlagener Speicherungssysteme gegenüber. Das Spektrum reicht von Dateisystemen über „lange Felder“ (BLOBs) in relationalen Datenbanksystemen bis hin zu erweiterbaren und objektorientierten Datenbanksystemen. Angefügt wird im fünften Kapitel eine Eigenentwicklung, die eine Speziallösung allein für MMOs bietet. Das Ziel dieses Beitrags ist ein möglichst umfassender und objektiver Vergleich (Kap. 6); statt eine einzige Lösung herauszustellen, sollen vielmehr die Kriterien entwickelt werden, die in einem konkreten Anwendungsfall eine Entscheidung für eine der vorgestellten Techniken ermöglichen. Dies wird in der abschließenden Zusammenfassung noch einmal verdeutlicht.

2 Multimediale Datenobjekte

Multimediale Datenobjekte (MMOs) sind aufzufassen als Zusammensetzung von Datenobjekten, die sich jeweils auf ein *einzelnes Medium* beschränken (englisch kann man hier von „single-media objects" oder SMOs sprechen). Schon diese SMOs sind erheblich komplexer als das, was man bisher in Anwendungen zu verwalten gewohnt war und was hier unter dem Begriff „formatierte Daten" zusammengefaßt werden soll. Formatierte Daten zeichnen sich dadurch aus, daß es zu ihnen umfangreiche Typ- und Strukturinformation gibt, die sehr viel über ihre Bedeutung aussagt. Beispiele sind einfache Werte, Satzstrukturen mit Feldern (Tupel) und auch komplexe Zeigerstrukturen. Dagegen handelt es sich bei den SMOs um *unformatierte Daten*, was bedeutet, daß sie aus (beliebig langen) Folgen von kleinen Elementen (Buchstaben, Bildpunkten, Lautstärkepegeln usw.) bestehen. Diese Folgen sind aus Systemsicht nicht weiter strukturiert, und ihre komplexe Bedeutung geht nicht aus den zugeordneten Namen hervor. Gerade das macht ihre maschinelle Verarbeitung so viel schwieriger als die der formatierten Daten.

Eine genauere Betrachtung der SMOs zeigt, daß sie niemals *nur* aus unformatierten Daten (z.B. Bildpixeln; Abtastwerten für Ton) bestehen, die als *Rohdaten* bezeichnet werden. Vielmehr enthalten sie stets auch noch formatierte Daten, die eine korrekte Interpretation und Identifikation der Rohdaten überhaupt erst ermöglichen. Diese *Registrierungsdaten* treten oft als „Header" auf. Ein typisches Beispiel sind die Angaben Höhe, Breite und Pixeltiefe zu einem Rasterbild, ohne die die Rohdaten nicht mehr wären als eine Bitsequenz. Erst die Registrierungsdaten erlauben die originalgetreue Reproduktion der SMOs auf einem Ausgabegerät. Sie sind deshalb obligatorisch und müssen mit den Rohdaten zusammen verwaltet werden; insbesondere darf die Änderung von Rohdaten und Registrierungsdaten nur aufeinander abgestimmt erfolgen. [Meye91]

Einige Anwendungen ergänzen die Rohdaten um weitere (formatierte oder unformatierte) Daten, die den Umgang mit den SMOs erleichtern sollen. Sie stellen beispielsweise Strukturen oder Inhalte der SMOs dar, die mit aufwendigen Verfahren (Bildanalyse, Texterschließung) aus den Rohdaten gewonnen oder auch vom Benutzer direkt eingegeben wurden. Dafür soll summarisch die Bezeichnung *Beschreibungsdaten* verwendet werden. Beispiele sind die Transkription einer Sprachaufnahme (Text) und die Sammlung von in einem Rasterbild erkannten Linien (Graphik). Beschreibungsdaten sind oft redundant. Der mit ihrer Erzeugung verbundene Aufwand ist jedoch so hoch, daß sich die explizite Abspeicherung lohnt. Speziell bei der Suche nach MMOs und bei ihrer Auswertung sind sie nützlich.

Tab. 1 zeigt die wichtigsten *Typen* von SMOs mit ihren Merkmalen; eine genauere Darstellung muß hier aus Platzgründen unterbleiben (vgl. [Meye91]). Wegen der Unterschiede erscheint eine einheitliche Behandlung nicht sinnvoll; mindestens die genannten fünf Typen sollten getrennt berücksichtigt werden. Es lassen sich sehr leicht noch Untertypen finden (z.B. Sprache bei Ton), die in bestimmten Anwendungen gesondert behandelt werden müssen; darauf wird hier verzichtet.

Die Unterscheidung der Typen spielt nicht nur bei der Abbildung auf die verfügbaren Speicher eine Rolle, sondern vor allem auch bei der Bereitstellung von *Operationen* auf den SMOs. Üblicherweise werden nacheinander folgende Klassen von Operationen auf SMOs realisiert:

- *Erzeugen* (aus einer Datei, aus Programmvariablen, von einem Gerät)
- *Ausgeben* (in eine Datei, in Programmvariable, auf ein Gerät)
- *Editieren*

- *Verknüpfen* (z.B. zu Dokumenten)
- *Weitergeben* (zugänglich machen, versenden)
- *Archivieren*
- *Auswerten* (Analysieren)
- *Vergleichen* (für die Suche)

Erzeugen und Ausgeben stellen das absolute Minimum dar, ohne das es keine sinnvolle Anwendung geben kann. Die konkreten Ausprägungen in den übrigen Klassen hängen sehr stark von den Bedürfnissen einzelner Anwendungen ab. Ein Speicherungssystem sollte aber stets die Gesamtheit möglicher Zugriffe unterstützen können.

Medium	*Inhalt*	*Zeitabhängigkeit*	*typische Größe*	*menschlicher Sinn*
Text	Folge von abdruckbaren Zeichen	nein	10 KB	visuell / akustisch
Graphik	Menge von Vektoren und Flächen	nein	10 KB	visuell
Rasterbild	Matrix von Bildpunkten	nein	1 MB (1024 x 1024)	visuell
Ton	Folge von Lautstärkepegeln oder Frequenzkomponenten	ja	600 MB (1 Stunde, Audio-CD)	akustisch
Bewegtbild (Video, Animation)	Folge von Rasterbildern oder Graphiken	ja	2 GB (30 min.)	visuell

Tabelle 1: Merkmale der wichtigsten Typen von Single-Media Objects (SMOs)

3 Anforderungen an die Speicherung

Die zentrale Aufgabe eines Multimedia-Speicherungssystems ist das *Speichern und Wiedergewinnen* von MMOs. Wiedergewinnen umfaßt dabei neben dem Auffinden bzw. Lokalisieren auch die Übergabe an die Anwendung oder den Benutzer. Hingegen muß das Ändern von MMOs nicht unbedingt in das System integriert werden – dies kann weiterhin den etablierten Spezialwerkzeugen vorbehalten bleiben, die für das Laden und Speichern auf das Archivsystem zurückgreifen sollten.

Da die Speicherungsproblematik für formatierte Daten bereits weitgehend beherrscht wird, sollten die dort als sinnvoll erkannten Anforderungen auch auf die Speicherung von MMOs übertragen werden. Neben den Forderungen nach Mehrbenutzerbetrieb, Fehlerbehandlung, Konsistenzerhaltung, Redundanzfreiheit und Versionierung sind in diesem Zusammenhang besonders die nach Datenunabhängigkeit und Anwendungsneutralität zu betrachten.

3.1 Datenunabhängigkeit und Anwendungsneutralität

Ein Multimedia-Speicherungssystem stellt den Anwendungen einen Zugang zu Externspeichern zur Verfügung. Für MMOs muß wegen des Datenvolumens und der Zeitbehaftung ein größeres Spektrum an Extern-

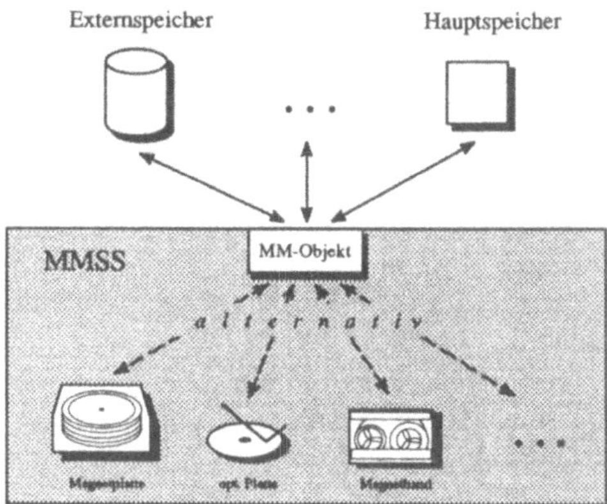

Abbildung 1: Geräteunabhängigkeit im Multimedia-Speicherungssystem

speichern zur Verfügung stehen als für formatierte Daten. Es umfaßt beispielsweise CD-ROM, analoge Bildplatte, DAT und Videoband. Die zugehörigen Speichergeräte verlangen eine von den konventionellen Magnetplattengeräten abweichende Ansteuerung. Diese den Anwendungen aufzubürden hieße, sie abhängig zu machen von derzeitiger Speichertechnik. Statt dessen sollte die MMSS-Schnittstelle eine Abstraktion dieser Technik anbieten und die Gerätedetails verbergen. Solche Abstraktionen sind beispielsweise „Read-Only Memory" (ROM) und „Write Once, Read Many Times" (WORM), die das MMSS auf verschiedene Speichergeräte abbilden kann, keineswegs nur auf CD-ROMs und WORM-Platten. Durch eine derartige MMSS-Schnittstelle wird eine *Geräteunabhängigkeit* der Anwendungen erreicht, die es erlaubt, Speichergeräte auszutauschen und so den rasanten technischen Fortschritt zu nutzen. Abb. 1 veranschaulicht die Situation. Daß sie nicht selbstverständlich ist, zeigt die Multimedia-Komponente MIM des objektorientierten Datenbanksystems ORION, die sogar eine Modellierung dieser Geräte und eine objektbezogene Geräteauswahl erlaubt [Woel87]. Geräteunabhängigkeit leistet also eine Entkopplung der Anwendung von den Externspeichergeräten und überläßt es dem MMSS, für beliebig große und u.U. zeitbehaftete Daten ein geeignetes Speichergerät zu auszuwählen.

Die Anwendungen bleiben damit aber noch für die Struktur (Codierung) dieser Daten verantwortlich. Für jedes Medium existieren zahlreiche verschiedene Datei- und Hauptspeicherformate, für Rasterbilder z.B. TIFF, GIF, Pixrect und XImage. Die Zusammensetzung von SMOs zu MMOs kann u.a. in Anlehnung an HyTime [Newc91] oder ODA/ODIF [Hora85] beschrieben werden. Und schließlich wird diese Vielfalt noch durch diverse Komprimierungsverfahren vergrößert. Zwar gibt es z.T. schon internationale Normen für die Codierung von Mediendaten, wie etwa JPEG für Rasterbilder [Wall91], doch setzen diese sich erst langsam durch. Auf absehbare Zeit muß ein MMSS davon ausgehen, daß verschiedene Anwendungen mit verschiedenen Formaten arbeiten, auch wenn sie MMOs gemeinsam benutzen.

Anstelle der einfachen Lösung, das bei der Abspeicherung vorliegende Format zu verwenden, dieses den Anwendungen beim späteren Zugriff zu nennen und ihnen die Interpretation (d.h. meist: die Konvertierung) selbst zu überlassen, sollte das MMSS das auf dem Externspeicher verwendete Format bestimmen und vor den Anwendungen verbergen. Es führt dann bei Ein- und Ausgabe ggf. selbst eine Konvertierung in das gewünschte Format durch, so daß alle Anwendungen mit ihrem eigenen Format arbeiten können. Dadurch wird eine *Formatunabhängigkeit* der Anwendungen erreicht. Abb. 2 veranschaulicht dieses Vorgehen.

Durch die nach außen angebotenen Formate ist grundsätzlich nicht festgelegt, wie und wo die MMOs systemintern abgespeichert werden. Je nach den anwendungsseitig vorwiegend nachgefragten Formaten können in-

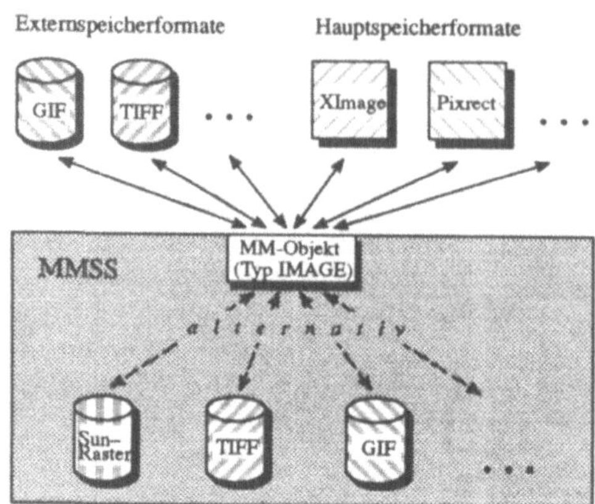

Abbildung 2: Formatunabhängigkeit am Beispiel des Datentyps IMAGE

tern ein oder mehrere Formate (und Komprimierungsverfahren) zur Speicherung verwendet werden. Auch die Auswahl des Speichergeräts nimmt das MMSS selbst unter Berücksichtigung der Zugriffsanforderungen vor. Beides muß für die Anwendungen transparent sein, damit sie unabhängig von der internen Plazierung und Darstellung der Daten auf die MMOs zugreifen können. Lediglich eine Änderung der Antwortzeit darf nach außen spürbar sein.

Geräte- und Formatunabhängigkeit sind nichts anderes als die besonderen Formen von *Datenunabhängigkeit*, die gerade für MMOs erforderlich sind. Formatunabhängigkeit ist des weiteren eine Voraussetzung für die *Anwendungsneutralität* des Datenbestandes: Die Speicherung der MMOs ist nicht mehr auf bestimmte Anwendungen zugeschnitten, sondern kann durch Modifikation (Erweiterung) des allgemeinen Zugriffsmechanismus (z.B. Hinzunahme weiterer Konverter) mit geringem Aufwand den Anforderungen neuer Anwendungen genügen. De facto hat man damit ein konzeptionelles Schema im Sinne der Drei-Schema-Architektur nach ANSI/SPARC [ANSI75] geschaffen. Dieses läßt sich auch in den Abb. 1 und 2 erkennen.

3.2 Abstrakte Datentypen für SMOs

Die im Kapitel 2 genannten Unterschiede zwischen den verschiedenen Arten von SMOs haben ebenso verschiedene Operationen zur Folge. Für jedes Medium muß daher ein eigener Typ mit spezifischen Operationen definiert und unter Berücksichtigung seiner besonderen Anforderungen implementiert werden. Die Realisierung solcher medienspezifischen Abstrakten Datentypen (MADTs) ist änderbar, ohne daß die Anwendungsprogramme davon betroffen sind (ADT-Konzept [Lisk 74]). Zudem wird dem Anwender eine Schnittstelle höherer Funktionalität zur Handhabung der SMOs angeboten. Allgemein umfaßt diese für alle MADTs Funktionen zum

- Speichern, Löschen, Lesen und Kopieren;
- Ändern;
- Abfragen von Eigenschaften und
- Vergleichen.

Es fällt derzeit schwer, einen festen Satz von Operationen eines MADTs für sämtliche Anwendungen anzugeben. Selbst die Menge der benötigten MADTs und ihre Beziehungen untereinander (z.B. in einer Typhierarchie) werden unterschiedlich festgelegt. Hier sollte einer konkreten Anwendung zumindest die Möglichkeit der Anpassung und Erweiterung gegeben werden. Andererseits reicht allein die Bereitstellung eines Mechanismus zur Definition beliebiger ADTs nicht aus, weil sie jedem Anwender die nicht triviale Erstellung der MADTs abverlangt. Statt dessen sollte ein initialer Satz von MADTs im System bereits vorhanden sein, den sich der Anwender durch Auswahl und Ergänzung auf seine spezifische Problemstellung zuschneiden kann.

3.3 Darstellung von Beziehungen zwischen und innerhalb von MMOs

SMOs stehen nicht für sich isoliert, sondern haben vielfältige Beziehungen zu anderen SMOs. Solche Beziehungen sollten in einem MMSS ebenfalls verwaltet werden, um Anwendungsneutralität, Konsistenzüberwachung und navigierende Suche zu erlauben. Mögliche Arten von Beziehungen sind:

- *Aggregation:* Diese Beziehungsart nimmt eine besondere Stellung ein, da allein durch sie MMOs entstehen. Dies kann entweder durch Beziehungen (Links) zwischen den SMOs, deren Graph dann als MMO interpretiert wird, geschehen oder durch die Spezifikation von (Teil-Ganze-) Beziehungen zwischen einem MMO-Repräsentanten und den beteiligten SMOs.
- *Inhaltliche Äquivalenz (Substitution):* Diese Beziehung spezifiziert, daß zwei Objekte inhaltlich mehr oder weniger das gleiche darstellen, z.B. zwei Fotos derselben Person, oder ein Text, der sowohl als Zeichenfolge als auch in Form einer Tonaufzeichnung vorliegt. Sollte das eine Objekt z.B. nicht verfügbar oder auf dem betreffenden Endgerät nicht präsentierbar sein, so kann das andere Objekt ohne (wesentlichen) Informationsverlust als Ersatzdarstellung dienen.
- *Synchronisation bei der Präsentation:* Sie dient zur Beschreibung der zeitlichen Abhängigkeit zwischen zwei Objekten, die z.B. „gleichzeitig" präsentiert werden müssen, wie eine Bildfolge und der zugehörige Ton.
- *Konsistenzerhaltung (im Rahmen des Änderungsdienstes):* Diese Beziehung zwischen zwei Objekten drückt aus, daß bei Änderung des einen auch das andere Objekt betroffen ist, z.B. zwischen einer Graphik und dem sie erläuternden Text innerhalb eines Dokuments.
- *Entstehungsgeschichte (Historie):* Diese Beziehung hält die historische Entwicklung fest, aus welchem Objekt bzw. welchen Objekten ein anderes hervorgegangen ist, z.B. verschiedene Versionen eines Objekts.
- *Attributierung:* Ein MMO kann als beschreibendes Merkmal eines Objektes verwendet werden, das durch (möglicherweise komplex strukturierte) formatierte Daten beschrieben wird, z.B. ein Auto mit den Attributen Hersteller, Modell, Farbe und Foto. Zwischen dem Objekt und dem MMO besteht dann eine Attributbeziehung.
- *Verweise:* Hierunter ist im wesentlichen das zu verstehen, was zur Zeit die meisten Hypertext- bzw. Hypermedia-Systeme ausmacht: eine vom Anwender „beschriftete" Kante, über die man von einem Objekt (Knoten) zu einem anderen navigieren kann, ohne daß die Kantenbeschriftung für das System interpretierbar ist.

Alle Beziehungsarten – mit Ausnahme der Verweise – sollten mit einer spezifischen, dem System bekannt zu machenden Semantik zu versehen sein, so daß das MMSS entsprechende Modifikationen von Operationen auf MMOs unter Berücksichtigung des Beziehungsumfeldes (Kontextes) durchführen kann. Diese Modifikationen können sehr vielfältiger Art sein. Wird z.B. die Ausgabe einer Tonaufzeichnung gewünscht und ist jedoch momentan kein akustisches Ausgabegerät verfügbar, so kann das MMSS nach einer Meldung automatisch einen als inhaltlich äquivalent spezifizierten Text am Bildschirm ausgeben. Oder bei Änderung einer Graphik wird der Anwender vom MMSS sofort informiert, welche anderen Objekte zur Konsistenzerhaltung ebenfalls geändert werden müssen, falls das System nicht selbst in der Lage ist, die Folgeänderungen zu vollziehen (was häufig der Fall sein wird).

3.4 Unterstützung der Suche

Da ein MMSS sehr viele MMOs verwalten soll, muß es mächtige Suchoperatoren anbieten. Neben dem direkten Zugriff über einen Identifikator umfassen diese Suchoperatoren die Abfrage von formalen Eigenschaften und vor allem des Inhalts, d.h. der in den MMOs dargestellten Information. Ebenso sollte die Suche nach einem MMO über die Spezifikation seines Beziehungsumfeldes möglich sein. Eine unmittelbar auf Wertgleichheit basierende Suche wie bei formatierten Daten wird hingegen keine große Bedeutung haben. Benötigt wird vielmehr die „unscharfe" Suche, bei der das Gesuchte nur mehr oder weniger genau umrissen wird (vgl. Information-Retrieval-Systeme, z.B. [Salt83]).

Inhaltsorientierte Suchanfragen sind prinzipiell in jedem beliebigen Medium formulierbar. Ein besonderes Problem ergibt sich jedoch bei der Formulierung von abstrakten, „unscharfen" Suchanfragen, die eine Umschreibung des Gesuchten erfordern. Wenn beispielsweise nach Fotos von alten Männern mit Hut gesucht werden soll, wäre dies nicht allein durch die „Vorlage" eines Fotos mit einem (bestimmten!) Mann mit Hut möglich, denn es ist nicht eindeutig, welche Eigenschaften des dargestellten Mannes für die Suchanfrage von Relevanz sind. Es bedarf daher eines Mediums, in dem Aussagen *über* Objekte getroffen werden können (Metaebene). Hierzu eignen sich letztendlich nur formale und natürliche Sprachen. Bei der Wahl einer solchen Sprache ist auf deren Mächtigkeit und die leichte Formulierbarkeit von Suchanfragen zu achten.

Bei der Bearbeitung von Suchanfragen stellt sich heute für alle komplexeren Medientypen das Problem, daß die vorhandenen Algorithmen zur Inhaltsanalyse noch nicht genügend weit fortgeschritten sind. Sie können Ergebnisse kaum in akzeptabler Zeit liefern (im interaktiven Betrieb), wenn überhaupt in brauchbarer Qualität. Hier kann eine gewisse Abhilfe durch die Einführung von Beschreibungsdaten geschaffen werden, die die für die Suche relevante Information in leicht auswertbarer Form darstellen. Die Bereitstellung der Beschreibungsdaten kann entweder durch den Offline-Einsatz medienbezogener Inhaltsanalyseverfahren geschehen oder durch den Anwender selbst. Hier stellt sich natürlich sofort das Problem der Normierung, denn gleiche Sachverhalte werden individuell verschieden interpretiert und ausgedrückt. Insbesondere aber können Beschreibungsdaten nur einen Ausschnitt der Information abbilden, der anwendungsabhängig festgelegt werden muß.

Zur Beschleunigung des Auffindens von MMOs können auch spezielle *Zugriffspfade* beitragen. Für formatierte Daten gibt es hier viele bewährte Strukturen (z.B. Bäume und Hashing), die auf Wertgleichheit und evtl. einer Ordnungsrelation beruhen. Sie lassen sich jedoch nicht auf unformatierte Daten übertragen, da bei diesen komplexe „Enthalten-in"-Operatoren wichtiger sind als Gleichheit und eine Ordnungsrelation nicht verfügbar ist. Bestenfalls kann man eine Suche nach syntaktischen Mustern unterstützen, ähnlich den Signaturdateien für den Zugriff auf Text [Falo85]. Für topologische Informationen ließen sich z.B. Grid-Files [Niev84] verwenden, aber auch damit wird nur ein kleiner Teil der Anfragen abgedeckt. Die Ausführungen in [Meye91] zeigen, daß für aussagekräftige Beschreibungsdaten und deren Vergleichsoperationen neuartige Zugriffspfade benötigt werden.

3.5 Verfügbarkeit und Kosten

Bei der Beurteilung eines Software-Systems ist neben den funktionalen Aspekten auch die Verfügbarkeit, d.h. die Frage, ob man es heute schon kaufen kann oder es sich noch in der Entwicklung befindet, von Bedeutung. Ebenso spielen der mit der Anschaffung und dem Einsatz verbundene Aufwand eine Rolle. Diese Kriterien haben aus der Sicht des Anwenders mindestens die gleiche Bedeutung wie die rein funktionale Bewertung eines Systems und sollten deshalb in die anschließende Betrachtung von Datenverwaltungssystemen mit einfließen.

4 Leistungen bekannter Datenverwaltungssysteme

Die Datenverwaltungssysteme spannen einen sehr weiten Rahmen vom einfachen Dateisystem bis zu verschiedenen Formen von Datenbanksystemen (DBS) auf. Diese Systeme bieten einen sehr unterschiedlichen Grad der Unterstützung bei der Speicherung und dem Wiedergewinnen von Daten, der hier genauer unter dem Aspekt der Verwaltung multimedialer Daten untersucht werden soll.

4.1 Dateisysteme

Dateien ermöglichen als universelle Speicherorganisationsform die Speicherung von Bitströmen, wahlfrei zugreifbaren Folgen von Blöcken fester Länge oder Sätzen fester bzw. variabler Länge, die über einen Schlüssel zugreifbar sind. In bestehenden MMSS werden die informationstragenden Rohdaten der SMOs, z.B. Pixel (bei Rasterbildern) oder Abtastwerte (bei Tonaufnahmen), meist in sequentiellen Dateien gespeichert, da für eine ausschnittsweise Bearbeitung von SMOs durch den wahlfreien Zugriff mittels einer (festen!) Blockeinteilung praktisch kein Bedarf besteht. Meistens wird auf die SMOs als Ganzes zugegriffen, was insbesondere für die vorhandenen Manipulationswerkzeuge gilt.

Dateien sind betriebssystemseitig nicht bezüglich ihres Inhalts getypt, d.h. daß das Dateisystem keinen Unterschied zwischen Dateien z.B. mit Bilddaten und solchen mit Sprechproben macht. Zudem wird bei den Rohdaten *eines* SMO-Typs nicht von verschiedenen Formaten abstrahiert, wie z.B. TIFF oder GIF bei Rasterbildern, so daß der Zugriff der Anwendung *formatabhängig* erfolgen muß. Einzige Hilfe sind hier Namenskonventionen, die z.B. den Rückschluß vom Suffix des Dateinamens auf das Dateiformat erlauben. Das ist sehr fehleranfällig, aber durchaus gängige Praxis. Häufig werden auch die Registrierungsdaten bzw. ein Teil davon als „Datei-Header" mit den Rohdaten zusammen gespeichert, was eine gewisse Unabhängigkeit im Zugriff ermöglicht – allerdings muß dieser Header korrekt interpretiert werden.

Das Dateisystem abstrahiert von der physischen Ansteuerung einzelner Speicherungsgeräte, aber die Charakteristika der Geräteklassen wie Magnetband, Platte, CompactDisk sind für den Benutzer sichtbar und bedingen auch eine unterschiedliche Form der Bedienung. Damit gewährleisten Dateisysteme keine vollständige *Geräteunabhängigkeit*.

Die einzige Möglichkeit, *Beziehungen* zu realisieren, liegt in der Verwendung des Dateinamens als Verweis, z.B. in Attributen bei einem relationalen DBS. Systemseitig erfolgt hier natürlich keinerlei Kontrolle, was u.a. bedeutet, daß beim Löschen einer Datei diese Verweise ins Leere zeigen. Außerdem gibt es keine *Konsistenzkontrolle* über mehrere Dateien hinweg.

Es wird nur die *Suche* nach Binärmustern in Dateien bzw. Dateiverzeichnisstrukturen unterstützt. Das Suchmuster wird bei Werkzeugen wie „grep" unter UNIX z.B. hexadezimal oder als Folge druckbarer Zeichen angegeben. Wegen der Datenabhängigkeit ist ein Suchen auf diese Weise nicht sehr effektiv. Ferner wird die dateiübergreifende Suche nicht unterstützt.

Dateisysteme sind *universell verfügbar*, d.h. im Lieferumfang eines jeden Betriebssystems inbegriffen, und verursachen damit keine zusätzlichen Anschaffungskosten. Sie bieten auf unterster funktionaler Ebene Persistenz von Daten mit der Möglichkeit des rechnergesteuerten Zugriffs. Ihr großer Vorteil liegt in ihrer Einfachheit und Effizienz. Ein Großteil der geforderten Funktionalität (Datenunabhängigkeit, Abbildung von Beziehungen, Suchen) muß aber vom Anwender selbst realisiert werden. Ratsam ist dann eine geeignete Modularisierung der Programme: die Verwaltung der MMOs und der Zugriff darauf sind in Unterprogrammbibliotheken zusammenzufassen. Diese Bibliotheken sollten von möglichst allen Anwendungen benutzt werden und zukünftige Änderungen am Speicherungssystem zulassen, also selbst eine gewisse Datenunabhängigkeit und Anwendungsneutralität garantieren. Das Problem übergreifender Anfragen und die Integritätsüberwachung kann aber auch auf diese Weise nicht anwendungsunabhängig gelöst werden. Außerdem kann das DBVS die BLOBs nicht weiter unterscheiden und verfügt somit über keine Anhaltspunkte, welche Speicherungsform im konkreten Fall am besten geeignet wäre.

4.2 Lange Felder in Datenbanksystemen

Die oben skizzierten Unzulänglichkeiten von Dateisystemen haben schon früh die Integration von SMOs in Datenbanksysteme nahegelegt. Hier liegt jedoch ein wesentliches Problem darin, daß herkömmliche Datenbankverwaltungssysteme (DBVS) für die Speicherung einfacher, kurzer Felder ausgelegt sind, d.h. daß insbesondere seitenübergreifende Sätze oft nicht vorgesehen sind und die Pufferverwaltung nicht auf mehrere MB umfassende Sätze eingerichtet ist. Dies führte zur Entwicklung von Non-Standard-DBS (z.B. für den CAD-Bereich), mit denen u.a. lange Felder, sog. Binary Large Objects (BLOBs), zusammen mit formatierten Daten verwaltet werden können [Hask81]. Kommerziell verfügbar sind beispielsweise die Systeme Informix, Oracle und Sybase.

Ein solches DBVS gewährleistet allgemein – und damit auch für die in den BLOBs gespeicherten Daten im besonderen – *Geräteunabhängigkeit*, d.h. daß Auswahl und Ansteuerung der Speichergeräte intern und transparent für den Benutzer abgewickelt werden. Oft wird aber tatsächlich nur ein einziger Gerätetyp, die Magnetplatte, unterstützt. Tupelbildung und aus Attributwerten ableitbare Beziehungen sind die einzigen Möglichkeiten, MMOs zu definieren.

Es liegt jedoch *Formatabhängigkeit* vor, da das DBVS die BLOB-Inhalte lediglich als Bitfolgen behandelt. Dem DBVS können weder Struktur- noch Formatierungsangaben mitgeteilt werden. Der Typ der Daten in den BLOBs und die auf sie anwendbaren Funktionen sind systemseitig unbekannt. Damit besteht nur die Möglichkeit der Speicherung und Wiedergewinnung als Ganzes. Alle anderen Manipulations- und Abfrageoperationen müssen in das Anwendungsprogramm verlagert werden. Es ist höchstens eine Vergleichsfunktion auf Bit-Basis verfügbar, deren Einsatz aber selten sinnvoll sein wird (Formatvielfalt!). Soll das DBVS dennoch eine Suche durchführen können, so müssen die erforderlichen Daten zusätzlich – in formatierter Weise – abgelegt werden.

Das DBVS ermöglicht die Tupelbildung, wobei ein Teil der Attribute als Primärschlüssel ein Tupel eindeutig kennzeichnet (relationales Datenmodell). Tupel können mittels der *Attributbeziehung* verknüpft, d.h. in Abhängigkeit von Attributwerten einander zugeordnet werden (Join). Hervorzuheben ist hier die *Fremdschlüsselbeziehung*, der systemkontrollierte Verweis eines Attributes auf ein anderes Tupel, das einen entsprechenden Primärschlüsselwert besitzt (Referentielle Integrität). Damit lassen sich Beziehungen allein als *Zuordnungen*, deren Semantik dem System unbekannt ist und nur dem vergebenen (Rollen-) Namen entnommen werden kann, ausdrücken.

Das DBVS kontrolliert die logische Konsistenz, wobei bestehende kommerzielle Systeme dies aber fast ausschließlich auf die Formulierung von Bedingungen zwischen den Attributwerten *eines* Tupels einschränken und eine Verletzung der Bedingung nur zu einer Verweigerung der DB-Operation führt (z.B. Integritätsbedingungen in Ingres [Ingr91]). Erst in letzter Zeit versucht man in Aktiven DBS, diese rein deskriptive Nutzung von Bedingungen z.B. über Trigger zu erweitern, so daß aus den Zugriffen systemintern Aktionen in Abhängigkeit von Bedingungen abzuleiten sind (z.B. ECA-Rules in HiPAC [McCa89]). Das bedeutet – je nach den bereitgestellten Ausdrucksmitteln – insbesondere die Veränderung von DB-Operationen in Abhängigkeit vom (momentanen) Datenbestand in der im Abschnitt 3.3 für MMOs geforderten Weise.

Das Transaktionskonzept mit den verschiedenen Sperrmodalitäten erlaubt nicht nur einen verfeinerten *Mehrbenutzerbetrieb*, sondern bietet auch besonderen *Schutz gegen Datenverlust* (einschließlich der BLOBs) bei Programmfehlern und Systemausfällen.

Die Einführung langer Felder ist damit ein einfacher Weg, größere Mengen von Binärdaten einem DBVS zu übergeben, um die Vorteile einer Datenbank nutzen zu können. Hierzu gehört nicht zuletzt eine einfachere Form der Systembedienung (als im Dateisystem) mit mächtigeren Operatoren (deskriptiver Zugriff statt Navigation auf Bit-Ebene). Der Grad der Integration der BLOBs in das DBVS ist allerdings sehr gering. Gerade weil MMOs sehr umfangreich und verschiedenartig sind, ist aber das reine Ablegen und Zurückholen ihrer Daten nicht ausreichend. Notwendig sind Mechanismen zur Datenabstraktion, z.B. über die Einführung von ADTs, so daß u.a. Eigenschaftsabfragen zur Suchunterstützung geboten werden können.

Ferner ist zumindest momentan das Antwortzeitverhalten von DBS im Vergleich zu Dateisystemen zu schlecht, auch wenn die größere funktionale Mächtigkeit der Benutzerschnittstelle berücksichtigt wird. Insbesondere besitzen sie noch keine Echtzeitfähigkeit, die für einige Medientypen bei der Präsentation unbedingt erforderlich ist (z.B. Video; vgl. Kap. 2). Verbesserte Verfahren zur Optimierung lassen hier auf Abhilfe hoffen. Es darf auch nicht vergessen werden, daß der Kauf eines DBVS eine größere Investition darstellt, die sich nur amortisieren kann, wenn die Möglichkeiten zur Datenabstraktion konsequent genutzt werden (können).

4.3 Erweiterbare Datenbanksysteme

Erweiterbare DBVS erlauben dem Benutzer u.a. die *Definition eigener Datentypen*. Diese neuen Typen können genau so verwendet werden wie die systemseitig vordefinierten. Wichtig ist die damit verbundene Erweiterung der Abfragesprache um typbezogene Funktionen.

Die Einführung neuer Datentypen kann auf zwei grundsätzlich verschiedene Arten erfolgen: Entweder existieren in der Datendefinitionssprache (DDL) des DBVS Anweisungen zur Definition neuer Wertebereiche und darauf anwendbarer Funktionen, so daß neue Abstrakte Datentypen ohne Änderungen am DBVS eingeführt werden können (z.B. Postgres [Ston87]). Oder man kann sog. DBVS-Generatoren einsetzen, die, ausgehend von einer Systembeschreibung, in der u.a. die vorgesehenen Typen festgelegt sind, ein speziell zugeschnittenes DBVS aus parametrisierten Systembausteinen konfigurieren (z.B. GENESIS [Bato90], EXODUS [Care90]). Bei EXODUS besteht darüber hinaus die Möglichkeit, alle Teile eines DBVS mit Ausnahme des Storage Managers völlig neu zu erstellen [Rich87]. Eine Zwischenstufe stellen Systeme wie Ingres dar, dessen Object Management Extension (OME) die Einführung neuer Domains durch die Programmierung von Kernel-Erweiterungen verlangt [Rela89], übrigens das momentan einzige kommerziell verfügbare System dieser Art.

Durch benutzerdefinierte ADTs wird volle *Datenunabhängigkeit* erreicht. Die Einführung neuer, medienbezogener Datentypen wie BILD, TON und VIDEO versetzt das DBVS in die Lage, die zugehörigen Daten adäquat zu behandeln und insbesondere intern die Bearbeitung typabhängig zu optimieren. Dadurch kann die Geräteunabhängigkeit für eine typabhängige Speicherung von SMOs genutzt werden.

Die Möglichkeiten zur Spezifikation von *Beziehungen* sind grundsätzlich dieselben wie beim „normalen" (relationalen) DBS, d.h. auf der Basis von Attributbeziehungen. Dies gilt auch für die Definition von MMOs.

Die Einführung entsprechender typbezogener Funktionen erlaubt es aber, Joins oder Restriktionen auf den Eigenschaften von MMOs zu spezifizieren, was vor allem die *Suche* erheblich vereinfacht. Suchanfragen können somit vollständig in der Datenmanipulationssprache (DML) formuliert und vom DBS bearbeitet werden wie bei den formatierten Daten.

Notwendig ist eine möglichst weitgehende Integration der neuen Datentypen in die internen Strukturen des DBVS, so daß z.B. auch geeignete *Zugriffspfade* spezifiziert werden können und eine korrekte Behandlung durch den Optimierer erfolgt. Systeme wie Postgres und Ingres/OME verlangen jedoch eine totale Ordnung auch auf den benutzerdefinierten Typen und die Angabe einer Transformation in einen systemdefinierten (formatierten) Datentyp, um die bisherigen Zugriffspfade nutzen zu können. Dies ist für Datentypen wie „Komplexe Zahl" problemlos zu leisten, für MMOs jedoch nur auf Umwegen, die die Nutzung in Zugriffspfaden sinnlos machen.

Bei den DBVS-Generatoren wie GENESIS und EXODUS, aber auch dem „Baukastensystem" Starburst, werden zwischen den Systembausteinen einheitliche Schnittstellen festgelegt (bei GENESIS z.B. auf der Basis von „stream rewrite rules" [Bato88]), so daß verschiedene Speicherungs- und Zugriffsstrukturen zum Einsatz kommen können, deren Verwendung in den Typdefinitionen geregelt wird. Ein wesentlicher Nachteil dieser Vorgehensweise liegt darin, daß für praktisch jede Anwendung ein dediziertes DBVS mit den erforderlichen Typen geschaffen werden muß, was jedoch eine spezifischere Optimierung ermöglicht.

Gehört die Einführung neuer ADTs zum Umfang der DDL, so ist eine internationale Standardisierung der Typdefinition leichter zu erreichen (z.B. als Erweiterung von SQL), wodurch der Forderung nach Portabilität Rechnung getragen wird. Die Angabe von Parametern zur Gestaltung der internen Speicherungs- und Zugriffsverfahren ist allerdings problematischer, da bislang keinerlei Standardisierung erfolgte.

4.4 Objektorientierte Datenbanksysteme

Die Objektorientierung ist eine Weiterentwicklung des ADT-Konzepts. Wie ein ADT stellt eine Klasse eine definitorische Verknüpfung dar von Daten, die den Zustand eines Objektes beschreiben (Instanzenvariablen), und Funktionen, mit denen Zugriff und Manipulation dieser Daten möglich sind (Methoden). Wesentliche Erweiterungen sind die Einführung der Objektidentität (im Unterschied zur Wertgleichheit) und des Vererbungskonzepts. Ferner ist die Komposition von Objekten zu beliebig geschachtelten komplexen Objekten möglich.

In objektorientierten Systemen werden die Objekte der realen Welt als *gekapselte* Einheiten repräsentiert, auf die nur mittels der Methoden zugegriffen werden kann. Die Repräsentationen sind nicht mehr offen bearbeitbar wie Tupel, bei denen nur die Attribute gekapselt sind, wie im Falle von relationalen DBS. Die Objekt-Kapselung unterstützt somit *Datenunabhängigkeit* auf höherer Ebene, leistet aber prinzipiell nicht wesentlich mehr, als schon ADTs bieten.

Die *Objektidentität* stellt als systemkontrolliertes, eindeutiges und unveränderliches Kennzeichen gegenüber dem (zusammengesetzten) Primärschlüssel bzw. Surrogat relationaler Systeme eine neue Qualität dar. Primärschlüssel sollen konzeptionell zwar eindeutig sein, werden aber in verfügbaren DBVS darauf zu selten überprüft. Allerdings gibt es inzwischen Normvorschläge für eine entsprechende Erweiterung von SQL. Nur obliegt die konsistente Verwaltung der Primär- und zugehörigen Fremdschlüssel dem Anwender – im Gegensatz zur Objektidentität von objektorientierten Datenbanksystemen.

Beziehungen zwischen Objekten werden in der Regel orthogonal zur Klassenhierarchie über den nach außen unsichtbaren Objektidentifikator hergestellt, der einzeln oder als Menge bzw. Liste eine Instanzenvariable bilden kann. Die Semantik unidirektionaler Beziehungen kann wie z.B. im System VODAK [Klas90] dadurch ausgedrückt werden, daß für jede Beziehungsart eine (Super-) Klasse definiert wird und deren Eigenschaften auf das Objekt, von dem die Beziehung ausgeht, vererbt werden. Von VODAK abgesehen, bleibt es aber auch in objektorientierten DBS (OODBS) bei den generischen Beziehungen. Ihre unterschiedliche Semantik wird zwar nicht mehr in der Anwendung, sondern in den Methoden der Objekte verwaltet, doch bleibt sie dem OODBS unbekannt. Dies erschwert eine Optimierung der Abspeicherung (z.B. Clustering) und des Zugriffs.

Es gibt keine besondere Unterstützung der *Suche*, da nur mit – objektbezogenen – Methodenaufrufen gearbeitet wird. Hier könnten in Systemklassen entsprechende Methoden vorgesehen werden, aber wie deren Zugriffe auf die zu untersuchenden Objekte effizient realisiert werden könnten, ist unklar.

Das *Vererbungskonzept* geht über Subtypenbildung hinaus. Die Vererbung von Attributen oder Methoden auf die Subklassen wird bei der Bildung von Generalisierungs- bzw. Klassifizierungshierarchien eingesetzt, wobei es allerdings je nach konkretem System grundsätzlich verschiedene Ausprägungen von Beziehungen zwischen Klassen und Objekten bzw. Superklassen gibt, was die Art der Weitergabe dieser deklarativen bzw. prozeduralen Eigenschaften betrifft (vgl. z.B. [Matt91]). Die Implementierung eigener Typen wird, ausgehend von vordefinierten Klassen, wesentlich erleichtert.

Einen weitereren Mangel stellen fehlende Zugriffsstrukturen zur Unterstützung der verschiedenartigen Beziehungen dar. Durch die Verwendung von Verweisen von einem Objekt auf das andere zur Darstellung von Beziehungen wird der durch relationale Systeme überwundene *navigierende Zugriff* wieder eingeführt. Abfragen und Manipulationen können oft nicht oder nur teilweise deskriptiv formuliert werden, so daß die Steuerung der Bearbeitungsschritte dem Benutzer obliegt.

5 Vorschlag eines speziellen Verwaltungssystems für MMOs

Die im vorhergehenden Kapitel aufgezeigten Defizite bestehender Speicherungssysteme haben am Lehrstuhl für Datenbanksysteme der Universität Erlangen-Nürnberg zur Entwicklung eines Experimentiersystems Multimedia-Object Manager (MOM) geführt. Um eine Fokussierung auf die neuartigen Aspekte von MMOs, insbesondere die Suche, die Beziehungen zwischen den MMOs und die Performance, zu erreichen, wurde bewußt auf die Speicherung formatierter Daten und auf dynamische Typdefinition verzichtet. Das resultierende Speicherungssystem kann später in ein (erweiterbares oder objektorientiertes) DBVS integriert werden oder weiterhin als eigenständiger, „interoperabler" Baustein an die bestehenden DBS gekoppelt werden.

Im ersten Ansatz sind die MADTs fest vorgegeben und disjunkt; in einer späteren Ausbaustufe sollen auch dynamische Typdefinitionen und Typhierarchien zugelassen werden. Realisiert werden derzeit die Typen TEXT, GRAPHICS, IMAGE, SOUND und VIDEO. Wie oben gefordert, gehören SMOs jeweils einem dieser MADTs an. Damit leistet MOM nicht nur die geforderte *Geräte-* und *Formatunabhängigkeit*, sondern auch noch eine differenzierte und adäquate Behandlung der SMOs auf allen Ebenen der Abstraktionshierarchie.

MOM verwaltet nur SMOs und deren Beziehungen (damit auch MMOs). Der Zugriff auf ein SMO erfolgt über einen systemvergebenen Identifikator, über die Beziehungen oder über den Suchmechanismus. Speziell für die *Suche*, aber auch allgemein für die Strukturierung des Gesamtbestandes an SMOs, wurde zusätzlich das Konzept der *SMO-Mengen* eingeführt. Zu jeder Suchanfrage wird die SMO-Menge angegeben, in der gesucht werden soll (der „Suchraum"). Wie in Abschnitt 3.4 herausgestellt, müssen inhaltsorientierte Suchanfragen wegen der Ausdrucksfähigkeit auf Metaebene im Medium Sprache formuliert werden. Dabei werden bestimmte Wörter durchaus unterschiedlich interpretiert, je nachdem, ob z.B. nach Röntgenbildern, Konzertaufnahmen, Gesetzestexten, Satellitenfotos oder Videoaufzeichnungen eines Crash-Tests gesucht wird. Das Konzept der SMO-Mengen trägt dem Rechnung, indem es zu jeder Menge ein eigenenes Wörterbuch [Meye91] vorsieht. SMO-Mengen können sich prinzipiell beliebig überlappen; eine strikte Teilmengenbeziehung und Disjunktheit sind jedoch als explizite Integritätsbedingungen formulierbar.

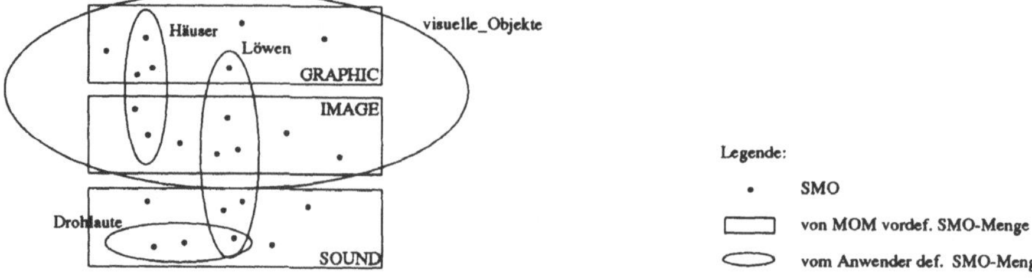

Abbildung 3: Beispiel für SMO-Mengen in MOM

Zu jedem MADT gibt es eine vordefinierte, nicht löschbare SMO-Menge, die alle SMOs dieses Typs enthält. Aus ihr können Elemente nur durch Löschen entfernt und durch Erzeugen eingefügt werden, wohingegen bei allen anderen, anwenderdefinierten SMO-Mengen die Zugehörigkeit dynamisch änderbar ist. Abb. 3 zeigt ein typisches Beispiel für die Verwendung von SMO-Mengen. Wie man sieht, können SMO-Mengen auch medienübergreifend definiert werden. Naheliegenderweise können die Bestandteile eines MMOs auch als Menge aufgefaßt werden, wobei das allein natürlich noch keine vollständige MMO-Definition darstellt.

Auf SMO-Mengen können die üblichen Operatoren der Mengenalgebra (Durchschnitt, Vereinigung, Differenz usw.) angewendet werden. Es gibt einen Zugriff auf alle SMOs einer Menge, einen Booleschen Elementoperator (SMO ε Menge?) und die Ermittlung sämtlicher Mengen, denen ein bestimmtes SMO angehört. Wegen der vordefinierten MADT-Mengen leistet dies zugleich auch die Typ-Feststellung zu einem gegebenen SMO-Identifikator.

MOM soll auch die *Beziehungen* zwischen SMOs verwalten, insbesondere die Aggregation zu MMOs (sowie deren Beziehungen). Dieser Teil der MOM-Funktionaltät ist derzeit noch in Arbeit. Es steht fest, daß es noch mehr geben muß als einen generischen Beziehungstyp, der außer Kardinalitätsrestriktionen keine weitere Semantik wiedergeben kann. Statt dessen sollen Beziehungstypen unterschieden und bei der Implementierung explizit berücksichtigt werden, mindestens die Aggregation, evtl. weitere der in Abschnitt 3.3 aufgezählten Arten. Hier ist ein Kompromiß zu schließen zwischen einer möglicherweise unübersichtlichen Vielfalt von Modellierungskonzepten einerseits und dem Optimierungspotential, das in einer differenzierten Behandlung liegt, andererseits.

Da MOM nur SMOs und MMOs verwalten kann, wird angenommen, daß die Anwendungen ein weiteres Speicherungssystem, z.B. ein relationales DBVS, für die formatierten Daten verwenden. Die Verknüpfung erfolgt dadurch, daß SMO-Identifikatoren (oder auch MMO-Identifikatoren oder SMO-Mengen-Identifikatoren) als Attributwerte in der relationalen Datenbank auftreten. Dazu sollte dort der Wertebereich „SMO-ID" definiert werden, idealerweise als ADT, notfalls als INTEGER. Jedem Attribut dieses Wertebereichs kann in MOM eine eigene SMO-Menge zugeordnet werden. Die in [Meye91] geforderte inhaltsorientierte Suche ist dann über eine entsprechende Suche in MOM, die eine Menge von SMO-IDs liefert, und den anschließenden Zugriff auf die Relation über diese SMO-IDs realisierbar (Abb. 4).

Die Trennung in zwei Datenhaltungssysteme erfordert zwar geeignete Mechanismen zur übergreifenden Transaktionssteuerung, erlaubt jedoch andererseits ein hohes Maß an Flexibilität bei der Realisierung von MOM. Änderungen an der Implementierung der MADTs werden erheblich erleichtert; deren Austausch und die Einführung neuer MADTs sind sogar im laufenden Betrieb denkbar.

Das Abstraktionsniveau der MOM-Schnittstelle gewährleistet Geräteunabhängigkeit und Anwendungsneutralität mindestens so gut wie alle anderen Speicherungssysteme. Das Spektrum der intern verwendbaren Speichergeräte, Komprimierungsverfahren und Zugriffspfade ist dagegen weit größer, da es nicht von den

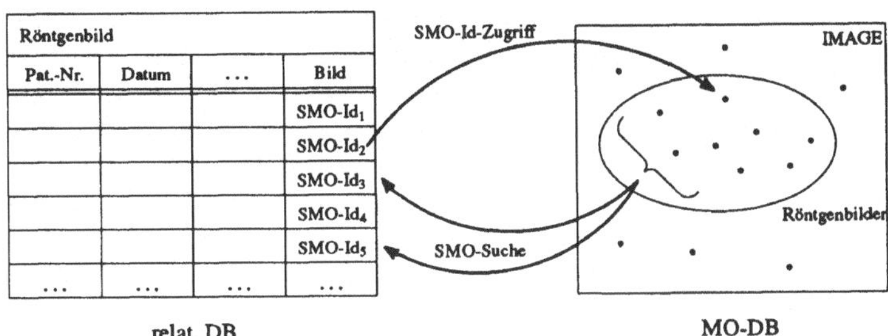

Abbildung 4: Beispiel einer Kopplung von MOM mit einem relationalen DBVS

Erfordernissen der Verwaltung formatierter Daten geprägt ist. Gleiches gilt für die Definition und Realisierung von Suchoperatoren. Das größte Manko von MOM ist seine Verfügbarkeit: Es handelt sich um einen Forschungsprototypen, der nur in Einzelfällen in den Praxiseinsatz gehen wird. Allerdings ist die geforderte Funktionalität auch in keinem marktgängigen Produkt verfügbar, und erklärtes Ziel der MOM-Entwicklung ist, für deren Weiterentwicklung wichtige Hinweise zu liefern.

6 Vergleich

In einer abschließenden Bewertung werden die vorgestellten Lösungsansätze anhand der in Kapitel 3 herausgearbeiteten Kriterien miteinander verglichen. Tab. 2 faßt die Bewertung der verschiedenen Speicherungssysteme zusammen. Zu einzelnen Tabelleneinträgen sind noch folgende Anmerkungen zu machen:

Das (Speicher-)*Gerätespektrum* ist bei Dateisystemen nur insoweit erweiterbar, als die Geräte bereits vorgesehen sind und über bestimmte Schnittstellen verfügen (z.B. CD-ROM). Davon abweichende Speicher (z.B. Videorecorder) können dagegen meist nicht über Dateizugriffe benutzt werden, sondern verlangen eine separate Behandlung (auf niedrigerem Abstraktionsniveau, im allg. Treiberebene). Was die *Geräteunabhängigkeit* angeht, so ist sie bei Dateisystemen und bei DBVS mit BLOBs zwar prinzipiell gewährleistet. Zugleich macht jedoch die mangelnde Flexibilität in der Geräteauswahl die Speicherung z.B. von Video-Aufnahmen *im* System praktisch unmöglich. Die Anwendungen, die dafür eine Lösung außerhalb des MMSS suchen müssen, sind also nur bei einem Teil ihrer Daten geräteunabhängig.

Die *Echtzeitfähigkeit* ist in OODBVS zwar prinzipiell realisierbar, wird aber in den meisten Systemen bisher nicht unterstützt, da die Information über die Zeitabhängigkeit bestimmter Objektklassen in den tieferen Schichten des Systems (Externspeicherverwaltung, Pufferverwaltung, Verwaltung physischer Sätze) nicht verfügbar ist. Entsprechende Anpassungsmechanismen, wie sie in erweiterbaren DBVS erprobt werden, können aber auf objektorientierte DBVS übertragen werden.

In summa sind die betrachteten MMSS vor dem Hintergrund von Tab. 2 wie folgt einzuschätzen:

Dateisysteme und Datenbanksysteme, die nur BLOBs unterstützen, gehen in ihrer Funktionalität bez. multimedialer Daten über das reine Abspeichern und Laden kaum hinaus, so daß für alle weiteren Anforderungen wie medientyp-spezifische Operationen, semantikbehaftete Beziehungen, Format- und u.U. auch Geräteunabhängigkeit der Anwender selbst verantwortlich ist. Der damit verbundene hohe Programmieraufwand läßt sich zwar durch die Bereitstellung von (einmal erstellten) Software-Bibliotheken in Grenzen halten, erlaubt aber keine umfassende, integrierte Kontrolle durch das System. BLOBs sind dagegen zumindest in das Recovery-Konzept des DBS einbezogen. Insgesamt werden Dateien und BLOBs nur mangels Alternativen, z.B. aufgrund begrenzter Ressourcen oder geringer Verfügbarkeit anderer Systeme, in Frage kommen.

Erweiterbare relationale und objektorientierte DBS dagegen erfüllen nahezu gleichermaßen bereits viele der aufgestellten Forderungen und unterscheiden sich im wesentlichen nur im zugrundeliegenden Datenmodell. Beide bieten medienspezifische ADTs und Zugriffspfade (bedingt), Datenunabhängigkeit sowie integrierte Kontrollmöglichkeiten und halten dadurch den Programmieraufwand für den Anwender gering. Jedoch fehlen ihnen (noch) die Unterstützung von Beziehungen, die mit einer funktionsbezogenen Semantik behaftet sind, und von beliebigen, inhaltsorientierten Suchanfragen, denen gerade bei multimedialen Datenobjekten eine besondere Bedeutung zukommt. Auf diesen Gebieten, aber auch auf dem der medienspezifischen Zugriffspfade, müssen noch zahlreiche Forschungs- und Entwicklungsleistungen erbracht werden.

Einen solchen Forschungsbeitrag soll das von uns zur Zeit entwickelte Experimentiersystem MOM leisten. Folglich soll es alle im Kapitel 3 aufgestellten Forderungen erfüllen und neue Verfahren insbesondere zur Suche und zur Spezifikation semantikbehafteter Beziehungen realisieren. Um dabei die Komplexität des Systems zumindest in den Anfangsstadien überschaubar zu halten, wird kein hierarchisches Typsystem unterstützt und die Speicherung formatierter Anwenderdaten einem separaten System überlassen.

Kriterium	*Lösung*				
	Dateien	*BLOBs*	*Erweit. DBVS*	*obj.-or. DBVS*	*MOM*
erweiterbares Gerätespektrum	nein	nein	ja (Starburst)	ja (ORION)	ja
Geräteunabhängigkeit	bedingt ja, z.B.Videorec.	bedingt ja, z.B. Videorec.	ja	bedingt ja	ja
Abbildung auf Speichergerät	Baum (UNIX), Extent-Tab.	?	Baum (EXODUS), Extents (Starburst)	Blockliste (ORION)	noch offen
Formatunabhängigkeit	nein	nein	ja	ja	ja
Typen	nein	nein	ja (hierarch.)	ja (hierarch.)	ja (flach)
verantwortlich für ADTs	Anwendung	Anwendung	System	System	System
Beziehungen	nein	nein	ja (ohne spez. Semantik)	ja (ohne spez. Semantik)	ja (mit spez. Semantik)
Zugriffspfade	nein	nein	generisch (Postgres), beliebig (Starburst)	generisch, falls überhaupt	spezifisch
formatierte Daten	nein	ja	ja	ja	nein
Echtzeitfähigkeit	machbar (Echtzeit-BS)	derzeit nicht	machbar	machbar	ja
Kosten	gering	mittel	hoch	hoch	mittel
Programmieraufwand für Anwender	sehr hoch	hoch	gering	gering	mittel
Verfügbarkeit	hoch	mittel	gering	gering	noch nicht

Tabelle 2: Vergleich der vorgestellten Lösungsansätze

7 Zusammenfassung

Ziel war es, die besonderen Anforderungen, die die Verwaltung von multimedialen Datenobjekten (MMOs) an Datenhaltungssysteme stellt, herauszuarbeiten. Dabei wurde das Augenmerk auf die Aspekte einer mediengerechten Datenmodellierung gerichtet, die ihrerseits eine Erfüllung der besonderen „technischen" Erfordernisse ermöglicht. Das Konzept der Abstrakten Datentypen wurde als das entscheidende Hilfsmittel für die Gewährleistung der Datenunabhängigkeit der Anwendungsprogramme, hier insbesondere der Geräte- und Formatunabhängigkeit, gefordert. Ferner wurden Möglichkeiten zur Darstellung von Beziehungen zwischen den und innerhalb der MMOs als wichtig erachtet, wobei es hier erst einmal um die Bereitstellung von allgemeinen Mechanismen geht, da die verschiedenen Arten von Beziehungen in ihrer vielfältigen Semantik noch nicht hinreichend geklärt sind. Den zentralen Aspekt jeder Archivierung bildet die Unterstützung der Suche. Hier stellen MMOs besondere Anforderungen hinsichtlich ihrer inhaltsorientierten Erschließung und der Bereitstellung von Zugriffspfaden. Neben diesem funktionsorientierten Anforderungskatalog müssen immer auch die Verfügbarkeit der Systeme und der mit der Umsetzung der Konzepte wie ihrem Einsatz verbundene Aufwand berücksichtigt werden.

Es wurde gezeigt, daß bei den verfügbaren Datenverwaltungssystemen die Flexibilität bezüglich der Abbildung auf Externspeichergeräte noch nicht ausreicht. Darunter leidet insbesondere die Echtzeitfähigkeit bei Datentypen wie Ton und Video. Ohnehin ist die Unterscheidung der Mediendatentypen und ihre spezifische Behandlung eine wichtige Voraussetzung für die qualifizierte Auswahl eines Speichergeräts. Aber auch die interne Erweiterbarkeit des Systems, also die Einbringung angepaßter Speicherungsstrukturen, ist für die Effizienz von entscheidender Bedeutung. Geräte- und Formatabhängigkeit der Anwendungen sind dafür notwendige Voraussetzungen.

Bei der Suchunterstützung, insbesondere der inhaltsorientierten Recherche, gibt es neuere Ansätze auf den Gebieten Mustererkennung und Information Retrieval, die vorrangig die Bereiche Wissenserkennung und -modellierung betreffen, aber noch verfeinert werden müssen. Vor allem das wichtige Gebiet der Zugriffspfade muß für diese neuen Repräsentationsformen weiter erforscht werden.

Ausgehend von diesen Feststellungen halten wir die Entwicklung des Speicherungssystems MOM als autonomes, aber nicht isoliertes System zur Archivierung von MMOs für notwendig. MOM soll auf der Basis eines modularen Aufbaus als Experimentiersystem zur Erprobung von dedizierten Konzepten für die Bewältigung der oben beschriebenen Problemkreise dienen.

Danksagung

Wir danken den Herren Prof. Dr. Hartmut Wedekind, Prof. Dr. Theo Härder und Prof. Dr. Winfried Lamersdorf sowie den anonymen Gutachtern für die hilfreichen Hinweise zur Verbesserung des Beitrags.

Literatur

ANSI75 ANSI/X3/SPARC Study on Data Base Management System, "Interim Report 75-02-08," *FDT-Bulletin of ACM-SIGMOD*, Vol. 7, No. 2, 1975.

Atki89 Atkinson, M., et al., "The Object-Oriented Database System Manifesto," *Proc. 1st Int. Conf. on Deductive and Object-oriented Database Systems* (Kyoto, Dec. 1989), Amsterdam 1989, pp. 40–57.

Bato88 Batory, D.S., Leung, T.Y., and Wise, T.E., "Implementation Concepts for an Extensible Data Model and Data Language," *ACM Transactions on Database Systems*, Vol. 13, No. 3, Sept. 1988, pp. 231–262.

Bato90 Batory, D.S., et al., "GENESIS: An Extensible Database Management System," in *Readings in Object-Oriented Database Systems*, eds. S.B. Zdonik and D. Maier, San Mateo 1990, pp. 500–518.

Care90 Carey, M.J., et al., "The EXODUS Extensible DBMS Project: An Overview," in *Readings in Object-Oriented Database Systems*, eds. S.B. Zdonik and D. Maier, San Mateo 1990, pp. 474–499.

Falo85 Faloutsos, C., "Access Methods for Text", *ACM Computing Surveys*, Vol. 17, No. 1, March 1985, pp. 49–74.

Hask81 Haskin, R.L., and Lorie, R.A., "On Extending the Functions of a Relational Database System," IBM Research Report RJ 3182, San Jose, CA, 1981.

Hora85a Horak, W., "Office Document Architecture and Office Document Interchange Formats: Current Status of International Standardization," *IEEE Computer*, Vol. 18, No. 10, Oct. 1985, pp. 50–60.

Ingr91 Ingres Corp., *INGRES/SQL Reference Manual for the UNIX and VMS Operating System, Rel. 6.4*; Alameda, Dec. 1991.

Kim90 Kim, W., et al., "Architecture of the ORION Next-Generation Database System," *IEEE Transactions on Knowledge and Data Engineering*, Vol. 2, No. 1, March 1990, pp. 109–124.

Klas90 Klas, W., Neuhold, E.J., and Schrefl, M., "Using an Object-Oriented Approach to Model Multimedia Data," *Computer Communications, Special Issue on Multimedia Systems*, Vol. 13, No. 4, May 1990, pp. 204–216.

Lisk74 Liskov, B., and Zilles, S., "Programming With Abstract Data Types", *ACM SIGPLAN Notices*, April 1974.

Masu87 Masunaga, Y., "Multimedia Databases: A Formal Framework," in *Proc. IEEE CS Office Automation Symposium* (Gaithersburg, MD, April 1987), IEEE CS Press, Washington, pp. 36–45.

Matt91 Mattos, N.M., Meyer-Wegener, K., and Mitschang, B., "Grand Tour of Concepts for Object-Orientation from a Database Point of View," SFB 124 Report No. 23/91, Universitiy of Kaiserslautern, Germany, 1991, also to appear in *Data & Knowledge Engineering*, 1993.

McCa89 McCarthy, D.R., and Dayal, U., "The Architecture Of An Active Data Base Management System," *ACM SIGMOD Record*, May 1989, pp. 215–224.

Meye91 Meyer-Wegener, K., *Multimedia-Datenbanken*, B.G. Teubner Verlag, Leitfäden der angewandten Informatik, Stuttgart 1991.

Newc91 Newcomb, S.R., Kipp, N.A., and Newcomb V.T., "The "HyTime" Hypermedia/Time-based Document Structuring Language," *Communications of the ACM*, Vol. 34, No. 11, Nov. 1991, pp. 67–83.

Niev84 Nievergelt, J., Hinterberger, H., and Sevcik, K.C., "The Grid File: An Adaptable, Symmetric Multikey File Structure," *ACM Transactions on Database Systems*, Vol. 9, No. 1, Jan. 1984, pp. 38–71.

Rela89 Relational Technology Inc., *INGRES Object Management Extension User Guide for the UNIX and VMS Operating System, Rel. 6.3*, Alameda, Nov. 1989.

Rich87 Richardson, J.E., and Carey, M.J., "Programming Constructs for Database System Implementation in EXODUS," in *Proc. ACM SIGMOD Annual Conf.* (San Francisco, May 1987), pp. 208–219.

Salt83 Salton, G., and McGill, M.J., *Introduction to Modern Information Retrieval*, McGraw-Hill Book Company, New York 1983.

Ston87 Stonebraker, M., and Rowe, L.A., "The Design of POSTGRES," *ACM SIGMOD Record*, Vol. 15, No. 2, June 1987, pp. 340–355.

Wall91 Wallace, G.K., "The JPEG Still Picture Compression Standard," *Communications of the ACM*, Vol. 34, No. 4, April 1991, pp. 30–44.

Woel87 Woelk, D., and Kim, W., "Multimedia Information Management in an Object-Oriented Database System," in *Proc. 13th Int. Conf. on VLDB* (Brighton, England, Sept. 1987), eds. P.M. Stocker and W. Kent, Morgan Kaufmann Publishers, Los Altos, CA, 1987, pp. 319–329.

Integrating Multimedia into the Distributed Office Applications Environment

J. Rückert, B. Paul
IBM European Networking Center (ENC)
P.O. Box 10 30 68
D-6900 Heidelberg

Abstract

The Distributed Office Applications Model (DOAM) provides the general framework for applications in the *office environment*. It is based on ISO Open System Interconnection communications model (OSI), especially on using the Association Control Service Element (ACSE), the Reliable Transfer Service Element (RTSE) and Remote Operations Service Element (ROSE). Using OSI, *openness* in a multi-vendor environment is achieved but at the same time the possibility to offer added-values concerning multimedia (audio, video) integration is blocked. This is mainly due to the restricted functionality of the OSI communications model that does not support communication services required by multimedia applications, e.g. isochronous data traffic. Using DOAM's Distinguished Object References (DOR) a solution to this problem can be offered: To transmit whole documents OSI communication is used; to transmit documents for immediate presentation or from real-time capturing control data is transmitted using OSI communication and multimedia data via a separate communication stack supporting isochronous communication services. Based on a prototype implementation of the DOAM conforming Document Filing and Retrieval (DFR) standard this solution is presented and the implemented prototype discussed.

1. Introduction

With the development of open communication systems adhering to international or de-facto standards (OSI, TCP/IP, etc.) it is possible to interconnect heterogeneous user groups. The openness due to standards usage allows users to spontaneously connect to others. Based on this openness different application layer services like virtual terminal (VT), message handling systems (MHS), file transfer and access (FTAM) or remote data base access (RDA) have been specified in standards. For some applications these standardized services are not sufficient but have to be extended to cover more application specific requirements. In the area of Distributed Office Applications (DOA) a model (DOAM) [4] has been standardized, giving the framework for standardized office applications. Document Filing and Retrieval (DFR) [3] is one standard within this DOAM framework. It defines the model of the document store with access and manipulation services that are necessary in the office environment and the according protocols to access them.

With the advance of new office applications, especially those using multimedia features [2; 9], new requirements arise. The main task for integrating multimedia is to handle audio and video as new data types in computer systems, including their special needs like synchronization, compression etc. [11].

Necessary steps toward a multimedia data integration into the office environment are the inclusion of these information types into the used

- office application platforms and document architectures
- document stores and data bases
- communication protocols and services.

Typical application scenarios for stored multimedia information are the browsing through large electronic multimedia libraries, technical manuals for various purposes, electronic encyclopedia and many more. In the office environment, the documents are letters, reports, minutes, notes, announcements together with multimedia annotation or integrated multimedia data. Typically they are stored in some central or distributed document store realized by a data base, onto which retrieval, document manipulation and handling functions can operate.

In the following section an overview of DOAM and DFR is given. Based on this, the integration requirements for multimedia into documents are considered. The chosen integration approach into standard based document filing and retrieval is presented and the experience with the implemented prototype discussed.

2. The DOAM and DFR Standards

The ISO standard DOAM [4] is the base for distributed office applications. It describes a general model for distributed office applications, its services and the protocols to access them.

Applications can be local or distributed over LANs or public networks. To achieve this, a general client-server model is defined. A client resides on the application program site and connects to a remote server providing the required service. Communication is based on the application layer services ACSE, RTSE (optional) and ROSE of OSI communication. Multiple servers can interact building a server system. Since this server system is transparent for the client, applications can operate on local or distributed data in the same way. Figure 1 shows this model for an application using Document Filing and Retrieval.

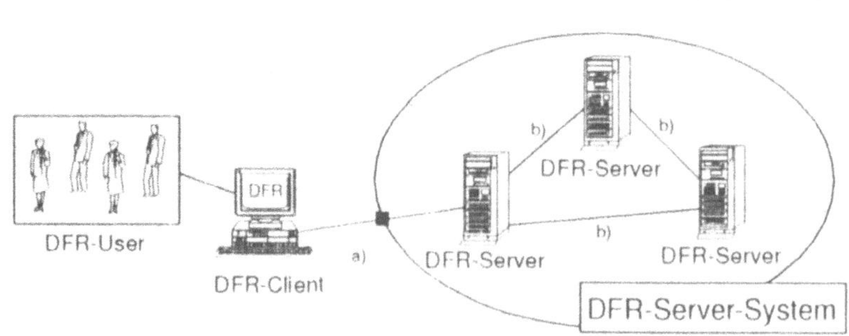

Figure 1. DFR as a DOA: a) DFR access protocol, b) DFR system protocol

Data items are treated as objects with a required minimum set of methods like create, read, modify, delete, copy etc. The base for all distributed handling of such objects is the definition of Distinguished Object References (DORs) that allows for handling of references to objects between distributed servers by Referenced Object Access (ROA). This reduces the need to copy data to a minimum. The model for such ROA operations is shown in figure 2.

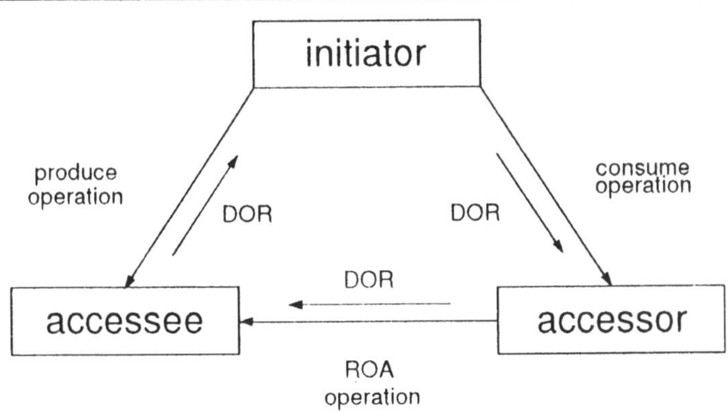

Figure 2. ROA: Referenced-object-access model

Accessor, accessee and initiator may reside on separate nodes. The shown scenario can be interpreted for DFR applications as follows: A DFR client (initiator) accesses a DFR server (accessee) to retrieve a document in the data base. Instead of requesting the found data itself, the DFR client may specify to get back as the result a reference (DOR) to the requested data. Therefore, this operation is named a *DOR produce operation*. The produced DOR may be given to another server, e.g. a print server for the document to be printed or transmitted as part of an electronic message for later access by the recipient. Since the DOR is "used up" this is a *DOR consume operation*. For performing the printing, the print server (accessor) starts the ROA operation accessing the DFR server (accessee), requesting the data the DOR refers to.

DFR [3] as the Document Filing and Retrieval in a DOA environment files documents as DFR objects separated in content and attributes, both to be stored e.g. in a data base. The attributes are used by DFR for handling, while the content is transparent to DFR. Besides documents, DFR supports groups of objects, enabling a hierarchically structured view onto the document store; references, enabling the membership of a DFR object in different groups; search-result lists, to keep results of retrieval operations. Attributes of DFR objects cover naming, versioning, date and time control, reservation, access and security as well as user defined attributes. Supported services performed as remote operations include creation, deletion, copying, moving, reading, modifying, listing, searching, reservation and service interruption.

From this, it is obvious that DFR meets the requirements of document storage and retrieval for the office environment by modelling the paper office document filing cabinet by its electronical counterpart. Even if originally not designed for multimedia information storage, the DFR concept of a strict separation of DFR objects into *attributes and content* allows it to handle multimedia information if the application using the DFR-client and the storage component of the DFR-server is able to do so. Problems arise, if the documents' internal time structure of such multimedia data becomes visible to the DFR server. Concerning communication requirements this is discussed in the next section.

3. Integration Requirements for Multimedia

In a distributed office environment, multimedia data require communication facilities capable to support the appropriate data traffic. Two different cases must be distinguished:

- *Transmission of multimedia documents from store to store.* This requires the transmission of the complete document as a single or multiple large files (bulk data transfer).
- *Transmission of multimedia for immediate presentation and/or real-time capturing.* In contrast to the above case, this requires isochronous data transmission for out of or into the data store, to allow interactive manipulation by the user (play, pause, stop etc.) and release from the need to send and store the whole data every time multimedia information is accessed.

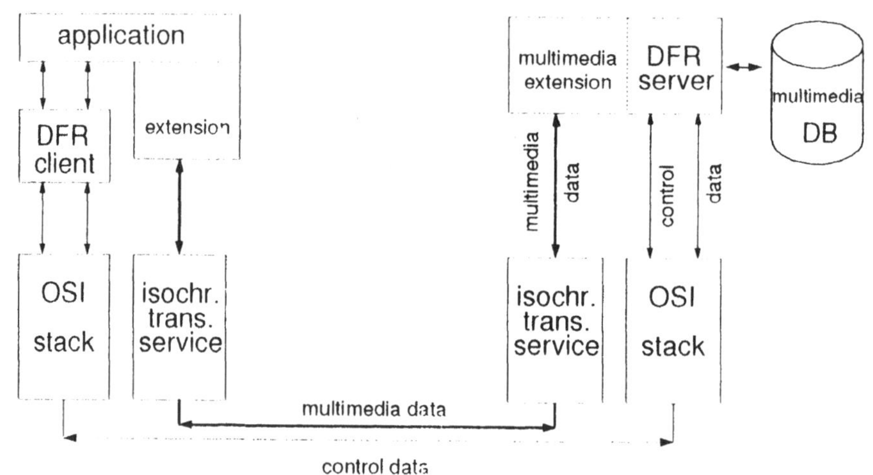

Figure 3. Dual-stack solution: Separated communication stacks for multimedia data and control.

To integrate such isochronous data communication services into the standardized DOAM, different solutions can be offered:

- The easiest way would be to drop the DOAM requirement of using OSI communications that is currently not capable of supporting isochronous data transmission. This requires standardization work in the DOAM environment with a small chance of success since standardized alternatives to OSI communication supplying isochronous data traffic are just under early development [10; 12].

- An alternative would be the incorporation of multimedia communication services into the OSI model. This also requires standardization work with small chances of success, since most applications currently using OSI do not require multimedia communications.
- The third alternative is a more technical approach, namely to separate multimedia communication into transmission of control and data and use the best suited communication services for each.

The general concept of using two different communication stacks is shown in figure 3. This approach is itself not standardized for this environment but uses standardized OSI communication wherever possible. It has the advantage of being *open* for the integration of new communication services as they become available and being *downward compatible* with DOAM applications that do not support or need multimedia capabilities. Its usage for DFR is described in the next section.

4. Approach and Realization

The approach presented in this paper uses the referencing possibilities of the DOAM model to integrate non-OSI communication into the DOAM environment, by the before described dual-communication stack solution. In fact, for the presentation of multimedia parts of documents a TCP/IP based communication stack has been used to transport isochronous data parts, whereas the OSI communication stack is used for control and other data. Since TCP/IP as is, does not support isochronous data traffic, a thin communication layer has been placed on top of it, managing a few buffers and a simple protocol mechanism to guarantee that buffers never run full or empty. Thus, on the presentation side the data portions can be delivered isochronously even if variances in the transmission delay occur. This simple approach works reasonably well for audio data even if the underlying communication system is heavily loaded. For more elaborated communication needs like high-quality audio, video or multiple connections other upcoming communication systems can be integrated using the same concept [10].

This technical solution has been integrated into DFR server and client prototypes. Applications capable to support both communication stacks can use the enhanced facilities of isochronous data transmission, others access the DFR server using OSI communications. Thus, standard DFR servers and enhanced multimedia capable DFR servers can be accessed by standard DFR clients. Of course, the data base used to store multimedia data must be capable to handle these multiple concurrent multimedia accesses.

A typical application scenario for DFR is searching documents in the store maintained by a DFR server. After identifying a specific document, the DFR-client reads the document specifying the result of the read operation to be the document's content, attributes or a DOR to the document. The DOR can be stored for later access to the referenced document, for transmission by electronic mail or other purposes. The multimedia application requiring isochronous data transmission services uses the DOR to access the document's data like shown in figure 4. It indicates the communication type to be used and the recipient's address in a special selector field of the DOR. The multimedia DFR server uses this address to establish an independent multimedia connection to the recipient and transmits the data. After successful transmission the initiator is acknowledged using OSI communication.

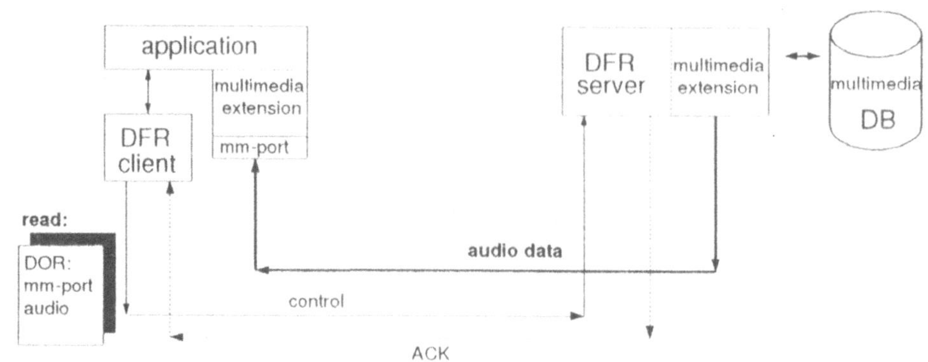

Figure 4. Multimedia-application: Accessing a multimedia DFR-server

5. The multimedia DFR Prototype

The described system has been implemented for audio document storage and retrieval. The system is coded in C on an IBM RS/6000 work station running IBM AIX 3.2. For the OSI communication the public available ISO development environment (ISO/DE) has been used. Multimedia communication is implemented as add-on to TCP/IP. Audio recording and play-back uses IBM's Audio Capture and Playback Adapter (ACPA), a plug-in board [1] that uses a standards based coding and decoding of digitized audio, therefore being open for audio data exchange in a heterogeneous environment. IBM RS/6000 work-stations have been interconnected by an IBM TokenRing that is also loaded by other data communications. Experiments with telephone quality audio with a bandwidth requirement of 5.5 KByte per second have been carried out. The delay from initiating the isochronous transmission to beginning of replay is approximately 0.5 seconds dependent on the process scheduling in the operating system and the number of buffers specified for the multimedia communication extensions. A buffering of 5.5 KByte adds one second delay. In the experiment no drop outs due to large data packet delays have been observed even if extensive bulk transfer is concurrently active. Currently the implementation supports audio for which transmission-times over LANs is negligible. It is to be extended to include video, as better suited and fast enough multimedia communication systems become available.

To demonstrate multimedia DFR a simple audio/visual information system on Heidelberg has been set up: A X-windows application connects to a remote DFR server by its local DFR client. It fetches a list of the digitized pictures of downtown Heidelberg. When the user selects a picture a short text description and the picture itself pops up and additional information is given as an audio play-back using the isochronous audio transfer described before. This scenario can easily be extended to a general purpose "information kiosk" to connect to various different DFR stores for information retrieval.

6. Prospect

The discussed DFR extension is a suitable way to incorporate multimedia into the *Distributed Office Applications Model* extending its applicability beyond the office arena. The chosen approach of using a dual communication stack model enables downward compatible solutions to extend the standards based data store DFR to cover isochronous multimedia data.

Demonstrating that audio can be transmitted over a LAN via TCP/IP is something already well known, but the goal of this work is to give the general concept how to *exploit upcoming isochronous communication services in a standardized environment* preserving compatibility with existing services. Since we also aim at video transmission, new communication stacks [7] supporting multimedia data will be integrated in the same way.

With the advance of such systems the *DFR server and its data base* must be able to store multimedia data allowing for retrieval on attributes or even the multimedia data itself. This requires new data base concepts, due to the large sized data and its requirements concerning hard- and soft-ware scheduling for connecting to isochronous communication services.

To *integrate video into existing systems* for presentation, solutions being able to compress and decompress video in real-time are needed to cut down exhaustive storage requirements. For homogeneous environments based on DOS or IBM OS/2 such hardware is already available with INTEL's DVI based Technology [6]. Software solutions do exist only for homogeneous or local environments like QuickTime (Apple) or Software Motion Picture (DEC), but standardized solutions are evolving [5].

The full integration of multimedia data into the information structure of DOAs like described in the introduction, requires *further work in the document architectures* concerning document structuring. This is being addressed by different standardization activities like HyperODA in the Open Document Architecture (ODA) arena and Standards like HyTime for the Standardized Generalized Markup Language (SGML) arena [8].

7. Acknowledgements

Our colleague H. Bunz had also been very active in implementing and promoting the DFR standard in the environment of ESPRIT PODA-II and PODA-SAX projects to store ODA documents. This work served as a base for the above described multimedia extensions to DFR, that T. Kröncke made a reality during his Diploma Thesis.

8. Literature

[1] *IBM Audio Visual Connection, Product Documentation,* IBM 1990.

[2] *Interactive Technologies,* CACM Vol.31, No. 7, July 1989.

[3] **ISO/IEC JTC 1/SC 18/WG 4,** *Information Technology - Text and office systems - Document filing and retrieval (DFR),* IS 10161, Juni 1991.

[4] **ISO/IEC JTC 1/SC 18/WG 4,** *Information technology. - Text and office systems - Distributed-office-applications-model,* IS 10031, Juni 1991.

[5] **D. LeGall,** *MPEG: A Video Compression Standard for Multimedia Applications,* CACM, Vol. 34, No. 4, April 1991, pp. 46-58.

[6] **K. Harney et. al.,** *The i750 Video Processor: A Total Multimedia Solution,* CACM Vol. 34, No. 4, April 1991, pp. 64-80.

[7] **D.B. Hehmann, M.G. Salmony, H.J. Stüttgen,** *Transport Services for Multimedia Applications on Broadband Networks,* Computer Communication, Vol. 13, No.4, May 1990.

[8] **S.R. Newcomb, N.A. Kipp, V.T. Newcomb,** *The "HyTime" Hypermedia/Time-based Document Structuring Language,* CACM Vol.34, No. 11, November 1991, pp. 67-83.

[9] **N. Naffah,** *Multimedia applications,* Computer Communications, Vol. 13, No. 4, May 1990.

[10] **Network Working Group,** *Experimental Internet Stream Protocol, Version 2 (ST-II),* CIP Working Group, C. Topolcic (Ed.), RFC 1190, 1990.

[11] **R. Steinmetz, J. Rückert, W. Racke,** *Multimedia-Systeme,* Das aktuelle Schlagwort, Informatik-Spektrum, Bd. 13, Heft 5, Oktober 1990, p.280.

[12] **K. Sauer, M. Tangemann,** *Performance of different Voice Integration Schemes applied to FDDI,* LAN 89, p. 167-172.

Integritätssicherung durch zusammengesetzte Objekte

Gerhard Koschorreck

Institut für Informatik, Universität Hannover
Lange Laube 22, D-W 3000 Hannover 1
gk@informatik.uni-hannover.de

1 Zielsetzung

Der Einsatz objekt-orientierter Techniken ermöglicht es heute, das Verhalten einzelner Objekte durch Programmiersprachenkonstrukte zu beschreiben. In der Programmiersprache Eiffel [Mey92] lassen sich Vor- und Nachbedingungen für die Ausführung von Methoden formulieren, so daß die Konsistenz der Einzelobjekte sichergestellt werden kann. In Datenbanksystemen muß aufgrund der langen Lebensdauer der Anwendungen vermieden werden, Prüfungen auf Integritätsverletzungen in Methoden zu "verstecken".

In Datenbank-Anwendungen ist das Konsistenzproblem von großer praktischer Bedeutung. Es muß nicht nur das Verhalten von Einzelobjekten, sondern auch von Beziehungen zwischen Objekten verschiedener Klassen beschrieben werden. Integritätsbedingungen (IBen) für solche zusammengesetzten Objekte werden deklarativ formuliert und im späteren Entwurfsprozeß in konsistenzerhaltende Methoden umgesetzt. Aufgrund der Langlebigkeit der betrachteten Objekte ist es außerdem erforderlich, bestehende Klassen in neu eingeführten Aggregationen benutzen zu können, ohne die "alten" Klassen verändern zu müssen.

Um später die Einhaltung von Integritätsbedingungen sicherstellen zu können, müssen sie bereits beim Datenbank-Entwurf berücksichtigt werden [Lip92]. In der realen Welt spielen gerade Beziehungen zwischen verschiedenen Objekten eine wichtige Rolle, so daß auf der konzeptionellen Ebene eine Möglichkeit bestehen sollte, solche Aggregationen angemessen zu modellieren. Hierfür soll eine Technik entwickelt werden, wie aus deklarativ formulierten IBen Implementierungen zur Integritätsüberwachung erhalten werden können. Betrachtet man die konzeptionellen Objekte, die Objekte der realen Welt repräsentieren, auch als die Einheiten der Integritätssicherung, so kann die Überwachung von IBen objekt-lokal durchgeführt werden. Auf einen globalen (und daher ineffizienten) Monitor kann verzichtet werden, wenn jedes Objekt die Information, welche Kontrollen durchgeführt werden müssen, in einem Methodenkontext enthält, der durch Meta-Methoden verändert werden kann.

2 Bisherige Ansätze

In objekt-orientierten Programmiersprachen lassen sich Beziehungen zwischen Objekten durch Attribute realisieren, die Referenzen auf andere Objekte enthalten. Diese Technik ist jedoch problematisch, da einerseits die Zeiger konsistent gehalten werden müssen, andererseits Beziehungen von Objekten in der Implementierung dieser Objekte festgeschrieben werden müssen. Die nachträgliche Einführung einer Beziehung kann somit nur durch Neuübersetzung verwirklicht werden (siehe

[Kil91]). Einige objekt-orientierte Datenbanksysteme bieten sog. *inverse relationships* an, mit denen Beziehungen zwischen Objekten verschiedener Klassen modelliert werden können (z.B. [AH90]).

Eine andere Möglichkeit, Beziehungen darzustellen, bietet das ER-Modell. Dort wird klar zwischen den beteiligten Objekten/Entities und den Beziehungen/Relationships unterschieden. Relationships sind jedoch keine Objekte und können daher nicht an anderen Beziehungen teilnehmen.

[AGO91] schlagen vor, sog. *Object-Relationships* zu benutzen, in denen zusammengehörige Objekte verwaltet werden. Die Object-Relationships sorgen für die Einhaltung von (vordefinierten) statischen und transitionalen Integritätsbedingungen. Es ist nicht möglich, eigene Integritätsbedingungen zu formulieren. Des weiteren können keine Methoden auf Object-Relationships definiert werden.

Mit den oben aufgeführten Ansätzen ist es nicht möglich, beliebige Integritätsbedingungen zu formulieren oder Relationships wiederum als Objekte zu behandeln. Problematisch ist zudem, daß die Implementierung von Integritätsbedingungen, die Objekte mehrerer Klassen betreffen, in objekt-orientierten Programmiersprachen auf alle teilnehmenden Klassen verteilt werden muß. Auch Bedingungen, die ein Objekt nur als Teil einer Aggregation betreffen, müssen in der Klassendefinition aufgeführt werden.

Ein weiteres Problem ist die Zuordnung von Methoden, die eine Aggregation betreffen. Meist gibt es kein Kriterium, in welcher der beteiligten Klassen eine solche Methode angesiedelt sein sollte.

3 Zusammengesetzte Objekte

Bei der Modellierung von Beziehungen der realen Welt im Rahmen des Datenbank-Entwurfs ist man bestrebt, die Spezifikation von Integritätsbedingungen, die eine (heterogene) Menge von Objekten betreffen, zwar im konzeptionellen Schema an einer Stelle zusammenzufassen, die Überwachung jedoch weitgehend objekt-lokal durchzuführen, um einen unnötigen Overhead zu vermeiden. Eine objekt-lokale Überwachung bietet sich gerade im objekt-orientierten Ansatz an; ein globaler Monitor wird dann nicht mehr benötigt.

Da die Unterscheidung zwischen Objekten und Aggregationen künstlich erscheint, können in einem allgemeineren Modell Aggregationen ebenfalls durch Objekte realisiert werden. Die Verweise, die sonst innerhalb von Objekten gespeichert werden, werden dann in einem zusammengesetzten Objekt zusammengefaßt. Aggregationen können wiederum Attribute und Methoden besitzen. Es lassen sich auch Aggregationen von Aggregationen modellieren, so daß sich z.B. auch Konstrukte des Higher-Order Entity-Relationship Modells (HERM) von [Tha90] nachbilden lassen. Das oben angeführte Zuordnungsproblem verschwindet, da Methoden für die Aggregation formuliert werden können.

Der Vorteil besteht darin, daß man konzeptionell nur Objekte und Klassen betrachten muß. Geht man davon aus, daß das Verhalten von Objekten durch Axiome beschrieben werden kann, so lassen sich in zusammengesetzten Objekten beliebige Integritätsbedingungen durch entsprechende Axiome formulieren. Diese Bedingungen können sich dabei auch auf Eigenschaften der Komponenten beziehen. Für die deklarativ angegebenen Integritätsbedingungen muß dann eine entsprechende Implementierung gefunden werden.

Das Verhalten zusammengesetzter Objekte wird zunächst durch eine Signatur und eine Menge von Integritätsbedingungen beschrieben. Als Beispiel sollen Mengen von Zählern zusammengefaßt werden, bei denen die Summe der Zählerstände kleiner als eine Maximalsumme (`max_sum`) ist. Ein Aggregationsobjekt kann dann z.B. die folgende Signatur besitzen:

```
objecttype COUNTER_SET (c: COUNTER) =
    sort  cs;
```

```
    method create :          -> cs;
    method max_sum :         -> int;
    method set_max_sum :     int -> ;
    method insert_counter :  c -> ;
    method remove_counter :  c -> ;
    method instances :       -> c set;
end;
```

Der Methodenaufruf `cs1.set_max_sum(100)` kann benutzt werden, um die Maximalsumme einer Zählermenge `cs1` zu setzen.

Die oben genannte Integritätsbedingung läßt sich folgendermaßen formulieren:

$$\forall(\mathtt{x} : \mathtt{cs})\ .\ \mathbf{sum_{bag}}\{\!\!\{\mathbf{apply}(\mathtt{show\_value}, \mathtt{instances})\}\!\!\} < \mathtt{max\_sum}$$

apply wende hierbei eine Methode auf eine Menge von Objekten an; $\mathbf{sum_{bag}}$ summiere alle Werte einer Multimenge.

Aus der angegebenen Integritätsbedingung kann nicht unmittelbar auf eine effiziente Implementierung geschlossen werden. Zu den Aufgaben des Datenbank-Entwurfs gehört es nun, die Spezifikationen der interessierenden Objekte schrittweise zu verfeinern und zu den deklarativ angegebenen IBen eine konkrete Implementierung in einer ausführbaren (Programmier-)Sprache zu finden. In [KL92] gehen wir näher auf diesen Aspekt ein.

Im obigen Beispiel besteht eine Möglichkeit der Prüfung darin, bei jeder Änderung der beteiligten Zählern alle Zählerstände aufzusummieren. Für die Überwachung von Integritätsbedingungen auf Aggregationen können jedoch auch die aus dem relationalen Modell bekannten Optimierungstechniken benutzt werden, z.B. [QW86]. Dies führt dazu, daß bei Änderungen ein (nach außen nicht sichtbares) Attribut `sum` des Aggregationsobjektes verändert wird. In `sum` ist dann die Summe der Zählerstände der beteiligten Komponenten gespeichert. Aus der zu Beginn formulierten IB können also zwei neue, äquivalente Bedingungen gewonnen werden. Die erste Bedingung betrifft den Wert des Summenattributes:

$$\forall(\mathtt{x} : \mathtt{cs})\ .\ \mathtt{sum} = \mathbf{sum_{bag}}\{\!\!\{\mathbf{apply}(\mathtt{show\_value}, \mathtt{instances})\}\!\!\}$$

Die zweite Bedingung legt den Zusammenhang zwischen dem Summenattribut und der Maximalsumme fest:

$$\forall(\mathtt{x} : \mathtt{cs})\ .\ \mathtt{sum} < \mathtt{max\_sum}$$

Diese Bedingungen für die Methodenausführung müssen in eine möglichst effiziente Implementierung umgewandelt werden.

Aggregationen mit Integritätsbedingungen können wiederum Komponenten in anderen Aggregationen sein. Faßt man die Zähler als Einzelpositionen eines Haushaltstitels auf, so können verschiedene solcher Haushaltstitel zu einem Haushaltsplan zusammengefaßt werden, für den dann wiederum IBen, d.h. Haushaltsregeln, aufgestellt werden können.

```
objecttype BUDGET (cs: COUNTER_SET) =
    sort   budget;
    method create :          -> budget;
    method title :           -> string;
    method budget_section :  -> cs set;

    constraint ...
end;
```

4 Überwachung von Integritätsbedingungen

Das Verhalten eines Objektes, das in einer Aggregation enthalten ist, kann durch den Zustand der anderen Komponenten beeinflußt werden, da alle Objekte zusammen Integritätsbedingungen erfüllen müssen. Um derartige kontextabhängige Bedingungen überwachen zu können, wurde von Turski vorgeschlagen, Aktionen von *pre-* und *postguards* zu kontrollieren ([Tur91], [Tur92]). Diese Methode kann für objekt-orientierte Systeme erweitert werden.

In objekt-orientierten Datenbanksystemen erfolgt die Überwachung von Integritätsbedingungen üblicherweise durch die Methoden der beteiligten Objekte. Führt man für Aggregationen keine eigenen Objekte ein, so steht man vor dem Problem, in einer Klasse Integritätsbedingungen formulieren zu müssen, die andere Klassen betreffen ([KLS91]). Klassen sind also nicht mehr voneinander unabhängig, was zu Problemen bei der Einführung neuer Aggregationen führt, da ggf. bestehende Klassendefinitionen verändert werden müssen.

Diese Schwierigkeiten lassen sich beseitigen, wenn man Aggregationen als eigenständige Objekte betrachtet, die die beteiligten Komponenten modifizieren können. Hierbei können die vom relationalen Modell her bekannten Triggermechanismen (z.B. [Kot89]) auf den objekt-orientierten Fall erweitert werden. Es ist zu prüfen, welche Methoden der an einer Aggregation beteiligten Objekte eine Integritätsverletzung hervorrufen können. Für diese Methoden muß eine Implementierung angegeben werden, die sicherstellt, daß die Integritätsbedingungen eingehalten werden. Hierbei kann die Implementierung Komponenten aus mehreren Klassen betreffen; es ist jedoch nicht sinnvoll, den Code auf diese Klassen zu verteilen, da er nur dann ausgeführt werden muß, wenn ein Objekt Teil einer Aggregation geworden ist.

Um dieses Ziel zu erreichen, wird der Methodenaufruf-Mechanismus modifiziert. Wird ein Objekt Teil einer Aggregation, z.B. durch Aufruf der Methode `insert_counter` im obigen Beispiel, so werden die Methoden, die eine Integritätsverletzung herbeiführen können, um einen *Methodenkontext* erweitert. Der Methodenkontext beinhaltet nun Aufrufe von Methoden, die im Aggregationsobjekt angegeben worden sind.

Die im Beispiel angegebene Integritätsbedingung läßt sich überprüfen, indem zunächst ein Vergleich mit dem privaten Attribut `sum` durchgeführt wird; falls die Bedingung nicht erfüllt wird, gelangt man in einen Ausnahmezustand, andernfalls muß `sum` entsprechend modifiziert werden.

Für die Überwachung der Integritätsbedingung und die Aktualisierung des Summenattributs werden zwei Methoden definiert:

```
pre_increment(x:int) is
  if x + sum > max
  then raise exception increment_failure
end;

post_increment(x:int) is
  sum := sum + x
end;
```

Wird ein Zähler Bestandteil einer Zählermenge, so muß der Methodenkontext dieses Objektes angereichert werden. Dies geschieht unter Verwendung von *Meta-Methoden*, die es erlauben, Objekte zu modifizieren. Analog gibt es Meta-Methoden, die den Methodenkontext eines Objektes reduzieren. Dies ist im Beispiel erforderlich, wenn ein Zähler aus einer Zählermenge entfernt wird.

```
insert_counter(c:counter) is
    ...
    enrich_pre_action(c, increment, pre_increment);
    enrich_post_action(c, increment, post_increment);
    ...
end;
```

Für einen Zähler c muß die increment-Methode kontrolliert werden; daher wird festgelegt, daß vor ihrer Ausführung die Methode pre_increment aufgerufen werden soll. Trat hierbei kein Fehler auf, soll nach Ausführung der increment-Methode das Summenattribut nachgeführt werden (post_increment).

Im allgemeinen Fall ist von den an einer Aggregation beteiligten Komponenten nur ihre Signatur bekannt, so daß nicht die konkrete Implementierung von Methoden verändert werden kann. Für jede Methode eines Objektes, das an einer Beziehung beteiligt ist, gibt es nun einen dynamisch veränderlichen Kontext, der angibt, welche Mengen von Operationen vor bzw. nach der eigentlichen Methode ausgeführt werden müssen. Dieser Kontext ändert sich, wenn das Objekt in eine neue Beziehung eintritt oder aus einer solchen entfernt wird.

Wird die Methode m eines Objektes o aufgerufen, so wird zunächst jede Methode der pre_actions ausgeführt. Falls hierbei eine Integritätsverletzung festgestellt wird, wird die Ausführung der Methode abgebrochen. Anschließend wird die Methode m selbst ausgeführt. Dann kommen alle Methoden der post_actions zur Ausführung. Die im Kontext benutzten Methoden müssen Parameter des gleichen Typs wie m besitzen.

Mit Hilfe des Methodenkontextes lassen sich sowohl optimistische wie auch pessimistische Verfahren implementieren. Für ein optimistisches Verfahren werden keine pre_actions angegeben; die Methode wird direkt ausgeführt. Anschließend kann in den post_actions die Prüfung auf Integritätsverletzungen durchgeführt werden. Bei pessimistischen Verfahren erfolgt die Prüfung auf Integritätsverletzungen vor der eigentlichen Methodenausführung.

Im Common Lisp Object System (CLOS) können Methoden aus Teilstücken zusammengesetzt werden. Durch diese *Methoden-Kombination* kann das Verhalten von Objekten angepaßt werden (siehe [GWB91]). Mit Hilfe des Meta-Objekt-Protokolls lassen sich Methodenkontexte für Objekte realisieren.

Ein Objekt kann an mehreren Beziehungen beteiligt sein, ohne daß an seiner Klassendefinition etwas geändert werden müßte:

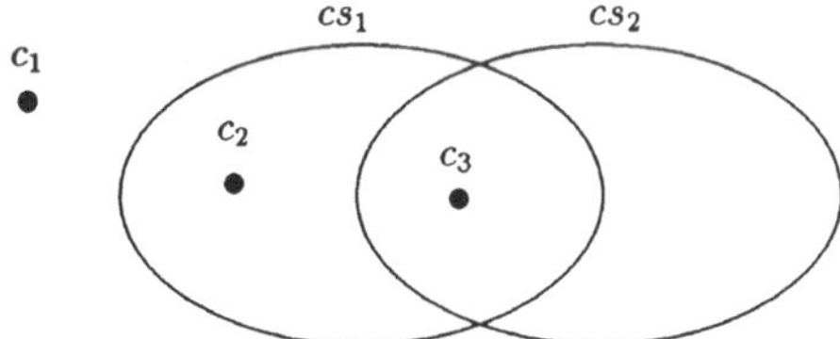

In dieser Situation braucht für den Zähler c_1 überhaupt keine Integritätsbedingung getestet werden, da das Objekt an keiner Aggregation teilnimmt; der Methodenkontext für die increment-Methode ist leer. Für c_2 muß eine Bedingung, für c_3 müssen zwei Bedingungen geprüft werden.

Neben den Methoden, die Zählerstände verändern, muß in der Aggregation natürlich auch geprüft werden, ob durch die Methode insert_counter die IB verletzt wird.

Falls statt einer maximalen eine minimale Summe sichergestellt werden soll, so muß neben dem Entfernen eines Zählers aus einer Zählermenge auch das Löschen eines Zählers überwacht werden. Ein Zähler darf solange nicht gelöscht werden, wie dadurch eine Integritätsverletzung auftritt.

Allgemein brauchen nur bei den Objekten Bedingungen geprüft werden, die auch an Aggregationen beteiligt sind. Der Aufwand, der z.B. im relationalen Modell dadurch entsteht, daß zunächst festgestellt werden muß, welche Tupel einer Relation nach einer Änderung überhaupt geprüft werden müssen, entfällt. Die Überwachung von Integritätsbedingungen kann also objekt-lokal durchgeführt werden. Ein globaler Monitor, der alle Einfügungen, Löschungen oder Änderungen überwacht, ist nicht erforderlich.

Während auf der konzeptionellen Ebene die Integritätsbedingungen für Aggregationen spezifiziert werden und dort auch der Code für die Überwachung zusammengefaßt wird, findet die Kontrolle auf Integritätsverletzungen zur Laufzeit in den beteiligten Komponenten statt. Dies stellt einen entscheidenden Vorteil zu bisherigen Ansätzen dar, da die Codierung von integritätssichernden Maßnahmen für Objekte mehrerer Klassen nicht auf verschiedene Klassen verteilt werden muß.

In unserem Ansatz werden zudem Klassendefinitionen nicht mit Implementierungsdetails überfrachtet, die einerseits möglicherweise gar nicht alle Objekte der Klasse betreffen und andererseits für die Verwendung der Objekte nicht erheblich sind.

Durch die Verwendung eines Methodenkontextes können Objekte auch zur Laufzeit noch in neue Aggregationen eingefügt oder aus ihnen entfernt werden, für die Integritätsbedingungen formuliert werden können. Dies ist insbesondere für Datenbank-Anwendung von Bedeutung, da die gespeicherten Informationen tendenziell langlebig sind. Die Erweiterbarkeit ist hier besonders wichtig.

5 Zusammenfassung und Ausblick

Während bei einer Implementierung mit Referenzen eine dynamische Änderung von Beziehungen nicht möglich ist, lassen sich diese durch zusammengesetzte Objekte problemlos modellieren. Gerade diese Flexibilität, Objekte zur Laufzeit in durch Integritätsbedingungen kontrollierte Aggregationen aufnehmen oder entfernen zu können, ermöglicht es, die reale Welt adäquat nachzubilden.

Objekte werden um einen Methodenkontext erweitert, der festlegt, welche Methoden vor bzw. nach dem eigentlichen Aufruf einer Methode auszuführen sind. In Aggregationen kann nun festgelegt werden, wie einzelne Methoden angereichert werden müssen, um Integritätsverletzungen auszuschließen. Es ist hierzu nicht erforderlich, die Klassendefinition der Komponenten zu modifizieren, so daß auch Objekte bereits bestehender Klassen Komponenten einer neu definierten Aggregation werden können.

Die Verwendung des Methodenkontextes erlaubt weiterhin eine effizientere Integritätsüberwachung als durch einen globalen Monitor, da nur bei den Objekten Integritätsprüfungen durchgeführt werden müssen, die auch an einer Aggregation beteiligt sind.

Die hier vorgestellte Methode eignet sich u.a. zur Überwachung dynamischer Integritätsbedingungen. Die Informationen, in welcher Situation sich ein Objekt in seinem Lebenslauf befindet, können in Aggregationsobjekten gehalten werden. Ziel weiterer Forschung wird daher sein, eine Methodik zu entwickeln, aus Transitionsgraphen ([Lip89]), die Objektlebensläufe beschreiben, Ansätze zur Implementierung integritätssichernder Methoden zu finden.

Zum anderen muß eine formale Semantik entwickelt werden, um die Umsetzung von Vor- und Nachbedingungen in entsprechende Methoden korrekt beschreiben zu können. Anzustreben ist eine Vorgehensweise, wie sie in [San90] beschrieben wird: Aus deklarativ angegebenen Integritätsbedingungen wird schrittweise, durch immer weitere Verfeinerung eine Implementierung abgeleitet, wobei für jeden Schritt die Korrektheit beweisbar sein sollte.

Literatur

[AGO91] A. Albano, G. Ghelli, R. Orsini: A Relationship Mechanism for a Strongly Typed Object-Oriented Database Programming Language. In G. M. Lohmann, A. Sernadas, R. Camps (eds.), *Proceedings of the 17th Int. Conf. on Very Large Data Bases - 1991*, 565–575, Morgan Kaufmann Publishers, 1991.

[AH90] T. Andrews, C. Harris: Combining Language and Database Advances in an Object-Oriented Development Environment. In S. Zdonik, D. Maier (eds.), *Readings in Object-Oriented Databases*, 186–196. Morgan-Kaufmann Publishers, 1990.

[GWB91] R. P. Gabriel, J. L. White, D. G. Bobrow: CLOS: Integrating Object-Oriented and Functional Programming. *Communications of the ACM 34:9 (September 1991)*, 28–38.

[Kil91] M. F. Kilian: A Note on Type Composition and Reusability. *OOPS Messenger 2:3 (April 1991)*, 24–32.

[KL92] G. Koschorreck, U. W. Lipeck: Integritätssicherung durch lokale Methoden. Interner Bericht, Institut für Informatik, Universität Hannover (eingereicht), 1992.

[KLS91] W. Kim, Y.-J. Lee, J. Seo: An Overview of Integrity Management in Object-Oriented Databases. *Data Engineering 14:2 (June 1991)*, 38–42.

[Kot89] A. Kotz: *Triggermechanismen in Datenbanksystemen*. Informatik-Fachberichte 201. Springer, 1989.

[Lip89] U. W. Lipeck: *Dynamische Integrität von Datenbanken: Grundlagen der Spezifikation und Überwachung*. Informatik-Fachberichte 209. Springer, Berlin, 1989.

[Lip92] U. W. Lipeck: Integritätszentrierter Datenbank-Entwurf. *EMISA Forum 2 (1992)*, 41–55.

[Mey92] B. Meyer: *Eiffel — The Language*. Prentice Hall, Hempel Hempstead, 1992.

[QW86] X. Qian, G. Wiederhold: Knowledge-based Integrity Constraint Validation. In *Proceedings of the 12th Int. Conf. on Very Large Data Bases — Kyoto, 1986*, 3–12, August 1986.

[San90] D. Sannella. Formal Programm Development in Extended ML for the Working Programmer, 1990. appeared: Proc. 3rd BCS/FACS Workshop on Refinement, Hursley Park, 1990. Springer Workshops in Computing, 99-130 (1991).

[Tha90] B. Thalheim: Extending the Entity-Relationship Model for a High-Level, Theory-Based Database Design. In J. W. Schmidt, A. A. E. Stogny (eds.), *Next Generation Information System Technology*, 161–184, Springer, 1990.

[Tur91] W. M. Turski: Prescribing Behaviours. *Theoretical Computer Science 90:1 (November 1991)*, 119–125.

[Tur92] W. M. Turski: Extending the Computing Paradigm. *Structured Programming 13:1 (1992)*, 1–9.

Eine Datenanfragesprache für den praktischen Umgang mit vorläufigen Daten in und zwischen eng kooperierenden Gruppen[1]

Thomas Kirsche
Universität Erlangen-Nürnberg
Martensstraße 3, 8520 Erlangen
kirsche@informatik.uni-erlangen.de

Zusammenfassung

Konventionelle Datenbanksysteme unterstützen kooperative Arbeit nur unzureichend. Defizite ergeben sich im Umgang mit vorläufigen Daten (Datenrepräsentation) und durch das klassische Transaktionskonzept (Datenverarbeitung). Die Gültigkeit der Daten wird durch committed und uncommitted festgelegt. Das Commit selbst trägt dabei die Bedeutung einer Freigabe und einer Festlegung gleichzeitig. Lange andauerende Entwurfszyklen, die die konsistenzerhaltende Auflösung der Isolation benötigen, sind nicht realisiert. Problemlösezyklen (problem solving activities, PSAs) legen einen Kooperationskontext fest, der lange dauern kann, konsistenzerhaltend ist und die Freigabe- und Festlegungsbedeutung des Commit entkoppelt. In diesem Beitrag wird das PSA-Daten- und -Verarbeitungsmodell vorgestellt, das die Kooperation in und zwischen eng kooperierenden Gruppen mit Hilfe der Datenanfragesprache CSQL (Cooperative SQL) ermöglicht. Ziel bei der Konzeption ist eine möglichst weitreichende Systemunterstützung für Datenbankbenutzer und -anwendungen.

1 Einleitung und Problemstellung

Datenbanken dienen der anwendungsneutralen Abspeicherung von Daten, die von vielen Benutzern oder Anwendungen gleichzeitig verwendet werden können. Das Datenbanksystem regelt den mehrfachen Zugriff in der Weise, daß keine inkonsistenten und veralteten Datenwerte für die einzelne Anwendung sichtbar werden. Dies wird durch die Realisierung eines Konzeptes erreicht, das unter dem Namen ACID-Transaktionskonzept (Atomarität, Konsistenz, Isolation, Dauerhaftigkeit) bekannt geworden ist [Gray81, HäRe83]. Das ACID-Konzept ist für ingenieurtechnische Anwendungen nur bedingt geeignet. Im Gegensatz z.B. zu Debit/Credit-Buchungen erstrecken sich die Phasen der technischen Produktentwicklung über Tage und Wochen. Weiterhin fallen während der Entwicklungsphase vorläufige und ungenaue Daten an, die in einer Projektdatenbank abgelegt werden sollen. Heute übliche Lösungen für solche technischen Datenbanken verfolgen einen stark anwendungsabhängigen Weg, der langandauernde Transaktionen außerhalb der Datenbank verwaltet und durch Zusatzinformationen die Gültigkeit der Projektdaten näher beschreibt. Die Interpretation von zusätzlicher Information allein in einer Anwendung (und nicht durch das Datenbanksystem) steht im Widerspruch zur postulierten Anwendungsneutralität. Gesucht sind daher Datenbankmechanismen, die diese Zusatzinformationen zum kontrollierten Austausch von vorläufigen Daten unterstützen. Die Mechanismen müssen dann in Form einer Datenanfragesprache zugänglich gemacht werden. Kapitel 2 dieses Beitrags stellt wesentliche Probleme bei der Repräsentation von vorläufigen Daten im relationalen Modell vor. In Kapitel 3 wird das Daten- und Verarbeitungsmodell eines Datenbanksystems zur Unterstützung der angesprochenen Problemstellungen umrissen. Kapitel 4 führt die Datenanfragesprache CSQL (Cooperative SQL) ein.

2 Repräsentation von unsicheren Daten im Relationenmodell

Bei der Interpretation von Queries auf vorläufigen bzw. unsicheren Daten in relationalen Datenbanken stehen nach [ImLi84] zwei Forderungen an die Anfragesprache im Mittelpunkt: Zum einen dürfen durch die (suk-

1. Teile der hier vorgestellten Arbeiten wurden im Rahmen des Sonderforschungsbereichs 182 "Multiprozessor- und Netzwerkkonfiguration" durchgeführt.

zessive) Anwendung der bereitgestellten Operatoren keine falschen Aussagen ableitbar sein. Zum anderen müssen die Operatoren aber so vollständig sein, daß alle sicher gültigen Aussagen auch tatsächlich abgeleitet werden können. In der ersten Forderung enthalten ist die semantisch korrekte Interpretation von Queries, die Tautologien enthalten: Auch wenn keinerlei Information über die Farbe eines Objekts vorliegt, ist es doch sicher, daß es sich in der Bedingung "WHERE farbe = 'rot' OR NOT (farbe = 'rot')" qualifiziert.

Codds klassischer Nullwert-Ansatz erfüllt diese Forderungen nicht. Die in [ImLi84] vorgestellten V-Tables mit unterscheidbaren Nullwerten kommen den aufgestellten Forderungen näher, weil sie alle Operationen bis auf die negative Selektion (Queries, die NOT enthalten) erlauben. Völlig erfüllt werden die Forderungen nur durch Conditional Tables, bei denen die Gültigkeit jedes Tupels durch eine Bedingung angegeben werden kann. Conditional Tables werden jedoch als theoretischer, nicht handhabbarer Ansatz bezeichnet ([ImLi84]). In der Neuauflage des Relationenmodells RM/V2, das sich intensiv mit Nullwerten auseinandersetzt ([Codd90], Kapitel 8 und 9), wird die Fehlinterpretation von Tautologien hingenommen. Einige Ansätze gehen von der Abgeschlossenheit des Modells unter der relationalen Operationen ab, indem "sichere" und "mögliche" Treffermengen von Queries ermittelt werden oder dem Benutzer die Interpretation des Ergebnisses überlassen (surely-Operator von [Lips79]). Eine aktuelle Übersicht über die Behandlung von unsicheren Daten in relationalen Systemen bietet [Morr90]. Die Erweiterung des Mengenbegriffs durch Fuzzy Sets erweitert die inhärenten Beschränkungen auch den neuen Modells RM/V2 in der Repräsentation (Übersicht in [YGBP92]). Außerhalb des Relationenmodells, aber mit ähnlichen Zielsetzungen in Repräsentation und Manipulation von vorläufigen Daten bewegen sich objektorientierte Datenmodelle. In [Zica90] werden unvollständige Schemata und Instanzen modelliert, sog. hypothetische Anfragen in [ImNV91] vorgestellt.

3 PSA-Daten- und -Verarbeitungsmodell

Der folgende Abschnitt geht auf die Merkmale des PSA-Daten- und -Verarbeitungsmodells für Problemlösezyklen ein. Dabei werden die Unterschiede zu den Ansätzen aus Kapitel 2 herausgearbeitet und die Besonderheiten des eingeschlagenen Wegs aufgezeigt. Die Merkmale des PSA-Modells ist der Verzicht auf Bewertungsmetriken für Unsicherheitsgrade, die systemüberwachte Veränderung der Daten hin zu "sichereren" Werten und die Einbeziehung der Datenbankbenutzer da, wo die einseitige, isolierte Bewertung durch das Datenbanksystem nicht mehr möglich ist. Daten- und Verarbeitungsmodell werden überblicksartig eingeführt. An anderer Stelle [JRRW90, JRRW91, Wede93] wird auf die theoretischen Grundlagen eingegangen und in [JBKR92] die Anwendung auf ein Szenario aus der Automobilentwicklung beschrieben.

3.1 Charakteristika

Die Bewertung von Ausprägungsalternativen mit einer Metrik, wie sie z.B. die Zugehörigkeitsfunktion in der Theorie der Fuzzy Sets vornimmt, erlaubt bei geeigneter Wahl der Operatoren die Kombination der Alternativen in einer abgeschlossenen Algebra. Damit sind Fragen nach der "wahrscheinlichsten" Ausprägung oder den "möglichen" Alternativen beantwortbar, vorausgesetzt, die elementaren Bewertungen reflektieren die modellierte Welt genügend. In der Praxis ist die numerische Gewichtung von Alternativen im Entwicklungszyklus jedoch selten ([JBKR92]). Sie werden eher durch unscharfe Termini wie "sicher" oder "vorgeschlagen" und in administrativen Freigabestufen voneinander abgegrenzt. Formales Gerüst für die unscharfe Prädikation von Aussagen (Datenausprägungen sind Aussagen) ist die Modallogik. Allerdings muß eine anwendungsnahe Interpretation geschaffen werden. Das PSA-Modell führt daher die Prädikate Zusicherung und Vorschlag ein, mit denen jeweils eine Menge von Alternativen auf Datenebene bewertet werden.

Eine weitere Beobachtung der technischen Entwicklungsarbeit ergab ([JBKR92]), daß die Bearbeitung von Entwicklungsaufgaben in Gruppen erfolgt. Während die Mitglieder einer Gruppe über (Teil-)Aufgaben und Ziele gegenseitig gut informiert sind, ist dies zwischen Mitgliedern verschiedener Gruppen nicht der Fall. Durch die enge Bindung der Gruppenmitglieder wird eine kooperierende Aufgabenbearbeitung möglich, bei der Schutzmechanismen eher hinderlich sind. Bei der gruppenübergreifenden Zusammenarbeit muß der Informationsaustausch jedoch in kontrollierter Weise erfolgen. An die Verläßlichkeit der Daten werden höhere Ansprüche gestellt. Das PSA-Modell trägt diesem Verhalten Rechnung, indem ein Gruppenbegriff eingeführt wird. Differenzierte, kontextabhängige Rechte regeln den Zugriff inner- und außerhalb der Gruppen auf unterschiedliche Weise.

Die Einbeziehung der Datenbankbenutzer findet im PSA-Modell durch Verhandlungen und durch Benachrichtigungen bei widersprüchlichen Datenentwicklungen statt. Wenn beispielsweise eine neue Zusicherung einer bestehenden Zusicherung widerspricht, können Verhandlungen ausgelöst werden. Der Ablauf der Verhandlung ist entweder automatisiert oder interaktiv. Eine Verhandlung ohne Zutun der Datenbankbenutzer wird mit installierten Verhandlungsstrategien realisert, das sind vor- oder benutzerdefinierte Funktionen, die Angebote bewerten und neue erzeugen. Interaktive Verhandlungen erfordern die Anwesenheit der Datenbankbenutzer und deren manuelle Reaktion innerhalb eines Zeitlimits. Benachrichtigungen lösen ähnlich wie Trigger bei Veränderungen eines spezifizierten Datums aus, kennen als einzige Aktion jedoch nur synchrone oder asynchrone Benachrichtigungen, z.B. per E-Mail.

3.2 Datenmodell (1)

Das PSA-Datenmodell für vorläufige Daten ist eine Erweiterung des relationalen Modells. Damit können die herkömmlichen Aussagen über Datenobjekte, nämlich committed oder uncommitted, durch Prädikate so verfeinert werden, daß verschiedene Gültigkeitsstufen ausdrückbar sind. Entscheidend ist, daß das Datenbanksystem die Semantik der Prädikate "kennt" und somit Kontrollen und Folgeaktionen in Zusammenhang mit der Gültigkeit der Daten durchführen kann.

Anleihen für das PSA-Datenmodell sind der Modallogik [HuCr68] entnommen (siehe unten). In der klassischen Modallogik werden vier Prädikate auf Aussagen eingeführt, die meist als notwendig, möglich, nicht notwendig und nicht möglich bezeichnet werden. Anstatt einfacher Aussagen der klassischen zweiwertigen Logik, die entweder falsch oder wahr sind, kann nun weiter differenziert werden, z.B. die Möglichkeit oder Notwendigkeit einer wahren oder falschen Aussage spezifiziert werden. Das PSA-Modell bleibt in der zweiwertigen Logik, verwaltet aber Prädikate auf der Ebene der elementaren Attributwerte: Einerseits können mit den Prädikaten nun differenzierte Aussagen hinsichtlich der Gültigkeit eines Datums formuliert werden, andererseits evaluieren Bedingungen über den Prädikaten in Queries zu TRUE oder FALSE. Die Abgeschlossenheit unter den Operationen ist so gewährleistet.

Das PSA-Modell erlaubt, inspiriert durch die Modallogik, Prädikate auf Datenwerten. Anders als in der Modallogik handelt es sich jedoch nicht um Metaprädikate, sondern primär um eine bestimmte Form der Darstellung vorläufiger Information auf Datenebene. Da zwischen den prädizierten Mengen aber auch Abhängigkeiten in Form von Integritätsbedingungen bestehen, sind die Prädikate sekundär zur Metaebene zu zählen. Als anwendungsnahe Interpretation der Prädikate werden "Zusicherung" und "Vorschlag" herangezogen. Die üblichen Basisdatentypen des Relationenmodells (Ganz- und Gleitkommazahlen, Zeichenketten, Datum, usw.) erhalten die Struktur aus Abbildung 1. Bei jedem Datum gibt die Menge der Zusicherungen an, in welchem Bereich der Datenwert liegen wird. Die Menge der Vorschläge enthält Elemente, die als mögliche Datenwerte betrachtet werden. Beide Mengen können den ganzen Wertebereich umfassen. Integritätsbedingungen sichern nach außen die Konsistenz des Datenobjektes. Beispielsweise muß ein Vorschlag immer in der Menge der erlaubten Werte (Zusicherungsmenge) sein. Die ein-elementige Zusicherungsmenge als Sonderfall drückt das Prädikat committed aus. Enthält die Zusicherungsmenge alle Elemente des Wertebereichs, ist das eine Form des uncommitted.

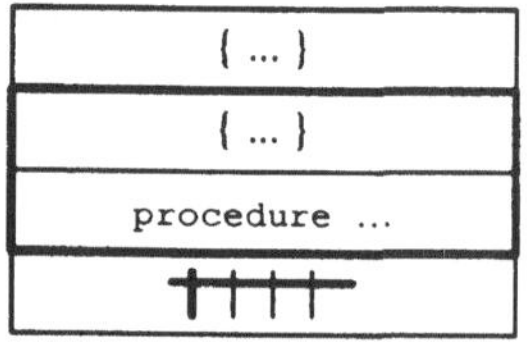

Abb. 1: Struktur eines Basisdatentyps

Die in Abbildung 1 zusätzlichen genannten Elemente Verhandlungsstrategie und Access Control List werden in Abschnitt 3.4 eingeführt.

3.3 Verarbeitungsmodell

Jedem Datenbanksystem liegt eine bestimmte Vorstellung über die Konsistenz der Datenbank zugrunde, d.h. in welchen logischen Einheiten Datenzugriffe möglich sind, wie der Zugriff mehrerer Benutzer geregelt ist, welche Ausfallsicherheit realisiert wird, usw. Das ACID-Konzept legt z.B. fest, daß alle Datenmanipulationen innerhalb von Transaktionen erfolgen und Änderungen erst am Ende der Transaktion sichtbar werden. Vorläufige Werte innerhalb einer laufenden Transaktion sind nicht sichtbar, um andere Transaktionen von der Nutzung dieser Daten abzuhalten und damit die Konsistenz der Datenbank nicht zu gefährden. Am Ende einer Transaktion werden meist mit den neuen Daten die alten Daten überschrieben, so daß der Eindruck entsteht, es können Daten geändert werden. Richtiger ist, daß eine neue Version erzeugt wird und die alte Version (im normalen Datenbankbetrieb) unwiederbringlich verloren ist. Jim Gray prangert in einem berühmt gewordenen Aufsatz die Gefährlichkeit des sog. Update-in-place als poison apple für die Fehlerbehandlung an, da die Änderungshistorie verloren geht ([Gray81]). Als weitere Konsequenz des Update-in-place erhält das Commit am Transaktionsende eine Doppelbedeutung, nämlich die *Freigabe* von Datenwerten zur Erzeugung einer neuen Version und die verbindliche *Festlegung* von Datenwerten als Ergebnis einer Transaktion.

Im PSA-Verarbeitungsmodell werden Freigabe und verbindliche Festlegung getrennt. Der Zugriff auf alle Daten erfolgt in einem genau spezifizierten Kontext, der als Problemlösezyklus (problem solving activity, PSA) bezeichnet wird. Der Kontext ist definiert in dem Sinne, daß stets klar ist, welche Datenwerte zu welchem Grad und von wem freigegeben oder festgelegt sind. An die PSA ist auch eine Gruppe von eng kooperierenden Benutzern gekoppelt. Benutzer der gleichen PSA haben andere Kooperationsmöglichkeiten als Anwendungen, die nicht zur PSA gehören. Verschiedene Problemlösezyklen bezeichnen verschiedene Kontexte. Sie sind nicht-atomare, konsistenz-erhaltende, nicht-isolierte, beliebig langandauernde und möglicherweise geschachtelte Kontrollsphären ([Davi78]), deren Datenänderungen erst an ihrem Ende dauerhaft werden. Problemlösezyklen unterstützen die Datenbankbenutzer systematisch beim Übergang von einer Version zur anderen, indem sie innerhalb von PSAs differenzierte Datenzustände zwischen alter und neuer Version erlauben und die Übergänge explizit überwachen. Während eine PSA den Kontext der Datenmanipulation festlegt, findet die eigentliche Datenmanipulation in kurzen, atomaren Arbeitseinheiten statt (atomic units of work, AUWs). AUWs sind ACID-Transaktionen mit der zusätzlichen Eigenschaft, daß die Kontrolle über die in der AUW benötigten Daten von der sie unmittelbar umgebenden PSA geholt werden und nach dem Commit (oder Abort) am Ende der AUW ausschließlich an sie zurückgegeben werden. Die PSA ermöglicht oder unterbindet die Weitergabe der Datenwerte an andere PSAs und schafft die Voraussetzungen für eine Kooperation zwischen PSAs. Alle Benutzer einer Datenbank arbeiten ausschließlich mit AUWs innerhalb von PSA-Kontexten auf dem Datenbestand. Das Ende einer AUW entspricht der Freigabe (die weiter differenziert wird, Abschnitt 3.4); das Ende einer PSA bedeutet eine Festlegung, d.h. Einbringung einer Version in die Datenbank.

3.4 Datenmodell (2)

Die Zusicherungsmenge einer PSA/AUW kann in einer anderen PSA/AUW verläßlich benutzt werden, wie ein mit commit freigegebener Wert am Ende einer ACID-Transaktion. Daher darf eine Zusicherung nur so geändert werden, daß die neue Zusicherung eine genauere Bestimmung der alten ist, d.h. eine Teilmenge. Die Änderung von Vorschlägen ist dagegen prinzipiell erlaubt, da keine Anwendung von deren Verläßlichkeit ausgehen darf. Um Änderungen von Vorschlägen differenziert einbringen zu können, wird über Annahme oder Ablehnung von Änderungswünschen mit Hilfe einer Verhandlungsstrategie (Abschnitt 4.6) entschieden, die bei jedem Datum installiert wird (Abbildung 1). Eine Verhandlungsstrategie ist ein Prozedur, die über die Annahme von Änderungsvorschlägen entscheidet. Damit kann so etwas wie die "Güte" von Vorschlägen unterschieden werden, indem die Annahme von Änderungen z.B. von der Einhaltung von Toleranzgrenzen abhängig gemacht oder die Teilmengeneigenschaft mit dem bisherigen Vorschlag überprüft wird.

Der Zugriff auf Daten wird üblicherweise durch zwei Mechanismen beschränkt. Zugriffsrechte, wie sie z.B. mit dem SQL-Befehl GRANT vergeben werden, spezifizieren die Möglichkeiten der Datenmanipulation. Ob der gewünschte Zugriff zu einem bestimmten Zeitpunkt innerhalb einer Transaktion möglich ist, hängt dann noch von der Kompatibilität mit evtl. gesetzten Sperren ab. Diese Vorstellungen werden im PSA-Datenmodell in zwei Richtungen erweitert. Zum einen werden Lese- und Schreibrechte nicht nur für das einzelne Datum geführt, sondern getrennt für Zusicherung, Vorschlag und Verhandlungsstrategie. Zum anderen wird ein verlängerter Sperrmechanismus realisiert, mit dem eine AUW Sperren von einer PSA erhalten und an eine PSA zurückgeben kann. Insbesondere können damit Rechte reserviert werden. Ein Datum kann z.B. innerhalb einer PSA über das Ende der AUW hinaus völlig gesperrt bleiben oder selektiv für Zusicherungen und Vorschläge zum Lesen und Schreiben für andere freigegeben werden. Damit werden neben Zusicherungen, Vorschlägen und Verhandlungsstrategien als viertes noch Zugriffsrechte und reservierte Rechte in einer Access Control List bei jedem Datum abgelegt (Abbildung 1).

4 Datenanfragesprache CSQL

Die Datenanfragesprache CSQL (Cooperative SQL) lehnt sich an SQL an, verfügt aber über zusätzliche Anweisungen, beispielsweise für den Umgang mit Problemlösezyklen und AUWs. CSQL ist für den eingebetteten Gebrauch in einer Wirtssprache entworfen. Die Datenanfragesprache wird nachfolgend anhand eines Beispiels eingeführt, indem eine Personalrelation erzeugt, mit einigen Tupeln gefüllt und abgefragt wird. Alle Datenmanipulationen finden innerhalb von PSAs bzw. AUWs statt. Der Kern von CSQL liegt in der Kooperation zwischen mehreren PSAs, die durch die Weitergabe von vorläufigen Daten, Verhandlungen und Benachrichtigungen charakterisiert ist.

In einem Prototyp wurde ein Präcompiler für die Wirtssprache C realisiert. Der auf den UNIX-Werkzeugen Lex und Yacc aufgebaute Präcompiler erzeugt Funktionsaufrufe der Wirtssprache, die aus Deklarationen, der eigentlichen Ausführungsanweisung und Funktionen zur Fehlerlokalisierung bestehen. Das PSA-System wurde in der Programmiersprache C unter dem Betriebssystem VAX/VMS realisiert. Es ist als Zusatzebene auf das relationale Datenbanksystem Rdb von Digital aufgesetzt.

4.1 Kooperationsmöglichkeiten in CSQL – Überblick

Die Kooperation zwischen Datenbankbenutzern wird in CSQL durch folgende Mechanismen und Ausdrucksmittel erreicht. An erster Stelle steht die Zuordnung alle DML-Anweisungen zu PSAs und AUWs und damit die Festlegung eines komplexen Ausführungskontextes. Mit der Unterteilung der Attribute in Zusicherungen, Vorschläge, Verhandlungsstrategien usw. kann wesentlich mehr Semantik als herkömmlich an die Datenwerte geknüpft werden, was die schrittweise Festlegung vorläufiger Werte ermöglicht. Benachrichtigungen dienen zur Einbeziehung von Benutzern bei nicht (vollständig) automatisierbaren Abläufen. Verhandlungsstrategien sind benutzerdefinierbare Funktionen zur automatisierten Verhandlungsführung. Eine Menge von Standardstrategien definiert bestimmte Kooperationsmuster beim Aushandeln von Datenwerten.

4.2 Verwaltung von PSAs und AUWs

Alle DML-Anweisungen werden in Problemlösezyklen bzw. atomare Arbeitseinheiten eingebettet. CSQL muß daher Ausdrucksmittel bereitstellen, um PSAs und AUWs in geeigneter Weise definieren und beenden zu können.

```
PSAId_Type pid;
EXEC CSQL BEGIN PSA USERS user2 ID INTO :pid;
EXEC CSQL CLOSE PSA :pid;
EXEC CSQL CONNECT TO PSA :pid DISPLAY "node_x";
EXEC CSQL DISCONNECT FROM PSA :pid;
EXEC CSQL BEGIN AUW IN :pid;
EXEC CSQL COMMIT AUW;
EXEC CSQL ABORT AUW;
```

Die PSA erhält vom Datenbanksystem bei BEGIN PSA eine eindeutige Identifikationsnummer, die in der Variablen :pid abgelegt wird. Mit der optionalen USERS-Klausel wird die Liste der Benutzer angegeben, die außer dem Erzeuger noch zur PSA gehören sollen. Für die spätere Kooperation zwischen Benutzern wird bei den Zugriffsrechten unterschieden, ob ein Benutzer zur PSA gehört oder nicht. Die PSA bleibt so lange erhalten, bis sie mit CLOSE PSA vollständig aus dem Datenbanksystem entfernt wird. Das CONNECT-Statement gibt an, daß die folgenden Anweisungen im Kontext der spezifizierten PSA ausgeführt werden. Ein Benutzer kann zu mehreren PSAs gleichzeitig Verbindungen geöffnet haben. Nach dem Schlüsselwort DISPLAY steht die Bezeichnung des Rechners, an dem Benachrichtigungen (Abschnitt 4.5) angezeigt werden. Nachrichten im Zusammenhang mit einer PSA werden nur solange ausgegeben, wie Verbindung zu dieser PSA besteht. Besteht keine Verbindung, werden alle Nachrichten gepuffert und bei der nächsten Verbindungsaufnahme angezeigt. Die Verbindung wird mit DISCONNECT wieder unterbrochen. Bei der Eröffnung einer AUW muß die PSA angegeben werden, zu der die AUW gehören soll. ABORT AUW und COMMIT AUW beenden offene AUWs mit der von ACID-Transaktionen bekannten Semantik. Schemaänderungen (DDL-Anweisungen) sind nie vorläufig und werden deshalb außerhalb von PSAs (und AUWs) durchgeführt.

4.3 Einfügen, Lesen und Ändern von Daten

Mit der INSERT-Anweisung wird in CSQL Zusicherungen, Vorschläge, Verhandlungsstrategien und Rechte explizit für ein neues Tupel gesetzt oder die Default-Werte für nicht spezifizierte Attributteile eingetragen. Im folgenden Beispiel werden zwei Tupel in eine Personal–Relation eingetragen. Da es sich um Bewerber handelt, können einige Attribute noch gar nicht, andere nur innerhalb gewisser Grenzen spezifiziert werden:

```
EXEC CSQL INSERT INTO personal ( name, gehalt, geburtsjahr )
ASSURANCES ( ,
             <3725.0,3987.5,[453.2,2676.4]>,
             <[1950,1964]> UNITE <[1967,1970]>)
PROPOSALS ( <"Anton","Hans">, <3987.5,[1000.00,2000.00]>, )
          DEFENDING LIKE ( :func2, :func1, )
PROTECTED RIGHTS (all, propose, none)
FOREIGN RIGHTS (:psaid1 all, :psaid2 propose, );

EXEC CSQL INSERT INTO personal ( name, gehalt ) VALUES ("Petra Heinl",675.9);
```

In der ersten Anweisung wird explizit keine Zusicherung für name gegeben, während die anderen beiden Attribute gehalt und geburtsjahr komplexe Zusicherungsmengen erhalten. Mengen werden in spitzen Klammern (< >) notiert. Es können Einzelelemente und bei skalaren Datentypen zusätzliche Intervalle angegeben werden. Die üblichen mengentheoretischen Operationen und Relationen stehen zur Verfügung. Für die Entscheidung über Annahme oder Ablehnung von Vorschlägen wurden für die Attribute gehalt und geburtsjahr zwei Verhandlungsstrategien mit dem Namen :func2 und :func1 installiert, die vorher im Programm deklariert sein müssen (Abschnitt 4.6). Für die PSA, in deren Kontext dieses INSERT-Statement ausgeführt wurde, werden für das Attribut name alle Rechte, für gehalt das Vorschlagsrecht und für geburtsjahr keine Rechte für die Zukunft reserviert. Außerdem werden der PSA :psaid1 alle Rechte und :psaid2 das Vorschlagsrecht eingetragen. Im zweiten Beispiel wird ein Tupel in die Personalrelation eingefügt, das für name den Vorschlag "Petra Heinl" und für gehalt den Vorschlag 675.9 enthält. Das Attribut geburtsjahr enthält als Default-Vorschlagsintervall und Default-Zusicherungsmenge den gesamten Wertebereich. Die installierte Default-Verhandlungsstrategie läßt alle Änderungen zu. Für die PSA :pid bestehen alle Zugriffsrechte, für andere PSAs keine. Ebenso hat die PSA :pid als Default keine Rechte für zukünftige Lese- und Schreiboperationen reserviert. Mit der SELECT-Anweisung kann nun aus der Personalrelation gelesen werden:

```
EXEC CSQL BEGIN DECLARE SET SECTION;
RealSetType var1, var 2;
char var3[max_length];
PSAId_Type var4;
EXEC CSQL END DECLARE SET SECTION;
[...]
EXEC CSQL SELECT
:var1 = ASSURANCE OF gehalt ASSURED,
:var2 = PROPOSAL OF gehalt,
:var3 = STRATEGY OF gehalt,
:var4 = RESPONSIBLE OF gehalt
FROM personal
WHERE PROPOSAL OF name SUPERSET OF <"Anton"> AND
      ASSURANCE OF gehalt PROPER SUBSET OF <[1500,2500]>;
```

In der SELECT-Anweisung qualifizieren sich die Tupel, die in der Vorschlagsmenge für name "Anton" und für die ein gehalt zwischen 1500 und 2500 zugesichert wurde. Es werden Zusicherung, Vorschlag, Verhandlungsstrategie und die PSA gelesen, in deren Kontext die Zusicherung gegeben wurde. Das Schlüsselwort ASSURED nach ASSURANCE OF gibt an, daß sich der Leser auf die Zusicherung verlassen will. Zusicherungen, auf die sich niemand verläßt, können zurückgenommen werden. Da eine Funktion schwer sinnvoll zurückgeliefert werden kann, wird in :var5 lediglich der Name der Verhandlungsstrategie abgelegt. In :var6 wird die Identifikation der PSA zurückgeliefert, die einen etwa vorhandenen Vorschlag für das Datum verwaltet. Diese Information wird intern für die Realisierung der interaktiven Verhandlungsstrategien benötigt und im Abschnitt 4.6 weiter erläutert. Die Verwendung eines Cursors ist nicht nötig, da es sich um ein Singleton-SELECT handelt, würde aber in Syntax und Struktur den SQL-Cursors entsprechen. Alle Elemente der Tupel können mit der UPDATE-Anweisung verändert werden.

```
EXEC CSQL BEGIN DECLARE FUNCTION SECTION;
negfunc : standard TEXT = "Es hat eine Verhandlung stattgefunden";
EXEC CSQL END DECLARE FUNCTION SECTION;
[...]
EXEC CSQL UPDATE personal
SET ASSURANCE OF geburtsjahr = <[1960,1970]"> RELIABLE
SET PROPOSAL OF geburtsjahr = <1966,1967]>
NEGOTIATING LIKE :negfunc
SET PROTECTED RIGHTS OF name = :mypsaid : none
SET FOREIGN RIGHTS OF name = :psaid5 : all;
WHERE PROPOSAL OF name EQUAL <"Petra Heinl">;
[...]
EXEC CSQL UPDATE personal
SET ASSURANCE OF name = <"Franz","Karl"> ASSURED
RELEASE RELY OF gehalt
WHERE RIGHTS OF gehalt CONTAIN PROPOSE FOR :psaid2;
```

Mit der ersten UPDATE-Anweisung werden Teile der Attribute geburtsjahr und name in den Tupeln verändert, deren Vorschlagsmenge gleich <"Petra Heinl"> ist. Die neue Zusicherung für geburtsjahr soll verläßlich eingetragen werden (optionales Schlüsselwort RELIABLE), d.h. im Falle nicht ausreichender Rechte oder widersprüchlicher Zusicherungen wird ein Fehler gemeldet. Ein erneutes Lesen des veränderten Datums um die Datenmanipulation zu kontrollieren, entfällt dadurch. RELIABLE ist auch nach SET PROPOSAL und SET PROTECTED/FOREIGN RIGHTS mit der gleichen Semantik möglich. Der neue Vorschlag für geburtsjahr wird mit der Verhandlungsstrategie :negfunc angegeben. Erzeugt die aktuell installierte Verhandlungsstrategie einen Gegenvorschlag, so wird mit :negfunc ein neuer Änderungsvorschlag erzeugt. Die bestehende Verhandlungsstrategie für geburtsjahr bleibt davon unberührt. Eine Reservierung von Rechten (SET PROTECTED RIGHTS) wird nicht vorgenommen und der PSA :psaid5 werden alle Rechte eingeräumt. In der zweiten Update-Anweisung werden alle Tupel der Relation personal manipuliert, für die :psaid2 das Vorschlagsrecht auf gehalt hat. Falls genügend Zugriffsrechte bestehen, wird die neue Zusicherung <"Franz", "Karl"> eingetragen. Die seit der INSERT-Anweisung bestehenden Vorschläge <"Anton", "Hans"> werden gelöscht, da sie keine Teilmenge der Zusicherung mehr darstellen. Die installierte Verhandlungsstrategie wird durch eine ersetzt, die jeden neuen Vorschlag akzeptiert. Wäre die Schnittmenge aus neuer Zusicherung und altem Vorschlag nicht leer, würde als Vorschlag die Schnittmenge eingetragen werden. Die Verhandlungsstrategie bliebe unberührt. ASSURED gibt an, daß sich die Anwendung semantisch auf die Zusicherungsmenge verläßt. ASSURED schließt RELIABLE ein. Mit RELEASE RELY wird angegeben, daß man sich auf die in der vorherigen SELECT-Anweisung gelesene Zusicherung nicht mehr verlassen will. Wenn kein weiterer Eintrag besteht, könnte die Zusicherung nun auf eine Zusicherungsmenge zurückgenommen werden, für die ein RELY besteht, ohne die Datenkonsistenz zu gefährden.

Die noch fehlenden Konstrukte zum Löschen von Tupeln und zur Manipulation des Datenschemas sind analog zu SQL gestaltet.

4.4 Spezifikation von Tupelmengen

In der CSQL-SELECT-, UPDATE- und DELETE-Anweisung können Tupelmengen verarbeitet werden. Die Qualifikation der Tupel geschieht durch eine WHERE-Klausel. Wie bei der Restriktion in SQL kann in der

WHERE-Klausel ein beliebiger boolescher Ausdruck stehen. Die Basiselemente sind Terme, die eine Menge von Tupeln über ihre Werte der Attributteile qualifizieren. Die Elementarbedingungen untergliedern sich daher auf Zusicherung, Vorschlag, Verhandlungsstrategie mit zuständiger PSA und Rechte. Ein Beispiel für die WHERE-Klausel in einer SELECT-Anweisung lautet:

```
WHERE
  ( PROPOSAL OF a1 PROPER SUBSET <23,] 30, 35[> AND
    STRATEGY OF a1 LIKE ALLOW ALL ) OR
  ( ASSURANCE OF a2 = SINGLE VALUE OR
    ASSURANCE OF a2 EQUAL <"Heinz", "Kurt", "Fritz"> ) AND
  RESERVED RIGHTS OF a2 CONTAINS NEGOTIATE FOR :your_psa
```

Weiterhin könnten die Attribute auch mit Relationennamen qualifiziert werden, um z.B. auch Verbundoperationen durchzuführen. Die Semantik der Vergleichsoperationen ist die gleiche wie oben; Vergleichbarkeit der Attributteile (z.B. Vorschlag, Zusicherung) ist dabei natürlich vorausgesetzt.

Da das bestehende PSA-System als Zusatzebene auf einem kommerziellen relationalen Datenbanksystem implementiert ist, bestehen so gut wie keine Möglichkeiten, die vom Optimierer erstellten Abarbeitungspläne zu beeinflussen. Insbesondere ist es nicht möglich, eigene Vergleichsfunktionen und damit auch Verbundoperationen für die neu definierten Datentypen zu ergänzen. In der jetzigen Implementierung wurde daher die Referenzierung von Tupeln ausschließlich über einen separat mitgeführten Primärschlüssel vorgenommen.

4.5 Benachrichtigung

Benachrichtigungen dienen dazu, den Benutzer über bestimmte Ereignisse in der Datenbank zu informieren. Benachrichtigungen sind die Grundlage für alle Arten von Diensten, die das Datenbanksystem nicht selbständig leisten kann. Interaktive Verhandlungen über Vorschläge sind hierfür ein Beispiel. Alle Benachrichtigungen haben entweder die Form von Fenstern, wenn der Benutzer gerade interaktiv mit dem Rechnersystem arbeitet, oder erreichen den Benutzer als E-Mails. Bei der Definition von Benachrichtigungen wird eine Liste der Benutzer angegeben, die vom Eintritt des Ereignisses benachrichtigt werden sollen. ALL (Default) informiert alle Benutzer dieser Liste, PRESENT nur die aus der Liste, die gerade interaktiv arbeiten. Mit FIRST wird nur der erste interaktive Benutzer der Liste informiert. Die Benachrichtigungen sind der Aktionsteil im üblichen ECA-Trigger-Schema [McDa89]. Als Auslöseereignisse sind möglich:

- RELY: Der Trigger löst aus, wenn in einer AUW z.B. SELECT ASSURANCE OF mit dem Prädikat ASSURED ausgeführt wurde und sich damit auf die gegebene Zusicherung verlassen wird.
- RELEASE RELY: Das Verlassen auf die Zusicherung wird zurückgenommen.
- PROPOSAL/ASSURANCE: Ein Vorschlag/eine Zusicherung wird gesetzt.
- PROPOSAL/ASSURANCE set: Ein Vorschlag/eine Zusicherung wird außerhalb der spezifizierten Menge set gesetzt.
- STRATEGY: Die Verhandlungsstrategie wird geändert.

Default-Ereignis ist PROPOSAL. Der Benachrichtigungszeitpunkt ist am Ende der AUW (DEFERRED, default) oder sofort (IMMEDIATE).

4.6 Verhandlungsstrategien

Verhandlungsstrategien sind im PSA-Modell Funktionen, die festlegen, ob ein Änderungswunsch für einen bestehenden Vorschlag angenommen, abgelehnt oder mit einem Gegenvorschlag neu verhandelt wird. Die Implementierung der Verhandlungsstrategie ist völlig beliebig. Sie kann algorithmisch sein oder die Interaktion mit Benutzer(n) enthalten. Das Datenbanksystem führt bei der Änderung eines Vorschlags lediglich die Prozedur aus, die beim Datenwert abgelegt ist und die Verhandlungsstrategie implementiert. Mit jedem Änderungswunsch ist eine zweite Verhandlungsstrategie (Angriffsstrategie) erforderlich, um evtl. Gegenvorschläge behandeln zu können. Verhandlungsstrategien, die zur Laufzeitbibliothek des PSA-Datenbanksystems gehören, sind:

```
EXEC CSQL BEGIN DECLARE FUNCTION SECTION;
func1 : ACCEPT ALL;
func2 : INTERSECTION TIMEOUT = 35;
func3 : STANDARD TEXT = "Fertigungskosten für Umfang > 30 beachten!"
        TIMEOUT = 300 ;
EXEC CSQL END DECLARE FUNCTION SECTION;
[...]
EXEC CSQL UPDATE personal:petra
SET STRATEGY OF geburtsjahr = :func2;
```

Die erste Strategie ACCEPT ALL akzeptiert jeden neuen Vorschlag, d.h. sie lehnt niemals einen Änderungswunsch ab und erzeugt auch keinen Gegenvorschlag. INTERSECTION bildet als Gegenvorschlag die Schnittmenge aus altem Vorschlag und Änderungswunsch und gibt sie an die Angriffsstrategie zurück. Erst nach Annahme des Gegenvorschlags wird dieser beim Datum abgelegt bzw. nach Ablauf der in TIMEOUT festgelegten Zeit wird der Änderungsvorgang abgebrochen. Der alte Vorschlag bleibt erhalten. STANDARD ist eine interaktive Verhandlungsfunktion. Die interaktive Verhandlung sollte idealerweise zwischen dem Benutzer, der den alten Vorschlag abgegeben hat, und dem, der den Änderungswunsch vorträgt, durchgeführt werden. Da die physische Anwesenheit beider Parteien bei der Verhandlung aber nicht gewährleistet ist, tritt eine PSA an die Stelle des Vorschlaghalters. Liegt ein Änderungswunsch vor, wird durch diese PSA ein interaktiver Benutzer ausgewählt, der Mitglied in der PSA und mit dem Änderer nicht identisch ist. In einem Bildschirmfenster werden alter Vorschlag und Änderungswunsch angezeigt. Von diesem Benutzer wird die Annahme, Ablehung oder ein Gegenvorschlag erwartet (Abbildung 2). Gibt es keinen entsprechenden interaktiven Benutzer, wird längstens für die Dauer der bei TIMEOUT spezifizierten Sekunden auf einen passenden interaktiven Benutzer gewartet bzw. nachher die Verhandlung mit einer Ablehnung des Änderungswunsches abgebrochen. Die Kennzeichnung der Verwalter-PSA für einen Vorschlag kann mit der SELECT RESPONSIBLE OF-Anweisung gelesen werden (Abschnitt 4.1).

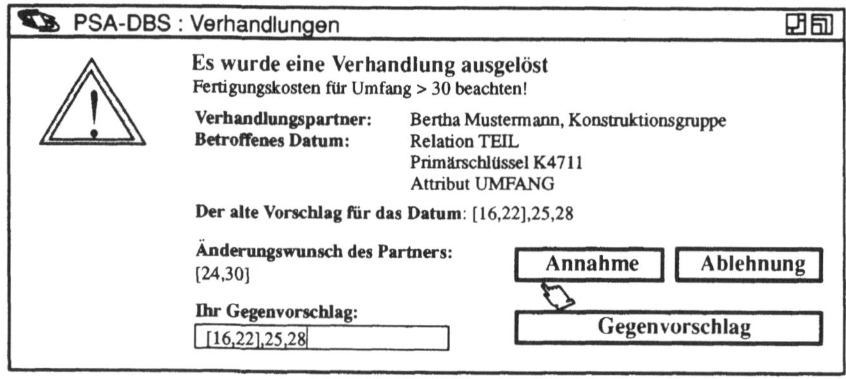

Abb. 2: Interaktive Verhandlung

Über die in das PSA-System integrierten Verhandlungsstrategien hinaus kann jede beliebige Funktion definiert werden, die aus altem Vorschlag und Änderungswunsch eine Annahme, Ablehnung oder einen Gegenvorschlag macht. Die Deklaration geschieht folgendermaßen:

```
EXEC CSQL BEGIN DECLARE FUNCTION SECTION;
myfunc : FUNCTION exe_file_spec INTERACTIVE | STANDALONE
        [ TIMEOUT = seconds] [ TEXT = string ];
EXEC CSQL END DECLARE FUNCTION SECTION;
```

Die Funktion wird in einer ausführbaren Datei abgelegt und vom PSA-System bei einer entsprechenden Verhandlung aufgerufen.

5 Ausblick

Die vorliegende Fassung des PSA-Modells ist sehr pragmatisch. In den weiteren Arbeiten wird daher die Kalkülisierung des Modells zu leisten sein, um die Fragen nach Korrektheit und Vollständigkeit beantworten zu können. Eine Neufassung des Datenmodells, in dem drei nahezu orthogonale Arten der Unsicherheit verwaltet werden, existiert daher bereits im Ansatz. Ebenso wird an einem geschlossenen und in das PSA-Verarbeitungsmodell integrierten Kooperationskonzept gearbeitet. Grundprinzip wird jedoch auch weiterhin die maximale Unterstützung, aber nicht die totale Anleitung der Datenbankbenutzer sein. Gerade im kreativen Feld der technischen Produktentwicklung scheinen die herkömmlichen, statischen Integrationsansätze wie z.B. Modellierungsvorschriften in CASE-Verfahren eher hinderlich.

Anerkennung verdient Petra Heinl, die im Rahmen ihrer Studienarbeit große Teile der Datenanfragesprache CSQL entworfen und den Präcompiler dafür implementiert hat.

Literatur

Codd90 Codd, E.F.: The Relational Model for Database Management - Version 2, *Addison-Wesley, Reading, Mass. u.a.*, 1990

Davi78 Davies, C.: Data Processing Spheres of Control, *IBM Systems Journal 17(2)*, 1978, S. 178-198

Gray81 Gray, J.: The transaction concept: Virtues and Limitations, *Proc. 7th VLDB (Cannes, September 9-11)*, 1981, S. 144-154

HäRe83 Härder, T., Reuter, A.: Principles of Transaction-oriented Database Recovery, *ACM Computing Surveys 15(4)*, 1983, S. 287-317

HuCr68 Hughes, G., Cresswell, M.: An Introduction to Modal Logic, *Methuen and Co, London*, 1968

ImNV91 Imielinski, T., Naqvi, S., Vadaparty, K.: Incomplete Objects - A Data Model for Design and Planning Applications, *Proc. ACM SIGMOD 91 Conf. (Denver, May 29-31)*, 1991, S. 288-297

ImLi84 Imielinski, T., Lipski, W.: Incomplete Information in Relational Databases, *Journal of the ACM 31(4)*, 1984, S. 761-791

JBKR92 Jablonski, S., Barthel, S., Kirsche, T., Rödinger, T., Schuster, H., Wedekind, H.: Datenbankunterstützung für kooperative Gruppenarbeit, 1992, *eingereicht zur Veröffentlichung*

JRRW90 Jablonski, S.; Reinwald, B.; Ruf, T.; Wedekind, H.: Von Transaktionen zu Problemlösezyklen: Erweiterte Verarbeitungsmodelle für Non-Standard-Datenbanksysteme, in: Härder, T.; Wedekind, H.; Zimmermann, G. (Hrsg.): *Entwurf und Betrieb verteilter Systeme*, Springer Informatik-Fachbericht 164, Berlin u.a., 1990, S. 221-247

JRRW91 Jablonski, S.; Reinwald, B.; Ruf, T.; Wedekind, H.: Supporting Cooperative Work in Database Systems by Data Release Modalities, *Interner Bericht des IMMD VI*, Universität Erlangen-Nürnberg, 1991

Lips79 Lipski, W.: On Semantic Issues Connected with Incomplete Information Databases, *ACM Transactions on Database Systems 4(3)*, 1979, S. 262-296

McDa89 McCarthy, D., Dayal, U.: The Architecture of an Active Database Management System, *Proc. ACM SIGMOD Conf. (Portland, May 31- June 2)*, 1989, S. 215-224

Morr90 Morrissey, J.: Imprecise Information and Uncertainty in Information Systems, *ACM Transactions on Database System 8(2)*, 1990, S. 159-180

Wede93 Wedekind, H.: Eine logische Analyse und Synthese des Begriffs "committed", *Informatik Forschung und Entwicklung 8(1), 1993*

YGBP92 Yazici, A., George, R., Buckles, B., Petry, F.: A Survey of Conceptual and Logical Data Models for Uncertainty Management, in: Zadeh, L., Kacprzyk, J. (eds.): *Fuzzy Logic for the Management of Uncertainty, John Wiley & Sons, New York u.a.*, 1992, S. 607-643

Zica90 Zicari, R.: Incomplete Information in Object-Oriented Databases, in: *SIGMOD Record 19(3)*, 1990

Benutzergesteuerte, flexible Speicherungsstrukturen für komplexe Objekte

Ullrich Keßler, Peter Dadam
Universität Ulm
Fakultät für Informatik
Abt. Datenbanken und Informationssysteme
Oberer Eselsberg, 7900 Ulm
e-mail: {kessler, dadam}@informatik.uni-ulm.de

Zusammenfassung

In der Vergangenheit wurden eine Reihe neuer Datenmodelle entwickelt, in denen komplex strukturierte Objekte unmittelbar dargestellt werden können. In der Regel werden hierbei für die logischen Strukturen eines Datenmodells bereits auch die physischen Speicherungsstrukturen festgelegt. Für die Wahl einer "optimalen" physischen Speicherungsstruktur - bei gegebener logischer Struktur - müßte jedoch die Art, in der auf die Daten später zugegriffen werden soll, mit berücksichtigt werden. Dies ist aber nur in einem System möglich, in dem die Abbildung der logischen Strukturen auf interne Speicherungsstrukturen frei definiert werden kann. Dazu werden in diesem Beitrag geeignete Basiskonstrukte für interne Speicherungsstrukturen sowie wesentliche Elemente und Parameter einer fiktiven Datendefinitionssprache diskutiert. Die hierbei vorgestellten Parameter sind zusammen so mächtig, daß mit ihnen explizit definiert werden kann, wie komplexe Objekte systemintern dargestellt werden sollen. Außerdem wird beschrieben, wie auch die Clusterung der Objekte gesteuert werden kann. Insgesamt wird dadurch eine Flexibilität erreicht, die so groß ist, daß sehr viele der in der Literatur vorgeschlagenen Speicherungsstrukturen nachgebildet werden können. Zusätzlich können eine große Zahl weiterer, noch nicht diskutierter Varianten und Mischformen beschrieben werden.

1. Einleitung und Problemstellung

Die sehr eingeschränkten Möglichkeiten, technisch-wissenschaftliche und sogenannte Non-Standard-Anwendungen mit traditionellen Datenmodellen zu modellieren, haben in der Vergangenheit zu einer Reihe von Vorschlägen für neuartige Datenmodelle, wie etwa Smalltalk-ähnliche, persistente objektorientierte Datenmodelle [Nier89], das Molekül-Atom-Datenmodell [Mits88] oder das NF^2-Datenmodell [ScPi82] bzw. dessen Erweiterung, das eNF^2-Datenmodell [PiAn86], geführt. Darauf aufbauend entstanden unterschiedliche DBMS-Prototypen, wie etwa O_2 [Banc88], AIM-P [Dada86], Prima [HMMS87], Orion [Kim89], XSQL [Lori85], GemStone [MSOP86], DASDBS [Paul87] und COCOON [ScSc90]. Diese Systeme unterstützen im Gegensatz zu herkömmlichen Datenbanksystemen die Speicherung komplex strukturierter Objekte unmittelbar, und zwar sowohl auf der Datenmodellebene als auch in den Anfragesprachen.

Gleichzeitig mit der Entwicklung neuer Datenmodelle und DBMS-Prototypen wurde auch diskutiert, wie komplexe Objekte auf Seiten des Hintergrundspeichers abgebildet werden können. Typische Vorschläge hierzu finden sich unter anderem in [Dada86], [DPS86], [HaOz88], [KFC90], [Kim89], [Lori85], [MSOP86] und [Sike88]. Daß es hierbei keine "beste" Abbildungsstrategie gibt, die in jedem Einzelfall das beste Ergebnis liefert, liegt auf der Hand. Wird ein komplexes Objekt in nur wenige "große" Speichereinheiten zerlegt, müssen auch bei der Bearbeitung von Anfragen[1], die nur kleine Teile eines komplexen Objektes betreffen, stets diese "großen" Speichereinheiten mit entsprechend vielen Seitenzugriffen gelesen werden. Umgekehrt ist eine Strategie, die ein komplexes Objekt in "viele" kleine Speichereinheiten zerlegt, auch nicht immer die beste Lösung. Beim häufigen Zugriff auf ganze Substrukturen komplexer Objekte müssen dann viele einzelne Speichereinheiten gelesen werden. Hierdurch summieren sich die beim Zugriff auf Speichereinheiten häufig zu beobachtenden langen Pfadlängen zu hohen Kosten. Sind die Speicherelemente zusätzlich nur ungenügend geclustert, kommt es auch noch zu vielen Seitenzugriffen. Eine gute Strategie müßte also häufig als Ganzes zugegriffene Substrukturen eines komplexen Objektes in eine oder wenige Speichereinheiten abbilden und selten gemeinsam zugegriffene Substrukturen separieren. Dieses Ziel kann aber, wie auch das nachfolgende Beispiel einer eNF^2-Roboterrelation zeigt, mit einer anwendungsunabhängigen Abbildungsstrategie, welche die Anwendungsprofile nicht berücksichtigt, nicht oder nur bedingt erreicht werden.

In Abb. 1 ist die stark vereinfachte Ausprägung einer eNF^2-Relation zu sehen, in der sowohl die für die Einsatzplanung von Robotern benötigten konstruktiven Daten als auch die für die Verwaltung benötigten administrativen Daten verschiedener Roboter gespeichert werden. Folgt man den oben genannten Vorschlägen, wird jede Achse eines Roboters auf 4 bis 8 Records verteilt. Werden die Daten der Achsen jedoch überwiegend im Zusammenhang gelesen, wäre eine Lösung, welche alle Daten einer Achse in einem einzigen Record speichert, wie dies in Abb. 1 für die Achse 1 durch den ▭-Rahmen angedeutet ist, vorzuziehen. Hierdurch würde die Zahl der Record-Zugriffe stark reduziert. Umgekehrt werden bei den obigen Heuristiken die Attribute "R_Nr", "Name" und "Beschreibung" meistens gemeinsam in einem Record abgelegt, obwohl sie unter Umständen besser auf mehrere Records verteilt werden sollten. Werden nämlich die Nummer und der Name eines Roboters wesentlich häufiger als dessen Beschreibung benötigt, könnte so vermieden werden, daß die unter Umständen lange Beschreibung jedesmal mit in den Hauptspeicher übertragen wird.

Ein zweites Optimierungspotential ist die Clusterung der Daten. Eine typische Heuristik in diesem Zusammenhang ist, alle Records eines komplexen Objektes auf benachbarten Seiten zu speichern (vgl. [BeDe89], [Dada86], [DPS86], [KFC90], [Kim87], [ScSi89]). Im Fall der Roboterrelation würde zum Beispiel versucht werden, alle Records eines Roboters auf der Platte benachbart zu speichern. Werden nun Teile der Daten häufig unabhängig von ihrer Objektzugehörigkeit gelesen, bewirkt diese Clusterung genau das Gegenteil. Ein Beispiel hierfür könnten die Einsatzdaten sein. Werden diese Werte für Abrechnungszwecke zumeist unabhängig von den übrigen Roboterdaten gelesen, wäre eine Clusterung, die sämtliche Einsatzdaten in einem einzigen objektübergreifenden Cluster speichert - wie dies in Abb. 1 durch die ░-Schattierung angedeutet ist - einer rein objektbezogenen Clusterung vorzuziehen.

Bei einer festen Abbildung logischer Konstrukte in physische Speicherungsstrukturen lassen sich Probleme dieser Art nur lösen, indem die logische - und damit auch die physische - Struktur der Objekte geändert wird. Dies hat allerdings zur Folge, daß auch

[1] Im folgenden wird der Begriff Anfrage als Synonym für Anfrage oder Datenmanipulationsauftrag verwendet.

{Roboter}										
R_Nr	Name	<Achsen>			{Einsatz}			{Effektoren}		Beschreibung
		Achs_Nr	<Positionsmatrix>		Produkt	{Leistung}		E_Nr	Aufgabe	
			Reihe	<Vektor>		Woche	Kosten			
R_1	Robi	1	1	<20,20,20,20>	Klappe	17	200	E_1	schweißen	Roboter ...
			2	<34,37,56,90>		30	300	E_2	nieten	
			3	<21,34,78,60>	Stange	16	400	E_3	pressen	
			4	<45,56,78,12>		29	100	E_4	kleben	
		2	1	<16,90,30,14>		41	500			
			2	<16,42,45,78>						
			3	<12,79,59,78>						
			4	<23,67,31,67>						
R_2	Bigi	...	...	...	...	...	...	...	...	...

Legende: Mengenbildung: {}, Listenbildung: <>

gewünschte Recordbildung:

gewünschte objektübergreifende Clusterung:

Abb. 1: Ausprägung einer eNF²-Roboterrelation

die - evtl. bereits existierenden - Anwendungsprogramme abgeändert werden müssen. Der bessere Weg, mit solchen Problemen umzugehen, ist eine Trennung zwischen logischer und physischer Struktur. Diesen Weg hat man bereits erfolgreich in einigen kommerziellen relationalen Datenbanksystemen eingeschlagen. In Ingres [Ingr90] kann der Anwender beispielsweise unter verschiedenen Methoden zur Speicherung der Relationen auswählen. In Oracle [Orac90] kann der Anwender die Clusterung der Relationen explizit definieren. Andere Beispiele sind das hierarchische Datenbanksystem IMS [Gee77] und Netzwerkdatenbanken, die eine Speicherbeschreibungssprache anbieten. In diesen Systemen hat der Anwender Möglichkeiten, in einer eigenen Sprache die internen Speicherungsstrukturen seinen Bedürfnissen anzupassen. Im Zusammenhang von komplexen Objekten gibt es jedoch erst wenige Vorschläge, wie die Speicherungsstrukturen und die Clusterungs-Strategien in Abhängigkeit von den Anwendungen definiert werden können. In [Scho92] werden zum Beispiel alternative Strategien zur Implementation von komplexen Objekten unter Verwendung eines Speichermanagers für hierarchische Strukturen diskutiert. In [BeDe89], [Kim87] und [ScSi89] wird gezeigt, wie die Daten in Abhängigkeit von den Anwendungen geclustert werden können.

Wie wir im folgenden am Beispiel des eNF²-Datenmodells zeigen werden, gibt es beim Entwurf von Speicherungsstrukturen für komplexe Objekte im wesentlichen zwei orthogonale Freiheitsgrade. Der erste Freiheitsgrad ist die Wahl einer Datenstruktur zur Implementation von Mengen, Listen und Tupeln. Der zweite Freiheitsgrad ist die Entscheidung, ob die Elemente von Mengen und Listen bzw. die Attribute von Tupeln direkt in diesen Datenstrukturen oder in referenzierten Records abgelegt werden. Um dem

Anwender die Kontrolle über diese Freiheitsgrade zu geben, reichen, wie wir ebenfalls zeigen werden, bereits drei einfache, orthogonale Parameter in einer entsprechenden Datendefinitionssprache aus. Mit ihnen kann die Abbildung eines komplexen Objektes auf Records annähernd frei definiert werden. Die Flexibilität, die diese Parameter bieten, ist dabei so groß, daß praktisch alle Vorschläge in den Papieren [Dada86], [DPS86], [HaOz88], [KFC90] und [Lori85] nachgebildet werden können. Darüber hinaus lassen sich viele weitere Varianten definieren. Im Extremfall kann ein vollständiges komplexes Objekt in einem einzigen Record gespeichert werden. Das andere Extrem, jeden atomaren Wert eines komplexen Objektes in einem eigenen Record zu speichern, ist ebenfalls möglich. Die logische Struktur der komplexen Objekte ist hiervon stets unbeeinflußt[2].

Darüber hinaus wird im weiteren Verlauf des Beitrags diskutiert, wie auch die Clusterung der Records gesteuert werden kann. Die diskutierten Techniken erlauben es, annähernd beliebige Records zu Clustern zusammenzufassen. So lassen sich beispielsweise beliebige Substrukturen komplexer Objekte gruppieren. Es ist aber auch möglich, Records unabhängig von ihrer Objektzugehörigkeit objektübergreifend in Clustern zusammenzufassen. Im Falle der Roboterrelation können beispielsweise die Achs- und Effektordaten objektbezogen jeweils in einem Cluster pro Roboter gespeichert werden. Gleichzeitig können die Einsatzdaten aller Roboter unabhängig von ihrer Objektzugehörigkeit in einem einzigen Cluster gespeichert werden.

Obwohl in diesem Beitrag mit dem eNF^2-Datenmodell ein rein disjunktes und nicht rekursives Datenmodell gewählt wurde, beschränkt sich die Anwendbarkeit der hier vorgestellten Verfahren nicht zwangsläufig auf Systeme, die auch an der Benutzerschnittstelle dieses Datenmodell anbieten (wie z.B. AIM-P). Für viele Systeme, die nach außen hin mächtigere Datenmodelle unterstützen, wurde vorgeschlagen, aus Effizienzgründen intern hierarchische Datenstrukturen zur Speicherung der komplexen Objekte zu verwenden. Beispielsweise wird in [BeDe89], [ScSi89] und [Kim87] ausführlich diskutiert, wie in O_2, Prima und in Smalltalk-ähnlichen Systemen, wie GemStone und Orion, deren komplexe Objekte, die nicht unbedingt hierarchisch aufgebaut sind, intern auf hierarchische Datenstrukturen abgebildet werden können. Eine ähnliches Ziel wird mit dem Speicherkernsystem DASDBS verfolgt. Auf einen Speichermanager, der ein hierarchisches Datenmodell anbietet, werden sowohl relationale Systeme [SPS87] als auch objektorientierte Systeme [Scho92] aufgesetzt. Der Grund ist, daß sich hierarchische Strukturen besonders gut zu Clustern zusammenfassen lassen, wodurch wiederum die Performanz eines Systems gesteigert werden kann.

Der Rest des Beitrages gliedert sich entsprechend der Idee, sowohl die Record-Struktur eines komplexen Objektes als auch dessen Clusterung frei definieren zu können. In Abschnitt 2 werden dazu kurz das hier zugrunde gelegte eNF^2-Datenmodell und eine Datendefinitionssprache mit einer stark vereinfachten Syntax eingeführt. In Abschnitt 3, dem Hauptteil dieses Beitrages, werden dann ausführlich die zwei Freiheitsgrade - Wahl einer Datenstruktur zur Implementation von Mengen, Listen und Tupeln und Entscheidung, ob Elemente bzw. Attribute materialisiert oder referenziert gespeichert werden - beim Entwurf von Speicherungsstrukturen für komplexe Objekte und die Kontrolle dieser

[2] Die nachträgliche Änderung der Speicherungsstrukturen eines Objektes erfordert unter Umständen eine interne Reorganisation des Objektes oder eine entsprechende Katalogverwaltung.

Freiheitsgrade durch Parameter einer Datendefinitionssprache diskutiert. In Abschnitt 4 wird beschrieben, wie die Clusterung der Records gesteuert wird. Abschnitt 5 faßt die Diskussion zusammen und gibt einen kurzen Ausblick.

2. Das eNF²-Datenmodell

Als Grundlage für die weiteren Diskussionen wird im folgenden das eNF²-Datenmodell nach [PiAn86] verwendet. An diesem Datenmodell wird exemplarisch gezeigt, wie die systeminterne Repräsentation und Clusterung von komplexen Objekten definiert werden können. Komplexe Objekte werden im eNF²-Datenmodell aus atomaren Werten und darauf rekursiv angewendeten Mengen-, Listen- und Tupelkonstruktoren gebildet. Typische atomare Wertebereiche sind Integer, Real und String. Abb. 2 veranschaulicht diesen Prozeß. Ein komplexes Objekt kann beispielsweise eine Menge von Mengen von Strings sein, aber auch nur ein einzelner Wert oder aber ein wesentlich komplexeres Objekt, wie die Roboter-Relation in Abb. 1. Jede Relation in erster Normalform ist ebenfalls ein Objekt des eNF²-Datenmodells.

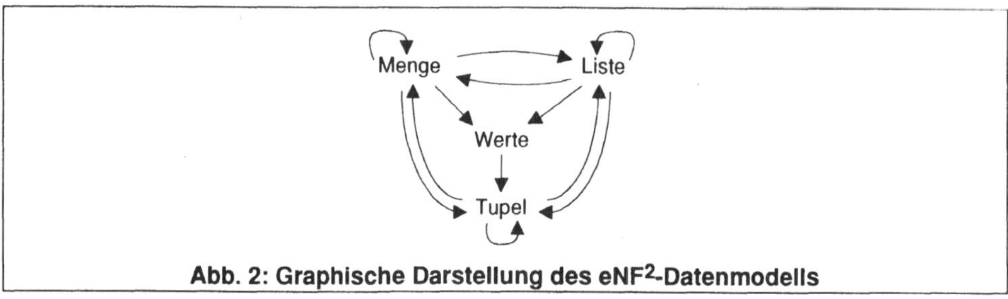

Abb. 2: Graphische Darstellung des eNF²-Datenmodells

Zur Definition des Typs und der Speicherungsstruktur eines komplexen Objektes wird in diesem Beitrag exemplarisch eine Datendefinitionssprache mit einer sehr einfachen Syntax verwendet, da hier die wesentlichen Prinzipien der Definition von Speicherungsstrukturen und nicht die syntaktischen Konstrukte einer solchen Sprache diskutiert werden sollen. Daher verzichten wir auch auf die eigentlich wünschenswerte Trennung zwischen Datendefinitions- und Speicherstruktursprache. Die vollständige Syntax dieser Sprache ist in der Abb. 9 im Anhang gegeben. Beschränkt man sich auf die reine Typdefinition, würde eine typische Mitarbeiterrelation mit den Attributen Pers_Nr., Name, Gehalt und Lebenslauf (s. Abb. 5) wie folgt definiert[3] (die Speicherstrukturbeschreibung wird später an den mit [...] gekennzeichneten Stellen eingetragen):

```
complex_object Mitarbeiter [...]
           set [...] of tuple (Pers_Nr.   [...]: integer,
                               Name       [...]: fix_string(30),
                               Gehalt     [...]: real,
                               Lebenslauf [...]: var_string)
```

3. Flexible Abbildung logischer Konstrukte in physische Speicherungsstrukturen

Beim Entwurf von physischen Speicherungsstrukturen für komplexe Objekte gibt es zwei wichtige Freiheitsgrade. Der erste Freiheitsgrad ist die Wahl der internen Speicherungsstrukturen zur Implementation von Mengen, Listen und Tupeln. Im folgenden werden

---

[3] Zum leichteren Verständnis werden in den Beispielen Schlüsselworte stets klein und frei zu wählende Bezeichner stets groß geschrieben.

diese internen Speicherungsstrukturen auch als "Konstruktordatenstruktur" bezeichnet. Zur Implementation einer Menge oder Liste kann zum Beispiel - ähnlich wie in Netzwerkdatenbanken - ein variabel langes Array oder eine verkettete Liste verwendet werden. Die Attribute eines Tupels können zusammenhängend in einem Record oder aufgeteilt auf mehrere gespeichert werden.

Der zweite Freiheitsgrad ist die Entscheidung, ob die Elemente einer Menge oder Liste bzw. die Attribute eines Tupels direkt in der Konstruktordatenstruktur gespeichert oder aber aus ihr heraus referenziert werden. Im folgenden werden diese Fälle auch als "materialisierte" bzw. "referenzierte" Speicherung bezeichnet. Für eine einfache Menge von atomaren Werten, die als Array implementiert ist, bedeutet dies: Bei einer materialisierten Speicherung enthält das Array die atomaren Werte. Bei der referenzierten Speicherung enthält das Array Referenzen auf Records mit den atomaren Werten. Graphisch ist dies in Abb. 3 für die Menge "{a, b, c}" dargestellt.

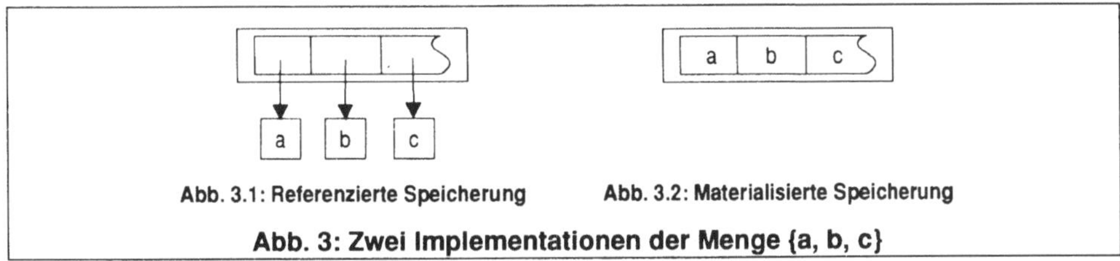

Abb. 3.1: Referenzierte Speicherung **Abb. 3.2: Materialisierte Speicherung**

Abb. 3: Zwei Implementationen der Menge {a, b, c}

Sind die Elemente einer Menge oder Liste bzw. die Attribute eines Tupels selbst komplex strukturiert, so ergeben sich weitere Möglichkeiten, das Objekt auf Records aufzuteilen. Dazu betrachte man beispielsweise die Menge

{{String_1, String_2}, {String_3, String_4}}.

In dieser Menge sind die Elemente "{String_1, String_2}" und "{String_3, String_4}" der äußeren Menge selbst wieder Mengen. Nun können sowohl die Elemente der äußeren als auch die Elemente der inneren Mengen referenziert oder materialisiert gespeichert werden. Die daraus resultierenden vier Speicherungsstrukturen[4] sind in der Abb. 4 graphisch dargestellt.

Abb. 4.1 zeigt die Speicherungsstruktur, in der sowohl die Elemente der äußeren als auch die Elemente der inneren Mengen referenziert gespeichert werden. Die Konstruktordatenstruktur der äußeren Menge enthält Referenzen auf Records mit den Konstruktordatenstrukturen der inneren Mengen. Diese wiederum enthalten Referenzen auf Records mit den Werten "String_1", ..., "String_4". In Abb. 4.2 wird angenommen, daß die Konstruktordatenstrukturen der Mengen "{String_1, String_2}" und "{String_3, String_4}" (= materialisierte Subobjekte) in demselben Record wie die Konstruktordatenstruktur der äußeren Menge gespeichert werden. Die Elemente "String_1", ..., "String_4" werden jedoch weiterhin in referenzierten Records abgelegt. Dieser Fall ist ein typisches Beispiel dafür, daß sich die Aussage: "ein komplexes Subobjekt wird materialisiert gespeichert" zunächst einmal nur auf die Speicherung der Konstruktordatenstruktur des betroffenen Subobjektes, nicht aber auf die Speicherung seiner Elemente bezieht. Abb. 4.3 zeigt den genau umgekehrten Fall: Die Elemente der

[4] Hierbei werden variabel lange Arrays als Konstruktordatenstrukturen angenommen. Werden zusätzlich auch verkettete Listen als Konstruktordatenstrukturen betrachtet, erhält man insgesamt 16 Varianten.

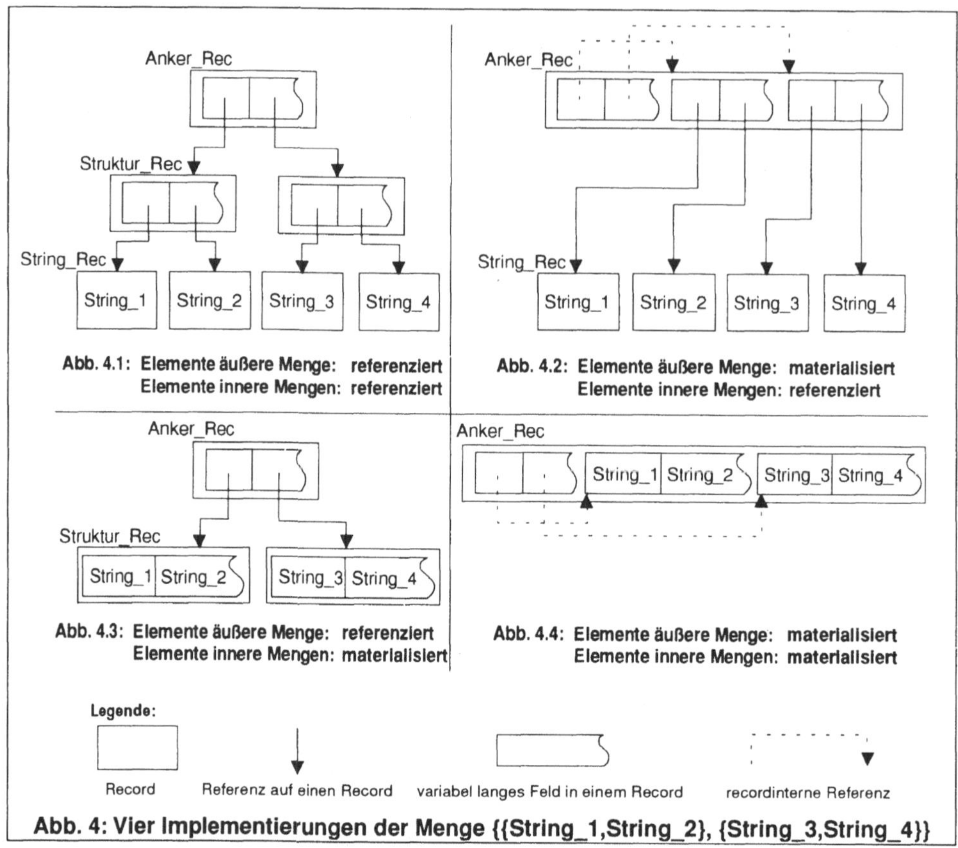

Abb. 4: Vier Implementierungen der Menge {{String_1,String_2}, {String_3,String_4}}

äußeren Menge werden referenziert, die Elemente der inneren Menge materialisiert. Daher enthält die Konstruktordatenstruktur der äußeren Menge Referenzen auf Records. Diese speichern die Konstruktordatenstrukturen der inneren Mengen zusammen mit den materialisierten Strings. Abb. 4.4 zeigt schließlich den letzten Fall, in dem sowohl die Elemente der äußeren als auch die Elemente der inneren Mengen materialisiert werden. Das vollständige Objekt wird daher in einem einzigen Record gespeichert.

Im folgenden werden nun orthogonale Parameter herausgearbeitet, mit denen diese Freiheitsgrade - Wahl einer geeigneten Konstruktordatenstruktur, Entscheidung zwischen referenzierter und materialisierter Speicherung - sowohl bei der Mengen- und Listenbildung als auch bei der Tupelbildung kontrolliert werden können. Mit diesen Parametern können unterschiedlichste Abbildungen der logischen Konstrukte des eNF^2-Datenmodells auf physische Speicherungsstrukturen beschrieben werden, so daß die Speicherungsstrukturen der Objekte auf die jeweiligen Anwendungen abgestimmt werden können. Dazu werden zunächst die Begriffe "Record" und "Record-Typname" etwas genauer eingeführt. Anschließend wird diskutiert, wie die Speicherungsstrukturen von Mengen und Listen definiert werden können. Hierbei werden unter anderem auch die 4 Speicherungsstrukturen aus Abb. 4 vollständig definiert. Danach wird die Tupelbildung betrachtet und diskutiert, wie sich dort die Speicherungsstrukturen beschreiben lassen.

3.1 Records und Record-Typnamen

Ein "Record" ist - so wie der Begriff in diesem Beitrag verwendet wird - ein logisches Speicherobjekt, das aus einer variablen Anzahl von Bytes besteht. Zur Identifizierung besitzt jeder Record einen eindeutigen Identifier. Je nach Größe der Records können sowohl mehrere Records in einer Seite des Hintergrundspeichers abgelegt als auch ein Record über viele Seiten verteilt werden.

Zur Speicherung eines komplexen Objektes wird mindestens ein Record benötigt. Dieser wird im folgenden auch als "Anker-Record" bezeichnet. Ist das komplexe Objekt lediglich ein atomarer Wert, so enthält der Anker-Record genau diesen Wert. Ist das komplexe Objekt hingegen eine Menge, Liste oder ein Tupel, so enthält der Anker-Record mindestens die gewählte Konstruktordatenstruktur. Über diesen Anker-Record können durch Verfolgung von Referenzen alle Subobjekte erreicht werden.

Um bei der Definition von Speicherungsstrukturen und insbesondere bei der Definition der Clusterung (s. Abschnitt 4) symbolisch auf Records Bezug nehmen zu können, werden Records mit semantisch äquivalentem Inhalt zu Record-Typen zusammengefaßt. Jeder Record-Typ erhält dazu bei der Definition der Speicherungsstrukturen einen eindeutigen, frei wählbaren "Record-Typnamen". Beispielsweise werden bei der Definition der Speicherungsstruktur in Abb. 4.1 die Record-Typnamen "Anker_Rec", "Struktur_Rec" und "String_Rec" vergeben. Dabei wird in der hier verwendeten Syntax der Record-Typname des Anker-Records in dem Parameter "anchor_record_type" vergeben (s. Anhang, Abb. 9 [1]). Die beiden anderen Record-Typnamen werden in den Definitionen der Mengen festgelegt.

3.2 Speicherungsstrukturen für Mengen - und Listenkonstruktoren

Entsprechend der vorangegangenen Diskussion gibt es bei der Implementation von Mengen und Listen zwei voneinander unabhängige Freiheitsgrade. Der erste Freiheitsgrad ist die Wahl der Konstruktordatenstruktur. Dies kann zum Beispiel ein variabel langes Array oder eine verkettete Liste sein; andere Implementationen sind aber auch denkbar. Der zweite Freiheitsgrad ist die Entscheidung, ob die Elemente direkt in der Konstruktordatenstruktur gespeichert werden oder ob diese nur Zeiger auf Records mit den Elementen enthält. Sollen beide Freiheitsgrade bei der Mengen- und Listenbildung unabhängig spezifiziert werden können, so werden hierfür in einer Datendefinitionssprache zwei entsprechende Parameter benötigt. In der hier verwendeten Syntax werden dazu in den Term zur Objektdefinition die Parameter "implementation" und "element_placement" integriert (vgl. Anhang Abb. 9, [2]-[7]):

```
object_type = ...
              /* Definition einer Menge. */
              set  [implementation     = implementation_type,
                    element_placement  = placement_type] of object_type |
              /* Definition einer Liste. */
              list [implementation     = implementation_type,
                    element_placement  = placement_type] of object_type |...
```

In dem Parameter "implementation" wird die gewünschte Implementation der Menge oder Liste ausgewählt. Kann in einem System eine Menge oder Liste durch ein Array oder eine verkettete Liste implementiert werden, so kann dieser Parameter die gültigen Werte "array" und "linked_list" annehmen (vgl. Abb. 9, [11]):

```
implementation_type = array | linked_list
```

Mit dem zweiten Parameter, hier "element_placement" genannt, wird bestimmt, ob die Elemente in der gewählten Konstruktordatenstruktur materialisiert oder aus ihr heraus referenziert werden. Als gültige Werte werden im folgenden verwendet (vgl. Abb. 9, [10]):

```
placement_type = inplace | referenced (record_type_name)
```

Wird in dem Parameter "element_placement " der Wert "inplace" angegeben, so werden die Elemente direkt in der Konstruktordatenstruktur gespeichert. Wird hingegen "referenced" verwendet, so wird für jedes Element der Menge oder Liste ein eigener Record vom Typ "record_type_name" angelegt. Beispielsweise werden die Elemente "String_1", ..., "String_4" der inneren Mengen der Menge "{{String_1, String_2}, {String_3, String_4}}" im Fall 1 entsprechend der nachfolgenden Definition in referenzierten Records mit dem frei gewählten Record-Typnamen "String_Rec" gespeichert (vgl. Abb. 4.1). Der gewählte Typname muß dabei innerhalb eines komplexen Objektes eindeutig sein. In die Konstruktordatenstruktur werden dann nur noch die Identifier dieser Records eingetragen.

Die Verwendung dieser Parameter sei am Beispiel der vier Speicherungsstrukturen für die Menge "{{String_1, String_2}, {String_3, String_4}}" aus Abb. 4 näher erläutert. Abb. 4.1 zeigt den Fall, daß sowohl die Elemente der äußeren als auch die Elemente der inneren Mengen referenziert gespeichert werden. Die vollständige Definition der Speicherungsstruktur lautet:

```
complex_object Menge_von_Mengen_von_Strings [anchor_record_type=Anker_Rec] 1
 set [implementation=array, element_placement=referenced (Struktur_Rec)A] of 2
   set [implementation=array, element_placement=referenced (String_Rec)B] of 3
       var_string.                                                           4
```

In Zeile 1 dieser Definition werden der Name "Menge_von_Mengen_von_Strings" des komplexen Objektes und der Record-Typname "Anker_Rec" des Anker-Records festgelegt. Zeile 2 besagt, daß das komplexe Objekt eine Menge ist. Zu ihrer Implementation wird ein Array verwendet. Die Elemente der Menge werden in referenzierten Records mit dem frei gewählten Record-Typnamen "Struktur_Rec" gespeichert. In Zeile 3 wird definiert, daß die Elemente der äußeren Menge selbst wieder Mengen sind. Auch diese inneren Mengen werden als Arrays implementiert. Die Elemente der inneren Mengen werden wiederum referenziert. Dazu werden sie in Records mit dem Typnamen "String_Rec" gespeichert. Zeile 4 besagt schließlich, daß die Elemente der inneren Mengen Strings variabler Länge sind.

Die Speicherungsstrukturen der Abb. 4.2, 4.3 und 4.4 können aus der Definition der Speicherungsstruktur der Abb. 4.1 durch Variation der Parameter "A" und "B" abgeleitet werden. Wird der Parameter "A" auf den Wert "element_placement = inplace" gesetzt, ergibt sich die Struktur der Abb. 4.2, in der die Elemente der äußeren Menge materialisiert, die der inneren aber referenziert werden. Umgekehrt ergibt sich die Struktur in Abb. 4.3, in der die Elemente der inneren Mengen materialisiert werden, nicht aber die Elemente der äußeren Menge, indem der Parameter "B" auf "element_placement = inplace" gesetzt wird. Schließlich erhält man die Struktur in Abb. 4.4, in der das gesamte komplexe Objekt in einem einzigen Record gespeichert wird, indem beide Parameter "A" und "B" auf "element_placement = inplace" gesetzt werden.

Bereits an diesem einfachen Beispiel sieht man den hohen Grad der Flexibilität, der durch den Parameter "element_placement" erreicht wird. Variiert man noch den

Parameter "implementation" von "array" nach "linked_list", kommen weitere zwölf Varianten zur Implementation der Menge von Mengen von Strings hinzu.

3.3 Speicherungsstrukturen für Tupelkonstruktoren

Nachdem im vorigen Abschnitt die Repräsentation von Mengen und Listen diskutiert wurde, wird nun dargestellt, wie sich die internen Speicherungsstrukturen von Tupeln beschreiben lassen. Prinzipiell existieren hierbei die gleichen Freiheitsgrade - Wahl einer Konstruktordatenstruktur, Entscheidung, ob Attribute referenziert oder materialisiert gespeichert werden - wie bei der Mengen- und Listenbildung. Im Falle der Tupelbildung entspricht der erste Freiheitsgrad der Entscheidung, ob ein Tupel - oder genauer gesagt seine Konstruktordatenstruktur - in einem Record oder auf mehrere Records verteilt gespeichert wird. Der zweite Freiheitsgrad ist die Entscheidung, ob die Attributwerte in der Konstruktordatenstruktur materialisiert gespeichert oder aus ihr heraus referenziert werden. Um diese beiden Freiheitsgrade ebenfalls unabhängig voneinander kontrollieren zu können, werden wiederum zwei Parameter gebraucht. Exemplarisch werden hierzu der neue Parameter "location" und der bereits bekannte Parameter "element_placement" in die Attributdefinition aufgenommen (vgl. Abb. 9, [8]-[9]):

```
attribute_description = attribute_name [location = location_type,
                                         element_placement=placement_type]: object_type
```

Mit dem Parameter "element_placement" wird wie bei Mengen und Listen definiert, ob ein Attributwert bzw. - wenn das Attribut eine Menge, Liste oder ein Tupel ist - dessen Konstruktordatenstruktur direkt in der Konstruktordatenstruktur des Tupels gespeichert oder aus ihr heraus referenziert wird. Dazu wird hier angenommen, daß ein Tupel durch eine Datenstruktur implementiert wird, die einem Record in einer Pascal-ähnlichen Programmiersprache gleicht. In dieser Datenstruktur wird für jedes Attribut ein Feld vorgesehen. Abhängig von dem Parameter "element_placement" enthält dieses Feld entweder den Attributwert oder eine Referenz auf einen Record mit dem jeweiligen Attributwert. Da der Parameter "element_placement" an die Attributdefinition gebunden ist, kann unabhängig für jedes Attribut entschieden werden, ob es materialisiert oder referenziert gespeichert wird.

Aus Optimierungsgründen, wenn zum Beispiel einige Attribute eines Tupels nur sehr selten zugegriffen werden, kann es nützlich sein, die Konstruktordatenstruktur eines Tupels auf mehrere Records aufzuteilen. Dazu wird sie im folgenden in einen Primärblock und optional mehrere Sekundärblöcke aufgeteilt. Sowohl dem Primär- als auch den Sekundärblöcken können hierbei mehrere Attribute zugeordnet werden. Jeder Sekundärblock wird in einem eigenen Record gespeichert. Die Referenzen auf diese Records werden in dem Primärblock gespeichert. Ob für den Primärblock ebenfalls ein Record angelegt wird, hängt davon ab, ob das Tupel selbst referenziert oder materialisiert gespeichert wird. Mit dem oben eingeführten Parameter "location" wird für jedes Attribut festgelegt, ob das zugehörige Feld in dem Primärblock oder in einem Sekundärblock lokalisiert wird. Der Parameter erhält dazu zwei zulässige Werte (Abb. 9, [12]):

```
location_type = primary | secondary (record_type_name)
```

Wird für ein Attribut "primary" angegeben, so wird das zugehörige Feld in dem Primärblock angelegt. Hat der Parameter hingegen den Wert "secondary (record_type_name)", so wird das Feld in einem Sekundärblock angelegt. Der Sekundärblock wird in einem Record vom Typ "record_type_name" gespeichert. Sollen mehrere Attribute in dem

Mitarbeiter			
Pers_Nr.	Name	Gehalt	Lebenslauf
77234	Maier	4000	Frau Bettina Maier ist am ...
77235	Schmidt	4400	Herr Fritz Schmidt ist am ...

Abb. 5: Ausprägung einer Mitarbeiterrelation

gleichen Sekundärblock gespeichert werden, so ist in "record_type_name" jeweils derselbe Record-Typname anzugeben.

Das Zusammenspiel der beiden Parameter "location" und "element_placement" soll nun an dem Beispiel der Mitarbeiterrelation in Abb. 5 verdeutlicht werden. Dabei nehme man an, daß die Relation sehr häufig verwendet wird, um aus dem Mitarbeiternamen die Personalnummer abzuleiten und umgekehrt. Auf das Gehalt und den Lebenslauf werde selten zugegriffen. Daher sollen der Name und die Personalnummer gemeinsam in dem Primärblock materialisiert gespeichert werden, das Gehalt und der Lebenslauf sollen hingegen in einem gemeinsamen Sekundärblock ausgelagert werden. Der unter Umständen lange Lebenslauf wird referenziert gespeichert. Um die Tupel der Relation zu verbinden, wird eine verkettete Liste verwendet. Eine Definition der Mitarbeiterrelation, die diese Eigenschaften hat, lautet dann:

```
complex_object Mitarbeiter [anchor_record_type=Link_Rec]
 set [implementation=linked_list, element_placement=referenced (Prim_Rec)]
  of tuple
  (Pers_Nr.   [location=primary, element_placement=inplace]: integer,
   Name       [location=primary, element_placement=inplace]: fix_string(30),
   Gehalt     [location=secondary (Sec_Rec),element_placement=inplace]: real,
   Lebenslauf [location=secondary (Sec_Rec),
               element_placement=referenced(Lebenslauf_Rec)]: var_string).
```

Die sich daraus ergebende Speicherungsstruktur ist in Abb. 6.1 dargestellt.

An diesem Beispiel ist gut zu erkennen, daß die Parameter "location" und "element_placement" beide benötigt werden und nicht redundant sind. Würde auf einen von beiden verzichtet, so könnte nicht ausgedrückt werden, daß die Referenz auf das Lebenslauf-Record zusammen mit dem Gehalt in einem Sekundärblock zu speichern ist. Es wäre nur noch möglich, für den Lebenslauf einen eigenen Sekundärblock anzulegen.

Ein Nachteil der dargestellten Speicherungsstruktur sind die vielen kleinen Link-Records, die jeweils nur einen Zeiger auf das nächste Tupel und den referenzierten Primärblock eines Tupels enthalten. Dieses Problem läßt sich aber leicht lösen, indem die Primärblöcke in den Link-Records materialisiert gespeichert werden. Dazu ist in der zweiten Zeile der Definition nur der Parameter "element_placement" von "referenced (Prim_Rec)" nach "inplace" umzusetzen:

```
complex_object Mitarbeiter [anchor_record_type=Link_Rec]
 set [implementation=linked_list, element_placement=inplace] of ...
```

Dies bewirkt, daß die Primärblöcke mit den Referenzen auf die Sekundär-Records und den Feldern für die Attribute Pers_Nr. und Name in den Link-Records materialisiert werden. Die sich jetzt ergebende Speicherungsstruktur ist in Abb. 6.2 dargestellt.

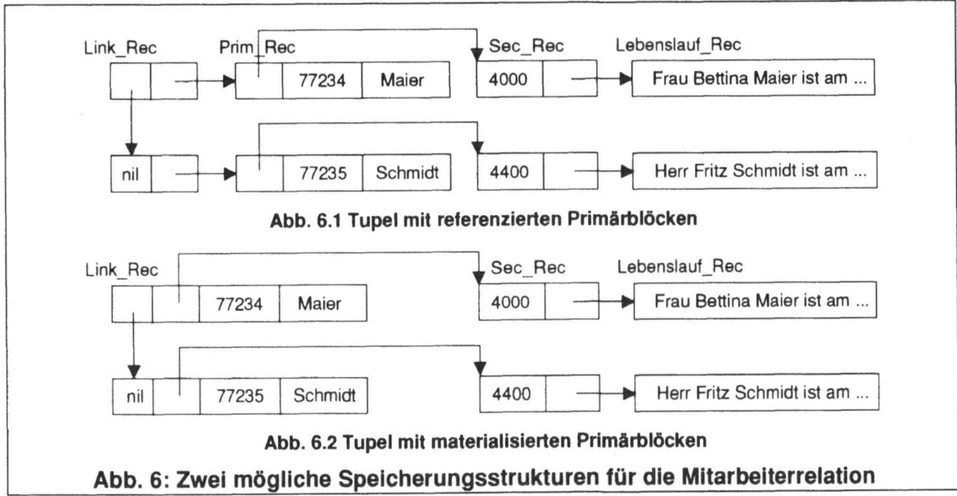

Abb. 6.1 Tupel mit referenzierten Primärblöcken

Abb. 6.2 Tupel mit materialisierten Primärblöcken

Abb. 6: Zwei mögliche Speicherungsstrukturen für die Mitarbeiterrelation

3.4 Vollständiges Beispiel einer Speicherungsstruktur für die Roboterrelation

Nachdem die Parameter "element_placement", "implementation" und "location" ausführlich diskutiert wurden, soll ihre Mächtigkeit noch einmal an dem Beispiel der eNF^2-Roboterrelation aus Abb. 1 demonstriert werden. Dazu ist im Anhang in Abb. 8 eine vollständige Definition des Typs und einer Speicherungsstruktur der Roboterrelation gegeben. Die Speicherungsstruktur wurde dabei entsprechend den Annahmen in der Einleitung entworfen. Häufig gemeinsam benötigte Daten wurden zusammengefaßt und selten gemeinsam benötigte Daten separiert. Die sich ergebende Record-Struktur ist im Anhang in Abb. 10 graphisch dargestellt.

Die folgenden Details sind an dieser Struktur besonders interessant. Die Konstruktordatenstruktur für die Robotertupel wurde auf einen Primär- und einen Sekundärblock aufgeteilt. Dies ist in [1], [2], [3], [13], [16] und [18] der Abb. 8 zu erkennen. So können die Konstruktionsdaten eines Roboters, wie Achsen und Effektoren, objektbezogen zu Clustern zusammengefaßt werden. Die hiervon separierten Einsatzdaten können hingegen objektübergreifend gespeichert werden. Nähere Einzelheiten dazu werden in Abschnitt 4 beschrieben werden. Die Daten einer Achse werden jeweils in einem "Achs-Record" zusammengefaßt ([5] - [12] in Abb. 8). Als Konstruktordatenstruktur für die Liste der Achsen wird ein Array ([4] in Abb. 8) verwendet. Dieses wird in dem "Sec_Rec"-Record materialisiert ([3] in Abb. 8). Diese Implementation einer Liste entspricht den Vorschlägen in DASDBS (vgl. [DPS86]), komplexe Objekte zu implementieren. Im Gegensatz dazu wird zur Implementation der Menge der Einsatzdaten eine Speicherungsstruktur gewählt, die der Strategie in AIM-P (vgl. [Dada86]) entspricht. Aus dem "Prim_Rec"-Record heraus wird ein Zeiger-Record referenziert ([13] in Abb. 8). Dieser enthält Referenzen auf Daten-Records mit den Namen der bearbeiteten Produkte und auf Records mit den Einsatzwochen und Kosten ([14], [15] in Abb. 8). Die Implementation der Menge der Effektoren entspricht schließlich den Vorschlägen zur Implementation von XSQL (vgl. [Lori85]). Die Elemente der Mengen werden durch Zwillingspointer verkettet ([17] in Abb. 8). Die umfangreichen Bedienungsanleitungen der Roboter werden in eigenen Records gespeichert werden ([18] in Abb. 8).

4. Benutzergesteuerte Clusterung komplexer Objekte

Mit den in Abschnitt 3 entworfenen Methoden können komplexe Objekte entsprechend den Anforderungen einer Anwendung auf Records aufgeteilt werden. Der zweite Schritt in einer optimierten Speicherung komplexer Objekte ist, häufig gemeinsam zugegriffene Records auf den gleichen oder benachbarten Seiten zu speichern. So können die Zahl der Seitenzugriffe und damit die Kosten, eine Anfrage auszuwerten, weiter reduziert werden. Auch hier gilt, daß eine feste Heuristik, wie zum Beispiel alle Records eines komplexen Objektes in einem Cluster zusammenzufassen (vgl. [BeDe89], [Dada86], [DPS86], [KFC90], [Kim87], [ScSi89]), in vielen, wenn nicht sogar in den meisten Fällen gut sein kann, aber auch manchmal versagt. Dann ist wieder die Kontrolle des Anwenders notwendig. Dazu führen wir nachfolgend die Begriffe "Segment" und "Cluster" ein und zeigen, wie der Anwender selbst bestimmen kann, welche Records in welchen Segmenten und Clustern gespeichert werden. Dabei wird hier eine Variante verfolgt, bei der für jeden Record-Typ festgelegt wird, in welchem Cluster seine Records abgelegt werden. Hierdurch wird unter anderem die Optimierung von Anfragen erleichtert, da bereits zur Übersetzungszeit die Clusterung der Records bekannt ist.

4.1 Segmente und Cluster

Als ein "Segment" wird im folgenden eine logisch zusammenhängende Einheit von Seiten auf dem Hintergrundspeicher bezeichnet. In einem dateigestützten System würde ein Segment auf eine oder mehrere Direktzugriffsdateien abgebildet werden. Zur Identifikation sollen Segmente eindeutige Namen haben. In dem folgenden Vorschlag wird jedes Segment in "Cluster" aufgeteilt. Jeder Cluster kann beliebig viele Records enthalten. Einem Cluster sollen dazu eine oder mehrere, nach Möglichkeit benachbarte Seiten eines Segmentes zugeordnet werden. Die Zahl der Cluster innerhalb eines Segmentes kann sich mit der gleichen Dynamik ändern, mit der Daten in die Datenbank eingefügt oder aus ihr herausgelöscht werden. Diese Aufteilung eines Segmentes in Cluster ähnelt sehr dem Verfahren zur Clusterung von Tupeln in dem kommerziellen Datenbanksystem Oracle [Orac90].

4.2 Objektbezogene und objektübergreifende Cluster

Bereits in der Einleitung wurde angedeutet, daß man zwei Arten von Clustern unterscheiden kann. Die hier als "objektbezogen" bezeichneten Cluster entsprechen im wesentlichen den "klassischen" Clustern. Sie werden verwendet, um Records entsprechend ihrer Objekt- oder Subobjektzugehörigkeit zusammenzufassen. Dazu wird für jede Ausprägung eines Objekt- oder Subobjekttyps ein (oder mehrere) Cluster eines (oder mehrerer) Cluster-Typs angelegt. In diesen Clustern werden die Records des Objektes oder Subobjektes gespeichert. Beispielsweise werden nachfolgend für jeden Roboter je ein "Sec_Rec_Cluster-i" und ein "Prim_Rec_Cluster-j" der Cluster-Typen "Sec_Rec_Cluster" und "Prim_Rec_Cluster" angelegt. In diesen werden die Records der Typen "Sec_Rec", "Achs_Rec", "Eff_Rec" und "Bes_Rec" entsprechend ihrer Objektzugehörigkeit eingefügt (vgl. -Schattierung in Abb. 10). Im Gegensatz dazu werden bei der als "objektübergreifende" Clusterung bezeichneten Methode die Records eines oder mehrerer Record-Typen unabhängig von ihrer Objektzugehörigkeit gemeinsam in einem Cluster gespeichert. Die -Schattierung in Abb. 10 deutet beispielsweise an, daß alle "Anker_Rec"- und "Prim_Rec"-Records in dem "Anker-Cluster" und alle "Pointer_Rec"-, "Produkt_Rec"- und "Leist_Rec"-Records in dem "Costs-Cluster" gespeichert werden.

Kombiniert man beide Methoden wie in Abb. 10, so ist es möglich, abhängig von der Anwendung gewisse Teile eines Objektes objektbezogen, andere objektübergreifend zu clustern. Zur Definition der Clusterung wird im folgenden, wie schon bei der Definition der Speicherungsstrukturen, wieder nur eine einfache Syntax verwendet. Sie besteht im wesentlichen aus einem Term mit zwei Alternativen (siehe Abb. 7).

4.2.1 Objektbezogene Cluster

Bei der objektbezogenen Clusterung werden Records entsprechend ihrer Objekt- oder Subobjektzugehörigkeit zusammengefaßt. Für jede Ausprägung eines Objekt- oder Subobjekttyps wird ein Cluster angelegt. Um diesen Zusammenhang zwischen Objekten und Clustern syntaktisch auf der Record-Ebene ausdrücken zu können, verwenden wir sogenannte "objektbezogene Cluster-Typen". Jeder objektbezogene Cluster ist eine Ausprägung eines solchen Typs. Zur Identifizierung der einzelnen Ausprägungen verwenden wir sogenannte "identifizierende" Records (identifying records). Die Idee ist dabei, daß alle Records eines Clusters direkt oder indirekt von dem "Identifying"-Record des Clusters abhängen müssen. Um einen objektbezogenen Cluster-Typ zu definieren, wird die erste Variante der Cluster-Definition (siehe Abb. 7) verwendet:

```
cluster_definition = object_cluster_type (cluster_type_name   = cluster_type_name,
                                          segment             = segment_name,
                                          identifying_records = record_type_name,
                                          member_records      = list_of_record_types)
```

Durch diesen Term wird ein Cluster-Typ mit dem Namen "cluster_type_name" definiert. Die Ausprägungen (= objektbezogene Cluster) des Typs werden in dem Segment "segment_name" angelegt. Diese Cluster werden durch Records identifiziert, deren Typ im Parameter "identifying_records" gegeben ist. Die Member-Klausel gibt an, welche Records welcher Record-Typen in diesen Clustern gespeichert werden. Diese Typen müssen dabei in einer direkten oder indirekten Eltern-Kind-Beziehung zu den "Identifying"-Records stehen. Außerdem können die "Identifying"-Records selbst Member-Records sein[5].

Das Verfahren der objektbezogenen Clusterung sei am Beispiel der Roboterrelation verdeutlicht. Entsprechend der Einleitung sollen die Achs- und Effektordaten jeweils in einem Cluster pro Roboter zusammengefaßt werden. Betroffen hiervon sind die Record-Typen "Sec_Rec", "Achs_Rec" und "Eff_Rec". Die entsprechende Definition des Cluster-Typs lautet:

```
object_cluster_type (cluster_type_name   = Sec_Rec_Cluster
                     segment             = Main,
                     identifying_records = Sec_Rec,
                     member_records      = (Sec_Rec, Achs_Rec, Eff_Rec))
```

Für jeden Record vom Typ "Sec_Rec" wird hierdurch im Segment "Main" ein Cluster angelegt. In Abb. 10 sind diese Cluster mit "Sec_Rec_Cluster-1" und "Sec_Rec_Cluster-2" bezeichnet. In diesen Clustern werden die Records der Typen "Sec_Rec", "Achs_Rec" und "Eff_Rec" entsprechend ihrer hierarchischen Abhängigkeit von den beiden "Sec_Rec"-Records gespeichert.

---

[5] Da ein "Identifying"-Record zunächst einmal nur als Identifier (über eine systeminterne Referenz) dient, ist es nicht zwingend notwendig, daß die "Identifying"-Records selbst Member-Records sind.

```
cluster_definition = /* Definition eines objektorientierten Cluster-Typs.   */
                     object_cluster_type (cluster_type_name   = cluster_type_name,
                                          segment             = segment_name,
                                          identifying_records = record_type_name,
                                          member_records      = list_of_record_types)|

                     /* Definition eines objektübergreifenden Clusters.     */
                     segment_cluster     (cluster_name        = cluster_name,
                                          segment             = segment_name,
                                          member_records      = list_of_record_types)

                       /* Liste von "member"-Record-Typen eines Clusters.   */
list_of_record_types = (record_type_name (, record_type_name)*)

cluster_type_name    = string /* Name eines objektorientierten Cluster-Typs. */

cluster_name         = string /* Name eines objektübergreifenden Clusters.   */

segment_name         = string /* Name eines Segmentes.                       */
```

Abb. 7: Term zur Zuordnung von Record-Typen zu Clustern

Bei der objektbezogenen Clusterung können Records einer beliebigen Hierarchiestufe als "Identifying"-Records verwendet werden. Damit können Records beliebiger Subobjekte geclustert werden. Außerdem ist es nicht notwendig, daß die "Identifying"-Records selbst in den Clustern (s. Fußnote 5), die sie identifizieren, gespeichert werden. Dies sei ebenfalls an einem Beispiel verdeutlicht:

```
object_cluster_type (cluster_type_name   = Prim_Rec_Cluster
                     segment             = Secondary,
                     identifying_records = Prim_Rec,
                     member_records      = (Bes_Rec))
```

Hier wird festgelegt, daß die "Bes_Rec"-Records in Clustern, die durch die "Prim-Rec"-Records identifiziert werden, im Segment "Secondary" gespeichert werden (vgl. Abb. 10 "Prim_Rec_Cluster-1" und "-2"). Die "Prim-Rec"-Records selbst werden aber, wie im folgenden definiert, in einem objektübergreifenden Cluster gespeichert werden.

4.2.2 Objektübergreifende Cluster

Objektübergreifende Cluster werden verwendet, um Records unabhängig von ihrer Objekt- und Subobjektzugehörigkeit in Clustern zusammenzufassen. Im Gegensatz zu objektbezogenen Clustern gibt es dabei stets nur eine Ausprägung eines objektübergreifenden Cluster(-Typs). Daher lassen sich diese Cluster auch durch eindeutige Namen identifizieren. Da es in einem Segment keine zwei objektübergreifenden Cluster mit demselben Namen gibt, werden sie im folgenden auch als segmentbezogene Cluster bezeichnet (vgl. Abb. 7). Ihre Verwendung sei ebenfalls am Beispiel der Roboterrelation näher erläutert.

In der Einleitung wurde angenommen, daß die Einsatzdaten häufig unabhängig von den Robotern zugegriffen werden. Es erscheint daher sinnvoll, alle Records der Typen "Pointer_Rec", "Produkt_Rec" und "Leist_Rec" unabhängig von ihrer Objektzugehörigkeit in einem Cluster zusammenzufassen. Dies wird durch den folgenden Term ausgedrückt. Alle Records der drei Typen werden hierdurch im Segment "Main" im Cluster "Costs_Cluster" (vgl. Abb. 10) gespeichert.

```
segment_cluster (cluster_name   = Costs_Cluster,
                 segment        = Main,
                 member_records = (Pointer_Rec, Produkt_Rec, Leist_Rec))
```

Ein anderes Beispiel sind die Records der Typen "Anker_Rec" und "Prim_Rec". Jeder Zugriff auf ein Objekt führt über diese Records. Daher sollen diese Records in einem - hier "Anker_Cluster" genannten (vgl. Abb. 10) - Cluster zusammengefaßt werden:

```
segment_cluster (cluster_name   = Anker_Cluster,
                 segment        = Main,
                 member_records = (Anker_Rec, Prim_Rec))
```

Mit dieser letzten Definition ist die Clusterung der Roboterrelation nunmehr vollständig beschrieben. Die Einsatzdaten der Roboter werden objektübergreifend in einem Cluster zusammengefaßt. Im Gegensatz dazu werden die Achs- und Effektordaten jeweils roboterbezogen geclustert. Hierdurch unterscheidet sich die Speicherungsstruktur von der sonst oft nur angebotenen (und auch hier möglichen) rein objektbezogenen Clusterung.

5. Zusammenfassung und Ausblick

In diesem Beitrag wurden zwei Freiheitsgrade - Wahl einer Konstruktordatenstruktur zur Implementation von Mengen, Listen und Tupeln, Entscheidung, ob Elemente bzw. Attribute materialisiert oder referenziert gespeichert werden - beim Entwurf von Speicherungsstrukturen für komplexe Objekte herausgearbeitet. Darauf aufsetzend wurden drei orthogonale Parameter entwickelt, die geeignet sind, diese Freiheitsgrade und damit die systeminterne Repräsentation komplexer Objekte zu definieren. Mit diesen Parametern kann die Aufteilung eines komplexen Objektes auf Records explizit kontrolliert werden. Es ist möglich, häufig gemeinsam zugegriffene Substrukturen komplexer Objekte in einem einzigen Record und damit in einer Zugriffseinheit zusammenzufassen. Umgekehrt können selten gemeinsam benötigte Substrukturen separat gespeichert werden. Die logische Struktur der Objekte ist hiervon stets unbeeinflußt. Anfragen können unabhängig von der gewählten Speicherungsstruktur formuliert werden. Die Wahl einer geeigneten oder ungeeigneten Speicherungsstruktur hat nur Auswirkungen auf die Performanz des Systems.

Für eine gute Performanz eines Systems ist auch eine sinnvolle Clusterung der Records notwendig. Sonst ist im ungünstigsten Fall für jeden Zugriff auf einen Record ein Plattenzugriff erforderlich. Im zweiten Teil dieses Beitrages wurde daher vorgestellt, wie die Clusterung der Records explizit definiert werden kann. Records können dabei objekt- bzw. subobjektbezogen, aber auch objektübergreifend zu Clustern zusammengefaßt werden. So können häufig gemeinsam zugegriffene Records wahlweise abhängig oder unabhängig von ihrer Objektzugehörigkeit gemeinsam in den gleichen Seiten des Hintergrundspeichers abgelegt werden. Die sonst übliche rein objektbezogene Clusterung wird damit durchbrochen.

Eine geeignete Speicherung komplexer Objekte ist allein jedoch noch kein Garant für eine gute Performanz. Zusätzlich muß auch die Optimierung von Anfragen auf die Objekt- und Speicherungsstrukturen abgestimmt sein. Dazu haben wir in [KeDa91] unterschiedliche Methoden zur Auswertung von Anfragen an komplex strukturierte Objekte mit Indexen diskutiert. Derzeit entwickeln wir Kostenformeln, um die hierbei generierten alternativen Anfragepläne in Abhängigkeit von der Speicherungsstruktur der Objekte bewerten zu können.

6. Literatur

Banc88 F. Bancilhon, G. Barbedette, V. Benzaken, C. Delobel, S. Gamerman, C.Lécluse, P. Pfeffer, P. Richard, F. Velez: *The Design and Implementation of O_2, an Object-Oriented Database System.* K.R. Dittrich (Ed.), Advances in Object-Oriented Database Systems, Proc. 2nd Int. Workshop on Object-Oriented Database Systems, Bad Münster, Lecture Notes in Computer Science 334, Springer-Verlag, pp. 1-22, 1988.

BeDe89 V. Benzaken, C. Delobel: *Dynamic Clustering Strategies in the O_2 Object-Oriented Database System. Altair*, BP105, 78153 Le Chesnay Cedex, France, pp. 1-27, 1989.

Dada86 P. Dadam, K. Kuespert, F. Andersen, H. Blanken, R. Erbe, J. Guenauer, V. Lum, P. Pistor, G. Walch: *A DBMS Prototype to Support Extended NF^2 Relations: An Integrated View on Flat Tables and Hierarchies.* ACM-SIGMOD, Proc. Int. Conf. on Management of Data Washington, D.C., pp. 356-367, 1986.

DPS86 U. Deppisch, H.-B. Paul, H.-J. Schek: *A Storage System for Complex Objects.* K. Dittrich, U. Dayal (Eds.), Proc. Int. Workshop on Object-Oriented Database Systems, Pacific Grove, pp. 183 - 195, 1986.

Gee77 W.C. McGee: *The information management system IMS/VS: Data base facilities.* IBM Systems Journal, Vol. 16, No. 2, pp. 96-123, 1977.

HaOz88 A. Hafez, G. Ozsoyoglu: *Storage Structures for Nested Relations.* IEEE Data Engineering, Vol 11, No. 3, Special Issue on Nested Relations, pp. 31 - 38, 1988.

HMMS87 T. Härder, K. Meyer-Wegener, B. Mitschang, A. Sikeler: *PRIMA - a DBMS Prototype Supporting Engineering Applications.* Proc. 13th Int. Conf. on Very Large Data Bases, Brighton, pp. 433 - 442, 1987.

Ingr90 *INGRES/Database Administrator's Guide.* Release 6.3, 1990.

KeDa91 U. Keßler, P. Dadam: *Auswertung komplexer Anfragen an hierarchisch strukturierte Objekte mit Pfadindexen.* H.-J. Appelrath (Ed), Proc. Datenbanksysteme in Büro, Technik und Wissenschaft, GI-Fachtagung, Springer-Verlag, Informatik-Fachberichte 270, pp. 218-237, 1991.

KFC90 S. Khoshafian, M.J. Franklin, M.J. Carey: *Storage Management for Persistent Complex Objects.* Information Systems, Vol. 15, No. 3, pp. 303-320, 1990.

Kim87 W. Kim, J. Banerjee, H.-T. Chou, J.F. Garza, D. Woelk: *Composite Object Support in an Object-Oriented Database System.* Proc. Int. Conf. on Object-Oriented Programming Systems, Languages and Applications (OOPSLA), pp. 118-125, 1987.

Kim89 W. Kim, N. Ballou, H.-T. Chou, J.R. Garza, D. Woelk: *Features of the ORION Object-Oriented Database System.* W. Kim, F.H. Lochovsky (Eds.), Object-Oriented Concepts, Databases, and Applications, ACM Press, Frontier Series, pp. 251-282, 1989.

Lori85 R. Lorie, W. Kim, D. McNabb, W. Plouffe, A.Meier: *Supporting Complex Objects in a Relational System for Engineering Databases.* W. Kim, D.S. Reiner, D.S. Batory (Eds.), Query Processing in Database Systems, Topics in Information Systems, Springer-Verlag, pp. 145-155, 1985.

Mits88 B. Mitschang: *The Molecule-Atom Data Model.* T. Härder (Ed.), The PRIMA Project Design and Implementation of a Non-Standard Database System, University Kaiserslautern, Report No. 26/88, Erwin-Schrödinger-Straße, 6750 Kaiserslautern, Germany, pp. 13-36, 1988.

MSOP86 D. Maier, J. Stein, A. Otis, A. Purdy: *Development on an Object-Oriented DBMS.* Proc. Int. Conf. on Object-Oriented Programming Systems, Languages and Applications (OOPSLA), pp. 472-482, 1986.

Nier89 O. Nierstrasz: *A Survey of Object-Oriented Concepts.* W. Kim, F.H. Lochovsky (Eds.), Object-Oriented Concepts, Databases, and Applications, ACM Press, pp. 3-21, 1989.

Orac90 *Oracle RDBMS Database Administrator's Guide*, Version 6.0, 1990.

Paul87 H.-B. Paul, H.-J. Schek, M. H. Scholl, G. Weikum, U. Deppisch: *Architecture and Implementation of the Darmstadt Database Kernel System.* ACM-SIGMOD, Proc. Int. Conf. on Management of Data, San Francisco, USA, pp. 196-207, 1987.

PiAn86 P. Pistor, F. Andersen: *Designing a Generalized NF2 Model with an SQL-Type Language Interface.* Proc. 12th Int. Conf. on Very Large Data Bases, Kyoto, Japan, pp. 278-285, 1986.

Scho92 M. H. Scholl: *Physical Database Design for an Object-Oriented Database System.* J.-C. Freytag, G. Vossen, D.E. Maier (Eds.), Query Processing for Advanced Database Applications, Morgan Kaufmann, to appear, 1993.

ScPi82 H.-J. Schek, P. Pistor: *Data Structures for an Integrated Data Base Management and Information Retrieval System.* Proc. Int. Conf. on Very Large Data Bases, Mexico City, pp. 197-207, 1982.

ScSc90 M. H. Scholl, H.-J. Schek: *A relational object model.* Proc. Int. Conf. on Database Theory (ICDT), Paris, Springer-Verlag, Lecture Notes in Computer Science 470, pp. 89-105, 1990.

ScSi89 H. Schöning, A. Sikeler: *Cluster Mechanisms Supporting the Dynamic Construction of Complex Objects.* Proc. 3rd Int. Conf. on Foundations of Data Organization and Algorithms (FODO), Paris, Springer-Verlag, Lecture Notes in Computer Science 367, pp. 31-46, 1989.

Sike88 A. Sikeler: *Key Concepts of the PRIMA Access System.* T. Härder (Ed.), The PRIMA Project Design and Implementation of a Non-Standard Database System, University Kaiserslautern, Rep.-No. 26/88, Erwin-Schrödinger-Straße, 6750 Kaiserslautern, Germany, pp. 69-99, 1988.

SPS87 M. H. Scholl, H.-B. Paul, H.-J. Schek: *Supporting Flat Relations by a Nested Relational Kernel.* Proc. 13th Int. Conf. on Very Large Data Bases, Brighton, England, pp. 137-146, 1987.

Anhang: Abbildungen

```
complex_object Roboter [anchor_record_type=Anker_Rec]
 set [implementation=array, element_placement=referenced(Prim_Rec)] of
  tuple(
   R_Nr    [location=primary, element_placement=inplace]: integer,                  [1]

   Name    [location=secondary(Sec_Rec), element_placement=inplace]: fix_string(30),  [2]

   Achsen  [location=secondary(Sec_Rec), element_placement=inplace]:                 [3]
     list [implementation=array, element_placement=referenced (Achs_Rec)] of         [4]
          tuple (                                                                    [5]
           Achs_Nr          [location=primary, element_placement=inplace]: integer,  [6]
           Positionsmatrix  [location=primary, element_placement=inplace]:           [7]
            list [implementation=array, element_placement=inplace] of                [8]
                 tuple (                                                             [9]
                  Reihe  [location=primary, element_placement=inplace]: integer,     [10]
                  Vektor [location=primary, element_placement=inplace]:              [11]
                   list [implementation=array,element_placement=inplace] of integer)), [12]

   Einsatz [location=primary, element_placement=referenced (Pointer_Rec)]:           [13]
    set [implementation=array, element_placement=inplace] of
        tuple (
         Produkt  [location=primary, element_placement=referenced (Produkt_Rec)]:    [14]
                   fix_string(30),
         Leistung [location= primary, element_placement=inplace]:
           set [implementation=array, element_placement=referenced (Leist_Rec)] of   [15]
               tuple (
                Woche  [location=primary, element_placement=inplace]: integer,
                Kosten [location=primary, element_placement=inplace]: integer)),

   Effektoren [location=secondary(Sec_Rec), element_placement=referenced (Eff_Rec)]: [16]
    set [implementation=linked_list, element_placement=inplace] of                   [17]
        tuple (
         E_Nr    [location= primary, element_placement=inplace]: fix_string(30),
         Aufgabe [location= primary, element_placement=inplace]: fix_string(30)),

   Beschreibung [location=secondary(Sec_Rec), element_placement=referenced (Bes_Rec)]: [18]
                var_string))).
```

Abb. 8: Typ und Speicherungsstruktur-Definition der eNF²-Roboterrelation

```
                      /* Definition eines komplexen Objektes. */
complex_object db_object_name [anchor_record_type = record_type_name] object_type [1]

                      /* Name eines komplexen Objektes. */
db_object_name       = string

                      /* Typname für Records mit semantisch äquivalentem Inhalt. */
record_type_name     = string

                      /* Rekursiver Aufbau eines komplexen Objekttyps. */
object_type          = /* Beispiel für atomare Wertebereiche. */                  [2]
                      integer | real | var_string | fix_string(length) |

                      /* Definition einer Menge. */
                      set  [implementation    = implementation_type,            [3]
                           element_placement = placement_type] of object_type | [4]

                      /* Definition einer Liste. */
                      list [implementation    = implementation_type,            [5]
                           element_placement = placement_type] of object_type | [6]

                      /* Definition eines Tupels mit einer Liste von Attributen. */
                      tuple (attribute_description {,attribute_description}*)   [7]

                      /* Länge eines Strings mit fester Länge. */
length               = integer

                      /* Definition eines Attributs eines Tupels. */
attribute_description = attribute_name [location          = location_type,      [8]
                                        element_placement = placement_type]: object_type [9]

                      /* Name eines Attributs. */
attribute_name       = string


        /* Parameter zur Definition der Speicherungsstruktur komplexer Objekte */

                      /* Angabe, ob ein Element einer Menge oder Liste bzw. ein */
                      /* Attribut eines Tupels referenziert oder materialisiert */
                      /* gespeichert wird. */
placement_type       = inplace | referenced (record_type_name)                   [10]

                      /* Implementierungstechniken für Mengen und Listen.*/
implementation_type  = array | linked_list                                        [11]

                      /* Angabe, ob ein Attribut in dem Primär- oder einem */
                      /* Sekundärblock gespeichert bzw. daraus referenziert wird. */
location_type        = primary | secondary (record_type_name)                    [12]
```

Abb. 9: Vereinfachte Syntax zur Beschreibung komplexer Objekte

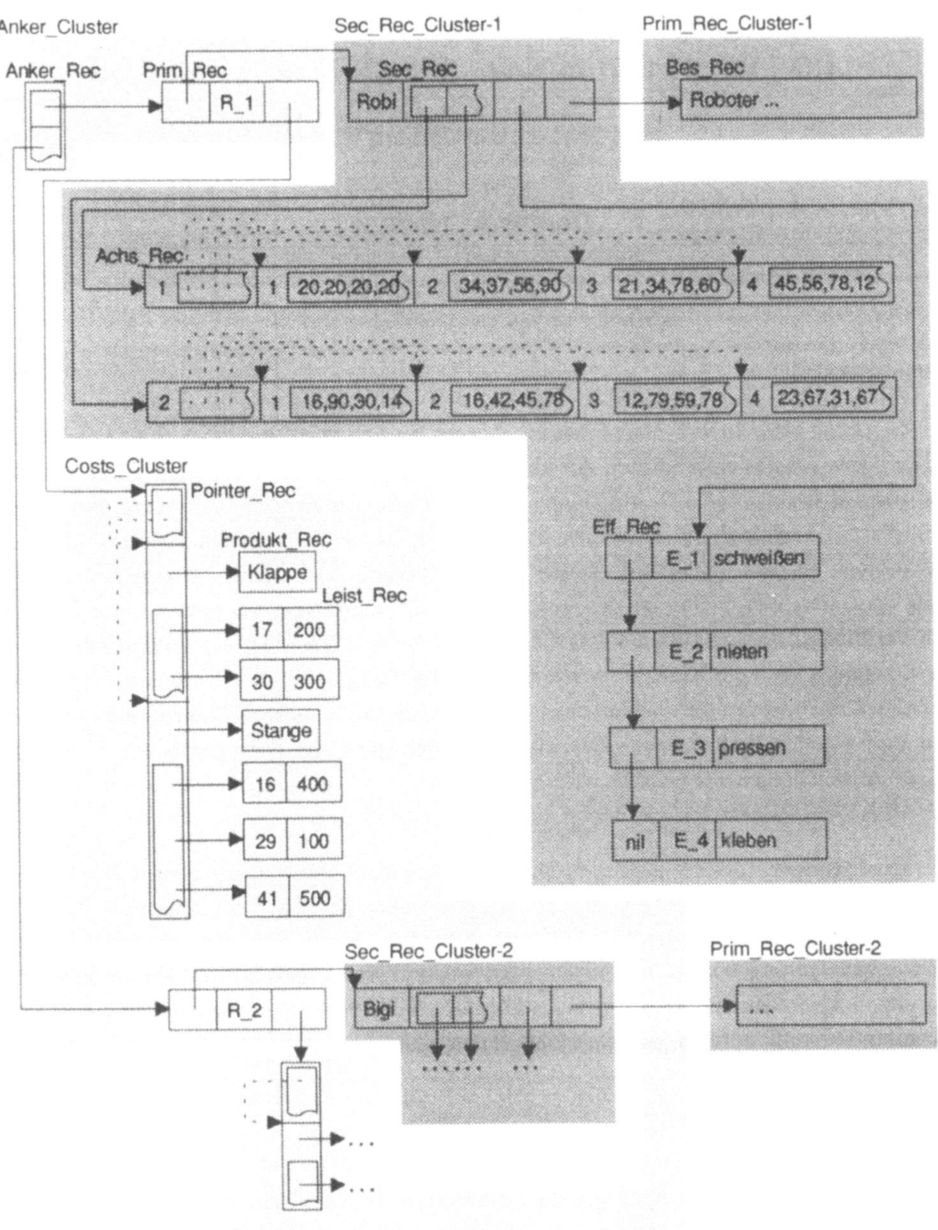

Legende: **objektbezogene Clusterung = 1 Cluster pro Objekt**

objektübergreifende Clusterung = 1 Cluster für alle Records, unabhängig von ihrer Objektzugehörigkeit

Abb. 10: Eine mögliche Speicherungsstruktur für die eNF^2-Roboterrelation

Datenpartitionierung zur Optimierung der I/O-Parallelität in Non-Standard-Anwendungen

Peter Zabback und Gerhard Weikum

ETH Zürich
Departement Informatik
Informationssysteme — Datenbanken
CH-8092 Zürich, Schweiz
E-Mail: {zabback,weikum}@inf.ethz.ch

Zusammenfassung

Disk-Arrays sind ein vielversprechender Ansatz zur Überwindung der viel zitierten "I/O-Krise". Der Einsatz einer großen Anzahl kleiner Plattenlaufwerke birgt ein hohes Potential zur Parallelisierung von I/O-Aufträgen und trägt damit entscheidend zur Reduzierung der Antwortzeit einzelner I/O-Aufträge bei. Der Schlüssel zum erfolgreichen Einsatz dieser Technologie für Non-Standard-Datenbanksysteme liegt in der Partitionierung und Verteilung der Daten über die Platten des Disk-Arrays. In diesem Beitrag stellen wir eine Methode zur Partitionierung von Dateien vor, die nicht nur auf die Minimierung der Antwortzeit abzielt, sondern auch die Einhaltung von Durchsatzanforderungen der Anwendungen berücksichtigt. Dabei werden die Größen der Partitionen für jede Datei individuell bestimmt. In einer umfassenden Performance-Evaluation auf der Basis von I/O-Traces aus Non-Standard-Anwendungen vergleichen wir unsere Methode der dateispezifischen Partitionierung mit einfacheren Methoden, bei denen die Partitionsgröße global festgelegt wird.

1 Einführung

Der dramatischen Entwicklung der Prozessorleistung steht eine vergleichsweise bescheidene Leistungssteigerung von I/O-Komponenten gegenüber. So geht man von einer jährlichen Verdopplung der Prozessorleistung aus, während bei der Positionierungsgeschwindigkeit von Magnetplatten nur etwa alle 10 Jahre eine Verdopplung erwartet wird [16]. Durch diese ständig wachsende Diskrepanz entwickelt sich das I/O-Subsystem zum entscheidenden Engpaß bei vielen Rechnerarchitekturen und Anwendungen.

Eine Möglichkeit zur Beseitigung dieses I/O-Engpasses besteht in der Ausnutzung von Parallelität. Voraussetzung dafür ist die entsprechende Konzeption des I/O-Subsystems, wobei Disk-Arrays einen vielversprechenden Ansatz darstellen [13][22][26][32]. Disk-Arrays bestehen aus einer großen Zahl kleiner, standardisierter (und damit kostengünstiger) Magnetplatten, die über einen leistungsfähigen Standardbus an einen Rechner angeschlossen sind. Werden nun die Anwendungsdaten geschickt über die Platten des Disk-Arrays verteilt, läßt sich durch Ausnutzung von I/O-Parallelität sowohl die Antwortzeit einzelner I/O-Aufträge reduzieren als auch der Durchsatz von I/O-Aufträgen erhöhen. Dies wird durch zwei Arten von I/O-Parallelität erreicht: erstens können einzelne (große) I/O-Aufträge parallelisiert werden, sofern die entsprechenden Daten über mehrere Platten verteilt sind, und zweitens können viele unabhängige I/O–Aufträge von verschiedenen Platten parallel bedient werden. Die erste Art der Parallelität heißt im folgenden Zugriffsparallelität, während die zweite Art mit Auftragsparallelität bezeichnet wird.

Klassische Datenbankanwendungen wie Buchungs– und Reservationssysteme können hierbei hauptsächlich von der Auftragsparallelität der I/O–Aufträge profitieren, da solche Systeme von einer großen Zahl kleiner I/O–Aufträge (typischerweise eine Seite der Größe 2–8 KBytes) dominiert werden. Durch Auftragsparallelität wird also der Durchsatz der I/O–Aufträge gesteigert, während die Antwortzeit eines einzelnen Auftrages nicht verbessert werden kann. Im Gegensatz dazu muß man bei Non–Standard–Anwendungen von wesentlich größeren I/O–Aufträgen ausgehen, da hierbei nicht nur einzelne (kleine) Tupel, sondern komplexe Objekte beliebiger Größe manipuliert werden. Beispiele für solche Objekte sind Bürodokumente innerhalb einer Büroablage, geometrische Daten beispielsweise aus dem CAD–Bereich, gerasterte Bilder wie beispielsweise Röntgenaufnahmen und Tomographien oder Videosequenzen in Multimediaanwendungen. In vielen Fällen wird gefordert, daß sowohl auf komplexe Objekte als Ganzes als auch auf selektierte Unterobjekte effizient zugegriffen werden kann. Daraus resultiert eine gemischte Last mit vielen großen als auch vielen kleinen I/O–Aufträgen, wobei häufig viele Benutzer gleichzeitig durch einen entsprechenden Datenbank–Server bedient werden sollen [1][4][6][11][12][29].

1.1 Datenpartitionierung

Der Schlüssel zum erfolgreichen Einsatz der Disk–Array–Technologie für dieses weite Anwendungsspektrum liegt in der Partitionierung und Verteilung der Anwendungsdaten. Für diese Partitionierung der Daten gibt es zwei grundsätzliche Alternativen:

- Dateien werden auf der Byte– bzw. Block–Ebene partitioniert. Der mit Abstand wichtigste Spezialfall der regelmäßigen byte–orientierten Partitionierung wird meist als *Striping* bezeichnet.
- Daten werden auf einer anwendungsorientierten Ebene partitioniert. Ein Beispiel dafür ist die Partitionierung von Tupelmengen in relationalen Datenbanksystemen.

Byte–orientierte Partitionierung hat gegenüber anwendungsorientierter Partitionierung den Vorteil, daß sie als generische Methode direkt im Speichersystem realisierbar ist und somit unmittelbar für alle denkbaren Anwendungen einsetzbar ist. Wir beschränken uns daher im folgenden auf diese Art der Partitionierung. Die zu partitionierenden Objekte sind also blockstrukturierte Byte–Folgen, die wir im folgenden kurz als "Datei" bezeichnen. Eine solche Datei entspricht beispielsweise einer einzelnen Relation oder einem Tablespace bzw. Indexspace in einem relationalen Datenbanksystem, einem komplexen Objekt oder einem physischen Speicher–Cluster in einem objektorientierten Datenbanksystem oder auch einem Bild, Video oder sonstigem "Blob" (Binary Large Object) in einer Multimediaanwendung.

Bei der byte–orientierten Partitionierung werden die zu partitionierenden Dateien in Bereiche von jeweils logisch aufeinanderfolgenden Bytes aufgeteilt. Bei dem mit Abstand wichtigsten Fall der regelmäßigen Partitionierung werden alle Bereiche gleich groß gewählt und reihum über alle Platten des Disk–Arrays verteilt. Eine naheliegende Abbildungsfunktion ist dabei $d = i \bmod N$, wobei i den i–ten Bereich bezeichnet, N die Anzahl der Platten im Disk–Array und d die berechnete Plattennummer ($0 \leq d \leq N-1$). Wegen des auf diese Weise entstehenden Streifenmusters über den Platten wird dieses Verfahren auch *Striping* genannt [17][28]. Die Größe eines Dateibereichs wird auch als *Striping–Granulat* bezeichnet. Das Striping–Granulat einer Datei ist also die größte Anzahl logisch aufeinanderfolgender Bytes (bzw. Blöcke), die auf eine Platte abgebildet werden.

1.2 Wahl des Striping–Granulates

Die Größe des Striping–Granulates hat einen entscheidenden Einfluß auf die Performance des Disk–Arrays. Ein sehr kleines Striping–Granulat führt zu einer starken Parallelisierung auch relativ kleiner I/O–Aufträge, was jedoch die Antwortzeit solcher I/O–Aufträge selbst im besten Fall nur unwesentlich reduziert und den maximal erreichbaren Durchsatz des Disk–Arrays sogar signifikant reduzieren kann. Kleine I/O–Aufträge sind nämlich durch die Positionierungszeit des Plattenarmes dominiert, während durch eine Parallelisierung der I/O–Aufträge nur die Übertragungszeit eines solchen Auftrages reduziert werden kann. Zusätzlich werden durch eine stärkere Parallelisierung auch mehr Zugriffsarme in Anspruch genommen, was die oben erwähnte Reduzierung des Durchsatzes zur Folge hat. Wird andererseits das Striping–Granulat zu groß gewählt, bleibt das vorhandene Potential zur Antwortzeitreduzierung ungenutzt, was für Anwendungen mit kritischen Antwortzeitanforderungen unakzeptabel sein kann.

In praktisch allen Produkten und Prototypen für Disk–Arrays und Disk–Array–basierte Dateisysteme wird das Striping–Granulat unabhängig von der Anwendung fest gewählt [15]. Typische Striping–Granulate sind ein Byte, ein Block (typischerweise 1–8KBytes), eine Spur (ca. 20–50 KBytes) oder ein Zylinder (ca. 200–500 KBytes). Konsequenterweise sind viele dieser Systeme nur für relativ eingeschränkte Anwendungsbereiche tauglich; ein Striping–Granulat von einem Byte etwa ist im Supercomputing–Bereich mit typischen Zugriffsgrößen im Megabyte–Bereich durchaus adäquat, für Datenbanksysteme aber unakzeptabel [9][10][21]. Wenn man den gesamten Bereich der Standard– und Non–Standard–Anwendungen von DBS mit einem einzigen Speichersystem abdecken möchte, ist es daher notwendig das Striping–Granulat an die jeweilige Anwendung anzupassen. Dies sollte automatisch durch das Speichersystem selbst erfolgen. Die Bestimmung des Striping–Granulats für eine gegebene Anwendung kann auf der Grundlage globaler Anwendungscharakteristika erfolgen oder auf der Grundlage der Zugriffscharakteristika einzelner Dateien. Im ersteren Fall haben alle Dateien das gleiche Striping–Granulat; im zweiten Fall ergeben sich dateispezifische Striping–Granulate.

In dieser Arbeit wird der Fall der dateispezifischen Striping–Granulate untersucht. Gerade Non–Standard–Anwendungen weisen häufig bezüglich der I/O–Auftragsgröße eine hohe Varianz auf [27], so daß eine dateispezifische Partitionierung signifikante Vorteile erwarten läßt. Eine Heuristik zur Bestimmung eines globalen, für alle Dateien identischen Striping–

Granulats wurde in [5] entwickelt; diese Heuristik läuft in praktisch allen Fällen auf ein Striping-Granulat von einer Spur hinaus. Der Ansatz der dateispezifisch optimierten Striping-Granulate wurde in [34][36] vorgeschlagen; er wird in der vorliegenden Arbeit weiterentwikkelt und auf der Basis realer I/O-Traces ausführlich evaluiert. Keine der bisherigen Arbeiten enthält derartige Leistungsuntersuchungen für reale Zugriffscharakteristika.

Abschnitt 2 enthält eine Beschreibung und Begründung unseres Optimierungsmodells zur Bestimmung dateispezifischer Striping-Granulate. Abschnitt 3 beinhaltet eine umfassende Evaluation der Methode auf der Basis von I/O-Traces aus den Anwendungsbereichen Büroablage und VLSI-Design. Abschnitt 4 diskutiert die inkrementelle Reorganisation bei Änderungen der Zugriffscharakteristika oder der verfügbaren Platten.

2 Eine heuristische Methode zur Datenpartitionierung

In diesem Abschnitt stellen wir unsere Methode zur optimalen Partitionierung von Anwendungsdaten vor. Wir verfolgen dabei zwei Ziele. Zum einen soll die Antwortzeit einzelner I/O-Aufträge minimiert werden, und zum andern sollen Mindestanforderungen bezüglich des Durchsatzes der I/O-Aufträge sichergestellt werden. Die Minimierung der Antwortzeit kann durch eine Parallelisierung von I/O-Aufträgen erreicht werden. Durch diese Parallelisierung einzelner I/O-Aufträge wird jedoch gleichzeitig die Plattenauslastung erhöht, was eine Durchsatzreduzierung zur Folge hat. Um nun bestehende Durchsatzanforderungen sicherstellen zu können, ist unter Umständen eine Reduzierung des Parallelitätsgrades notwendig.

Gemäß diesen Überlegungen erfolgt die Bestimmung des optimalen Striping-Granulats in zwei Schritten. Zunächst wird für eine Datei das Striping-Granulat so bestimmt, daß die Antwortzeit für einen typischen I/O-Auftrag bezüglich dieser Datei minimal wird. Bei diesen Überlegungen wird zunächst Einbenutzerbetrieb angenommen, d.h. Durchsatzüberlegungen und Warteschlangen an den Platten werden ignoriert. Erst im zweiten Schritt wird das zuvor berechnete Striping-Granulat den Durchsatzerfordernissen angepaßt.

2.1 Minimierung der Antwortzeit

Betrachten wir eine neu zu allozierende Datei der Größe S Blöcke, mit einer mittleren Auftragsgröße von R Blöcken. Für viele Anwendungen ist R a priori bekannt. In einem Buchungs- oder Reservationssystem zum Beispiel können wir von einer mittleren Auftragsgröße von einem Block ausgehen. Handelt es sich bei der neuen Datei um ein Bild aus einer Multimediaanwendung, so können wir meist davon ausgehen, daß immer auf das ganze Bild zugegriffen wird, also $R=S$ gilt. Sollte zum Allokationszeitpunkt keine Schätzung für R vorliegen, so kann zunächst ein Standardwert angenommen werden (z.B. die mittlere Auftragsgröße aller existierenden Dateien); die Datei kann später reorganisiert werden, wenn eine genauere Schätzung für R vorliegt.

Wird nun ein I/O-Auftrag der Größe R von P Platten bearbeitet, so ergibt sich die Antwortzeit $t_{resp}(R,P)$ wie folgt:

$$t_{resp}(R,P) = t_{seek}(P) + t_{rot}(P) + t_{trans}(R,P), \quad (1)$$

wobei $t_{seek}(P)$ die Positionierungszeit und $t_{rot}(P)$ die Rotationsverzögerung der "langsamsten" unter den beteiligten Platten darstellen sowie $t_{trans}(R,P)$ die Übertragungszeit ist. Formel (1) macht deutlich, daß $t_{seek}(P)$ als auch $t_{rot}(P)$ vom Parallelitätsgrad P abhängen, während $t_{trans}(R,P)$ sowohl durch die Größe des I/O–Auftrages R als auch durch den Parallelitätsgrad P bestimmt wird. Bei den folgenden Überlegungen gehen wir davon aus, daß alle Platten im Disk–Array vom gleichen Typ sind.

Wird ein I/O–Auftrag von P Platten parallel bedient, so ist für die Antwortzeit des Auftrages die längste Positionierungszeit aller beteiligten Platten maßgebend. Gehen wir davon aus, daß die Platten des Disk–Arrays bezüglich der Armposition unabhängig voneinander sind, so ergibt sich nach [2] für die maximale Anzahl Zylinder Z_{max}, die von der längsten Positionierung überwunden werden müssen:

$$Z_{\max} = \left[1 - \prod_{i=1}^{P} \frac{2i}{2i+1}\right] \times Z , \quad (2)$$

wobei Z die Anzahl der Zylinder einer Platte bezeichnet. Für die Positionierungszeit $t_{seek}(P)$ der langsamsten Platte ergibt sich damit:

$$t_{seek}(P) = a \times Z_{\max} + b, \quad (3)$$

mit geeigneten Konstanten a und b (Eine lineare Approximation der Positionierungszeit ist hier zulässig, da wir bei diesen Mittelwertbetrachtungen von einer großen Zahl zu überquerender Zylinder ausgehen müssen, und wir uns dadurch immer im linearen Bereich der Positionierungszeitfunktion bewegen [10]).

Analoge Überlegungen lassen sich auch für die Rotationsverzögerung anstellen. Sind P Platten an einem I/O–Auftrag beteiligt, müssen wir für die Antwortzeit wiederum die Rotationsverzögerung der langsamsten Platte berechnen [25][34]:

$$t_{rot}(P) = \frac{P}{P+1} \times t_{rot}, \quad (4)$$

wobei t_{rot} die Zeit für eine volle Plattenumdrehung darstellt.

Mit wachsendem Parallelitätsgrad steigen also sowohl die maximale Positionierungszeit als auch die maximale Rotationsverzögerung signifikant an, was gerade bei relativ kleinen I/O–Aufträgen, deren Antwortzeit durch diese zwei Komponenten dominiert ist, eine Erhöhung der Antwortzeit bewirkt.

Die einzige Antwortzeitkomponente, die mit zunehmendem Parallelitätsgrad eine Reduzierung erfährt, ist die Übertragungszeit $t_{trans}(R,P)$. Nehmen wir an, daß mit einer vollen Plattenumdrehung gerade eine Spur übertragen werden kann, so gilt:

$$t_{trans}(R,P) = \frac{t_{rot}}{B} \times \frac{R}{P}, \quad (5)$$

wobei B die Kapazität einer Plattenspur in Blöcken ist. Wir gehen hier vereinfachend davon aus, daß bei der Übertragung der $\lceil R/P \rceil$ Blöcke von einer Platte weder Spur- noch Zylinderwechsel notwendig werden. In dem ausführlicheren Modell in [34] werden sowohl Wahrscheinlichkeiten für Spur- und Zylinderwechsel als auch die notwendige Zeit dafür berücksichtigt.

Die Kombination der Formeln (1) bis (5) führt schließlich auf:

$$t_{resp}(R,P) = a \times \left[1 - \prod_{i=1}^{P} \frac{2i}{2i+1} \right] \times Z + b + \frac{P}{P+1} \times t_{rot} + \frac{R}{P \times B} \times t_{rot} \,. \qquad (6)$$

Analytisch läßt sich der optimale Parallelitätsgrad P_{opt}, bei dem die Antwortzeit $t_{resp}(R,P_{opt})$ minimal wird, durch die Lösung der folgenden Gleichung bestimmen:

$$\frac{dt_{resp}}{dP}(P_{opt}) = 0 \qquad (7)$$

Um die erste Ableitung von $t_{resp}(R,P)$ bezüglich P berechnen zu können, wird Formel (2) durch die logarithmische Funktion

$$Z_{\max} \approx (1 - e - f \times \ln(P)) \times Z, \qquad (8)$$

mit entsprechenden Konstanten e und f, approximiert [18]. Damit ergibt sich Formel (7) zu

$$\frac{t_{rot}}{P_{opt}+1} - \frac{a \times Z \times f}{P_{opt}} - \frac{P_{opt} \times t_{rot}}{(P_{opt}+1)^2} - \frac{R \times t_{rot}}{P_{opt}^2 B} = 0 \,. \qquad (9)$$

Dies führt schließlich auf eine kubische Gleichung mit zwei negativen Lösungen und einer positiven Lösung, die gerade den gesuchten optimalen Parallelitätsgrad P_{opt} liefert [34].

Das optimale Striping-Granulat SG_{opt}, bei dem die Antwortzeit eines I/O-Auftrages minimal wird, läßt sich jetzt sehr einfach aus der typischen Auftragsgröße R und dem optimalen Parallelitätsgrad P_{opt} bestimmen. Es ergibt sich nämlich aus:

$$SG_{opt} = \left\lceil \frac{R}{P_{opt}} \right\rceil \,. \qquad (10)$$

Abbildung 1 zeigt SG_{opt} für verschiedene Auftragsgrößen R. Zugrundegelegt wurden dabei die Leistungsparameter einer Platte vom Typ Fujitsu M2624SA [8]. Für Auftragsgrößen bis zu R=20 KBytes gilt $SG_{opt} = R$, d.h. solche Aufträge sind von der Positionierungszeit und Rotationsverzögerung dominiert, so daß eine Parallelisierung keine Antwortzeitgewinne bringt. Mit wachsender Auftragsgröße R steigen natürlich die durch eine Parallelisierung möglichen Antwortzeitgewinne, so daß SG_{opt} entsprechend kleiner wird.

2.2 Berücksichtigung von Durchsatzanforderungen

Bei den bisherigen Überlegungen zur Antwortzeitminimierung sind wir davon ausgegangen, daß sich die I/O-Aufträge gegenseitig nicht behindern, also keine Warteschlangen und damit Wartezeiten an den Platten entstehen. In einem Mehrbenutzersystem ist dieser Fall eher die

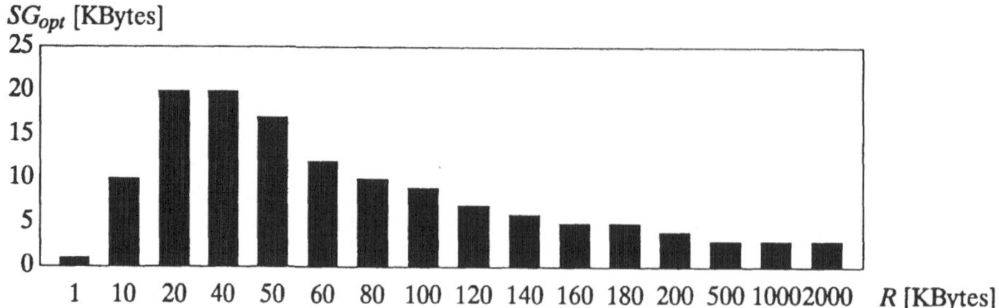

Abbildung 1: Optimales Striping–Granulat SG_{opt} für verschiedene Auftragsgrößen R

Ausnahme, so daß wir bei entsprechend hoher Ankunftsrate eigentlich davon ausgehen müssen, daß I/O–Aufträge eine Platte belegt vorfinden und auf das Freiwerden der Platte warten müssen. Für den Fall, daß I/O–Aufträge nur von einer Platte bedient werden, ist dieses Szenario analytisch wohlverstanden und kann beispielsweise durch ein M/G/1–Warteschlangenmodell modelliert werden [14]. Für ein Szenario, bei dem ein I/O–Auftrag von mehreren Platten bedient wird und die Anzahl der Platten von Auftrag zu Auftrag variiert (sogenannte Fork–Join–Synchronisation [19][24]), ist ein solches analytisches Modell nicht bekannt. Lediglich für den Fall das immer zwei Platten in einen I/O–Auftrag involviert sind, ist eine exakte analytische Lösung bekannt [7]. Daher gehen wir in unserem Ansatz in zwei Schritten vor und lassen zunächst Warteschlangen an den Platten unberücksichtigt.

Um zu einer Abschätzung für den maximal erreichbaren Durchsatz zu gelangen, ist neben der Anzahl der Platten im System D und einiger Hardware–Kenngrößen auch die Kenntnis der mittleren Auftragsgröße $\overline{R}$ (gemittelt über alle Aufträge auf alle Dateien) notwendig. Werden die Aufträge im Mittel von $\overline{P}$ Platten bedient, so gilt für den maximal erreichbaren Durchsatz $T_{max}(\overline{P},\overline{R})$:

$$T_{max}(\overline{P},\overline{R}) = \frac{D}{\overline{P}\left(L + \frac{t_{rot}}{B} \times \frac{\overline{R}}{\overline{P}}\right)}, \tag{11}$$

wobei L die mittlere Positions– und Rotationsverzögerung einer Platte darstellt.

Abbildung 2 zeigt den maximal erreichbaren Durchsatz (bei einer Plattenauslastung von 100%) in einem System mit $D=16$ Platten und einer mittleren Auftragsgröße von $\overline{R}=100$ KBytes in Abhängigkeit vom mittleren Parallelitätsgrad $\overline{P}$. Dabei wird der maximale Durchsatz für $\overline{P}=1$ erreicht, also gerade dann, wenn alle Aufträge von genau einer Platte bedient werden. In diesem Fall weist die Summe der Plattenbelegungszeiten keine "unproduktiven" Zeiten auf, so daß das System bezüglich des Durchsatzes am effektivsten genutzt wird.

Daß für $P=1$ der Durchsatz maximal ist, gilt zumindest für den Fall, bei dem die Aufträge über alle Platten gleichverteilt sind. Im Falle einer "schiefen" Zugriffsverteilung wird die Platte mit den meisten Aufträgen frühzeitig zum Engpaß und limitiert somit den Durchsatz des Gesamtsystems [20]. Unter Umständen reicht daher ein einfaches Allokationsschema (z.B.

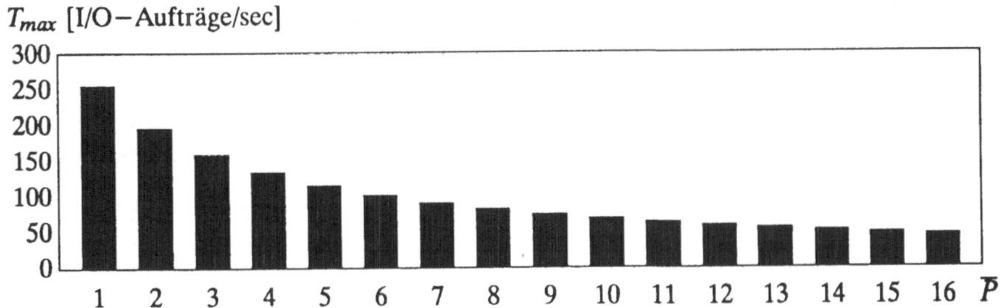

Abbildung 2: Maximal erreichbarer Durchsatz T_{max} ($D=16, \overline{R}=100$) in Abhängigkeit von $\overline{P}$

Round-Robin) nicht aus, um eine gute Balancierung der I/O-Last sicherzustellen. Überlegungen und Algorithmen zur (dynamischen) Lastbalancierung, durch die eine Gleichverteilung der Aufträge über alle Platten erreicht werden kann, finden sich in [30][35].

Aus diesen Überlegungen läßt sich nun ableiten, daß zur Minimierung der Antwortzeit einzelner I/O-Aufträge eine starke Parallelisierung wünschenswert sein kann, dies im Mehrbenutzerbetrieb jedoch zu einer zu starken Limitierung des Durchsatzes führen kann. Liegen von Seiten der Anwendung Durchsatzanforderungen vor, so ist der Parallelitätsgrad einzelner I/O-Aufträge auf Kosten der Antwortzeit zu reduzieren. Ist ein Durchsatz λ_{max} gefordert, so ist $\overline{P}_{max}$ so zu bestimmen, daß

$$T_{max}(\overline{P}_{max}, \overline{R}) \geq \lambda_{\max} \tag{12}$$

gilt. Darüber hinaus wird häufig gefordert, daß die mittlere Plattenauslastung im Disk-Array einen bestimmten Wert (z.B. 0.5) nicht überschreitet, da sonst die Antwortzeiten aufgrund zunehmender Warteschlangenbildung unakzeptabel werden. Soll ein Durchsatz λ_{max} bei einer Plattenauslastung von ϱ erreicht werden, so muß gelten

$$T_{max}(\overline{P}_{max}, \overline{R}) \geq \frac{\lambda_{\max}}{\varrho}, \tag{13}$$

und damit

$$\overline{P}_{max} \leq \frac{D \times \varrho}{\lambda_{max} \times L} - \frac{t_{rot} \times \overline{R}}{B \times L}. \tag{14}$$

Dabei wird zur Vereinfachung optimale Lastbalancierung im Disk-Array angenommen. Unsere Heuristik zur Bestimmung des optimalen Striping-Granulats SG_{opt} einer Datei geht nun folgendermaßen vor. Zunächst wird aufgrund der mittleren I/O-Auftragsgröße R der Datei der Parallelitätsgrad P_{opt} so bestimmt, das die Antwortzeit minimal wird. Weiterhin läßt sich aus der Anzahl Platten im System D, der Durchsatzanforderung λ_{max}, der gewünschten mittleren Plattenauslastung ϱ und der mittleren I/O-Auftragsgröße $\overline{R}$ der maximale Parallelitätsgrad $\overline{P}_{max}$ bestimmen, der nicht überschritten werden darf, wenn der geforderte Durchsatz λ_{max} eingehalten werden soll. Der effektive Parallelitätsgrad P_{eff} eines I/O-Auftrages der Größe R ergibt sich dann aus dem Minimum von P_{opt} und $\overline{P}_{max} \times R/\overline{R}$. Für I/O-Aufträge, die größer sind als $\overline{R}$, ist ein höherer Parallelitätsgrad zulässig, während Aufträge, die kleiner als $\overline{R}$ sind, einen entsprechend kleineren Parallelitätsgrad aufweisen sollten.

3 Leistungsevaluation

In diesem Abschnitt wird die Leistung der in Abschnitt 2 beschriebenen Methode zur optimalen Datenpartitionierung mittels trace-getriebener Simulation evaluiert. Gemäß den Optimierungszielen des Modells sind die Antwortzeit und der maximal erreichbare Durchsatz der I/O-Aufträge die zentralen Leistungsmaße der Evaluation. Die Evaluation basiert auf dem prototypisch implementierten Filesystems FIVE [35]. FIVE ist ein vollständiges Filesystem für parallele Platten, welches auf Unix "Raw Disks" aufsetzt. Die Geräteebene von FIVE erlaubt es auch, Disk-Array-Konfigurationen zu simulieren, die über die real verfügbare Konfiguration hinausgehen. Die detaillierte Simulation von Disk-Arrays ist mit Hilfe des Simulationspakets CSIM [31] realisiert. In der im folgenden vorgestellten Evaluation haben wir mit dieser Disk-Array-Simulation gearbeitet, um nicht durch die uns real zur Verfügung stehende Plattenanzahl (von 8 Platten) limitiert zu sein. Abbildung 3 gibt einen Überblick über die Leistungsparameter des simulierten Hardware-Konfiguration. Die Kenngrößen einer einzelnen Platte entsprechen dabei denen einer Platte vom Typ Fujitsu M2624SA [8].

Anzahl Platten	32	Kapazität einer Platte	539 MBytes
Blockgröße	1024 Bytes	Kapazität des Disk-Array	17.2 GB
Spurgröße	35 Blöcke	Rotationsgeschwindigkeit	4400 U/min
Anzahl Spuren pro Zylinder	11	mittlere Positionierungszeit	12 msec
Anzahl Zylinder pro Platte	1435	Transferrate pro Platte	2.44 MBytes/sec

Abbildung 3: Leistungsparameter des simulierten Disk-Arrays

Die folgenden Striping-Strategien wurden verglichen:

- *Opt*: dateispezifisch optimierte Striping-Granulate entsprechend unserer Heuristik von Abschnitt 2
- *Track*: ein globales Striping-Granulat von einer Spur (35KBytes)
- *Cyl*: ein globales Striping-Granulat von einem Zylinder (385KBytes)
- *Block*: ein globales Striping-Granulat von einem Block (1KBytes)
- *Clustered*: Dateien werden überhaupt nicht partitioniert (verschiedene Dateien werden aber wohl über verschiedene Platten verteilt); dieser Fall entspricht quasi einem unendlich großen Striping-Granulat

Als Allokationsstrategie für die aus der Partitionierungsentscheidung resultierenden Dateipartitionen wird in allen Fällen eine Greedy-Heuristik verwendet, die eine gleichmäßige Verteilung der I/O-Last über alle Platten anstrebt [30][35]. Die in diese Heuristik einfließenden Zugriffshäufigkeiten der Dateien und der Blöcke innerhalb einer Datei wurden durch Vorabanalyse der zugrundeliegenden I/O-Traces ermittelt.

Abschnitt 3.1 beschreibt zwei I/O-Traces — aus den Bereichen Büroablage und VLSI-Design — die in der Simulation verwendet wurden. Abschnitt 3.2 stellt die Ergebnisse der

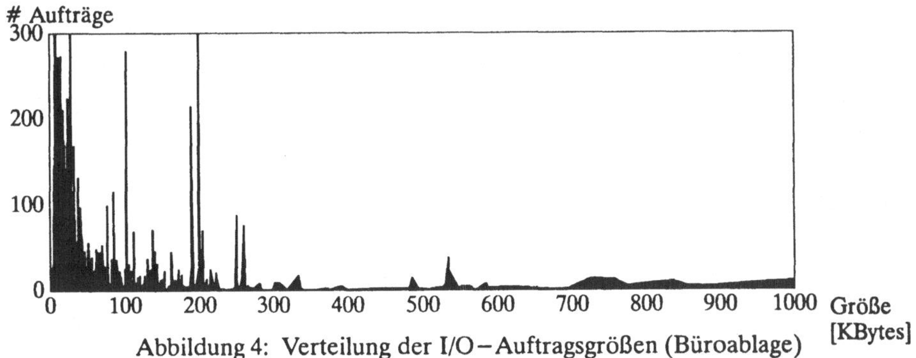

Abbildung 4: Verteilung der I/O–Auftragsgrößen (Büroablage)

Evaluation vor. In Unterabschnitt 3.1.1 wird zunächst nur die Optimierung der Datenpartitionierung bezüglich der Antwortzeit betrachtet. Bei diesen Experimenten ist die Ankunftsrate der I/O–Aufträge niedrig genug, um Warteschlangen an den Platten auszuschließen. In Unterabschnitt 3.1.2 werden die von der Anwendung vorgegebenen Durchsatzanforderungen berücksichtigt.

3.1 Anwendungslast

3.1.1 Büroablage

Bei der Anwendung Büroablage handelt es sich um die Aufzeichnung des Benutzungsmusters auf Dateien des Desktop–Publishing–Systems Interleaf TPS unter Unix. Zu diesem Zweck wurde auf dem System ein Sampling–Prozeß installiert, der in regelmäßigen Abständen die Inodes der betroffenen Dateien inspizierte und alle vorgefundenen Änderungen protokollierte. Bei dem betrachteten Desktop–Publishing–System entspricht jedes Dokument einer Datei. Dokumente werden immer komplett in den virtuellen Speicher geladen und in eine zur Bearbeitung geeignete Repräsentation konvertiert. Bei Änderungen werden Dokumente immer komplett zurückgeschrieben, und zwar periodisch und am Sitzungsende. Da Dokumente in der Regel wachsen, sind Write–Aufträge größer als Read–Aufträge.

Anzahl I/O–Aufträge im Trace	13501
Anzahl Create–Aufträge	2475 (18.3 %)
Anzahl Read–Aufträge	6624 (49.1 %)
Anzahl Write–Aufträge	2310 (17.1 %)
Anzahl Delete–Aufträge	2092 (15.5 %)
mittlere Größe eines Read–Auftrags	144.70 KBytes
mittlere Größe eines Write–Auftrags	245.11 KBytes
mittlere Auftragsgröße	166.32 KBytes

Abbildung 5: Anwendungscharakteristika Büroablage

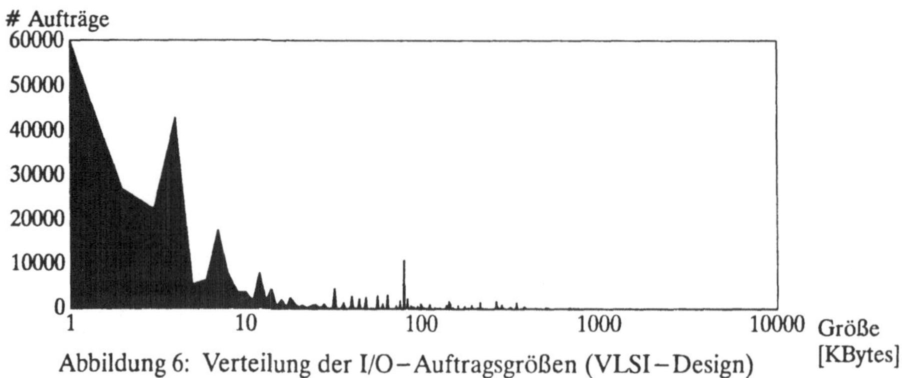

Abbildung 6: Verteilung der I/O-Auftragsgrößen (VLSI-Design)

Der von uns implementierte Sampling-Prozeß liefert also praktisch einen kompletten I/O-Trace dieser Anwendung. Abbildung 4 zeigt die Verteilung der Dokumentgrößen, die gleichzeitig der Verteilung der I/O-Auftragsgrößen entspricht. Abbildung 5 zeigt weitere Lastcharakteristika.

3.1.2 VLSI-Design

Bei der Anwendung VLSI-Design handelt es sich um einen Trace aus einer an der University of California at Berkeley durchgeführten Studie über das I/O-Verhalten der dortigen Rechnerkonfiguration [3]. Details über die verwendeten Protokollierungsverfahren, die untersuchte Systemkonfiguration und eine ausführliche Analyse der Trace-Daten finden sich in [3]. Für unsere Simulationen benutzen wir einen 48 Stunden langen Trace, dessen Charakteristika in Abbildung 6 und Abbildung 7 wiedergegeben sind. Der Trace beinhaltet in erster Linie VLSI-Design-Programme und VLSI-Simulationen mit I/O-Auftragsgrößen von bis zu 20 MBytes. Darüber hinaus führen weitere Anwendungen wie Textverarbeitung, Programmentwicklung und Debugging zu einer hohen Varianz der I/O-Auftragsgröße über alle Dateien. Insgesamt weist dieser Trace also ein für bestimmte Non-Standard-Datenbankanwendungen typisches Zugriffsmuster auf.

Anzahl I/O-Aufträge im Trace	431218
Anzahl Create-Aufträge	4305 (1.0 %)
Anzahl Read-Aufträge	373389 (86.6 %)
Anzahl Write-Aufträge	52216 (12.1 %)
Anzahl Delete-Aufträge	1308 (0.3 %)
mittlere Größe eines Read-Auftrags	107.50 KBytes
mittlere Größe eines Write-Auftrags	103.94 KBytes
mittlere Auftragsgröße	107.06 KBytes

Abbildung 7: Anwendungscharakteristika VLSI-Design

3.2 Ergebnisse

3.2.1 Optimierung der Antwortzeit

Büroablage

Abbildung 8 zeigt die mittlere Antwortzeit von I/O-Aufträgen verschiedener Größe für die verschiedenen Striping-Methoden. Für Auftragsgrößen bis 10 KBytes schneidet die Methode *Block* am schlechtesten ab. Die Ursache ist eine zu starke Parallelisierung der Aufträge, wodurch die maximale Positionierungszeit und Rotationsverzögerung signifikant erhöht, die Transferzeit bei diesen Auftragsgrößen aber nur unwesentlich reduziert wird. Alle anderen Methoden verhalten sich bei diesen Auftragsgrößen praktisch gleich. In diesen Fällen wird ein I/O-Auftrag von genau einer Platte bedient, wodurch in allen Fällen zu einer Antwortzeit von ca. 17 msec erreicht wird. Auffällig ist in jedem Fall die im Vergleich zu unserem analytischen Modell niedrige Antwortzeit. Nach dem Modell sollte die mittlere Antwortzeit für Aufträge bis zu einer Größe von 10 KBytes bei ca. 20 msec liegen. Dieses Modell geht jedoch bei der Berechnung der Positionierungszeit von einer mittleren Armpositionierungszeit von 12 msec aus (siehe Abbildung 3). Aufgrund der relativ hohen Lokalität bei den Zugriffen, liegt die tatsächlich beobachtete mittlere Armpositionierungszeit jedoch bei 6 msec. Dieses Phänomen bewirkt eine Überbewertung der Positionierungszeit in unserem Modell zur Bestimmung des optimalen Striping-Granulates.

Für Auftragsgrößen bis 100 KBytes beträgt die Verbesserung von *Opt* oder *Block* gegenüber *Clustered* einen Faktor von 1.2 – 1.3 und gegenüber *Track* immerhin 1.14. Mit wachsender Auftragsgröße steigt auch der Gewinnfaktor. So beträgt für Aufträge bis 500 KBytes der Gewinnfaktor 3.8 (*Clustered/Opt*) bzw. 1.3 (*Track/Opt*). Bis zu dieser Größe verhalten sich *Cyl* und *Clustered* gleich. In beiden Fällen wird bis zu dieser Auftragsgröße praktisch ein Parallelitätsgrad von 1 benutzt. Für sehr große Aufträge hat die Verbesserung einen Faktor von 10.5 (*Clustered/Opt*) bzw. 1.6 (*Clustered/Cyl*). Dies geht aus Darstellungsgründen aus Abbildung 8 nicht hervor (Für Aufträge bis zu 1 MBytes betrug die Antwortzeit für *Clustered* mehr als 320 Millisekunden). Für Auftragsgrößen größer 100 KBytes verhalten sich die Methoden *Opt* und *Block*

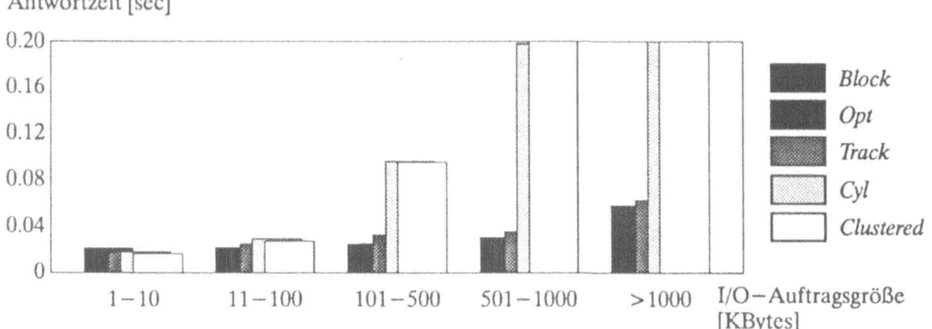

Abbildung 8: Antwortzeit für verschiedene I/O-Größen und Striping-Methoden (Büroablage)

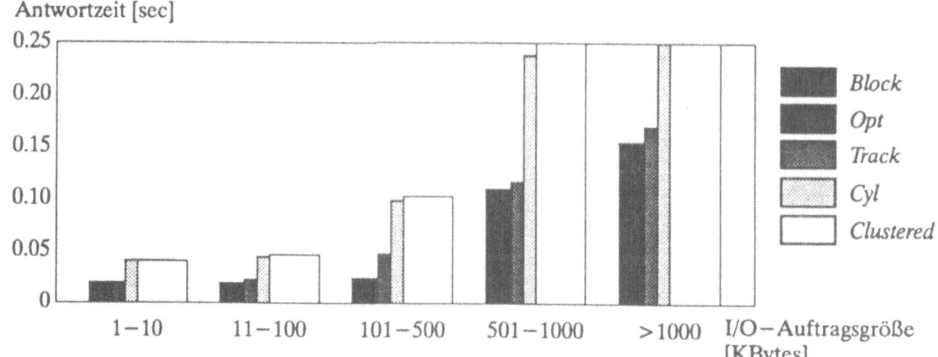

Abbildung 9: Antwortzeit für verschiedene I/O-Größen und Striping-Methoden (VLSI-Design)

im wesentlichen gleich. Beide Verfahren parallelisieren diese Aufträge sehr stark, so daß ab einer Auftragsgröße von ca. 160 KBytes immer alle Platten an dem Auftrag beteiligt sind.

VLSI-Design

Das gleiche Experiment haben wir für die Anwendung VLSI-Design wiederholt (Abbildung 9). Dabei läßt sich ein sehr ähnliches Verhalten der Methoden beobachten. Auffällig ist im Vergleich zum vorhergehenden Experiment das schlechte Abschneiden der Methoden *Cyl* und *Clustered* für kleine I/O-Aufträge bis 10 KBytes. Dies ist auf eine ungleiche Verteilung der I/O-Last bei diesen Methoden zurückzuführen, die bei dieser Anwendung stärker zum Tragen kommt, da die Ankunftsrate im Original-Trace deutlich höher liegt.

Durch eine höhere Varianz der Auftragsgrößen wird bei dieser Anwendung auch der Vorteil der dateispezifischen Partitionierung (Methode *Opt*) gegenüber der global partitionierenden Methode *Track* deutlicher. Für I/O-Aufträge bis 100 KBytes beträgt der Verbesserungsfaktor *Track*/*Opt* 1.2 und für Auftragsgrößen bis 500 KBytes sogar 2.0.

3.2.2 Berücksichtigung von Durchsatzanforderungen

Bei den bisherigen Untersuchungen sind wir von einer vergleichsweise niedrigen Ankunftsrate der I/O-Aufträge ausgegangen, so daß die Partitionierungsentscheidung ausschließlich im Hinblick auf minimale Antwortzeiten gefällt wurde. Diese Ankunftsraten können von dem System auch bei starker Parallelisierung einzelner Aufträge bewältigt werden, ohne daß signifikante Warteschlangen an den Platten auftreten. Um das Verhalten bei höherer Last zu untersuchen, wurden zusätzliche Simulationen durchgeführt, bei denen die Zwischenankunftszeiten der I/O-Aufträge im Trace um einen bestimmten "Lastfaktor" verkürzt wurden.

Büroablage

Abbildung 10 zeigt die mittlere Antwortzeit (gemittelt über alle I/O-Größen) für die verschiedenen Partitionierungsmethoden. Schon bei relativ geringen Ankunftsraten erreicht die Methode *Clustered* ihren maximalen Durchsatz und führt zu unakzeptablen Antwortzeiten,

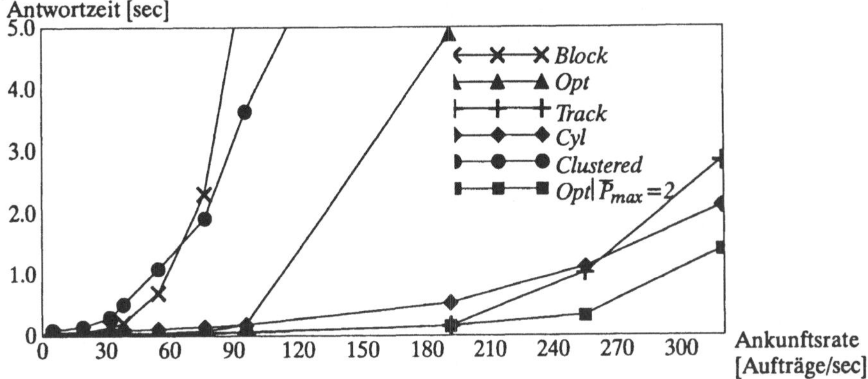

Abbildung 10: Antwortzeit bei verschiedenen Partitionierungsmethoden in Abhängigkeit von der Ankunftsrate (Büroablage)

verursacht im wesentlichen durch Warteschlangenbildung. Aufgrund der theoretischen Überlegungen von Abschnitt 2.2 sollte *Clustered* eigentlich den höchsten Durchsatz erreichen, da in diesem Fall keine Parallelisierung einzelner Aufträge vorgenommen wird und dadurch die Plattenbelegungszeit minimiert wird. Tatsächlich ist das schlechte Abschneiden von *Clustered* in diesem Fall auf eine starke Unbalanciertheit der I/O–Last zurückzuführen. Zwei der Platten tragen einen großen Teil der Gesamtlast und werden so frühzeitig zu einem limitierenden Faktor des Systems. Die Partitionierung der Dateien bei den Striping–Methoden trägt also auch wesentlich zur Lastbalancierung bei, indem sie der für die Allokation verwendeten Greedy–Heuristik mehr Freiheitsgrade verschafft.

Bei der Methode *Block* ist der Grund für die frühzeitige Sättigung des I/O–Systems in der zu starken Parallelisierung der kleinen Aufträge (bis 10 KBytes) zu suchen. Dies führt nicht nur zu unnötig hohen Antwortzeiten schon bei niedriger Ankunftsrate (vergleiche Abbildung 8) sondern auch zu hohen Plattenbelegungszeiten und damit sehr frühzeitig zu Warteschlangenbildung an allen Platten.

Mit steigender Ankunftsrate ist für die Methoden *Track* und *Cyl* ein besseres Verhalten gegenüber *Opt* zu beobachten. Bei *Opt* ist das primäres Ziel die Minimierung der Antwortzeit. Dies führt im Vergleich zu den anderen Methoden zu einem höheren mittleren Parallelitätsgrad $\overline{P}$ (für *Opt* gilt $\overline{P}=9.7$, für *Track* $\overline{P}=3.9$ und bei *Cyl* ist $\overline{P}=1.3$). Dies muß sich natürlich auf die Antwortzeiten bei hohen Ankunftsraten auswirken. In allen Fällen tritt bei einer Ankunftsrate von $\lambda \approx 250$ Aufträgen pro Sekunde eine Sättigung des I/O–Systems ein, d.h. wir beobachten sehr hohe mittlere Plattenauslastungen (je nach Methode zwischen 70–90%) und damit Warteschlangenbildung einhergehend mit signifikant erhöhten Antwortzeiten. Durch eine Beschränkung des mittleren Parallelitätsgrades auf $\overline{P}_{max}=2$ können jedoch auch für $\lambda \approx 250$ akzeptable Antwortzeiten sichergestellt werden (Methode *Opt*| $\overline{P}_{max}=2$), wobei in diesem Fall die mittlere Plattenauslastung etwas über $\varrho=0.5$ liegt. Erkauft wird diese

Durchsatzerhöhung durch etwas erhöhte Antwortzeiten bei niedrigen Ankunftsraten, da nun das Parallelisierungspotential nicht mehr voll ausgeschöpft wird.

VLSI-Design

Das gleiche Experiment haben wir für die Anwendung VLSI-Design durchgeführt (Abbildung 11). Wie schon bei der Anwendung Büroablage erreicht auch hier die Methode *Clustered* ihren maximalen Durchsatz bei sehr niedrigen Ankunftsraten. Der Grund liegt wiederum in einer extremen Unbalanciertheit der Auftragsverteilung. So hatte z.B. die "heißeste" der 32 Platten ca. 18 % der Gesamtlast zu tragen. Wir haben zwar auch hier eine Vorabanalyse des Traces durchgeführt und bei der Allokation der Dateien auf eine möglichst ausgeglichene I/O-Lastverteilung geachtet. Die Ungleichverteilung der Aufträge über die Dateien der Anwendung war jedoch so heftig, daß zumindest bei der Methode *Clustered* keine gute Lastbalancierung möglich war. Erst durch die Partitionierung der Dateien und die Verteilung der "heißesten" Partitionen über verschiedene Platten konnte die vorzeitige Sättigung einzelner Platten ausgeschlossen werden. Dies ist z.B. bei der Methode *Block* der Fall. Hier wird jede Datei so fein partitioniert, daß bei der mittleren Auftragsgröße von $\overline{R}=107$ KBytes (vergleiche Abbildung 7) alle Platten an der Auftragsbearbeitung beteiligt sind. Die Auslastung der Platten ist hier nahezu perfekt balanciert. In diesem Fall ist die Sättigung des I/O-Systems bei einer Ankunftsrate von ca. 100 Aufträgen pro Sekunde auf die hohen Plattenbelegungszeiten aufgrund der zu starken Parallelisierung zurückzuführen.

Wie schon bei der Anwendung Büroablage ist auch bei der Anwendung VLSI-Design bei hoher Ankunftsrate die starke Parallelisierung der Aufträge bei der Methode *Opt* für Warteschlangenbildung und damit erhöhte Antwortzeiten verantwortlich. Auch hier kann durch die Beschränkung des Parallelitätsgrades ($Opt|\overline{P}_{max}=2$) ein im Vergleich zu den globalen Partitionierungsmethoden *Track* und *Cyl* besseres Antwortzeitverhalten bei hoher Ankunftsrate erzielt werden.

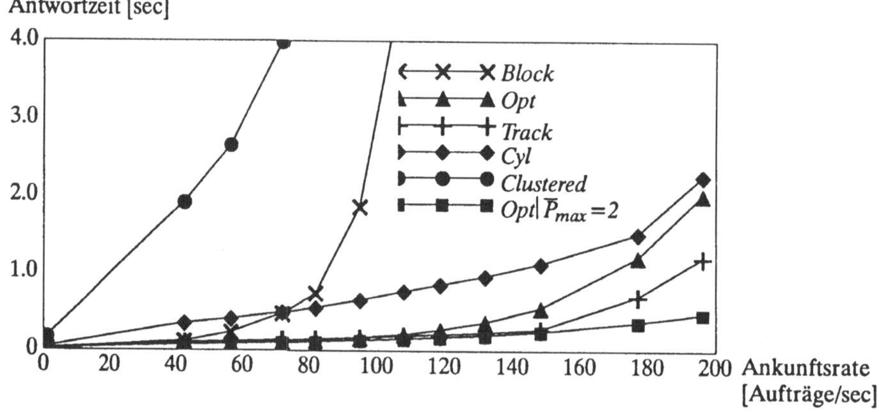

Abbildung 11: Antwortzeit bei verschiedenen Partitionierungsmethoden in Abhängigkeit von der Ankunftsrate (VLSI-Design)

4 Inkrementelle Reorganisation

Dateispezifische Striping–Granulate erlauben es, die Datenpartitionierung an Veränderungen der Zugriffscharakteristika oder der Hardwarekonfiguration durch inkrementelle Reorganisation anzupassen. Der Vorteil dieser Flexibilität wird anhand des folgenden Szenarios klar. Ein Disk–Array werde zur Erhöhung der Leistung (also nicht etwa aufgrund von Platzkapazitätsüberlegungen) um zusätzliche Platten erweitert. Um dieses zusätzliche Leistungspotential auszunutzen, müssen nun existierende Daten repartitioniert werden. Bei einem System mit einem festen, globalen Striping–Granulat müßten dazu alle Daten komplett reorganisiert werden. Bei großen Datenvolumen und Anwendungen mit hohen Verfügbarkeitsanforderungen wäre eine entsprechende Offline–Reorganisation unakzeptabel, und eine vollständige Online–Reorganisation im laufenden Betrieb würde die Leistung der regulären I/O–Aufträge stark beeinträchtigen.

In unserem Ansatz der dateispezifischen Striping–Granulate dagegen ist es möglich, nur die wichtigsten Dateien — also wegen der typischerweise sehr ungleichmäßigen Verteilung der Zugriffshäufigkeiten nur einen Bruchteil der Daten — zu reorganisieren, um so bereits wesentliche Leistungsverbesserungen zu erzielen. Das folgende Experiment demonstriert die möglichen Leistungssteigerungen anhand des I/O–Trace für den Anwendungsbereich Büroablage. Das ursprünglich aus 32 Platten bestehende Disk–Array wird auf 64 Platten erweitert. Die x % am häufigsten referenzierten Dateien werden repartitioniert und potentiell über alle 64 Platten verteilt, während die übrigen 100–x % der Dateien unberührt bleiben und damit auch keinerlei Reorganisationskosten verursachen. Danach wird die mittlere Antwortzeit der I/O–Aufträge aus dem Trace auf der veränderten Konfiguration für verschiedene Ankunftsraten gemessen. Die Resultate sind für x = 0, 1, 2 und 5 in Abbildung 12 dargestellt. Der Fall x = 0 — ohne jede Reorganisation also — entspricht gerade der alten Konfiguration mit 32 benutzten Platten. Es zeigt sich, daß bereits bei Repartitionierung von nur 2 % der Daten fast schon der maximal möglich Nutzen erreicht wird; dieser Fall ist fast so gut wie der Fall x = 5, und für x > 5 ergibt sich praktisch keine weitere Verbesserung. Die im Fall x = 2 erzielte Ver-

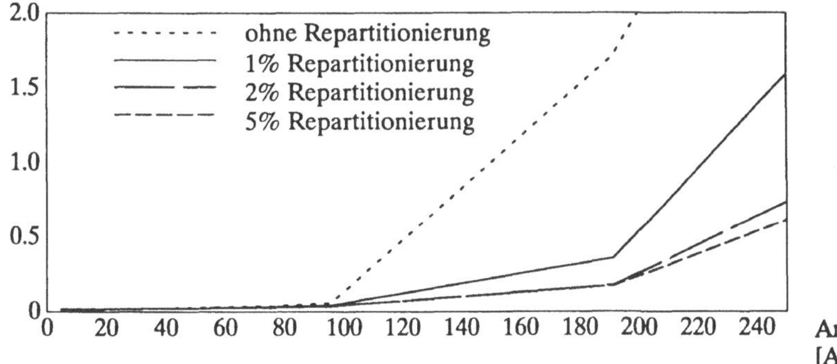

Abbildung 12: Antwortzeitverbesserung durch inkrementelle Reorganisation

besserung der mittleren Antwortzeit gegenüber der alten Konfiguration beträgt bei hoher Ankunftsrate ungefähr einen Faktor von 10.

5 Ausblick

In diesem Beitrag haben wir eine Methode zur Partitionierung von Daten zur Ausnutzung von I/O–Parallelität vorgestellt und evaluiert. Dabei hat sich gezeigt, daß in den betrachteten Non–Standard–Anwendungen eine dateispezifische Partitionierung signifikante Vorteile gegenüber einfacheren Methoden mit globaler Partitionierung hat.

Zusätzlich zu den Leistungsvorteilen hat die dateispezifische Partitionierung den Vorteil, daß existierende Datensammlungen inkrementell reorganisiert werden können. Beispielsweise können bei einer Erweiterung eines Disk–Arrays um zusätzliche Platten Leistungsverbesserungen erzielt werden, indem nur die wichtigsten Daten repartitioniert werden. Analog können bei Änderungen der Zugriffscharakteristika (z.B. steigende Durchsatzanforderungen) drohende Leistungseinbußen durch inkrementelle Reorganisation weitgehend vermieden werden. Diese Eigenschaften sind zentral für die "Skalierbarkeit" und Anpaßbarkeit eines Speichersystems für Disk–Arrays. Kommerzielle Disk–Arrays und Filesysteme für Disk–Arrays, die mit einem globalen Striping–Granulat arbeiten, besitzen diese Flexibilität nicht.

Die in dieser Arbeit diskutierte und im Prototyp FIVE implementierte Datenpartitionierungsmethode zur Optimierung der I/O–Parallelität ist Teil eines von uns entwickelten Pakets von heuristischen Algorithmen zur Datenplazierung in Disk–Arrays und allgemeineren verteilten Speichersystemen. Dieses Paket beinhaltet zusätzlich Methoden zur Datenallokation und adaptiven Lastbalancierung [30][35] sowie Algorithmen zur Datenreorganisation. Schließlich ist in FIVE auch ein Spektrum von konfigurierbaren Fehlertoleranzmechanismen für Disk–Arrays realisiert [23][37].

Die Arbeiten zur Datenpartitionierung, –allokation und –reorganisation gehören zum COMFORT–Projekt an der ETH Zürich [33]. Dieses Projekt verfolgt das Langzeitziel, das Leistungs–Tuning von Datenbanksystemen für komplexe Anwendungen so weit wie möglich zu automatisieren. Wir erwarten, daß künftige Non–Standard–Datenbanksysteme wegen der breiten Palette der zu unterstützenden Anwendungsklassen mit stark variierenden Lastcharakteristika noch mehr Tuning–Optionen und Systemparameter anbieten werden, als dies bereits heute bei kommerziellen Datenbanksystemen der Fall ist. Es ist daher essentiell, Systemadministratoren bei der zunehmend komplexer werdenden Aufgabe des Leistungs–Tunings zu unterstützen. Die in dieser Arbeit vorgestellte automatische Datenpartitionierung zur Optimierung der I/O–Parallelität ist ein kleiner Schritt in diese Richtung.

Literatur

[1] Abramowicz, K., Dittrich, K.R., Längle, R., Ranft, M., Raupp, T., Rehm, S., DAMOKLES — Architektur, Implementierung, Erfahrungen, *Informatik Forschung und Entwicklung*, Band 6, Heft 1, 1991, pp. 1–13

[2] Bitton, D. and Gray, J.N., Disk Shadowing, *Proceedings of the 14th International Conference on Very Large Data Bases*, 1988, pp. 331–338

[3] Baker, M.G., Hartman, J.H., Kupfer, M.D., Shirriff, K.W., and Ousterhout, J.K., Measurements of a Distributed File System, *Proceedings of the 13th ACM Symposium on Operating System Principles*, 1991, pp. 198–212

[4] Cattell, R.G.G. (Ed.), Special Section on Next–Generation Database Systems, *Communications of the ACM*, Vol. 34, No. 10, 1991

[5] Chen, P.M. and Patterson, D. A., Maximizing Performance in a Striped Disk Array, *Proceedings of the 17th International Symposium on Computer Architecture*, 1990, pp. 322–331

[6] Dadam, P., Linnemann, V., Advanced Information Management (AIM): Advanced Database Technology for Integrated Applications, *IBM Systems Journal*, Vol. 28, No. 4, 1989, pp. 661–681

[7] Flatto, L. and Hahn, S., Two Parallel Queues Created by Arrivals with Two Demands I, *SIAM Journal of Applied Mathematics*, Vol. 44, No. 5, 1984, pp. 1041–1053

[8] Fujitsu, Product Information Fujitsu M262X, 1991

[9] Garcia–Molina, H. et. al, Disk Arrays: Are they of Use for Database Processing (Panel), *Proceedings of the 1st International Conference on Parallel and Distributed Information Systems*, 1991, pp. 117–118

[10] Gray, J.N., Horst B., and Walker, M., Parity Striping of Disk Arrays: Low–Cost Reliable Storage with Acceptable Throughput, *Proceedings of the 16th International Conference on Very Large Data Bases*, 1990, pp. 148–161

[11] Härder, T. (Ed.), The PRIMA Project: Design and Implementation of a Non–Standard Database System, Technischer Bericht 26/88, Sonderforschungsbereich 124, Universität Kaiserslautern, 1988

[12] Härder, T., Reuter, A., Architektur von Datenbanksystemen für Non–Standard–Anwendungen, in: Blaser, A., Pistor, P. (Hrsg.), *Datenbanksysteme für Büro, Technik und Wissenschaft*, GI–Fachtagung, Karlsruhe, 1985, Informatik–Fachbericht 94, Springer–Verlag, 1985

[13] Hennessy, J.L. and Patterson, D.A., *Computer Architecture: A Quantitative Approach*, Morgan Kaufmann, San Mateo, CA, 1990

[14] Highleyman, W., Performance Analysis of Transaction Processing Systems, *Prentice Hall*, 1989

[15] Infotech SA Inc., *The Mass Storage Report '92*, Silver Spring, Maryland, 1992

[16] Katz, R.H., Gibson, G.A., and Patterson, D.A., Disk System Architectures for High Performance Computing, *Proceedings of the IEEE*, Vol. 77, No. 12, 1989, pp. 1842–1858

[17] Kim, M.Y., Synchronized Disk Interleaving, *IEEE Transactions on Computers*, Vol. C–35, No. 11, 1986, pp. 978–988

[18] Kim, M.Y. and Tantawi, A.N., Asynchronous Disk Interleaving: Approximating Access Delays, *IEEE Transactions on Computers*, Vol. 40, No. 7, 1991, pp. 801–810

[19] Lee, E.K. and Katz, R.H., An Analytic Performance Model of Disk Arrays and its Application, *Technical Report No. UCB/CSD 91/660*, University of California Berkeley, 1991

[20] Livny, M., Khoshafian, S., and Boral, H., Multi–Disk Management Algorithms, *Proceedings of the International Conference on Measurement and Modeling of Computer Systems*, 1987, pp. 69–77

[21] Merchant, A., Yu, P.S., Performance Analysis of a Dual Striping Strategy for Replicated Disk Arrays, *Proceedings of the 2nd International Conference on Parallel and Distributed Information Systems*, San Diego, 1993

[22] Moad, J., Relief for Slow Storage Systems, *Datamation*, Vol. 36, No. 17, 1990, pp. 20–28

[23] Muntz, R.R. and Lui, J.C.S., Performance Analysis of Disk Arrays Under Failure, *Proceedings of the 16th International Conference on Very Large Data Bases*, 1990, pp. 162–173

[24] Nelson. R. and Tantawi, A.N., Approximate Analysis of Fork/Join Synchronisation in Parallel Queues, *IEEE Transactions on Computers*, Vol. 37, No. 6, 1991, pp. 739–743

[25] Ng, S., Some Design Issues of Disk Arrays, *Proceedings of the IEEE Compcon Spring Conference*, 1989, pp. 137–142

[26] Patterson, D.A., Gibson, G., and Katz, R.H., A Case for Redundant Arrays of Inexpensive Disks (RAID), *Proceedings of the SIGMOD International Conference on Management of Data*, 1988, pp. 109–116

[27] Reuter, A., Performance and Reliability Issues in Future DBMSs, *Proceedings of the International Symposium on Database Systems of the 90s*, Lecture Notes in Computer Science 466, Springer, 1990, pp. 294–315

[28] Salem, K. and Garcia–Molina, H., Disk Striping, *Proceedings of the 2nd International Conference on Data Engineering*, 1986, pp. 336–342

[29] Schek, H.–J., Paul, H.–B., Scholl, M.H., Weikum, G., The DASDBS Project: Objectives, Experiences, and Future Prospects, *IEEE Transactions on Knowledge and Data Engineering*, Vol. 2 No. 1, 1990, pp. 25–43

[30] Scheuermann, P., Weikum, G., and Zabback, P., Automatic Tuning of Data Placement and Load Balancing in Disk Arrays, In *Database Systems for Next–Generation Applications — Principles and Practice, Advanced Database Research and Development Series*, Word Scientific Publications, 1992

[31] Schwetman, H., CSIM Reference Manual (Revision 16), MCC Technical Report ACA–ST–252–87, Rev. 16, *Microelectronics and Computer Technology Corporation*, Austin, 1992

[32] Sierra, H.M., An Introduction to Direct Access Storage Devices, *Academic Press*, 1990

[33] Weikum, G., Hasse, C., Mönkeberg, A., Zabback, P., The COMFORT Project (Project Synopsis), *Proceedings of the 2nd International Conference on Parallel and Distributed Information Systems*, San Diego, 1993

[34] Weikum, G., Zabback, P., and Scheuermann, P., Dynamic File Allocation in Disk Arrays, Technical Report No. 147, Computer Science Department, ETH Zurich, 1991

[35] Weikum, G., Zabback, P., and Scheuermann, P., Dynamic File Allocation in Disk Arrays, *Proceedings of the SIGMOD International Conference on Management of Data*, 1991, pp. 406–415

[36] Weikum, G. and Zabback, P., Tuning of Striping Units in Disk–Array–Based File Systems, *Proceedings of the 2nd International Workshop on Research Issues on Data Engineering: Transaction and Query Processing (RIDE–TQP)*, 1992, pp. 80–87

[37] Weikum, G. und Zabback, P., I/O–Parallelität und Fehlertoleranz in Disk–Arrays, Manuskript, ETH Zürich, 1992, erscheint in: Informatik–Spektrum

Object-Oriented Access to Relational Database Systems

U. Hohenstein, C. Körner

Siemens AG, ZFE BT SE 33, Otto-Hahn-Ring 6, W-8000 München 83

Abstract

A C++ interface is presented that provides an adequate coupling to relational database systems dispensing with embedded SQL approaches. The interface reaps the benefits of an extended Entity-Relationship approach having powerful modelling features. The concepts of the data model are directly reflected by the interface thereby providing an abstract view of information even in the context of access and manipulation. Special emphasis is put on the inclusion of associative queries. To this end an SQL-like query language is integrated to formulate complex queries in a comfortable way.

The essential aspects of the implementation of the interface are discussed. A layered architecture allows for a quick and simple implementation and facilitates an easy coupling to other systems.

1 Introduction

Programming interfaces for relational DBMSs (database management systems) mostly rely on an embedded SQL concept. On the one hand, this approach is general enough to provide a coupling to several languages. But on the other hand, the handling is cumbersome and makes application programs difficult to write and hard to read. In fact, a coupling to C++ [Str91] can be done the same way. However, instead of going the conventional way of an embedded SQL, the class concept of C++ allows for better solutions. The easiest one is representing each relation as a C++ class, which gets the same attributes (as far as the relational attribute domains are directly representable in C++). Access is encapsulated in methods (called member functions in C++).

However this approach has some disadvantages. At first, the relational model lacks of semantic expressiveness. It is commonly agreed that more sophisticated modelling concepts are needed in most applications. Furthermore, some important features of C++, in particular inheritance, are not used for such "database classes", although they are for free in C++.

In this paper we rectify these shortcomings. We pick up ideas developed for object-oriented systems and propose a corresponding C++ interface for relational DBMSs. We make use of more sophisticated modelling features leading to data model, which incorporates object-oriented concepts [ABD+89] like object identity, subtyping, and complex objects into an Entity-Relationship (ER) model. A corresponding interface for C++ to the relational DBMS is proposed that is based on the data model retaining the higher abstraction level. Thus, manipulating and accessing data is completely done on a more abstract level in terms of ER concepts, handling entities and relationships. Moreover, invoking database functionality from C++ programs is done in a natural and smoothly fitting way. In particular, the coupling of C++ with the database functionality can be done without running into the "impedance mismatch".

Having an underlying relational DBMS, we would commit a sin by not using the relational query mechanism. We would thoughtless renounce lots of investigations in the field of query optimization, experience that is too valuable to get lost. Consequently, we emphasize on associative query facilities passing over the full use of relational SQL to the interface. Deficiencies of querying, often recognized in object-oriented systems, could thus be avoided.

The overall result behaves as an object-oriented DBMS, which has been implemented on top of a relational system. However while commercially available systems use the data model of C++, our approach provides more modelling primitives like complex objects or an explicit relationship concept.

In the following we present the essential concepts of our approach. We firstly define in section 2 an object-oriented data model based on the Entity-Relationship (ER) approach. Based upon this data model, an abstract object-oriented data manipulation facility is presented in section 3 that provides a comfortable and C++ conform way to access the data. Besides some features for navigating through the database, a powerful associative access is provided by using an SQL-like ER query language.

We place particular emphasis on easing the implementational effort and portation. The section 4 outlines the most important parts of the implementation elucidating the efficiency and simplicity of the approach. There is no need for developing a new C++ compiler or precompiler due to a simple generative approach. We let the C++ compiler do the work as much as possible. Consequently, the approach can be implemented very quickly and easily. Moreover, a well-structured and layered implementation is proposed that makes the database interface portable so that it could quite simply be coupled with other platform systems. Especially a portation to a relational, an NF^2, ER or object-oriented system is possible with low effort. Furthermore the layering opens the door to adapt the interface for other programming languages.

We conclude the paper with some remarks about possible improvements and future research topics.

2 Extended Entity-Relationship Model

The C++ database interface we want to present is based upon an Entity-Relationship (ER) approach similar to [EGH+92]. It enhances Chen's ER model [Che76] with the notions of object identity, subtyping and inheritance, multivalued attribute and components. Every object of an entity type possesses an *object identity* that is independent of any properties and globally unique in the database. *Subtyping* is provided for both entity types and relationship types. This concept is a simple form of ISA relationship supporting inclusion semantics: Instances of a subtype also belong to their supertype. Attributes and the participation in relationships are inherited from supertypes to subtypes. Attributes may be *multivalued*, i.e, set-, bag-, or list-valued. Bags retain duplicates of an element in contrast to sets. Thus, an element may occur multiple in a bag. The elements of a list are enumerated so that the i-th element in a list can directly be referenced. Besides some predefined attribute domains, *complex domains* like **date** are also available. The domain **longfield** is used for the database representation of a file in the sense of 'binary large objects'). *Components* can be understood as object-valued attributes and describe complex structured entity types, whose entities are composed of other entities. They model a "stronger" form of association than relationships. Similar to [KBG89], components can be specified as dependent and/or exclusive. Dependency affects the propagation of operations: Roughly speaking, deleting an object also requires the deletion of its dependent components. Exclusivity is a property that determines whether the sets of referenced objects must be disjoint or not. In the later case, sharing on type and instance level is possible. All these features make the data model "structurally" object-oriented [Dit88]. Relating the extended ER model to object-oriented data models, it provides explicit *n-ary relationships*. Associations between objects do not need to be expressed as references or pointers [Deux90, LLOW91], they are an own relationship concept having its own behaviour and its own operations [GeD91]. In this regard we agree with [Rum87, AGO91] who argument that relationships are conceptually higher than just references and should be supported directly. Relationships are symetrical and may have attributes. In contrast to objects, relationships do not possess an identity on their own, since their identity can be derived from the the objects involved in a relationship. The entity types participating in a relationship type can be given role names and cardinalities.

The following figure gives an example of a simple schema, modelling parts of a software component.

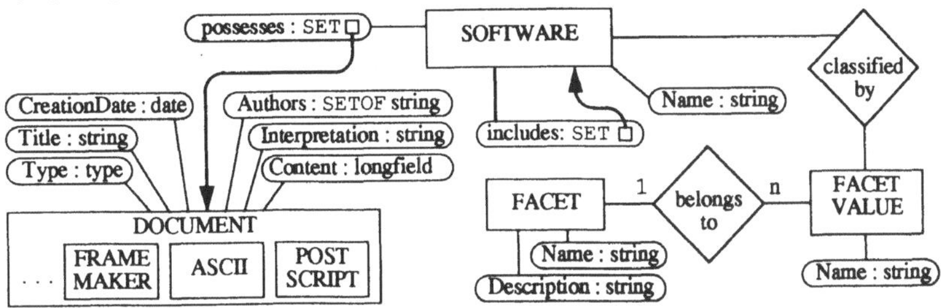

We make the data model "fully" object-oriented by allowing user-defined methods for entity types to be added in the schema definitions. Implementing the methods must be done in C++. As usual, some predefined generic operations described in the next section can be used for definition.

3 The C++ Database Interface

The data model provides an abstract view to the data stored in the relational database. We now present a database interface that directly reflects the abstract view of modelling concepts. It provides a coupling of the programming language C++ [Str91] with database functionality in a comfortable way that smoothly fits to C++. Handling both persistent and transient data is only done in C++. The way to deal with data resembles much of commercially available object-oriented DBMSs, especially ObjectStore [LLOW91]. But in contrast to them, we do not just provide a persistent programming language. We rather retain the abstract data model. In fact, we have to struggle with the "impedance mismatch", because the extended ER model provides more concepts to model data than can be done in C++. However, we avoid the impedance mismatch to a large degree, since we directly reflect the ER modelling concepts in C++ by using the class concept.

Essentially we use the ideas produced in [OdH91], however brought into line with the ER model presented here. The simple but fundamental principle of our approach is called *generative*: Given a database schema, several C++ classes are automatically generated, the methods (member functions in C++) of which yield the database functionality. The resulting classes are called **DML** (**D**ata **M**anipulation **L**anguage) **classes**, because their (generic) functions provide the data manipulation facilities. Each entity type and relationship type has a corresponding C++ class. The type hierarchy of the database schema is directly reflected by the C++ inheritance hierarchy. Some additional classes are needed to represent attribute domains that are not available in C++ like **longfield**. Parameterized "template" classes like `SETOF<...>` are generated for constituting sets of integers or lists of entities. User-defined methods will automatically be included in these classes.

The C++ classes **ET** related to entity types ET represent the structural properties (attributes) and provide the functionality to manipulate persistent objects by means of predefined functions. C++ objects, which are C++ placeholders for database objects, can be created by **new**. At the beginning, they are just transient. But objects may be stored in the database by explicitly invoking the **MakePersist** function. If the object already exists, it will be overwritten. Any entity type can consequently have both persistent and transient objects, and the ordinary C++ capabilities can be used to handle both. Hence, attribute values can be set, e.g., by applying the C++ reference operator '->'. Some of the attribute domains like **int** or **float** are already available in C++ so that no special treatment is necessary. On the other hand, complex attribute domains like **date** or **longfield** are represented by corresponding C++ classes providing the related functionality. For instance, the class `Longfield` enables copying in a file (**CopyIn**), copying out into a file (**CopyOut**), and checking whether an associated file exists. Multivalued attributes and components (`SETOF(<domain>)`, `LISTOF(<ET>)` etc.) are represented by parameterized C++ classes. Functions can be used to insert values into or delete values from a set or list and to iterate on them. The function **Delete** deletes an object and all the relationships it is involved in from the database. **Delete** is a propagating operation, deleting all subobjects in the sense of complex objects [KBG89]. Similarly, operations to produce a **DeepCopy**, i.e. all the objects building a complex object are copied, and to make a **ShallowCopy**, copying the object and establishing references to the direct subobjects [ABD+89].

Similar to the classes **ET**, classes **RT** reflect the structure and functionality associated with relationship types RT. Please note that relationships are quite different from objects in the model and possess their own functionality. Particularly, individual relationships are not treated as C++ objects. Naturally, relationships can be established between objects or deleted. The participating objects as well as possible attribute values are given as parameters. Relationships possess a persistence concept on their own. A relationship can be established between temporary objects. If all the participating objects are persistent, the relationship is automatically made persistent. Navigation through the database by following relationships from object to object is possible in an easy way.

```
SOFTWARE *sw = new SOFTWARE;                      // C++ object                        (1)
sw->Name = new String("MyComponent");             // set attribute value
POSTSCRIPT *ps = new POSTSCRIPT;
ps->Authors = new SETOF<String>;                  // insertion into
ps->Authors->Insert("Uwe");                       // set-valued attribute 'Authors'
ps->Authors->Insert("Christian");
ps->Content->CopyIn("/home/hackers/file.ps");    // copy file into Longfield
sw->possesses->Insert(ps);                        // ps becomes component of sw
```

```
sw->MakePersist();                            // insert objects sw and ps into DB  (2)
. . .
FACET_VALUE *value = 0;                       // navigation :                      (3)
classified_by cursor (sw,value);              //      cursor for 'classified_by'
for (cursor.First(); !cursor.EOS(); cursor.Next())
    { cout << cursor.FACET_VALUE->Name;
      SETOF<FACET> *fset = belongs_to::Get_FACET(cursor.FACET_VALUE);
      FACET *f = fset->First(); cout << "for facet " << f->Name << endl; };   (4)
```

This is a short sketch about using the DML interface. Obviously, the application programs are not aware of an explicit database language, since all the manipulation is done in pure C++. Hence, the code correctly runs through any commercial C++ compiler.

(1) demonstrate how to create C++ objects. Both variables *sw and *ps point to these objects. The C++ objects are now transient, they are just container for database objects and consequently not stored in the database so far. Transient and persistent C++ objects can be manipulated by using the ordinary C++ facilities, e.g., setting attribute values - more precisely data fields - with the reference operator '->'. A predefined function is used to insert concrete authors into the set-valued attribute 'Authors'. Inheritance takes place the same way as in C++. Hence 'CreationDate' and 'Authors', which both are attributes of the supertype DOCUMENT, can be accessed. Afterwards the object *ps is made a component of *sw. We are again confronted with inheritance, because 'possesses' really expects a DOCUMENT rather than a POSTSCRIPT object.

(2) makes the complex object consisting of *sw and its component *ps explicitly persistent. Persistent objects get a unique object identifier automatically.

The navigational principle relies on the concept of relationship types. The piece of code presented in (3) prints out the classification of a software component, i.e., its facet values and the facets they belong to. A cursor concept is applied for navigation. Several cursors can be defined for each relationship type. The initialization defines what relationships in a type should be traversed: If none of the roles is set, i.e., if the parameters refer to the null pointer 0, then the whole extent of the relationship type is fetched. If one role refers to a given object, then all the relationships related with this object are retrieved. The cursor only contains the first relationship including the participating objects just as the attribute values of the relationship. An access to them is possible, e.g., `cursor.FACET_VALUE` yields the participating facet value. Cursors can be moved on to the next relationship by the function **Next**. If the relationship type is exhausted, a special flag **EOS** is set.

Instead of navigating through relationships in the above mentioned way, a simpler way is provided by using **Get_ET** functions. This function yields all the objects of a given role ET that are related to the other participating objects.

Those result sets are represented by `SETOF<ET>` classes are available for each entity type ET. The ordinary set operations are possible, e.g., compatible sets can be merged or intersected. New objects, no matter whether database objects or C++ objects, can be inserted into a set. Existing elements can be deleted, however, not deleting the object itself but only its occurrence in the set. In contrast to ObjectStore [LLOW91] or O_2 [Deux90], we do not introduce iterators like '**for each**' or '**for x in ...**' for traversing sets, because these constructs require a new compiler. We only rely on C++ by just providing a **First** or **Next** function to traverse through a set object by object (cf. (4)). Exhausted sets are indicated by a flag **EOS**.

Comparing the achieved functionality with the one of object-oriented DBMS, we loose some flexibility because the persistence of objects is strictly related to entity types; it is not possible to make arbitrary C++ objects persistent. On the other hand, our approach has an advantage by supporting complex objects in the sense of [KBG89], which in spite of being well-known are rather rarely provided.

Special attention is dedicated to enhance the associative query capabilities. While [OdH91] only uses a simple functional approach, we bid up to strength the capabilities of the underlying relational query language. For querying objects from the database, the **ET** classes possess a comfortable **Find** function. A single parameter of type **char*** denotes a character sequence that describes a formula being subject to an associative query language. That formula specifies a selection condition that restricts the occurrences of the extent of the entity type to all instances satisfying this condition. The actual parameter can be a variable that contains a query specification, thus allowing for dynamic queries that are evaluated at run-time. The result will be a set or bag of instances belonging to the entity type.

Example 1 *Select all the Framemaker design documents having 2 authors one of both is Uwe*

```
char* query1 = "select fm from fm in FRAMEMAKER
                where  'Uwe' in fm.Authors and fm.Interpretation = Design";
                       and cnt(fm.Authors) = 2";
BAGOF<FRAMEMAKER> *result = FRAMEMAKER::FIND(query1);
```

The associative query language is an SQL/EER subset [HoE92] adapted to our data model. Similar to other SQL extensions, like HDBL [PiD89] proposed for a NF^2 data model or the ER language CERMoQL [ScR89], the query language naturally supports all the modelling concepts like multivalued attributes, components and subtyping with inheritance in an adequate manner. Furthermore, concepts like aggregate functions or nesting/unnesting are orthogonally integrated.

The result of such an associative query generally constitutes a set of objects, here represented by the variable *result of type `SETOF<FRAMEMAKER>`. Duplicates are retained but can be eliminated by declaring *result as `BAGOF<FRAMEMAKER>`. Please note selecting the instances of a type generally also considers all the instances of its subtypes. If this is not desired, the operator `instances(ET)` can be applied taking only into account the instances of the type itself.

By declaring `FRAMEMAKER *fm` and using `fm = result->Next()`, all objects in the set can be accessed. It is worth mentioning that each entity of the result can be used for further navigation in the database, for instance to access the 'CreationDate' attribute in the usual way `fm->CreationDate`.

Find requires that only objects of one type can be selected. But neither projections nor joins are possible. Consequently only those queries can be used in the Find function that select whole entities, i.e. have the form `select x from x in ET where` ϕ.

In order to pass the full functionality of relational SQL over to the querying facility, just another possibility formulating associative queries is provided. It allows defining the query result as a C++ class, possibly being structured. However, these classes are not DML classes and consequently query results cannot be stored in the database.

Example 2 *Given a document, select its authors and all the reusable components related to it*

```
class Query2 { char* author,
               SETOF<SOFTWARE> *comp; };
/* DOCUMENT *doc  should refer to an object of type DOCUMENT */
char* query2 = select a , (select sw from sw in SOFTWARE
                           where  sw possesses d)
               from   d in DOCUMENT , a in d.Authors
               where  d = @doc";
SETOF<Query2> *result = new SETOF<Query2> (query2,doc);
Query2 *tuple = result->First(); cout << tuple->comp->First()->Name << endl;
```

The class Query2 defines the structure of the result, which is filled with C++ objects by invoking the **new** operator of C++. Similar to the Find function, the passed parameter string specifies the query. The correctness of the query, i.e., whether the result of the query matches the class structure can only be done at run time due to the dynamic execution of queries. However it is important that no precompiler is necessary to check the consistency of both owing to the use of the Meta Information Protocol [BKS92]: This tool provides type information about C++ classes at run-time so that a check can easily be done. Please note that we put up with the obvious gap due to a lack of "closeness" [HeS91]: The structure of a query result is defined by a C++ class, rather than an entity type following the ER rules. Consequently the result does not consist of entities; it contains several tuples, the parts of which can be entities certainly. However, our main goal providing a powerful query facility justifies this disadvantage for the moment.

Considering query2, we see that (sub-) queries of the form `select-from-where` are special kinds of terms. Thus, they can be used as target terms. This allows us to formulate nested queries known from the NF^2 model ([ScS89]). Quite a useful extension of SQL/EER allows one to involve C++ objects in queries: The special symbol '@' here denotes a C++ variable. The above query thus has the effect of an parameterized query: For the document represented by the C++ variable *doc, the query is evaluated. Even more, relations between navigational and associative access via variables can be established.

4 Implementational Aspects

The design of the database interface presented in the previous section is guided by the overall goal to make the implementation quite easy and portable to other DBMSs.

The main strategy is to avoid building a precompiler or extending the C++ compiler for achieving the coupling; just an ordinary C++ compiler is used and is made do as much as possible work. This leads to the principle of automatically generating C++ classes that provide the database functionality.

In the sequel, we investigate the most important aspects of the implementation in more detail elaborating the advantages of the general approach. Subsection 4.2 discusses the generative process, while 4.3 elucidates on how aiming at portability leads to a layered architecture. We figure out the basic constituents needed to be implemented: The **DDL compiler** generating the DML classes (the interface) and the **Basic Access Layer** that performs the mapping onto the relational system and attends to portability. Beforehand, we prepare the discussion by presenting an abstract view of the implementation in subsection 4.1. Finally, the openness of the approach is clarified (subsection 4.4).

4.1 Functional View

Using an underlying relational DBMS implies a transformation of the ER concepts onto relational ones. This holds for both the data model and the operations. The usual proceeding can be described as follows: a **model transformation 'M**: ER model→ REL model' maps each ER schema into an equivalent relational (REL) schema = M(ER schema). Having the resulting REL schema installed on a concrete system, the operations and queries can be transformed into corresponding relational ones by means of an **operation transformation Op(M)** and **query transformation Qu(M)**. Both transformations are strictly dependent on the mapping M denoted as Op(M) and Qu(M), respectively. Afterwards, the relational statements can be executed on the relational system.

The model transformation is done very straightforward essentially following [EHH+89]. Entity types ET and relationship types RT are transformed to corresponding relations R(ET) and R(RT) [Che76]. Each relation R(ET) gets an identifying surrogate key attribute 'ET$'. The values of this attribute 'ET$' are generated and controlled by the relational database system. Similarly, the relations R(RT) get a key consisting of (rolename) attributes '$n_i$$: $ET_i$$' to express the relationship between the participating entity types. Subtypes get an additional attribute relating the tuples (objects or relationships) to the tuples in the supertype relation.

Non-multivalued attributes are directly derived from the corresponding entity type or relationship type. Components are treated as attributes, except the fact that they receive the surrogates. We establish an additional relation R(a) for each multivalued attribute 'a'. 'a' itself becomes an attribute of R(a). Furthermore, R(a) gets an attribute 'a$' referring to the surrogate of R(ET). This makes it possible to join both relations R(ET) and R(a) to reestablish their connections. If 'a' is bag- or list-valued, we add the numbering attribute 'a#' "implementing" the multiplicity of bags or ordering of lists, respectively.

Based upon this prerequisite step, the complete DML proposed for the ER model, i.e., operations (C++ member functions) and associative queries, can be translated into relational statements.

The operation transformation Op(M) is closely related to the principle of M. If we want to insert one entity into an entity type ET, we have to insert one entity tuple into the relation R(ET) and possibly several tuples into relations R(a) representing multivalued attributes. Handling complex objects is more difficult, because we are concerned with propagation of insertion, deletion and deep or shallow copies. Consequently, several entities in different entity types (or corresponding relations) must be manipulated. If we want to insert a new (concrete) relationship, we have to insert the tuples of surrogate values corresponding to the participating entities. Deletion is quite similar.

The query transformation Qu(M) can logically be subdivided into four successive logical steps in order to become flexible with respect to ER and relational query languages.

Q_1 **Elimination of sophisticated concepts:** At first, we map the associative query language into an *ER standard form* by eliminating sophisticated concepts, e.g., inheritance or some language-specific features like keywords. The result is a representation of an ER calculus expression [GoH91]. This transformation step is easy and can generally be done one-to-one. Furthermore, some logical conversions are performed, e.g., eliminating the connective `implies` or the quantifier `for all`, because both are generally not available in relational languages.

Q_2 **Data model shift:** This step is in charge of the data model shift; consequently it is dependent on the data model transformation M. More precisely, this step is the only part that depends on M. The ER standard form is mapped into a relational counterpart. The resulting "*relational standard form*" is an extension of the "classical" relational calculus because it offers aggregate functions and nested queries. But it is still based upon relational concepts, i.e., relations and (datavalued) attributes. The extended relational calculus enables us to carry out the step as one-to-one. Every associative query results in exactly one relational query. What we have to do in this step is to transform concepts that are exclusively available in the EER calculus. This means that we have to "implement" features that are non-relational modelling primitives like terms and formulas containing components, multivalued attributes, or relationships.

Q_3 **Conversion into a concrete relational query language:** Finally, the relational calculus is mapped into a relational query language like SQL or QUEL. Due to the powerfulness of the relational calculi, this step cannot be performed one-to-one. For example, SQL provides no possibility to compute the average of sums in one only query. We need at least features to generate intermediate relations keeping interim results.

Q_4 **Re-interpretation of result:** Finally, the flat tuples resulting from the relational query must be interpreted in terms of the ER model. For example, previously eliminated nestings must be established and object identifiers hidden in surrogates must be managed.

This stepwise transformation of queries is advantageous with regard to:

- Complexity: The four single steps are easier to handle than the whole query transformation.
- Modularity: We can easily replace one ER query language with another one by only changing step Q_1. Consequently, several associative languages can be offered in order to support different styles or several degrees of functionality. Similarly, the underlying relational query language can be exchanged by only adapting Q_3. This proceeding increases the portability because we can implement our query language(s) on any relational database system. Moreover, only the second step is dependent on the underlying model transformation M. All the other steps are independent from changes on this transformation. Hence, several strategies for model transformations can be offered with only affecting the step Q_2.
- Theoretically sound definition: The first two steps can formally be defined, e.g., using attribute grammars. Indeed, this has been done for the steps Q_1 [HoE92] and Q_2.

The principle works for any kind of ER query language and relational query language.

4.2 Generative Approach

The substantial principle of our generative approach is given by a mechanism to generate C++ classes for a given database schema. These DML classes represent the structural properties of entity types and relationship types as well as providing the DML functionality associated with them. The task of generation is done by a so-called **DDL Compiler**. The generation is based on a mixture of macro instantiation, C++ templates and direct output of C++ code. Hence it is easily possible to include the code of user-defined methods into entity type classes. Given a database schema, the generated output consists of C++ *header files* (".h"), which contains the C++ class definitions including the signatures of the member functions, and *implementation files* (".cc") implementing the member functions. Some other files are predefined as they contain C++ templates (producing generic `SETOF` or `LISTOF` classes) and predefined classes like `Longfield` or `Date` that are independent of the schema. All these files (i.e., C++ classes) are compiled and linked into application programs. Hence, There is no need extending or modifying a C++ compiler: The ordinary C++ compiler is used as far as possible, especially for type checking and inheritance. The main database task is hidden in the DDL Compiler.

Furthermore, the DDL compiler makes available the schema information itself to application programs in special predefined C++ classes. Hence, the whole schema information is hold in special C++ classes and corresponding functions can be used to navigate through the schema information.

The generation of the header files is quite easy and fairly straightforward, due to the close correspondence between the ER schema definitions and C++ classes. The implementation of the member functions must principally call the relational SQL interface in order to establish the connection. Before doing that, an equivalent relational schema must be established, mapping entity types and relationship types onto relations. The DDL compiler thus has to perform the model transformation M and to install the resulting equivalent relational schema.

4.3 Layering of Implementation

The code of the implementation files, implementing the functions of the DML classes, must principally use the interface given by the relational system. However, we put another layer, called **Basic Access (BA) layer**, between the platform system and the DML classes. The BA layer depend neither on the data model nor on the database schema. The advantages are obvious: First, this layer needs to be implemented only once due to the independence of the schema. Second, the implementation of the DML functions can use BA functions, which finally are implemented by using relational features. Consequently the code to be generated becomes shorter, since the handling of relational operations is extracted into this additional layer. Second, the BA layer abstracts from the physical storage platform and concentrates the platform dependence on as small as possible parts of the implementation. Moreover the new BA layer allows the environment to switch to another platform without changing the implementation of the DML since the BA functions are platform-independent. Hence the implementation consists of a *three-level* architecture building two layers upon the platform system:

The *DML layer* implements the data manipulation interface to the application programs, i.e., C++ classes for manipulating objects and relationships, and invokes the BA functions. The BA functions are the same for any platform system and implemented in the *Basic Access layer*, which consequently abstracts from the platform. Finally, the *Relational Platform System* is used as a persistent storage server providing the basic functionality like concurrency control, transaction mechanisms, or recovery.

Let us now discuss the basic blocks of the layers by addressing some special problems in more detail.

The DML layer implements the DML for the programs, i.e., C++ DML classes that allow manipulating entities and relationships in C++. The implementation of the DML on top of the BA layer is mainly very straightforward. The member functions can directly be mapped onto corresponding BA function calls. Furthermore, the DML is responsible for some specific points:

- One application may have *different* C++ variables pointing to the *same* database object, e.g., if this object is fetched into different C++ objects. Hence synchronisation of modifications is necessary. This achieved by an in-memory *object cache*, which maintains consistent updates of objects in an application.
- Management of complex objects is based on *lazy* retrieval, i.e., the complete complex object is just fetched when explicitly requested. This is more efficient since not all parts of a complex structure are generally interesting. In the same way, set traversal is also performed in a lazy manner.
- Generally, DML functions related to complex objects are handled here, e.g., making complex objects persistent or deleting them. Some functions like the deletion of an object from a subtype without deleting it occurrence in the supertype requires a special handling due to the different semantics in C++.

The Basic Access layer provides functionality for communicating objects (including sets/longfields) and relationships between C++ object representations and the relational system. It operates as an *Object Manager* and a *Relationship Manager* providing functions to cater for storage and retrieval of objects and relationships. In fact, both perform the task of the operation transformation Op(M). Consequently, the implementation of the BA functions is obviously dependent on the model transformation M. However, these functions are independent of the schema and furthermore do not rely on the model transformation M. The interface is always the same for any kind of transformation.

Another functional component is dedicated to the query evaluation. Associative queries (which are specified in an SQL/EER subset [HoE92]) are communicated to the *Associative Query Interpreter (AQI)* for evaluation to take advantage of special platform capabilities. The associative language is mapped onto a corresponding language in the platform, i.e., each ER query will be translated into a relational SQL query, according to the query transformation Qu(M). The implementation of the associative language, the AQI, is dependent on the platform capabilities. However, we have shown in subsection 4.1 how to design a modular query evaluation. The AQI makes use of two important features. First, the Meta Information Protocol (MIP) [BKS92] is used to check whether the result of an associative query matches the definition of the `Query` class that describe the structure of the result. This requires that type information about those query classes is available, which is exactly provided by the MIP. Second, we use the templates of the C++ version 3.0 one more time to create generic `SETOF` or `LISTOF` classes. Consequently, the `SETOF<Query>` C++ classes containing query results are automatically generated by the C++ compiler.

4.4 Openness

The layered architecture separates functionality in such a way that both extensibility *downwards* (towards other DBMS platforms) as well as *upwards* (towards other programming languages) is facilitated. No components of the architecture put special requirements on platform functionality.

Establishing a C++ coupling to another platform system requires a modification of the model transformation M, in fact only if the platform system relies on a different data model. The other parts of the DDL Compiler, especially the generation of DML classes, are not concerned.

Furthermore, a re-implementation of the Basic Access layer is necessary. This layer is essentially just a storage server, and the transition to any reasonable platform is fairly straightforward for the operation transformation Op(M). The SQL-like associative query *language* is platform independent, but its *implementation* (the Associative Query Interpreter) is dependent on the platform capabilities. Thus, this mapping needs to be changed. The stepwise proceeding of the query transformation Qu(M) simplifies this task. If another relational system is used, only the step Q_3 must be adapted to the new system-specific characteristics. Changing the type of system also involves the step Q_2.

Upward independence concerns the desire to access a database from *different* programming languages - [Sto90] states that the DBMS should support "persistent X" for a variety of programming languages X. Making the DML connectable to multiple programming languages is facilitated by modifying the DDL Compiler to emit code for another language, rather than C++ code, and which interface to the BAL functionality. In fact, specifying user-defined methods must then be done in the new programming language.

5 Conclusions

In this paper, we have described a coupling of C++ with a relational database management system. The work was strongly influenced by current object-oriented database systems, and thus the presented C++ interface is quite similar to use. While most object-oriented systems rely on the data model of the programming language C++ and thus provide a notion of pointers (possibly with automatically maintained inverses) only, we use an extended Entity-Relationship model. Having the concept of explicit relationships is believed to provide valuable and flexible modelling capabilities.

The coupling is easy and quickly to implement causing only low expenses. In particular, there is no need for developing a new C++ compiler or precompiler due to a simple generative approach. We just need a DDL compiler to install a conceptual schema on the platform system and to create some C++ classes. The remaining work is done by ordinary C++ compilers. We make intensive use of the C++ Compiler of AT&T, version 3.0, which provides so-called "templates" in the sense of parameterized classes. Using the Meta Information Protocol, which provides meta information about classes used in a C++ program, helps doing without a precompiler approach even for querying.

For the time being, we have finished the design of the interface as described in this paper. The implementation of the DML will be soon started on SUN4 workstations in AT&T C++ version 3.0. Owing to an adequate architecture, the implementation on top of the relational DBMS is rather simple and fast to make. Moreover, the chosen architecture is open to portability, allowing an easy switch to other relational systems. Even NF^2, ER or object-oriented systems may be used as underlying platform providing an adequate query facility is available. Other database systems having quite a different nature can be used, too. However, some more effort is needed to perform the query evaluation.

Essentially, future research will be done in the following directions:

- The data model should be enhanced with further modelling concepts. Problems might arise due to their representations in C++. In particular, a *versioning mechanism* as part of the data model implies that special support in the search and manipulation process may be provided.
- *Dynamic schema modifications* should be possible. As a first step, incremental schema extensions will be supported, allowing to extend a schema step by step.
- Support for *(local) subdatabases/workspaces*, i.e. some protection mechanism on type and instance level. This also relates to access right mechanisms.

Finally, we envisage having a uniform DML layer for several different DBMSs. Anyway, the DML layer will not be affected, but the query evaluation will.

References

[ABD+89] M. Atkinson / F. Bancilhon / D. DeWitt / K. Dittrich / D. Maier / St. Zdonik: *The Object-Oriented Database System Manifesto.* In: Proc. of DOOD '89, Kyoto (Japan) 1989.

[AFS89] S. Abiteboul / P.C. Fischer / H.-J. Schek (eds.): *Nested relations and Complex Objects in Databases.* Springer Verlag, 1989. Lecture Notes in Computer Science No. 361.

[AGO91] A. Albano / G. Ghelli / R. Orsini: *A Relationship Mechanism for a Strongly Typed Object-Oriented Database Programming Language.* In: Proc. of 16th Int. Conf. on Very Large Databases, Barcelona, Spain (VLDB '91) 1991 (565–575)

[BKS92] F. Buschmann / K. Kiefer / M. Stal: *A Runtime Type System for C++.* In G. Heeg / B. Magnusson / B. Meyer (eds.): Technology of Object-Oriented Languages and Systems - TOOLS 92, Dortmund 1992

[CDV88] M.J. Carey / D. DeWitt / S.L. Vandenberg: *A Data Model and Query Language for EXODUS.* Proc. of the ACM SIGMOD Int. Conf. on Management of Data 1988, Chicago

[Che76] P.P. Chen: *The Entity-Relationship Model - Towards a Unified View of Data.* ACM Transactions on Database Systems 1976, 1(1) (9 - 36)

[Deux90] O. Deux et al: *The Story of O_2.* IEEE Transactions on Knowledge and Data Engineering 1990, 2(1)

[Dit88] K. Dittrich: *Advances in Object-Oriented Database Systems.* In: Proc. of the 2nd Int. Workshop on Object-Oriented Systems 1988, Springer LNCS No. 334.

[EGH+92] G. Engels / M. Gogolla / U. Hohenstein / K. Hülsmann / P. Löhr-Richter / H.-D. Ehrich: *Conceptual Modelling of Database Applications Using an Extended ER Approach.* Data & Knowledge Engineering 1992, Vol. 9 (157–204)

[EHH+89] G. Engels / U. Hohenstein / K. Hülsmann / P. Löhr-Richter / H.-D. Ehrich: *CADDY: Computer-Aided Design of Non-Standard Databases.* In N. Madhavji / H. Weber / W. Schäfer (eds.): Int. Conf. on System Development Environments & Factories. Berlin, May 1989. Pitman Publ., London 1990

[GeD91] A. Geppert / K. Dittrich: *Objektstrukturen in Datenbanksystemen. Oder: Auf der Suche nach voller Objektorientierung.* In H.-J. Appelrath (ed.): Datenbanksysteme in Büro, Technik und Wissenschaft, Kaiserslautern 1991 (421–429)

[GoH91] M. Gogolla / U. Hohenstein: *Towards a Semantic View of an Extended Entity-Relationship Model.* ACM Transactions on Database Systems 16 (3), 1991

[HeS91] A. Heuer / M. Scholl: *Principles of Object-Oriented Languages.* In H.-J. Appelrath (ed.): Datenbanksysteme in Büro, Technik und Wissenschaft, Kaiserslautern 1991 (178 - 197)

[HoE92] U. Hohenstein / G. Engels: *SQL/EER : Syntax and Semantics of an Entity-Relationship Based Query Language.* Information Systems 1992, 17 (3) (209 - 242)

[KBG89] W. Kim / E. Bertino / J. Garcia: *Composite Objects Revised.* In J. Clifford / B. Lindsay / D. Maier (eds.): Proc. of the 1989 ACM SIGMOD Int. Conf. on the Management of Data, Portland 1989. SIGMOD RECORD 1989, 18(2) (337 - 347)

[LLOW91] Ch. Lamb / G. Landis / J. Orenstein / D. Weinreb: *The ObjectStore Database System.* Communications of ACM, 34(10), October 1991 (50–63)

[OdH91] E. Odberg / U. Hohenstein: *Data Model and Database Interface Specification.* Technical Report (Deliverable D1.2.B1, No. REBOOT-7046.7), December 1991.

[PiD89] P. Pistor / P. Dadam: *The Advanced Information Management Prototype.* In: [AFS89]

[Rum87] J. Rumbaugh: *Relations as Semantic Constructs in an Object-Oriented Language.* In: Proceedings of the Conf. on Object-Oriented Systems, Languages and Applications (OOPSLA), Orlando (Florida), 1987 (466–481)

[ScR89] B. Schiefer / S. Rehm: *Eine Anfragesprache für ein strukturell-objektorientiertes Datenmodell.* In Th. Härder (ed.): Datenbanksysteme in Büro, Technik und Wissenschaft, Zürich 1989 (373 - 388)

[ScS89] H.-J. Schek / M.H. Scholl: *The Two Roles of Nested Relations in the DASDBS Project.* In: [AFS89]

[Str91] B. Stroustrup: *The C++ Programming Language.* 2nd edition, Addison-Wesley 1991

[Sto90] M. Stonebraker (The Committee for Advanced DBMS Function). *Third-Generation Database System manifesto.* SIGMOD RECORD 1990, 19(3).

Implementing a Design Management and Cooperation Model on the Basis of KRISYS

Cirano Iochpe, Fernando de Ferreira Rezende, Maria Aparecida Castro Livi
*Informatics Institute, Universidade Federal do Rio Grande do Sul**

Nelson Mendonça Mattos
*IBM Database Technology Institute***

Joachim Thomas
*Department of Computer Science, Universität Kaiserslautern****

Abstract: After describing both the design management and cooperation model of the STAR Design Environment and the transaction manager of the KRISYS Knowledge Representation System, this article explains how the former is being realized on the basis of the latter.

1 Introduction

In the last ten years much effort has been spent by researchers to extend database technology in order to cope with new requirements posed by so-called non-standard applications. Especially design applications need new, more expressive data models as well as present processing models which are not supported by conventional transaction systems.

In order to support long-duration as well as collaborative work in the design environment, new database transaction models were proposed [Ioch89] which give up the transaction properties of atomicity and isolation. Although such models can prevent long-duration work to be completely undone in case of either user or system failure and support the exchange of temporary results among designers, they cannot rely on serializability to maintain database correctness. Therefore, so-called cooperation models ([Kaef90], [Cast92]) were proposed which aim at capturing application semantics to identify when the database (DB) is correct as well as in which cases temporary results can be seen by other transactions.

To completely cope with the requirements of design processing models and maintain DB correctness, the database system (DBS) must integrate both a long-duration transaction with a cooperation model.

This paper presents part of the research work which aims at realizing the project management and cooperation model of the AMPLO/STAR design environment [Wagn92] on the basis of KRISYS's transaction manager [Reze92].

The rest of the article is organized as follows. Section 2 briefly describes STAR's project management and cooperation model. KRISYS's architecture and transaction model is

---

* P.O.Box 15064, 91501-970 Porto Alegre, RS, Brazil, e-mail: iochpe@inf.ufrgs.br

** 555 Bailey Avenue, San Jose, CA, 95150 USA, e-mail: mattos@stlvm14.ibm.com

*** P.O.Box 3049, D-6750 Kaiserslautern, Germany, e-mail: thomas@informatik.uni-kl.de

presented in Section 3. The strategy used to implement the project and cooperation model integrated with the transaction model is discussed in Section 4. Section 5 concludes the paper.

2 STAR's Design Management and Cooperation Model

STAR's Design Management and Cooperation Model (DMCM) supports two views of the evolutionary character of design applications: object construction and design process development ([Ioch91],[Cast92]). Relying on the cooperation model proposed in [Kaef90], design objects are specified to the system by means of their (future) features which should be realized during the design process. The latter is modeled as a partial order of design steps. Each design step manipulates a set of objects and implements some of their (expected) features. Design steps incrementally change object states until objects reach their final states, that is, states in which objects incorporate all features declared in their specifications. Figure 2.1 depicts DMCM's basic elements and their relationships.

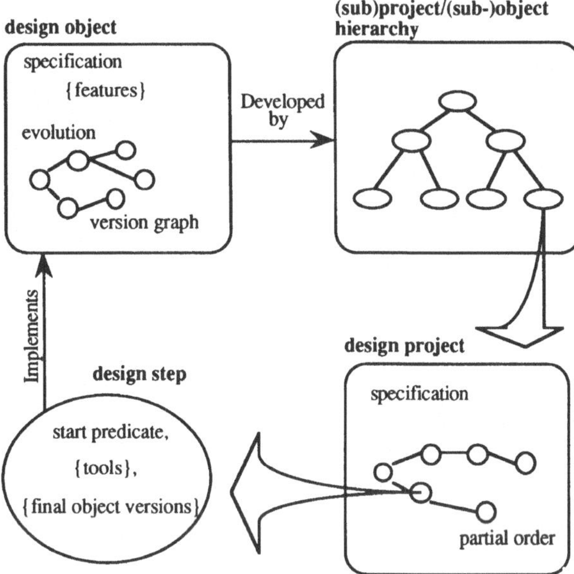

Figure 2.1: Modeling the Design Process

2.1 Object Specification and Object Design Evolution

The specification of a design object includes a set of features that represents the set of characteristics which must be present in the object at the end of the design process. Object features express design decisions about form, performance, functions, and correctness criteria. They can also represent the ocurrence of either a test or a simulation of an object. Moreover, the object specification can either establish or estimate values for the features (e.g. the area of a chip must end up between 2 and 3 cm^2). An object specification can be updated at any time. New features can be added to as well as existing features can be deleted from it. Designers can also change expected feature values at any time.

Object design evolution is captured by a partial order of object versions. Each version expresses one of the states which were already reached by the object due to the design process. Each state is represented by a specific set of (realized) object characteristics. Therefore, versions of a same object differ from one another either in the set of features they incorporate or in the values they set to them.
The model supposes a three-level DB hierarchy: private DB (DBpr), project DB (DBpj) and public DB (DBpu). The location in the database hierarchy of a specific object version depends on its actual development state which can be classified as either in-work, or stable, or consolidated. DBpu stores the consolidated versions which can be neither updated nor deleted. Stable versions are those which realize a reasonable number of the expected object features and can be exchanged among designers of the same project. They are kept in their respective project databases. In-work object versions are those which do not aggregate enough features to be considered stable. They are kept in the private databases of their respective creators.

2.2 Project Specification and Design Process Evolution

DMCM views a design project as a hierarchy of design (sub)tasks (i.e. subprojects), each one of which develops one or more (sub)objects. The latter are integrated to form the final product of the design project (e.g. the design of a cpu could include the design of a main memory component, the one of a bank of registers, that of an ALU, and the bus design).

Each (sub)project is modeled by means of a set of object specifications and a project specification. Object specifications describe the goals of the project. The project specification defines the way the goals should be achieved. A project specification consists of a partial order of design steps (DS). Each DS expresses a set of design activities which have a common meaning (e.g. form a specific design phase) for the application. During its execution, a design step can implement new object characteristics, test already existing ones, and inform designers about object design evolution.

An DS is responsible for the execution of a set of application-oriented design tools (e.g. editors, compilers, and simulators) each one of which accesses existing object versions and can generate new ones. The model supports human intervention which can be represented as an application tool inside the step.

DMCM allows designers to define an execution order for the tools inside an DS. In addition, designers must point out the subset of object versions to be created inside a design step that must be kept in the database at the end of its execution.

At DS definition time, designers must declare specific object versions as either input to or output of design tools. Relying on this information, the project manager can infer the exact point in time when a specific version will be needed for cooperation. It can also infer when it will be produced as well as in which DS it will occur.

Not only its relative position in the partial order of design steps determines when an DS must be started. Designers can associate a start predicate to every design step. Such a predicate can relate the execution of its associated step to the realization of any object characteristic as well as to the evaluation of any query against the database. The project manager can control design process evolution by keeping information about the directed graph of design steps as well as evaluating the start predicates of steps which are ready to execute.

DMCM allows step specifications to be updated at any time. Moreover, the model enables designers to suspend, resume, and abort step executions. Any of these operations on one DS can force the project manager to abort or compensate for those design steps which depend upon that one and either already finished or are still executing.

2.3 Object-Transfer Operations

Cooperation among designers of the same project is supported by the design management and cooperation model on the basis of both object characteristics and object-transfer operations.

Any designer can access object versions stored in the public database. Object versions in a DBpj can be accessed only by designers working on the respective project. Finally, versions stored in a private DB can be accessed by its owner only.

Since DMCM allows the design of an object to be carried out by more than one designer, a transfer of an object version between the private databases of two of its creators has not the same semantics as a transfer operation which lends a copy of an object version to a non-creator designer. While the prior operation prevents the first creator to continue working with the version, the latter prevents the user of the version to update it, while the creator can continue designing the object (i.e. producing new versions of it). Therefore, transfer operations between creators transfer object versions from one DBpr to another. On the other hand, object-transfer operations between creators and users send copies of object versions from project databases to private ones.

Since new object versions can be created in parallel to the use of some older version of a same object, the project manager must keep track of exchanged version copies. New versions should eventually substitute older ones at user sites. Object versions either composed by or whose design relies upon borrowed versions cannot be consolidated in the DBpu before those borrowed versions are. In addition, the project manager must identify those design steps (of any existing project specification) which relied on any object version created inside an DS that has been aborted or compensated for. Responsible designers must decide whether affected design steps should be rolled back or not.

The end of a cooperation at the project level is usually decided by designers responsible for the project specification that borrowed the object version(s). A cooperation can either remain until the end of the whole project or be cancelled due to either DS abortion or version deletion.

3 KRISYS' Architecture and Transaction Model

3.1 Overview of the Architecture

KRISYS' architecture is based on a workstation/server computer configuration. It is organized as a hierarchy of software modules. Some of these modules are located at the server node while others execute at the workstation (see Figure 3.1).

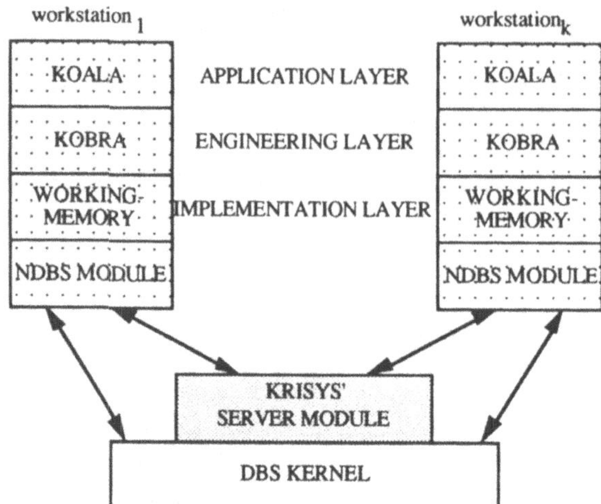

Figure 3.1: A simplified Version of KRISYS' Architecture

The application layer implements the KOALA Processing System which realizes KRISYS' application interface [Dess89]. This layer provides the end user with an abstract view of the knowledge along with operations to support knowledge base (KB) design as well as KB access and manipulation.

The engineering layer realizes the knowledge model of KRISYS, named KOBRA (KRISYS Object-Centered Representation Model). KOBRA views the application domain as a graph of structured objects. Objects are modeled through schemas that support the representation of entities, classes, sets, instances, elements, and aggregates.

The implementation layer is composed of the Working-Memory System, the NDBS Module, the KRISYS' Server Module, and the DBS Kernel. The working-memory (WM), i.e. a main storage structure which works like an application buffer to temporarily store KB objects, enables fast access with low costs (i.e. equivalent to the access through pointers [Matt91]).

The NDBS Module handles both the communication between workstation and server as well as the mapping of WM objects onto KB ones, and vice-versa. In addition, this module iteracts with the Server Module in order to realize KRISYS' transaction model.

The Server Module controls the communication between users as well as between user transactions, the actual state of those transactions, and the access to well defined parts of the knowledge base, i.e. worlds (see Section 3.3).

The DBS Kernel is responsible for the KB non-volatile storage. In the actual implementation, this module is represented by the INGRES relational database system.

3.2 The Transaction Model

KRISYS realizes a long-duration transaction model. A User Transaction (UT) [Reze92] encapsulates either the whole user work or, at least, well-defined parts of it. User operations (e.g. KOALA queries, KOBRA statements) are submitted from inside her/his

UT which can take hours, days, and even weeks to be concluded. UTs are neither atomic nor isolated but they must be consistent as well as durable.

Inside an UT, work can be distributed into a set of Short Transactions (STs). Although the actual implementation of KRISYS supports serial execution of STs only, short transactions shall be able to execute concurrently in the future. They will represent units of isolation inside an UT. The durability of a committed short transaction depends on its UT's fate. If the UT aborts (i.e. is aborted by the user), its executing STs are aborted and its committed STs are compensated for.

KRISYS realizes the concept of a Savepoint. Savepoints can be issued either from inside an UT or from inside an ST. The scope of a savepoint is the transaction inside which it was defined. It is no longer valid after transaction commit or abort. Savepoints allow users to delimit phases of their work as well as to establish security points during the processing of their transactions. To return the state of her/his work back to a previously defined savepoint, the user issues a Partial Rollback statement.

As required by long-duration work, the transaction model supports also the concepts of Suspend and Resume. The Suspend statement causes the interruption of an UT for an undefined period of time. On the other hand, the Resume statement causes the restart of a previously suspended UT.

KRISYS' transaction model enables user transactions to exchange knowledge. The realized knowledge transfer concept is explained in the following section.

3.3 Overview of Knowledge Transfer in KRISYS

To explain knowledge transfer in KRISYS, it is necessary to introduce the concept of Worlds [Thom91]. A world can be defined as a set of objects that represent together a logically and referentially consistent closed unit. The knowledge base as a whole is viewed as the union of all existing worlds. One important point is that users do not see the whole KB at once (what could lead to problems due to inconsistencies among worlds), but one world at a time (according to their access rights). KRISYS helps maintaining application consistency by imposing that each KOBRA statement as well as KOALA query access KB objects of one world only. Nevertheless the same UT can access any number of worlds (through the Change-To-World statement). Worlds accessed by an UT remain related to it until its end and cannot be accessed by any other UT during this time.

KRISYS' transaction model supports knowledge transfer between two worlds by means of the Transfer statement. A user can issue a transfer operation from inside her/his UT. The transaction must be already related to the world containing the knowledge to be (copied and) transferred.

Depending on the values of its parameters (which are informed by the user), the Transfer statement can exchange knowledge between user transactions in different ways [Reze92] (see Figure 3.2). Regarding the relationship between sender and receiver worlds, the transfer may be performed as either independent, or dependent, or even mutually dependent. An UT which receives a knowledge base object by means of an independent Transfer operation can handle it as its own object regardless of the fate of the UT which sent the object. On the other hand, an UT which receives an object by means of a dependent Transfer operation must remove that object from its associated world in case the sending UT aborts or rolls back to some savepoint issued before the execution of the operation. In addition, in the mutually dependent Transfer operation the sending UT, too, must rollback work in case the receiving UT either aborts or (partially) rolls back.

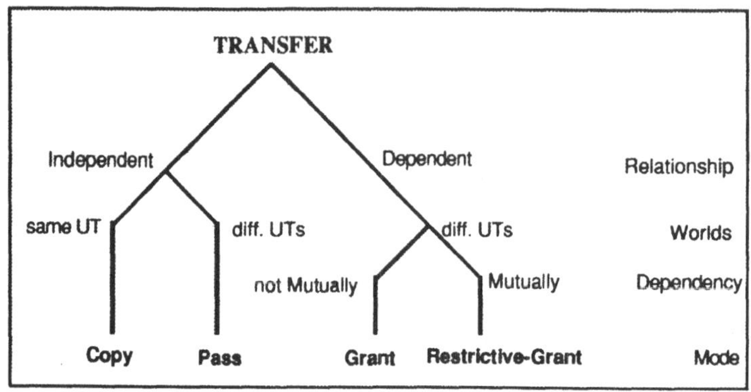

Figure 3.2: Alternatives of Object-Transfer Operations in KRISYS

The process of either aborting or rolling back an UT may become complicated, since it involves the decision of more than one user. To cope with this situation, KRISYS offers the Nullify command. It authorizes the transaction manager to eliminate any dependencies between UTs. The Nullify statement is an exception to the treatment of dependencies because it transforms a dependent Transfer operation (i.e. grant or restrictive-grant) into an independent one (i.e. pass). It represents an important feature which helps solving either conflicts or misunderstandings among users.

4 Mapping Databases onto Worlds and Steps onto UTs

The key idea of implementing STAR's Design Management and Cooperation Model on the basis of KRISYS is to use both the concept of Worlds to realize STAR's database hierarchy and the transaction model to support the implementation as well as management of design steps. In the following, we explain the actual implementation in more details.

4.1 Implementing Databases as Worlds

Each database instance of the hierarchy (i.e. DBpu, DBpj, and DBpr) is implemented in KRISYS as one world. Figure 4.1 shows an example. To help maintaining DBpr's consistency, a new world (DBstep) is created every time a design step is initiated and the former is related to the latter.

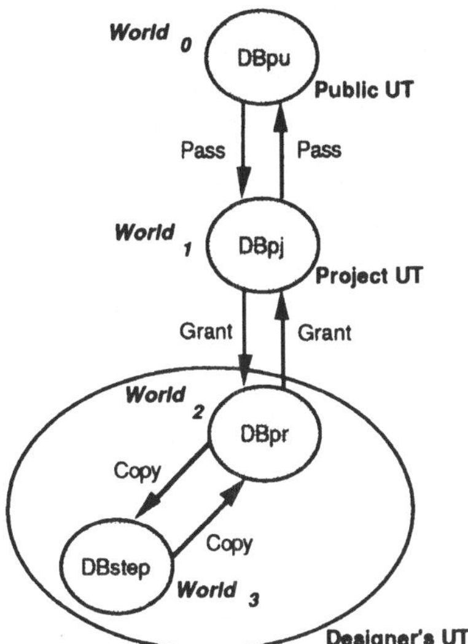

Figure 4.1: Mapping the Database Hierarchy onto a Set of Worlds

In Figure 4.1, before an application tool is started from inside the design step W3 is created and all the necessary input object versions are copied from W2 to W3. The tool accesses as well as creates objects in W3 only. At the end of the design step, the project manager issues copy commands to bring the significant results of the step into W2. In case the step must be aborted, W3 is simply deleted from the knowledge base.

Object versions are exchanged between project databases and DBpu by means of Transfer-Pass operations. The Pass command is appropriate in such situations since objects cannot be removed from DBpu and, on the other hand, DBpu is not dependent upon object deletion in project databases.

To make an object version stable, the project manager copies it from the DBpr where it was created into the respective DBpj. It must be done through a Transfer-Grant operation. DBpj is kept dependent upon DBpr for the former cannot keep the received version in case either it or the object it represents is removed from DBpr, or the designer's transaction is aborted. On the other hand, when DBpr receives an object from DBpj the opposite dependency must be applied for this object was created in another DBpr and granted to DBpj's UT.

Object versions are transferred between DBstep and DBpr by means of the Copy command since both these databases are associated with the same UT and no dependency is needed between them.

4.2 Applying User Transactions to Control Design Step Execution

One could think of implementing a partial order of design steps as a user transaction and the steps themselves as short transactions. The problem with this strategy is that KRISYS does not allow Transfer operations from inside STs. Therefore, before starting a design step STAR's project manager would have to bring into DBpr's new created world all input object versions of all tools whose execution must take place inside the step. None of the tools would be started as long as, at least, one of those versions could not be granted.

We considered another strategy. Partial orders will be known and controlled by STAR's project manager only. They have no counterpart in KRISYS. Design steps are delimited in the user transaction by means of savepoints and application tools are each encapsulated into a ST. By choosing such a strategy, we give up the possibility of executing non-dependent design steps of a same partial order in parallel. We plan to change to the first presented strategy as soon as KRISYS is modified to allow Transfer operations to be issued from inside short transactions.

Figure 4.2 illustrates how a design step is mapped onto an UT. At the beginning of a step, the project manager issues a savepoint. In case the step must be aborted, the project manager asks KRISYS' transaction manager to return UT's state to this savepoint. A new DBstep (W3) is created and messages can be sent to the UT controlling DBpj as to ask for Transfer operations. Similarly, the project manager issues copy operations to transfer object versions from DBpr (W2) to DBstep.

When all input objects of $tool_1$ are already stored in DBstep, a short transaction is started which encapsulates the execution of $tool_1$. As the application program accesses STAR objects, the latter are mapped onto KRISYS objects and access operations are issued from the ST. If $tool_1$ aborts, the project manager aborts ST. Otherwise ST can commit.

After all application tools which are specified in the design step have executed, the project manager starts copying the final object versions produced by the step from DBstep to DBpr.

Step as well as partial order suspension and resumption are implemented by means of UT suspension and resumption, respectively.

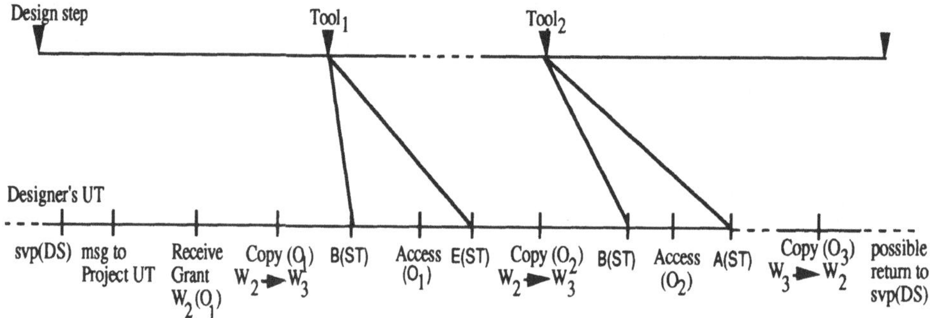

Figure 4.2: Controlling the Execution of a Design Step from Inside a User Transaction

5 Conclusion

This paper briefly presented the Project Management and Cooperation Model of the STAR design environment as well as the world and transaction models of the KRISYS knowledge base system. Relying on these models, a strategy of realizing STAR's project manager on the basis of KRISYS was explained in more detail. The implementation of this strategy is under way and we expect to have a running prototype by the end of 1992. The prototype will help us to validate both the cooperation and the long-duration transaction models. In parallel, a new architecture of KRISYS is being designed which allows concurrent short transactions and Transfer operations to be issued from inside them.

6 References

[Cast92] M. A. Castroz L., C. Iochpe: Design and Cooperation Management Through Design Steps and Object Characteristics. 18th Latin-American Conference on Informatics, Aug 1992, Las Palmas de Gran Canaria, España.

[Dess89] S. Dessloch, N. M. Mattos: KOALA, An Interface for Knowledge Based Management Systems. Research Report, Universitaet Kaiserslautern, 1989.

[Ioch89] C. Iochpe: Database Recovery in the Design Environment: Requirements Analysis and Performance Evaluation. Ph. D. Thesis, Universitaet Karlsruhe, Karlsruhe, 1989.

[Ioch91] C. Iochpe, M. A. C. Livi: Cooperation Support in a CAD Environment. 6th Brazilian Symposium on Database Systems, May 1990, Manaus. (In Portuguese).

[Kaef90] W. Kaefer: A Framework for Version-based Cooperation Control. Research Report, Universitaet Kaiserslautern, 1990.

[Matt 91] N. M. Mattos: An Approach to Knowledge Base Management. Lecture Notes in Artificial Intelligence, Berlin, v. 513, 1991.

[Reze92] F. F. Rezende: A Transaction Model to Support the Concept of Worlds in KRISYS. Master Dissertation, CPGCC-UFRGS, 1992. (In Portuguese).

[Thom91] J. Thomas: An Approach for the Representation of Worlds and Viewpoints in the KBMS KRISYS. Diplomarbeit, Universitaet Kaiserslautern, 1991. (In German).

[Wagn92] F. R. Wagner et al.: Design Version Management in the STAR Framework. 3rd IFIP Workshop on Electronic Design Automation Frameworks, Bad Lippspringe, Germany, March 1992.

Query Optimization in an OODBMS

Christian Rich, Marc H. Scholl
Computer Science Department, University of Ulm
e–mail: {rich, scholl}@informatik.uni–ulm.de

Abstract

It is clearly crucial for the success of object–oriented databases to find efficient implementations that improve on the performance of relational systems, rather than being powerful in terms of modeling and features, but just too slow to be used. This paper describes the mapping of COCOON to DASDBS, a nested relational database kernel system, as an example OODBMS mapping to a complex storage system. We describe 1) choices for physical designs that make use of the complex storage model and 2) the generation of efficient, set–oriented execution plans for object–oriented database queries, using rule–based query optimization techniques. We use hierarchical clustering and embedded (sets of) object references, and show how to explore them for efficient path traversals expressed in queries involving complex objects. Prototypes of both, a physical design tool and a query optimizer have been implemented. Preliminary results show feasibility, and execution time improvements of an order of magnitude.

1. Introduction

The design of Objectbase Systems, which map object oriented–, semantic– or knowledge representation models to an underlying database kernel system, in order to close the gap between application and database system, are currently considered as candidates for future database architectures. Query optimization in COCOON, an object oriented database project following this kernel architecture approach, will be sketched in this report.

OODBMSs have been designed based on the observation that today's databases supporting simply structured data are quite successful in commercial areas, but future applications need the support for more complex structures, with complex integrity constraints built into the model and with powerful, set–oriented query interfaces. The rationale of the COCOON project is to build an object–oriented model (COCOON), supporting flexibility through powerful structuring primitives, rich semantics, and encapsulation, as well as a powerful query and update language (COOL), on top of a database kernel (DASDBS), which efficiently supports common database operations, such as storage of and access to complex database records (see Figure 1.1). A similar approach is followed e.g. by Härder et al. [6].

One of the fundamental innovations of the relational approach to databases are the non–procedural query languages, which offers high level, set–oriented database access as well as efficiency through optimizations performed by the DBMS as key advantages. Provided that we accept the requirements of new applications to continue to work with such high–level languages in OODBMSs, we have to: (i) extend "relational–style" languages properly, so as to adopt them to the more powerful models, and (ii) extend "relational–style" query processors to efficiently execute these new query languages.

It is clearly crucial for the success of OODBMSs to find efficient implementations that improve on the performance of relational systems, rather than being powerful in terms of modeling and features, but

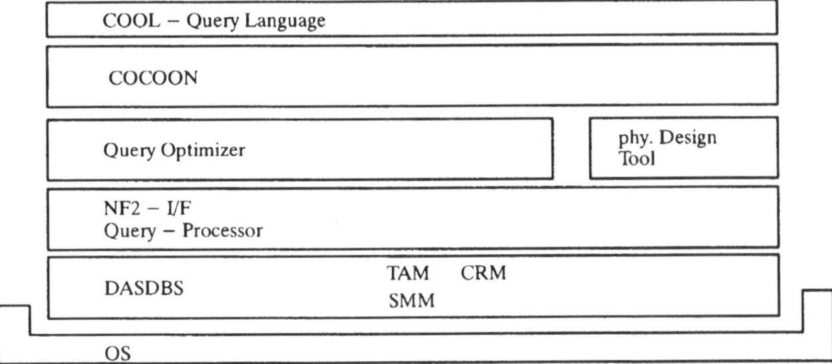

Figure 1.1: The COCOON – DASDBS Architecture

just too slow to be used. Up to now, no final conclusion can be drawn on how the architecture of an OODBMS should look. It is, however, a common anticipation that relational systems as the underlying storage engine would be to slow. Further, even though the large body of relational query optimization techniques can be used as a starting point for object–oriented query optimization, obviously, to fully exploit the object–oriented paradigm, special optimization techniques are needed.

The flexibility concerning the modeling and processing inherent in the object models and query languages poses a high demand on the implementation. On one hand, even more so than in traditional databases, the conceptual structure of the database is hardly ever also an efficient, internal one. Rather, data representing the conceptual objects may be structured completely different for performance reasons. Therefore, the mapping of objects of the model into the structures of the DBMS kernel system, has to be considered with great care. The most favorable internal representation is dependent on the type and frequency of expected queries, that is, the transaction load faced. On the other hand, in order to support efficient application execution, all issues related with query evaluation and optimization as well as general considerations about the mapping of functionality onto the kernel system have to receive special attention.

We used DASDBS, our prototype database kernel system, which supports flexible structures with operators that go beyond relational queries, as the target platform for the research described below. A query optimization methodology is specified, and a first query optimizer has been implemented accordingly. It was one of the main objectives of the COCOON project to reach some (at least preliminary) conclusions on the feasibility and performance trade–offs of this approach. DASDBS was chosen as the storage system, because of its support for complex storage structures. First of all, the support of nested relations allows for the storage of hierarchically clustered data. That is, we have hierarchical access structures with an arbitrary level of nesting, as well as the opportunity to define nested join indices. This can be very useful to store COCOON objects and the "relationships" between them. Second, the DASDBS interface offers powerful data retrieval and manipulation operations. The system has a set–oriented, algebraic interface with efficient operations on complex objects. All operations performed in the kernel are executed in a single scan through the data [22, 26]. Operations that are not single scan processible are performed outside the kernel, in the higher–level query processor. The query processor's ability of processing on complex nested structures, further improves processing, like for reassembling complex object structures [25].

The overall architecture of the COCOON implementation on top of the DASDBS kernel system is shown in Figure 1.1. The two aspects of this architecture, structure mapping and operations mapping, are realized in the physical design tool and the query optimizer, respectively. Physical design uses the COCOON schema, statistics about cardinalities and distribution, and a description of a transaction load to propose a good internal storage structure expressed in terms of nested DASDBS relations. At transaction processing time, the optimizer has to translate COOL operations down to operations on these physical NF^2 structures. The execution plans generated consist of physical NF^2–algebra operators, some of which, such as joins, are implemented in the high–level query processor, others are DASDBS kernel calls.

The paper is structured as follows: Section 2 gives a short description of COCOON and introduces a running example, before we describe physical design choices in Section 3. In Section 4 we present the translation of queries onto the physical level, and the optimization of query execution plans. Section 5 compares with related work, before we conclude in Section 6.

2. COCOON

Essentially, the COCOON model as described in [31, 32] is an object–function–model. Its constituents are objects, functions, types and classes. COCOON offers a variety of structuring capabilities to model complex objects. Class and type hierarchies (i.e. classification and generalization), the abstraction concepts of aggregation and association, and derived methods offer a flexible modeling framework. The query language, COOL, offers object–preserving as well as object–generating generic query operators plus generic update operators. The key objective in the design of COOL was its set–oriented, descriptive characteristics, similar to a relational algebra. COCOON is a core object model, basically we have objects (concrete and abstract) and one type constructor, namely set. Other features can be added later due to the orthogonality of the language.

Objects are instances of abstract data types (ADTs). They can be manipulated only by means of their interface, a set of functions. **Data** are instances of concrete types (such as numbers, strings) and constructed types (such as sets). The distinction from objects is similar to [2].

Functions are described by a name and signature (i.e., domain and range types). Functions can be single– or set–valued, they are the interface operations of types. A useful feature is the capability of defining inverses of functions. This integrity constraint is enforced by the system during updates.

Types are described by their name and the set of functions that are applicable to their instances. Types are arranged in a *subtype hierarchy*, where subtypes inherit functions from their supertypes. Objects can be instances of more than one type at the same time ("multiple instantiation")

Classes are typed collections of objects (sometimes called "type extends"). Classes are arranged in a *subclass hierarchy* that is exactly the set inclusion between the sets of objects they represent. Objects are "members of" classes, possibly more than one at a time ("multiple class membership"). Particularly, superclasses contain all members of their subclasses.

As an example, we will use an architectural design application throughout this paper. The COCOON graphical representation is given in Figure 2.1 In this application we are mainly dealing with rooms, furnishings and areas. All of them are design–objects. Rooms are described by their name, orientation, position, size, etc. Between certain rooms there is a neighborhood–relationship. Each room contains a set of furnishings, which are described by their name, price, width, length, height, etc. Each room be-

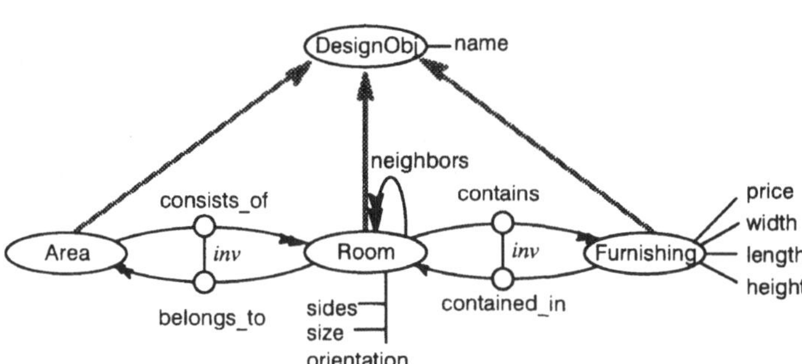

Figure 2.1: Our example DB–World

longs to some areas, and each area consist of some rooms. That is, the room 'Office1' could be part of the area 'working–area', and may contain furnishings like 'Wooden Desk' and 'Computer'. A COOL query asking for offices, having no 'computer' is given below:

Q := select [name = "Office"
and select [name = "Computer"] (contains) = {}] (Room);

3. Physical Database Design

In this section we discuss the mapping of COCOON schemas to nested relations (DASDBS) [30]. That is, given a COCOON database schema, what are the alternatives for the internal DB layouts, and further, given a transaction load, which internal DB layout results in the least overall cost of transaction execution. This optimization task is performed by the physical design tool.

Because COCOON (like almost all OODBMS) offers a variety of structuring capabilities to model complex objects, it is not at all trivial to find good, that is, efficient, storage structures that support the variety of operations on objects reasonably well. Objects may be hierarchically composed of subobjects, several objects may share common subobjects, objects may appear as (attribute) values of other objects, different objects can be related to each other by functions, methods, or relationships. Type (or class) hierarchies introduce another dimension of object interrelation: an object of one class also "appears" in all its superclasses; again, with multiple inheritance, this need not be a strict hierarchical inclusion. Computed values (attributes, methods) may be used to derive, rather than store, data that are associated with objects.

3.1 Alternatives for Physical DB Design

In order to explain the alternatives for mapping COCOON database schemas to nested relations at the physical level, we proceed by stepping through the basic concepts of the COCOON object model, and showing the implementation choices. Since the choices for each of the concepts combine orthogonally, this spans a large decision space that is investigated by the physical database design tool (next section).

Implementing Objects

According to the object–function paradigm of COCOON, an object itself is sufficiently implemented by a unique identifier (OID), that is generated by the system. All data related to an object in one way or the other will refer to this identifier (see below). We denote for each object type *A*, attributes of internal relations containing the OID of objects of type *A* by *AID*.

Implementing Functions

In COCOON, functions are the basic way of associating information (data values or other objects) to objects. In principle, we can think of each function being implemented as a binary relation, with one attribute for the argument OID and the other for the result value (data item or OID). In case of set-valued functions the second attribute will actually be a subrelation of unary subtuples, containing one result (OID or data value) each. So, in principle, each single-valued function as well as each multi-valued function would be implemented in a binary relation. For example, in our architectural design application, the functions *size* and *furnishings* of *Rooms* would result in two relations, *Room_size(RID, size)* and *Room_furnishings(RID, furnishings(FID))* respectively. Obviously, there are some choices. The decision space as far as function implementations are concerned includes the following alternatives in our current approach:

Bundled vs. Decoupled: Each function defined on a given domain object type might either be stored in a separate (binary) relation as shown above: the *decoupled* mode. Alternatively, we can *bundle* functions together with the relation implementing the type.
In the example above, the bundled implementation of *Room size* and *Room furnishings*, would yield the following type table : *Room(RID, size, furnishings(FID))*.

Logical vs. Physical Reference: A function returning a (set of) object(s), not (a) data value(s), can be implemented by storing just OIDs (*logical reference*) of result objects or by including a TID (*physical reference*) as well. Continuing on the above example (bundled), inclusion of physical references for the *neighbors* function, would result in: *Room(RID, size, furnishings(FID, @F))*. Notice the naming convention: (physical) reference attributes have @ as a prefix.

Oneway vs. Bothway References: A function can be implemented by a forward reference only (*oneway*), or it can be implemented with backpointers (*bothway*). For example, in case the *contained_in* function of *furnishings* would not be present in the conceptual schema, we could nevertheless decide to implement it, to have the *contains* function of *Rooms* supported with backpointers as well.

Reference vs. Materialized: Functions returning (possibly sets of) objects, not data values, can be implemented by the various forms of references discussed up to now. Alternatively, however, we can directly *materialize* the object-tuple(s) representing the result object(s) within the object-tuple representing the argument object. This is a way of achieving physical neighborhood (clustering). In our example, the decision to materialize the *furnishings* function of *Room* objects would generate a nested type table that contains the type table for *furnishings* as a subrelation: *Room(RID, size,... furnishings(FID,name, ...))*. Obviously, we need no backward references in this case. Furthermore, this alternative is free of redundancy only if the materialized function is *1:n*, that is, it's inverse is single-valued.

Computed vs. Materialized: Finally, an additional option is to materialize derived (computed) functions. Assuming that some function can be computed, we could nonetheless decide to internally materialize it, if retrieval dominates updates to the underlying base information significantly. The more retrieval dominates updates, and the more costly the computation is, the more likely is the case that materialization pays off. For example, the *size* function of *Rooms* is derived from the actual geometry of the Room. But computing the *size* incurs quite some effort and if object shapes rarely change, materializing the *size* function clearly is a good strategy (see also [10]).

Implementing Types, Classes, and Inheritance

The COCOON model separates between types and classes, this results in having two inheritance hierarchies: one between types (organizing structural, function inheritance), and one between classes (organizing set inclusion). Since classes are always bound to a particular (member–) type, physical design for types is the larger grain approach, whereas design for individual classes would be the finer grain approach (remember, there may be more than one class per type). Currently, we do the physical design on a type basis, that is, all objects of a given type are physically represented in the same way (even if they belong to several classes). Classes are implemented as views over their underlying type table. This results in the following choices w.r.t. types, classes, and inheritance:

Types: Each object type is mapped to a type table with at least one attribute, containing the OID. Additional attributes are present in case of any bundled functions and/or materializations of object functions. The type table T may itself be a subrelation of some other table, if type T was materialized w.r.t. a function returning T–objects.

Classes: Each class C is implemented as a view over its underlying type table. If the class is defined by a predicate ("all"–classes and views in COCOON), this predicate is used as the selection condition. If the class is defined to include manually added member objects ("some"–classes in COCOON), the underlying type table is extended by a Boolean attribute C that is set to true, if the object is a member of this class C.

Inheritance: Subtyping is implemented by having one type table per subtype. Three possibilities are considered:

- an object–tuple is included in each supertype's table. In case there are any bundled or materialized functions, these are not repeated in the subtypes' tables. In this case, object–tuples in subtype tables might optionally include physical references to supertype tuples.
- an object–tuple is included only in one type's table, that of the most specific subtype. In case of any bundled or materialized functions in supertypes, these are also included in the subtype's table.
- an object–tuple is included in each supertype's table. In case of any bundled or materialized functions in supertypes, these are also included in the subtype's table.

3.2 The Default Physical Design

In order to have a starting point for the implementation of COCOON on top of DASDBS, we have identified a default physical design that includes the following choice of implementation strategies:

Functions: All functions are bundled with their type table. Object–valued functions are implemented as references, with physical references and backpointers. Multi–valued functions become subrelations.

Inheritance: Objects are present in all supertype tables, inherited functions are repeated in subtype tables. No backpointers to supertype tuples are included.

The default physical design for our architectural example world, given in the beginning (Figure 2.1), is shown in Figure 3.1.Further, we show an alternative physical design, where the object valued function *furnishing* is materialized, in Figure 3.2. Both designs will be used later on, when describing the query optimization task.

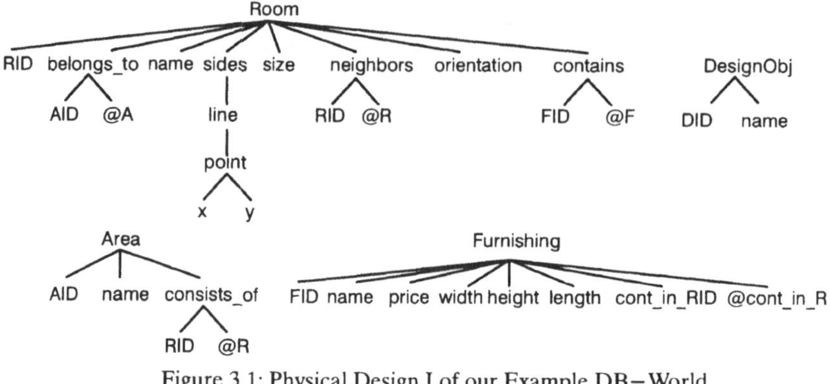

Figure 3.1: Physical Design I of our Example DB–World

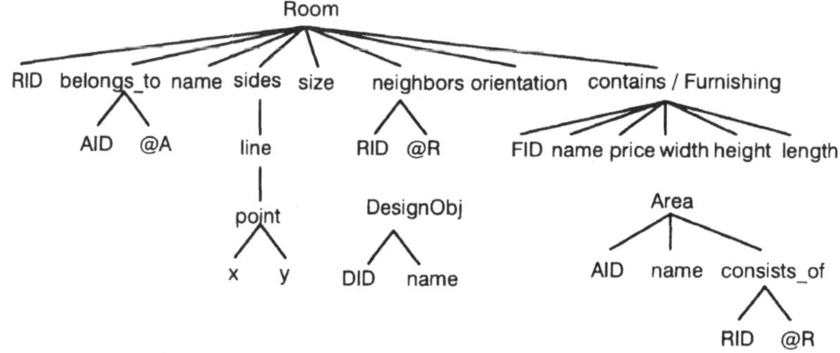

Figure 3.2: Physical Design II of our Example DB–World

3.3 Physical Design Tool

In order to exploit the options given above, we have a first prototype implementation of a "physical DB design expert system" (considering some of the above alternatives) running. The system takes as input a COOL schema, a description of the anticipated (or observed) transaction load, and information on the cardinality and size of the DB objects. The output is a (set of) proposed physical designs for use with DASDBS, together with cost estimates for the transaction mix obtained from a cost model. The system is implemented in Prolog, and will be extended to consider a wider choice of storage schemas, especially those including access paths and more general forms of redundancy in the future.

4. Query Optimization

In this section, we discuss the transformation and optimization of queries that are given to the system in terms of the COCOON database schema. It is the task of the query optimizer to map these COOL queries down to the physical level by: (i) transforming them to the nested relational model and algebra as available at the DASDBS kernel interface, and (ii) select a good (if not the best) execution strategy.

Because COCOON's query language, COOL, is pretty similar to a nested relational algebra, a straightforward transformation from COOL expressions down to a nested relational algebra expression against any fixed implementation on the internal level (e.g., the default physical design) is rather easily done. Complications arise from the fact that the mapping of data structures is very flexible, and that, depending on the chosen design, operations have to be optimized substantially.

We have investigated two competitive approaches to query transformation and optimization. The first one is a purely algebraic one, comparable to what we did with the relational to nested relational mapping [27]: COCOON classes would be defined as 'views' over the stored nested relations, COOL queries would be transformed to the nested relational level by 'view substitution', and finally, algebraic transformations within the nested relational algebra could be applied, so as to eliminate redundant subexpressions. Quite a few redundant joins would have to be removed in case of materialized functions (hierarchical clustering). This has exactly been the problem addressed in [29].

Example 4.1: Given the COOL query

Q_1 := extract [name, orientation, size,
extract[name] (neighbors),
extract[name, price, width, length] (contains)
] (Room);

and assuming the default physical design (Figure 3.1) in the transformation of this query to the NF^2 level, this results in the query

Q_c := PROJECT[name, orientation, size,
PROJECT [name] (neighbors),
PROJECT [name, price, width, length] (contains)]
(JOIN [Room.contains.FID=Furnishing.FID]
(JOIN [Room.nbrs.RID=Room.RID] (Room, Room), Furnishing))

However, if the internal physical design is the one given in Figure 3.2, that is the function *contains* is materialized, one join operation can be removed by optimization, resulting in the query Q_i. Notice, that further optimization could be performed, which is not shown here.

Q_i := PROJECT[name, orientation, size,
PROJECT[name] (neighbors),
PROJECT [name, price, width, length] (contains)]
(JOIN [Room.nbrs.RID=Room.RID] (Room, Room))

The second approach directly uses the information about the physical database schema in the transformation of a given COOL query into a nested relational algebra representation. No redundant joins are created, that would have to be removed in the following optimization phase. Thus we have a more direct transformation. In Example 4.1 above, this would result in transforming query Q_1 directly onto the physical schema, that is, into query Q_i.

We have chosen this second approach in our current implementation. The optimization phase following the transformation chooses the specific execution strategy, e.g. the ordering of operators, as well as the best implementation strategies. For example, whether a nested loop or a sort merge join is selected. This leads to the architecture of our query optimization process, given in Figure 4.1.

In the first step, the transformation task, we use a "Class Connection Graph". We will elaborate more on that in the following. The second step, that is, the optimization phase, we use a rule–based algebraic query optimizer, generated with the EXODUS Optimizer Generator [8].

4.1 Transforming COOL–Queries onto the Physical Schema

The input to the optimizer is a COOL–query expressed on the conceptual schema, while the transformations apply to execution plans, i.e., on the physical schema. The first step is to do the translation to an algebraic query representation on the physical schema. To do this, we use a Class Connection Graph similar to the one proposed in [17].

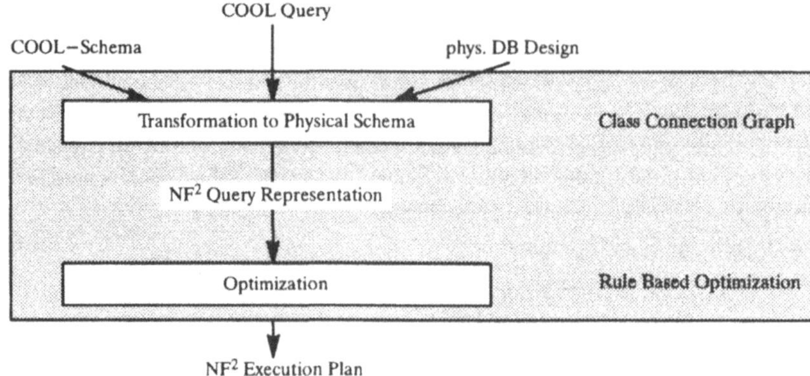

Figure 4.1: Optimizer Architecture

After the input query is parsed, the optimizer scans at the same time the query graph (a graph representing the given query) and a physical schema graph. From these, the class connection graph is constructed. A possible physical schema graph is given in Figure 4.2. This schema graph corresponds to our physical design, shown earlier in Figure 3.2. The nodes are files, which may implement
– a single class extension (e.g. A implements Areas and D implements DesignObjects)
– several class extensions (e.g. R implementing Room and Furnishings)
– a part of a class extension, when a class extension is vertically fragmented.

The arcs denote the kind of function implementation. Solid arcs denote materialized functions (e.g. contains). Dashed arcs are functions stored as references to subobjects inside the instance of the owner object.

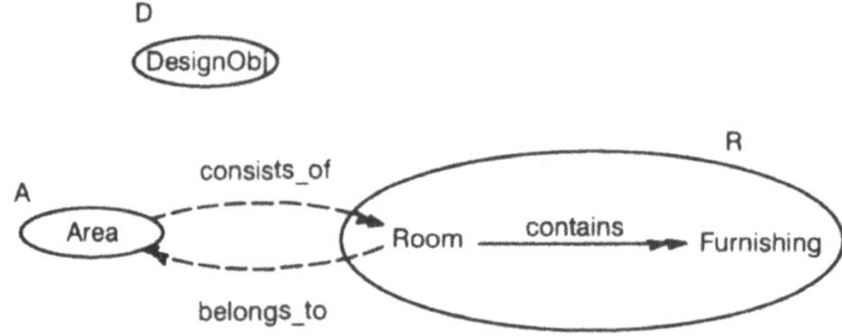

Figure 4.2 : A sample Physical Schema Graph

Now let us look at the transformation of a sample query. Suppose we have a physical schema graph as shown in Figure 4.2 and the following query:

Query Q2 :
extract [name, orientation, size,
extract [name] (neighbors),
extract [name, price] (select [name = "computer"] (contains))
]
(RoomC)

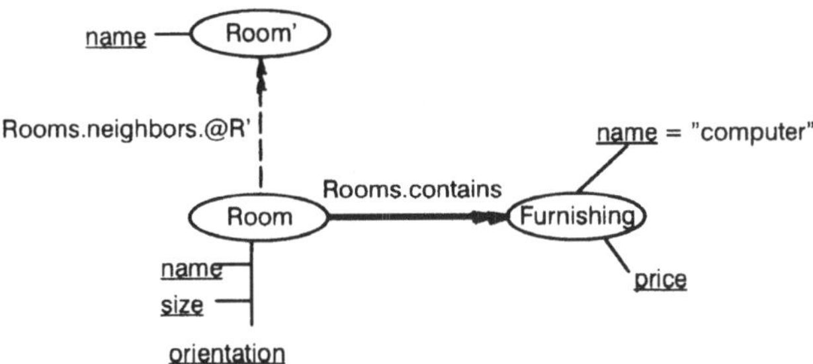

Figure 4.3: A sample Class Connection Graph

Figure 4.3 shows the Class Connection Graph constructed for that query. The nodes of the class connection graph represent classes which are affected by the given query. The edges are the functions involved in the query, connecting classes via implicit or explicit joins. There are three different kinds of edges, depending on the physical representation of these functions, i.e. did we store logical OIDs, physical references, or is this object function materialized. In our example, the *contains* function of *Room* objects is materialized, and the *neighbors* function is supported by pointers. The use of the *neighbors* function results in a second occurrence of class Room, here denoted as *Room'*. In case a class extension would be stored vertically fragmented, this would result in having a class for each fragment, all of them connected with corresponding arcs. Further, we see the selection predicates (name = "computer") and the printable attributes, which shall be displayed (name, size, and orientation of Rooms).

A class connection graph represents a given query, without any hints on execution orders, that is, all possible execution plans can be generated from the class connection graph. For example, we have the choice to perform forward or backward traversals, or to start in the middle of a path, as well as to interleave other operations with the traversal (cf. [21]).

4.2 Optimization of Query Execution Plans

In this section we describe the model of execution offered by the base system (DASDBS kernel and query processor) and how query execution plans are represented. Then, we describe the opportunities for optimization, give some example transformation rules defining the search space, and show how to explore it. Further, we will give some example queries and demonstrate how they are optimized by our system.

4.2.1 Model of Execution

The DASDBS kernel interface is set–oriented, with efficient operations on complex objects. Due to the support of nested relations, complex objects may be hierarchically clustered. However, there will be the need to reassemble objects, which are not clustered in one nested relation, as well as to perform operations on these reassembled objects. These tasks are performed in the query processor (see Figure 1.1). The resulting model of execution is as follows: the run–time system consists of a limited set of procedures, the physical algebra operators. Each procedure transforms a data stream according to an argument which was derived from the original query. For example a selection operator is removing tuples of a data stream, not satisfying the corresponding predicate given in the query. Complex queries result in nesting these procedures, i.e. the output of one procedure will be the input of another one.

The transfer of data between these procedures is done by streams [7], to avoid unnecessary writing of intermediate results. All operators are performed within a single operating system process, to prevent operating system scheduling and inter–process communication, as it is much more expensive than procedure calls.

Our approach to describe the nesting of base system procedures, is to use processing trees. A processing tree represents the execution plan for a given query. Two possible processing trees are given in Figure 4.4. The leaf nodes, which represent complex operations on one DASDBS relation, are performed (in a set–oriented way) by the DASDBS kernel. Internal nodes are performed in the COOL–specific query processor (in a streaming mode). Again, it is obvious, that the initial tree which is derived from the original query, will probably not be the optimal to execute. It is the optimizers task to find the cheapest equivalent execution plan, which then will be executed.

Figure 4.4: Two equivalent Processing Trees

4.2.2 Which Potential for Optimization do we have?

Given a query, obviously there are many equivalent processing trees, that is, alternatives to execute the query. These alternatives result from a number of open choices, some of which are listed in the following.

Join Ordering. A sequence of join operations is freely reorderable, this results in many alternatives. In order to reduce the number of orderings to consider, one may exclude the ones resulting in Cartesian products, or restrict the join orderings to the ones resulting in linear join trees, instead of considering all possible, bushy ones (this is the well–known problem studied, for example, in [33, 20, 39, 38]. The reason for join operations to occur is the following: First, reassembling objects from several relations requires a join operation for each partition. Object partitioning is introduced for example, in the mapping of inheritance hierarchies. Second, each application of an object valued function (which is not materialized) results in a corresponding join. Reordering these joins corresponds to changes to the order of function application, that is whether we do forward or backward traversals, or starting in the middle of a path query [3]. Notice, that these implicit joins may be supported by link fields (see Section 3.1), and therefore enable efficient pointer based join algorithms [36].

Pushing Selections. Selections may be performed at various times. For example, one could perform a given selection before or after applying an object valued function (move selection into join, or vice versa). Additionally, selections with conjunctively combined selection predicates may be split into two selections (or vice versa), and the order of selections, as well as the order of the terms in selection predicates, may be changed.

Pushing Projections. Projections, in the same way as selections, may be performed at various times. In addition, the order of applying projections and selections may be changed.

Method Selection. For each logical operation there may be several methods, that is physical implementations. For example, a join operation may be performed by nested loops join, hash join, or sort merge join. In addition, for implicit joins which are supported by link fields, pointer based join versions may be selected. Further, selections may be performed by using indexes, or by performing a relation scan, followed by predicate testing.

Index Selection. If a selection is supported by multiple indices, one has the opportunity to use all, some, or just one of the available indices.

Almost all of the choices given above, can be combined orthogonally, such that the number of equivalent processing trees grows extremely fast with increasing query complexity.

4.2.3 How to find the Optimal Execution Plan

A query optimizer should find a good (if not the best) execution plan as fast as possible, i.e. without considering as many as possible alternative execution plans, which will (at least with high probability) not lead to the optimal one. As indicated in the context of extensible DBMS, a rule–based approach to query optimization benefits from two circumstances: first, this allows rather flexible extensions to the underlying equivalences or transformation rules, and second, a combination of equivalence–based transformations (i.e., algebraic optimization) with cost–based transformation rules can easily be obtained in this framework. Due to the fact that a rule based query optimizer is one of the most intricate subsystems of a database system, it is desirable not to start an implementation from scratch. Therefore, we decided to use the EXODUS optimizer generator [8] for the implementation of the COOL optimizer. Without going into detail, a cost model to estimate the quality of execution plans, as well as rules to describe possible transformations have to be defined by the implementor of the optimizer, the search strategy is provided by EXODUS.

The cost functions for methods are fairly standard, similar to the ones of System R [33]. They had to be adapted to the nested relational model. These functions are based on information about the stored data, like tuple and page cardinalities for each relation, and the number of distinct values for each attribute. Further improvements, like including information about data distribution, as well as taking indexes into account, are planned for the future.

To specify rules describing possible transformations of processing trees, that is, of nested relational algebra expressions, we utilized transformation rules known from the (flat) relational model and the (complex) rules defined for the nested model in [29, 28] as a starting point. Roughly, 1NF rules are applicable in the NF^2 model on relations and on the subrelations, having additional constraints and more complex argument transfer functions. NF^2 rules handle complex operations e.g. nest, unnest and complex select–project–join queries. To handle object–oriented paradigms, such as set valued object functions, inverse functions, or link supported functions, special rules are necessary. For example object reassembly, involving set–valued object functions results in (multiple) joins. Here, the classical join enumeration problem does no longer apply, we have to solve a hierarchical join scheduling problem. The result of a join operation is a hierarchical view on the same set of objects, having an additional nesting. Object reassembly results in one additional nesting for each set valued function. Therefore, changing the join order according to the commutativity and associativity rule, as known from the relational model, may not be correct anymore. A survey of transformation and implementation rules used, can be found in [24].

The EXODUS optimizer generator was designed with the intention to be extendible, that is, it should support query optimization without making restrictive assumptions about the data model, the query language, or the run time system. So using the EXODUS optimizer is in principle quite easy. Looking deeper into it, it turned out that due to the enhanced complexity of the rule set, in addition with more sophisticated constraints and "argument transfer functions", a considerable amount of additional work has to be done by the optimizer implementor.

Example rule: The rule how two project operations can be combined into one project operation, can be formulated in the relational model in the following way:

$\pi\ [A]\ (\pi\ [B]\ (E)) \equiv \pi\ [A]\ (E)$ (Obviously, $A \subseteq B$ has to be fulfilled, to have a correct expression on the left side.)

This rule leads to several rules in the NF^2 model, each having an increased complexity. One resulting rule is given below:

$$\pi[...\sigma_{F_2}(A)...]\ \pi[...\sigma_{F_1}(A)...]\ (E) \equiv \pi[...\sigma_{F_2}\sigma_{F_1}(A)...]\ (E)$$

Using the notation enforced by EXODUS, this rule is not expressible, rather it has to be formulated in the following way (actually, in the same way as the relational rule):

$$\pi\ 1\ (\ \pi\ 2\ (E)) \equiv \pi\ 1\ (E)$$

But this rule is rather incomplete, the missing parts have to be supplied in so-called support functions, that is, the condition code (to check whether the rule is applicable) and argument transfer functions.

4.3 Example Transformation and Optimization

In the following we will give one more example COOL query, and demonstrate how the query is mapped to an execution plan for the query processor, and where performance gains are achieved.

A query asking for offices without a computer, is formulated in COOL in the following way.

Q_3 := select [name = "Office"
and select [name = "Computer"] (contains) = {}]
(Room) ;

Assuming the physical design I (Figure 3.1), the translation to the physical schema results in a processing tree as given below.

```
SELECT [ Room.name = "Office"
   |     AND SELECT [Furnish.name = "Computer"] ( contains ) = { } ]
   |
JOIN [..., Furnish.FID = Room.contains.FID ]
   /\
  /  \
Furnish   Room
```

Note that due to the use of the *contains* function (which is not materialized), a join operation is inserted. Because there is no partitioning or subtyping, no additional joins are necessary in this example. The '...' after the keyword *JOIN* indicate, that (up to now) no specific join method has been selected. After optimization, the resulting execution plan looks like:

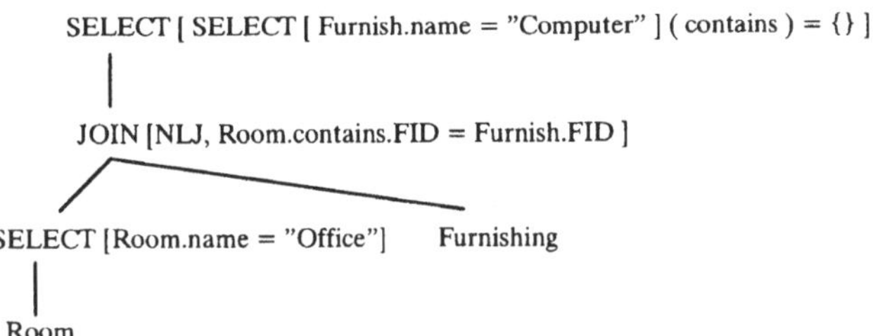

Obviously it improves performance, to split the selection and move one part into the join, that is, to apply the *name* function first to *Room* objects, before following the set of links (*Room.contains*) to *Furnishings*, to check whether there is no *Computer* in that *Room.* Assuming an index on *name* of *rooms,* and physical links, this will be quite efficient, much more efficient, than in a flat relational approach. There the *Room–Furnishing* relationship is modeled by taking the primary key of *Rooms* into *Furnishings* (as a foreign key). However, if the physical design is the one given in Figure 3.2, query Q_3 results in

```
SELECT [ Room.name = "Office"
   |        AND SELECT [Furnish.name = "Computer"] ( contains ) = {} ]
 Room
```

This execution plan does not even need any join operation, and can be executed within one (single scan) kernel operation.

4.4 Experience

A first prototype optimizer has been implemented [15, 9], and integrated [41, 19] into the COCOON–DASDBS system. COOL queries are passed from the COOL interface to the optimizer, and after translation onto the physical schema and optimization, execution plans can be passed to the query processor to execute the query on the DASDBS kernel. The query processors functionality includes Nested Loop–, Nested Block–, and Sort Merge Joins, as well as pointer–based variants of these join algorithms, which had been implemented similar to [36]. However notice, all join algorithms perform on nested storage structures, and are therefore variants of the algorithms as known from the relational model. The functionality of the query optimizer includes removal of redundant operations, the combination of operations, and select–project–join ordering, on nested relations. Since our goal was to evaluate the advantages and cost of using a complex record (DASDBS) instead of flat record (RDBMS) storage manager, the main emphasis has been on the effects of hierarchical clustering and embedded references; indexes played only a supporting role; future improvements should include indexes as well.

The implementation of COOL on top of DASDBS has been completed (to the described level) only recently. After evaluating single components, first experiments have been carried out using the entire system. In the following, we will summarize some of the most interesting preliminary results. All experiments were run on a Sun 3/80, without other users.

In order to evaluate the advantages of embedded (sets of) references and hierarchical clustering, we ran the following experiment: We consider a COOL query that accesses two classes, *Rooms* and *Furnishings*, and compare object reassembly times, if 1) no physical pointers, 2) physical pointers, and 3) materialization can be exploited. The cardinality of class *Room* is fixed to 100 tuples, so as to model a selection that has already been evaluated. The number of furnishings per Room, that is, the number of subtuples in the subrelation *Room.contains* is drawn from a uniform distribution over the range of a) 1–5, b) 5–10, c) 10–50 and d) 50–100. This results in a number of 300 to 7500 subtuples in total. We evaluated Nested Loop–, Nested Block–, and Sort Merge Joins, as well as their pointer–based variants.

Figure 4.5 compares the best join strategy for either of the three alternatives of physical support (plain value–based, with pointers, materialization). As expected, Sort Merge join performs much better than Nested Loops join, for medium to large relation sizes, both, with and without pointers. We see that storing (sets of) physical object references within the referencing objects, substantially speeds up object reassembly (a factor of 2–3 was observed). This is because the referenced tuples of the second relation can be fetched directly, without scans, index lookups, or sorting. Finally, materializing object functions, as expected, performs best. The cost function is a linear function of the relation cardinality, compared to e.g. a logarithmic function for Sort Merge join. The improvement increases with the relation cardinality, and ranged in our experiment from a factor 5 to 7 over pointers and 10 to 20 over value–based joins (see also [40]).

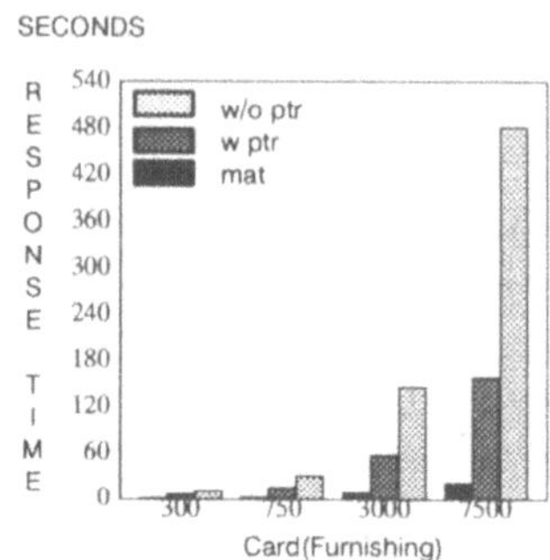

Figure 4.5: Comparrison of Logical References, Physical References and Materialization

We also investigated how much effort had to be spent during the optimization phase. First, we consider the number of nodes created in the search tree for a sample query, relative to the number of joins, as the number of nodes mainly determines the search time. In Figure 4.6, we see that the number of nodes does not increase exponentially, the search time was less than a tenth of a second for each query. Second, we see in Figure 4.7 the estimated execution cost before and after the transformations had been applied, as delivered by EXODUS.

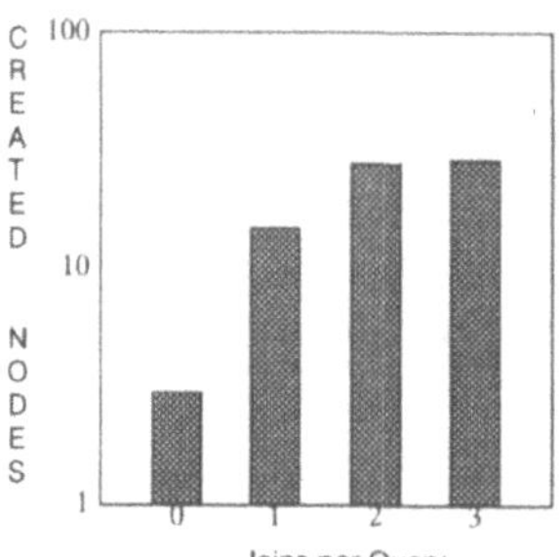

Figure 4.6: MASH Size

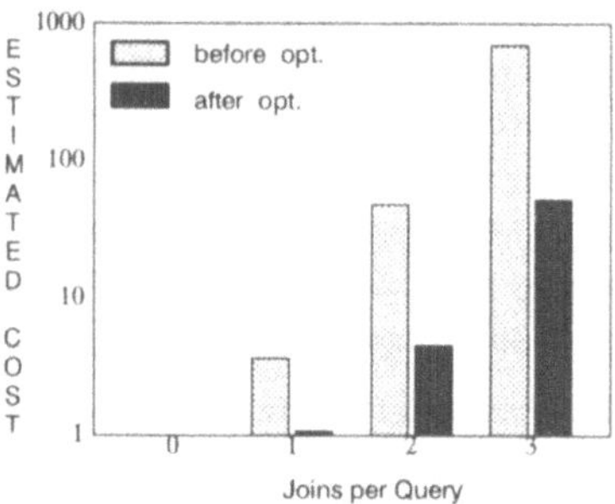

Figure 4.7: Plan Cost before and after Transformations

Our optimization approach, using rule based optimization techniques, showed to handle the optimization task, generating efficient execution plans in a reasonable time. Due to the exploitation of hierarchical clustering and embedded (sets of) object references this result in substantial execution time improvements.

The use of DASDBS storage structures (nested relations) and corresponding query processing strategies required a substantial amount of coding (for "argument transfer functions") in addition to the generated optimizer. This is because the EXODUS rule language was oriented towards a flat algebra.

We plan to include more sophisticated query evaluation plans into the optimizers repertoire, for example hierarchicalized join plans [25]. This will, however, require even more hand coding. So, EXODUS might no longer be the tool best suited for this purpose.

The next step is to compare the relative performance of the DASDBS implementation with an implementation based on a commercial platform: Oracle, as a relational system that can emulate two–level nesting (via Oracle "Clusters"). The details of these experiments are beyond the scope of this paper. In a nutshell, the results we obtained so far are: as expected, with the same query processing strategy Oracle performs up to a few times faster than DASDBS. However, one–to–many joins supported by hierarchical clustering in DASDBS outperforms Oracle clusters. Further, many–to–many relationships supported by hierarchical clustering of sets of object references in DASDBS (resulting in just one join operation for reassembling object structures) outperforms Oracle (where two joins are needed, one of them can be supported by a cluster) as well.

5. Related Work

Much work in query optimization for OODBMS, has concentrated on optimizing path traversals. Index structures tailored for accessing objects along a reference chain, leading from one object to another via single valued or set valued attributes are considered in e.g. [18, 11, 12, 4, 1, 13, 35]. These proposed strategies are important pieces to enhance performance for path expressions, using supporting index structures. However, our approach does not focus on index structures for path traversals. Rather, we specified a query optimization methodology for exploring object references stored inside the owner object, as well as hierarchical clustering, corresponding to the direct storage model. In addition, our approach tries to exploit set–oriented processing strategies, whereas others, e.g. Kemper's term representation for queries [12] is typically oriented towards nested iteration schemes.

Query rewrite approaches, like [34, 37, 5, 23] are more general then focusing on path traversals, but study query optimization just on the logical level. Choices for physical object representation as well as method implementations are not considered. This precludes the specification of cost based optimization strategies. We consider a variety of physical designs and the resulting costs for complex object processing [40], and are therefore able to estimate the effect of each transformation, based on a cost model. This is similar to [16], which focussed on recursive queries.

In the COCOON project, we study a new query optimization approach, that incorporates features not found in earlier approaches. No other approach we are aware of, has analogs to our unified treatment of handling (set valued) object relationships, which may be supported by logical references, physical references or materialization. As queries involving path expressions are very common in object oriented databases, it is important to recognize that certain path traversals can be expressed as joins. These have several possible execution orders, and several possible implementation strategies, depending on the physical database layout. The choice of an efficient strategy is performed by an optimizer constructed using the EXODUS optimizer generator [15]. Notice that dealing with path traversals as joins is related to the transformation of nested SQL queries [14].

6. Conclusions

We described the mapping of COCOON to DASDBS, a nested relational database kernel system, as an example OODBMS mapping to a complex storage system. We described 1) choices for physical designs that make use of the complex storage model and 2) the generation of efficient, set-oriented execution plans for object-oriented database queries, using rule-based query optimization techniques.

We use hierarchical clustering and embedded (sets of) object references, as features supported by DASDBS. Therefore, we are able to avoid breaking the complex structures of the objects into small pieces in order to store them in (flat) relations, as this would result in large join queries, for queries against the object-oriented schema. Further, storing (sets of) physical object references, allows efficient pointer-based join algorithms. This results in being superior in performance, due to more flexible physical database layouts and more efficient query processing algorithms. A query optimization approach is described, which handles the required optimization task.

A first physical design tool and a first query optimizer have been implemented. Preliminary results show feasibility, and execution time improvements of an order of magnitude. In the future, we will – among others– compare our approach to a mapping onto a commercial flat record (RDBMS) storage manager.

References

1. O. Deux et al., "The O2 System", *CACM,* vol. 34, no. 10, p. 34, October 1991.
2. C. Beeri, "Formal Models for Object Oriented Databases", *Proc. DOOD,* Kyoto, 1989.
3. E. Bertino, "Optimization of Queries using Nested Indices", in *Proc. EDBT,* LNCS, vol. 416, pp. 44–59, Springer 1990.
4. E. Bertino and W. Kim, "Indexing Techniques for Queries on Nested Objects", *IEEE Trans. on Knowledge and Data Eng.*, vol. 1, no. 2, p. 196, June 1989.
5. S. Cluet and C. Delobel, "A General Framework for the Optimization of Object-Oriented Queries", *Proc. SIGMOD*, p. 383, San Diego, California., June 1992.
6. S. Dessloch, T. Härder, F.-J. Leick, N.M. Mattos, C. Laasch, C. Rich, M.H. Scholl, and H.-J. Schek, "COCOON and KRISYS: A Comparison", in *Objektbanken für Experten*, ed. R. Bayer, T. Härder, and P.C. Lockemann, Informatik Aktuell, Springer Verlag, 1992.
7. G. Graefe, "Volcano, An Extensible and Parallel Dataflow Query Processing System", July 1990, *to appear in IEEE Trans. Knowledge and Data Engineering.*
8. G. Graefe and D.J. DeWitt, "The EXODUS Optimizer Generator", *Proc. ACM SIGMOD*, pp. 160–171, San Francisco, CA., May 1987.
9. J. Hofmann, "Evaluierung eines COOL-Anfrageoptimierers", *Semesterarbeit*, ETH Zurich, Departement Informatik, Zurich, 1992.
10. A. Kemper, C. Kilger, and G. Moerkotte, "Function Materialization in Object Bases", *Proc. ACM SIGMOD*, p. 258, Denver, CO, May 1991.
11. A. Kemper and G. Moerkotte, "Advanced Query Processing in Object Bases Using Access Support Relations", *Proc. VLDB*, p. 290, Brisbane, Australia, 1990.
12. A. Kemper and G. Moerkotte, "Access Support in Object Bases", *Proc. ACM SIGMOD*, p. 364, Atlantic City, NJ, May 1990.

13. U. Kessler and P. Dadam, "Auswertung komplexer Anfragen an hierarchisch strukturierte Objekte mittels Pfadindexen", *Proc. BTW*, Kaiserslautern, Germany, March 1991.
14. W. Kim, "On Optimizing an SQL-like Nested Query", *ACM TODS*, vol. 7, no. 3, September 1982.
15. T. Laes, "Generierung und Evaluierung eines Anfrageoptimierers", *Diplomarbeit*, ETH Zurich, Departement Informatik, Zurich, 1991.
16. R. Lanzelotte, P. Valduriez, and M. Zait, "Optimization of Object-Oriented Recursive Queries Using Cost-Controlled Strategies", *Proc. ACM SIGMOD*, San Diego, California., June 1992.
17. R. Lanzelotte, P. Valduriez, M. Ziane, and J.J. Cheiney, "Optimization of Nonrecursive Queries in OODBs", *Proc. DOOD-2*, Munich, Germany, December 1991.
18. D. Maier and J. Stein, "Indexing in an Object-Oriented DBMS", *Proc. Int'l Workshop on Object-Oriented Database Systems*, p. 171, Pacific Grove, CA, September 1986.
19. O. Mayer, "Abbildung und Integration von COOL-DDL auf NF2", *Semesterarbeit*, ETH Zurich, Departement Informatik, Zurich, 1992.
20. K. Ono and G.M. Lohman, "Extensible Enumeration of Feasible Joins for Relational Query Optimization", *IBM Research Report*, RJ 6625 (63936), San Jose, CA, December 1988.
21. G. Pathak and J.A. Blakeley, "Query Optimization in Object-Oriented Databases", *Proc. Workshop on Database Query Optimization*, OGC, CS Technical Report 89-005, Beaverton, OR., May 1989.
22. H.B. Paul, H.J. Schek, M.H. Scholl, G. Weikum, and U. Deppisch, "Architecture and Implementation of the Darmstadt Database Kernel System", *Proc. ACM SIGMOD*, p. 196, San Francisco, CA, May 1987.
23. H. Pirahesh, W. Hasan, and J. Hellerstein, "Extensible/Rule Based Query Rewrite Optimization in Starburst", *Proc. ACM SIGMOD*, p. 39, San Diego, California., June 1992.
24. C. Rich, "Query Rewrite and Plan Optimization in COCOON, using Hierarchical Algebra Transformations", *University of Ulm, Dept. of Computer Science, Technical Report*, 1992 (in Preparation).
25. A. Rosenthal, C. Rich, and M.H. Scholl, "Reducing Duplicate Work in Relational Join(s): A Unified Approach", *Submitted for publication, also Technical Report NR:172, ETH Zurich, Dept. of Computer Science*, 1992.
26. H.J. Schek, H.B. Paul, M.H. Scholl, and G. Weikum, "The DASDBS Project: Objectives, Experiences, and Future Prospects", *IEEE Trans. on Knowledge and Data Eng.*, vol. 2, no. 1, March 1990.
27. M.H. Scholl, H.B. Paul, and H.J. Schek, "Supporting Flat Relations by a Nested Relational Kernel", *Proc. VLDB*, p. 137, Brighton, England, August 1987.
28. M.H. Scholl, "The Nested Relational Model --- Efficient Support for a Relational Database Interface", *Ph.D. Thesis, Dept. of Computer Science, TU Darmstadt*, 1988 . (in German)
29. M.H. Scholl, "Theoretical Foundation of Algebraic Optimization Utilizing Unnormalized Relations", in *Proc. ICDT*, LNCS, vol. 243, pp. 380-396, Springer, Rome, Italy, September 1986.
30. M.H. Scholl, "Physical Database Design for an Object Oriented Database System", in *Query Processing for Advanced Database Applications*, ed. J.C. Freytag, G. Vossen, and D. Maier, Morgan-Kaufman, San Mateo, CA, 1993, To appear.
31. M.H. Scholl and H.-J. Schek, "A Relational Object Model", in *Proc. ICDT*, LNCS, vol. 470, pp. 89-105, Springer, Paris, December 1990.
32. M.H. Scholl and H.-J. Schek, "A Synthesis of Complex Objects and Object-Orientation", *Proc. IFIP TC 2 Working Conference on Database Semantics: Object Oriented Databases -Analysis, Design and Construction*, Windermere, U.K., July 1990.

33. P.G. Selinger, M.M. Astrahan, D.D. Chamberlin, R.A. Lorie, and T.G. Price, "Access Path Selection in a Relational Database Management System", *Proc. ACM SIGMOD*, pp. 23–34, Boston, MA., May–June 1979.
34. G.M. Shaw and S.B. Zdonik, "A Query Algebra for Object–Oriented Databases", *Proc. IEEE Data Eng.*, p. 154, Los Angelos, CA, February 1990.
35. E. Shekita and M. Carey, "Performance Enhancement Through Replication in an Object–Oriented DBMS", *Proc. ACM SIGMOD*, p. 325, Portland, OR, May–June 1989.
36. E.J. Shekita and M.J. Carey, "A Performance Evaluation of Pointer–Based Joins", *Proc. ACM SIGMOD*, p. 300, Atlantic City, NJ., May 1990.
37. D.D. Straube, "Queries and Query Processing in Object–Oriented Database Systems", *University of Alberta, CSD Technical Report 90–33*, Edmonton, Canada, December 1990.
38. A. Swami, "Optimization of Large Join Queries: Combining Heuristics and Combinatorial Techniques", *Proc. ACM SIGMOD*, p. 367, Portland, OR, May–June 1989.
39. A. Swami and A. Gupta, "Optimizing Large Join Queries", *Proc. ACM SIGMOD*, pp. 8–17, Chicago, IL., June 1988.
40. W.B. Teeuw, C. Rich, M.H. Scholl, and H.M. Blanken, "An Evaluation of Physical Disk I/Os for Complex Object Processing", *Proc. IEEE Conf. on Data Eng.*, Vienna, Austria, April 1993, To appear. A more detailed version is available as Technical Report 183, ETH Zurich, Dept. of Computer Science, 1992.
41. D. Wilhelm, "Query–Schnittstelle für DASDBS", *Diplomarbeit*, ETH Zurich, Departement Informatik, Zurich, 1991.

Integration heterogener relationaler Datenbankschemata mittels eines objektorientierten Datenmodells

Jürgen Frohn* und Georg Lausen

Fakultät für Mathematik und Informatik
Universität Mannheim, W-6800 Mannheim, Deutschland
{frohn, lausen}@pi3.informatik.uni-mannheim.de

Zusammenfassung

Ein Hauptproblem bei der Integration heterogener Datenbanken ist die Auflösung der unterschiedlichen Darstellung sich überlappender Realweltausschnitte. Im folgenden wird eine Strategie vorgestellt, um strukturelle und semantische Heterogenität mittels der objektorientierten, regelbasierten Datenbank-Sprache Frame-Logik aufzulösen. Insbesondere werden dabei termbasierte Objektidentitäten und parametrisierte Klassen verwendet, um möglicherweise mehrfach auftretende Objekte über alle lokalen Datenbanken hinweg eindeutig identifizieren zu können. Bei nicht auflösbaren semantischen Konflikten erlaubt der Vererbungsmechanismus die Priorisierung der Semantik einer bestimmten lokalen Datenbank.

1 Einführung

Die Möglichkeit zur Integration heterogener Datenbanken wird zunehmend als eine der wichtigsten Voraussetzungen für effiziente und konsistente Informationssysteme erkannt. Die Schlagworte sind hier *federated databases, interoperability of heterogeneous databases*, oder auch *interoperability of multidatabases*[Hsi92]. Für so charakterisierte Datenbanken ist es typisch, daß Anwendungen Daten aus unterschiedlichen Datenbanken benötigen. Falls dabei sich überlappende oder sogar identische Realweltausschnitte in den beteiligten Datenbanken unterschiedlich dargestellt werden, liegt eine Heterogenität der einzelnen Schema vor. Aspekte der Integration heterogener Datenbanken[1] in diesem Sinn sind der Inhalt dieser Arbeit. Wir beschränken uns auf den Fall relationaler Datenbanken; die entwickelten Techniken sind in analoger Weise auf den allgemeineren Fall der Integration von Datenbanken mit unterschiedlichen Datenmodellen anwendbar.

Der Integrationsansatz dieser Arbeit basiert auf einem *globalen* Schema, das die Zusammenhänge aller betrachteten *lokalen* Schemata enthält. Geeignete Abbildungen ermöglichen, daß Anfragen an das globale Schema, die Daten in unterschiedlichen Datenbanken betreffen, für den Benutzer transparent ausgeführt werden können. Ansätze, die auf einem globalen Schema beruhen, finden sich auch in anderen Arbeiten, wobei nicht objektorientierte Ansätze z.B. in [SL90, KLK91, Hsi92] und objektorientierte z.B. in [Ken91, UW91, SN88, SN90] unterschieden werden können. Objektorientierte Datenmodelle bieten dabei den Vorteil der besseren Strukturierbarkeit des Integrationsprozesses. Wir verwenden als Grundlage *Frame-Logik*, eine objektorientierte Regelsprache [KL89, KLW90]. Durch

*Die Arbeit dieses Autors wird unterstützt von der Deutschen Forschungsgemeinschaft, Aktenzeichen La 598/3-1.

[1] Der Einfachheit wegen reden wir im folgenden nur von *Heterogenität*, obwohl *Schemaheterogenität* exakter wäre.

die Verwendung von Termen als Objektidentitäten, Regeln, parametrisierbaren Klassen mit datenabhängig definierten Signaturen und Instanzen, Klassenhierarchien mit Vererbung und der Fähigkeit, Daten und Metadaten in derselben Sprache zu verarbeiten, lassen sich viele Aspekte der Integration der einzelnen lokalen Schemata in das globale Schema einfach und elegant ausdrücken. Ähnlichkeiten bestehen zu den Arbeiten [KLK91, Ken91]. [KLK91] verwenden eine Hornklauselsprache, die Ausdrücke einer Logik höherer Ordnung ermöglicht, jedoch nicht objektorientiert ist. Frame-Logik hat einen vergleichbaren Sprachumfang und ist zusätzlich objektorientiert. Insbesondere termbasierte Objektidentitäten erleichtern den Integrationsprozeß, da dadurch die Vorkommen derselben Objekte in verschiedenen Datenbanken unterschieden werden können. Entstehen durch das Auftreten derselben Objekte in mehreren Datenbanken Konflikte der Methodenanwendung, so werden diese mittels des Vererbungsmechanismus auf einer entsprechenden Klassenhierarchie gelöst. In [Ken91] wird eine funktionale objektorientierte Sprache verwendet, die, wie für funktionale Sprachen typisch, Ausdrücke höherer Ordnung manipulieren kann. Darüberhinaus werden für die Integration objektorientierte Konstrukte nicht ausgenutzt, insbesondere wird beispielsweise nicht auf die Möglichkeit zurückgegriffen, mittels Klassenhierarchien den Integrationsprozeß zu strukturieren. Gegenüber dem semantischen Modell in [UW91] und den dabei angedeuteten Import- und Exportprozeduren zur Schematransformation erlaubt unser Ansatz durch die regelbasierte Sprache und die parametrisierbare Klassen eine kompakte Darstellung und Transformation der Metadaten. Die Trennung von struktureller und semantischer Heterogenität erleichtert die Schemaintegration. Der Parametrisierung von Klassen entspricht das "Object-coloring" in [SN88]. Während dort sich entsprechende Klassen über eine Aufwärtsvererbung in einer globalen Generalisierung zusammengefaßt werden, bietet die Integration mittels Regeln in Frame-Logik eine höhere Flexibilität. Insbesondere erlaubt unser Ansatz die Auflösung von semantischen Konflikten aufgrund sich widersprechender Informationen in den einzelnen lokalen Datenbanken durch eine Priorisierung mittels der Definition einer Klassenhierarchie der entsprechenden lokalen Objekte und des Überschreibens der entsprechenden Methode.

Die Arbeit ist folgendermaßen strukturiert: In Kapitel 2 werden verschiedene Formen der Heterogenität erläutert. Kapitel 3 gibt eine kurze Begründung des Einsatzes von Frame-Logik und anschließend eine Einführung in die benötigten Sprachkonstrukte. Im Kapitel 4 werden die einzelnen Schritte der Integration lokaler Schemata in ein globales Schema im Zusammenhang behandelt. Kapitel 5 faßt die bisher am Beispiel diskutierten Schritte zu einer Methode zusammen und diskutiert Architekturaspekte. In Kapitel 6 erfolgt eine Bewertung der Ergebnisse.

2 Integrationsprobleme bei heterogenen Datenbanken

In der Regel liegen Informationen aus verschiedenen Datenbanken in unterschiedlichen Darstellungen vor. Folgende verschiedene Formen der Heterogenität können dabei auftreten (vgl. [SL90]):

Namenskonflikte: Verschiedene Bezeichner für gleiche Realweltobjekte nennt man *Synonyme*; gleiche Bezeichner für verschiedene Realweltobjekte nennt man *Homonyme*.

Strukturelle Konflikte (Schema-Konflikte): Gleiche Attribute können verschiedene Typen haben, z.B. eine Angestelltennummer kann in einer Datenbank als STRING, in einer anderen als INTEGER abgelegt sein. Ebenso kann die gleiche Information in verschiedenen Strukturen gegeben sein, z.B. kann die Information, die einmal in einem Attribut enthalten ist, in einer anderen Datenbank eine eigene Relation bilden.

Semantische Konflikte: Selbst strukturell sich entsprechende Informationen können noch eine unterschiedliche Bedeutung haben. Ursache dafür sind zusätzliche implizite Informationen der Daten bzw. Attribute, wie z.B. die Einheit, in der ein Wert gespeichert wird. Auch nichtnumerische Werte können eine zusätzliche Information besitzen, die nicht explizit in der Datenbank angegeben ist. So kann beispielsweise das Attribut `aktie` Aktien im allgemeinen, oder nur frei handelbare Aktien meinen. Ziel ist es durch geeignete semantische Transformationen, wie z.B. arithmetische Umformungen bei verschiedenen Einheiten, diese semantischen Konflikte zu lösen.

Wir konzentrieren uns im folgenden im wesentlichen auf strukturelle und semantische Konflikte bei der Integration. Das Problem der Homonyme und Synonyme liegt mehr in ihrer Erkennung als in ihrer Behandlung. Das folgende leicht modifiziert aus [KLK91] übernommene Aktienmarktszenario bildet die Grundlage unserer Ausführungen. Wir betrachten drei Datenbanken `db_1`, `db_2`, `db_3` mit insgesamt drei Aktien `sun`, `ibm`, `dec`. Die entsprechenden Relationenschemata der drei Datenbanken enthalten jeweils Informationen darüber, wie hoch der Verkaufspreis `preis` von durch ihren Name `name` repräsentierten Aktien zu interessierenden Zeitpunkten `dat` ist:[2]

```
db_1:  relation danapr(dat/DATUM, name/STRING, preis/INTEGER).
db_2:  relation dasid(dat/DATUM, sun/INTEGER, ibm/INTEGER, dec/INTEGER).
db_3:  relation sun(dat/DATUM, preis/INTEGER).
       relation ibm(dat/DATUM, preis/INTEGER).
       relation dec(dat/DATUM, preis/INTEGER).
```

Jedes Tupel in Relation `danapr` gibt pro Datum und Name den jeweiligen Preis an; wir nehmen an, daß die Werte von `name` gerade die Namen der betreffenden Aktien sind, d.h. `sun`, `ibm`, `dec`. Die Relation `dasid` enthält pro Aktie ein eigenes Attribut und gibt pro Tupel für alle Aktien pro Datum den jeweiligen Preis an (als Attributwert des entsprechenden Namen-Attributes); db_3 schließlich enthält für jede Aktie eine eigene Relation, sodaß die einzelnen Tupel gerade die entsprechenden Datum-Preis Angaben enthalten. Jede der Datenbanken enthält im Prinzip dieselbe Information, jedoch in anderen Strukturen. Es liegen somit offensichtlich strukturelle Konflikte vor. Semantische Konflikte können ebenfalls existieren, z.B. können die Preise in unterschiedlichen Währungen vorliegen, oder auch kann in einer Datenbank Preis Eröffnungspreis und in einer anderen Abschlußpreis bedeuten.

Der wesentliche Schritt der Integration ist die Übertragung der Zusammenhänge der lokalen Schemata in das globale Schema, bei gleichzeitiger Auflösung struktureller und semantischer Konflikte. Das Datenmodell des globalen Schemas ist Frame-Logik. Der erste Schritt der Integration ist die Umformulierung der relationalen lokalen Schemata in Frame-Logik.

Die relationale Struktur der lokalen Schemata soll dabei beibehalten werden; gleichzeitig erlaubt dies die Ausnutzung der sprachlichen Möglichkeiten von Frame-Logik zur Auflösung der jeweiligen Konflikte. Sei db_i eine lokale Datenbank; die Umformulierung in Frame-Logik bezeichnen wir dann mit oodb_i:

```
oodb_1:  danapr[tupel =>> {ELEM[dat => DATUM; name => STRING;
                                preis => INTEGER]}].
```

[2] Die Typen der Attribute sind jeweils durch einen Schrägstrich abgetrennt.

db_1		
danapr		
dat	name	preis
3.3.93	sun	150
4.3.93	ibm	160

db_2			
dasid			
dat	sun	ibm	dec
3.3.93	150	151	152
4.3.93	153	154	155

db_3			
sun		ibm	
dat	preis	dat	preis
3.3.93	160	3.3.93	159
4.3.93	158		

oodb_1: danapr[tupel ↠ {e_1[dat → 3.3.93; name → sun; preis → 150],
e_2[dat → 4.3.93; name → ibm; preis → 160]}].

oodb_2: dasid[tupel ↠ {e_4[dat → 3.3.93; sun → 150; ibm → 151; dec → 152],
e_5[dat → 4.3.93; sun → 153; ibm → 154; dec → 155]}].

oodb_3: dapr[relation ↠ {sun[tupel ↠ {e_6[dat → 3.3.93; preis → 160],
e_7[dat → 4.3.93; preis → 158]}],
ibm[tupel ↠ {e_8[dat → 3.3.93; preis → 159]}]}].

Abbildung 1: Lokale Datenbanken und Objekte ihrer objektorientierten Sicht.

oodb_2: dasid[tupel ⇒⇒ {ELEM[dat ⇒ DATUM; sun ⇒ INTEGER;
ibm ⇒ INTEGER; dec ⇒ INTEGER]}].

oodb_3: dapr[relation ⇒⇒ {AKTIE[tupel ⇒⇒ {ELEM[dat ⇒ DATUM;
preis ⇒ INTEGER]}]}].

danapr, dasid werden hier als Objekte betrachtet, auf denen jeweils eine Methode tupel definiert ist mit der entsprechend angegebenen Signatur. tupel ist offensichtlich ein überladener Bezeichner. In beiden Fällen ist tupel mengenwertig; die Anwendung auf die beiden Objekte ergibt die jeweilige Relation, hier als eine Menge von Objekten mit Identifikatoren vom Typ ELEM. Für dapr wird zunächst eine Methode relation definiert, die als Ergebnis die Menge der Relationen der betreffenden Aktien liefert. AKTIE, ELEM sind Klassen; AKTIE enthalte gerade die betrachteten Aktiennamen sun, ibm, dec; ELEM enthalte eine hinreichend große Menge von Objektidentifikatoren für die einzelnen Tupel der Relationen.

Das Resultat der bisherigen Umformung bezeichnen wir als *objektorientierte Sicht* auf die lokalen Datenbanken. Die einzelnen Objekte einer objektorientierten Sicht sind als virtuelle Objekte zu verstehen, das heißt, sie werden bei Bedarf aus den Tupeln in den lokalen Datenbanken berechnet. Bei der strukturellen Nähe zu den entsprechenden lokalen Schemata ist dies beispielsweise mittels SQL-Ausdrücken einfach möglich. Aspekte der Anfragestellung an das integrierte globale Schema, und damit das Problem der Berechnung der virtuellen Objekte, behandeln wir genauer im Kapitel 5. Abbildung 1 zeigt konkrete Relationen und die entsprechenden virtuellen Objekte der objektorientierten Sichten.

3 Frame-Logik als Grundlage der Integration

Die Integration mehrerer Datenbanken, denen eventuell verschiedene Datenmodelle zugrundeliegen, macht ein globales Datenmodell erforderlich, in dem die Integration erfolgt [SL90]. Die Anforderungen an das globale Datenmodell umfassen eine hohe Ausdrucksfähigkeit, um komplexe Sachverhalte darzustellen, und eine hohe semantische Anpassungsfähigkeit, um die verschiedenen konzeptuellen Schemata und jeweilige Semantik der diversen Datenbanken verknüpfen zu können. In [SCGS91] wird daraus gefolgert, daß funktionale oder objektorientierte Datenmodelle als globale Datenmodelle besonders geeignet sind. Ein wichtiges Argument hierbei ist, daß diese Datenmodelle auf einem einzigen vereinheitlichenden Strukturierungskonzept beruhen und nicht, wie beim ER-Modell, durch eine Vielfalt der Konzepte die Komplexität der Integration erhöhen. Frame-Logik bezieht hier eine extreme Position, da nicht nur als alleiniges Strukturierungskonzept Objekte angeboten werden, d.h. es wird nicht zwischen *entities* und *relationships* wie im ER-Modell unterschieden, sondern auch Metakonzepte wie Klassen und Methoden als Objekte betrachtet werden. Mittels seiner Syntax höherer Ordnung und Beibehaltung einer Semantik erster Ordnung erscheint Frame-Logik als Datenmodell zur Integration heterogener Datenbanken gut geeignet.

Eine detaillierte Beschreibung von Frame-Logik ist in [KLW90], bzw. [LM91] gegeben. Aus Platzgründen sei Frame-Logik hier nur an einem Beispiel erklärt.

STAMMAKTIE : AKTIE. aktie(sun) : AKTIE. ibm $\doteq$ big_blue.

aktie(sun)[preis @ 3.3.93 $\rightarrow$ 170; besitzer $\twoheadrightarrow$ {peter, paul}].

AKTIE[preis @ DATUM $\Rightarrow$ {INTEGER}; besitzer $\Rightarrow\!\!\!\Rightarrow$ {ANGESTELLTER}].

X : AKTIONÄR $\longleftarrow$ aktie(Y)[besitzer $\twoheadrightarrow$ {X}].

Objektidentitäten (OIDs) sind in Frame-Logik variablenfreie Terme, die mittels Objektkonstruktoren[3] gebildet werden, welche dabei wie Funktionssymbole behandelt werden[4]. Beispiele für OIDs sind ibm, aktie(sun), AKTIE. Obwohl Objekte, z.B. ibm, und Klassen, z.B. AKTIE, formal nicht unterschieden werden, werden zur Verdeutlichung verschiedene Schreibweisen benutzt[5]. Terme, die aus Objektkonstruktoren und Variablen gebildet sein können, werden als *ID-Terme* bezeichnet, z.B. X, aktie(Y), besitzer.

Klassenzugehörigkeit von Objekten, z.B. aktie(sun) : AKTIE, und ebenso Klassenhierachie, z.B. STAMMAKTIE : AKTIE, werden durch *ISA-F-Terme* ausgedrückt. *Daten-F-Terme* beschreiben das Ergebnis einer Methode, gegebenenfalls mit Argumenten, angewendet auf ein Objekt. Dabei wird zwischen funktionalen ($\rightarrow$) und mengenwertigen ($\twoheadrightarrow$) Daten-F-Termen unterschieden. Durch aktie(sun)[preis @ 3.3.93 $\rightarrow$ 170]. wird z.B. ausgedrückt, daß die funktionale Methode preis angewendet auf das Objekt aktie(sun) mit dem Argument 3.3.93 das Ergebnis 170 liefert. *Signatur-F-Terme* schreiben zu einer Methode in Abhängigkeit des Objektes und gegebenenfalls der Argumente bestimmte Ergebnisklassen vor. AKTIE[besitzer $\Rightarrow\!\!\!\Rightarrow$ {ANGESTELLTER}]. z.B. definiert die Methode besitzer für alle Objekte der Klasse AKTIE mit dem geforderten Ergebnistyp ANGESTELLTER.

Zusätzlich zu F-Termen sind in Frame-Logik auch Prädikate zugelassen. Ein ausgezeichnetes Prädikat ist die Gleicheit, z.B. ibm $\doteq$ big_blue. Die Klassenzugehörigkeit von Objekten und die betreffende Klassenhierachie lassen sich auch mittels Regeln definieren. Beispielsweise besagt die Regel X : AKTIONÄR $\longleftarrow$ aktie(Y)[besitzer $\twoheadrightarrow$ {X}]., daß jeder ID-Term, der in der Ergebnismenge der Methode besitzer enthalten ist, zu einem Element der Klasse AKTIONÄR wird.

[3]Objektkonstruktoren der Stelligkeit 0 werden auch als Konstanten bezeichnet.

[4]Wir betrachten den Fall uninterpretierter Funktionen, so daß Terme genauer Herbrand-Terme sind.

[5]Klassen werden in SMALL-CAPITALS, Objekte in Typewriter beginnend mit einem Kleinbuchstaben, Variablen in Typewriter beginnend mit einem Großbuchstaben dargestellt.

Die Methode `besitzer` wird dabei auf alle OIDs angewendet, die durch eine Variablenersetzung in `aktie(X)` entstehen.

4 Integration der lokalen Schemata

Grundlage zur Auflösung der bestehenden Konflikte zwischen den einzelnen Schemata sind die jeweiligen objektorientierten Sichten auf die lokalen Datenbanken. Vor der eigentlichen Konfliktauflösung müssen zuerst die Objekte des globalen Schemas bestimmt werden. In unserem Beispiel sind die interessierenden Objekte offensichtlich die einzelnen Aktien. Wir definieren eine Klasse AKTIE, die alle OIDs zur Identifikation der relevanten Aktien enthält, sowie eine geeignete Signatur für diese Klasse:

```
aktie(sun), aktie(ibm), aktie(dec) : AKTIE.
AKTIE[name ⇒ STRING, preis @ DATUM ⇒ INTEGER].
```

Zum einfacheren Verständnis des Beispiels haben wir als OIDs gerade die Namen der Aktien, umgeben mit dem Objektkonstruktor `aktie`, gewählt. Im realistischeren Fall einer großen, möglicherweise nicht bekannten Menge von Aktien kann die Menge der OIDs durch eine Regel bestimmt werden. Weiterhin wird die Signatur der Klasse AKTIE definiert, die die beiden Methoden `name`, `preis` enthält. Die Methode `preis` besitzt ein Argument des Typs DATUM und gibt den Aktienpreis des entsprechenden Tages an. Dabei können die Werte-Paare, die sich aus dem Datum und dem Aktienpreis ergeben, als eigene Relation bzgl. einer bestimmten Aktie betrachtet werden. Die Menge der Objekte der Klasse AKTIE kann somit als eine unnormalisierte Relation aufgefaßt werden.

4.1 Lokale kanonische Schemata

Mit der bisherigen Klasse AKTIE geht jedoch jegliche Information über die Herkunft der einzelnen Objekte verloren. Wenn z.B. die Aktie `sun` als Objekt sowohl in der Datenbank `db_1`, als auch in der Datenbank `db_2` enthalten ist, müssen beide Versionen unterscheidbar sein, da semantische Konflikte möglich sind. Daher ist es vorteilhaft, nicht nur Klassen für das globale Schema zu betrachten, sondern für die lokalen Schemata gesonderte, entsprechend parametrisierte Klassen einzuführen. In unserem Beispiel führen wir zunächst eine Klasse DATENBANK ein, um die einzelnen lokalen Datenbanken unterscheiden zu können und danach die Klasse AKTIE entsprechend zu parametrisieren:

```
db_1, db_2, db_3 : DATENBANK.
aktie(X,Y) : AKTIE(X) ⟵ aktie(Y) : AKTIE ∧ X : DATENBANK.
AKTIE(X)[name ⇒ STRING, preis @ DATUM ⇒ INTEGER] ⟵ X : DATENBANK.
```

Man beachte, daß durch die Erweiterung des Objektkonstruktors `aktie` um ein weiteres Argument Aktien lokaler Datenbanken jetzt über alle Datenbanken hinweg eindeutig identifiziert werden können. Die letzte der obigen Regeln definiert dann eine entsprechend angepaßte Signatur für die parametrisierte Klasse AKTIE(X).

Mit diesen Regeln sind nun alle Vorbereitungen getroffen, um die Integration der lokalen Schemata in das globale Schema vorzunehmen. Ausgangspunkt sind die objektorientierten Sichten der ursprünglich relationalen Schemata. In einem ersten Schritt definieren wir zunächst die Objekte sogenannter *lokaler kanonischer Schemata*. Kanonisch soll hier ausdrücken, daß die als verbindlich festgelegte Objektstruktur, in unseren Beispiel AKTIE, als Grundlage gewählt wird. In einem zweiten Schritt werden dann die Objekte des *globalen kanonischen Schemas* mit aufgelösten semantischen Konflikten erzeugt.

Wir benötigen noch eine auf den einzelnen Objekten der Klasse DATENBANK definierte Methode, die uns zu jeder lokalen Datenbank die (virtuellen) Objekte bzgl. des lokalen kanonischen Schemas liefert. Die Signatur einer solchen Methode **aktienbestand** ist wie folgt:

```
X[aktienbestand ⇒⇒ {AKTIE(X)}]  ←  X : DATENBANK.
```

Es folgen die Regeln zur Definition der Objekte des jeweiligen lokalen kanonischen Schemas:[6]

```
db_1[aktienbestand →→ {aktie(db_1,X)[name → X, preis @ Z → Y]}
        ←  danapr[tupel →→ {E[dat → Z, name → X, preis → Y]}].
```

Die Methode `tupel` angewendet auf das Objekt **danapr** liefert eine Menge von Objekten. Jedes Objekt in dieser Menge definiert eine Ersetzung der Variablen `E,X,Y,Z`; d.h., für jedes solche Objekt kann der Rumpf der Regel wahr gemacht werden. Eine bezüglich einer solchen Variablenersetzung vorgenommene Regelanwendung liefert für die `db_1`-Version der betreffenden Aktie mit Namen `X` einen Eintrag in die durch die Methode `preis` beschriebene Relation. Man beachte, daß jeder solche Eintrag eindeutig über alle Datenbanken mittels der **aktie**-OID und des jeweiligen Datums identifiziert ist.

```
db_2[aktienbestand →→ {aktie(db_2,X)[name → X, preis @ Z → Y]}
        ←  dasid[tupel →→ {E[dat → Z, X → Y]}] ∧¬ X ≐ dat.
```

Die Besonderheit hier ist, daß die Methodennamen in `dasid` gerade die Aktiennamen sind. Da formal in Frame-Logik auch Methoden Objekte sind, kann die Variable `X` in derselben Regel sowohl an einer OID-Position als auch an einer Methodenposition stehen. Man beachte desweiteren, daß die Variable `X` durch alle Methodennamen außer `dat` ersetzt werden kann, und somit eine Aufblähung des Regelrumpfes auf alle in `dasid` definierten Aktien-Methoden überflüssig wird.

```
db_3[aktienbestand →→ {aktie(db_3,X)[name → X, preis @ Z → Y]}
        ←  dapr[relation →→ {X[tupel →→ {E[dat → Z, preis → Y]}]}].
```

Die Variable `X` wird hier wiederum durch Aktiennamen ersetzt, die jedoch im Unterschied zu `dasid` für Relationen stehen.

Mittels der obigen drei Regeln haben wir nun alle strukturellen Konflikte aufgelöst; jeweils bezüglich der entsprechenden lokalen Datenbank befinden sich alle Aktienobjekte in ihrer kanonischen Form. Als nächstes können wir mit der Auflösung der semantischen Konflikte beginnen.

4.2 Globales kanonisches Schema

In der Literatur werden verschiedene Formen semantischer Konflikte betrachtet, z.B. [Ken91, UW91]. Uns interessiert hier neben der Auflösung von Konflikten insbesondere die Handhabung der zueinander in Konflikt stehenden Methoden bzgl. der unterschiedlichen lokalen Schemata. Wir begnügen uns

[6] Die folgenden Regeln sind aufgrund des gemeinsamen Beispiels auf den ersten Blick ähnlich zu [KLK91]. Der entscheidende Unterschied ist, daß durch die Verwendung von OIDs, Methoden und Klassen in unserem Ansatz eine semantisch adäquatere Formulierung erreicht wird, die später auch die Anwendung von Vererbung ermöglichen wird.

somit mit zwei Arten von semantischen Konflikten. Der erste Typ sind Umrechnung von Maßeinheiten, allgemein Situationen, in denen eine Bijektion zwischen Wertemengen angegeben werden kann. In unserem Beispiel können die Preise der Aktien in unterschiedlichen Währungen angegeben sein. Dieser Fall läßt sich einfach durch Hinzufügen von geeigneten Prädikaten zu dem Rumpf der betreffenden Regeln erreichen. Sei die verbindliche Währung DM und sei die Währung in db_1 \$, dann führt der folgende Regelrumpf für die db_1-Regel die Umrechnung durch:

$$\longleftarrow \texttt{danapr[tupel} \twoheadrightarrow \texttt{\{E[dat} \rightarrow \texttt{Z, name} \rightarrow \texttt{X, preis} \rightarrow \texttt{Y1]\}]} \wedge \texttt{Y = \$toDM(Y1)}.$$

Durch Hinzufügen von (bijektiven) Prädikaten können ebenso Namensumbenennungen vorgenommen werden, z.B. ibm zu big_blue.

Die zweite Situation, die wir betrachten wollen, ist etwas komplizierter. Nehmen wir an, in db_1 und db_2 sei der Preis einer Aktie jeweils der Tagesabschlußpreis, und in db_3 der Tageseröffnungspreis. In diesem Fall können wir eine Konfliktauflösung erreichen, indem wir pro Datum und Aktie den jeweiligen Preis in db_3 durch den Preis des Folgetages ersetzen. Intererssanter wird das Problem, wenn Preis der Tageshöchstpreis ist; ein Anpassen wie im vorherigen Fall ist jetzt nicht mehr möglich. Der einzige verbleibende Ausweg ist, die Unterschiedlichkeit der Semantik zu tolerieren und im Falle von überlappenden lokalen Datenbanken eine Auswahl unter den Methoden zu treffen, z.B., wird die Aktie sun sowohl in db_1 als auch in db_3 geführt, so kann entweder erstere oder letztere lokale Datenbank durch Berücksichtigung ihrer Methode preis priorisiert werden.

Fragen dieser Art werden auch in [KLK91, Ken91, SN88, SN90] behandelt. In [KLK91] werden solche Priorisierungen explizit ausprogrammiert; in [Ken91] werden drei Varianten vorgeschlagen zur Behandlung der unterschiedlichen Ergebnisse der Methoden: Betrachtung aller Resultate, Auswahl eines Resultates, Aggregierung über alle Resultate. In [SN88] wird jedem globalen Objekt mittels des "Object coloring" durch die Aufwärtsvererbung das Verhalten einer bestimmten lokalen Klasse zugeordnet, so daß das Problem unterschiedlicher Ergebnisse vermieden wird. [SN90] lösen dieses Problem durch "Message forwarding", d.h. Methoden, die nicht direkt von einem (globalen) Objekt behandelt werden können, werden an ein semantisch verwandtes (lokales) Objekt weitergeleitet und dort aufgerufen. Falls eine Methode an mehrere Objekte weitergeleitet wird, erfolgt eine Aggregierung der Ergebnisse der einzelnen Methoden.

Im folgenden zeigen wir, wie mittels der sprachlichen Möglichkeiten von Frame-Logik der Vererbungsmechanismus zur Methodenauswahl ausgenutzt werden kann, um ein eindeutiges Resultat auszuwählen. Dadurch wird eine semantisch adäquatere Behandlung ermöglicht. Das Problem kann so formuliert werden, daß bzgl. einer gegebenen Menge von aus verschiedenen Datenbanken stammenden Versionen desselben Objektes im Falle von überladenen Methoden mittels des Vererbungsmechanismus die gewünschte zur Anwendung gelangt. Dies kann erreicht werden, indem die Objektversionen in eine entsprechende Ordnung gebracht werden, sodaß die Auswahl über das Überschreiben von Methoden erreicht wird. Man beachte hierbei, daß in Frame-Logik hierarchische Beziehungen zwischen Objekten erlaubt sind, da formal nicht zwischen Objekten und Klassen unterschieden wird. In unserem Beispiel sind folgende Versionen der Objekte gegeben: aktie(db_1,X), aktie(db_2,X), aktie(db_3,X). Nehmen wir an, daß der entsprechende Index gerade der Priorität entspricht. Dies ergibt die folgende Klassenordnung, wobei eine höhere Priorität einer niedrigeren Hierarchiestufe entspricht:

$$\texttt{aktie(X)} : \texttt{aktie(db\_3,X)} : \texttt{aktie(db\_2,X)} : \texttt{aktie(db\_1,X)} \longleftarrow \texttt{aktie(X)} : \text{AKTIE}.$$

```
aktie(db_1,ibm)[preis @ 4.3.93 → 160].
   ↓
aktie(db_2,ibm)[preis @ 4.3.93 → 153].  ─┐
   ↓                                      │ Vererbung
aktie(db_3,ibm).                          │
   ↓                                      │
aktie(sun)[preis @ 3.3.93 → 153].       ←┘
```

Abbildung 2: Priorisierung durch Überschreiben der Methoden bei Unvollständigkeit.

Durch die OIDs, die sich durch Ersetzung der Variablen `X` in **`aktie(X)`** ergeben, werden die Objekte des globalen kanonischen Schemas bezeichnet. Diese erben die Methoden eines entsprechenden Objekts aus einem lokalen kanonischen Schema, wobei durch die Klassenordnung und das Überschreiben von Methoden die Priorität berücksichtigt wird.

Insbesondere ermöglicht diese Vorgehensweise flexible Prioritäten, die im allgemeinen abhängig von beliebigen Werten definiert sein können. Die beiden folgenden F-Terme definieren z.B. verschiedene Prioritäten für verschiedene Aktien:

```
aktie(sun) : aktie(db_3,sun) : aktie(db_2,sun) : aktie(db_1,sun).
aktie(ibm) : aktie(db_1,ibm) : aktie(db_2,ibm) : aktie(db_3,ibm).
```

Als letzten Schritt können jetzt die Objekte des globalen kanonischen Schemas wie folgt definiert werden:

```
db[aktienbestand ->> {aktie(X)}]  <--  D[aktienbestand ->> {aktie(D,X)}].
```

`db` sei hier das die globale (virtuelle) Datenbank repräsentierende Objekt. Man beachte, daß im Rumpf der Regel über alle Aktienobjektversionen quantifiziert wird; die Methoden **`name`**, **`preis`** können im Regelkopf und -rumpf entfallen, da sie aufgrund der Klassenordnung vererbt werden, wobei die Anwendung der priorisierten Methoden garantiert ist.

Man beachte auch die Auswirkung der Vererbung für den Fall, daß in der Datenbank mit der höchsten Priorität nur für bestimmte Tage ein Aktienpreis vorliegt. Für alle anderen Tage wird automatisch der Aktienpreis der Datenbank mit der nächstniedrigeren Priorität übernommen, sofern für den jeweiligen Tag der Aktienpreis in dieser Datenbank gegeben ist. Abbildung 2 demonstriert diesen Prozeß, wobei für die **`ibm`**-Aktie am **`4.3.93`** in **`db_3`** kein Preis vorliegt. Möchte man dies jedoch vermeiden, und nur die Aktienpreise der Datenbank mit der höchsten Priorität betrachten, so muß die Methode **`preis`** auf der Klassenebene definiert werden, so daß nicht die Werte, sondern die Berechnungsvorschriften vererbt werden.

5 Integrationsmethode und Architekturaspekte

In den vorangehenden Kapiteln haben wir an einem Beispiel gezeigt, wie die Integration heterogener relationaler Schemata unter Zuhilfenahme von Frame-Logik so vorgenommen werden kann, daß eine gemeinsame Nutzung der Daten der lokalen Datenbanken möglich wird. Mittels Frame-Logik wird eine Auflösung der strukturellen und semantischen Konflikte erreicht; die eigentlichen Daten bleiben in den lokalen Datenbanken. Frame-Logik ermöglicht in der Terminologie eines globalen kanonischen Schemas eine konfliktbereinigte Sicht auf die lokalen Datenbanken. Im folgenden sollen die einzelnen Schritte in einen mehr methodischen Rahmen gebracht werden und die Einbettung in eine Architektur vorgestellt werden. Im Vergleich z.B. mit dem in [SL90] vorgestellten Fünf-Schichten-Modell entspricht in unserem Ansatz ein relationales Schema einer zu integrierenden Datenbank dem *local schema*, unser lokales kanonisches Schema dem *component schema* bzw. dem *export schema*, welche hier zusammenfallen, da jeweils die komplette Schema–Information bei der Integration betrachtet wird, und das globale kanonische Schema dem *federated schema*. Ein *external schema* als eine benutzerabhängige Einschränkung des globalen Schemas kann ebenfalls mittels Regeln der F-Logik definiert werden, worauf hier jedoch nicht näher eingegangen werden soll.

Schritt 1. Definition der objektorientierten Sichten auf die lokalen Datenbanken: Es werden die relationalen Schemata in Frame-Logik umformuliert. Dies ist die Voraussetzung, um mittels des vollen Sprachumfangs von Frame-Logik weiterarbeiten zu können. Aufgrund der einfachen Struktur relationaler Schemata und der sprachlichen Flexibilität von Frame-Logik ist eine entsprechende Transformation einfach automatisierbar.

Schritt 2. Definition des globalen kanonischen Schemas: Hier wird die für das globale kanonische Schema verbindliche Struktur festgelegt. Dies heißt im wesentlichen, daß die Signaturen der Klassen und ihre Instanzen angegeben werden.

Schritt 3. Definition der lokalen kanonischen Schemata: Das kanonische Schema wird hier zunächst mit den Namen der lokalen Datenbanken parametrisiert, sodaß bei Überlappungen der lokalen Datenbanken unterschiedliche Versionen der Objekte auseinandergehalten werden können. Basierend auf den objektorientierten Sichten werden Regeln angegeben, die die entsprechenden Objekte der lokalen Schemata definieren. Da die lokalen kanonischen Schemata (modulo der Parametrisierung) bereits dem globalen kanonischen Schema entsprechen, wird hier bereits eine Auflösung der strukturellen Konflikte erreicht.

Schritt 4. Auflösen der semantischen Konflikte: Hier werden die die Objekte definierenden Regeln so ergänzt, bzw. erweitert, daß semantische Konflikte soweit möglich bereinigt werden. Im Falle, daß dies nicht vollständig erreicht werden kann, kann durch Anordnung der betreffenden Klassen in eine Klassenhierarchie mittels des Vererbungsmechanismus eine Priorisierung der zueinander in Konflikt stehenden Methodendefinitionen erreicht werden.

Schritt 5. Definition der Objekte des globalen Schemas: Da alle Konflikte aufgelöst sind, ist hier praktisch lediglich ein Einsammeln der einzelnen Objekte erforderlich.

Zum Abschluß soll noch kurz beispielhaft aufgezeigt werden, wie in unserem Rahmen mittels geeigneter Architekturkompenenten eine gemeinsame Nutzung der Daten verschiedener lokaler Datenbanken ermöglicht werden kann. Es lassen sich grob drei Komponenten unterscheiden. Der **Schema-Integrator** enthält das globale kanonische Schema und die die betreffenden Objekte definierenden Regeln (einschließlich der die strukturellen und semantischen Konflikte auflösenden Regeln). Der **Lokale-Schema-Importeur** erzeugt die objektorientierten Sichten auf die lokalen Datenbanken und bildet somit die Eingabe für die Schemaintegrator. Der **Globale-Schema-Exporteur** macht die durch den Schema-Integrator definierten Objekte Anwendungen verfügbar. Zur Ermöglichung von SQL-Anwendungen ist hier eine Transformation des globalen kanonischen Schemas in das relationale Datenmodell erforderlich. Eine solche Transformation ist analog zu der Bildung der objektorientierten Sichten auf die relationalen Datenbanken möglich. Ein konkreter Benutzerauftrag wird in der so skizzierten Architektur analog zu einem Auftrag an eine (nicht permanente) Sicht einer Datenbank behandelt. Der Aufwand der Abbildung der Frame-Logik-Objekte in die Relationen der lokalen Datenbank ist im wesentlichen durch den Schema-Integrator bestimmt.

6 Zusammenfassung

In dieser Arbeit wird die Integration heterogener relationaler Datenbankenschemata mittels eines objektorientierten Datenmodells diskutiert. Aufgrund seiner Eigenschaften scheint Frame-Logik ein geeigneter Kandidat eines Datenmodells für die Integration heterogener Schemata zu sein. Die Fähigkeit, unterschiedliche Versionen von Objekten betrachten zu können, Klassen einschließlich ihrer Signaturen regelbasiert definieren zu können, und insbesondere Konfliktauflösungen durch Priorisierung einer Methode mittels Vererbungshierarchien vornehmen zu können, trägt sehr zur Klarheit und Kompaktheit des Integrationsprozesses bei.

Literatur

[Hsi92] David K. Hsiao. Federated Databases and Systems: Part I - A Tutorial on Their Data Sharing. *VLDB Journal*, 1:127 - 179, 1992.

[Ken91] William Kent. Solving domain mismatch and schema mismatch problems with an object-oriented database programming language. In *Proceedings of the Intl. Conference on Very Large Data Bases*, pages 147 - 160, 1991.

[KL89] Michael Kifer and Georg Lausen. F-logic: A higher-order language for reasoning about objects, inheritance and scheme. In *Proceedings of the ACM SIGMOD Conference on Management of Data*, pages 134 - 146, 1989.

[KLK91] Ravi Krishnamurthy, Witold Litwin, and William Kent. Language features for interoperability of databases with schematic discrepancies. In *Proceedings of the ACM SIGMOD Conference on Management of Data*, pages 40 - 49, 1991.

[KLW90] Michael Kifer, Georg Lausen, and James Wu. Logical foundations of object oriented and frame-based languages. Informatik Berichte 3/1990, Universität Mannheim, june 1990.

[LM91] Georg Lausen and Beate Marx. Eine Einführung in Frame-Logik. In Gottfried Vossen and Kurt-Ulrich Witt, editors, *Entwicklungstendenzen bei Datenbanksystemen*, pages 173 - 202. Oldenbourg Verlag, 1991.

[SCGS91] F. Saltor, M. Castellanos, and M. Garcia-Solaco. Suitability of data models as canonical models for federated databases. *SIGMOD RECORD 20(4): Special issue: Semantic Issues in Multidatabase Systems*, 20(4):44 - 48, December 1991.

[SL90] Amit P. Sheth and James A. Larson. Federated database systems for managing distributed, heterogeneous, and autonomous databases. *ACM Computing Surveys*, 22(3):183 - 236, September 1990.

[SN88] Michael Schrefl and Erich J. Neuhold. Object class definition by generalization using upward inheritance. In *Proceedings of the Intl. Conference on Data Engeneering*, pages 4 - 13, 1988.

[SN90] Michael Schrefl and Erich J. Neuhold. A knowledge-based approach to overcome structural differences in object-oriented database integration. In *Artificial Intelligence in Databases and Information Systems (DS-3)*, pages 265 - 304. North Holland, 1990.

[UW91] Susan D. Urban and Jian Wu. Resolving semantic heterogeneity through the explicit representation of data model semantics. *SIGMOD RECORD 20(4): Special issue: Semantic Issues in Multidatabase Systems*, 20(4):55 - 58, December 1991.

Objektidentifikation in Heterogenen Datenbanksystemen

oder: Was tun, wenn die globale Schnittstelle "zu mächtig" wird?

Martin Härtig, Klaus R. Dittrich
Forschungsbereich Datenbanktechnologie, Institut für Informatik der Universität Zürich
Winterthurerstrasse 190, CH-8057 Zürich, Schweiz
email: {haertig, dittrich}@ifi.unizh.ch

Kurzfassung

Heterogene Datenbanksysteme (HDBS) bieten an ihrer Schnittstelle ein globales Datenmodell an, das Anwendern einheitlichen und integrierten Zugriff auf die Daten verschiedener, autonomer Datenhaltungssysteme gewährt. Die an sich wünschenswerte große Mächtigkeit eines globalen Datenmodells kann dazu führen, daß nicht mehr alle seine Konzepte auf Basis beliebiger zu integrierender lokaler Systeme realisiert werden können. Das Papier diskutiert diese Problematik für Objektidentität als zentrales Konzept objektorientierter Datenmodelle, die sich besonders als globale Datenmodelle eignen. Als Lösung wird vorgeschlagen, verschiedene Alternativen für die Integration "fremder" Daten vorzusehen. Jede Alternative ist einerseits charakterisiert durch Anforderungen an die Identifizierbarkeit von Daten im lokalen System und andererseits durch die Datenbankfunktionalität, die für diese Daten global verfügbar ist. Die Idee besteht darin, selektiv nur diejenige auf Objektidentität basierende Funktionalität sichtbar zu machen, die auf einem konkreten lokalen System realisierbar ist. Das vorgestellte Konzept ist Bestandteil des ZOO_{IFI}-Systems, das durch Anwendung objektorientierter Technologie die Konstruktion eines HDBS unterstützt.

1 Einleitung und Motivation

In vielen Unternehmen und Organisationen existieren umfangreiche Datenbestände mit hoher wirtschaftlicher Bedeutung, die zwar unabhängig entstanden sind und eigenständig verwaltet werden, aber über ein gemeinsames leistungsfähiges Netzwerk erreichbar sind. In dieser Situation müssen Anwendungen in zunehmendem Maße auf Daten zugreifen, die auf unterschiedliche, autonome Datenbanksysteme (DBS) und Dateisysteme "zersplittert" sind. Der immer drängender werdende Wunsch nach Unterstützung für solche Anwendungen führte zu beträchtlichen Forschungsanstrengungen auf dem Gebiet der sogenannten *Heterogenen (Föderativen) Datenbanksysteme* (HDBS) [Brig92], [Shet90]). Ein HDBS vereint mehrere *lokale* Datenhaltungssysteme (einschließlich der existierenden Datenbestände) unter einem gemeinsamen Dach. Es soll eine homogenisierende (Software-) Schicht zur Verfügung stellen, die (*globalen*) Anwendern die integrierte, einheitliche Nutzung der verschiedenen heterogenen Datenbestände erlaubt und ihnen die Illusion eines homogenen DBS zu vermitteln sucht. Dabei soll die Autonomie der lokalen Datenhaltungssysteme erhalten werden, auf denen insbesondere existierende Anwendungen unverändert lauffähig bleiben müssen.

Von zentraler Bedeutung für HDBS ist das *globale Datenmodell* (gDM), das die einheitliche Schnittstelle zu den integrierten lokalen DBS bildet und somit deren (Datenmodell-) Heterogenität verbirgt. Es dient der einheitlichen Repräsentation der lokalen Daten, die von den lokalen DBS verwaltet werden und in *lokalen Schemata* mit Hilfe der verschiedenen *lokalen Datenmodells* beschrieben sind. Dazu werden die lokalen Schemata in sogenannte *Komponentenschemata* in termini des gDM transformiert. Die Datenmanipulationssprache (DML) des gDM wird von globalen Anwendungen für den Zugriff, die Kombination und Manipulation der lokalen Daten benutzt und entlastet diese somit vom Umgang mit verschiedenen lokalen DML. Daneben ist das gDM auch Grundlage der *Schemaintegration*, deren Ziel es ist, ausgehend von den Komponentenschemata durch Ausräumen von Diskrepanzen und Redundanzen eine konsistente Sicht auf den Daten zu konstruieren. Schließlich dient es auch dazu, neue Informationen (die in keiner der existierenden Datenbasen vorhanden sind) zu modellieren, die insbesondere bei der Beschreibung von Zusammenhängen zwischen den bislang isolierten lokalen Daten anfallen.

Die zentralen Qualitäten, die für ein gDM bei dessen Entwicklung angestrebt werden, sind seine Eignung für die Schemaintegration sowie hohe "semantische Ausdrucksfähigkeit", um die Konzepte eines möglichst breiten Spektrums von (lokalen) Datenmodellen auf globaler Ebene repräsentieren zu können [Salt91]. Gerade aus der letzteren Anforderung resultiert der Trend, daß meist sehr hochentwickelte Datenmodelle mit mächtigen Konzepten als gDM vorgeschlagen werden. Diese Sichtweise läßt außer acht, daß jedes an der globalen Schnittstelle angebotene Konzept letztendlich auf Basis (der Anwenderschnittstelle) der lokalen Systeme realisiert werden muß. Entsprechend kann für den *Datenbankintegrator* (DBI), der ein konkretes (lokales) Datenbanksystem X in ein HDBS einzubringen hat, die "Anhäufung" von mächtigen Konzepten im gDM zu einem gravierenden Problem werden. Es kann nun nämlich passieren, daß Konzepte des gDM, die auch auf die globalen Repräsentationen von in X gespeicherten Daten (von globalen Anwendern) angewandt werden können, kein (geeignetes) Gegenstück im lokalen DBS X haben und deshalb nicht (oder nur schwer) durch den DBI realisierbar sind.

In jüngerer Zeit hat sich die Erkenntnis durchgesetzt, daß sich objektorientierte Datenmodelle sehr zur Verwendung als gDM eignen [Salt91]. Dabei tritt allerdings das eben geschilderte prinzipielle Problem mächtiger gDM insbesondere im Zusammenhang mit dem Konzept der Objektidentität auf, das einerseits zentral für objektorientierte Datenmodelle ist und auf dem auch weitere Konzepte basieren (z.B. komplexe Objekte), für dessen Realisierung auf globaler Ebene (im Rahmen des HDBS) aber andererseits von vielen gängigen DBS nur unzureichende Unterstützung geboten wird. Soll man nun im objektorientierten gDM das Konzept der Objektidentität weglassen (mit gravierenden Folgen auch für andere Konzepte), oder aber gängige DBS ohne ausreichende Unterstützung für Objektidentität von der Aufnahme in das HDBS ausschließen? Beide Wege sind sicherlich keine Lösung.

Als Ausweg aus diesem Dilemma schlagen wir in diesem Papier vor, verschiedene Alternativen für die Integration eines lokalen DBS in ein HDBS mit objektorientiertem gDM einzubauen. Aus realisierungs-("integrations-")technischer Sicht (DBI) entsprechen diese Alternativen jeweils einem unterschiedlichen Grad an Unterstützung, den ein lokales System im Hinblick auf globale Objektidentität bietet. Im gDM manifestieren sich die Alternativen in dem Grad, in dem Objektidentität auf globaler Ebene ausgenutzt werden kann, was sich i.w. in den anwendbaren Operationen sowie der dauerhaften (globalen) "Referenzierbarkeit" zeigt. Zu diesem Zweck bietet das gDM die Möglichkeit, die *"Verwendbarkeit"* von Klassen bzw. deren Instanzen zu spezifizieren (einzuschränken). Die Idee besteht darin, Objektidentität auf globaler Ebene für alle Klassen (der Komponentenschemata) bzw. deren Objekte zu realisieren, aber nur jeweils *den* Teil der auf Objektidentität basierenden Funktionalität der globalen Schnittstelle für den Anwender verfügbar zu machen, der auf Basis des lokalen Systems *realisierbar ist*, das die Instanzen dieser Klasse letztlich verwaltet. Die Möglichkeit zur Spezifikation der Verwendbarkeit von Klassen erlaubt außerdem, Zugriffsbeschränkungen, die lokale Systeme aufgrund ihrer Autonomie erlassen können, auch global zu repräsentieren sowie die Arbeit des DBI auf das im konkreten Fall tatsächlich notwendige Maß zu reduzieren.

Die in dem vorliegenden Beitrag diskutierte Problematik der Objektidentität in HDBS und der hierfür vorgeschlagene Lösungsansatz ist ein Aspekt des ZOO_{IFI}[1]-Projekts. Dessen Ziel ist es, durch die Anwendung objektorientierter Technologie ein System (gleichen Namens) zu entwickeln, das weitgehende Unterstützung für die Integration beliebiger Datenhaltungssysteme (einschließlich der von diesen verwalteten, bereits existierenden Datenbestände) in ein HDBS bietet. Dabei sollen an der globalen Schnittstelle nicht nur lesende, sondern auch ändernde Operationen sowie die "permanente" Verknüpfung von bislang isolierten lokalen Daten (durch neue, noch in keinem lokalen System vorhandene Datenobjekte bzw. Beziehungen) unterstützt werden.

2 Ein Überblick über ZOO_{IFI}

Die Integration eines lokalen DBS (mit gegebenem lokalen Schema und Datenbasis) in ein HDBS erfolgt i.w. in zwei (Abbildungs-) Schritten. Zum einen muß für das lokale Schema eine Repräsentation in termini des globalen Datenmodells erzeugt werden (Abbildung des lokalen Datenmodells in das gDM). Zum anderen muß die DML des gDM auf die DML des lokalen Systems "abgebildet" werden (Realisierung der Homogenisierungsschicht). In den meisten Ansätzen beruht der letztere Schritt auf einer *Übersetzung* der DML des gDM in die des lokalen Modells. In ZOO_{IFI} realisieren wir diesen Schritt dagegen, indem die Operationen der globalen DML für jedes lokale System *implementiert* werden. [Bert89] bezeichnet diese Vorgehensweise als *"operational mapping"* und demonstriert deren hohe Flexibilität bei der Integration.

Das ZOO_{IFI}-Projekt macht sich für die geschilderten Aufgaben objektorientierte Konzepte aus dem Datenbankbereich, aber insbesondere auch aus dem Bereich der objektorientierten Software-Entwicklung zunutze. Zum einen verwenden wir ein objektorientiertes gDM, zum anderen wird die homogenisierende Software-Schicht eines HDBS in objektorientierter Weise realisiert. Damit wird es möglich (letztlich wegen der ereichbaren hohen Wiederverwendbarkeit von Software), große Teile der für die Kopplung lokaler Systeme notwendigen Software in dieser Schicht im voraus zur Verfügung zu stellen, so daß die Integration eines konkreten Systems nur noch vergleichsweise wenig Aufwand erfordert und auf die Bearbeitung der für dieses System spezifischen Aspekte beschränkt bleibt. Insbesondere werden gleiche Aufgaben nicht immer wieder bei der Integration weiterer Systeme von neuem realisiert.

In diesem Kapitel wird zunächst kurz das objektorientierte gDM von ZOO_{IFI} [Härt92a] vorgestellt, das die weithin anerkannten Konzepte objektorientierter Datenmodelle [Atki89] für die Zwecke der Integration einsetzt und nötigenfalls (siehe Kapitel 3) erweitert. Anschließend wird die Schemaarchitektur von ZOO_{IFI} beschrieben. Dann gehen wir auf die Realisierung der Integrationsschicht ein, welche auf der Idee der sogenannten objektorientierten *"Frameworks"* basiert.

[1] Zurich object-oriented integration framework for building Heterogeneous Database Systems.

2.1 Das objektorientierte globale Datenmodell

Objekte sind charakterisiert durch eine Objektidentität (siehe Kapitel 3), einen internen Zustand (Wert, Struktur) sowie die auf sie anwendbaren Operationen. Klassen dienen der gemeinsamen Beschreibung gleichartiger Objekte (Intension) und fassen diese in einer Menge (Extension) zusammen (ein Beispiel für eine Klassendefinition wird später (Bild 2) gegeben). Der Zustand eines Objekts wird mit Attributen beschrieben. Attribute haben einen atomaren Wertebereich (integer, string, etc.) oder beschreiben Assoziationen mit anderen Objekten; ferner lassen sich mit Hilfe von (mehrstufig anwendbaren) Konstruktoren (Mengen, Listen, Tupel) komplexe Attribute ausgehend von atomaren Werten und Assoziationen bilden. Bei Assoziationen unterscheiden wir zwischen Referenzen und Unterobjektbeziehungen. Letztere erlauben den Aufbau *komplexer Objekte*, die andere eigenständige Objekte als Komponenten enthalten und sich als eine Einheit (z.B. bei Operationen) verhalten. Während Unterobjektbeziehungen eine spezielle (vom DBS ausgenutzte) Semantik tragen und eine sehr starke Bindung zwischen Objekten ausdrücken, dienen Referenzen der Modellierung allgemeiner Beziehungen. Der Anwender hat die Möglichkeit, die für eine Klasse charakteristischen Operationen (Methoden) zu definieren. Methoden, die ein Objekt oder eine Menge von Objekten als Ergebnis liefern, können zur Definition des Zustandes eines (komplexen) Objekts herangezogen werden. Ein komplexes Objekt besteht somit nicht nur aus den direkt und indirekt über die Unterobjektbeziehungen erreichbaren, sondern auch aus den über solche Methoden (dynamisch) *berechneten* Komponentenobjekten.

In der Klassendefinition wird zwischen öffentlichen und privaten Eigenschaften (Attributen und Methoden) unterschieden. Nur die öffentlichen Eigenschaften sind Benutzern der Objekte einer Klasse direkt zugänglich, während die privaten verborgen bleiben (Einkapselung). Die Klassen sind in einer Hierarchie angeordnet (Taxonomie). Subtypen ererben die Eigenschaften ihrer Obertypen (mehrfache Vererbung). Eng damit verbunden ist die Möglichkeit, geerbte Operationen im Rahmen eines Subtyps zu redefinieren. Dies wiederum zieht das Überladen von Operatoren (Polymorphismus) und dynamisches Binden nach sich.

Die DML unseres Datenmodells bietet generische Operationen an, die sich auf Objekte bzw. Klassen beziehen (z.B. Erzeugen, Löschen, Kopieren, Vergleich auf Gleichheit/Identität etc.), die (einfache) Suche in der Extension einer Klasse basierend auf Attributwerten ermöglichen, das Lesen und Modifizieren der Attribute eines Objektes erlauben sowie die üblichen mit den Konstruktoren verbundenen Operationen. Schließlich hat der Anwender die Möglichkeit, einzelne Objekte mit einem Namen zu belegen, über den er diese (oft als "Einstiegspunkte" bezeichneten) Objekte wieder auffinden kann.

Wir wollen an dieser Stelle noch einen Begriff einführen, der später (und allgemein bei objektorientierten DBS) eine Rolle spielt. Unter der *Aktivierung* eines Objektes verstehen wir den Vorgang (zur Laufzeit), eine lokale Dateneinheit vom lokalen DBS anzufordern, deren globale Repräsentation, also das zugehörige globale Objekt zu erstellen und dieses über die globale Schnittstelle in Anwendungen zur Bearbeitung bereitzustellen (z.B. als Ergebnis einer Leseoperation). Das Objekt ist dann *aktiv*, solange es für die Anwendung(en) zur Bearbeitung zur Verfügung steht. Die genaue Ausgestaltung des Aktivierungsmechanismus (explizite oder implizite Aktivierung/Passivierung etc.) ist weitgehend eine Frage der Einbettung in eine Programmiersprache und braucht hier nicht weiter betrachtet zu werden.

2.2 Die Schemaarchitektur

Ein *Komponentenschema* beschreibt in termini des objektorientierten gDM die relevanten Daten eines lokalen Datenbanksystems, das Teil der Föderation ist. Es entsteht durch Transformation des lokalen Schemas des betreffenden lokalen Systems, welches in termini des jeweiligen lokalen Datenmodells die lokale Datenbasis beschreibt. Im *föderierten Schema* wird die Gesamtsicht auf alle beteiligten Datenbasen beschrieben, wie sie den globalen Anwendungen präsentiert wird. Dazu werden zum einen die Komponentenschemata der beteiligten lokalen Systeme importiert (die Klassendefinitionen werden damit Bestandteil des föderierten Schemas) und zum anderen können hier weitere, sogenannte *Anreicherungsklassen* beschrieben werden. Diese dienen dazu, (persistente) "Beziehungen" zwischen den bislang isolierten lokalen Daten zu definieren oder andere zusätzliche Daten zu beschreiben. Im Gegensatz zu den Klassen der Komponentenschemata, die der "nachträglichen" Beschreibung existierender Daten dienen, werden Instanzen der Anreicherungsklassen erst im Zuge des Aufbaus des HDBS neu erzeugt und in einem speziellen (internen) Datenbanksystem von ZOO_{IFI} abgelegt.

Wir werden im weiteren Verlauf Typen in lokalen Schemata als *lokale Typen* bezeichnen (auch wenn es sich um Klassen eines objektorientierten lokalen DBS handeln kann), während ihre globalen Repräsentationen (ebenso wie Anreicherungsklassen) mit dem Begriff *globale Klassen* belegt werden.

2.3 Der Integrationsrahmen: Objektorientierte Realisierung der Integrationssoftware

Die Realisierung der homogenisierenden Schicht basiert in ZOO_{IFI} auf der Idee der sogenannten *"Frameworks"* [John88], [Wirf90]. Diese gehen über die für objektorientierte Systeme charakteristischen, wiederverwendbaren und mittels Überschreiben adaptierbaren Klassenbibliotheken hinaus und verwirklichen Wiederverwendbarkeit auf der Entwurfsebene. Frameworks sind ein abstrakter Entwurf für die Lösung einer Familie ähnlicher Probleme. Dazu definieren sie in Form von interoperierenden abstrakten und konkreten Klassen die Struktur eines gesamten Programm- bzw. Subsystems einschließlich des wesentlichen Kontroll- und Datenflusses. Diese "generische Applikation" wird dann zur Lösung eines konkreten Problems zu einem spezifischen System verfeinert, indem an dafür vorgesehenen Stellen Subklassen abstrakter Klassen gebildet und dort Methoden (die in den vorgegebenen Klassen (abstrakt) definiert sind) überschrieben werden.

Diese Technologie wenden wir für unsere "Problemfamilie", die Integration verschiedener, autonomer DBS in ein HDBS, an und realisieren die Homogenisierungsschicht als Framework, dem "Integration Framework" oder *Integrationsrahmen*[2]. Dieser bietet als Schnittstelle für den globalen Anwender das objektorientierte gDM in Form einer Klassenhierarchie an, in der die generischen Operationen (der DML) als Methoden definiert sind. Benutzerklassen (des föderierten Schemas) werden als Subklassen in diese vorgegebene Hierarchie eingehängt (vgl. Kapitel 3) und erben so die generischen Operationen.

Der Integrationsrahmen enthält eine vorgefertigte Implementierung des gDM (der generischen Operationen), die auf einer abstrakten Schnittstelle zu den lokalen Systemen basiert, welche durch sogenannte *"Kopplungsklassen"* mit abstrakten Methoden beschrieben ist. Solche abstrakte, von der Implementierung benutzte Methoden (*"Primitive"*) iterieren beispielsweise über die Extension einer (lokalen) Klasse, transformieren eine lokale Dateneinheit in den Wert eines globalen Objekts (oder umgekehrt) oder liefern einen Identifikator für ein lokales Objekt, auf dem innerhalb des Integrationsrahmens die Realisierung einer globalen Objektidentität aufgebaut werden kann. Die Integration eines lokalen DBS entspricht der Bildung von geeigneten Subklassen der Kopplungsklassen, in denen eine Implementierung der Primitive bereitgestellt werden muß. Die auf diese Weise realisierte Kopplung gilt für alle Klassen des zu diesem lokalen DBS gehörigen Komponentenschemas. Über diese "generische" Kopplung hinaus bietet der Integrationsrahmen auch die Möglichkeit der *klassenspezifischen* Kopplung. Durch erneute Subklassenbildung können die Primitive nochmals individuell für jede Klasse des föderierten Schemas überschrieben werden. Dies ist zum einen notwendig, falls die Kopplung (bzw. Teile davon) nicht oder nur sehr schwierig generisch für ein gesamtes lokales System gestaltet werden kann. Auf der anderen Seite bietet sich hier die Möglichkeit, für einzelne Klassen eine von der "Standardintegration" (evtl. nur in wenigen Aspekten) abweichende Einbindung in das HDBS zu verwirklichen.

Insgesamt stellt der Integrationsrahmen erhebliche Unterstützung für die Integration eines lokalen Systems bereit, da der DBI "lediglich" einige Primitive implementieren muß. Im übrigen kann er natürlich auch von Software, die bei bereits durchgeführten Kopplungen anderer Systeme erstellt wurde, profitieren. Er muß also genau den für "sein" System spezifischen Teil der Kopplung implementieren. Außerdem bietet der Integrationsrahmen mit der klassenspezifischen Kopplung sehr hohe Flexibilität.

3 Realisierung von Objektidentität in HDBS durch Einführung von Integrationsalternativen

Die Verwendung eines objektorientierten Datenmodells als gDM wirft für den DBI das in der Einleitung bereits angedeutete Problem auf, daß für ein im gDM angebotenes Konzept oftmals kein (geeignetes) Gegenstück im lokalen System existiert. Der DBI ist für die Realisierung (globaler) Objektidentität letztlich (d.h. auch wenn auf globaler Ebene teilweise nachgebessert werden kann) auf Leistungen (Dienste) der lokalen Systeme angewiesen.

Die Diskussion dieses Problems und die Vorstellung der in ZOO_{IFI} entwickelten Lösung ist Gegenstand dieses Kapitels. Wir führen dazu zunächst in die Problematik der Objektidentität in HDBS ein und arbeiten dann die in ZOO_{IFI} angewandte Lösung heraus, mehrere Integrationsalternativen anzubieten und hierzu die Verwendbarkeit von Klassen (bzw. deren Instanzen) im Schema spezifizierbar zu machen. Nach einer Betrachtung, wie die Anforderungen der einzelnen Alternativen an die lokalen Systeme (bzw. Typen) befriedigt werden können, werden weitere Anwendungen der Spezifikation der Verwendbarkeit von Klassen in ZOO_{IFI} dargestellt.

3.1 Das Problem der Objektidentität in HDBS

Objektidentität [Khos86] ist die Eigenschaft, die ein Objekt von allen anderen Objekten unterscheidet und unabhängig ist vom aktuellen Zustand des Objektes. Änderungen im Zustand eines Objekts ergeben somit immer dasselbe Objekt. Objektidentität beruht (zumindest konzeptionell) auf einem systemvergebenen, unveränderbaren Schlüssel, dem sogenannten *Surrogat*, das eine eindeutige Identifizierbarkeit aller Objekte im System ermöglicht. Ob das

[2] Eine umfassende Beschreibung des Integrationsrahmens ist nicht Gegenstand dieses Papiers; siehe hierzu [Härt92b]. Dort wird auch die Einbettung des gDM in und die Realisierung des Integrationsrahmens mit C++ beschrieben.

Surrogat für den Anwender sichtbar ist oder nur systemintern benutzt wird, wird in existierenden objektorientierten DBS unterschiedlich gehandhabt.

Objektidentität ist ein zentrales Konzept objektorientierter DBS ([Atki89], [Khos86]), das u.a. als Grundlage für Assoziationen dient, die Semantik von Änderungsoperationen definiert, Gleichheit und Identität zweier Objekte unterscheidbar macht etc. Um Objektidentität an der (objektorientierten) globalen Schnittstelle eines HDBS zu verwirklichen, muß jedes globale Objekt go, das eine lokale Dateneinheit lo repräsentiert, (konzeptuell) ein Surrogat oid_{global} besitzen. Nun kann in einem HDBS dieses Surrogat nicht wie in einem homogenen DBS *bei der Generierung* von go ("ein für alle mal") zugewiesen (und z.B. mit der physischen Repräsentation von go gespeichert) werden, da diese im lokalen System erfolgt. Vielmehr muß jedesmal, wenn (innerhalb derselben oder verschiedenen Sitzungen) eine bestimmte lokale Dateneinheit lo über die globale Schnittstelle zugegriffen wird, dasselbe globale Objekt go mit Surrogat oid_{global} aktiviert werden. Umgekehrt muß bei gegebenem globalen Objekt go (bzw. oid_{global}) das zugehörige lokale Objekt lo eindeutig lokalisierbar sein (über einen geeigneten Identifikator id_{local}). Dies wird z.B. notwendig, wenn go auf globaler Ebene referenziert oder als Unterobjekt benutzt wird (vgl. Kapitel 2.1). Insgesamt muß also das HDBS eine bidirektionale Abbildung zwischen globalen Surrogaten und lokalen Identifikatoren halten (vgl. auch [Elia91]). Der Identifikationsmechanismus des lokalen Systems muß dabei eine "sichere" Identifikation der lokalen Daten über deren gesamte Lebensdauer gewährleisten, was letztlich ein *extern sichtbares* Surrogat erfordert (das Konzept der Objektidentität allein genügt nicht!). Dabei ist es ausreichend, ein Surrogat zu haben, welches innerhalb eines Typs (Datenbasis) eindeutig ist. Die systemweite Eindeutigkeit kann dann innerhalb des HDBS sichergestellt werden (z.B. durch geeignete Konkatenation einer Typ-/Datenbasisidentifikation).

Der überwiegende Teil von existierenden Datenbanksystemen erfüllt diese Bedingung nicht. In der Literatur beschriebene Lösungsvorschläge gehen dieses Problem in zweierlei Weise an. Ein Teil der Ansätze versucht, den lokal vorhandenen Identifikationsmechanismus zu einem Surrogatmechanismus "aufzuwerten" (siehe z.B. [Elia91]), indem man z.B. davon ausgeht, daß das lokale System Änderungen eines wertbasierten Identifikationsschlüssels an das HDBS meldet (vgl. auch Kapitel 3.3). Während hier im gDM Objektidentität im strengen Sinne beibehalten wird, wird sie in anderen Ansätzen gelockert (siehe z.B. [Bert89]). Meist ist dabei Objektidentität nur während der Dauer einer Sitzung gewährleistet und Daten im lokalen System müssen auch nur während dieser Zeit eindeutig identifizierbar sein; man spricht auch von "session object identifiers". In diesem Fall müssen Abstriche bei der im gDM verfügbaren Funktionalität in Kauf genommen werden (z.B. können keine neuen permanenten Assoziationen verwaltet werden). In beiden Fällen ist als gravierender Nachteil zu vermerken, daß viele gängige DBS nicht integrierbar sind, deren Zahl besonders im ersten Fall erheblich ist.

3.2 Spezifikation der Verwendbarkeit von Klassen

Die vorangehende Diskussion hat das Dilemma aufgezeigt, daß man entweder Abstriche hinsichtlich der global verfügbaren Datenbankfunktionalität hinnehmen muß oder nicht alle DBS integrieren kann. Als Ausweg schlagen wir vor, verschiedene Alternativen für die Integration lokaler Systeme in das HDBS einzubauen. Dazu "kategorisieren" wir die (mit der Objektidentität zusammenhängende) Funktionalität des gDM nach den Anforderungen an die Identifizierung der lokalen Dateneinheiten. Jede der auf diese Weise entstehenden Integrationsalternativen ist somit gekennzeichnet durch

- die Datenbankfunktionalität, die an der globalen Schnittstelle in dieser Alternative zur Verfügung steht (Sicht des globalen Anwenders), und
- die Anforderungen, die hinsichtlich der (eindeutigen) Identifizierung von Daten im lokalen System bestehen (Sicht des DBI).

Diese Alternativen spiegeln das Wechselspiel wider zwischen der Unterstützung seitens des lokalen Systems und der im HDBS realisierbaren Funktionalität des gDM. Die Identifizierbarkeit lokaler Daten hängt allerdings nicht immer nur vom lokalen System, sondern oftmals auch von deren lokalen Typ ab. Deshalb muß in ZOO_{IFI} (wie bereits in Kapitel 2.3 angedeutet) eine Integrationsalternative nicht unbedingt für ein gesamtes lokales System festgelegt werden, sondern kann individuell für jeden lokalen Typ (bzw. dessen globaler Repräsentation) gewählt werden.

In ZOO_{IFI} bieten wir drei Alternativen an. Sie orientieren sich nicht in erster Linie an den verschiedenen Identifizierungs*mechanismen* (Surrogat, wertbasierter Schlüssel, etc.), sondern an der *Dauer*, für die (für den Integrationsrahmen) eine eindeutige Identifizierung einer lokalen Dateneinheit gewährleistet ist. Dieses Kriterium resultiert gerade aus den Anforderungen, die bei der Realisierung des objektorientierten gDM (auf Basis der Funktionalität der lokalen Systeme) entstehen. Die Alternativen sind:

A. Permanente Objektidentifikation

B. Temporäre Objektidentifikation

C. Imaginäre Objektidentifikation

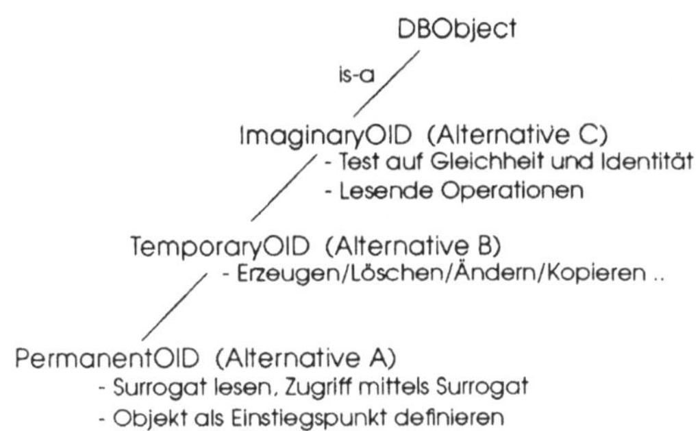

Bild 1. Vorgegebene Klassenhierarchie (mit generischen Operationen) zur Spezifikation der Verwendbarkeit von Klassen

Wir charakterisieren zunächst die jeweiligen Anforderungen an das lokale System (bzw. Typ), um dann die in den Alternativen an der globalen Schnittstelle verwendbare Datenbankfunktionalität zu beschreiben. Alternative A verlangt, daß eine lokale Dateneinheit dauerhaft eindeutig lokalisierbar ist. In anderen Worten, der Zusammenhang zwischen globalem Objekt (bzw. dessen Surrogat) und dem lokal gespeicherten Datum, das es repräsentiert, muß (wie im vorigen Kapitel beschrieben) für die gesamte Lebensdauer des Objekts im HDBS (ab dem Zeitpunkt seiner ersten Aktivierung an der globalen Schnittstelle) gewährleistet sein. Dagegen muß in Alternative B dieser Zusammenhang nur solange bestehen, wie das Objekt aktiv ist (d.h. an der globalen Schnittstelle für den Anwender zur Verfügung steht; vgl. Kapitel 2.1). In der dritten Alternative (C) schließlich braucht nach der "Erstellung" des globalen Objekts aus der lokalen Dateneinheit letztere nicht mehr lokalisierbar sein.

Die starke Forderung von Alternative A an die lokalen Systeme (bzw. Typen) ergibt sich genau dann, wenn auch auf *globaler* Ebene eine dauerhafte (ein Programm überdauernde) Identifizierung eines Objekts benötigt wird. Dies ist der Fall, wenn das Surrogat für den globalen Anwender extern verfügbar gemacht wird (d.h. durch eine entsprechende Operation gelesen werden kann), wenn ein Objekt als Einstiegspunkt verwendbar sein oder in einer Assoziation mit einer Anreicherungsklasse teilnehmen soll (als Unterobjekt oder Ziel einer Referenz einer Anreicherungsklasse).

Alternative B wurde im Hinblick auf Operationen eingeführt, die Modifikationen in der lokalen Datenbasis bewirken. Um nämlich in einem (aktiven) globalen Objekt vorgenommene Änderungen auch im lokalen Gegenstück nachvollziehen zu können[3], muß letzteres lokalisierbar sein, während das globale Objekt aktiv ist. Da eine lokale Dateneinheit erst einmal als globales Objekt aktiviert sein muß, damit die Löschoperation dafür aufgerufen werden kann, erzwingt analog auch die Realisierung dieser Operation die Lokalisierbarkeit lokaler Objekte, solange ihre globalen Repräsentationen aktiv sind.

In der Alternative C, bei der der Zusammenhang zwischen lokaler Dateneinheit und globalem Objekt sofort nach der Aktivierung verlorengeht (verlorengehen kann), sind nur lesende Zugriffe erlaubt. Es ist zu beachten, daß (aus der Sicht des globalen Anwenders) in dieser Alternative bei jeder Aktivierung eines lokalen Objektes ein "neues" globales Objekt mit (konzeptionell) neuem Surrogat entsteht. Während deshalb in den ersten beiden Alternativen die Operation zum Test auf Identität zweier Objekte immer den boolschen Wert "true" liefert, falls sie auf zwei Objekte angewandt wird, die *dieselbe* lokale (evtl. "mehrfach aktivierte") Dateneinheit repräsentieren, wird die Operation "false" als Ergebnis haben, wenn "dieselbe" lokale Dateneinheit mehrfach aktiviert wird. Im Falle der temporären Objektidentifikation wird das korrekte Ergebnis der Operation u.a. dadurch sichergestellt, daß man auf der globalen Ebene dem Anwender keine Möglichkeit gibt, sich die Identität eines Objekts über die Aktivierung hinaus zu "merken" (direkt über das Surrogat, als Einstiegspunkt, durch eine Referenz etc.) und dann z.B. in einer späteren Sitzung in einem Identitätsvergleich zu verwenden. Dies ist nur in der Alternative mit permanenter Objektidentifikation möglich.

Zur Vermeidung von Mißverständnissen sei darauf hingewiesen, daß die starken Anforderungen der ersten Alternative (A) nur von Klassen erfüllt werden müssen, die an Assoziationen mit Anreicherungsklassen (vgl. Kapitel 2.2) teilnehmen. Dagegen können in Assoziationen *innerhalb eines Komponentenschemas* auch beliebige Klassen parti-

[3] Wie dies genau geschieht, ist wiederum i.w. eine Frage der Einbettung des gDM in die Wirtssprache. Wir gehen im weiteren der Einfachheit halber davon aus, daß Änderungen eines globalen Objekts als Ganzes (auf explizite Anforderung des Anwenders oder implizit bei Transaktionsende) im lokalen System nachvollzogen werden.

```
CLASS Employee
INHERITS PermanentOID
RESTRICTIONS NO_CREATE NO_DELETE
PUBLIC
    name : string (30);
    METHOD Number_of_children () : integer;
    METHOD RaiseSalary (amount : integer) : void;
    colleagues : SET ( REF(Employee) );
    ...
PRIVATE
    salary : integer;
    children : LIST (Kids); /* Komponentenobjekte */
    ...
END Employee
```

Bild 2. Beispiel für eine Klassendefinition mit Spezifikation ihrer Verwendbarkeit

zipieren, die nach einer der Alternativen B oder C integriert wurden, denn solche Assoziationen repräsentieren lokale Strukturen, die auch innerhalb des lokalen Systems verwaltet werden.

Die Festlegung einer Alternative für eine globale Klasse erfolgt auf folgende Weise. Im gDM werden die verschiedenen Alternativen dargestellt, indem man jede in Form einer Klasse repräsentiert und diese wie in Bild 2 gezeigt in einer (strengen) Hierarchie anordnet. Jede solche Klasse definiert die generischen Operationen als Methoden[4], die zusätzlich zu den bereits ererbten in dieser Alternative erlaubt sind. Obwohl für das bloße Generieren eines Objektes nicht die Anforderungen der zweiten Alternative an lokale Systeme erhoben werden müssen, siedeln wir aus "Symmetriegründen" diese Operation bei TemporaryOID an. Jede benutzerdefinierte Klasse wird (direkt oder indirekt) in diese vorgegebene Hierarchie eingehängt und auf diese Weise wird die *Verwendbarkeit* jeder Klasse (individuell) spezifiziert (Bild 1 zeigt ein Beispiel; die darin enthaltene RESTRICTIONS-Klausel wird später erläutert). Zum einen können nur die ererbten generischen Operationen auf die Klasse bzw. ihre Instanzen angewandt werden, d.h. daß z.B. nur solche Objekte gelöscht, geändert etc. werden können, deren Klassen von TemporaryOID erben. Zum anderen dürfen nur solche Klassen in Assoziationen mit Anreicherungsklassen teilhaben, die PermanentOID als Oberklasse besitzen. Dies wird nicht nur im föderierten Schema, sondern auch zur Übersetzungszeit in Anwendungsprogrammen und Methoden durch Typprüfungen bei den Aufrufen der generischen Operationen gewährleistet.

Die beschriebene Idee zur Lösung der Problematik von Objektidentität in HDBS ist also zusammenfassend dadurch charakterisiert, daß sie Objektidentität für alle Objekte verwirklicht, aber (für eine globale Klasse) nur diejenige auf Objektidentität basierende Datenbankfunktionalität für den globalen Anwender sichtbar macht, die auf dem konkreten lokalen System (bzw. Typ) im Rahmen des HDBS realisierbar ist. Im Unterschied zu anderen Ansätzen sind also mehrere Alternativen für die Integration lokaler DBS in ZOO_{IFI} eingebaut sind, die ein breites Spektrum lokaler Systeme zu integrieren gestatten.

3.3 Identifizierbarkeit von Daten in lokalen Systemen

Bislang haben wir einen dritten Aspekt der im vorigen Unterkapitel erläuterten Integrationsalternativen übergangen, nämlich die Erfüllbarkeit der an die lokalen DBS (bzw. Typen) gestellten Anforderungen hinsichtlich der Identifizierbarkeit der lokalen Dateneinheiten (d.h. in welche Alternative reihen sich gängige DBS ein?). Prinzipiell ist hier zu diskutieren, welche lokalen Systeme die Anforderungen einer Alternative "direkt" befriedigen und welche Nachbesserungen ggf. im Rahmen der Integrationssoftware durch den DBI vorgenommen werden können.

Bei der Repräsentation eines lokalen Typs durch eine Klasse mit imaginärer Objektidentifikation bestehen offensichtlich keine Anforderungen an die Lokalisierung einzelner Instanzen des lokalen Typs. Insbesondere können deshalb auch z.B. Typen integriert werden, deren Instanzen nicht materialisiert sind. Dies ist etwa der Fall, wenn das lokale Schema ein externes Schema (view) eines DBS ist oder es sich bei dem lokalen System um kein Datenhaltungssystem, sondern etwa um ein "beliebiges" Programm handelt, und der lokale Typ gerade dessen dynamisch berechnetes Ergebnis beschreibt.

Auf den ersten Blick mag die Beobachtung erstaunen, daß objektorientierte DBS, die das Konzept der Objektidentität unterstützen, meist nicht den Forderungen der Alternative A genügen, die permanente Objektidentifikation an der globalen Schnittstelle verwirklicht. Dies liegt einfach daran, daß sie das (intern vorhandene) Surrogat von Ob-

[4] Aus Gründen der Übersichtlichkeit unterscheiden wir in der Hierarchie in Bild 2 nicht zwischen Methoden, die für Objekte und solchen, die für Klassen aufgerufen werden.

jekten nicht extern verfügbar machen. Meist erlauben diese Systeme eine sichere Identifikation ihrer Objekte, solange man in Form von Variablen eines Anwendungsprogramms (die Integrationssoftware ist ein solches!) einen "handle" für ein Objekt besitzt. Hier handelt es sich um die bereits erwähnten "session object identifiers" [Bert89], [Elia91]. Damit erfüllen sie die Anforderungen der oben erläuterten zweiten Alternative, sofern die Integrationssoftware (DBI) dafür sorgt, daß ein solcher "handle" gehalten wird, solange ein Objekt an der globalen Schnittstelle aktiv ist. Auch lokale Typen, die einen identifizierenden (wertbasierten) Schlüssel für ihre Instanzen definieren, lassen sich mit dieser Alternative integrieren, wenn die Integrationssoftware in Zusammenarbeit mit dem lokalen System eine Änderung dieses Schlüssels verhindern kann, solange die zugehörigen globalen Objekte aktiv sind. Hierfür bietet sich der Rückgriff auf die Isolationseigenschaft von Transaktionen an (falls im lokalen System verfügbar). Indem man nämlich die Transaktion (auf dem lokalen System), in der die lokale Instanz gelesen wurde, erst wieder nach der Inaktivierung des zugehörigen globalen Objekts beendet, sorgt man dafür, daß der identifizierende Schlüssel nicht verändert wird. Alternativ können auch andere Konzepte verwendet werden, die eine Änderung der identifizierenden Attribute über einen bestimmten Zeitraum ausschließen (z.B. Schutzkonzepte, explizite Sperren).

Die schärfste Anforderung nach unveränderbaren Schlüsseln (Alternative A) wird unmittelbar nur von DBS erfüllt, die ein Surrogat extern zur Verfügung stellen (z.B. DAMOKLES [Ditt87] oder XSQL [Hask82]). Allerdings kann man auch lokale Typen in dieser Alternative integrieren, die einen aufgrund seiner "Semantik" unveränderlichen, wertbasierten Schlüssel besitzen (z.B. eine AHV-Nummer (Schweizer Version einer Sozialversicherungsnummer)). Dies zu entscheiden, ist Aufgabe des DBI.

Darüberhinaus ist es auch möglich, durch geeignete zusätzliche Maßnahmen im Rahmen der Integrationssoftware auf Basis veränderlicher (aber eindeutiger) Schlüssel eine sichere Identifizierung lokaler Dateneinheiten zu erreichen. Dazu muß das HDBS über Änderungen eben dieser Schlüssel auf dem laufenden gehalten werden. [Elia91] schlägt hierfür vor, ein spezielles "update log" für lokale Typen, die global zur Verfügung gestellt werden, im lokalen System zu führen und dem HDBS zugänglich zu machen oder dem HDBS Zugriff auf das normale Transaktions-Log zu gewähren. Auch aktive Mechanismen [Kotz88] können - sofern im lokalen System vorhanden - für diesen Zweck genutzt werden.

Eine weitere Idee besteht darin, für jeden lokalen Typ, der nach Alternative A integriert werden soll, aber hierfür keine ausreichende Unterstützung bietet, einen zusätzlichen Typ im lokalen (!) System anzulegen, der eine Indirektionstabelle realisiert (Bild 3). Diese enthält für jede (jemals global aktivierte) Instanz des betreffenden lokalen Typs einen Eintrag, der sich aus einem eindeutigen, unveränderlichen Identifikator (der dann vom HDBS benutzt wird) und einem "Verweis" auf die lokale Instanz zusammensetzt. Die "Kunst" besteht nun darin, diesen Verweis aktuell zu halten. Dazu ist man wiederum auf Dienste des lokalen Systems angewiesen. Bei relationalen DBS greift man hierzu auf die referentielle Integrität zurück (falls sie im konkreten DBS unterstützt wird). Die Indirektionstabelle entspricht hier (Bild 3a) einer zusätzlichen Relation (RR), die den erwähnten Verweis als Fremdschlüssel (R#) implementiert, für den referentielle Integrität verlangt wird (REFERENCES R). Ändert sich der Primärschlüssel einer lokalen Dateneinheit (Tupel aus R), wird der Fremdschlüssel automatisch nachgeführt (ON UPDATE CASCADE); bei einem Löschvorgang wird der Fremdschlüssel auf NULL gesetzt. Die gleichen Maßnahmen lassen sich auch durch einen aktiven Mechanismus verwirklichen. In objektorientierten DBS (ohne extern verfügbares Surrogat) wird die Indirektionstabelle als (lokale) Klasse definiert (Bild 3b), in der der Verweis abhängig vom lokalen Datenmodell als Referenz (local_object) o.ä. realisiert wird. In beiden Fällen implementiert die Indirektionstabelle ein extern sichtbares, "lokales Surrogat", das von ZOO_{IFI} zur Realisierung der Alternative A herangezogen wird. Beidesmal ist es auch charakteristisch, daß nur durch eine *im lokalen System* angelegte Tabelle das die Aktualität (des Verweises) garantierende lokale Konzept (referentielle Integrität bzw. Objektidentität) ausgenutzt werden kann. Die Verwaltung

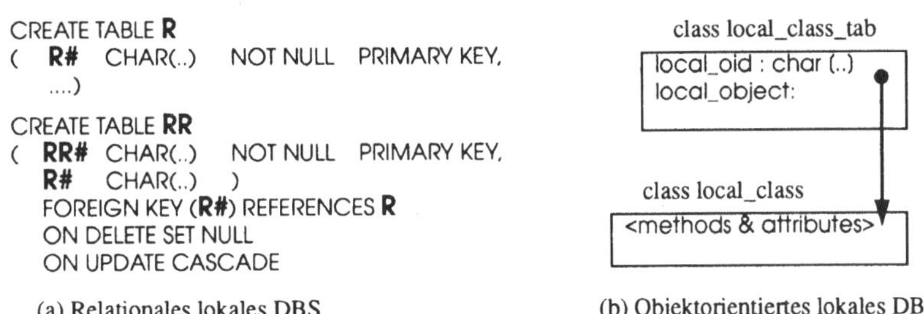

(a) Relationales lokales DBS

(b) Objektorientiertes lokales DBS

Bild 3. Identifikation lokaler Daten über eine Indirektionstabelle

der Tabelle (Einfügen von Elementen, Ausnutzung zur Identifikation lokaler Daten etc.) ist Teil der Integrationssoftware und Aufgabe des DBI.

Die vorstehende Diskussion hat gezeigt, daß eine *klassenspezifische* Wahl der Integrationsalternative dringend erforderlich ist, da oftmals die Erfüllbarkeit von Anforderungen an die Identifizierbarkeit von Daten von deren (lokalem) Typ abhängt (z.B. müssen nicht alle lokale Typen überhaupt einen identifizierenden Schlüssel besitzen). Ferner ist deutlich geworden, daß man im Rahmen der Integrationssoftware durch zusätzliche Maßnahmen eine "höherwertige" Integrationsalternative erreichen kann als die durch das lokale System unmittelbar unterstützte, um dadurch mehr Funktionalität an der globalen Schnittstelle anbieten zu können. Zwar ist damit meist auch eine Beeinträchtigung der Autonomie des lokalen Systems verbunden, die jedoch keinen Eingriff in dessen Software mit sich bringt, sondern lediglich dessen Schnittstelle ausnutzt, und daher durchaus tolerabel sein kann.

Gerade die "Zusatzmaßnahmen" zur Realisierung einer höherwertigen Alternative betreffen viele Stellen in der Integrationssoftware (man denke z.B. an die oben erläuterte Indirektionstabelle). Diese Beobachtung unterstreicht die Bedeutung (Vorteile!) des Integrationsrahmen-Ansatzes in ZOO_{IFI}. Dort können diese Maßnahmen bereits durch vorgefertigte Software basierend auf geeigneten Primitiven (vgl. Kapitel 2.3) (vor-)implementiert werden. Der DBI benötigt dann nicht eine vollständige Kenntnis des Aufbaus der Integrationssoftware und wird insbesondere von der Betrachtung des Kontrollflusses entlastet; er muß lediglich die Primitive überschreiben und braucht sich nicht mehr darum zu kümmern, wo diese in der Integrationssoftware aufgerufen werden müssen und wie sie zusammenwirken. Eine Realisierung der obigen Maßnahmen durch vom DBI vorgenommene *Änderungen* in der Integrationssoftware (im Unterschied zu deren Ergänzung) wäre nicht akzeptabel.

3.4 Weitere Anwendungen der Spezifikation der Verwendbarkeit von Klassen in ZOO_{IFI}

Über die Problematik der Objektidentität hinaus gibt es weitere Gesichtspunkte, die in einem HDBS Einfluß auf die Verwendbarkeit von Klassen bzw. deren Instanzen haben. Aufgrund der Autonomie der lokalen Systeme können diese Einschränkungen für den Zugriff auf ihre Daten durch das HDBS verfügen, die auf globaler Ebene ausdrückbar sein müssen. Dies ist umso wichtiger, wenn das lokale System keine oder unzulängliche Mittel zur Durchsetzung dieser Einschränkungen besitzt. Auf der anderen Seite ist es aber ebensogut möglich, daß an der Schnittstelle des HDBS auf bestimmten (lokalen) Daten nicht die gesamte Funktionalität des gDM benötigt wird. Kann dies an der globalen Schnittstelle spezifiziert (und durchgesetzt) werden, läßt sich der Aufwand (des DBI) für die Integration der entsprechenden lokalen Typen (Systeme) erheblich reduzieren, da die nicht benötigte Funktionalität nicht zu realisiert werden braucht - vorausgesetzt die Architektur des HDBS sieht wie in ZOO_{IFI} geeignete Möglichkeiten hierfür vor. Darauf werden wir nochmals zurückkommen.

In einem konkreten Fall muß also nicht unbedingt die "maximale" Integrationsalternative für eine Klasse (die basierend auf dem lokalen System bzw. des lokalen Typs prinzipiell realisierbar wäre) gewählt werden. Zudem erlauben wir in ZOO_{IFI}, daß bestimmte ererbte generische Operationen (Erzeugen, Löschen und Ändern von Objekten) für ein Klasse explizit verboten werden können. Dies wird notwendig, wenn man aus einem der eben geschilderten Gründe einzelne Operationen nicht anbieten möchte oder wenn man z.B. Objekte zwar global permanent referenzieren, aber keine Änderungen in der lokalen Datenbasis zulassen möchte. Im Beispiel aus Bild 2 (RESTRICTIONS-Klausel) können Instanzen der Klasse Employee über das gDM nicht gelöscht oder eingefügt, wohl aber geändert werden.

An dieser Stelle soll nochmals die Wichtigkeit der klassen*individuellen* Integration (und damit verbundenen Spezifikation der Verwendbarkeit) betont werden. Zum einen ist es meist nicht nur vom lokalen System, sondern auch vom konkreten lokalen Typ abhängig, welche Integrationsalternative unterstützt werden kann (so daß ohne die Möglichkeit der klassenspezifischen Integration für alle Klassen eines Komponentenschemas die "minimale", d.h. für alle Klassen realisierbare Alternative gewählt werden müßte). Dies ist etwa der Fall, wenn nicht alle lokalen Typen überhaupt über einen eindeutigen Schlüssel verfügen oder wenn die Unveränderbarkeit eines wertbasierten Schlüssels nur für wenige Typen garantiert ist. Zum anderen möchte man auch den in 3.3 beschriebenen Zusatzaufwand bei der Nachbesserung im Rahmen der Integrationssoftware nur betreiben, falls das aus globaler Sicht auch wirklich notwendig ist. So ist es oftmals ausreichend, Objekte bestimmter Klassen als Einstiegspunkte definieren zu können oder in Assoziationen teilhaben zu lassen (da z.B. die weitere Navigation ausschließlich innerhalb eines Komponentenschemas erfolgt) und eben nur für diese Klassen den notwendigen Zusatzaufwand für die permanente Objektidentifikation zu investieren. Die Wahl einer geeigneten Integrationsalternative kann als Teil eines "Datenbankentwurfs für das HDBS" angesehen werden.

Die Spezifikation der Verwendbarkeit von Klassen wird im Integrationsrahmen von ZOO_{IFI} bei der Realisierung der Kopplungssoftware für ein lokales System (durch den DBI) in der folgenden Weise ausgenutzt. Ausgehend von einer solchen Spezifikation läßt sich bestimmen, welche Primitive (vgl. Kapitel 2.3) vom DBI zu überschreiben sind, um die von globalen Anwendern (überhaupt) benutzbare Funktionalität auf Basis des lokalen Systems zu realisieren.

Wir wollen nochmals ins Gedächtnis rufen, daß hierbei einzelne Aspekte einer generischen (d.h. für ein gesamtes lokales System realisierten) Kopplung für einzelne Klassen überschrieben bzw. erweitert werden kann. Beispielsweise kann eine Klasse, für die im Gegensatz zu den anderen Klassen eines Komponentenschemas permanente Objektidentifikation verwirklicht werden soll, die (generischen) Transformationen zwischen lokalem Datenmodell und gDM, die deskriptive Suche in der Extension einer Klasse etc. von der "Standardkopplung" erben, muß aber im Rahmen einer geeigneten Subklasse im Integrationsrahmen weitere Methoden überschreiben (z.B. eine, die den (lokalen) identifizierenden Schlüssel liefert). Insgesamt wird durch den Ansatz von ZOO_{IFI} erreicht, daß durch Vermeidung unnötiger Arbeiten genau der in einer konkreten Situation notwendige Aufwand für die Integration eines DBS in das HDBS investiert wird. Ferner kann der Zusammenhang zwischen der Definition einer Klasse im Komponentenschema und den hierfür zu realisierenden Primitiven als Anleitung für die Arbeit des DBI genutzt werden.

4 Zusammenfassung und Ausblick

Die Verwendung eines mächtigen Datenmodells als gDM eines HDBS kann zu dem Problem führen, daß nicht mehr die gesamte im gDM verfügbare Funktionalität auf allen (lokalen) Daten tatsächlich realisierbar ist. Wir haben dies in dem vorliegenden Papier für ein objektorientiertes gDM und das für das objektorientierte Paradigma zentrale Konzept der Objektidentität gezeigt, die von gängigen DBS in unterschiedlicher Weise unterstützt wird. Anschließend wurde die in ZOO_{IFI} verwendete Lösung dieses Problems beschrieben, die auf der Erkenntnis beruht, daß der Ausweg aus dem Dilemma, entweder viele Systeme nicht integrieren zu können oder Abstriche an den Konzepten des gDM zu machen, in der Bereitstellung verschiedener Integrationsalternativen liegt.

Jede der diskutierten Alternativen ist einerseits gekennzeichnet durch die Anforderungen, die sie an die (Dauer der) Identifizierbarkeit lokaler Dateneinheiten stellt, und andererseits durch die Datenbankfunktionalität, die dann an der globalen Schnittstelle benutzt werden kann. Indem man in diesem Sinne die Verwendbarkeit von Klassen spezifizierbar macht, kann man Objektidentität im gDM verankern, aber nur den Teil der auf diesem Konzept beruhenden Datenbankfunktionalität dem Anwender zugänglich machen, der jeweils auf dem betreffenden lokalen System (bzw. Typ) auch realisierbar ist. Der Preis für diese Vorteile besteht darin, daß das "glatte" objektorientierte gDM (Kapitel 2.1) um ein zusätzliches Konzept erweitert werden mußte.

Wie in vielen anderen Gebieten der neueren Datenbankforschung wird durch die Spezifikation der Verwendbarkeit von Klassen "mehr Semantik dem (H)DBS bekannt gemacht". Diese wird in ZOO_{IFI} ausgenutzt, um den Aufwand für die Integration eines lokalen Systems klein zu halten, indem das Schreiben unnötiger Kopplungssoftware für global nicht verwendete Funktionalität vermieden wird.

Der hierzu vorgeschlagene Integrationsrahmen wird momentan mit C++ und dem objektorientierten DBS ObjectStore implementiert. Zugleich arbeiten wir an einer Umgebung, die basierend auf dem Integrationsrahmen die Kopplung eines lokalen Systems unterstützt.

Literatur

[Atki89] Atkinson, M.; Bancilhon, F.; DeWitt, D.; Dittrich, K.; Maier, D.; Zdonik, S.: The Object-Oriented Database System Manifesto (A Political Pamphlet). Proc. DOOD 89, Kyoto/Japan, December 1989

[Bert89] Bertino, E. et al.: Integration of Heterogeneous Database Applications Through an Object-Oriented Interface. Information Systems, Vol. 14, No. 5, 1989

[Brig92] Bright, M.W.; Hurson, A.R.; Pakzad, S.H.: A Taxonomy and Current Issues in Multidatabase Systems. IEEE Computer, Volume 25, No. 3, March 1992

[Ditt87] Dittrich, K.R.; Gotthard, W.; Lockemann, P.C.: DAMOKLES - a Database System for Software Engineering. Lecture Notes in Computer Science, Vol. 244, Springer, 1987

[Elia91] Eliassen, F.; Karlsen, R.: Interoperability and Object Identity. SIGMOD Record, Vol. 20, No. 4, December 1991

[Härt92a] Härtig, M.: Das objektorientierte globale Datenmodell von ZOO_{IFI}. Technischer Bericht, Institut für Informatik der Universität Zürich, 1992.

[Härt92b] Härtig, M.; Dittrich, K.R.: An Object-Oriented Integration Framework for Building Heterogeneous Database Systems. Proc. IFIP DS-5 Conference on Semantics of Interoperable Database Systems, Lorne, Australia, Nov. 1992

[Hask82] Haskin, R.L.; Lorie, R.A.: On Extending the Functions of a Relational Database System. SIGMOD 82

[John88] Johnson, R.E.; Foote, B.: Designing Reusable Classes. Journal of Object-Oriented Programming, Vol.1, No. 2, 1988

[Kent91] Kent, W.: The Breakdown of the Information Model in Multi-Database Systems. SIGMOD RECORD, Vol. 20, No.4, December 1991

[Khos86] Khoshafian, S.N.; Copeland, G.P.: Object Identity. Proc. 1st OOPSLA Conf., 1986

[Kotz88] Kotz, A.; Dittrich, K.R.; Muelle, J.A: Supporting Semantic Rules by a Generalized Event/Trigger Mechanism. Proc. EDBT 88

[Salt91] Saltor, F.; Castellanos, M.; Garcia-Solaco, M.: Suitability of data models as canonical models for federated databases. SIGMOD Record, Vol. 20, No. 4, December 1991

[Shet90] Sheth, A.P.; Larson, J.A.: Federated Database Systems for Managing Distributed, Heterogeneous, and Autonomous Databases. ACM Computing Surveys, Special Issue on Heterogeneous Databases, Vol. 22, No. 3, September 1990

[Wirf90] Wirfs-Brock, R.J.; Wilkerson, B.; Wiener, L.: Designing Object-Oriented Software, Prentice-Hall, 1990

Zur Entwicklung eines klassenlosen Objekt-Modells

M. Groß-Hardt, G. Vossen
FB Mathematik, AG Informatik
Justus-Liebig-Universität Gießen
Arndtstraße 2
W-6300 Gießen

1 Einführung

Klassenlose Objekt-Modelle werden als Alternative zu klassen-basierten in prototypischen Programmiersprachen diskutiert. Wir motivieren, aus welchen Gründen derartige Modelle auch für bestimmte Datenbank-Anwendungen sinnvoll sind, und skizzieren ein spezielles klassenloses Modell sowie eine Deklarationssprache für dieses. Das Modell wird von uns als Grundlage für eine experimentelle Systementwicklung verwendet.

Das Paradigma der Objekt-Orientierung basiert generell auf folgenden fünf Prinzipien [3]:

1. Jede Entität der abzubildenden Realwelt wird als *Objekt* modelliert, welches eine eigenständige Existenz hat; letztere wird manifestiert mittels eines eindeutigen *Identifikators*, welcher vom Wert des Objekts verschieden ist.

2. Jedes Objekt *kapselt Struktur* und *Verhalten*; erstere wird beschrieben über Attribute, deren Werte zusammen den Zustand des Objekts darstellen und wiederum Objekte sein können (so daß komplexe Objekte via Aggregation modellierbar werden), letzteres besteht aus einer Menge von *Methoden*, d.h. Prozeduren, die auf dem Objekt ausführbar sind.

3. Der Zustand eines Objekts ist ausschließlich durch das Verschicken von *Nachrichten* (Messages) zugreifbar oder veränderbar, welche die Ausführung entsprechender Methoden veranlassen.

4. Objekte mit gemeinsamer Struktur und gemeinsamem Verhalten werden in *Klassen* zusammengefaßt; jedes Objekt ist Instanz einer Klasse.

5. Eine Klasse kann definiert werden als Spezialisierung einer oder mehrerer anderer Klassen und *erbt* in diesem Fall Struktur und Verhalten von diesen.

Dieses Paradigma hat in den letzten Jahren unter anderem im Datenbank-Bereich zunehmende Bedeutung erlangt; eine Reihe objekt-orientierter Datenbank-Systeme ist bereits kommerziell verfügbar. Diese Entwicklung wurde angestoßen durch die Erkenntnis, daß relationale Systeme speziell in technisch-wissenschaftlichen Anwendungen etwa im Hinblick auf adäquate Modellierung an ihre Grenzen stoßen. Man interessiert sich daher in zunehmendem Maße für *objekt-orientierte Datenmodelle* bzw. für *Objekt-Modelle*, wobei bisherige Vorschläge [1, 2, 6, 10, 11, 21] ausnahmslos auf dem Klassen-Konzept basieren. Speziell in Entwurfs-Umgebungen stellt sich jedoch heraus, daß die Flexibilität dieser Modelle noch immer eingeschränkt ist, und es wird seit einiger Zeit vermutet

[15, 18, 20], daß das Klassen-Konzept hierfür (mit-) verantwortlich ist. Dies legt die Entwicklung eines *klassenlosen* Objekt-Modells nahe.

In diesem Kurzbericht wollen wir zunächst in Abschnitt 2 genauer eingehen auf bisher unzureichend gelöste Aspekte bei der Modellierung von Objekten. Dies soll motivieren, warum die Beschäftigung mit einem klassenlosen Modell sinnvoll ist. Ein solches Modell wird sodann in Abschnitt 3 einführend skizziert, wobei wir uns hier auf den strukturellen Teil beschränken. In Abschnitt 4 deuten wir die zentralen Elemente einer Deklarationssprache für dieses Modell an, wobei wir uns auf die Erzeugung von Objekten und die Definition von *Kollektionen* beschränken. Abschnitt 5 gibt einen kurzen Überblick über den Stand unseres Projekts sowie einen Ausblick auf weitere Arbeiten.

2 Grenzen existierender Objekt-Modelle

Formale Datenmodelle für objekt-orientierte Datenbanken folgen in ihrem Aufbau meist der folgenden Linie [20]: Ausgehend von Basistypen lassen sich komplexe Typen bilden unter Anwendung von Konstruktoren wie "tuple", "set" oder "list"; die Zulassung von Klassennamen als Typen ermöglicht sodann die Bildung komplexer Aggregationen, in welchen Teil- oder Unterobjekte wiederverwendet werden können. Die Mächtigkeit eines solchen Modells wird im allgemeinen im Hinblick auf Nonstandard-Datenbank-Anwendungen (z. B. CAD, CASE, CIM) hin entworfen, jedoch bleibt praktisch immer der Nachweis aus, daß gerade diese Bereiche damit adäquat unterstützt werden. Dies liegt nach unserer Auffassung daran, daß bisherige Modell-Vorschläge eine Reihe wichtiger Aspekte meist nicht abdecken:

1. Entitäten können in mehreren Rollen gleichzeitig auftreten oder Rollen besitzen, welche sich im Laufe der Zeit verändern. Z. B. Kann eine Person zu einem Zeitpunkt ein Student, zu einem anderen ein Angestellter, oder eine Person kann diese und weitere Rollen gleichzeitig haben.

2. Objekte können sich in unterschiedlichen Entwicklungsstadien befinden. So ist es z. B. in einer Entwurfs-Anwendung wichtig, unvollständige Entwürfe zu speichern, also Objekte, deren Typ im Laufe der Zeit vervollständigt wird.

3. Klassen können "zu wenige" Instanzen besitzen. Will man etwa in einer Anwendung zahlreiche Einzeleigenschaften von individuellen Objekten als Unterscheidungsmerkmal verwenden, kann dies zu einer kombinatorischen Explosion der Anzahl zu verwendender Klassen-Namen [18] führen, wobei jede einzelne nur wenige Instanzen besitzt, und dies obwohl es ausreicht, die Methoden zu kennen, auf die ein Objekt reagieren kann.

4. Objekte und ihre Klassen können in "umgekehrter Reihenfolge" entstehen. Speziell in Entwurfs-Anwendungen "denken" Designer im allgemeinen nicht in Klassen, sondern in Objekten, und zwar ohne sich über Struktur- bzw. Verhaltens-Deklaration vollständig Klarheit verschafft zu haben.

Erste Ansätze zur Berücksichtigung dieser Aspekte in Objekt-Modellen werden bereits in der Literatur beschrieben [4, 9, 14, 15, 22]. Vielversprechend erscheint insbesondere der Verzicht auf ein Klassen-Konzept als zentrales Modellierungs-Konstrukt und die Einbeziehung von Konzepten prototypischer objekt-orientierter Programmiersprachen [12, 19], welche das Vererbungs-Konzept durch das Prinzip der Delegation ersetzen. Wir gehen als nächstes kurz auf die wesentlichen bisher gemachten Vorschläge ein; diese fallen im wesentlichen in zwei Kategorien:

Einerseits wird in einigen Vorschlägen der Aspekt veränderbarer oder multipler Typisierung sowie Objekt-Evolution behandelt. Die Auffassung, daß mehrfache, veränderliche Rollen typisch sind für Objekte mit langer Lebensdauer und daß Möglichkeiten, dies zu modellieren, für zukünftige

Informationssysteme wesentlich sein wird, steht etwa hinter den Entwurfs-Zielen des *Melampus*-Projekts bei IBM Almaden [4]. Das Datenmodell dieses Systems verwendet sogenannte *Aspekte* [14] zur Unterstützung von Typ-Veränderungen bei Objekten bzw. zur Modellierung von Objekten mit multiplen Typen. Ebenso erlaubt das Datenmodell des Systems Iris [22], Typen dynamisch anzunehmen oder zu verlieren. Ein weiterer Vorschlag zur Struktur-Veränderung von Objekten, welcher auf einem speziellen Sichten-Konzept basiert, findet sich im MORE-Datenmodell [17]. In [9] wird das Konzept der *OR-Objekte* eingeführt, welche es ermöglichen, unvollständige Spezifikationen zu modellieren, für die während eines Entwurfs-Prozesses noch Entscheidungen zu fällen sind.

Andererseits werden bereits Konzepte prototypischer Programmersprachen im Datenbank-Kontext berücksichtigt: In [15] werden Objekte der realen Welt in sogenannten *Objekt-Hierarchien* modelliert. Jedes Objekt in einer solchen Hierarchie beinhaltet gewisse Informationen über das Ganze und hat ein bestimmtes Verhalten; empfängt es eine Message, die es nicht versteht, so delegiert es diese an sein Vater-Objekt. Prototypische Programmiersprachen [12, 19] basieren generell auf der Idee, Anwendungen *ohne* eine Klassifikation zu modellieren, welche die Welt in Mengen von "zusammengehörige" Entitäten zerlegt. Ein Prototyp wird dort verstanden als ein "Default-Verhalten" für ein bestimmtes zu modellierendes Konzept, und neue Objekte können bereits vorhandenes Wissens wiederverwenden dadurch, daß sie angeben, wodurch sie sich von einem Prototypen unterscheiden. Die Untersuchung solcher *klassenloser* Modelle im Datenbank-Kontext erscheint angemessen insbesondere für Entwurfs-Umgebungen wie CAD oder CASE.

3 Struktur im klassenlosen Modell CLOOD

3.1 Einführung

Das CLOOD[1]-Modell ist gedacht als dediziertes Daten-Modell für Entwurfs-Anwendungen. Dementsprechend betonen wir in diesem Modell die Sicht, daß Objekte im Vordergrund der Betrachtung stehen (und nicht die Klassen, in denen sie in anderen Modellen als Instanzen enthalten sind). Objekte haben eine unabhängige Existenz (manifestiert durch einen eindeutigen Identifikator) und einen Wert; darüber hinaus sollen sie versionierbar sein und Methoden ausführen können, worauf wir jedoch hier nicht eingehen werden (Einzelheiten entnehme man [7]). Objekte stehen ferner miteinander in Beziehung (via Aggregation). Werte sind nach wie vor Elemente bestimmter Domains, welche wiederum durch Typen beschrieben werden (und Methoden sind Programme, deren Signatur sich ebenfalls dieser Typen bedient). Typen können hierarchisch angeordnet werden.

Während nun Objekt-Populationen in unserem Ansatz ohne Einschränkungen erzeugt werden können und existieren dürfen, ist für ein deklaratives Anfragen, wie man es sich für Datenbanken im allgemeinen wünscht, mehr nötig. Diesem Zweck dienen sogenannte *Kollektionen*, Mengen von Objekten, welche beliebig oder anhand vorgegebener Selektions-Bedingungen zusammengesetzt werden können. Kollektionen sind das Grundkonstrukt, an welches Anfragen zu richten sind.

Wir werden am Ende dieses Abschnitts andeuten, daß sich wenigstens auf der Ebene von Instanzen ein klassen-basierter Ansatz als Spezialfall unseres Konzeptes ergibt: Klassen (-Extensionen) sind Kollektionen mit der Eigenschaft, daß alle Elemente gleiche Struktur (und gleiches Verhalten) haben. Kollektionen, die unter Aggregation abgeschlossen sind, werden wir in Anlehnung an [5] *Konstellationen* nennen.

3.2 Objekte und Werte

Wir unterstellen die Verfügbarkeit folgender endlicher und paarweise disjunkter Mengen:

- Eine Vereinigung **D** unterschiedlicher Mengen atomarer Werte (integers, strings etc.),

[1]Class-Less Object-Oriented Data model

- eine Menge $\mathbf{A}$ von Attribut-Namen,
- eine Menge $\mathbf{O}$ von Objekt-Identifikatoren.

Für eine Teilmenge $O \subseteq \mathbf{O}$ definieren wir sodann eine Menge $V(O)$ von *Werten* über O wie folgt:

(i) $\mathbf{D} \subseteq V(O)$,

(ii) $O \subseteq V(O)$,

(iii) $\mathtt{nil} \in V(O)$,

(iv) gilt $v_1, \ldots, v_n \in V(O)$, $A_1, \ldots, A_n \in \mathbf{A}$ mit $A_i \neq A_j$ für $i \neq j$, $n \geq 1$, so ist $[A_1 : v_1, \ldots, A_n : v_n] \in V(O)$,

(v) gilt $v_1, \ldots, v_n \in V(O)$, so ist $\{v_1, \ldots, v_n\} \in V(O)$.

Wir beschränken uns momentan auf die Betrachtung von Tupel- und Mengen-Werten (neben den genannten Formen (i)–(iii) atomarer Werte). Das Universum aller Werte sei $\mathbf{V} := V(\mathbf{O})$.

Da Objekte Werte haben sollen, führen wir eine *Wert-Zuweisung* ein als Abbildung der Form

$$\text{val} : \mathbf{O} \rightarrow \mathbf{V};$$

und verlangen, daß jedes Objekt einer aktuell betrachteten Menge von Objekten einen Wert hat, der die entsprechende Werte-Menge respektiert:

$$(\forall\, O \subseteq \mathbf{O})\ (\forall\, o \in O)\ (\exists\, v \in V(O))\ \text{val}(o) = v \qquad (1)$$

Als laufendes Beispiel verwenden wir die folgende Menge von Objekten:

val(*john*) = [*name*: 'john smith', *age*: 35]
val(*mary*) = [*name*: 'mary price', *age*: 27, *children*: { *peter*, *laura* }]
val(*peter*) = [*name*: 'peter', *age*: 2, *favToy*: *bear*]
val(*bear*) = [*name*: 'balu', *owner*: *peter*]
val(*laura*) = [*name*: 'laura', *age*: 6, *favToy*: *puppet*]
val(*puppet*) = [*name*: 'henna', *owner*: *laura*]
val(*sam*) = [*name*: 'sam miller', *age*: 42, *job*: 'programmer',
worksFor: *ibm*, *salary*: 40.000]
val(*liza*) = [*name*: 'liza meier', *age*: 24, *major*: 'cs', *univ*: *nyu*, *gpa*: 2.4]
val(*ibm*) = [*cname*: 'ibm corp.', *headq*: 'ny', *employees*: { *sam* }]
val(*nyu*) = [*uname*: 'new york univ.', *loc*: 'manhattan', *students*: { *liza* }]

Wir unterstellen also die Verfügbarkeit der üblichen atomaren Werte; Objekt-Identifikatoren können vom Benutzer vergeben werden. Ferner nehmen wir o.B.d.A. an, daß jedes Objekt tupelwertig ist mit möglicherweise genesteten anderen Werten.

Wie das Beispiel bereits andeutet, können Objekte einander über *Aggregations-Links* referenzieren. Zur Präzisierung dessen seien $O \subseteq \mathbf{O}$, $o, o' \in O$. Wir schreiben dann $o \rightarrow o'$, falls der Wert von o ein Attribut A enthält, dessen Wert o' ist oder enthält. Mit $\rightarrow^*$ sei die transitive Hülle von $\rightarrow$ bezeichnet. In obigem Beispiel gilt etwa *mary* $\rightarrow$ *peter* $\leftrightarrow$ *bear*, *mary* $\rightarrow$ *laura* $\leftrightarrow$ *puppet*, *sam* $\leftrightarrow$ *ibm*, *liza* $\leftrightarrow$ *nyu*.

Im folgenden heiße eine Menge $O \subseteq \mathbf{O}$ *konsistent*, falls sie unter Aggregation abgeschlossen ist, d.h. $(\forall\, o \in O)\ o \rightarrow^* o' \implies o' \in O$. Jede des weiteren betrachtete Objekt-Menge soll in diesem Sinne konsistent sein.

Da wir oben vorausgesetzt haben, daß jedes Objekt tupelwertig ist, können wir von den Attributen eines Objekts sprechen; es bezeichne attr(o) die Menge aller Attribut-Namen, die auf oberster Nestungsstufe in val(o) vorkommen für jedes Objekt o. Im Beispiel ist also etwa attr(*john*) = { *name, age* }, attr(*ibm*) = { *cname, headq, employees* }

3.3 Typen und Domains

Werte in dem oben eingeführten Sinne können unsinnig sein, was wir ausschließen durch die Einführung von Typen sowie die Forderung, daß Werte "korrekt getypt" sind: Eine Menge $T(\mathbf{A})$ von *Typen* über einer gegebenen Menge $\mathbf{A}$ von Attribut-Namen wird wie folgt definiert:

(i) $B \subseteq T$, wobei B eine endliche Menge von Basistypen ist;

(ii) $\mathtt{oid} \in T$;

(iii) $\mathtt{none} \in T$;

(iv) sind A_i verschiedene Attribute aus $\mathbf{A}$ und $t_i \in T$, $1 \leq i \leq n$, so ist
$[A_1 : t_1, \ \ldots, \ A_n : t_n] \in T$;

(v) ist $t \in T$, so ist $\{t\} \in T$.

Wir schreiben auch T anstelle von $T(\mathbf{A})$, falls $\mathbf{A}$ unerheblich ist. Typen sollen wie üblich als Beschreibungen von Domains dienen; zu diesem Zweck definieren wir eine Abbildung dom wie folgt: Für $O \subseteq \mathbf{O}$ sei

$$\text{dom} : T(\mathbf{A}) \rightarrow 2^{V(O)}$$

rekursiv wie folgt definiert:

(i) $(\forall\, b \in B)\ (\exists!\ d \subseteq \mathbf{D})\ \text{dom}(b) = d$;

(ii) $\text{dom}(\mathtt{oid}) = O$;

(iii) $\text{dom}(\mathtt{none}) = \mathtt{nil}$;

(iv) $\text{dom}([A_1 : t_1, \ \ldots, \ A_n : t_n])$
$:= \{[A_1 : v_1, \ldots, A_n : v_n] \mid (\forall\, i, 1 \leq i \leq n)\ v_i \in \text{dom}(t_i)\}$;

(v) $\text{dom}(\{t\}) := \{\{v_1, \ \ldots, \ v_n\} \mid (\forall\, i, 1 \leq i \leq n)\ v_i \in \text{dom}(t)\}$.

Unsinnige Werte werden dann vermieden durch die folgende Forderung:

$$(\forall\, O \subseteq \mathbf{O})\ (\forall\, o \in O)\ (\exists!\ t \in T)\ \text{val}(o) \in \text{dom}(t) \qquad (2)$$

Diese Bedingung erlaubt es, vom *Typ eines Objekts* zu sprechen: Für $O \subseteq \mathbf{O}$ sei $o \in O$ ein Objekt mit Wert val(o). Dann existiert ein eindeutiger Typ $t \in T$ mit val(o) $\in$ dom(t); dieses t wird als der Typ von o festgelegt, d.h. type(o) $:= t$. Im Beispiel gilt etwa type(*john*) = [*name*: **string**, *age*: **int**]. In analoger Weise sprechen wir auch vom *Typ eines Attributs*, was mit type(A) für ein Attribut A bezeichnet wird. Es ist z. B. type(*name*) = **string** in Gegenwart des Typs [*name*: **string**, *age*: **int**]. Für einen gegebenen Typ $t \in T$ und eine Menge $O \subseteq \mathbf{O}$ können wir weiter von allen Objekten vom Typ t sprechen:

$$\text{objects}(t, O) := \{\ o \in O \mid \text{type}(o) = t\ \}$$

3.4 Subtypisierung

Wie die obigen Beispiele bereits zeigen, kann ein Objekt eine Spezialisierung eines anderen Objekts sein, insbesondere dann, wenn sein Typ detaillierter ist als der Typ des anderen Objekts. Dies erfassen wir durch eine Subtypen-Beziehung wie folgt: Sei T eine Menge von Typen. Eine Relation $\leq \subseteq T \times T$ sei wie folgt definiert:

(i) $t \leq t$ für jedes $t \in T$,

(ii) $[A_1 : t_1, \ldots, A_n : t_n] \leq [A'_1 : t'_1, \ldots, A'_m : t'_m]$, falls

  (a) $(\forall A'_j, 1 \leq j \leq m)(\exists A_i, 1 \leq i \leq n)\ A_i = A'_j \wedge t_i \leq t'_j$,

  (b) $n \geq m$,

(iii) $\{t\} \leq \{t'\}$, falls $t \leq t'$,

(iv) $t \leq$ **none** für alle $t \in T$.

"$\leq$" definiert also eine baumstrukturierte Hierarchie mit Wurzel **none**. In unserem Beispiel gilt etwa [*name*: **string**, *age*: int, *favToy*: oid] $\leq$ [*name*: **string**, *age*: int] oder type(*sam*) $\leq$ type(*john*).

3.5 Kollektionen

Im Datenbank-Kontext ist es stets wünschenswert, deklarativ Anfragen stellen zu können, d. h. spezifizieren zu können, welchen Bedingungen ein Anfrage-Ergebnis genügen sollte, ohne eine Berechnungsvorschrift für dieses Ergebnis mitliefern zu müssen. Diesem Wunsch tragen wir Rechnung durch die Einführung von Kollektionen, welche in beliebiger Weise aus vorhandenen Objekten zusammengesetzt sein können: Für $O \subseteq \mathbf{O}$ heißt jede Teilmenge $K \subseteq O$ eine *Kollektion*. Beispiele für Kollektionen sind die folgenden:

$$\begin{aligned} K_1 &= \{\ mary,\ sam,\ liza\ \} \\ K_2 &= \{\ sam,\ nyu\ \} \\ K_3 &= \{\ peter,\ bear\ \} \\ K_4 &= \{\ john,\ mary\ \} \end{aligned}$$

Während man allgemein Kollektionen über Selektions-Bedingungen konstruieren wird, ist es sinnvoll, gewisse Kollektionen mit speziellen Eigenschaften auszuzeichnen; wir stellen als nächstes drei solcher Arten vor und beginnen mit der Reformulierung eines ursprünglich in [5] eingeführten Begriffs:

Eine Kollektion K heißt *Konstellation*, falls K unter Aggregation abgeschlossen ist, ein ausgezeichnetes Wurzel-Objekt enthält, für welches diese Aggregation gebildet wurde, und keine "hängenden" Objekte umfaßt, d.h.

(i) $(\forall\, o \in K)\ o \rightarrow^* o' \quad \Longrightarrow \quad o' \in K$;

(ii) $(\exists\, o \in K)\ (\forall\, o' \in K \setminus \{o\})\ o \rightarrow^* o'$.

Beispiele für Konstellationen sind

$$\begin{aligned} K_5 &= \{\ mary,\ peter,\ bear,\ laura,\ puppet\ \} \\ K_6 &= \{\ liza,\ nyu\ \} \end{aligned}$$

Wichtiger erscheint uns ein zweiter Spezialfall, *Klassen*, welchen wir als nächstes definieren. Hierzu benötigen wir folgendes: Ist K eine beliebige Kollektion, so sei

$$\text{types}(K) := \textstyle\bigcup_{o \in K} \text{type}(o)$$

Eine Kollektion $K \subseteq O$ heißt *Klasse*, falls alle Objekte in K denselben Typ t haben und K bzgl. dieses Typs abgeschlossen ist, d.h.

(i) $|\text{types}(K)| = 1$;

(ii) $\text{types}(K) = \{t\} \Longrightarrow K = \text{objects}(t, O)$

Diese Definition, welche für Verhalten noch zu ergänzen ist [7], hat eine Reihe von Konsequenzen: Erstens ist eine Klasse in unserem Sinne bzgl. "ihres" Typs abgeschlossen. Damit sind Klassen also mit Typen assoziiert, und nicht etwa umgekehrt wie in klassen-basierten Modellen, und keine zwei Klassen können vom gleichen Typ sein. Zweitens gilt, da der Typ einer Klasse eindeutig ist, daß sich die $\leq$ - Halbordnung auf Klassen fortsetzt: Sind K, K' Klassen, so gelte

$$K \leq K' \quad :\Longleftrightarrow \quad \text{types}(K) \leq \text{types}(K')$$

(Man beachte, daß beide types-Mengen hier einelementig sind.) Die folgenden Kollektionen sind Beispiele für Klassen: $K_7 = \{\ \textit{mary}\ \}$, $K_8 = \{\ \textit{john}\ \}$, $K_9 = \{\ \textit{peter, laura}\ \}$. Ferner gilt $K_7 \leq K_8$.

Ein wesentlicher Unterschied zu Klassen in anderen Objekt-Modellen [1, 6, 10, 11, 20, 21] besteht darin, daß wir Klassen als reine Anfragehilfsmittel verstehen; sie sind zur Deklarationszeit einer Datenbank unbekannt (da nicht vordefiniert) und somit auch nicht Ergebnis eines Entwurfsprozesses. Damit unterscheiden wir uns auch von Arbeiten wie [16] oder [13], in welchen die Ansicht vertreten wird, Entwurfs-Anwendungen benötigen dedizierte Klassen-Bibliotheken, falls eine Datenbank-Unterstützung gewünscht wird.

Es sei abschließend bemerkt, daß sich auch in unserem Modell unter Verwendung der oben eingeführten Subtypen-Beziehung IS-A-Zusammenhänge nachbilden lassen; auf Einzelheiten hierzu sei verzichtet.

4 Zur Deklarationssprache des Modells

Wir deuten in diesem Abschnitt die Grundzüge einer Sprache an, mit welcher man Objekte erzeugen und unterschiedliche Kollektionen definieren kann; weitere Einzelheiten hierzu findet man in [8].

Grundsätzlich kann ein neues Objekt dadurch erzeugt werden, daß man ihm einen Identifikator gibt und es mit einem Wert versieht; hierzu dient das Kommando

create *o-name* **value** *val*;

Hierbei steht *o-name* für einen benutzer-definierten Identifikator und *val* für den mit *o-name* assoziierten Wert. Zur Gewährleistung der Konsistenz im weiter oben definierten Sinne muß mit jedem neuen o ein Wert val(o) assoziiert werden, welcher aus der Menge $V(O)$ entnommen ist, wobei O alle bisher existierenden Objekte umfaßt. Um nun Aggregationen konstruieren zu können, in welchen z. B. zyklische Referenzen vorkommen, muß eine Möglichkeit bestehen, auf Objekt-Namen Bezug zu nehmen, bevor diese vollständig bekannt sind. Dazu erlaubt das Kommando

create *list-of-o-names*;

die Einführung lediglich neuer Identifikatoren, welchen jeweils der Wert `nil` zugeordnet wird. Dieser Wert kann zu einem späteren Zeitpunkt durch einen "realen" Wert ersetzt werden durch das Kommando

update *o-name* **set value** *val*;

Man beachte, daß es damit möglich ist, den Typ eines Objekts zu verändern, denn ein existierender Wert kann durch einen völlig neuen ersetzt werden; insbesondere kann ein Objekt-Wert auf `nil` gesetzt werden. Schließlich erlauben wir Veränderungen von Attribut-Werten innerhalb von Tupel-Werten durch das Kommando update *o-name* set *attr-name := val*;

Diese Sprachelemente ermöglichen bereits ein flexibles Arbeiten mit Objekten; insbesondere können Tupel-Werte um neue Attribute ergänzt werden, Attribute können aus solchen Werten gelöscht werden, und ebenso können Mengen-Werte verändert werden. Genauere Untersuchungen zur Mächtigkeit der Sprachelemente stellen wir in [8] an.

Es ist allerdings nicht in jeder Anwendung wünschenswert, für jedes verwendete Objekt den Identifikator vom Benutzer festlegen zu lassen. Daher sehen wir auch vor, daß solche Identifikatoren system-generiert sind, und zwar durch Deklaration einer "oid-Variablen" und einer Zuweisung gemäß folgender Syntax:

declare *var-name*;
var-name := create_object [value *val*];

Hierbei bezeichnet *var-name* eine Variable, welche durch die Zuweisung eine nach außen nicht sichtbare Oid und, falls kein Wert *val* deklariert wird, den Wert nil erhält; eine Verwendung dieser Variablen im Wert eines anderen Objekts setzt deren aktuellen Wert an die betreffende Stelle.

In unserem Beispiel sind die folgenden Kommandos gültige Statements:

```
create puppet, bear;
create john value [ name:'john smith',
                    age:35 ];
create peter value [name:'peter',
                    age:2,
                    favToy:bear ];
```

Die Benutzung von Variablen illustriert folgendes Beispiel:

```
declare o; o := create_object;
create puppet value [ name:  'henna', owner:  o ];
```

Beim *Löschen* von Objekten müssen wir sicherstellen, daß ausgehend von einer konsistenten Objektmenge nach dem Löschen die resultierende Menge wieder konsistent ist. Die Syntax für das Löschen von Objekten lautet:

delete *list-of-o-names;*

Auf die Semantik dieser Operation und im Zusammenhang damit zu lösende Probleme wird in [8] genauer eingegangen.

Wir gehen abschließend kurz auf die Definition von Kollektionen ein. Kollektionen sind beliebig zusammengesetzte Mengen von Objekten. Die Syntax des entsprechenden Definitions-Kommandos lautet

let collection *coll-name* [be { *setOfObjects* | *select-stmt* }];

Wir unterstellen, daß alle aktuell existierenden Objekte in einer implizit definierten Kollektion *Objects* zusammengefaßt sind. Im einfachsten Fall kann durch das let-Kommando eine Kopie von *Objects* erzeugt werden, oder es kann aus *Objects* eine Teilmenge selektiert werden. Eine solche Selektion kann explizit, d. h. durch Auflistung der gewünschten Elemente, oder implizit über ein select-Statement angegeben werden. Letzteres hat die allgemeine Form

select { *path expression* | * }
[from <*list-of-collections*>]
[where *condition*];

Die Verwendung von Pfad-Ausdrücken, welche nur für objektwertige Attribute erlaubt sind, erläutern wir hier lediglich an folgendem Beispiel: Das Kommando

```
select children.favToy from Objects;
```

selektiert von allen Objekten mit dem Attribut *children* die *favToys* der Objekte, die von diesem Attribut referenziert werden. Eine entsprechende Kollektion wird also insgesamt definiert durch

```
let collection toys be select children.favToy from Objects;
```

Als Bedingungen (conditions) sind Ausdrücke der Form "A" oder "A cop v" erlaubt, wobei A ein Attribut, v ein Wert und cop ein Vergleichsoperator sind; außerdem dürfen elementare Bedingungen durch logisches Und, Oder und Nicht verbunden werden. Beispiele für die Definition von Kollektionen sind:

- `let collection myObjects;` (*erzeugt eine Kopie von *Objects* *)
- `let collection persons be`
  `select * from Objects where name and age;`
- `let collection oldPersons be`
  `select * from persons where age > 60;`
- `let collection students be`
  `select * from persons where major and not salary;`

Eine Klasse wird durch

let class *className* **be** { *o-name* | *type* };

definiert. Es wird eine Klasse mit dem Namen *className* erzeugt, welche entweder das Objekt *o-name* und alle weiteren Objekte desselben Typs oder alle Objekte des angegebenen Typs *type* enthält. Als Beispiel diene das zulässige Statement

```
let class persons be john;
```

Ein entsprechendes Sprachkonstrukt ist zur Definition von Konstellationen vorgesehen; Einzelheiten entnehme man [8].

5 Zusammenfassung und Ausblick

In diesem Kurzbericht haben wir versucht zu motivieren, warum für bestimmte Anwendungsbereiche speziell in der Technik, genauer in Entwurfs-Umgebungen, eine Abkehr von herkömmlichen klassenbasierten Objekt-Modellen sinnvoll sein kann. Eine Analyse bisher vorgeschlagener Alternativen läßt klassenlose Modelle, wie sie auch in prototypischen Programmiersprachen Verwendung finden, geeignet erscheinen, jedoch fehlt bisher eine Beschreibung eines formalen derartigen Modells. Wir haben hier die strukturellen Grundzüge eines solchen Modells beschrieben und den ersten Entwurf einer entsprechenden Deklarationssprache skizziert. Ziel unseres Projekts CLOOD ist die Realisierung eines experimentellen Systems, welches auf dem Modell basiert und diese Sprache bereitstellt.

Das CLOOD-Modell ist de facto ausdrucksstärker als hier beschrieben; insbesondere ist ein Versions-Konzept direkt in das Modell eingebaut: Objekte können in mehreren Versionen existieren, und Objekt-Versionen können zu *Konfigurationen* zusammengesetzt werden. Auf diese Weise wird es möglich, in CLOOD Rollenspiel, Unvollständigkeit, Zeitveränderlichkeit etc. adäquat zu erfassen.

Literatur

[1] S. Abiteboul, P.C. Kanellakis: The Two Facets of Object-Oriented Data Models; IEEE Data Engineering Bulletin 14 (2) 1991, 3–7

[2] E. Bertino et al.: An Object-Oriented Data Model for Distributed Office Applications; Proc. ACM Conference on Office Information Systems 1990, 216–226

[3] E. Bertino, L. Martino: Object-oriented Database Management Systems: Concepts and Issues; IEEE Computer 24 (4) 1991, 33–47

[4] F. Cabrera et al.: The Melampus Project: Toward an Omniscient Computing System; IBM Research Report RJ7515, San Jose 1990

[5] W. Cellary, G. Vossen, G. Jomier: Multiversion Object Constellations for CAD Databases; Bericht Nr. 9105, AG Informatik, Univ. Gießen, November 1991

[6] O. Deux et al.: The Story of O_2; IEEE TKDE 2, 1990, 91–108

[7] M. Groß-Hardt, G. Vossen: CLOOD: A Class-Less Model for Object-Oriented Design Databases; Bericht Nr. 9208, AG Informatik, Univ. Gießen, November 1992

[8] M. Groß-Hardt, G. Vossen: CQL: A Manipulation Language for the CLOOD Object Model; Bericht in Vorbereitung, AG Informatik, Univ. Gießen

[9] T. Imielinski et al.: Incomplete Objects -- A Data Model for Design and Planning Applications; Proc. ACM SIGMOD 1991, 288–297

[10] A. Kemper et al.: GOM: A Strongly Typed Persistent Object Model with Polymorphism; Proc. BTW 1991, Springer IFB 270, 198–217

[11] C. Lecluse, P. Richard: Foundations of the O_2 Database System; IEEE Data Engineering Bulletin 14 (2) 1991, 28–32

[12] H. Liebermann: Using Prototypical Objects to Implement Shared Behavior in Object Oriented Systems; Proc. ACM OOPSLA 1986, 214–223

[13] G.T. Nguyen et al.: An Object Model for Engineering Design; Proc. ECOOP 1992, Springer LNCS 615, 233–251

[14] J. Richardson, P. Schwarz: Aspects: Extending Objects to Support Multiple, Independent Roles; Proc. ACM SIGMOD 1991, 298–307

[15] E. Sciore: Object Specialization; ACM TOIS 7, 1989, 103–122

[16] E. Siepmann, G. Zimmermann: On Object-Oriented Datamodel for the VLSI Design System PLAYOUT; Proc. 26th ACM/IEEE Design Automation Conference 1989, 814–817

[17] K. Tsuda et al.: MORE: An Object-Oriented Data Model with a Facility for Changing Object Structures; IEEE TKDE 3, 1991, 444–460

[18] J.D. Ullman: A Comparison of Deductive and Object-Oriented Database Systems; Proc. 2nd DOOD 1991, Springer LNCS 566, 263–277

[19] D. Ungar, R. Smith: Self: The Power of Simplicity; Proc. ACM OOPSLA 1987, 214–242

[20] G. Vossen: On Formal Models for Object-Oriented Databases; EMISA Forum 2/1992, 22–40

[21] G. Vossen, K.U. Witt: Objectbase Schemata and Objectbases in the FOOD Model; Techn. Report 9101, AG Informatik, Univ. Gießen, Juni 1991

[22] K. Wilkinson et al.: The Iris Architecture and Implementation; IEEE TKDE 2, 1990, 63–75

Fixpoint Evaluation with Subsumption for Probabilistic Uncertainty

Werner Kießling[1] Gerhard Köstler[1] Ulrich Güntzer[2]

[1] Fakultät für Informatik,
Technische Universität München,
Orleansstr. 34, 8000 München 80,
Germany
{wk | koestler}@informatik.tu-muenchen.de

[2] Wilhelm-Schickard-Institut,
Universität Tübingen,
Sand 13, 7400 Tübingen 1,
Germany
guentzer@informatik.uni-tuebingen.de

Abstract

The deep complexity of uncertain data modelling has resisted to general solutions so far. Instead, a diversity of modelling approaches has been proposed over the years, but few systems actually have been built. The DUCK calculus is one recent ambitious rule-based attempt to model uncertainty on the grounds of established probability theory as typically used e.g. in medical diagnosis. This paper describes how deductive database technology can be exploited for prototyping of a system for uncertain reasoning.

In particular we discuss the issues of ADT-ideas in Datalog by using interpreted predicates. Moreover we show that for safety reasons logic programming and current Datalog optimizers must be upgraded to deal with semantic optimization in form of subsumption. New differential least fixpoint operators, customized for subsumption optimization, are provided. Finally we outline the design and implementation of DUCK-Demonstrator/1.1 which serves as a research vehicle for ongoing studies of uncertain reasoning phenomena and for optimization of vague queries.

1 Introduction

The importance of uncertainty modelling in information systems for advanced applications has been recognized in AI for quite a while, whereas the field of databases has been busy with handling certain information efficiently. Recently the need for a confluence of both areas seems to attract more and more attention ([Lag90], [UMI92]) — a situation which does not look unlike the days when databases and logic programming began to merge. Consequently this paper targets at an audience which has shared interests and some familiarity with uncertainty concepts within AI (see e.g. [KSH91], [Pea88] for an overview) and from deductive databases ([Ull89]).

Currently there is no such thing as one uniform data model for uncertainty, instead a variety of models, divided in non-numerical and numerical approaches, have been proposed. Buzzwords from the latter line of research are Dempster-Shafer theory, Fuzzy sets and various probabilistic methods, including the relatively wide-spread Bayesian networks. These Bayesian networks are quite popular in AI because — in contrast to most other methods — implemented systems are available which are used in several medical decision support expert systems (see e.g. [AWFA87]).

The DUCK approach (**D**eduction of **U**n**C**ertain **K**nowledge), as introduced in [GKT91], [KTG92] and [TGK92], is a representative of the probability approach to uncertainty, too. Our interest here is to study computational aspects (issues of formal semantics of probabilistic reasoning are studied in [Bac90] and [NS92]). As pointed out in [TGK92], there are choices available to the implementor of an uncertainty calculus between global linear/nonlinear programming and local computation models.

This paper aims to elaborate how deductive database technology can serve as a prototyping platform for uncertainty.

The rest of the paper is organized as follows. In Section 2 we review the DUCK calculus as required for the purposes here and we provide an example from medical diagnosis, which cannot be done with other existing systems. Section 3 is concerned with a fixpoint evaluation of the DUCK calculus. Emphasizing the need of ADTs we give a direct specification in terms of a quite complex, non-linearly recursive Datalog^{func}-program. The main obstacles for immediate execution on available deductive database systems being unsafety, we investigate the semantic notion of subsumption. This study enables us to derive an implementation of DUCK on the level of extended relational algebra (ERA) by means of customized differential fixpoint iteration respecting subsumption. Section 4 gives an overview description of DUCK-Demonstrator/1.1, a first version implementing the full functionality of the DUCK calculus. Finally section 5 summarizes our results and points out areas of ongoing research.

2 The DUCK-Approach for Uncertain Inference

2.1 The DUCK Calculus

The uncertainty data model of DUCK rests on the solid foundations of axiomatic probability theory, permitting subjective as well as objective interpretation. Specifically *conditional* probabilities serve to describe uncertain situations. The salient features of the DUCK model comprise

(1) uncertain rules quantified by probability intervals,

(2) explicit conditional independence information,

(3) comparative probabilities,

(4) no need to provide complete probability information,

(5) plausible reasoning with facts and uncertain rules.

This expressiveness makes the DUCK-approach strictly more powerful than the popular Bayesian networks and systems like SIMUNC ([vR90]) employing linear programming techniques. DUCK is also capable of modelling *nonmonotonic* reasoning by considering different contexts [KTG92]. First of all we want to give some notations and definitions.

Definition 2.1

a) **Conditional probability:**

Let A, B be events with a probability measure P and let AB denote the intersection of A and B. If $P(A) > 0$, then the *conditional probability* of B given A is defined as $P(B|A) = P(AB)/P(A)$.

The equivalent rule-based interpretation is: $A \xrightarrow{P(B|A)} B$.

b) **Uncertain rule:**

Let $C_1, C_2, \ldots, C_k$ be events. C_l and its complement $\overline{C_l}$, $1 \leq l \leq k$, are called (positive and negative) basic events. We consider conjunctive events $A = A_1 \cdots A_n$, $B = B_1 \cdots B_m$, where $n, m \geq 0$ and A_i, B_j are basic events. A conjunctive event $D = D_1 \cdots D_n$ with $n = 0$ is denoted by Ω.

Let A and B be conjunctive events with $P(A) > 0$. An *uncertain rule* consists of an upper and a lower bound for a conditional probability:

$$A \xrightarrow{x_1, x_2} B \quad \text{iff} \quad 0 \leq x_1 \leq P(B|A) \leq x_2 \leq 1.$$

If lower and upper bound coincide we simply write $A \xrightarrow{x} B$. An immediate consequence of the definition of the conjunctive event Ω is $A\Omega = A$.

c) **Conditional independence:**

Let A, B and C be conjunctive events. C is *independent* of A under condition B, denoted $I(A,B,C)$, iff $P(C|BA) = P(C|B)$. *Unconditional independencies* are represented by $I(A,\Omega,C)$.

d) **Comparative probabilities:**

Let A, B and C conjunctive events with $P(A) > 0$. Assertions like $P(C|A) \geq k \cdot P(B|A)$ or $P(C|A) \leq k \cdot P(B|A)$ are called *comparative probabilities* and will be denoted by

$$A \xrightarrow{\theta k[B]} C, \qquad \theta \in \{\geq, \leq\}$$

DUCK as a rule-based approach to uncertain reasoning applies inference rules to deduce new uncertain rules and independencies from a set of given ones.

Definition 2.2 (Inference mechanism)

Let $\mathcal{R}$ be a set of uncertain rules, conditional independencies or comparative probabilities, let A and B be conjunctive events.

$$\mathcal{R} \vdash A \xrightarrow{x_1,x_2} B \quad \text{iff} \quad A \xrightarrow{x_1,x_2} B$$

can be generated, given $\mathcal{R}$, by the following inference rules $\mathcal{I}$ in a finite number of steps.

Inference Rules $\mathcal{I}$:
(Subsequently only those are listed which are needed in our running example. For the rest of $\mathcal{I}$ see appendix A.1).
Let A, B and C denote conjunctive events and let F denote a basic event.

(S) Sharpening:

$$\{A \xrightarrow{x_1,x_2} B,\, A \xrightarrow{y_1,y_2} B\} \vdash A \xrightarrow{z_1,z_2} B,$$

$$z_1 = \max(x_1,y_1),\; z_2 = \min(x_2,y_2)$$

(PRC2) Precise Rule Chaining 2:

(a) $\{A \xrightarrow{u_1,u_2} F, AF \xrightarrow{x_1,x_2} C, A\overline{F} \xrightarrow{y_1,y_2} C\}$
$\vdash A \xrightarrow{z_1,z_2} C$

$$z_1 = \begin{cases} u_1 \cdot x_1 + (1-u_1) \cdot y_1 & \text{if } x_1 > y_1 \\ u_2 \cdot x_1 + (1-u_2) \cdot y_1 & \text{otherwise} \end{cases}$$

$$z_2 = \begin{cases} u_2 \cdot x_2 + (1-u_2) \cdot y_2 & \text{if } x_2 > y_2 \\ u_1 \cdot x_2 + (1-u_1) \cdot y_2 & \text{otherwise} \end{cases}$$

(b) $\{A \xrightarrow{u_1,u_2} F, AF \xrightarrow{x_1,x_2} C, A\overline{F} \xrightarrow{y_1,y_2} C,$
$x_1 > 0 \text{ or } y_1 > 0\} \vdash AC \xrightarrow{z_1,z_2} F$

$$z_1 = \begin{cases} 1 & \text{if } u_1 = 0, y_2 = 0 \\ \frac{u_1 \cdot x_1}{u_1 \cdot x_1 + (1-u_1) \cdot y_2} & \text{otherwise} \end{cases}$$

$$z_2 = \begin{cases} 0 & \text{if } u_2 = 1, x_2 = 0 \\ \frac{u_2 \cdot x_2}{u_2 \cdot x_2 + (1-u_2) \cdot y_1} & \text{otherwise} \end{cases}$$

(I) Invariance:

(a) $\{B \xrightarrow{x_1,x_2} C,\, I(A,B,C)\} \vdash AB \xrightarrow{x_1,x_2} C$

2.2 Specification of Extended Bayesian Networks

As a demonstration of the expressiveness of the DUCK-calculus we will show the deduction of probabilities in Bayesian networks. As a difference to the well-known approach of using these networks ([Pea88]) we allow the use of probability intervals and denote this kind of network as *extended Bayesian network*. It should be emphasized that none of the existing expert system tools for uncertain reasoning known to us can handle the following example. Bayesian network tools like HUGIN ([AOJJ89]) only allow *point* probabilities but no intervals. SIMUNC [vR90] can't cope with conditional independencies as encoded in the topology of a Bayesian network.

Example 2.3 (Metastatic Cancer)

We extend a fictious medical example (given by [Spi86]) by using probability intervals:

> *Metastatic cancer is a possible cause of a brain tumour, and is also an explanation for increased total serum calcium. In turn, either of these could explain a patient falling into a coma. Severe headache is also possibly associated with a brain tumour.*

This scenario can be modeled by the Bayesian network of Fig. 1, where nodes are binary random variables, e.g. $\tilde{A}$ has the discrete values A and $\overline{A}$. The edges of this network may be labelled by the

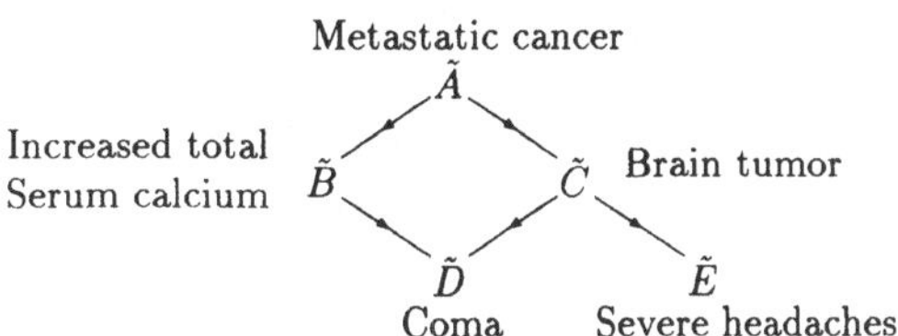

Figure 1: Bayesian network for metastatic cancer.

following probability intervals:

$$
\begin{array}{ll}
\Omega \xrightarrow{0.2,0.25} A & \\
A \xrightarrow{0.8,0.85} B & \overline{A} \xrightarrow{0.2,0.25} B \\
A \xrightarrow{0.2,0.25} C & \overline{A} \xrightarrow{0.05,0.10} C \\
BC \xrightarrow{0.8,.85} D & \overline{B}C \xrightarrow{0.8,0.85} D \\
B\overline{C} \xrightarrow{0.8,.85} D & \overline{B}\,\overline{C} \xrightarrow{0.05,0.10} D \\
C \xrightarrow{0.8,0.85} E & \overline{C} \xrightarrow{0.6,0.65} E
\end{array}
$$

An important feature of Bayesian networks is that the probability of a node — given its parents — does not depend on its other ancestors (ancestors with respect to a total ordering of the nodes compatible with the partial one given by the graph). There are many implicit conditional independencies encoded in the topology of the network, e.g.

$$
\begin{array}{llll}
I(B,A,C), & I(\overline{B},A,C), & \ldots & I(\overline{B},\overline{A},\overline{C}) \\
I(A,BC,D), & I(\overline{A},BC,D), & \ldots & I(\overline{A},\overline{B}\,\overline{C},\overline{D}) \\
I(ABD,C,E), & I(\overline{A}BD,C,E), & \ldots & I(\overline{A}\,\overline{B}\,\overline{C},\overline{C},\overline{E})\ .
\end{array}
$$

Uncertain queries like $D \overset{?}{\longrightarrow} A$, $E \overset{?}{\longrightarrow} A$ or $DE \overset{?}{\longrightarrow} A$ can be answered by applying the DUCK inference rules (Ia), (PRC2a) and (PRC2b) yielding (the results were computed by the DUCK-Demonstrator/1.1 that will be introduced in section 4):

$$D \xrightarrow{0.33,0.53} A \qquad E \xrightarrow{0.19,0.28} A \qquad DE \xrightarrow{0.31,0.56} A$$

This kind of reasoning from symptoms to causes is often used in medical statistics. The probabilities of having metastatic cancer are deduced dependent on the outcome of clinical test, e.g. under the premises of falling into a coma, having severe headaches or having both of the symptoms.

3 Fixpoint Evaluation of the DUCK Calculus

In this section we describe the implementation of the DUCK calculus which is based on the use of extended deductive database technology. We introduce an efficient representation for conjunctive events and transform the DUCK inference rules into a recursive Datalog^{func}program with external interpreted predicates. As it will turn out this program isn't safe in the traditional sense and therefore cannot be executed by standard deductive database systems. This leads us to a semi-naive delta-iteration scheme, extended by a subsumption mechanism, to compute the fixpoint.

3.1 Representation of Conjunctive Events

Conjunctive events may be regarded as an abstract data type (ADT). This ADT could be implemented straightforwardly by representing a conjunctive event as the set or list of its basic events as described by [GKT91]. A much more efficient solution is to realize conjunctive events by bitstrings and to use the operations manipulating the bitstrings as external predicates and functions in a Datalog^{func}program.

The ADT *Conjunctive events* is based on two types: *basic events* and *conjunctive events*, whereby *basic events* is a sub-type of *conjunctive events*. The positive basic events $C_1, \ldots, C_n$ of Def. 2.1 b) are constants (or operations of arity 0) of type *basic event*, Ω is a constant of type *conjunctive events*.

a) Operations on *basic events*:

- **Basic-event-p**(A) checks whether A is a basic event.
- **Negate-basic-event**(A) maps a basic event A to its negation, i.e. C_i to $\overline{C_i}$ or $\overline{C_i}$ to C_i.

b) Operations on *conjunctive events*:

- **Conjunct-events**(A, B) maps event $A = A_1 \cdots A_n$ and event $B = B_1 \cdots B_m$ to the event $A_1 \cdots A_n B_1 \cdots B_m$.
- **Common-sub-event**(A, B) yields the basic events occuring in both A and B.
- **Event-minus**(A, B) yields the basic events occuring in A but not in B.
- **Disjunct-events-p**(A, B) checks whether $A = A_1 \cdots A_n$ and $B = B_1 \cdots B_m$ don't contain basic events A_i and B_j with $A_i = B_j$ or $A_i = \overline{B_j}$.
- **Sub-event-p**(A, B) checks whether all basic events of an event A occur in an event B, too.
- **Differ-in-complementary-event-p**(A, B) checks whether two events are identical except one basic event which is complementary, e.g. $A = A_1 \cdots A_n$ and $B = \overline{A_1} \cdots A_n$.

Additionally the ADT obeys some algebraic laws like

$$\textsf{sub-event-p}(B, A) \Longrightarrow \textsf{conjunct-events}(A, B) = A \ .$$

The implementation of the ADT *Conjunctive events* is based on the interpretation of positive integers as bitstrings whereby even (odd) bit positions represent positive (negative) basic events. The operations on basic and conjunctive events are realized by applying bit operations on these integers. Thus we get an efficient realization of the ADT avoiding the problems of the set representation, e.g. the need of set unification. Indeed, using bit operations we get a linear complexity for all the operations of the ADT. (See the extended version of this paper [KKG92] for a Common Lisp implementation of some ADT-operations).

3.2 Canonical Forms for Uncertain Rules

Uncertain rules $A \xrightarrow{x_1,x_2} B$ as defined in 2.1 b) contain two conjunctive events: the premise and the conclusion. It can easily be seen that not every combination of two events makes sense. For example it is not necessary to regard uncertain rules with a basic event contained in both the premise and the conclusion. By definition of uncertain rules this rule is equivalent to one with this basic event omitted in the conclusion. Also uncertain rules with both a basic event and its complement occuring in the premise or in the conclusion are meaningless for this probability equals zero all the time. These observations lead us to the definition of canonical forms for uncertain rules.

Definition 3.1 (Canonical forms for uncertain rules)

Let $A \xrightarrow{x_1,x_2} B$ with $A = A_1 \cdots A_n$ and $B = B_1 \cdots B_m$ be an uncertain rule. This rule is said to be in canonical form, iff

(CF1) there are no different basic events C_i and C_j,
$C_i, C_j \in \{A_1, \ldots, A_n, B_1, \ldots, B_m\}$, with $C_i = C_j$

(CF2) there are no different basic events C_i and C_j,
$C_i, C_j \in \{A_1, \ldots, A_n, B_1, \ldots, B_m\}$, with $C_i = \overline{C_j}$.

We suppose that all uncertain rules in the knowledge base obey these canonical forms and have to ensure that all inference rules produce rules in canonical form only. Indeed, if the equality test $A \neq C$ in the inference rules (WCL), (CRb), (WCR), (WCRN) and (PRC1) is implemented as *disjunct-events-p(A,C)*, the canonical forms are maintained.

An important implication of using rules in canonical form is that the number of basic events of the premise and of the conclusion of a uncertain rule in canonical form can't exceed the number of positive basic events k, what is important for the termination of the fixpoint iteration performed to deduce the consequences of a knowledge base.

3.3 Mapping the DUCK calculus onto Datalog^{func}

One possibility to implement our approach to uncertainty reasoning is to use deductive database technology. In this section we show that the DUCK calculus can be mapped onto Datalog with functions (but without negation) using the operations of the ADT *conjunctive events* as external interpreted predicates and functions. First of all we have to determine the predicates occuring in this logic program.

Let $\mathcal{R}$ be a knowledge base with uncertain rules, conditional independencies and comparative probabilities. $\mathcal{R}$ may be given by a knowledge engineer to model an application domain. The information of $\mathcal{R}$ is represented by three extensional relations:

$$
\begin{array}{lll}
br(A,B,X1,X2) & :\Longleftrightarrow & A \xrightarrow{X1,X2} B \in \mathcal{R} \\
bi(A,B,C) & :\Longleftrightarrow & I(A,B,C) \in \mathcal{R} \\
bc(A,\theta,k,B,C) & :\Longleftrightarrow & A \xrightarrow{\theta k[B]} C \in \mathcal{R}
\end{array}
$$

We should emphasize that logic programming systems based on term unification (as all Prolog systems) may run into serious difficulties here, since $X1, X2$ are real numbers.

The uncertain rules and conditional independencies deduced by the inference mechanism are realized as intensional relations where the deduced uncertain rules are represented by *two* mutually recursive intensional relations for reasons explained below. Relation *sr* represents uncertain rules contained in the knowledge base or generated by the inference rules except for sharpening (S) and *dr* represents the uncertain rules deduced by applying sharpening to *sr*. Thus we define:

$$
\begin{array}{lll}
sr(A,B,X1,X2) & :\Longleftrightarrow & br(A,B,X1,X2) \vee dr \underset{\mathcal{I}_{UR}}{\vdash} A \xrightarrow{X1,X2} B \\
di(A,B,C) & :\Longleftrightarrow & bi(A,B,C) \vee \mathcal{R} \underset{\mathcal{I}_{IND}}{\vdash} I(A,B,C)
\end{array}
$$

where $\mathcal{I}_{UR}$ are all inference rules of the DUCK calculus generating uncertain rules except for the sharpening rule (S) and $\mathcal{I}_{IND}$ is the set of inference rules generating independencies, i.e.

$$
\begin{array}{ll}
\mathcal{I}_{UR} = & \{(C),(BI),(CL),(WCL),(CR),(WCR),(CRN),(WCRN), \\
& (N),(I),(CP),(PRC1),(PRC2)\} \\
\mathcal{I}_{IND} = & \{(SYM),(DEC),(WU),(CON)\}\ .
\end{array}
$$

Hereby we interprete the relation *dr* as the set of uncertain rules encoded by the tuples of *dr*. $Sr(A,B,X1,X2)$ is only an auxiliary, virtual relation. Application of the sharpening rule (S) to tuples of *sr* yields the relation

$$
dr(A,B,X1,X2)\ :\Longleftrightarrow\ sr \underset{S}{\vdash} A \xrightarrow{X1,X2} B\ .
$$

Again in this definition we interprete the relation *sr* as the set of uncertain rules encoded by the tuples of *sr*. The reason for introducing the relation *sr* is to ensure that to all newly deduced uncertain rules the sharpening rule (S) is applied immediately. This helps to avoid useless deductions by the subsumption mechanism in section 3.6. Some inference rules (see appendix A.1), like (CL), (WCL), (WCRN), (SYM) and (PRC1) use bidirectional uncertain rules $A \overset{x_1,x_2}{\underset{y_1,y_2}{\longleftrightarrow}} B$ in their hypothesis. This is just an abbreviation for two uncertain rules $A \xrightarrow{x_1,x_2} B$ and $B \xrightarrow{y_1,y_2} A$. To avoid three- and four-fold recursion in the evaluation of these inference rules we regard this abbreviation as a kind of (pseudo) inference rule

(BID) Bidirectional Rule definition

$$
\{A \xrightarrow{x_1,x_2} B, B \xrightarrow{y_1,y_2} A\} \vdash A \overset{x_1,x_2}{\underset{y_1,y_2}{\longleftrightarrow}} B
$$

Thus we get an intensional relation of bidirectional uncertain rules

$$
2dr(A,B,X1,X2,Y1,Y2)\ :\Longleftrightarrow\ dr \underset{BID}{\vdash} A \overset{X1,X2}{\underset{Y1,Y2}{\longleftrightarrow}} B
$$

With these definitions it is immediate that the direct mapping of the DUCK inference rules results in a Datalog^{func} program which has the predicate connection graph, depicted by Fig. 2, with a recursive clique $\{sr, dr, 2dr, di\}$ of cardinality 4.

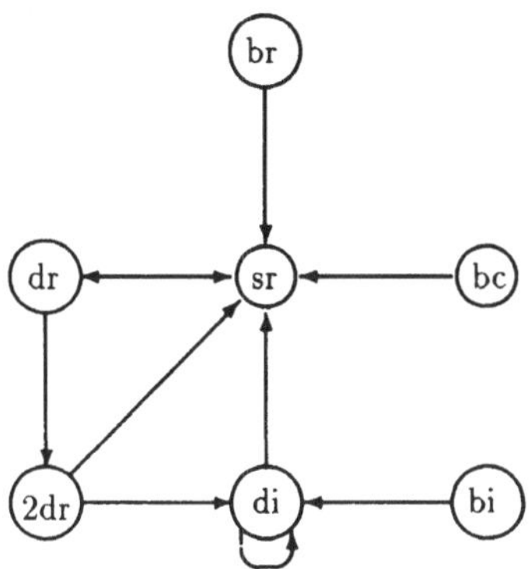

Figure 2: Predicate connection graph of DUCK.

As an example we translate some of the DUCK inference rules into a nonlinearly recursive Datalog^{func} program given in an LDL-like notation (see [NT89]). Hereby we regard operations of the ADT *Conjunctive events* as predicates, too.

```
% Axioms
sr(A,B,X1,X2)    ←   br(A,B,X1,X2)
di(A,B,C)        ←   bi(A,B,C)

% Some inference rules from I_UR

% Chaining (a)
sr(A,C,Z1,Z2)    ←   dr(A,BC,X1,X2), dr(A,NotBC,Y1,Y2),
                     differ-in-complementary-event-p(BC,NotBC),
                     common-sub-event(BC,NotBC,C),
                     Z1 = X1 + Y1, Z2 = min(1, X2 + Y2).
% Conjunction Left (a)
sr(AB,C,Z1,Z2)          ←   2dr(A,B,U1,U2,V1,V2), dr(A,BC,X1,X2),
                            (U1 > 0; V1 > 0),
                            sub-event-p(B,BC),
                            event-minus(BC,B,C),
                            conjunct-events(A,B,AB),
                            Z1 = X1/U2,
                            Z2 = if X2 = 0 then 0
                                 elsif X2 > 0 and U1 > 0
                                           then min(1, X2/U1)
                                 else 1.
```

```
% Conjunction Right (a)
sr(A,BC,Z1,Z2)          ←  dr(A,B,X1,X2), dr(AB,C,Y1,Y2),
                           conjunct-events(A,B,AB),
                           conjunct-events(B,C,BC),
                           Z1 = X1 * Y1, Z2 = X2 * Y2.
% Negation
sr(A,NotB,Z1,Z2)        ←  dr(A,B,X1,X2),
                           basic-event-p(B),
                           negate-basic-event(B,NotB),
                           Z1 = 1 - X2, Z2 = 1 - X1.
% Invariance (a)
sr(AB,C,X1,X2)   ←  dr(B,C,X1,X2), di(A,B,C),
                    conjunct-events(A,B,AB).

% Pseudo Inference rule (BID)
2dr(A,B,X1,X2,Y1,Y2)  ←  dr(A,B,X1,X2), dr(B,A,Y1,Y2).

% The sharpening inference rule (S)
dr(A,B,Z1,Z2)  ←  sr(A,B,X1,X2), sr(A,B,Y1,Y2),
                  Z1 = max(X1, Y1), Z2 = min(X2, Y2).
```

Note the use of the ADT operations **differ-in-complementary-event-p** as join predicate, **sub-event-p** as selector predicate and **negate-basic-event** as projector predicate.

3.4 Safety by Subsumption

In the last section we outlined the transformation of the DUCK calculus to a logic program. Unfortunately the program is not safe ([SV89]), i.e. the computed fixpoint of this program isn't finite. This can be demonstrated by a simple example.

Example 3.2 (Potential unsafety)

Let $\mathcal{R} = \{A \xrightarrow{x_1,x_2} B, A \xrightarrow{y_1^0,y_2^0} BC, 0 < x_1 < x_2, 0 < y_1^0\}$ be a knowledge base. By applying the inference rules (BIb), the pseudo inference rule (BID) and (CLa) we get $AB \xrightarrow{z_1,z_2} C$ with $z_1 = \frac{y_1^0}{x_2}$ and $z_2 = \min(1, \frac{y_2^0}{x_1})$. Applying (CRa) results in

$$\{A \xrightarrow{x_1,x_2} B, AB \xrightarrow{z_1,z_2} C\} \underset{(CRa)}{\vdash} A \xrightarrow{y_1^1,y_2^1} BC$$

$$y_1^1 = \tfrac{x_1}{x_2} \cdot y_1^0 < y_1^0$$
$$y_2^1 = \min(1, \tfrac{x_2}{x_1} \cdot y_2^0) \geq y_2^0$$

That is we derive an uncertain rule $A \longrightarrow BC$ with a worse lower bound and a worse or equal upper bound. This deduction can be repeated and we get

$$A \xrightarrow{y_1^n,y_2^n} BC, \quad y_1^n = (\frac{x_1}{x_2})^n \cdot y_1^0, \quad y_2^n = \min(1, (\frac{x_2}{x_1})^n \cdot y_2^0)$$

after n steps. (y_1^n, y_2^n) converges to $[0,1]$ without reaching it after a finite number of steps. Thus the DUCK calculus isn't safe unless special countermeasures are taken. □

Obviously $A \xrightarrow{y_1^0,y_2^0} BC$ subsumes $A \xrightarrow{y_1^n,y_2^n} BC$ for $n > 0$, i.e. it has a tighter probability interval. Therefore nothing is lost if all rules subsumed by others are ignored. Standard logic programming systems based on a lattice structure with respect of set inclusion can't cope with such a situation. We define a subsumption ordering between uncertain rules and use this ordering to remove all subsumed tuples during fixpoint iteration. Subsumption was introduced as a powerful means to semantic query optimization for deductive databases with integrity constraints by [CGM88]. In our context with DUCK's own semantics it is defined as:

Definition 3.3 (Subsumption ordering)

Let r_1, r_2 with $r_1 := A \xrightarrow{x_1,x_2} B$ and $r_2 := A \xrightarrow{y_1,y_2} B$ be two uncertain rules. r_2 ***subsumes*** r_1, denoted by $r_1 \sqsubseteq r_2$, iff $y_1 \geq x_1$ and $y_2 \leq x_2$.

Note that $\sqsubseteq$ is a partial ordering on the set of all uncertain rules. It can be extended to sets of uncertain rules similarly to [BK89].

Definition 3.4 (Subsumption on sets)

Let R_1 and R_2 be two sets of uncertain rules. R_2 subsumes R_1, denoted by $R_1 \sqsubseteq R_2$, iff

$$\forall r_1 \in R_1 \, \exists r_2 \in R_2 \colon r_1 \sqsubseteq r_2$$

On sets of uncertain rules $\sqsubseteq$ is only a preorder (antisymmetry is missing), because the sets could contain rules subsumed by other ones. Like [BK89] we regard only *reduced sets* with no redundant (subsumed) uncertain rules.

Definition 3.5 (Reduced sets)

a) A set of uncertain rules R is called *reduced*, if no $A \xrightarrow{x_1,x_2} B \in R$ is subsumed by a different $A \xrightarrow{y_1,y_2} B \in R$.

b) The reduced version of a finite set of uncertain rules R, denoted by $\mathrm{red}(R)$, is gained by taking only the maximal rules with respect to $\sqsubseteq$.

On reduced sets $\sqsubseteq$ is antisymmetrical and therefore a partial ordering.

By reducing the set of generated rules after each deduction step we solve the unsafety problem described in example 3.2. The converging but subsumed sequence of rules $A \xrightarrow{y_1^n,y_2^n} BC$ in example 3.2 is pruned in the deduction tree, because they are subsumed by the rule $A \xrightarrow{y_1^0,y_2^0} BC$ in the knowledge base. In the next section a special differential fixpoint iteration with a subsumption mechanism is introduced for this reason. This mechanism generalizes the optimization technique known as "*push selection by certainty*" of [SSG+89] and is based on the fact that tighter probability intervals for the hypotheses generate tighter intervals for the conclusions, i.e. DUCK is monotonic with respect to subsumption as shown in lemma 3.10.

The subsumption ordering can be extended to bidirectional rules in a canonical way: a bidirectional rule r_2 subsumes another bidirectional rule r_1, iff both of the uncertain rules constituting r_2 subsume the corresponding uncertain rules of r_1. Subsumption on sets and reduced sets for bidirectional rules are then defined in an analogous way.

3.5 Mapping DUCK to Extended Relational Algebra

We argued in the last section that standard deductive database systems are not able to directly evaluate the Datalog^{func}program of section 3.3. Of course this prohibits a very rapid prototyping of a fully functional running prototype. Nevertheless, circumventing the current weakness of deductive compilers by accessing the lower level of extended relational algebra with fixpoint operators will bring us to our goal sufficiently fast.

First we have to translate the Datalog program to extended relational algebra (ERA), using the external operations of the ADT *conjunctive events* as selection and projection functions and as join predicates. One advantage of implementing the calculus on this level is that we have control on the join order and the indices. Moreover we will show that translating Datalog automatically to ERA would not be as efficient as done manually. For example translating the sharpening inference rule (S) to ERA results in

$$F_S(SR) := SR *_S SR := \prod_{A_1,B_1,\max(X_1,Y_1),\min(X_2,Y_2)} (SR(A_1,B_1,X_1,X_2) \underset{A_1=A_2,B_1=B_2}{\bowtie} SR(A_2,B_2,Y_1,Y_2))$$

The inference rules $\mathcal{I}_{UR}$, $\mathcal{I}_{IND}$ and (BID) as defined above can be mapped to ERA expressions $F_{\mathcal{I}_{UR}}(DR, DI, 2DR)$, $F_{\mathcal{I}_{IND}}(DI, 2DR)$ and $F_{BID}(DR)$ in a similar way as shown for (S). This yields the following equational system for the clique of cardinality 4:

$$\begin{array}{lcl} SR & = & F_{UR}(DR, DI, 2DR) \\ DR & = & F_S(SR) \\ DI & = & F_{IND}(DI, 2DR) \\ 2DR & = & F_{BID}(DR) \end{array} \qquad (1)$$

with

$$\begin{array}{lcl} F_{UR}(DR, DI, 2DR) & := & BR + F_{\mathcal{I}_{UR}}(DR, DI, 2DR) \\ F_{IND}(DI, 2DR) & := & BI + F_{\mathcal{I}_{IND}}(DI, 2DR) \end{array}$$

Obviously the relations DR and SR are mutually recursive, i.e. there is an implicit sequential ordering between the relations. We perform another optimization to make this ordering explicit:

$$\begin{array}{lcl} DR & = & F_S(F_{UR}(DR, DI, 2DR)) \\ DI & = & F_{IND}(DI, 2DR) \\ 2DR & = & F_{BID}(DR) \end{array} \qquad (2)$$

The following lemma shows that this was a correct optimization.

Lemma 3.6

The least fixpoint of (1) is the least fixpoint of (2).

Proof. See the extended version of this paper [KKG92]. □

Thus it is sufficient to evaluate the simpler equational system (2), an optimization that cannot be done by any current Datalog optimizer. In the following we concentrate on the fixpoint iteration for the equation

$$DR = F(DR, DI, 2DR)$$

with $F(DR, DI, 2DR) := F_S(F_{UR}(DR, DI, 2DR))$ and use the abbreviation $\mathbf{D} := (DR, DI, 2DR)$. Computing the least fixpoint of this equation — applying differential delta-iteration — results in all uncertain rules deducible from the knowledge base. In such iteration schemes one has to compute efficiently the difference $F(\mathbf{D} + \mathbf{\Delta}) \setminus F(\mathbf{D})$ where $\mathbf{\Delta} := (\Delta DR, \Delta DI, \Delta 2DR)$ and + is set union canonically extended to vectors. This can be done by *auxiliary functions* $\mathrm{Aux}_F(\mathbf{D}, \mathbf{\Delta})$ with $\mathrm{Aux}_F(\mathbf{D}, \mathbf{\Delta}) \setminus F(\mathbf{D}) = F(\mathbf{D}+\mathbf{\Delta}) \setminus F(\mathbf{D})$. Auxiliary functions are obtained by symbolic differentiation (see [GKB87]). Thus we get as auxiliary function for F:

$$\begin{array}{lcl} \mathrm{Aux}_F(\mathbf{D}, \mathbf{\Delta}) & = & \mathrm{Aux}_{F_{UR}}(\mathbf{D}, \mathbf{\Delta}) *_S F_{UR}(\mathbf{D}) + \\ & & F_{UR}(\mathbf{D}) *_S \mathrm{Aux}_{F_{UR}}(\mathbf{D}, \mathbf{\Delta}) + \\ & & \mathrm{Aux}_{F_{UR}}(\mathbf{D}, \mathbf{\Delta}) *_S \mathrm{Aux}_{F_{UR}}(\mathbf{D}, \mathbf{\Delta}) \end{array}$$

Taking into account that sharpening is symmetrical — another semantic optimization — the second term can be obmitted. Nevertheless we have a multiplicator $F_{UR}(\mathbf{D})$ in the auxiliary function, implying an expensive application of $\mathcal{I}_{UR}$ to the entire relations of $\mathbf{D}$. Fortunately this can be bypassed by the following lemma.

Lemma 3.7

Let $Aux_F(\mathbf{D}, \mathbf{\Delta})$ be the auxiliary function of F. Then

$$\begin{aligned} Aux_F(\mathbf{D}, \mathbf{\Delta}) \setminus F(\mathbf{D}) &= (Aux_{F_{UR}}(\mathbf{D}, \mathbf{\Delta}) *_S F(\mathbf{D}) + \\ &\quad Aux_{F_{UR}}(\mathbf{D}, \mathbf{\Delta}) *_S Aux_{F_{UR}}(\mathbf{D}, \mathbf{\Delta})) \setminus F(\mathbf{D}) \end{aligned}$$

Proof. See the extended version of this paper [KKG92]. □

Instead of the expensive multiplicator $F_{UR}(\mathbf{D})$ we can take $F(\mathbf{D})$ that is computed as $DR + \Delta DR$. This *semantical* optimization could not be done by an automatic Datalog to ERA compiler either.

3.6 Delta-iteration with Subsumption

The main reason for going down to the ERA level was the need for a subsumption mechanism in the delta iteration scheme (on the other hand it allowed us to apply a lot of semantic optimizations). We will customize standard differential fixpoint iteration.

Definition 3.8 (Delta-iteration scheme)

The standard delta-iteration scheme is given by:

Initialization: $(S_0, \Delta_1) := (\emptyset, F(\emptyset))$

Iteration: $(S_{t-1}, \Delta_t) \longrightarrow (S_t, \Delta_{t+1}) :=$

$$(S_{t-1} + \Delta_t, \mathrm{Aux}_F(S_{t-1}, \Delta_t) \setminus (S_{t-1} + \Delta_t)) \quad t \geq 1$$

The operations $+$ and $\setminus$ are the right ones with respect to set inclusion but must be replaced if a more general subsumption ordering $\sqsubseteq$ on sets is used. We define two new operations $\oplus$ and $\ominus$.

Definition 3.9 (Union and difference with subsumption)

Let A and B be two finite sets of uncertain rules.

a) The operation $A \oplus B$ is defined as the reduced version (see def. 3.5) of $A + B$.

b) The operation $A \ominus B$ is defined as the reduced version of $\{a \in A \mid \nexists b \in B : a \sqsubseteq b\}$.

Substituting $\oplus$ for $+$ and $\ominus$ for $\setminus$ and taking the reduced version of $F(\emptyset)$ as first delta we get a new differential fixpoint iteration scheme denoted as ***delta iteration with subsumption.*** In this iteration scheme we consider only the maximal uncertain rules, i.e. the reduced versions of sets. This is reasonable because the ERA expression $F(\mathbf{D})$ is monotonic with respect to subsumption as shown by the following lemma.

Lemma 3.10 (Monotonicity w.r.t. $\sqsubseteq$)

Let $\mathbf{D_1} = (DR_1, DI_1, 2DR_1)$ and $\mathbf{D_2} = (DR_2, DI_2, 2DR_2)$ be two vectors of sets of uncertain rules, independencies and bidirectional rules, let $\mathbf{D_1} \sqsubseteq \mathbf{D_2}$ be an abbreviation for $DR_1 \sqsubseteq DR_2$, $DI_1 \subseteq DI_2$, $2DR_1 \sqsubseteq 2DR_2$ and let $F(\mathbf{D})$ be the ERA expression as defined in section 3.5. Then

$$\mathbf{D_1} \sqsubseteq \mathbf{D_2} \Longrightarrow F(\mathbf{D_1}) \sqsubseteq F(\mathbf{D_2})$$

Proof. We show the monotonicity property only for the inference rule (CRN). Checking it for the remaining rules is straightforward.

Let $A \xrightarrow{x_1^1, x_2^1} C, A \xrightarrow{y_1^1, y_2^1} FC \in DR_1$. DR_1 is subsumed by DR_2, i.e. there exist uncertain rules $A \xrightarrow{x_1^2, x_2^2} C, A \xrightarrow{y_1^2, y_2^2} FC \in DR_2$ with $A \xrightarrow{x_1^1, x_2^1} C \sqsubseteq A \xrightarrow{x_1^2, x_2^2} C$ and $A \xrightarrow{y_1^1, y_2^1} FC \sqsubseteq A \xrightarrow{y_1^2, y_2^2} FC$. By definition of $\sqsubseteq$ this implies $x_1^2 \geq x_1^1$, $x_2^2 \leq x_2^1$, $y_1^2 \geq y_1^1$ and $y_2^2 \leq y_2^1$. With $z_1^i = \max(0, x_1^i - y_2^i)$ and $z_2^i = \min(1, x_2^i - y_1^i)$ we get $z_1^2 \geq z_1^1$ and $z_2^2 \leq z_2^1$ and therefore $A \xrightarrow{z_1^1, z_2^1} \overline{F}C \sqsubseteq A \xrightarrow{z_1^2, z_2^2} \overline{F}C$ implying $F_{CRN}(DR_1) \sqsubseteq F_{CRN}(DR_2)$. □

Based on this lemma it is possible to consider reduced sets only and we get the following theorem:

Theorem 3.11

Let DR_t^1, $t \geq 0$, be the sequence of relations generated by standard delta-iteration for the DUCK equational system (2) and let DR_t^2, $t \geq 0$, be the sequence of relations generated by delta-iteration with subsumption. Then $red(DR_t^1) = DR_t^2$.

Proof. See the extended version of this paper [KKG92]. The proof is based on the monotonicity of F w.r.t. the subsumption relation. □

An immediate consequence of this theorem is: if Δ_t^2 is empty in the delta-iteration scheme with subsumption, then DR_{t-1}^2 is the reduced version of the fixpoint of the equation. Note that there exist infinite sequences of deduced uncertain rules r_i with $r_1 \sqsubseteq r_2 \sqsubseteq r_3 \sqsubseteq \ldots$. Applying the subsumption mechanism r_i is replaced by r_{i+1}. Thus though we have no termination in such a case, the cardinality of the relations DR_t^2 is bound and we can arbitrarily approximate the limits of the probability interval and then stop. This property is denoted as *weak safety* (see [SV89]) in contrast to safety that also requires termination.

The new operations $\oplus$ and $\ominus$ depend on the subsumption ordering. Using subsumption for bidirectional rules, new operations for sets of bidirectional rules can be defined substituting the operations $+$ and $\setminus$. This yields a subsumption mechanism for bidirectional rules, too.

4 The DUCK-Demonstrator/1.1

The implementation ideas sketched in the last section were integrated in a prototypical realization of the DUCK calculus we call the DUCK-Demonstrator/1.1. In this section we sketch the computational complexity inherent in uncertain reasoning and describe the features and architecture of this running experimental system.

4.1 Complexity of Probabilistic Reasoning

As shown by theoretical work probabilistic reasoning is a task with deep computational complexity. Cooper [Coo90] proves that probabilistic reasoning in Bayesian networks is NP-complete. The kind of reasoning the DUCK approach offers is an even more general one (e.g. the use of probability intervals and explicit conditional independencies) and thus probabilistic reasoning using the DUCK calculus must be NP-complete, too. In [FH91] the complexity of probabilistic propositional logic is proved to be NP-complete, likewise, what in a sense is the best one can hope for. This shows the demand for further semantical optimization and powerful query-guided heuristics for the deduction process. Nevertheless, the DUCK Demonstrator is a fruitful device for our research studies especially for developing this kind of heuristics.

4.2 Features and Architecture

The DUCK-Demonstrator/1.1 was prototypically implemented in Common Lisp using the extended relational algebra interface R-Lisp ([Sch90]). The demonstrator contains modules for implementing the ADT *Conjunctive events* and the DUCK calculus as R-Lisp expressions, comprising about 16,000 lines of Lisp code. The probabilities are realized by an unbounded rational arithmetic but could also be done by a floating point arithmetic with unlimited precision. The new delta-iteration scheme with subsumption can be customized by a suitable subsumption ordering. User interaction is managed by a graphical interface using the Common Lisp–Motif interface CLM. The most important features of the demonstrator are:

- The inference rules used in the deduction process may be chosen and also be changed during computation.

- An incremental computation is possible adding new knowledge during deduction.
- It offers a large scale of queries using wildcards at any position, e.g. $* \xrightarrow{?} B$, $A \xrightarrow{?} *$ and $?\,I(*, B, *)$.
- The consistency of the knowledge base (i.e. for no uncertain rule the upper limit is less than the lower limit) is permanently checked.
- The deduction graph for a query can be reconstructed and visualized by an explanation module.

5 Summary and Outlook

In this paper we examined the use of deductive database technology for rapid prototyping of a system for uncertain reasoning based on the DUCK calculus. Mapping the calculus onto Datalog^{func}we emphasized the importance of semantic optimization — especially of a subsumption mechanism to obtain at least weak safety. By describing a delta-iteration scheme with subsumption, filtering the relations on the fly, we pointed out features needed for the development of more sophisticated compilers and optimizers for deductive databases. This kind of subsumption (and of course the use of real numbers) can hardly be done by Prolog-based systems. Moreover we presented some feasible semantic optimizations.

The expressiveness of our approach was demonstrated by modelling a medical example beyond the possibilities of other expert system tools for uncertain reasoning that we know. Finally the DUCK-Demonstrator/1.1 was introduced — a fully running system that implements all rules of the calculus and offers many features, e.g. incremental deduction and explanation facilities. It serves as a research vehicle to develop more techniques of semantic optimization.

Our long term goal is to identify subclasses of DUCK knowledge bases and queries allowing fast (i.e. polynomial) uncertainty reasoning. Nevertheless —as we sketched — there are tough cases with an inherent exponential complexity. An important research topic is therefore the search for acceptable heuristics (as nowadays exist for many NP-complete problems of practical importance as e.g. for the travelling salesman) that efficiently control the deduction process.

Acknowledgement

We would like to thank Helmut Thöne for many helpful comments and suggestions.

References

[AOJJ89] Stig K. Andersen, Kristian G. Olesen, Finn V. Jensen, and Frank Jensen. HUGIN — a shell for building Bayesian belief universes for expert systems. In *Proc. of the 11 th IJCAI*, pages 1080–1085, Detroit, MI, 1989.

[AWFA87] S. Andreassen, M. Woldbye, B. Falck, and S. K. Andersen. MUNIN — a causal probabilistic network for interpretation of electromyographic findings. In *Proc. of the 10 th IJCAI*, pages 366–372, Milan, Italy, 1987.

[Bac90] Fahiem Bacchus. *Representing and Reasoning with Probabilistic Knowledge: a logical approach.* The MIT Press, Cambridge (USA), 1990.

[BK89] F. Bancilhon and S. Khoshafian. A calculus for complex objects. *Journal of Computer and System Sciences*, 38:326–340, 1989.

[CGM88] U.S. Chakravarthy, J. Grant, and J. Minker. Foundations of semantic query optimization for deductive databases. In J. Minker, editor, *Foundations of Deductive Databases and Logic Programming*, pages 243–274. Morgan Kaufmann, Los Altos, 1988.

[Coo90] Gregory F. Cooper. The computational complexity of probabilistic inference using Bayesian networks. *Artificial Intelligence*, 42:393–405, 1990.

[FH91] Ronald Fagin and Joseph Y. Halpern. Uncertainty, belief, and probability. *Computational Intelligence*, 7(3):160–173, 1991.

[GKB87] Ulrich Güntzer, Werner Kießling, and Rudolf Bayer. On the evaluation of recursion in (deductive) database systems by efficient differential fixpoint iteration. In *Proceedings of the 3rd International Conference on Data Engineering*, pages 120–129, Los Angeles, California, 1987.

[GKT91] Ulrich Güntzer, Werner Kießling, and Helmut Thöne. New directions for uncertainty reasoning in deductive databases. In *Proceedings ACM SIGMOD International Conference on Management of Data*, pages 178–187, Denver, USA, 1991.

[KKG92] Werner Kießling, Gerhard Köstler, and Ulrich Güntzer. Fixpoint evaluation with subsumption for probabilistic uncertainty. Technical Report TUM-I9237, Fakultät für Informatik, Technische Universität München, Dec. 1992.

[KSH91] Rudolf Kruse, Erhard Schwecke, and Jochen Heinsohn. *Uncertainty and Vagueness in Knowledge Based Systems.* Artificial Intelligence. Springer, Berlin, 1991.

[KTG92] Werner Kießling, Helmut Thöne, and Ulrich Güntzer. Database support for problematic knowledge. In *Proc. Int. Conf. on Extending Database Technology (EDBT)*, pages 421–436, Vienna, Austria, 1992.

[Lag90] Database systems: Achievements and opportunities. In *Lagunita Beach Report of the NSF Invitational Workshop on Future Directions in DBMS Research*, Palo Alto, 1990.

[NS92] R.T. Ng and V.S. Subrahmanian. Empirical probabilities in monadic deductive databases. In *8th Conference on Uncertainty in Artificial Intelligence*, pages 215–222, Stanford, USA, 1992.

[NT89] S. Naqvi and S. Tsur. *A Logical Language for Data and Knowledge Bases.* Computer Science Press, New York, 1989.

[Pea88] Judea Pearl. *Probabilistic Reasoning in Intelligent Systems.* Morgan Kaufmann, San Mateo, 1988.

[Sch90] Heribert Schütz. R-Lisp — eine erweiterte relationale Algebra in Lisp. Technical Report TUM-I9049, Institut für Informatik, Technische Universität München, 1990.

[Spi86] David J. Spiegelhalter. Probabilistic reasoning in predicitive expert systems. In L.N. Kanal and J.F. Lemmer, editors, *Uncertainty in Artificial Intelligence*, pages 47–68. Elsevier Science Publishers B.V. (North-Holland), 1986.

[SSG+89] H. Schmidt, N. Steger, U. Güntzer, W. Kießling, R. Azone, and R. Bayer. Combining deduction by certainty with the power of magic. In *Proceedings 1st International Conference on Deductive and Object-Oriented Databases*, pages 205–224, Kyoto, Japan, 1989.

[SV89] Y. Sagiv and M. Y. Vardi. Safety of datalog queries over infinite databases. In *Proceedings ACM SIGACT-SIGART-SIGMOD Symposium on Principles of Database Systems*, pages 160–171, Philadelphia, USA, 1989.

[TGK92] Helmut Thöne, Ulrich Güntzer, and Werner Kießling. Towards precision of probabilistic bounds propagation. In *8th Conference on Uncertainty in Artificial Intelligence*, pages 315–322, Stanford, USA, 1992.

[Ull89] J. Ullman. *Principles of Database and Knowledge-Base Systems*, volume 1,2. Computer Science Press, New York, 1988,1989.

[UMI92] Uncertainty in information systems: From needs to solutions. In *UMIS, Two-Meeting Invitational Workshop*, Palma de Mallorca, Sept. 1992.

[vR90] M. von Rimscha. The determination of comparative and lower probability. In *Workshop Uncertainty in Knowledge-Based Systems, FAW-B-90025*, volume 2, pages 344–376, Ulm, Germany, 1990. FAW Ulm.

Appendix

A.1 The Inference Rules

(Let A, B, C denote conjunctive events and let F denote a basic event.)

(C) Chaining:

(a) $\{ A \xrightarrow{x_1,x_2} FC,\ A \xrightarrow{y_1,y_2} \overline{F}C \} \vdash A \xrightarrow{z_1,z_2} C,$

$z_1 = x_1 + y_1,\ z_2 = \min(1, x_2 + y_2)$

(b) $\{ A \xrightarrow{x_1,x_2} BC \} \vdash A \xrightarrow{x_1,1} C$

(c) $\{ A \xrightarrow{x_1,x_2} BC,\ C \xrightarrow{1} B \} \vdash A \xrightarrow{x_1,x_2} C$

(d) $\{ A \xrightarrow{x_1,x_2} BC,\ A \xrightarrow{1} B \} \vdash A \xrightarrow{x_1,x_2} C$

(PRC1) Precise rule chaining 1:

$$\{ A \overset{u_1,u_2}{\underset{v_1,v_2}{\longleftrightarrow}} B,\ B \overset{x_1,x_2}{\underset{y_1,y_2}{\longleftrightarrow}} C,\ A \neq C \} \vdash A \xrightarrow{z_1,z_2} C$$

$$z_1 = \begin{cases} \max(0, u_1 \cdot (1 - \frac{1}{v_1} \cdot (1 - x_1))) & \text{if } v_1 > 0 \\ u_1 & \text{if } v_1 = 0,\ x_1 = 1 \\ 0 & \text{otherwise} \end{cases}$$

$$z_2 = \begin{cases} \min(1, \frac{u_2 x_2}{v_1 y_1}, u_2(1 - \frac{x_2}{v_1}(1 - \frac{1}{y_1})), \\ \qquad 1 - u_1(1 - \frac{x_2}{v_1}), \frac{x_2}{y_1(v_1 - x_2) + x_2}) & \text{if } v_1 > 0,\ y_1 > 0 \\ \min(1, 1 - u_1(1 - \frac{x_2}{v_1})) & \text{if } v_1 > 0,\ y_1 = 0 \\ 1 - u_1 & \text{if } v_1 = 0,\ x_2 = 0 \\ u_2 & \text{if } v_1 = 0,\ y_1 = 1 \\ 1 & \text{otherwise} \end{cases}$$

(CL) Conjunction Left:

(a) $\{ A \overset{u_1,u_2}{\underset{v_1,v_2}{\longleftrightarrow}} B,\ u_1 > 0 \vee v_1 > 0,\ A \xrightarrow{x_1,x_2} BC \}$

$\vdash AB \xrightarrow{z_1,z_2} C,$

$z_1 = \frac{x_1}{u_2},$

$$z_2 = \begin{cases} 0 & \text{if } x_2 = 0 \\ \min(1, \frac{x_2}{u_1}) & \text{if } x_2 > 0, u_1 > 0 \\ 1 & \text{otherwise} \end{cases}$$

(b) $\{ AB \xrightarrow{x_1,x_2} C,\ A \xrightarrow{y} C,\ y = 0 \vee y = 1 \} \vdash AB \xrightarrow{y} C$

(WCL) Weak Conjunction Left:

$\{ A \underset{v_1,v_2}{\overset{u_1,u_2}{\longleftrightarrow}} B,\ u_1 > 0 \vee v_1 > 0,\ B \xrightarrow{x_1,x_2} C, A \neq C\}$

$\vdash AB \xrightarrow{z_1,z_2} C,$

$$z_1 = \begin{cases} 1 & \text{if } x_1 = 1 \\ \max(0, 1 - \frac{1-x_1}{v_1}) & \text{if } x_1 < 1, v_1 > 0 \\ 0 & \text{otherwise} \end{cases}$$

$$z_2 = \begin{cases} 0 & \text{if } x_2 = 0 \\ \min(1, \frac{x_2}{v_1}) & \text{if } x_2 > 0, v_1 > 0 \\ 1 & \text{otherwise} \end{cases}$$

(CR) Conjunction Right:

(a) $\{ A \xrightarrow{x_1,x_2} B,\ AB \xrightarrow{y_1,y_2} C \} \vdash A \xrightarrow{z_1,z_2} BC,$

$z_1 = x_1 \cdot y_1,\ z_2 = x_2 \cdot y_2$

(b) $\{ A \xrightarrow{x_1,x_2} B,\ B \xrightarrow{y} C, A \neq C \}$

$\vdash A \xrightarrow{z_1,z_2} BC,$

$$z_1 = \begin{cases} 0 & \text{if } y = 0 \\ x_1 & \text{if } y = 1 \end{cases},\quad z_2 = \begin{cases} 0 & \text{if } y = 0 \\ x_2 & \text{if } y = 1 \end{cases}$$

(WCR) Weak Conjunction Right:

$\{ A \xrightarrow{x_1,x_2} B,\ A \neq C \} \vdash A \xrightarrow{0,x_2} BC$

(N) Negation:

$\{ A \xrightarrow{x_1,x_2} F \} \vdash A \xrightarrow{z_1,z_2} \overline{F},$

$z_1 = 1 - x_2,\ z_2 = 1 - x_1$

(CRN) Conjunction Right with Negation:

$\{ A \xrightarrow{x_1,x_2} C,\ A \xrightarrow{y_1,y_2} FC \} \vdash A \xrightarrow{z_1,z_2} \overline{F}C,$

$z_1 = \max(0, x_1 - y_2),\ z_2 = x_2 - y_1$

(WCRN) Weak Conjunction Right with Negation:

$\{ A \underset{v_1,v_2}{\overset{u_1,u_2}{\longleftrightarrow}} F,\ v_1 > 0,\ \ F \underset{y_1,y_2}{\overset{x_1,x_2}{\longleftrightarrow}} C,\ y_1 > 0,\ A \neq C \}$

$\vdash A \xrightarrow{0,z_2} \overline{F}C,$

$$z_2 = \min(1, (1 - y_1) \cdot \tfrac{u_2 \cdot x_2}{v_1 \cdot y_1}, 1 - u_1,$$
$$(1 - y_1) \cdot \tfrac{x_2}{v_1 \cdot y_1 + (1 - y_1) \cdot x_2})$$

(BI) Bidirectional Rule:

(a) $\{ A \overset{x_1,x_2}{\underset{0}{\longleftrightarrow}} B \} \vdash A \overset{0}{\longrightarrow} B$

(b) $\{ B \overset{x_1,x_2}{\longrightarrow} A,\ x_1 > 0 \} \vdash A \overset{0,1}{\longrightarrow} B$

(OI) Omega Inclusion:

(a) $\{ \Omega \overset{x_1,x_2}{\longrightarrow} A,\ x_1 > 0 \} \vdash A \overset{1}{\longrightarrow} \Omega$

(b) $\{ A \overset{y_1,y_2}{\longrightarrow} B \} \vdash A \overset{1}{\longrightarrow} \Omega$

(I) Invariance:

(b) $\{ AB \overset{x_1,x_2}{\longrightarrow} C,\ I(A,B,C) \} \vdash B \overset{x_1,x_2}{\longrightarrow} C$

(SYM) Symmetry:

$\{ I(A,B,C),\ B \overset{x_1,x_2}{\underset{y_1,y_2}{\longleftrightarrow}} C,\ x_1 > 0 \text{ or } y_1 > 0\} \vdash I(C,B,A)$

(DEC) Decomposition:

$\{ I(FB,C,D),\ I(\overline{F}B,C,D) \} \vdash I(B,C,D)$

(WU) Weak Union:

$\{ I(FB,C,D),\ I(\overline{F}B,C,D) \} \vdash I(F,BC,D)$

(CON) Contraction:

$\{ I(A,BC,D),\ I(B,C,D) \} \vdash I(AB,C,D)$

(CP) Comparative Probabilities:

(a) $\{ A \overset{x_1,x_2}{\longrightarrow} B,\ A \overset{\geq k[B]}{\longrightarrow} C \} \vdash A \overset{z_1,1}{\longrightarrow} C,$
$z_1 = min(1, k \cdot x_1)$

(b) $\{ A \overset{x_1,x_2}{\longrightarrow} B,\ A \overset{\leq k[B]}{\longrightarrow} C \} \vdash A \overset{0,z_2}{\longrightarrow} C,$
$z_2 = min(1, k \cdot x_2)$

Handling Temporal Knowledge in a Deductive Database System

Michael Böhlen and Robert Marti
Institut für Informationssysteme
ETH-Zentrum
8092 Zürich, Switzerland
e-mail: (boehlen|marti)@inf.ethz.ch

Abstract

We describe the design and implementation of a temporal deductive database system which supports (1) the storage of facts annotated with a time interval to indicate their perceived time of validity in the real world and (2) deduction rules which express temporal dependencies between (stored or derived) facts. The system features a logic-based query language in which even complex temporal queries can be expressed fairly concisely. We show how formulas involving temporal conjunction, disjunction, and negation can be translated into temporal extensions of the operators of relational algebra and into the database language SQL. A vital step in this translation is an implicit temporal normalization of intermediate results to avoid a redundant representation of temporal information which can even lead to incorrect results in certain cases.

Keywords: Temporal Databases, Temporal Knowledge, Temporal Reasoning, Valid Time, Logic Programming, Deductive Databases, Relational Databases, Relational Algebra, SQL.

1 Introduction

In most application areas, the contents of a database mirror the perceived state of a part of the real world (the universe of discourse) at a specific point in time, usually the present. Changes in the universe of discourse are reflected by replacing the corresponding part of the database contents, by adding to them, or by removing from them. However, there are many application areas where not only the present state of the universe of discourse is of interest, but also the history leading up to the present state and/or one or even several possible future scenarios. This is especially true in many banking applications where one is interested in the development of stock and money markets or even in political developments (see e.g. [Fischer 91]). Other areas where time plays an important role are ticket reservation systems, expert systems monitoring the functioning of complex technical equipment, and planning applications.

In present-day database management systems, there is practically no support for applications involving the time dimension. Typically, data which is superseded by more recent information is simply discarded. At best, commercial database systems support the keeping of an undo-log which records all database operations together with timestamps indicating the time of their execution. In the literature on temporal databases, these timestamps model what is called *transaction time* (see e.g. [Snodgrass et al. 85]). Such an undo-log makes it possible to reconstruct previous database states from the current database state by rolling back all transactions which committed since a specific point in time. Apart from the apparent inefficiency to answer queries pertaining to previous database states, this approach is in many cases insufficient because one can only make statements and ask queries about the actual execution of database operations. This may certainly be of interest, for example when auditing a database. However, in the kinds of applications mentioned above, one must be able to make statements about when certain events occurred in the universe of discourse and when future events are expected to occur. This notion of time in databases is typically called *valid time*, and we shall concentrate on this aspect of time in the rest of this paper[1].

Since current database systems do not support the notion of valid time, database administrators or even application programmers are forced to develop their

[1] Note that we use the term *temporal* database even though we do not consider transaction time in this paper. [McKenzie et al. 91] propose the use of the term *historical* database instead.

own ad-hoc solutions outside of the DBMS. This has the following drawbacks:

- Without a standard representation and standard operators to handle time, there are likely to be many different and incompatible solutions to the problem, aggravating the integration of separately designed databases and applications.
- Temporal operations, i.e., temporal conjunction, disjunction and negation, are rather tedious to express in current (non-temporal) database languages such as SQL. Therefore, the formulation of temporal queries is error-prone. (As it turns out, this is even true if the underlying storage manager and its query language are extensible with user-defined abstract data types, a facility provided by some post-relational and object-oriented DBMSs.)
- Without knowledge concerning the representation and processing of temporal data, a DBMS cannot do a good job of optimizing temporal queries which are often rather expensive.

Current approaches to deal with temporal data typically extend the relational algebra with a temporal join operator. In our work, we introduce temporal operators for first-order predicate logic instead. We show how temporal conjunctions can be translated into temporal join operators and/or selections. Similarly, temporal disjunctions can be mapped to a temporal union operator, while temporal negations are computed using a temporal difference operator. Finally, an existentially quantified temporal formula can be expressed as a projection.

It is important to note that with the exception of the temporal join, these temporal operators cannot always be expressed as a single expression in standard relational algebra, because their application can lead to results which contain redundancies with respect to the temporal dimension. Even worse, these redundancies can in turn induce incorrect answers to certain types of queries, for example, queries about the duration of events. Hence, the results of these operators must be converted into temporal normal form [Gabbay et al. 91].

Our declarative, logic-based approach extends nicely to the specification of deductive rules involving temporal dependencies. Temporal rules often allow a sizeable reduction of the amount of extensional data (facts) required to model certain real-world situations. As an example, consider an across-the-board salary raise of 5% to adjust for inflation in a company with a workforce of 10'000 as of a specific date. Instead of adding 10'000 facts, we can simply add a single rule which expresses the fact that everyone's salary at that date must be multiplied by 1.05.

The paper is structured as follows: In the next section, we motivate our approach to temporal information in deductive databases by giving a simple example. Section 3 then introduces the syntax to express facts, rules, and queries involving temporal aspects. In section 4, we briefly explain the translation of non-temporal formulas to relational algebra. Subsequently, we define the semantics of temporal formulas by specifying their translation to operators of a temporal relational algebra. In section 5, we show how the operations of the temporal relational algebra introduced in section 4 can be implemented on top of a relational DBMS using SQL statements embedded in a procedural language such as C. Section 6 presents an extended example to demonstrate the power of our temporal deductive database system while section 7 briefly discusses related work. Note that in the following, we assume the reader to be familiar with the basic definitions of deductive databases.

2 Motivation

The primary goal of our work is to provide concepts to store and process a large amount of both extensional and intensional time-varying information. However, we would also like to emphasize a secondary goal, namely, to support a high-level temporal query language which attempts to relieve users from having to specify implicit temporal connections between the atoms of a temporal logical formula. To achieve this, we always calculate the time range during which a temporal formula is valid automatically. This reduces the complexity of a large number of typical queries and in some sense enhances the expressive power of the query language. Let us illustrate this by considering a simple stock exchange example:

$/*\ share(CompanyName, Price)\ */$
$share('UBS', 4100)@[1991/1/3]$
$share('UBS', 3900)@[1991/1/4]$
$share('UBS', 3725)@[1991/1/5]$
$share('UBS', 3980)@[1991/1/6]$
$share('UBS', 3970)@[1991/1/7]$
$share('UBS', 3910)@[1991/1/8]$
$share('UBS', 4010)@[1991/1/9]$
$share('UBS', 3920)@[1991/1/10]$
$share('UBS', 4330)@[1991/1/11]$

To retrieve the time periods when the price of the *UBS* share was below 4000 SFr we issue the query

$$?\!-\{ValidTime\}\ \exists Price(share('UBS', Price) \wedge Price < 4000)$$

which returns the result

```
ValidTime
-------------------
[1991/1/10]
[1991/1/4-1991/1/9]
```

The curly braces denote a temporal query (cf. next section). Inside these braces we simply introduce a name for the resulting temporal interval. Note that the explicit quantification of the price forces a temporal normalization ([Gabbay et al. 91]). I.e. several tuples must be collapsed into a single one. One may argue that this is just pure cosmetic for the user's convenience. This is not true as we can easily show:

$?\text{–}\{\exists ValidTime: duration(ValidTime) > 3\,day\}$
$\exists Price(share(\text{'}UBS\text{'}, Price) \wedge Price < 4000)$

```
yes
```

This query returns yes or no depending on whether the price of the *UBS* share dropped below 4000 SFr. for more than three consecutive days. The ***duration*** function computes the length of a time interval and relies on a normalized data representation which eliminates the multiple storage of one fact with overlapping or adjacent time intervals. Without this normalization, the answer to the above query had been *no*.

3 Syntax

In this section we define the syntax of a temporal deductive database. It is based on the syntax of traditional deductive database languages as explained for example in [Ceri et al. 90], [Lloyd 87] and [Wüthrich 91].

Variables and *predicates* are represented by character strings starting with a letter. It is clear from the context whether a name represents a variable or a predicate. There are two kinds of variables, temporal and non-temporal ones. Besides numbers and strings we introduce temporal constants to model time intervals, e.g. [1989/3/5-1990/2/6]. The formal definition of such constants can be found in the syntax definition in the appendix. Here, we only mention that for user convenience we also support short forms of intervals. For example the temporal constant [1990] covers all events that took place during the year 1990. This interpretation is in our opinion the most natural one because it catches the meaning of a natural language statement.

Conjunction ($\wedge$), disjunction ($\vee$), negation ($\neg$) and implication ($\rightarrow$) are the *logical operators* that can be used to connect predicates. We also allow quantifiers ($\exists, \forall$) inside a formula. Parentheses are used to override the default precedences.

A *(temporal) term* is a (temporal) variable or a (temporal) constant. If p is an n-ary predicate, $t_1, \ldots, t_n$ are terms and T is a temporal term, then $p(t_1, \ldots, t_n)@T$ is a ***temporal atom***. The meaning of such an atom is, that $p(t_1, \ldots, t_n)$ is valid at time T. As we mentioned above, we allow the quantification of variables. Temporal variables can be quantified as any other variable. For user convenience it is also possible to omit this variable. So instead of $\exists T(sick(Emp)@T)$ we can just write $sick(Emp)$. Variable-free terms and atoms are called ground as usual. *Formulas* are defined recursively: Every atom is a temporal formula. If F and G are formulas then so are $\neg F$, $F \wedge G$, $F \vee G$ and $F \rightarrow G$. If F is a formula and x is a variable then $\exists x F$ and $\forall x F$ are formulas as well.

Besides the user defined predicates there exist also some predefined evaluable predicates for numbers and strings ($=, \neq, >, <, \geq, \leq$) with their standard interpretation. The predefined predicates for temporal terms are *before, after, precedes, follows, overlaps,...* as suggested in [Allen 83]. A complete list of these builtins and their graphical representation is listed in the appendix.

A ***temporal restriction*** is a formula that is built from temporal ground terms, a temporal variable, the predefined temporal predicates and the standard logical operators. It is used to restrict the temporal variable. Its use will become clear when we introduce temporal rules and queries below. A typical temporal restriction is for example $T\,before\,[1980] \vee T\,after\,[1990]$. Here we exclude all intervals T, valid anywhere between 1980 and 1990.

A ***temporal deductive database*** consists of a finite set of temporal and nontemporal facts and rules. A ***(temporal) fact*** is a (temporal) ground atom. $p(t_1, \ldots, t_n)@T \leftarrow \{Res\}\ W$ is a ***temporal rule*** with head $p(t_1, \ldots, t_n)@T$ and body W, if $p(t_1, \ldots, t_n)@T$ is a temporal atom and W is a formula. *Res*, a temporal restriction for T, can be used to put some constraints onto the resulting time range of W. Note that T is always instantiated to the resulting time interval of the temporal formula W. This interval is computed automatically to cut down the complexity of W and to enhance the expressive power of our language as we outlined in section 2. An example of a temporal rule is $r(X)@T \leftarrow \{T\,after[1990]\}\ p(X) \wedge q(X)$. In a temporal rule, all logical connectives have temporal semantics (see next section). If a rule does not contain a temporal restriction, the logical connectives have the usual (non-temporal) semantics ([Lloyd 87],[Burse 92]).

A ***temporal query*** has the form $?\text{–}\{T: Res\}\ W$, where W is a formula and Res is a temporal restriction for the variable T. Again T is automatically instantiated to the resulting time interval of W. The name T is arbitrary except that it may not occur in W. If we are not interested in the resulting interval we can quantify T or omit it completely (cf. syntax definition in the appendix). Again the presence respectively absence of the temporal restriction decides whether the query gets a temporal or non-temporal semantics.

4 Semantics

A temporal predicate p is represented as a "normal" predicate p' with an additional argument which denotes the time interval during which a fact of p is valid. For example, a (ground) fact $p(c)@t$ is represented as $p'(t,c)$. The set of facts belonging to the predicate p' is in turn represented as a relation P'.

Hence, the semantics of formulas in our temporal logic language can be defined in terms of the operators of relational algebra, namely, projections of the form $\pi_{attrs}R$, selections ($\sigma_{cond}R$), cartesian products ($R_1 \times R_2$) or natural joins ($R_1 \bowtie R_2$), union ($R_1 \cup R_2$), and set difference ($R_1 \setminus R_2$).

As a reminder, we will first define the semantics of formulas in "classical" (non-temporal) deductive databases. In order to do so, we assume that all formulas are normalized into what we call or-free parts normal form (similar to the miniscope form of [Bry 89], see [Bursc 92] for details). Moreover, we assume that constants only occur in built-in (evaluable) predicates. Formulas which do not fulfill the above requirements can easily be rewritten: A formula of the form $p(\ldots, const, \ldots)$ must be replaced by the formula $\exists Var_i\ (p(\ldots, Var_i, \ldots) \wedge Var_i = const)$.

Under these assumptions, it suffices to give the (somewhat informal) correspondences between formulas and relational algebra expressions below. Following [Ullman 88, p.100 ff], p and q denote user-defined predicates while P and Q denote the corresponding (extensional or intensional) relations. Moreover, F stands for an evaluable predicate (e.g. =, <), while $\vec{x}$ and $\vec{y}$ denote vectors of variable names. Finally, by abuse of mathematical notation, $\vec{x} \cup \vec{y}$ stands for a vector consisting of the union of the variable names occurring in $\vec{x}$ and $\vec{y}$ in some selected order. Similarly, we define $\vec{x} \cap \vec{y}$ as an intersection and $\vec{x} \setminus \vec{y}$ as a set difference of the respective variable names of $\vec{x}$ and $\vec{y}$.

(ground instances) of	are elements of	remarks
$p(\vec{x}) \wedge q(\vec{y})$	$\pi_{\vec{x}\cup\vec{y}}(P \bowtie Q)$	(1)
$p(\vec{x}) \vee q(\vec{y})$	$P \cup Q$	(2)
$p(\vec{x}) \wedge \neg q(\vec{y})$	$P \setminus \pi_{\vec{x}}(P \bowtie Q)$	(1), (3)
$p(\vec{x}) \wedge F(\vec{y})$	$\sigma_{F(\vec{y})}P$	(1), (3)
$\exists \vec{y}\ p(\vec{x})$	$\pi_{\vec{x}\setminus\vec{y}}P$	(3)

(1) The join condition is derived from the common variable names, $\vec{x} \cap \vec{y}$.
(2) $\vec{x}$ and $\vec{y}$ must contain the same variable names.
(3) $\vec{y}$ must be a subset of $\vec{x}$.

Note that restrictions (2) and (3) are enforced by the so-called allowedness ([Lloyd 87, p.89]) and safety ([Ceri et al. 90, p.208 ff]) conditions that have been defined for deductive databases.

Temporal logical connectives are a generalization of their non-temporal counterparts in that they do not only compute truth values but also the time intervals during which the resulting formula is perceived as being true. As we will see, a specific operation on time intervals is implicitly associated with every temporal logical connective, namely set intersection with conjunction, set union with disjunction, and set difference with negation.

4.1 Temporal Conjunction

The temporal conjunction selects a subset of the crossproduct of two relations P' and Q'. The resulting tuples are valid if and only if the tuples (ground atoms) of p and q are valid at the same time. Therefore, every ground instance of the formula

$$\{T\}\ p(\vec{x}) \wedge q(\vec{y})$$

which is an abbreviation for

$$\{T\}\ \exists T_p, T_q\ (p(\vec{x})@T_p \wedge q(\vec{y})@T_q)$$

is a member of the relation constructed by the following relational algebra expression:

$$\pi_{T,\vec{x}\cup\vec{y}}(\sigma_{T=T_p\cap T_q \wedge T\neq\emptyset}(P' \bowtie Q'))$$

where P' and Q' are joined according to the common variable names occurring in $\vec{x}$ and $\vec{y}$.

In other words, a ground instance of $p(\vec{x}) \wedge q(\vec{y})$ is true during a non-empty time interval T if

1. the corresponding ground instance of $p(\vec{x})$ is true during the interval T_p
2. the corresponding ground instance of $q(\vec{y})$ is true during the interval T_q
3. T is the (non-empty) intersection of T_p and T_q

This operation is equivalent to the temporal join that has been investigated in several papers on temporal relational databases (see e.g. [Elmasri 90], [Leung et al. 90]). The graphical representation of Fig. 1 shows a simple example of such a temporal conjunction. To simplify the illustration, we only show two facts $p(a)$ and $q(a)$ with their associated temporal arguments represented as a Boolean valued function of time, i.e., we show the time intervals when $p(a)$,

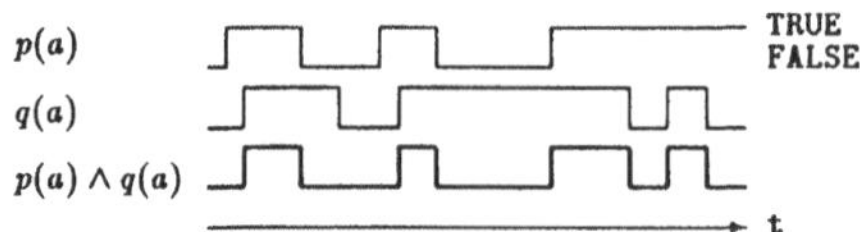

Fig. 1. The temporal conjunction

$q(a)$ respectively $p(a) \wedge q(a)$ hold and when they do not.

4.2 Temporal Disjunction

The temporal disjunction, as shown in Fig. 2, is a

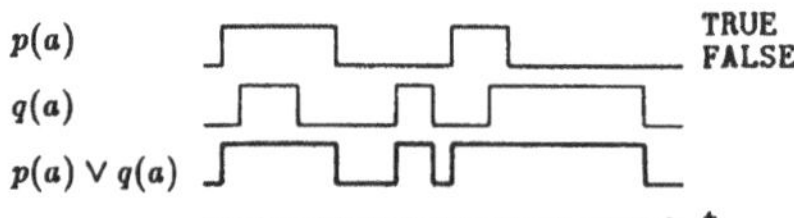

Fig. 2. The temporal disjunction

straightforward generalization of the non-temporal disjunction defined above: Every ground instance of the formula

$$\{T\}\ p(\vec{x}) \vee q(\vec{y})$$

which is an abbreviation for

$$\{T\}\ \exists T_p, T_q\ (p(\vec{x})@T_p \vee q(\vec{y})@T_q)$$

is a member of the relation

$$\nu(\pi_{T,\vec{x}}(\sigma_{T=T_p}P' \cup \sigma_{T=T_q}Q'))$$

The ν-operator ensures that the resulting relation is temporally normalized. We would like to emphasize that this operation is not within the realm of standard relational algebra. This means that the above expression cannot be implemented as a single database operation (see next chapter).
Following the above definitions, a ground instance of $p(\vec{x}) \vee q(\vec{y})$ is true during a time interval T if

1. the corresponding ground instance of $p(\vec{x})$ is true during the interval T_p
2. the corresponding ground instance of $q(\vec{y})$ is true during the interval T_q
3. T is (a subset of) the union of T_p and T_q

4.3 Temporal Negation

The temporal negation $p(\vec{x}) \wedge \neg q(\vec{y})$, illustrated in Fig. 3, restricts the time range of $p(\vec{x})$ to those periods

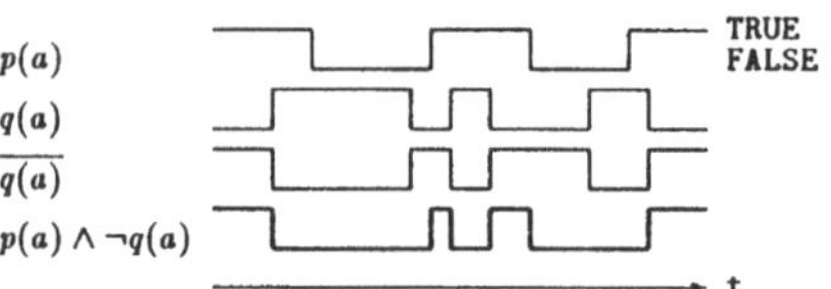

Fig. 3. The temporal negation

when $q(\vec{y})$ does not hold. This is equivalent to the temporal conjunction of $p(\vec{x})$ and $\overline{q(\vec{y})}$, where $\overline{q(\vec{y})}$ denotes the temporal complement of $q(\vec{y})$. Formally, every formula

$$\{T\}\ p(\vec{x}) \wedge \neg q(\vec{y})$$

which is an abbreviation for

$$\{T\}\ \exists T_p(p(\vec{x})@T_p) \wedge \neg\exists T_q(q(\vec{y})@T_q)$$

is defined as

$$\{T\}\ \exists T_p(p(\vec{x})@T_p \wedge \overline{\exists T_q(q(\vec{y})@T_q)})$$

In other words a ground instance of $p(\vec{x}) \wedge \neg q(\vec{y})$ is true during a time interval T if

1. the corresponding ground instance of $p(\vec{x})$ is true during the interval T_p
2. the corresponding ground instance of $q(\vec{y})$ is *not* true during the interval T_q
3. T is (a subset of) the set difference $T_p \setminus T_q$

4.4 Evaluable Predicates

Every ground instance of the formula

$$\{T\}\ p(\vec{x}) \wedge F(\vec{y})$$

which is an abbreviation for

$$\{T\}\ \exists T_p(p(\vec{x})@T_p) \wedge F(\vec{y})@[-\infty, +\infty]$$

where F is either a non-temporal evaluable predicate such as $<$ and $=$ or a temporal evaluable predicate such as *before* or *during*, is a member of the relation constructed by the relational algebra expression

$$\pi_{T,\vec{x}}(\sigma_{F(\vec{y})}P')$$

In order to compare temporal terms we provide the operators proposed by [Allen 83] (see appendix).

It should be obvious that temporal evaluable predicates, like the *duration* function we mentioned earlier, require a temporal normal form of the relations. Temporal predicates evaluated over an unnormalized relation can yield quite different results compared with the results we get evaluating them over a normalized relation.

4.5 Existential Quantification

Temporal existential quantification (which we often call somewhat imprecisely "temporal projection") is defined as in the non-temporal case in that ground instances of the formula

$$\{T\}\ \exists\vec{y}\,(p(\vec{x}))$$

which stands for

$$\{T\}\ \exists\vec{y}, T_p\,(p(\vec{x})@T_p)$$

are members of the relation

$$\nu(\pi_{T_p,\vec{x}\setminus\vec{y}}P')$$

Note that both variables holding temporal and non-temporal values can be existentially qualified. As with set union, the quantification of variables may result in overlapping or touching time intervals of tuples being equal in all other arguments which means that an additional normalization of the resulting tuples is necessary.

5 Implementation

In this section, we describe our implementation of a database manager which supports the temporal logic query language and operators introduced in sections 3 and 4. We have opted to do this by building a front-end to a commercial relational DBMS which supports standard SQL. This front-end is implemented entirely in Prolog and consists of modules for lexical and syntactic analysis, type inferencing, normalizing logic formulas, checking the allowedness of normalized formulas, translating them into SQL statements, and evaluating these statements in a correct order. (See [Marti et al. 89, Wüthrich 91] for a description of a similar front end for a deductive DBMS.)
The principal reason for basing our implementation on relational technology is that it allows a gradual transition from existing non-temporal databases servicing only SQL-based applications into an environment with both temporal and non-temporal information and applications. Clearly, an approach based on post-relational or object-oriented technology also appears feasible. We would like to emphasize, however, that merely adding a new abstract data type with operations to deal with (sets of) time intervals is not equivalent to our approach, since our temporal query language relieves the user of the burden to explicitly specify these operations in most cases.
Following [Gadia et al. 85, Navathe et al. 88], we represent a temporal interval as a pair of (integer) values t_s for its start point and t_e for its end point. Note that the intervals are closed at their lower but open at their upper end. So t_s belongs to the interval whereas t_e does not. Consequently, an empty interval is represented by a pair for which $t_s \geq t_e$ holds.
Clearly, a fact such as $p(a)$ can be true in the intervals $[t_{s_1}, t_{e_1}], [t_{s_2}, t_{e_2}], \ldots, [t_{s_n}, t_{e_n}]$, where $t_{e_{i-1}} < t_{s_i}$ for all $1 < i < n$, and false at all other points in time. Since a relational DBMS does not support structured attributes we have to store n tuples of the form $p(a)@[t_{s_i}, t_{e_i}]$. Moreover, in order to guarantee correct answers to temporal queries, we also have to ensure that no temporal information is stored redundantly, in that all overlapping and touching time intervals for a single fact $p(a)$ must be merged into one single time interval. As a result, the system should perform corresponding integrity checks whenever temporal information is updated. Moreover, as we shall see in the following subsections, the temporal operators have to guarantee the absence of temporal redundancy as well.
In order to simplify the following illustrations of the generated SQL statements, we assume that all predicates have one single non-temporal argument which is mapped to an SQL table with an attribute named c. As discussed above, the time interval is mapped to two attributes named t_s and t_e.

5.1 Intersection of Intervals

As mentioned in the introduction, the intersection of intervals (as required by the temporal conjunction) has been studied by several other authors and is quite well understood. The advantage of this operation is that it can be translated into a single closed relational algebra expression. Therefore several temporal extensions of relational database systems support this operation.

```
select greatest(p.ts, q.ts), least(p.te, q.te), p.c
from p, q
where p.c = q.c
and greatest(p.ts, q.ts) < least(p.te, q.te)
```

The condition $greatest(p.t_s, q.t_s) < least(p.t_e, q.t_e)$[2] restricts the join to those tuples overlapping in the temporal argument. Otherwise empty intervals ($t_s \geq t_e$) would be selected as well.
[Leung et al. 90] studied this operation in depth. They also motivated some alternatives to the conventional nested-loop join method, to improve the performance of a join. We don't consider such optimization techniques. Our goal here is, to find a translation of all temporal operators into equivalent standard relational expressions.

5.2 Temporal Normalization

In section 4.2 we showed that temporal disjunctions lead to the union of time intervals. Since this is not a closed operation, corresponding tuples with touching or overlapping time intervals must be merged into a single tuple. (As it turns out, the same is true if variables are explicitly quantified.) This process is called a temporal normalization. In both cases we can get tuples that are equal up to their time range and overlap in their temporal argument:

$$r(a)@[1981-1983]$$
$$r(a)@[1982-1987]$$
$$r(a)@[1987-1989]$$

The normalization merges these tuples into a single one; in this case:

$$r(a)@[1981-1989]$$

The importance of the temporal normalized form can be easily seen, if we consider the query $?\!- r(a)@T \wedge duration(T) < 6\ year$. In the unnormalized set, all three tuples satisfy the query, while the normalized tuple does not. This illustrates that the answer set can be quite different for normalized and unnormalized set of tuples.
The basic idea of the temporal normalization is the following: we iteratively generate new tuples from two overlapping ones until no more new tuples are generated. Such an iteration is a well known technique in deductive databases. It is used to calculate the least fixpoint of recursive queries ([Bancilhon et al. 86]). One problem with such iterations is the number of iteration steps that have to be performed until the fixpoint is reached. In our case the number of iteration steps are bounded by $O(\log n)$ where n is the number of tuples in the temporal unnormalized relation.

Proof: Let r be an unnormalized relation (eg. after having merged tuples of p and q in r). If we add the union of two overlapping (or touching) intervals in every iteration step, there remain only half as many intervals to be merged as before. This gives raise to a sequence as shown below:

r : n *intervals to be merged*
r^1 : $n/2$ *intervals to be merged*
r^2 : $n/4$ *intervals to be merged*
r^3 : $n/8$ *intervals to be merged*
r^4 : $n/16$ *intervals to be merged*
r^5 : $n/32$ *intervals to be merged*

⋮

r^x : $n/2^x$ *intervals to be merged*

$$n/2^x = 1 \Rightarrow n = 2^x \Rightarrow x = {}^2\log n$$ □

Figure 4 illustrates this process for $n = 8$. Note that not only the shown intervals are generated. If we join

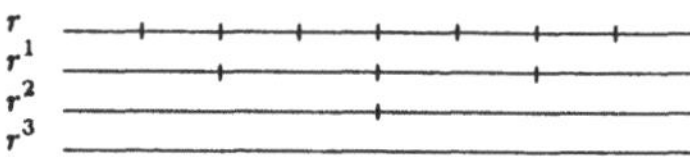

Fig. 4. The iteration process for n=8

all touching intervals in every step we get all possible subintervals (eg. intervals of length three) as well.
In reality the situation is even better than outlined in the proof above. We seldom can collapse all n tuples of a relation into one single tuple. Actually we could restrict n to be the greatest number of tuples in a chain of temporally overlapping or touching tuples. This is often much less than the number of tuples in the relation.
Let's now turn to the translation of a single iteration step. Again we assume that r is the relation that has to be normalized. The merging of two overlapping or touching intervals is translated into:

[2] *greatest* and *least* are not standard SQL functions. They are ORACLE builtins. It's possible to replace them by an equivalent standard SQL expression:

```
SELECT q.ts, p.te, p.c
    FROM p, q
    WHERE p.c = q.c
    AND q.ts ≤ p.ts AND p.ts < q.te AND q.te < p.te
UNION SELECT p.ts, q.te, p.c
    FROM p, q
    WHERE p.c = q.c
    AND p.ts ≤ q.ts AND q.ts < p.te AND p.te ≤ q.te
UNION SELECT p.ts, p.te, p.c
    FROM p, q
    WHERE p.c = q.c
    AND p.ts > q.ts AND p.te < q.te
UNION SELECT q.ts, q.te, p.c
    FROM p, q
    WHERE p.c = q.c
    AND q.ts > p.ts AND q.te < p.te
```

```
insert into r
  select a0.ts, a1.te, a0.c
    from r a0, r a1
    where a0.c = a1.c
    and a0.ts < a1.ts
    and a1.ts ≤ a0.te
    and a0.te < a1.te
  minus select * from r
```

Note the minus part in the select statement. It prevents the multiple insertion of the same tuple during the iteration. Because duplicates are not deleted automatically from ORACLE, we must do it by hand, otherwise the iteration (cf. below) will never terminate.
Now this SQL statement must be repeated until no more new tuples are added. In a procedural language this results in a simple control loop around the insert statement shown above:

```
repeat
    insert...
      :
until 'no tuples inserted'
```

After having constructed and added all desired intervals by merging touching or overlapping ones, we must delete the original tuples, since they are now contained in the larger ones:

```
delete from r a0
where exists (
    select *
      from r a1
      where a0.c = a1.c
      and (a0.ts > a1.ts and a0.te ≤ a1.te
           or a0.ts ≥ a1.te and a0.te < a1.c1))
```

Example: To clarify the temporal normalization we will give now a small example. The first table below shows the original table r, containing five tuples (Note that such a table can always result after a union or a projection). The second table illustrates the iteration process. The first iteration step adds three tuples, the second step one tuple to the original table r. The third iteration step yields no more tuples and so the iteration process terminates. After the deletion of those tuples contained in larger ones we get the two required tuples, displayed in the last table.

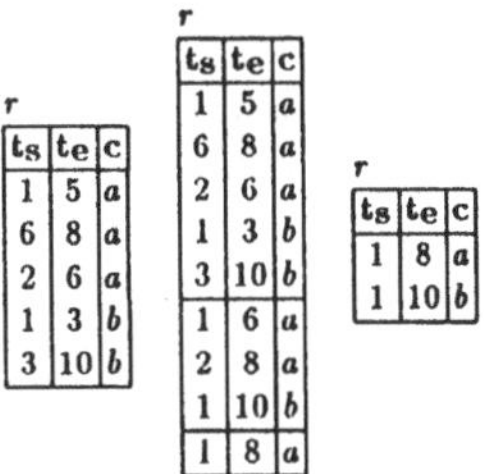

r

ts	te	c
1	5	a
6	8	a
2	6	a
1	3	b
3	10	b

r

ts	te	c
1	5	a
6	8	a
2	6	a
1	3	b
3	10	b
1	6	a
2	8	a
1	10	b
1	8	a

r

ts	te	c
1	8	a
1	10	b

5.3 Subtraction of Intervals

The temporal negation was defined in the previous section by the temporal complement. Out of two temporal adjacent intervals we constructed a temporal complement interval (cf. Fig. 3). In a relational database system it is quite cumbersome and expensive to get two adjacent intervals because relations are not ordered. Therefore we avoid the explicit construction of the temporal complement. Instead, we use interval subtraction to implement the temporal negation.
Let us first have a closer look at the interval subtraction. Figure 5 illustrates three cases of this subtraction for two overlapping intervals (we omitted those cases yielding an empty interval). The most interesting case is the one in the middle: it illustrates that interval subtraction can result in *two* intervals (This is the case when the interval T_2 is completely contained in T_1). Therefore, the result of an interval difference can be obtained by at most two steps. First, we construct the earlier (lower) interval by issuing an operation designated $\backslash_L$, resulting in $T_1 \backslash_L T_2$. Then, we construct the later (upper) interval by issuing an operation designated $\backslash_U$.

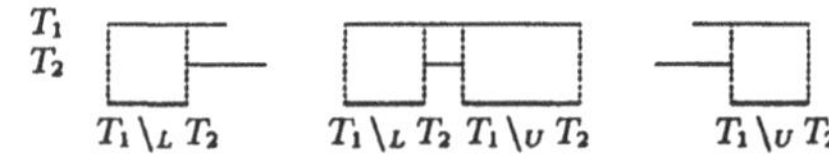

Fig. 5. Subtraction of intervals

Using these two operators, the temporal negation $p(c)@T_p \wedge \neg\exists T_q(q(c)@T_q)$ can be solved in three steps now.

First step: We take those tuples from p that overlap with some tuples of q such that $T_p \backslash_L T_q$ is not empty. Then we add to p the tuples $p(c)@[T_p \backslash_L T_q]$. In SQL this looks as follows:

```
insert into p
    select p.t_s, q.t_s, p.c
    from p, q
    where p.c = q.c
    and q.t_s ≥ p.t_s and q.t_s < p.t_e
```

Second step: Step two is symmetric to step one. We take those tuples from p that overlap with some tuples of q such that $T_p \setminus_U T_q$ is not empty. Then we add the tuples $p(c)@[T_p \setminus_U T_q]$ to p. The SQL statement looks quite similar as well:

```
insert into p
    select q.t_e, p.t_e, p.c
    from p, q
    where p.c = q.c
    and q.t_e > p.t_s and q.t_e ≤ p.t_e
```

If we look at these two statements it seems very natural to take them together into a single one where both select parts are connected by a union command. This is not possible because there may exist tuples in p that are overlapped at both interval ends by tuples of q. If we perform the two steps sequentially we catch these cases as well.

Third step: In the first two steps we only added tuples to p. The old ones, from which we computed the new ones by cutting the range of the temporal argument, were not removed. So we must delete now those tuples still overlapping with some tuples of q to get the required result:

```
delete from p
where exists (
    select *
        from q
        where p.c = q.c
        and(p.t_s ≥ q.t_s and p.t_s < q.t_e
        or q.t_s ≥ p.t_s and q.t_s < p.t_e))
```

Example: The first two tables below show the starting point, with p containing two and q containing three tuples. The third table illustrates the effect of the two insert statements explained above: the first one adds two tuples, the second one five tuples to p. After having deleted those tuples from the third table that overlap with some tuples of q we get the three result tuples displayed in the fourth table.

p

ts	te	c
2	10	a
12	16	a

q

ts	te	c
1	3	a
5	6	a
8	12	a

p

ts	te	c
2	10	a
12	16	a
2	5	a
2	8	a
3	10	a
3	5	a
3	8	a
6	10	a
6	8	a

p

ts	te	c
3	5	a
6	8	a
12	16	a

6 An Extended Example

In the following, we illustrate some of the expressive power of our query language by considering the consolidation of companies within a banking application. We assume that the knowledge base contains the following facts:

```
/* earnings(Company, Amount) */
earnings('BBC', 2.2)@[1980/3 – 1981/2]
earnings('BBC', 1.9)@[1981/3 – 1982/2]
earnings('BBC', 2.6)@[1982/3 – 1983/2]
earnings('ASEA', 10.3)@[1980/10 – 1981/9]
earnings('ASEA', 14.3)@[1981/10 – 1982/9]
earnings('ASEA', 13.9)@[1982/10 – 1983/9]
earnings('ABB', 22.9)@[1990/3 – 1991/2]
```

In a first step, we compute for each company their earnings per time unit. The resulting predicate is called *adjEarnings* and is useful for adding and comparing earnings of different companies later on:

```
adjEarnings(Company, AdjAmount)@Period
    ←
        earnings(Company, Amount)@Period ∧
        AdjAmount = Amount/duration(Period)
```

In order to be able to compute the consolidated earnings of the companies *BBC* and *ASEA* before they merged into the single company *ABB*, we can introduce the following (recursive!) rule:

```
adjEarnings('ABB', TotalAmount)@Period
    ←{Period}
        adjEarnings('BBC', AmountBBC) ∧
        adjEarnings('ASEA', AmountASEA) ∧
        TotalAmount = AmountBBC + AmountASEA
```

Note the implicit use of temporal conjunction in the above rule as a result of the temporal restriction *Period*. This allows us to handle business years which span different time periods. As a result, a user of the system who inquires about the earnings of *ABB* for the last 10 years does not have to be aware that it originally consisted of two independent companies which merged during the time period in question. This is illustrated by the following queries:

?– $\exists NormEarn($
$comp('ABB', NormEarn)@Time \wedge$
$RealEarn = NormEarn * duration(Time))$

RealEarn	Time
4.58	[1980/10-1981/2]
6.74	[1981/3-1981/9]
5.97	[1981/10-1982/2]
9.27	[1982/3-1982/9]
6.05	[1982/10-1983/2]
22.9	[1990/3-1991/2]

?– $\exists NormEarn($
$comp('ABB', NormEarn)@Time \wedge$
$AnnualEarn = NormEarn * 1\,year)$

AnnualEarn	Time
13.61	[1980/10-1981/2]
13.38	[1981/3-1981/9]
17.74	[1981/10-1982/2]
18.41	[1982/3-1982/9]
17.97	[1982/10-1983/2]
24.82	[1990/3-1991/2]

?– $\exists NormEarn, Time($
$comp('ABB', NormEarn)@Time \wedge$
$[1981/7]\ during\ Time \wedge$
$Earn\_July\_81 = NormEarn * 1\,month)$

Earn_July_81
1.11

7 Related Work

In the last decade there has been a considerable interest in temporal extensions of databases. HTQuel ([Gadia et al. 85]), TSQL ([Navathe et al. 88]) and TQuel ([Snodgrass 84]) support temporal extensions of popular relational database query languages. The main goal of these languages was a temporal extension of the base query languages (Quel, SQL) in such a way that non-temporal queries and updates were still handled. Due to this restriction, all these languages don't provide the full functionality of the temporal relational algebra. None of these approaches can deal with temporal disjunction or negation. Another drawback is the missing power in the deduction of new knowledge.

Other authors proposed temporal extensions of (extended) entity-relationship models. These models allow a greater flexibility in the representation of temporal intervals. For example if set valued arguments are supported, one can choose set of intervals as his base type ([Gadia et al. 91, Elmasri 90]).

A closely related work is [Gabbay et al. 91]. Gabbay and McBrien studied the translation of the five temporal relational algebra operators to nontemporal ones and to SQL as well. They showed that it's not possible to encode the temporal union and difference in terms of the standard relational algebra ([Gabbay et al. 91, p.427, table 3.1]). As a possible solution they suggested an extension of the relational algebra by these two operators. We have shown here how these operations can be implemented if we embed the relational algebra in a procedural language, providing a simple loop mechanism.

8 Conclusions

We have described the translation of temporal formulas to temporal relational algebra and to standard SQL expressions. Straightforward solutions exist for the temporal conjunction. More sophisticated methods are required to solve temporal negation and disjunction. They can't be implemented completely within the framework of the relational algebra. Several standard relational algebra operations are needed to implement these operations. We proved that the costs to do this are logarithmic in the number of tuples (temporal disjunction) or even constant (temporal negation).

Future work will investigate the integration of temporal and nontemporal operators. We have considered here only temporal logical operators. But there exist cases where we would like to perform just standard logical operations without doing any temporal computation. Two different approaches are possible to solve this problem. On one side we can try to enhance the semantics of our temporal operators to catch these cases. On the other side we can allow both sets of operations: temporal and nontemporal ones. The user must then select in every case the appropriate operation.

9 Acknowledgements

We would like to thank J. Burse, A. Dittrich, R. Gross, D. Schmidt, H. Walther and the referees for their helpful comments on earlier drafts of this paper.

References

[Allen 83] J.F.Allen. *Maintaining Knowledge about Temporal Intervals*. Communications of the ACM, Vol. 16, Number 11, November 1983.

[Allen 85] J.F.Allen. *A Common-Sense Theory of Time.* Proceedings of the International Joint Conference on Artificial Intelligence, 1985.

[Bancilhon et al. 86] F.Bancilhon, R.Ramakrishnan. *An Amateur's Introduction to Recursive Query Processing Strategies.* ACM SIGMOD Conference, 1986.

[Benthem 83] J.F.A.K. van Benthem. *The Logic of Time.* D.Reidel Publishing Company, 1983.

[Bry 89] F.Bry. *Towards an Efficient Evaluation of General Queries: Quantifier and Disjunction Processing Revisited.* Proc. ACM SIGMOD Int. Conf. on Management of Data, 1989, pp. 193-204.

[Burse 92] J.Burse. *ProQuel: Using Prolog to Implement a Deductive Database System.* Technical report. Institut für Informationssysteme ETH Zürich, 1992.

[Ceri et al. 90] S.Ceri, G.Gottlob, L.Tanca. *Logic Programming and Databases.* Surveys in Computer Science, Springer Verlag, 1990.

[Elmasri 90] R.Elmasri. *A Temporal Model and Query Language for ER Databases.* IEEE Data Engineering Conference, 1990.

[Fischer 91] M.C.Fischer. *Knowledge-based Simulation and Country Risk Assessment in Commercial Banking.* Ph.D. Thesis Nr. 9543, ETH Zürich, 1991.

[Gabbay et al. 91] D.Gabbay, P.McBrien. *Temporal Logic & Historical databases.* Proceedings of the 17th International Conference on Very Large Databases, 1991.

[Gadia et al. 85] S.K.Gadia, J.H.Vaishnav. *A Query Language for a Homogeneous Temporal Database.* ACM SIGMOD-SIGACT, Principles of Database Systems, 1985.

[Gadia et al. 91] S.K.Gadia, C.Yeung. *Inadequacy of Interval Timestamps in Temporal Databases.* Information Sciences, Nr. 54, 1991.

[McKenzie et al. 91] L.E.McKenzie, R.T.Snodgrass. *Evaluation of Relational Algebras Incorporating the Time Dimension in Databases.* ACM Computing Surveys, Vol. 23, No. 4, December 1991.

[Leung et al. 90] C.Leung, R.Muntz. *Query Processing for Temporal Databases.* Proceedings of the 6th International Conference on Data Engineering, 1990.

[Lloyd 87] J.W.Lloyd. *Logic Programming.* Symbolic Computation, Springer Verlag, 1987.

[Marti et al. 89] R.Marti, C.Wieland, B.Wüthrich. *Adding Inference to a Relational Database Management System.* Datenbanksysteme in Büro, Technik und Wissenschaft, Springer Verlag, Informatik-Fachbericht Nr. 204, 1989.

[Navathe et al. 88] S.B.Navathe, R.Ahmed. *TSQL: A Language Interface for History Databases.* Temporal Aspects in Information Systems. C.Rolland, F.Bodart, M.Leonard (Editors). Elsevier Science Publishers B.V., 1988.

[Snodgrass 84] R.Snodgrass. *The Temporal Query Language TQuel.* Proceedings of the 3rd ACM SIGMOD Symposium on Principles of Database Systems, Waterloo Canada, April 1984.

[Snodgrass et al. 85] R.Snodgrass, I.Ahn. *A Taxonomy of Time in Databases.* ACM SIGMOD, International Conference on Management of Data, May 1985.

[Ullman 88] J.D.Ullman. *Principles of Database and Knowledge-Base Systems.* Volume I, Computer Science Press, 1988.

[Wüthrich 91] B.Wüthrich. *Large Deductive Databases with Constraints.* Ph.D. Thesis Nr. 9401, ETH Zürich, 1991.

A Temporal Relations

For completeness we show here the possible relations between time intervals that are permitted. Note that not all relations shown in [Allen 83] are provided. We omit the inverse of the last three, rarely used relations, for example. For a thorough discussions of these relations the reader is referred to [Allen 83, Allen 85].

- I_1 `before` I_2
- I_1 `after` I_2
- I_1 `preceds` I_2
- I_1 `follows` I_2
- I_1 `during` I_2
- I_1 `contains` I_2
- I_1 `equal` I_2
- I_1 `overlaps` I_2
- I_1 `starts` I_2
- I_1 `ends` I_2

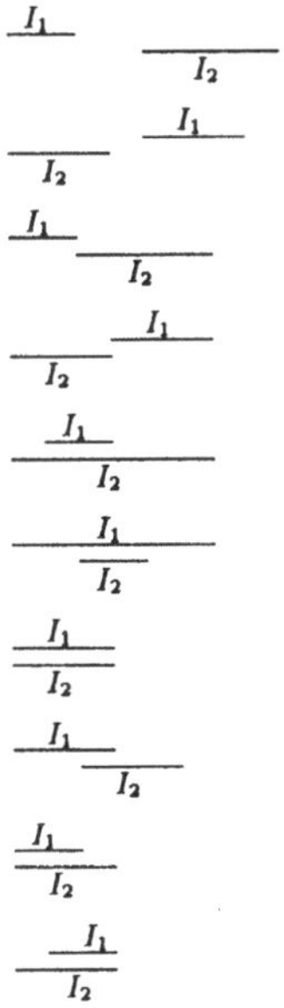

B Syntax Definition

We present a simplified version of the EBNF syntax of our temporal deductive database system ProQuel. Some features, such as the insertion and the deletion of tuples or the creation and the dropping of tables have been omitted. We focused on those aspects that are heavily affected by the temporal concepts, eg. queries, rules and facts.

Note also that we abstracted from the actual key sequence that has to be entered on the keyboard, to get a more readable syntax.

```
query     = "?-"["("var[":"tRes]")"] formula.
rule      = atom "←"["("tRes")"] formula.
fact      = atom.

formula   = disj["→"disj].
disj      = conj{"∨"conj}.
conj      = subform{"∧"subform}.
subform   = {"¬"|("∃"|"∀")var}literal.
literal   = "("formula")"|evalPred|atom.
evalPred  = expr relOp expr.
atom      = ident["("expr{","expr}")"]
            ["@"interval].

expr      = ["-"]term{("+"|"-")term}.
term      = factor{("*"|"/"|"mod"|"div")
            factor}.
factor    = "("expr")"|string|integer|float|
            var|interval|"duration("tTerm")".

relOp     = ">"|"<"|"="|"≤"|"≥"|"≠"|tRelOp
tRelOp    = "before"|"after"|"precedes"|
            "follows"|"during"|"contains"|
            "overlaps"|"starts"|"ends"|
            "equal".

tTerm     = interval|var.
interval  = "["timept["-"timept]"]".
timept    = ∞ | Year["/"Month["/"Day[
                "/"Hour"/"Minute[
                "/"Second]]]]].

tRes      = tDisj["→"tDisj].
tDisj     = tConj{"∨"tConj}.
tConj     = tLit{"∧"tLit}.
tLit      = "("tRes")"|"¬"tLit|
            tTerm tRelOp tTerm.
```

Regelgestützte Generalisierung von Gebäudegrundrissen in geographischen Datenbanken

Ralf Bill
Institut für Photogrammetrie
Universität Stuttgart
Keplerstr. 11
7000 Stuttgart 1

Marko Krause
Mozartstr. 36
7053 Kernen 1

Andreas Reuter
Institut für Parallele und
Verteilte Höchstleistungsrechner
Universität Stuttgart
Breitwiesenstr. 20–22
7000 Stuttgart 80

Keywords: Generalisierung, rechnergestützte Kartographie, Geo-Informationssysteme, regelbasierter Ansatz, relationale Datenbank, geometrische Manipulation, Graphmanipulation, topologische Manipulation

Zusammenfassung

Die Bearbeitung raumbezogener Daten zwecks Darstellung in Landkarten wird zunehmend mit Computerunterstützung durchgeführt. Für den Prozeß der kartographischen Generalisierung, in dem die darzustellenden Gegebenheiten aufgrund von Platzmangel in der Darstellung vereinfacht bzw. modifiziert werden, existieren noch keine Verfahren, die den vielfältigen Anforderungen dieses Vorgangs gerecht werden. Es wird ein regelbasierter Ansatz vorgestellt, der sowohl der heuristischen Natur dieses Vorgangs entspricht als auch der geforderten Flexibilität gerecht wird, die es erlaubt, ihn unterschiedlichen Anforderungen anzupassen.

1 Problembeschreibung

Jede Karte ist als Modell der Wirklichkeit eine vereinfachte und generalisierte Darstellung, denn schon bei der Datenerhebung erfolgt eine Klassifizierung und Auswahl der aufzunehmenden Objekte (nach [G. Hake (1982)]). Diese Art der Generalisierung wird im folgenden Beitrag allerdings nicht behandelt. Statt dessen wird untersucht, wie Karteninformationen, die in einer Datenbank gespeicherten sind, beim Übergang von einem großen Maßstab (z. B. 1:5000 als Ausgangsmaßstab) in einen kleinreen Maßstab (z. B. 1:25000 als Folgemaßstab) automatisch so aufbereitet werden können, daß das Ergebnis trotz des geringeren Platzangebots im Zielmaßstab gut lesbar bleibt und gleichzeitig möglichst wenig verfälscht wird. Man bezeichnet dies als Generalisierung zum Zwecke kartographischer Wiedergabe, die kartographische Generalisierung im engeren Sinne. Die vorliegende Arbeit behandelt davon ausschließlich einen Teilaspekt: die Generalisierung von Gebäudegrundrissen. Im Gegensatz zu den bisher bekannten Ansätzen ist sie aber nicht auf einen bestimmten Maßstabsübergang fixiert. Sie basiert auf Ergebnissen einer Studienarbeit an der Fakultät Informatik der Universität Stuttgart ([M. Krause (1992)]).

Kartographische Generalisierung ist ein Vorgang, der üblicherweise von einem ausgebildeten Kartographen manuell durchgeführt wird. Die Notwendigkeit zur Generalisierung ist aufgrund des geringeren Platzangebots im Zielmaßstab gegeben und ihr Hauptziel ist, eine *lesbare* Darstellung zu erzielen. Dieses Prinzip der *Lesbarkeit* widerspricht den Prinzipien der *geometrischen Richtigkeit* und der *Vollständigkeit*, die ebenfalls zu berücksichtigen sind. Im Einzelfall muß also zwischen diesen drei Prinzipien vermittelt werden. Der Kartograph wendet beim Generalisieren sieben elementare Vorgänge an, die kartenlogisch konsequenten Konventionen unterliegen und in Abb. 1 (links) beispielhaft dargestellt sind. Eine ausführliche Einführung in die kartographische Generalisierung findet sich in [G. Hake (1982), Kap. 4.4].

Elem. Vorgang	Ausgangs- darstellung	Generali- sierung	Folgedar- stellung
1. Verein- fachen			
2. Ver- größern			
3. Ver- drängen			
4. Zus.- fassen			
5. Aus- wählen			
6. Klassi- fizieren, Typi- sieren			
7. Bewer- ten			

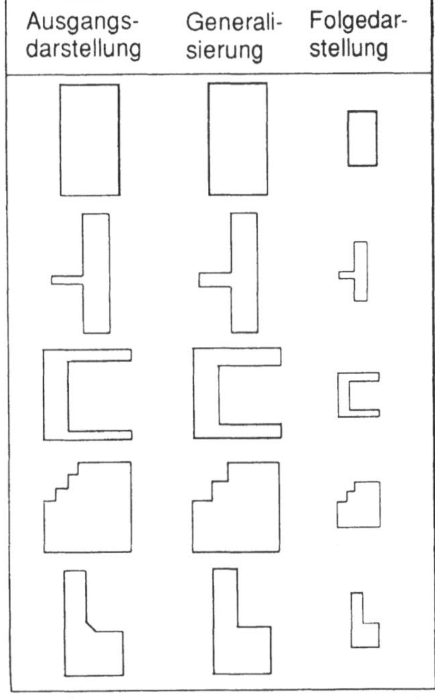

Abbildung 1: links: Elementare Vorgänge der kartographischen Generalisierung [G. Hake (1982)]
rechts: Beispielhafte Generalisierung an Einzelgebäuden

Die Vorgänge Vereinfachung und Vergrößerung sind rein geometrische Operationen; Verdrängung, Zusammenfassung und Auswahl sind geometrische und quantitative Methoden. Typisierung und Bewertung sind qualitative Maßnahmen und dienen der inhaltlichen Hervorhebung.

Die Bedeutung der *automatischen* kartographischen Generalisierung nimmt mit der Verfügbarkeit raumbezogener Daten und der Systeme zu ihrer Verarbeitung, Analyse und Präsentation, sogenannter Geo-Informationssysteme (GIS, s. [R. Bill, D. Fritsch (1991)]), zu. Im Vordergrund dieser Arbeit steht nur der Teilaspekt der Generalisierung von Grundrissen einzelner Gebäude, der auch kurz **Gebäudegeneralisierung** genannt wird. Die Begriffe Grundriß und Gebäude sind im folgenden austauschbar. Gebäudegeneralisierung erfolgt durch Transformation der in der Datenbank gespeicherten geometrischen Gebäudedaten bezogen auf den größten (genauesten) Maßstab. Um festzustellen, an welchen Stellen eines Gebäude Veränderungen erforderlich sind, werden Seitenlängen, Abstände, Flächen- und Winkelmaße mit gewissen Minimalmaßen verglichen, die vom Zielmaßstab abhängen. Werden Minimalmaße unterschritten, so muß eine Transformation stattfinden, die diese Gegebenheit beseitigt, um Lesbarkeit zu gewährleisten. Wie diese Transformation im Einzelfall aussieht, beruht auf Intuition und mehr oder weniger verbindlichen Konventionen. Gerade diese heuristische Vorgehensweise legt die Modellierung der kartographischen Generalisierung durch einen regelbasierten Ansatz nahe. Abb. 1 (rechts) zeigt beispielhaft einige Gebäudedarstellungen und daraus abgeleitete generalisierte Darstellungen.

Folgend wird kurz der Stand der Technik auf dem Gebiet der automatischen Generalisierung skizziert. Seit nunmehr zwanzig Jahren beschäftigt Geodäten dieses Thema. [W. Staufenbiel (1973)] formuliert eine Reihe von geometrischen Gegebenheiten, die jeweils, wenn sie für einen Gebäudeteil zutreffen, auf diesen die Anwendung einer Aktion auslösen, die ihn aufgrund wohldefinierter Berechnungsvorschriften verändert. Die Aktionen stellen lokale Generalisierungsmaßnahmen dar; die Reihenfolge ihrer Anwendung wird von einem festen Ablaufschema vorgegeben, das von der konkreten Gebäudeform unabhängig ist. Staufenbiels Implementierung erreicht bei 90% üblicher Gebäudeformen befriedigende Ergebnisse. Die geometrischen Gegebenheiten, die sich im wesentlichen an graphischen Mindestgrößen im Folgemaßstab orientieren, lassen sich informal folgendermaßen wiedergeben:

- Gebäudeseiten, die kleiner sind als der Längengrenzwert G (z. B. 0,3 mm), müssen verändert werden.
- Gebäudeteilflächen (Vorbauten, Einsprünge), die kleiner sind als der Flächengrenzwert F (z. B. 0,09 mm^2), müssen verändert werden.

Unterschreiten Gebäudeseiten oder -teilflächen ihre Mindestdimension, so werden sie geeignet weggelassen oder so verändert, daß sie ihre Mindestdimension erhalten. Auf der Grundlage von Staufenbiels Ansatz existiert auch eine Softwarelösung, die als Bestandteil des photogrammetrisch-kartographischen Systems PHOCUS ([K. Menke (1992)]) am Markt kommerziell angeboten wird.

Einen ganz anders gearteten Ansatz präsentiert [U. Meyer (1989)], der auf der Basis der Mustererkennung in Rasterdaten Gebäude als ganzes zu L-, Z- und T-Formen klassifiziert. Bei einer kleinen Anzahl möglicher Gebäudeformen ist dieser Ansatz gut geeignet; bei komplizierten Formen werden lediglich signaturhafte Ergebnisse erzielt. Der Ansatz erfordert die Wandlung von Vektordaten in Rasterdaten und umgekehrt, wobei letztere Konversion nicht ohne weiteres möglich ist.

Der in [M. Krause (1992)] bearbeitete Ansatz ähnelt dem von W. Staufenbiel, versucht jedoch eine Loslösung von den geometrischen Details hin zur Behandlung graphisch-begrifflicher Konfigurationen, die durch abstrakte Begriffe, wie den der visuellen Ähnlichkeit von Strecken, Winkeln und Gebäudeteilen, bestimmt werden. Darüber hinaus ist auch thematisches, vom Zweck der zu erstellenden Karte abhängiges Generalisieren möglich, das außer der bloßen Erscheinungsform der Objekte deren Bedeutung mit berücksichtigt. Dies ist im Zusammenhang mit GIS wichtig. Im Gegensatz zu Staufenbiels Ansatz werden die Regeln der Generalisierung nicht fest ins System eingebaut, sondern als Parameter eingegeben, was ihm die gewünschte Flexibilität verleiht. Die Vorteile der regelorientierten Generalisierung werden auch in [B. Butterfield, R. McMaster, Ed. (1991)] diskutiert.

2 Ein regelbasierter Ansatz zur Gebäudegeneralisierung

2.1 Das Datenbankschema

Das dem Ansatz zugrunde liegende Datenbankschema modelliert die Struktur von polygonalen Gebäudegrundrissen durch einen gerichteten Graphen. Knoten entsprechen darin den Polygonecken, Kanten den Polygonseiten. Die Knoten tragen die Koordinaten der Polygonecken als Attribute. Die Orientierung der Kanten, die einen Grundriß begrenzen, ist so gewählt, daß die begrenzte Fläche stets auf der rechten Seite ist. Mit dieser Konvention ist die Interpretation von Attributen eindeutig, die von der Orientierung der Kanten abhängen, wie beispielsweise der Winkel, den eine Kante mit der x-Richtung des Koordinatensystems einschließt (der sog. Richtungswinkel t). Haben zwei Grundrisse eine Seite gemeinsam, so wird diese für jeden Grundriß extra durch eine Kante repräsentiert, die einander entgegen gerichtet sind. Die damit verbundenen Knoten sind für beide Gebäude jedoch identisch. (s. Abb. 2 links). In diesem Modell begrenzt eine Kante genau einen Grundriß und hat, bezogen auf diesen Grundriß, genau eine Nachfolgerkante. Gemeinsam bilden sie darauf einen Winkel, dessen Attribute vereinbarungsgemäß der ersten Kante zugeordnet werden. Damit können Winkel repräsentiert werden, ohne dafür eine eigene Relation zu verwalten. Das im folgenden zugrundegelegte

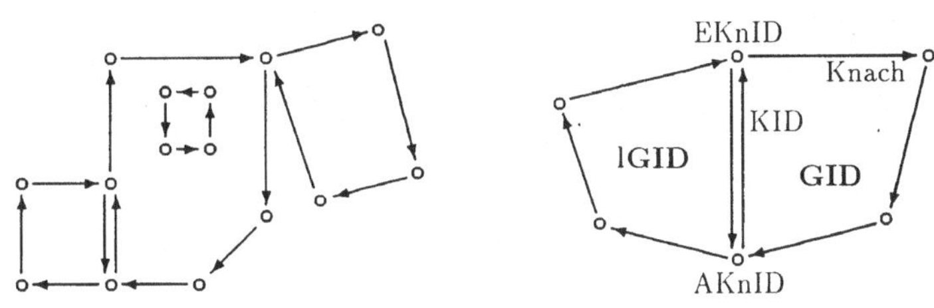

Abbildung 2: Beispielgraphen zur Repräsentation von Grundrissen

Relationenschema mit einigen abgeleiteten Attributen sieht folgendermaßen aus:

Gebäude(**GID**, Flächenmaß, ...)
Kante (**KID**, **GID**, **AKnID**, **EKnID**, lGID, Knach, Länge, Kat, S, t, w, WKlasse, ...)
Knoten (**KnID**, **X**, **Y**, ...)

Die fett gedruckten Attribute sind ausreichend, um die Grundrißgeometrie vollständig zu beschreiben. Die restlichen Attribute sind daraus ableitbar und werden allein aus Leistungsgründen mitgeführt. Knach und lGID dienen dem einfachen Zugriff auf Kanten, die durch den Knoten EKnID mit der Kante KID inzident sind, ohne daß dabei die Knotenrelation benötigt wird (s. Abb. 2 rechts). Die restlichen Attribute sind aus den Koordinaten X und Y ableitbar. Die Bedeutung der Attribute soll kurz erläutert werden (s. auch folgenden Abschnitt):

GID: Gebäude-Identifikator (in Kantenrelation Fremdschlüssel für die Gebäuderelation)
KID: Kanten-Identifikator
AKnID,EKnID: Knoten-Identifikator des Anfangs- bzw. Endknotens der Kante KID (Fremdschlüssel für die Knotenrelation)
lGID: Identifikator des links von der Kante liegenden Gebäudes (Fremdschlüssel für die Gebäuderelation); NULL, falls kein angrenzendes Gebäude vorhanden ist
Knach: Identifikator für die Nachfolgekante im Gebäudezyklus (Fremdschlüssel für die Kantenrelation)
Flächenmaß: Größe des Grundrisses (aus X und Y aller zu GID gehörenden Knoten abgeleitet)
Länge: Kantenlänge (aus X und Y von AKnID und EKnID abgeleitet)
Kat: Längenkategorie; Größenordnung der Kantenlänge (aus Länge abgeleitet)
S: Ähnlichkeitswert; erlaubt zu bestimmen, ob zwei verschiedene Kanten einem Betrachter als etwa gleich lang erscheinen (aus Kat abgeleitet)
t: Richtungswinkel; Winkel zwischen der Kantenrichtung und der x-Richtung des Koordinatensystems (aus X und Y von AKnID und EKnID abgeleitet)
w: Innenwinkel zwischen KID und Knach (aus t von KID und Knach abgeleitet)
WKlasse: Größenordnung des Winkels w (z. B. gestreckt, mittelstumpf, halbstumpf, rechtwinklig, halbspitz,...; aus w, Kat und Kat von Knach abgeleitet)

Der folgende Abschnitt beschreibt einige Attribute ausführlicher. Das Regelsystem ist so entworfen, daß die hier vorgeschlagenen Attribute und deren Ableitungsfunktionen leicht durch andere ersetzt werden können. Insofern stellen sie ein Musterbeispiel dar, das nach Bedarf erweitert und modifiziert werden kann.

2.2 Prädikate und Attribute zur Beschreibung von Regelbedingungen

In unserem Ansatz verwenden wir ein vorwärtsverkettendes Regelsystem, dessen Arbeitsweise am Vorbild der Programmiersprache OPS_5 nachzuvollziehen ist ([Krickhahn (1987)]). Die Regeln haben darin die Form: **Wenn** <*Bedingung*> **dann** <*Aktion*>. Findet das Regelsystem Daten, die die Bedingung einer Regel erfüllen, so wird ggf. die zugehörige Aktion darauf angewendet. Diese Vorgehensweise heißt **Vorwärtsverkettung** und bildet den Gegensatz zu **Rückwärtsverkettung**, die beispielsweise der Programmiersprache PROLOG zugrunde liegt. Durch übergeordnete heuristische Auswahlregeln wird bei Vorwärtsverkettung der Weg zu einem Endzustand, der durch die Regelanwendungen erreicht werden soll, gesucht. Für die kartographische Generalisierung ist Vorwärtsverkettung die geeignete Strategie, da für Rückvärtsverkettung der Zielzustand selbst bekannt sein muß; hier kennen wir nur dessen Eigenschaften. Die genauen Unterschiede zwischen Vorwärts- und Rückwärtsverkettung sowie die Kopplung von Regelsystemen mit Datenbanken werden in [Krickhahn (1987), N. M. Matthos (1989), A. Reuter (1986)] dargelegt.

Das Regelwerk beschreibt auf der Grundlage der Gebäudegeometrie, wie Gebäudeteile, die im Zielmaßstab nicht mehr erkennbar sind, verändert werden müssen, damit auch der resultierende Umriß im kartographischen Sinne korrekt ist. Die Menge dieser gesuchten geometrischen Situationen wird ausschließlich durch die Regelbedingungen bestimmt, wobei jede Bedingung Aussagen macht über Merkmale der gesuchten Zielobjekte. Formal sind diese Aussagen über Merkmale Prädikate, die auf Attribute angewendet werden. Die umgangssprachliche Bedingung „X ist ein Gebäude und das Flächenmaß von X ist kleiner als $50\,\mathrm{m}^2$" wird dabei durch 'Gebäude(X) $\wedge$ X.Flächenmaß $\leq 50\,\mathrm{m}^2$' ausgedrückt. Das erste Prädikat bestimmt, daß das Objekt X vom Typ Gebäude sein soll, das zweite legt dessen maximale Grundfläche fest. Der Ausdruck '$50\,\mathrm{m}^2$' läßt sich dabei als ein global verfügbares Attribut mit konstantem Wert auffassen. Die Regelbedingungen in diesem Ansatz bestehen ausschließlich aus Prädikaten, die auf Attribute (und Konstanten) angewendet werden und die logisch mit „und" verknüpft sind.

$$\mathrm{P}_1(X_{10}.\mathrm{A}_{10},\ldots,X_{1m_1}.\mathrm{A}_{1m_1}) \wedge \ldots \wedge \mathrm{P}_n(X_{n0}.\mathrm{A}_{n0},\ldots,X_{nm_n}.\mathrm{A}_{nm_n})$$

Jedes A_{ik} ist dabei ein Attribut, das für die zugehörigen Objekte X_{ik} definiert ist; statt $X_{ik}.\mathrm{A}_{ik}$ kann auch ein konstanter Attributwert eingesetzt werden. Der Rest dieses Abschnitts stellt Attribute und Prädikate vor, die für Regelbedingungen in unserem Ansatz verwendet werden.

In dem eingangs definierten Relationenschema sind nur drei Objektklassen vorhanden: Gebäude, Kanten und Knoten. Andere Objekttypen, wie z. B. Winkel, werden nicht explizit in Relationen repräsentiert. Eine Ausnahme bilden diejenigen Winkel, die von benachbarten Seiten eines Grundrisses gebildet werden: ihre Attribtue (w und WKlasse) sind der linken Seite vom Gebäudeinnern aus betrachtet zugeordnet und befinden sich deshalb in der Kantenrelation. Da sie häufig benötigt werden, ist es sinnvoll, sie nicht in einer eigenen Relation zu verwalten. Dies sollte jedoch nicht zu Verständnisproblemen führen.

Objekte vom Typ Knoten tragen die einzigen lagebeschreibenden Attribute, die Koordinaten **X, Y** des repräsentierten Punktes. Die einzigen vom Maßstab der Koordinaten abhängigen Attribute der Kante sind ihre **Länge** und ihr **Richtungswinkel t** Aus den Richtungswinkeln zweier beliebiger Kanten läßt sich leicht der von ihnen eingeschlossene Winkel berechnen, ohne daß die Koordinaten der Endpunkte und damit die Knotenrelation benötigt werden.

Die Attribute X, Y, Länge und Richtungswinkel dürfen von Regelbedingungen nicht unmittelbar verwendet werden, da sie absolute, allein von der Metrik und vom Maßstab der Koordinaten abhängige Größen sind. Es macht keinen Sinn solche Größen zu verwenden, da sie den Zielmaßstab sowie die visuellen Bedingungen, unter denen die generalisierte Darstellung betrachtet werden soll, nicht berücksichtigen. Die folgenden Attribute stellen abstraktere Begriffe dar, die unmittelbar für Generalisierung relevant sind. Sie hängen wesentlich von einem Parameter ab, in den sowohl die Betrachtungsverhältnisse als auch der Zielmaßstab eingehen: der Mindestlänge ℓ_0. Das ist diejenige Länge, die eine Polygonseite in der Zieldarstellung mindestens haben muß, um noch gut sichtbar zu sein. Abhängig von ℓ_0 werden nun die folgenden Attribute definiert.

Die **Längenkategorie Kat** (oder kurz Kategorie) stellt die Größenordnung einer Länge bzgl. ℓ_0 dar und ist folgendermaßen definiert:

$$X.\text{Kat} = \log_{\sqrt{2}} \frac{X.\text{Länge}}{\ell_0} \qquad \text{mit Kante}(X)$$

Die Kategorie abstrahiert von konkreten Seitenlängen; eine Seite der Länge ℓ_0 hat die Kategorie 0. Abb. 3 (links) demonstriert den Zusammenhang zwischen Länge und Kategorie: Haben zwei Kanten das Längenverhältnis $\sqrt{2}$, so unterscheiden sich ihre Kategorien um 1. Für die Kategorie ist das Prädikat **Kleinseite** definiert, daß erfüllt ist, wenn sie kleiner als Null ist.

Ein weiteres bedeutendes Kantenattribut ist der **Ähnlichkeitswert S**. Er erlaubt es, die visuelle Ähnlichkeit der Längen zweier Kanten quantitativ anzugeben: Je mehr sich ihre Ähnlichkeitswerte unterscheiden, desto weniger sind sie einander ähnlich. Der von uns verwendete Ähnlichkeitswert wächst logarithmisch mit der Kategorie, so daß eine Länge der Kategorie 0 den Ähnlichkeitswert 0 erhält. Damit wird der visuellen Wahrnehmbarkeit der Variation einer Länge um einen festen Prozentsatz Rechnung getragen, die umso größer ist, je größer die Länge ist. Unserer Definition liegt jedoch keine umfangreiche Untersuchung zugrunde, da sie nicht grundlegend für die Entwicklung eines geeigneten Regelsystems ist. Bedeutend ist, daß dieser Begriff überhaupt definiert ist. Damit läßt sich nun ein Prädikat definieren: Zwei Kanten sind **ähnlich**, wenn sich ihre Ähnlichkeitswerte um höchstens 1 unterscheiden.

Oftmals benötigt man in Regelbedingungen Aussagen über Winkelgrößen. Die Forderung, daß ein Winkel α rechtwinklig sein soll, wird nicht befriedigend durch '$\alpha = 100^g$' ausgedrückt, schließlich kann man einen Winkel von $100{,}1^g$ mit bloßem Auge nicht von einem rechten Winkel unterscheiden. Die Forderung besagt, daß ein Winkel visuell als rechter Winkel wahrgenommen wird, auch wenn er in gewissen Grenzen von 100^g abweicht. Das Intervall, in dem sich α befinden kann, so daß er als rechtwinklig empfunden wird, ist abhängig von der Mindestlänge ℓ_0 und den Kategorien seiner Schenkel. Das Attribut **Winkelklasse (WKlasse)**, das für Winkel definiert ist, leistet das Gewünschte: Es ordnet jeden Winkel eindeutig in eine von 13 Klassen ein, die in Abb. 3 (rechts) veranschaulicht sind. Die genaue Definition kann hier der Kürze halber nicht wiedergegeben werden. Es ist aber offensichtlich, daß eine Abweichung von einem Winkel um einen bestimmten Betrag umso deutlicher wird, je näher er an 100^g oder 200^g liegt. Winkel um 50^g bzw. 150^g sind gegenüber Variationen am unempfindlichsten.

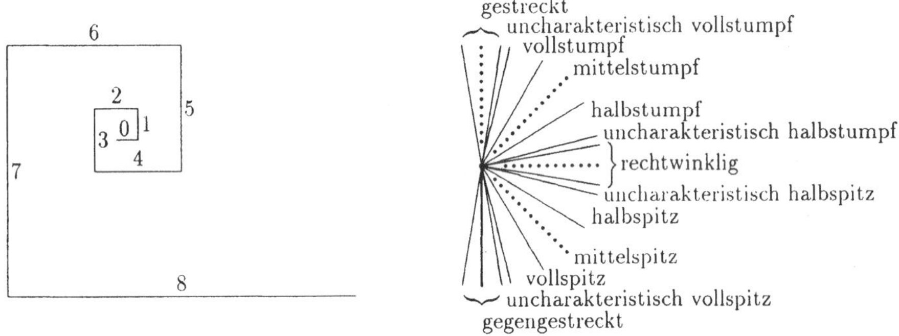

Abbildung 3: links: Beispielstrecken und ihre Kategorien für $\ell_0 = 3\,\text{mm}$
rechts: Schema der Aufteilung eines Halbkreises in Winkelklassen

Zuletzt soll noch erwähnt werden, daß in Regelbedingungen die Attribute von Kanten auch auf Strecken zwischen beliebigen Knoten anwendbar sind, auch wenn diese nicht durch eine Kante verbunden sind. Diese Attribute sind zwar nicht in den Relationen enthalten, werden jedoch automatisch, ohne daß es in der Regel erklärt werden muß, aus den dort verfügbaren abgeleitet. Dasselbe gilt für

Winkel, die nicht von Schenkeln gebildet werden, die Kanten sind. Auch für sie sind die Attribute w und WKlasse verwendbar. Solche Attribute, die automatisch aus den Basisattributen abgeleitet werden, heißen **virtuelle Attribute**.

2.3 Beispiel für einen einfachen Fall

Die im vorigen Abschnitt vorgestellten Attribute und Prädikate sollen nun anhand einer einfachen Beispielregel veranschaulicht werden, die in Abb. 4 dargestellt ist. Der untere Teil der Abbildung zeigt ihre Bedingung und Aktion, der obere skizziert den von der Bedingung definierten Gebäudeteil sowie seine gestrichelt dargestellte gewünschte Form, die von der Aktion erzielt wird. Die Bedingung

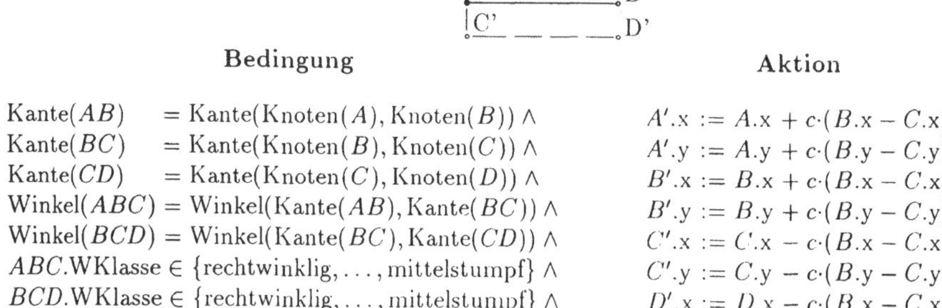

Bedingung

$$
\begin{aligned}
&\text{Kante}(AB) = \text{Kante}(\text{Knoten}(A), \text{Knoten}(B)) \wedge \\
&\text{Kante}(BC) = \text{Kante}(\text{Knoten}(B), \text{Knoten}(C)) \wedge \\
&\text{Kante}(CD) = \text{Kante}(\text{Knoten}(C), \text{Knoten}(D)) \wedge \\
&\text{Winkel}(ABC) = \text{Winkel}(\text{Kante}(AB), \text{Kante}(BC)) \wedge \\
&\text{Winkel}(BCD) = \text{Winkel}(\text{Kante}(BC), \text{Kante}(CD)) \wedge \\
&ABC.\text{WKlasse} \in \{\text{rechtwinklig}, \ldots, \text{mittelstumpf}\} \wedge \\
&BCD.\text{WKlasse} \in \{\text{rechtwinklig}, \ldots, \text{mittelstumpf}\} \wedge \\
&\text{Kleinseite}(BC) \wedge \\
&\neg\text{Kleinseite}(AB) \wedge \neg\text{Kleinseite}(CD) \wedge \\
&ABC.\text{w} \cdot BCD.\text{w} < 0 \wedge \\
&\text{ähnlich}(BC.\text{S}, 0)
\end{aligned}
$$

Aktion

$$
\begin{aligned}
A'.\text{x} &:= A.\text{x} + c\cdot(B.\text{x} - C.\text{x}) \\
A'.\text{y} &:= A.\text{y} + c\cdot(B.\text{y} - C.\text{y}) \\
B'.\text{x} &:= B.\text{x} + c\cdot(B.\text{x} - C.\text{x}) \\
B'.\text{y} &:= B.\text{y} + c\cdot(B.\text{y} - C.\text{y}) \\
C'.\text{x} &:= C.\text{x} - c\cdot(B.\text{x} - C.\text{x}) \\
C'.\text{y} &:= C.\text{y} - c\cdot(B.\text{y} - C.\text{y}) \\
D'.\text{x} &:= D.\text{x} - c\cdot(B.\text{x} - C.\text{x}) \\
D'.\text{y} &:= D.\text{y} - c\cdot(B.\text{y} - C.\text{y})
\end{aligned}
$$

$$\text{mit } c = \tfrac{1}{2}(\ell_0 - BC.\text{Länge})$$

Abbildung 4: Beispielregel für bedeutende Seitenversprünge ($\overline{BC}$) mit Prinzipskizze

legt fest, daß der Gebäudeteil aus zwei langen Seiten $\overline{AB}$ und $\overline{CD}$ sowie aus einer kurzen Seite $\overline{BC}$ besteht. Die langen Seiten sind im Gegensatz zur kurzen Seite keine Kleinseiten, d. h. ihre Kategorien sind mindestens Null, so wie es oben definiert wurde. $\overline{BC}$ muß zusätzlich zu einer Seite mit dem Ähnlichkeitswert 0 (der Länge ℓ_0) ähnlich sein, damit die Verfälschung durch die Aktion nicht zu groß ist, die sie auf die Länge ℓ_0 streckt. Die Winkel ABC und BCD müssen nicht rechtwinklig sein, sie müssen jedoch einander entgegen orientiert und dürfen nicht zu stumpf sein. Wie man an der Skizze ablesen kann, verschiebt die Aktion die Seiten $\overline{AB}$ und $\overline{CD}$ parallel und streckt die Seite $\overline{BC}$ bis zur Länge ℓ_0.

Diese Regel behandelt einen Gebäudeteil, der aus einer *festen* Anzahl von Kanten besteht. Es ist jedoch manchmal notwendig, Regeln für Gebäudeteile mit *beliebiger* Kantenzahl zu formulieren. Wenn beispielsweise Teilflächen aufgrund ihrer geringen Fläche zu behandeln sind, so muß auf die Fläche eines Gebäudeteils Bezug genommen werden, der prinzipiell beliebig viele Kanten haben kann. Um auf ähnliche Weise wie in der Beispielregel Aussagen über solche komplexen Objekte machen zu können, ist das **Pfadkonzept** entwickelt worden, von dem hier aus Platzgründen lediglich die Grundidee mitgeteilt werden kann: Es definiert, wie Attribute von Gebäudeteilen mit variabler Kantenzahl (Pfaden), z. B. deren Umfang oder Fläche, rekursiv berechnet werden können. Damit ist es möglich sie sukzessiv beim Durchlaufen des Pfades durch eine Schleife zu berechnen, ohne daß komplizierte verschachtelte Datenbankanfragen erforderlich sind.

3 Implementierungsaspekte

Die Realisierung des vorgestellten Ansatzes verlangt im wesentlichen zwei Systemkomponenten: Ein Datenbanksystem, das die zu bearbeitenden Objekte verwaltet und ein Regelanwendungssystem, das auf der Grundlage des Datenbanksystems Generalisierungsregeln zur Anwendung bringt. Idealerweise sollte das Datenbanksystem komplexe Objekte verwalten können und einen effizienten raumbezogenen Zugriff auf sie ermöglichen. Bearbeitung und Zugriff sollten außerdem mengenorientiert möglich sein und auf den Anwendungszweck abgestimmt werden können. Das Datenbanksystem INGRES, ein relationales System mit SQL-Schnittstelle, das wir auf UNIX-Workstations mit Einbindung in C-Programmierung verwendet haben, entspricht nicht diesem Idealbild, bildet aber ein portables Standardsystem, das für unseren Zweck ausreicht: Es soll gezeigt werden, daß ein regelorientierter Ansatz den Erfordernissen der Generalisierung gut gerecht wird; Effizienzüberlegungen standen dabei im Hintergrund.

Das Regelanwendungssystem besteht aus zwei Teilen: Einer behandelt die Bedingung, der andere die Aktion einer Regel. Letztere ist eine Transformation auf dem von der Regelbedingung beschriebenen Gebäudeteil, die die Datenbank in den Zustand mit den gewünschten Eigenschaften überführt. Daß die Integrität der Daten dabei erhalten bleibt, wird dadurch gewährleistet, daß Änderungen der Daten nur durch bereitgestellte Transformationsprozeduren möglich sind. Unsere Implementierung richtet sich primär auf die Behandlung von Regelbedingungen. Soll eine Regel angewendet werden, so müssen zunächst alle Gebäudeteile gefunden werden, die ihre Bedingung erfüllen. Diesen Vorgang nennt man **Instanziierung** der Regel; die dabei gefundenen Gebäudeteile heißen **Instanziierungen.** Wir betrachten eine Instanziierung als eine Folge benachbarter Kanten *eines* Gebäudes und nennen ihn **Gebäudeteilkontur** oder kurz Kontur. Zur Darstellung des Grundprinzips ist diese Einschränkung ausreichend, da gebäudeübergreifende Regeln lediglich benötigt werden, wenn nach der Generalisierung einzelner Gebäude diese mit ihren lokalen Nachbarn in Einklang gebracht werden, indem sie zueinander ausgerichtet oder zusammengefaßt werden. Unser Ansatz sieht auch die Behandlung diese Fälle vor, was hier der Kürze wegen nicht dargelegt wird. Der folgende Abschnitt stellt ein Verfahren vor, das mit der eben genannten Einschränkung zu einer gegebenen Bedingung die Menge aller möglichen Instanziierungen findet.

3.1 Erzeugung und Verwaltung von Regelinstanziierungen

Die Instanziierungen zu einer Regel werden jeweils durch ein Tupel in einer eigenen Relation, der Instanzrelation, repräsentiert. Ein Instanztupel ist die Aneinanderreihung derjenigen Tupel, die die Instanziierung bilden bzw. die entsprechenden Objekte repräsentieren. Dies hat den Vorteil, daß bei Ausführung einer Aktion ohne Zugriff auf die Basisrelationen alle benötigten Attributwerte in *einem* Tupel vorliegen. Um die verschiedenen Knoten und Kanten eines Instanztupels unterscheiden zu können, werden ihre Attribute durch angehängte Indizes eindeutig gemacht: Die X-Koordinate des i-ten Knotens der Teilkontur (vom Anfangsknoten mit 0 beginnend durchnumeriert) lautet damit Xi und die Länge der Kante, die Knoten j mit Knoten k verbindet, heißt Längejk. Abb 5 veranschaulicht eine Instanziierung graphisch und zeigt darunter das Schema der Instanzrelation. Die Punkte '...' stehen für alle Attribute des Objekts, das durch das vorhergehende Attribut identifiziert wird. Das Attribut BedNr ist ein Identifikator für die Regelbedingung, um Instanziierungen verschiedener Bedingungen unterscheiden zu können. Die durch ein Instanztupel repräsentierte Kontur kann auch weniger als 8 Kanten haben (die Maximalzahl 8 ist willkürlich gewählt); in diesem Fall sind dann die Attributwerte der unbenutzten Kanten und Knoten NULL.

Mit Hilfe der Attributnamen der Instanzrelation können nun Regelbedingungen verkürzt formuliert werden: Statt des Ausdrucks 'Knoten(A) $\wedge$ Knoten(B) $\wedge$ Kante(AB) $\wedge$ AB.Kat $<$ 2' kann man auch einfach 'KID01.Kat $<$ 0' schreiben. Die Lage der betreffenden Kante innerhalb der gesuchten Teilkontur ist damit implizit festgelegt; in diesem Fall ist sie darin die erste. Wird in derselben Bedingung noch die Kante KID12 verwendet, so ist sie die Nachfolgerkante von KID01, mit der sie

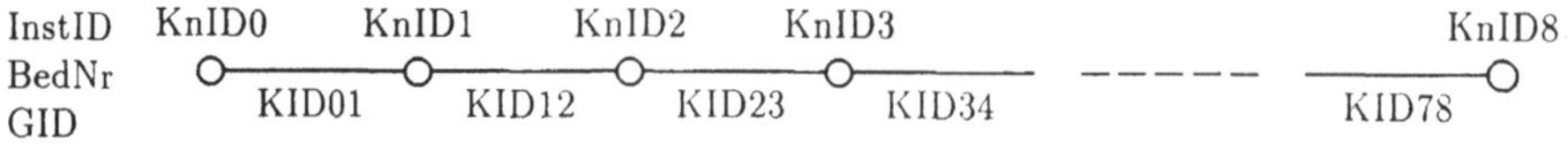

```
InstID  KnID0     KnID1     KnID2     KnID3                    KnID8
BedNr   O---------O---------O---------O-------  -----  --------O
GID        KID01     KID12     KID23     KID34              KID78
```

Instanz(<u>InstID</u>, GID, BedNr,
KnID0,...,KID01,...,KnID1,...,KID12,..., ... ,KnID7,...,KID78,...,KnID8,...)

Abbildung 5: Struktur einer Instanziierung mit zugehöriger Relation 'Instanz'

durch den Knoten KnID1 inzident ist.

Folgende Insert-Anweisung erzeugt die Instanziierungen für die Bedingung (B1). Die letzte Zeile darin muß durch SQL-Ausdrücke ersetzt werden, die die Prädikate P_1 und P_2 realisieren und die eigentliche Selektion darstellen, die durch die Bedingung ausgedrückt wird.

(B1) $P_1(KID23) \wedge P_2(KID34)$

```
insert into Instanz
       ( BedNr,    GID,
         KnID2,    X2,      Y2,     .., KID23,     lGID23,     Kat23,     ..,
         KnID3,    X3,      Y3,     .., KID34,     lGID34,     Kat34,     ..,
         KnID4,    X4,      Y4,     .. )
select 1,          KA23.GID,
         KN2.KnID, KN2.X, KN2.Y,.., KA23.KID, KA23.lGID, KA23.Kat,..,
         KN3.KnID, KN3.X, KN3.Y,.., KA34.KID, KA34.lGID, KA34.Kat,..,
         KN4.KnID, KN4.X, KN4.Y,..
from     Knoten KN2, Kante KA23, Knoten KN3, Kante KA34, Knoten KN4
where    KA23.Knach = KA34.KID     and     KN2.KnID = KA23.AKnID
and      KN3.KnID = KA34.AKnID     and     KN4.KnID = KA34.EKnID
and      P1(...) and P2(...)
```

Für jeden Knoten der Kontur nimmt die Knotenrelation einmal am Verbund teil, jeweils mit einem anderen Correlation-Namen zur eindeutigen Identifikation. Dasselbe gilt für die Kanten, wobei die Verbundbedingung für aufeinanderfolgende Kanten durch das Hilfsattribut Knach realisiert wird. Grundsätzlich werden alle Attribute der gesamten Kontur in die Instanzrelation kopiert, auch wenn nicht alle in der Bedingung auftauchen, damit der Aktion der zugehörigen Regel eine vollständige Beschreibung für ihre Transformation zur Verfügung steht. Zu unserer Implementierung gehört ein Generator, der eine Bedingung in der oben erwähnten Kurzform einliest und daraus eine Insert-Anweisungen gemäß obigem Beispiel generiert, mit der alle zu der Bedingung existierenden Instanziierungen erzeugt werden können. Da sich die Regelbedingungen während der Laufzeit nicht verändern, können die zugehörigen SQL-Anweisungen schon vorher übersetzt und optimiert werden.

Es ist klar, daß bei Bedingungen, die viele Kanten umfassen, die Komplexität der erzeugten Insert-Anweisung so groß sein kann, daß sie nicht mehr (effizient) verarbeitet werden kann. Der Generator ist darum so einstellbar, daß durch die erzeugte Insert-Anweisung zunächst nur nach einem Ausschnitt der Kontur gesucht wird, wobei nur diejenigen Teilbedingungen verwendet werden, die sich auf den betrachteten Teilausschnitt beziehen. Dadurch werden also Instanziierungen erzeugt, die noch unvollständig sind, aber alle gesuchten enthalten. Das hat den Vorteil, daß weniger Verbundoperationen nötig sind. Der Generator erzeugt nun weiter eine Reihe von Update-Anweisungen, durch die die Instanziierungen schrittweise vervollständigt werden, wobei jeweils ein weiterer Teilausschnitt der Kontur betrachtet wird. Davon sind nur diejenigen Instanziierungen betroffen, die die Teilbedingungen für den jeweils betrachteten Teilausschnitt erfüllen. Die restlichen werden durch Delete-Anweisungen gelöscht.

4 Ausblick

Das hier vorgestellte Verfahren ist ein erster Schritt zur Realisierung von Geo-Informationssystemen, die in flexibler und erweiterbarer Art Anwendungswissen in die Methoden zur Datenverwaltung und -präsentation einzubeziehen erlauben. Die Ergebnisse sind ungeachtet der Performance, die nicht Gegenstand dieser Arbeit war, insgesamt sehr ermutigend. Zum einen wird praktisch nachvollziehbar demonstriert, daß mit traditionellen Techniken Aufgaben gelöst werden können, die eigentlich in den Bereich der Mustererkennung gehören: Generalisierung redet ja stets davon, wie bestimmte Formen und Konturen, unabhängig von ihrer Lage und Größe, zu behandeln sind. Aus den Beschränkungen, die bei der Verfolgung des Ansatzes deutlich werden, ergeben sich auch Hinweise für weitere Untersuchungen auf diesem Gebiet: Es ist offensichtlich, daß Erweiterungen des Regelkalküls erforderlich sind, um angemessener über komplexe Konturen reden zu können. Nahliegend ist hier ein zumindest zweistufiges Regelsystem, das zunächst in aller Allgemeinheit z. B. den Begriff „Gebäudeteil" definiert und dann in verfeinernden Regeln bestimmte Arten von Gebäudeteilen (Erker u. ä.) charakterisiert. In dieser Richtung laufen bereits weiterführende Arbeiten.

Literatur

[R. Bill, D. Fritsch (1991)] *Grundlagen der Geo-Informationssysteme*
Band 1: Hardware, Software und Daten.
Wichmann. Karlsruhe. 429 Seiten.

[B. Butterfield, R. McMaster, Ed. (1991)] *Rule based cartographic generalization*
London, Longman.

[G. Hake (1982)] *Kartographie I*
de Gruyter. Sammlung Göschen 2165. Berlin–New York.

[M. Krause (1992)] *Entwicklung und Implementierung eines regelbasierten Ansatzes zur automationsgestützten Generalisierung von Gebäudegrundrissen*
Studienarbeit 1099
Fakultät Informatik, Universität Stuttgart.

[Krickhahn (1987)] *Die Wissensrepräsentationssprache OPS_5: Sprachbeschreibung und Einführung in die regelorientierte Programmierung*
Wiesbaden: Vieweg, 1987

[N. M. Matthos (1989)] *An Approach to Knowledge Base Management*
Dissertationsschrift
FB Informatik, Universität Kaiserslautern.

[K. Menke (1992)] *PHOCUS for Cartographic Applications*
Schriftenreihe des Instituts für Photogrammetrie an der Universität Stuttgart, Heft 15, S. 115–121.

[U. Meyer (1989)] *Generalisierung der Siedlungsdarstellung in digitalen Situationsmodellen*
Wissenschaftliche Arbeiten der Fachrichtung Vermessungswesen der Universität Hannover.

[A. Reuter (1986)] *Kopplung von Datenbank- und Expertensystemen*
it, No. 3, S. 164–175

[W. Staufenbiel (1973)] *Zur Automation der Generalisierung topographischer Karten mit besonderer Berücksichtigung großmaßstäbiger Gebäudedarstellungen*
Wissenschaftliche Arbeiten der Lehrstühle für Geodäsie, Photogrammetrie und Kartographie der Universität Hannover.

Eine Speicher- und Zugriffsarchitektur zur effizienten Anfragebearbeitung in Geo-Datenbanksystemen

Thomas Brinkhoff, Holger Horn, Hans-Peter Kriegel, Ralf Schneider

Institut für Informatik, Universität München, Leopoldstr. 11 B, 8000 München 40

Zusammenfassung

Im Bereich geographischer Datenbanksysteme liegen aufgrund der Komplexität der Objekte und Anfragen sowie der extrem großen Datenvolumina besondere Anforderungen an die Speicher- und Zugriffsarchitektur in bezug auf eine effiziente Anfragebearbeitung vor. In den letzten Jahren wurden eine Reihe von Konzepten, wie räumliche Indexstrukturen, Approximationen, Objektzerlegung und Mehrphasen-Anfragebearbeitung als einzelne Bausteine vorgeschlagen und analysiert, um die Leistungsfähigkeit von Geo-Datenbanksystemen zu steigern. In dieser Arbeit beschreiben wir eine globale Speicher- und Zugriffsarchitektur, die sich modular aus obigen Bestandteilen zusammensetzt. Um einen mengenorientierten Zugriff großräumiger Bereichsanfragen effizient zu unterstützen, haben wir unsere Geo-Architektur um das neue Konzept einer Szenen-Organisation erweitert. Ein experimenteller Leistungsvergleich zeigt, daß sich durch diese Szenen-Organisation massive Leistungssteigerungen, insbesondere für große Bereichsanfragen erzielen lassen.

1 Einführung und Motivation

Die rechnergestützte Verwaltung, Darstellung und Auswertung raumbezogener Information hat in den letzten Jahren immer größer werdende Bedeutung erlangt. So kommen geographische Informationssysteme in steigendem Maße in öffentlicher Verwaltung, Wissenschaft und Wirtschaft zum Einsatz. In vielen Anwendungsfeldern wie Raumplanung, Katasterwesen, Umweltüberwachung sind sie die Basis von entscheidungsunterstützenden Systemen [Bar 89].

Kern geographischer Informationssysteme (GIS) sind *geographische Datenbanken*. Im Gegensatz zu betriebswirtschaftlich-administrativen Anwendungen, die auf Standard-Datenbanken basieren, sind solche Datenbanksysteme für geographische Anwendungen ungeeignet [Wid 91]. Die unzureichende Ausdrucksstärke beispielsweise relationaler Systeme führt zu unnatürlicher Datenmodellierung und unzureichender Effizienz.

In den letzten Jahren haben daher verschiedene Forschungsgruppen eine Vielzahl von Konzepten und Techniken entwickelt, um einzelnen Anforderungen geographischer Datenbanksysteme gerecht zu werden. Beispiele dafür sind räumliche Datenmodelle, effiziente Geo-Indexstrukturen usw.

In den folgenden Abschnitten schlagen wir eine Speicher- und Zugriffsarchitektur für Geo-Datenbanksysteme *(Geo-Architektur)* vor, die aufzeigt, wie eine Reihe verschiedener Konzepte in eine Gesamtarchitektur integriert werden können. Dabei soll jedoch weder ein vollständig neues Datenbanksystem noch ein neuentwickelter Datenbankkern präsentiert werden. Vorschläge für solche Systeme sind DASDBS [SW 86], EXODUS [CDRS 86], GRAL [Gue 89] oder POSTGRES [SR 86]. Statt dessen kombinieren wir verschiedene Konzepte und Techniken zu einem effizienten Mechanismus für die räumliche Anfragebearbeitung, der in o. g. Systeme integriert werden kann. Dabei kommen neben bekannten Techniken auch neue Konzepte zum Einsatz, beispielsweise die *Szenen-Organisation*, die bei großräumigen Bereichsanfragen zu massiven Leistungssteigerungen führt.

In Abschnitt 2 stellen wir zunächst die Objekte und Operationen vor, die in geographischen Anwendungen auftreten. Daraus leiten wir wichtige Basisanfragen ab, die durch unsere Architektur effizient bearbeitet werden sollen. Im dritten Abschnitt teilen wir die Bearbeitung der Anfragen in Phasen ein. Algorithmen und Verfahren zur effizienten Unterstützung der einzelnen Phasen werden im vierten Abschnitt vorgestellt. Diese werden Bestandteil unserer Speicher- und Zugriffsarchitektur. Abschnitt 5 evaluiert das Leistungsverhalten der Architektur und geht dabei insbesondere auf das hier neu vorgestellte Konzept der Szenen-Organisation ein. Den Abschluß bilden Zusammenfassung und Ausblick.

2 Objekte und Operationen in einem Geo-Datenbanksystem

In dieser Arbeit schlagen wir eine konzeptionelle Architektur zur Objektspeicherung und Anfragebearbeitung in geographischen Datenbanksystemen vor. Für die Entwicklung einer solchen Architektur sind der Typ der zu verwaltenden Objekte sowie die Art der gewünschten Operationen von entscheidender Bedeutung. Dies gilt um so mehr, je höher die Anforderungen in bezug auf Laufzeit- und Speicherplatzeffizienz sind. In den folgenden Abschnitten geben wir daher zunächst eine Spezifikation der betrachteten Objekte und Operationen.

2.1 Objekte

Die in einer geographischen Datenbank gespeicherten Objekte *(Geo-Objekte)* modellieren einen bestimmten Ausschnitt der Erdoberfläche in bezug auf eine oder mehrere Eigenschaften (Themen). Dementsprechend sind die Objekte durch eine *geometrische Komponente* und eine *thematische Komponente* charakterisiert. Während die geometrische Komponente Ort und Ausdehnung des Realitätsbereiches beschreibt, der durch das Objekt repräsentiert wird, enthält die thematische Komponente eine qualitative oder quantitative thematische Charakterisierung.

Geometrische Komponente

Die geometrische Komponente der Objekte besteht jeweils aus einem der topologischen Grundelemente der Ebene, dem *Punkt*, der *Linie* oder der *Fläche*.

Punkte lassen sich einfach unter Angabe ihrer Koordinaten bezogen auf ein gegebenes Koordinatensystem beschreiben. Um linienartige Gebilde zu modellieren, finden sowohl Polygonzüge als auch freiformbare Kurven (Bézier/B-Spline) Verwendung. Der Darstellung flächiger Objekte kommt in Geo-Datenbanksystemen sehr große Bedeutung zu; auf sie wollen wir uns im folgenden konzentrieren. Zur Modellierung von Flächen existieren zwei grundsätzlich verschiedene Ansätze: das *Rastermodell* und das *Vektormodell*, für die in der Literatur jeweils eine Fülle spezifischer Vor- und Nachteile aufgeführt werden. Das Vektormodell weist eine sehr gute Skalierbarkeit auf und hat i. allg. einen geringeren Speicherplatzbedarf als das Rastermodell. Weiterhin bleiben die Objekte beim Vektoransatz individuell zugreifbar und sind damit einfacher indizierbar. Aus diesen Gründen wird in den letzten Jahren das Vektormodell innerhalb geographischer Datenbanksysteme favorisiert.

Für unsere Architektur sind *einfache Polygone mit Löchern (EPL)* die Objektklasse zur Flächenmodellierung. Ein EPL besteht aus einem einfachen, d.h. nicht selbstüberlappenden, Polygon, aus dem einfache Polygone als Löcher herausgeschnitten sein können (vgl. Bild 1). Die Klasse der EPL ist für geographische Anwendungen gut geeignet. Sie erlaubt eine Flächenbeschreibung in beliebiger Genauigkeit und berücksichtigt explizit die in geographischen Gegebenheiten häufig auftretenden "Lochbereiche" wie Seen oder Enklaven.

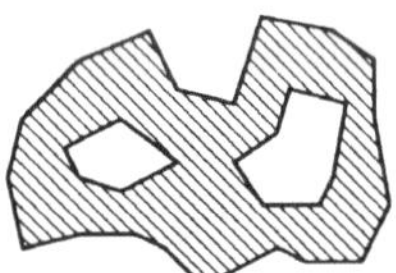

Bild 1: Einfaches Polygon mit Löchern

Thematische Komponente

Die thematische Komponente eines Objektes charakterisiert den durch seine Geo-Komponente modellierten Realitätsausschnitt in bezug auf ein oder mehrere Themen qualitativ bzw. quantitativ, z.B. in bezug auf Flächennutzung oder Niederschlagsmenge. Dazu finden i. allg. einfache Zahlen oder Zeichenketten, die in ihrer Kombination einen Attributvektor (Tupel) bilden, Verwendung.

Objektmodell

Die zu entwickelnde Speicher- und Zugriffsarchitektur für geographische Datenbanksysteme soll in der Lage sein, Mengen von Objekten bestehend aus geometrischer (EPL) und thematischer (Vektor einfacher Datentypen) Komponente zu verwalten. Bild 2 gibt ein Beispiel.

Bild 2: Karte europäischer Verwaltungsbezirke modelliert als Menge von EPL

Beide Komponenten erfordern eine völlig unterschiedliche Handhabung durch die Geo-Architektur. Für die Verwaltung von Vektoren einfacher Datentypen (Tupel) existiert in relationalen Datenbanksystemen eine Vielzahl erprobter und effizienter Datenstrukturen und Algorithmen. Demgegenüber erfordert die Organisation der Geo-Komponente neuartige Strukturen, die in der Lage sind, die beliebig komplexe geometrische Beschreibung so zu verwalten, daß Anfragen, die sich auf Lage und Geometrie der Objekte beziehen, möglichst effizient bearbeitet werden können.

Neben diesen grundsätzlichen Eigenschaften der Geo-Objekte sind für den Entwurf der Architektur zwei weitere Aspekte von entscheidender Bedeutung. Eine möglichst genaue Charakterisierung der Objekte aus realen Anwendungen und eine Spezifikation der auf den Objektmengen auszuführenden Anfragen und Operationen.

2.2 Charakteristika der Objekte

Eine allgemeingültige exakte Beschreibung der Objektmengen, wie sie in Geo-Datenbanksystemen auftreten, läßt sich nicht geben. Zu unterschiedlich sind die Anforderungen aus dem breiten Spektrum geographischer Anwendungen. Eine grobe grundsätzliche Charakterisierung in bezug auf eine Reihe von Eigenschaften ist aber möglich.

Komplexität und Variabilität der Daten

- *Anzahl der Objekte und Datenvolumen*

  Die Anzahl der Objekte in einer geographischen Datenbank hängt sehr stark vom Anwendungsbereich ab, für den sie entworfen wurde sowie von den Eigenschaften des modellierten Ausschnittes der Erdoberfläche. Nach [Fra 91] und [Cra 90] treten in realen Anwendungen Objektmengen mit einer Größe bis zu 10^9 Datensätzen auf. Beim Datenvolumen ist mit bis zu 1 TerraByte zu rechnen. Die zu entwickelnde Geo-Architektur muß in der Lage sein, derartige Datenvolumina (auf dem Sekundärspeicher) zu verwalten.

- *Variabilität in Objekten und Mengen*

  Daten in realen geographischen Anwendungen zeichnen sich durch eine sehr große Variabilität der Objekte und Objektmengen aus [Fra 91]. Dies bezieht sich vorrangig auf:

  - *Objektausdehnung*
    Sie variiert nach [Fra 91] in einer Spanne von $1 : 10^6$, wobei die größten Objekte den gesamten Datenraum umfassen können.

  - *Objektform*

- *Speicherplatzbedarf*
  In der World Data Bank II [GC 87] beispielsweise variiert der Speicherplatzbedarf von Polygonen innerhalb einer Spanne von 0,5 KB bis über 1,1 GB.
- *Verteilung der Objekte in der Ebene*
  Die Anzahl der Objekte pro Flächeneinheit (Dichte) variiert in realen Anwendungen nach [Fra 91] in einer Spanne von $1 : 10^4$.

Insbesondere ist zu beachten, daß es prinzipiell weder für die Objektausdehnung, die Komplexität der Objektstruktur, den Speicherplatzbedarf noch für die Dichte der Objekte Obergrenzen gibt. Bei Auswahl bzw. Entwicklung von Datenstrukturen und Algorithmen für eine Geo-Architektur ist dies zu beachten.

Dauerhafte Speicherung des Datenbestandes in schwach dynamischer Umgebung

Die Erfassung des Datenbestandes eines geographischen Datenbanksystems ist ungleich aufwendiger als bei Standardsystemen im betriebswirtschaftlich-administrativen Bereich. Als Datenbasis liegen oft Tausende von Papierkarten vor, die aufwendig digitalisiert und nahtlos in eine Gesamtdatenbank integriert werden müssen. Dieses weitgehend manuelle Vorgehen ist eine Quelle von Ungenauigkeiten und Inkonsistenzen, die durch aufwendige Konsistenzprüfungen auf der Datenbank entdeckt und beseitigt werden müssen. Eine weitere Quelle geometrischer Daten sind Satellitenaufnahmen von der Erdoberfläche, die aufbereitet und in das Vektorformat konvertiert werden. Insgesamt macht die Datengewinnung und Konsistenzerhaltung ca. 80% der Betriebskosten eines geographischen Datenbanksystems aus [Arn 90].

Ist der Datenbestand einmal erfaßt, so wird er persistent gespeichert und langfristig genutzt. Dabei bleiben die Daten i. allg. jedoch nicht statisch, sondern unterliegen noch Veränderungen durch die nachträgliche Korrektur von Fehlern oder Inkonsistenzen und durch Veränderungen im modellierten Weltausschnitt. Insgesamt ist der Datenbestand als schwach dynamisch zu charakterisieren.

Die aufgeführten Merkmale der Geo-Objekte und die im folgenden beschriebenen Anfragen und Operationen bilden gemeinsam eine Art Anforderungsdefinition für die zu entwickelnde Speicher- und Zugriffsarchitektur.

2.3 Anfragen und Operationen

Aufgrund der sehr unterschiedlichen Anwendungssituationen, in denen geographische Datenbanksysteme eingesetzt werden, ist es nicht möglich einen standardisierten Satz von Anfragen und Operationen anzugeben, der allen Anforderungen genügt [SV 89]. Statt dessen unterscheiden wir 4 Basis-Operationsklassen und benennen jeweils typische Vertreter, die durch die Zugriffsarchitektur unterstützt werden sollen.

1) Modifikationen

Analog zu Standard-Datenbanksystemen stehen in einem Geo-Datenbanksystem Operationen zur Verfügung, die Datensätze zur Datenbank hinzufügen, sie löschen oder modifizieren.

2) Selektionen

Grundsätzlich lassen sich zwei Arten von Selektionen unterscheiden; solche, die sich auf die räumliche, und solche, die sich auf die thematische Komponente der Objekte beziehen.

a) Räumliche Selektionen:

Bei den räumlichen Selektionen werden Objekte anhand ihrer räumlichen Lage und Ausdehnung aus einer Menge von Objekten selektiert.

- *Ortsbezogene Selektion: Punktanfragen*
  Für einen gegebenen Anfrageort (Punkt) *P* und eine gegebene Objektmenge *M* liefert eine Punktanfrage *(Point Query)* alle Objekte aus *M*, die sich am Ort *P* befinden, die *P* also geometrisch enthalten (siehe Bild 3(a)).
- *Bereichsbezogene Selektion: räumliche Bereichsanfragen*
  Für eine gegebene polygonale Anfrageregion *R* und eine gegebene Objektmenge *M* liefert die *Region Query* alle Objekte aus *M*, die die Anfrageregion *R* schneiden. Ein Spezialfall der Region Query ist

die *Window Query*, bei der die Anfrageregion durch ein achsenparalleles Rechteck gebildet wird (vgl. Bild 3(b)).

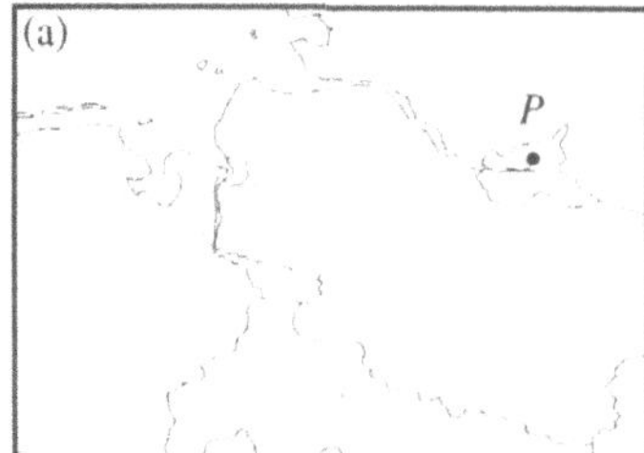

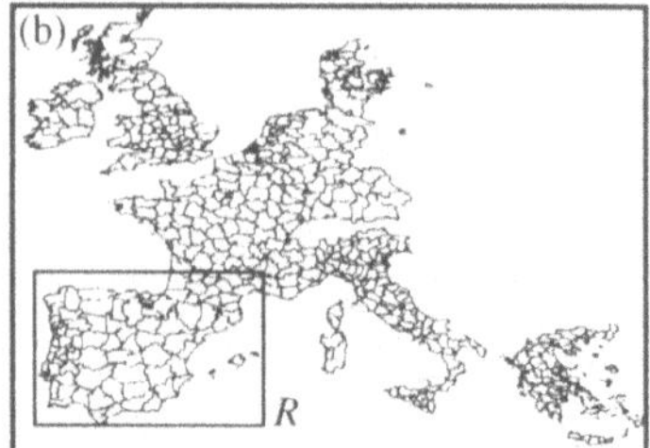

Bild 3: Beispiele für ortsbezogene und bereichsbezogene Selektion

b) Thematische Selektionen:

Bei den thematischen Selektionen werden Objekte anhand bestimmter Eigenschaften ihrer thematischen Komponente aus einer Menge von Objekten selektiert. In diesem Abschnitt konzentrieren wir uns zunächst auf die geometrische Komponente der Objekte. Die Unterstützung thematischer Selektionen wird in Abschnitt 4.5 betrachtet.

3) Kombinationen

- *Spatial Join*
  Die räumliche Join-Operation liefert für zwei Objektmengen A und B alle Paare (a, b), $a \in A, b \in B$, deren geometrische Komponenten sich schneiden. Für jedes Objekt $a \in A$ sind also gerade die Objekte in B zu finden, die sich mit a überlappen. Für die effiziente Ausführung des Spatial Joins ist ein geometrisch selektiver Zugriff auf die Objekte notwendig [BKS 93c].
- *Map Overlay*
  Der Map Overlay ist eine der wichtigsten Operationen in einem Geo-Informationssystem [Bur 86]. Er kombiniert zwei (oder mehr) Mengen von Geo-Objekten. Diese Verknüpfung wird über eine Overlay-Funktion gesteuert, die bestimmt, welche Schnittobjekte in welcher Form zur Ergebnismenge gehören. Der Map Overlay basiert somit auf dem Spatial Join bzw. dessen Varianten. Zusätzlich zum Spatial Join müssen die tatsächlichen Schnittobjekte zwischen zwei Ausgangsobjekten berechnet oder benachbarte Objekte, die die gleiche Thematik besitzen, miteinander verschmolzen werden [KBS 91].

4) Auswertungen

Den Selektionen bzw. Kombinationen bestehender Objektmengen sind innerhalb von Anwendungsprogrammen häufig weitere Verarbeitungsschritte nachgeschaltet. Die dazu notwendigen Operationen und Verfahren sind sehr spezifisch für die jeweilige Anwendung und deshalb selbst nicht Teil einer allgemeinen Speicher- und Zugriffsarchitektur. Grundsätzlich unterscheiden lassen sich aber:

- *automatische Analyse*
  In die Klasse der Analysefunktionen fallen Berechnungen, die auf der geometrischen und oder der thematischen Komponente der Objekte durchgeführt werden. Typische Vertreter sind z.B. Durchschnittsberechnungen von Fläche oder Umfang von Objekten, Berechnung von Abständen und Wegelängen zwischen Objekten, Ermittlung von Minimum oder Maximum bestimmter thematischer Attribute usw.
- *Visualisierung*
  In vielen Fällen ist die automatische Analyse eines Datenbestandes nicht möglich, sondern es sind manuelle Zwischenschritte durch den Benutzer zur vollständigen Analyse erforderlich. Dafür ist eine Visualisierung der Daten auf graphischen Ausgabemedien (i.d.R. Bildschirm) erforderlich.

Die Aufstellung macht deutlich, daß den räumlichen Selektionen innerhalb der Anfragen und Operationen eine besondere Bedeutung zukommt. Sie sind nicht nur eine eigenständige Anfrageklasse, sondern fungieren auch als wichtigste Basisoperationen der Klassen 2 - 4. Ihre effiziente Realisierung ist daher notwendige Voraussetzung für ein gutes Leistungsverhalten des gesamten geographischen Datenbanksystems.

3 Ein Phasenmodell für die geometrische Anfragebearbeitung

Nachdem wir sowohl Objekte als auch Anfragen und Operationen klassifiziert und ihre Charakteristika beschrieben haben, soll jetzt eine Architektur zur Speicherung der Geo-Objekte und zur Bearbeitung der Anfragen aufgebaut werden. Vorrangige Aufgabe dieser Architektur ist die *effiziente* Bearbeitung der geometrischen Anfragen und Operationen. Daher betrachten wir diese Anfragen näher, unterscheiden verschiedene Phasen in ihrer Bearbeitung und geben Algorithmen und Verfahren zur Unterstützung der einzelnen Phasen an.

Wie im vorangegangenen Kapitel beschrieben, sind die räumlichen Selektionen die wichtigsten Basisoperationen bei der Bearbeitung geometrischer Anfragen. Ihre Durchführung läßt sich in verschiedene Schritte einteilen.

Schritt 1: Einschränkung des Datenraumes

Bei räumlichen Selektionen ist es möglich, die Suche nach Objekten auf einen geometrischen Bereich einzuschränken, in dem überhaupt nur Kandidaten liegen können, die die Anfrage erfüllen.

Soll die Einschränkung des Datenraumes möglichst effizient erfolgen, ist der Einsatz von Zugriffspfaden erforderlich, die die Objekte entsprechend ihrer räumlichen Lage und Ausdehnung im Datenraum indizieren und schnell zugreifbar machen. Alle Objekte, die eine Anfrage erfüllen, liegen wegen der geometrischen Selektivität stets auch räumlich benachbart zueinander. Um einen effizienten Objektzugriff zu unterstützen, sollten räumlich nahe beieinanderliegende Objekte daher durch den Zugriffspfad auch möglichst physisch nahe beieinander gespeichert werden, d.h. *geclustert* werden.

Wegen der bereits beschriebenen Komplexität der Geo-Objekte ist es nicht möglich, über die vollständige Ausdehnungsinformation der Objekte zu indizieren. Ein Zugriffspfad kann daher auch nicht das exakte Ergebnis einer Anfrage liefern, sondern nur einen möglichst großen Teil der Objekte sofort von der Ergebnismenge ausschließen. Es verbleibt eine Menge von Kandidaten, die in der Ergebnismenge liegen können und an Schritt 2 der Anfragebearbeitung weitergeleitet werden. Diese Art der zweistufigen Anfragebearbeitung ist aus [Ore 89] unter den Begriffen *Filter- und Verfeinerungsschritt* bekannt.

Schritt 2: Genauere Untersuchung der Objekte

In Schritt 2 der Anfragebearbeitung werden die Kandidaten daraufhin untersucht, ob sie die Anfrage tatsächlich erfüllen. Dazu ist die Auswertung eines geometrischen Prädikates wie z.B. das Enthaltensein eines Punktes im Objekt, das Überschneiden mit einem Rechteck o.ä. zu überprüfen. Ganz analog zu Schritt 1 der Anfragebearbeitung können dabei verschiedene Teilschritte unterschieden werden. Zunächst wird die Untersuchung des Objektes auf die für den Test notwendigen lokalen Teile beschränkt. Bild 4 zeigt dazu ein Beispiel: Um zu entscheiden, ob das Anfragefenster den Voltasee schneidet, ist nur dessen nordwestliche Spitze näher zu untersuchen.

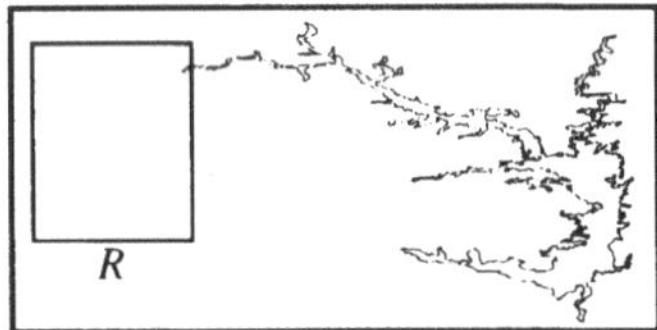

Bild 4: Test eines Anfragebereichs gegen den Voltasee

Wegen der Komplexität der Objekte einerseits und der geometrischen Selektivität der Anfragen andererseits, ist es sinnvoll, die komplexen Objekte lokal zu strukturieren und die entstehenden Strukturelemente bezüglich ihrer Lage und Ausdehnung räumlich zu organisieren. Auf den für die jeweilige Anfrage tatsächlich relevanten Objektteilen wird dann der geometrische Test durchgeführt. Dazu kommen Verfahren aus dem Gebiet der algorithmischen Geometrie zum Einsatz, die schließlich entscheiden, ob ein Objekt die Anfrage tatsächlich erfüllt oder nicht.

Schritt 3: Ausgabe des Objektes zur Weiterverarbeitung

Ist ein Objekt als Teil des Ergebnisses identifiziert, so muß es möglichst schnell als Gesamtobjekt verfügbar gemacht werden, z.B. um weiterverarbeitet zu werden. Dies macht eine physisch zusammenhängende Speicherung aller zum Objekt gehörenden Teile erforderlich, die durch eine spezielle Speicherungsorganisation realisiert werden muß [Wei 89].

4 Eine Architektur für die Anfragebearbeitung in Geo-Datenbanksystemen

Nach der abstrakten Beschreibung des Phasenmodells in der geometrischen Anfragebearbeitung geben wir im folgenden algorithmische Techniken zur Unterstützung der einzelnen Phasen an. Sie kommen später als Bausteine zur effizienten Durchführung der einzelnen Schritte in unserer Gesamtarchitektur zum Einsatz.

4.1 Räumliche Indexstrukturen

Indexstrukturen als elementarer Bestandteil der internen Ebene eines Datenbanksystems dienen dazu, eine dynamische Menge von Objekten so auf einem seitenorientierten Sekundärspeicher zu organisieren, daß eine Menge von Anfragen und Operationen auf dem Datenbestand effizient, d.h. unter möglichst geringem Bedarf an Sekundärspeicherzugriffen und CPU-Zeit bearbeitet werden kann.

In Standard-Datenbanksystemen kommen für solche Zwecke vornehmlich B-Baum-Varianten zum Einsatz. Mit ihnen lassen sich linear geordnete Schlüssel von N Objekten so organisieren, daß für eine Modifikation oder exakte Suche nur auf $\log(N)$ Seiten zugegriffen werden muß.

Für geographische Datenbanksysteme sind B-Bäume und andere eindimensionale Indexstrukturen jedoch nicht geeignet. Hier sind vielmehr Strukturen gesucht, die in der Lage sind, flächige geometrische Objekte (einfache Polygone mit Löchern) bezüglich ihrer Lage und Ausdehnung in der Ebene zu indizieren. Beliebige einfache Polygone mit Löchern sind jedoch zu komplex, um ihre gesamte Lage und Ausdehnungsinformation, d.h. die gesamte Objektbeschreibung, bei der Indizierung berücksichtigen zu können. Statt dessen betrachten wir zunächst die räumliche Indizierung einfacherer Flächenobjekte. Übersichten über räumliche Indexstrukturen sind z.B. in [Sam 90] und [Wid 91] enthalten.

Die einfachste Klasse ausgedehnter Geo-Objekte sind *achsenparallele Rechtecke*. Für diese Objektklasse existiert bereits eine Reihe von Indexstrukturen mit dem *R-Baum* [Gut 84] als einem bekannten Vertreter. Der R-Baum faßt soviele räumlich nahe beieinanderliegende Objekte (Rechtecke) zusammen, wie auf eine (Daten-) Seite passen, speichert sie dort gemeinsam ab und umschreibt sie mit einem *minimal umgebenden achsenparallelen Rechteck (MUR)*. Eine Menge derartiger Rechtecke wird ihrerseits auf einer (Directory-) Seite gespeichert und wiederum mit einem MUR umschrieben. So wird die gesamte Objektmenge stufenweise räumlich zusammengefaßt und es entsteht ein baumartiges Directory aus Rechtecken (Bild 5).

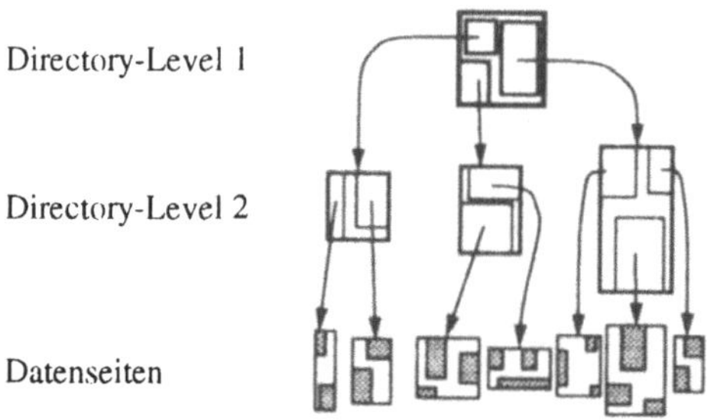

Bild 5: Schematische Darstellung eines R*-Baumes

Eine besonders effiziente Version des R-Baumes ist der *R*-Baum* [BKSS 90], der eine ausgefeilte Strategie zur Partitionierung von Seitenregionen verwendet und bei Bedarf auch Umstrukturierungen im Baum vornimmt.

Diese Art räumlicher Organisation der Rechtecke erlaubt eine effiziente Bearbeitung von Punkt- und kleinräumigen Bereichsanfragen [BKSS 90], allerdings eben nur auf Mengen achsenparalleler Rechtecke oder anderer sehr einfacher Objekte, die in eine Datenseite passen. In realen Anwendungen ist es jedoch notwendig, sowohl komplexere Objekte speichern als auch größere Bereichsanfragen effizient bearbeiten zu können. Für komplexere Objektklassen und großräumigere Anfragen existieren bislang nur sehr wenige Vorschläge für Indexstrukturen. Die im späteren Teil dieses Kapitels vorgestellte Zugriffsarchitektur wird in der Lage sein, Mengen einfacher Polygone mit Löchern zu speichern und auch großräumige Anfragen effizient zu beantworten.

4.2 Approximationen

Zur Ergebnismenge einer geometrischen Anfrage gehören all die Objekte einer Objektmenge, die ein geometrisches Prädikat erfüllen, also z.B. einen Punkt enthalten, von einem gegebenen Objekt geschnitten werden o.ä.. Wie im vorangegangenen Abschnitt beschrieben, dienen räumliche Indexstrukturen dazu, möglichst viele Objekte von vornherein von der Ergebnismenge auszuschließen. Es verbleiben Kandidaten, die genauer geometrisch getestet werden müssen. Dies ist bei sehr komplexen Objekten (Polygonen mit sehr vielen Eckpunkten) außerordentlich zeitaufwendig [KHS 91]. So liegt es nahe, dem eigentlichen Test auf dem Objekt einen Vortest voranzustellen, um für möglichst viele Kandidaten schon dort zu entscheiden, daß sie die Anfrage sicher erfüllen oder sicher nicht erfüllen.

Für einen derartigen Vortest eignet sich das Konzept der *Objektapproximation*. In [Kri 91] ist eine detaillierte Klassifikation verschiedener Approximationen gegeben. Eine Approximation hat eine im Vergleich zum Objekt einfache Beschreibung und nähert das Objekt möglichst gut an - zwei offensichtlich konkurrierende Kriterien. Um Objektapproximationen für einen geometrischen Vortest effizient nutzen zu können, muß das Objekt vollständig in der Approximation enthalten sein *(konservative Approximation)* [Sch 92]. Beispiele für konservative Approximationen sind achsenparallele Rechtecke, konvexe n-Ecke, Ellipsen usw. (Bild 6).

Bild 6: Verschiedene konservative Approximationen

Für eine Punktanfrage beispielsweise wird dann innerhalb der Anfragebearbeitung für alle Kandidatenobjekte zunächst getestet, ob ihre Approximation den Anfragepunkt enthält. Aufgrund der Einfachheit der Approximationsobjekte ist dieser Test sehr schnell durchführbar. Fällt der Test negativ aus, d.h. enthält die Approximation den Punkt nicht, so kann ihn auch das Objekt nicht enthalten und der Kandidat wird verworfen. Ein teurer Punkt-In-Polygon-Test kann so eingespart werden. Nur im Falle eines positiven Vortests ist der Test auf dem Objekt selber noch durchzuführen. Von seinem Ergebnis hängt endgültig ab, ob das Objekt zur Ergebnismenge gehört oder nicht. Wegen ihrer einfachen Beschreibbarkeit eignen sich Approximationsobjekte gut für die Speicherung in räumlichen Indexstrukturen (vgl. Abschnitt 4.2).

In [BKS 93a] werden Approximationsverfahren für geometrische Objekte ausführlich beschrieben und ihre Eignung anhand von Datenbanken aus realen Anwendungen evaluiert. Das minimal umgebende Fünfeck hat sich dabei als bester Kompromiß zwischen Approximationsgüte und Speicherplatzbedarf erwiesen. Weiterhin wird gezeigt, daß sich der R*-Baum auch gut zur Organisation anderer Approximationen als minimal umgebender Rechtecke eignet.

4.3 Objektzerlegungen

Während die Objektapproximation das Ziel hat, möglichst häufig geometrische Tests auf den Polygonen ganz zu verhindern, dienen *Objektzerlegungen* dazu, diese Tests zu vereinfachen, d.h. schneller ausführbar zu machen.

Betrachten wir wieder den Test, ob ein Polygon einen gegebenen Anfragepunkt enthält. Zur Durchführung dieses Tests ist ein Algorithmus mit in der Zahl der Polygonpunkte linearer Laufzeit erforderlich [PS 88]. Bei detailreichen Polygonen mit vielen tausend (reellwertigen) Polygonpunkten führen solche Tests zu erheblichen Laufzeiten. Andererseits fällt auf, daß für die Entscheidung des Tests nur ein sehr kleiner lokaler Teil des Objektes wirklich relevant ist. Diese Beobachtung legt es nahe, die Objekte in einfache lokale Bereiche einzuteilen und für die Durchführung des Tests möglichst nur einen dieser lokalen Bereiche zu betrachten. Dies führt zum Konzept der *Objektzerlegung*, bei dem ein Polygon in eine Menge einfacherer lokal beschränkter Teilkomponenten zerlegt wird. In [KHS 91] und [Kri 91a] wird der Zerlegungsansatz für einfache Polygone mit Löchern ausführlich vorgestellt und diskutiert. Als Teilkomponenten kommen einfache Objektklassen wie Dreiecke, Trapeze, konvexe Polygone usw. in Frage.

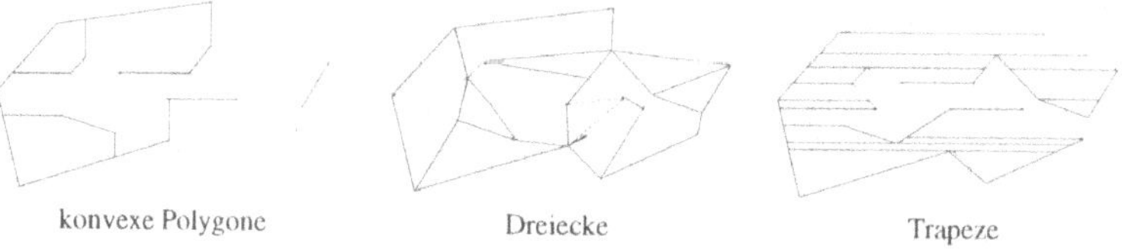

Bild 7: Verschiedene Zerlegungsverfahren für einfache Polygone mit Löchern

Geometrische Tests werden dann z.B. lediglich auf einem Trapez durchgeführt, was wesentlich effizienter ist, als das gesamte Polygon für den Test zu betrachten. Um effizient entscheiden zu können, welche Komponente oder Komponenten für den jeweiligen Test tatsächlich relevant sind, werden sämtliche Teilkomponenten eines Objektes in einem speziellen R*-Baum - *TR*-Baum* genannt - räumlich organisiert abgespeichert. Der TR*-Baum ist eine Hauptspeicher-Indexstruktur zur Repräsentation eines Objektes, die zur Durchführung des Tests vollständig in den Hauptspeicher geladen wird. In [SK 91] zeigen wir, daß der TR*-Baum verschiedene geometrische Anfragen und Operationen effizient unterstützt.

4.4 Szenen-Organisation

Eine wichtige Anforderung an Geo-Datenbanksysteme ist die *Mengenorientierung*. Neben kleinräumigen Anfragen muß ein Geo-Datenbanksystem in der Lage sein, großräumige Anfragen effizient zu bearbeiten. Bei solchen Anfragen werden große Datenmengen vom Sekundärspeicher in den Hauptspeicher übertragen. Die bisher in diesem Beitrag vorgestellten Konzepte unterstützen durch selektiven Objektzugriff insbesondere Punkt- und kleinräumige Bereichsanfragen; großräumige Anfragen erfahren durch diese Ansätze keine besondere Effizienzsteigerung. Daher benötigen wir in unserer Architektur ein Konzept, das eine Mengenorientierung unterstützt; wir werden es später als *Szenen-Organisation* bezeichnen.

Betrachten wir die bisherige Speicherorganisation und die zu speichernden Geo-Objekte, so können folgende Beobachtungen gemacht werden:

- Die Geo-Objekte sind oft im Vergleich zu den Seiten, auf denen die Objekte gespeichert werden, sehr groß. Oft passen nur wenige Objekte in eine Seite. Etliche Objekte benötigen auch bei einer Seitenkapazität von 4 KByte mehrere Seiten Speicherplatz (vgl. Abschnitt 2.2).
- Die Seiten werden räumlich unabhängig voneinander auf dem Sekundärspeicher abgelegt; d.h. räumlich benachbarte Seiten sind nicht physisch nah gespeichert. Größere Bereichsanfragen lesen aber eine Reihe räumlich benachbarter Seiten in den Hauptspeicher ein. Folglich müssen die Seiten auf dem Sekundärspeicher von verschiedenen Stellen "zusammengesammelt" werden. Dadurch entsteht ein erheblicher Leistungsverlust.

Die in diesem Abschnitt präsentierten Konzepte stellen somit nur eine *lokale Ordnung* innerhalb von Seiten sicher [Wid 91]. Um die Mengenorientierung geeignet zu unterstützen, ist eine *globale Ordnung* notwendig, d.h. größere räumlich zusammenhängende Bereiche der Geo-Daten werden physisch nahe gespeichert.

Um größere Speicherbereiche zu handhaben, lassen sich unterschiedliche Wege gehen. In [Wei 89] werden die *Nutzung größerer Seiten*, *Seiten mit variabler Größe*, *verschiedene Pufferstrategien* und *physikalische Clusterung von Seiten* kombiniert mit einer *mengenorientierten Seitenschnittstelle* zur Handhabung großer komplexer Objekte detailliert diskutiert. Innerhalb dieser Arbeit wird die physikalische Clusterung von Seiten favorisiert und bietet sich als adäquater Ansatz zur Speicherung sog. *Szenen* (Begriffsdefinition folgt) innerhalb unserer Geo-Architektur an. Um diesen Ansatz praktisch umzusetzen, wird eine mengenorientierte Schnittstelle zwischen Datenbanksystem und Sekundärspeichermedium benötigt. Ein derartiges Interface erlaubt den effizienten Transfer von Mengen physikalisch benachbarter Seiten vom Sekundär- in den Hauptspeicher. Die Implementierung eines solchen Interfaces soll hier allerdings nicht weiter erörtert werden.

In [HSW 88] wurde vorgeschlagen, den Erhalt der globalen Ordnung geometrischer Punktdaten über *dynamisches z-hashing* zu realisieren. Dieser Ansatz wurde in [HWZ 91] auf räumliche Daten mit Ausdehnung übertragen. Dabei wird allerdings nur die globale Ordnung bezüglich der Approximationen sichergestellt. Außerdem ist dieser Ansatz für Hash-Verfahren und nicht für Verfahren mit beliebiger Raumaufteilung einsetzbar. Daher haben wir ein Konzept entwickelt, das auf der Partitionierung des Raumes durch den R*-Baum beruht.

Der Aufbau der Szenen-Organisation

Wie bereits erwähnt, nutzen wir den R*-Baum wegen seines guten Leistungsverhaltens und seiner Robustheit als integrale Komponente unserer Geo-Architektur. Der R*-Baum verwendet ein sehr effizientes Schema zur Partitionierung, ohne die Objekte zu clippen oder in einen anderen Raum zu transformieren. So liegt die Idee nahe, Partitionen, d.h. ausgewählte Teilbäume des R*-Baumes als Einheiten der physikalischen Clusterung zu verwenden. Im folgenden ist eine *Szene* als ein Teilbaum des R*-Baumes definiert und physikalisch auf dem Sekundärspeicher geclustert. Eine Szene besteht aus einer größeren Menge physisch benachbarter Seiten, die alle zugehörigen Geo-Objekte umfaßt.

Benötigt ein Geo-Objekt mehrere Seiten Speicherplatz, so werden diese Seiten innerhalb der Szene physisch zusammenhängend abgespeichert. Damit kann auch ein einzelnes, größeres Objekt durch eine Operation vom Sekundärspeicher vollständig in den Hauptspeicher übertragen werden (vgl. Schritt 3 im Phasenmodell). Ansonsten unterliegen die Seiten innerhalb einer Szene keiner Ordnung. Sie werden wie bisher vom R*-Baum verwaltet.

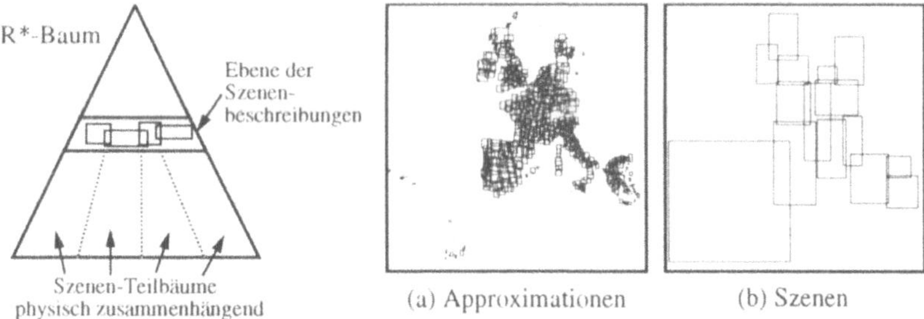

Bild 8: Schematische und beispielhafte Darstellung der Szenen-Organisation

Neben einer schematischen Darstellung der Szenen-Organisation zeigt Bild 8 den Szenenaufbau an einem Beispiel. Die Daten sind die Verwaltungsbezirke der EG (siehe Bild 1). In einem R*-Baum sind die Polygone, die diese Bezirke geometrisch modellieren, deren Teilkomponenten und die Objektapproximationen (Bild 8 (a)) organisiert. Bild 8 (b) zeigt die Partitionierung des R*-Baumes auf einer höheren Directory-Ebene; diese Rechtecke beschreiben die Szenen im Baum; die zugehörigen Teilbäume sind physisch zusammenhängend gespeichert.

Anfragebearbeitung

In einer Szenen-Organisation können sowohl klein- als auch großräumige Anfragen effizient bearbeitet werden. Kleinräumige Anfragen werden wie bisher seitenweise abgearbeitet. Besitzt eine Bereichsanfrage hingegen einen größeren Anfragebereich, werden die betroffenen Szenen, die den Anfragebereich schneiden, vollständig in den Hauptspeicher gelesen. Dieses kann sehr effizient erfolgen, da die Seiten der Szene physisch benachbart sind. Damit ist auf dem Plattenspeicher nur eine Suchoperation notwendig, um die Szene einzulesen. Ohne die Szenen-Organisation müßte jede Seite einzeln angesteuert werden. Allerdings kann eine Szene auch eine Reihe von Geo-Objekten umfassen, die die Anfrage nicht erfüllen *(Fehltreffer, "False Hits")*. Dieses führt dazu, daß das Übertragungsvolumen bei der Szenen-Organisation ansteigt. Eine relativ kleine Zahl von False Hits beeinträchtigt die Effizienz aber nicht wesentlich, da der Aufwand für die Suche einer Seite den Aufwand für die Übertragung einer Seite bei weitem übersteigt [PH 90]. Zusätzlich kann die Größe des Schnittbereiches mit dem Anfragebereich als Maß für die Entscheidung dienen, ob eine Szene vollständig eingelesen wird oder ob die Anfrage ohne Nutzung der Szenen-Organisation über den R*-Baum abläuft. Eine genauere Untersuchung des Leistungsverhaltens der Szenen-Organisation folgt in Abschnitt 5.1.

Nachdem die Szene in den Hauptspeicher eingelesen wurde, kann die Anfragebearbeitung in der bisherigen Form weiter ablaufen. Eine detaillierte algorithmische Beschreibung der dynamischen Organisation der Szenen-Architektur findet sich in [Sch 92] und [BKS 93b]. Die Ergänzung der bisherigen Techniken zur Anfragebearbeitung um eine Szenen-Organisation erlaubt sowohl eine effiziente kleinräumige Selektion als auch eine Unterstützung großräumiger Bereichsanfragen.

4.5 Einbindung thematischer Attribute

Die bisher vorgestellten Techniken sind vollständig auf die Unterstützung räumlicher Anfragen ausgerichtet. Neben räumlichen Anfragen spielen aber auch Anfragen bezüglich thematischer Attribute eine wichtige Rolle in geographischen Informationssystemen. Die thematischen Attribute (vgl. Abschnitt 2.1) sind in unserem Ansatz der geometrischen Komponente zugeordnet.

Um thematische Anfragen effizient unterstützen zu können, benötigen wir somit neben dem räumlichen Index *Sekundärindizes* (z.B. B-Bäume) für die relevanten thematischen Attribute. Der R*-Baum bestimmt in Verbindung mit der Szenen-Organisation den Ort der physischen Speicherung. Damit dies losgelöst von den Sekundärindizes erfolgen kann, benötigen wir eine *Link-Tabelle*. Die Link-Tabelle ordnet jedem Geo-Objekt, repräsentiert durch ein eindeutiges *Surrogat*, eine Datenseite im R*-Baum zu. Wenn sich nun die Datenseite des Geo-Objektes ändert, wird nur der Eintrag in der Link-Tabelle geändert; Änderungen in den Sekundärindizes sind nicht notwendig. Damit der Zugriff auf die Link-Tabelle vom Raumindex aus erfolgen kann, müssen die Einträge der Geo-Objekte in den Datenseiten um das Surrogat erweitert werden.

Bild 9 zeigt im Rahmen der Gesamtarchitektur das Konzept zur Einbindung von Sekundärindizes über Link-Tabellen und Surrogate. In [Kri 91b] und [Sch 92] wird dieses Konzept ausführlicher erläutert.

4.6 Die Geo-Architektur

Bisher haben wir eine Reihe von prinzipiellen Konzepten und Techniken zur effizienten Anfragebearbeitung in Geo-Datenbanken vorgestellt. Diese betten wir nun in eine Gesamtarchitektur, unsere *Geo-Architektur*, ein. Bild 9 stellt die gesamte Architektur schematisch dar.

Die Basis unserer Architektur bildet der R*-Baum. Er organisiert die Daten seitenweise auf dem Sekundärspeicher und ermöglicht eine effiziente räumliche Indizierung. Damit kann der Suchbereich von räumlichen Anfragen eingeschränkt werden.

Eine räumliche Anfrage durchläuft bei der Wurzel beginnend den R*-Baum. Dabei trifft sie auf eine oder mehrere Szenenbeschreibungen. Übersteigt die Größe des Schnittbereiches von Anfrageregion und Szene einen Schwellenwert, wird eine Szene vollständig in den Hauptspeicher geladen und die weitere Anfragebearbeitung läuft im Hauptspeicher ab; damit entfallen aufwendige Suchoperationen auf dem Sekundärspeicher. Anderenfalls werden die erforderlichen Datenbereiche seitenweise in den Hauptspeicher transferiert.

Die nächste Stufe in der Architektur bilden die Approximationen. Sie unterstützen eine einfache Vorauswahl, ob ein Geo-Objekt eine Anfrage erfüllt oder nicht. Dazu wird die Approximation in den Einträgen der Datenseiten gespeichert, z.B. das minimal umgebende Fünfeck.

Erfüllt die Approximation eines Geo-Objektes die Anfragebedingung, muß das Objekt weiter untersucht werden. Dazu befindet sich in jedem Objekteintrag ein Verweis auf die exakte Geometrierepräsentation. Diese wird durch den TR*-Baum verwaltet. Er strukturiert die Zerlegungskomponenten des Geo-Objektes räumlich. Damit kann die Lokalität von Anfragen ausgenutzt und auf die entscheidenden Teilkomponenten direkt zugegriffen werden. Anhand dieser einfachen geometrischen Teilobjekte kann die Anfragebedingung überprüft werden. Dieses Vorgehen erspart den aufwendigen Test mit dem Gesamtobjekt.

Abgerundet wird die Architektur durch Sekundärindizes für thematische Attribute. Eine thematische Anfrage läuft den B-Baum ab. Dadurch erhält man einen oder mehrere Surrogate. Über das Surrogat greift man auf die Link-Tabelle zu und erhält die Nummer der Datenseite, die den zugehörigen Objekteintrag enthält.

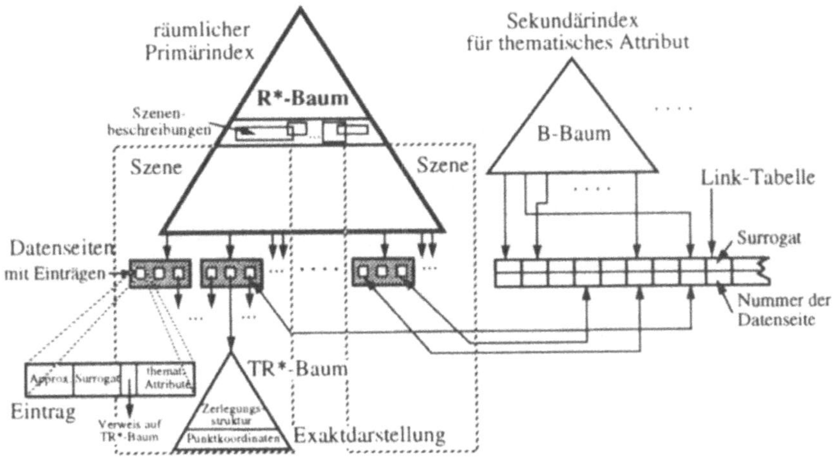

Bild 9: Integration einzelner effizienter Bausteine in unsere Geo-Architektur

5 Empirische Evaluierung der Geo-Architektur

Die Techniken, die in der von uns vorgeschlagenen Architektur für Geo-Datenbanksysteme verwendet werden, wurden bereits intensiv empirisch untersucht. Die Basis des Systems ist der R*-Baum. Leistungsdaten wurden in [BKSS 90] vorgestellt und zeigen gegenüber anderen R-Baum-Varianten einen beträchtlichen Leistungsgewinn. Ein Leistungsvergleich mit dem R^+-Baum und dem PMR-Quadtree findet sich in [HS 92]. Die unterschiedlichen Approximationen haben wir in [BKS 93a] auf ihre Eignung untersucht und das minimal umgebende Fünfeck als die beste Approximation ermittelt.

Den Zerlegungsansatz haben wir in [Kri 91a] und [KHS 91] untersucht. Insbesondere für kleinräumige Anfragen konnten für die konvexe und die Trapez-Zerlegung entscheidende Leistungsgewinne gegenüber dem unzerlegten Ansatz erzielt werden. Die integrierte Repräsentation eines in Trapeze zerlegten Geo-Objektes durch einen TR*-Baum wurde von uns in [SK 91] betrachtet. Dabei zeigte sich der R*-Baum als Hauptspeicherversion mit niedrigen Verzweigungsgrad geeignet, verschiedenste Anfrage- und Operationstypen gleichmäßig effizient zu bearbeiten.

Die Organisation der Geo-Objekte in Szenen wurde dagegen bisher noch nicht untersucht. Daher wollen wir im folgenden die Szenen-Organisation näher betrachten und sie innerhalb eines Leistungsvergleiches detailliert beurteilen.

5.1 Evaluierung der Szenen-Organisation

Prinzipiell lassen sich drei Ansätze für die Speicherung von Geo-Objekten unterscheiden:

1.) Speicherung der Exaktdarstellung außerhalb der Datenseiten (Ansatz 1)

In den Datenseiten der Indexstruktur befinden sich neben den Approximationen nur Verweise auf die Exaktdarstellung der Geo-Objekte. Die Exaktdarstellung wird außerhalb der Speicherungsstruktur, nicht räumlich organisiert gespeichert, z.B. in sequentiellen Dateien. Dieser Ansatz wird beispielsweise bei Quadtrees verwendet [HS 92]. Anders formuliert stellt die räumliche Indexstruktur für die Approximationen einen Primärindex und für die eigentlichen Geo-Objekte einen Sekundärindex dar. Bild 10 zeigt den Ansatz schematisch. Ein Vorteil dieses Ansatzes ist, daß eine hohe Zahl von Approximationen gemeinsam in einer Datenseite gespeichert wird, d.h. es wird eine maximale lokale Ordnung auf den Approximationen hergestellt. Außerdem gibt es keine prinzipielle Größenbeschränkung für die exakte Repräsentation der Geo-Objekte. Wesentlicher Nachteil ist, daß die Ordnungserhaltung sich nur auf die Approximationen bezieht. Folglich ist auch bei Bereichsanfragen für jeden Zugriff auf die exakte Objektrepräsentation ein zusätzlicher Seitenzugriff notwendig, da diese nicht räumlich organisiert wird.

2.) Speicherung der Exaktdarstellung innerhalb der Datenseiten (Ansatz 2)

Die exakte Repräsentation der Objekte wird zusätzlich zu den Approximationen innerhalb der Datenseiten gespeichert. Damit sind auch diese physisch nah gespeichert und können bei Anfragen gemeinsam in einem Zugriff in den Hauptspeicher eingelesen werden [Wid 91]. Die Indexstruktur ist im Gegensatz zum ersten Ansatz damit ein Primärindex, der die physische Speicherung bestimmt. Wesentlicher Nachteil dieses Ansatzes ist, daß so nur wenige Objekte in eine Seite passen und häufig räumlich benachbarte Geo-Objekte in verschiedene Datenseiten fallen. In Abschnitt 2.2 wurde aufgezeigt, daß in Geo-Datenbanken sehr große Objekte auftreten können, die mehrere Seiten Speicherplatz benötigen. Solche Objekte lassen sich durch diesen Ansatz nur schwer organisieren.

3.) Speicherung der Objekte in einer Szenen-Organisation (Ansatz 3)

Diesen Ansatz haben wir in Abschnitt 4.4 vorgestellt. Hierbei werden größere Teile der Daten in physisch zusammenhängenden, aber nur lokal sortierten Speicherbereichen zusammengefaßt und über den R*-Baum organisiert.

Bild 10 zeigt die drei Ansätze schematisch:

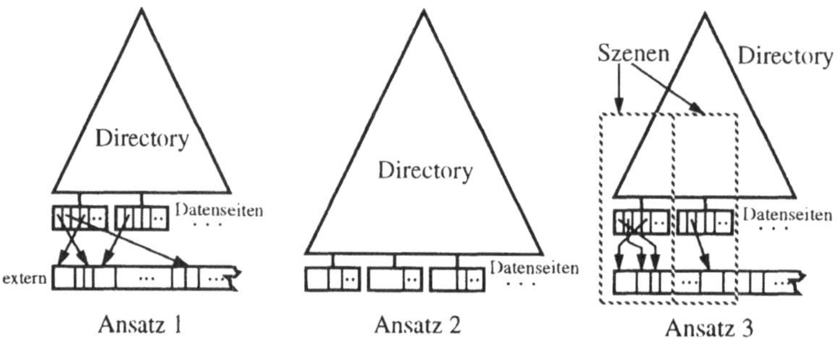

Bild 10: Ansätze zur Speicherung von Geo-Objekten

Die Szenen-Organisation ist für die Unterstützung großräumiger Bereichsanfragen entworfen. Für solche mengenorientierten Anfragen stellen sich zwei Fragen, die im folgenden näher untersucht werden:

- Welches Leistungsverhalten zeigt jeder der drei Ansätze? Kann durch die Szenen-Organisation gegenüber den beiden anderen Speicherungsverfahren ein entscheidender Leistungsgewinn erzielt werden ?
- Bei welcher Szenengröße zeigt die Architektur das beste Leistungsverhalten? Hängt diese Größe stark von der Größe der Bereichsanfragen ab ?

Testumgebung

Um diese Fragestellungen beantworten zu können, haben wir die drei Ansätze in empirischen Untersuchungen miteinander verglichen. Testdaten waren reale Daten vom US Bureau of the Census [Bur 89], die die Verwaltungsgrenzen, Straßenzüge, Eisenbahnlinien und Flüsse von vier kalifornischen Counties repräsentieren. In dieser Datenbasis befanden sich 119.151 Linienzüge, die jeweils aus 2 bis 349 Punkten bestehen. Jede Koordinate wird durch eine Real-Zahl von 8 Byte dargestellt, so daß sich ein Gesamtdatenvolumen von 15,9 MByte ergibt. Approximiert wurden diese Linienzüge durch minimal umgebende Rechtecke, für deren Repräsentation 16 Byte zur Verfügung stehen. Diese Rechtecke sind in Bild 11 (a) dargestellt.

Aus diesen Daten wurden gemäß der drei Ansätze R*-Bäume erzeugt. Die Seitenkapazität betrug dabei 4 KByte.

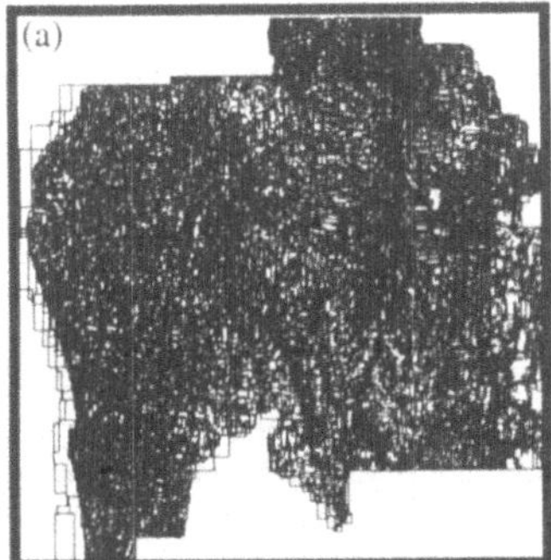

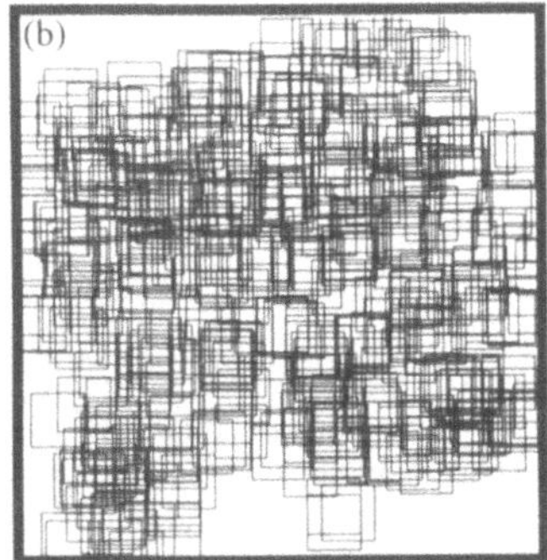

Bild 11: Darstellung der Testdaten und -anfragen

Um Aussagen über das Leistungsverhalten der Verfahren für größere Bereichsanfragen zu gewinnen, haben wir vier Testserien mit unterschiedlich großen Anfragebereichen untersucht. Jede Testserie bestand aus 464 quadratischen Bereichsanfragen (Window Queries), die über den von Objekten überdeckten Datenraum gleichverteilt waren. Die Größe der Anfragebereiche variiert zwischen 0,25% und 16% der Fläche des Gesamtdatenraumes. Bild 11 (b) zeigt die Anfragen bei einer Fläche von 1%. In Tabelle 1 sind die Anfragen der vier Testserien genauer spezifiziert.

Testserie	Größe der Anfragen (Prozent vom Gesamtdatenraum)	pro Testserie		durchschnittlich pro Anfrage	
		eingelesene Datensätze	eingelesene Daten (KByte)	eingelesene Datensätze	eingelesene Daten (KByte)
I	0,25 %	189.229	29.392	408	63
II	1 %	714.937	105.521	1.541	227
III	4 %	2.687.648	382.483	5.792	824
IV	16 %	9.462.455	1.315.236	20.393	2.835

Tabelle 1: Charakteristika der Testserien

Für die Bewertung der Effizienz der Verfahren wird ein Maß zur Beschreibung des Zugriffsaufwandes benötigt. Wie bereits erwähnt, lassen sich für einen Seitenzugriff die Zeit für die Suche der Seite auf dem Sekundärspeicher und die Zeit für das Lesen und den Transfer der Seite vom Sekundärspeicher in den Hauptspeicher unterscheiden. Für die Bestimmung des Gesamtaufwandes bewerten wir im folgenden den Aufwand für die Suche im Vergleich zum Übertragungsaufwand im Verhältnis 10 zu 1. Dieses Verhältnis entspricht in etwa realen Magnetplattenspeichern [PH 90]. Ist N_S die Anzahl der Suchoperationen und N_T die Anzahl der Transfers, gilt für den Zugriffsaufwand A:

$$A = 10N_S + N_T$$

Für Bereichsanfragen sind die Zugriffskosten, die durch den R*-Baum verursacht werden, im Verhältnis zu den Kosten für die Zugriffe auf exakte Repräsentationen gering. Daher betrachten wir im folgenden nur die Zugriffe, die durch das Einlesen der exakten Darstellung der Geo-Objekte entstehen.

Testergebnisse

Tabelle 2 zeigt den Zugriffsaufwand bei Speicherung der Linienzüge außerhalb der Datenseiten (Ansatz 1). Die Anzahl der Suchoperationen (N_S), die Zahl der Transfers (N_T) und der Zugriffsaufwand A sind dort gerundet in Tausend dargestellt. Durch das Runden ergibt sich A in den folgenden Tabellen nicht genau aus N_S und N_T.

Testserie I (0,25 %)			Testserie II (1 %)			Testserie III (4 %)			Testserie IV (16 %)		
N_S	N_T	A	N_S	N_T	A	N_S	N_T	A	N_S	N_T	A
189	189	2.082	715	715	7.864	2.688	2.689	29.585	9.462	9.463	104.088

Tabelle 2: Zugriffsaufwand Ansatz 1 (in Tausend, gerundet)

Bedingt durch den Ansatz, die Exaktdarstellung auszulagern, ist für jeden angefragten Datensatz mindestens eine (teure) Suchoperation notwendig, da die exakten Repräsentationen nicht räumlich organisiert sind. Nach jeder Suchoperation ist mindestens ein Transfer notwendig. Die Tatsache, daß die Transferzahl nicht wesentlich höher als N_S ist, resultiert aus der geringen Zahl von Datensätzen, die größer als eine Seite sind.

In Tabelle 3 sind die Ergebnisse für das zweiten Speicherverfahren angegeben, bei dem die Linienzüge innerhalb der Datenseiten gespeichert werden.

Testserie I (0,25 %)			Testserie II (1 %)			Testserie III (4 %)			Testserie IV (16 %)		
N_S	N_T	A	N_S	N_T	A	N_S	N_T	A	N_S	N_T	A
16	16	175	52	52	573	180	180	1.985	610	610	6.710

Tabelle 3: Zugriffsaufwand Ansatz 2 (in Tausend, gerundet)

Gegenüber dem ersten Ansatz kommt diese Vorgehensweise mit deutlich weniger Suchoperationen aus. Dies ist dadurch bedingt, daß mehrere Linienzüge in einer Datenseite gespeichert werden und durch einen Zugriff eingelesen werden. Der Gewinn hängt nur unwesentlich von der Größe der Bereichsanfragen ab. Da es in den Testdaten kaum Datensätze gibt, deren Größe die Seitengröße übersteigt, ist N_T praktisch genauso groß wie N_S.

Bei der Szenen-Organisation sind die Ergebnisse wesentlich von der durchschnittlichen Größe der Szenen abhängig. Während beim ersten Ansatz die exakte Darstellung nur dann eingelesen wird, wenn sie aufgrund der Anfrage benötigt wird, werden beim zweiten Ansatz am Rand von Anfragen unweigerlich auch Exaktrepräsentationen eingelesen, die die Anfrageregion nicht berühren *(Fehltreffer)*. Sehr große Szenen kommen mit sehr wenig Suchoperationen aus, benötigen aber dafür um so mehr Operationen zum Transfer vom Sekundärspeicher in den Hauptspeicher, da die Zahl der Fehltreffer mit zunehmender Szenengröße steigt. Je kleiner die Szenen werden, desto mehr steigt der Aufwand zum Suchen und desto geringer wird der Übertragungsaufwand. Um diesen Effekt näher zu untersuchen, haben wir unterschiedliche Szenengrößen getestet. Die Ergebnisse sind in Tabelle 4 aufgeführt; die Einträge mit dem geringsten Zugriffsaufwand sind dunkel unterlegt.

Wie erwartet, sinkt N_S mit zunehmender Szenengröße, während N_T steigt, je größer die Szenen sind. Dabei bildet sich je nach Größe der Anfragebereiche ein Optimum beim Zugriffsaufwand, das etwa zwischen 25 und 100 KByte liegt. Je größer die Anfragen sind, desto größer ist die optimale Szenengröße. Allerdings ist die Abhängigkeit nicht sehr einschneidend: Während 64 der Faktor zwischen Testserie I und IV bezüglich der Größe der Anfragebereiche ist, beträgt der Faktor zwischen den entsprechenden optimalen Szenengrößen nur rund 4. Außerdem verläuft die Aufwandsfunktion im Bereich dieser Optima bei allen Testserien sehr flach, so daß mit rund 77 KByte eine für alle Testserien nahezu optimale Szenengröße bestimmt werden kann.

durchschnittl. Szenengröße (Byte)	Testserie I (0,25 %)			Testserie II (1 %)			Testserie III (4 %)			Testserie IV (16 %)		
	N_S	N_T	A	N_S	N_T	A	N_S	N_T	A	N_S	N_T	A
1.852.750	1,1	698	709	1,2	781	794	1,6	943	959	2,1	1.666	1.188
757.943	1,2	275	287	1,6	343	345	2,4	505	529	4,1	837	877
273.357	1,5	128	144	2,3	185	208	4,2	324	365	8,6	638	725
140.124	1,8	78	96	3,0	123	153	6,0	238	298	14,1	528	669
91.619	2,2	62	84	3,9	103	142	8,5	214	299	20,8	503	711
79.027	2,1	51	72	3,9	90	130	8,8	191	280	22,7	474	701
63.402	2,3	46	70	4,5	85	130	10,4	187	291	27,5	467	742
33.283	3,2	36	68	6,7	70	137	17,3	167	340	48,8	447	936
18.610	4,2	26	68	10,0	57	158	27,8	151	429	82,8	432	1.260
10.716	6,1	23	84	15,4	54	209	45,6	153	609	140	452	1.853
8.367	6,8	21	87	18,2	52	235	55,6	152	708	175	460	2.210

Tabelle 4: Zugriffsaufwand Szenen-Organisation (Ansatz 3) (in Tausend, gerundet)

Zusammenfassung

In Tabelle 5 ist der Zugriffsaufwand für alle drei untersuchten Speicherungsansätze dargestellt. Dabei ist der Aufwand auf das erste Verfahren auf 1 normiert; bei den beiden anderen Ansätzen ist der Faktor angegeben, um den sich der Aufwand vermindert hat. Die durchschnittliche Szenengröße für Ansatz 3 beträgt 79.027 Byte.

Ansatz	Verbesserung des Zugriffsaufwands A (Faktoren)			
	I (0,25 %)	II (1 %)	III (4 %)	IV (16 %)
1: Geometrie außerhalb der Datenseite	1,0	1,0	1,0	1,0
2: Geometrie innerhalb der Datenseite	11,9	13,7	14,9	15,5
3: Szenen-Organisation	28,9	60,5	105,7	148,5

Tabelle 5: Verbesserung des Zugriffsaufwandes der Ansätze 2 und 3 im Vergleich zu Ansatz 1

Die Ergebnisse lassen sich wie folgt vergleichen und zusammenfassen:

- Der Ansatz, die Exaktdarstellung innerhalb der Datenseiten zu speichern, ist in unseren Tests dem ersten Ansatz, die exakte Repräsentation auszulagern, um einen Faktor von rund 12 bis 15 überlegen. Die Größe der Anfragebereiche spielt dabei nur eine untergeordnete Rolle.

  Bei diesem Ergebnis ist allerdings ein wichtiger Aspekt zu berücksichtigen: Die untersuchten Geo-Objekte sind im Vergleich zu der Größe der Datenseiten relativ klein. In realen Karten treten häufig wesentlich umfangreichere Objekte auf (vgl. Abschnitt 2.2). Das heißt, daß bei solchen Daten die

Objekte zwangsläufig ausgelagert werden müssen. In Folge wird dieser Ansatz sich bei einem größeren Anteil umfangreicher Objekte stark an das Leistungsverhalten des ersten Verfahrens annähern.

- Eindeutiger Gewinner dieses Vergleiches ist die Szenen-Organisation. Bereits bei kleinen Anfragebereichen tritt ein erheblicher Leistungsgewinn ein. So ist die Szenen-Organisation um einen Faktor von knapp 30 besser als der Auslagerungsansatz. Bei größeren Anfragebereichen steigt dieser Faktor sogar auf 106 und 148.

Eine weitere wichtige Beobachtung ist, daß eine nahezu optimale Szenengröße weitgehend unabhängig von der Größe der Anfragebereiche ist. Damit ist der Deckungsbereich für eine Implementierung mit einer festgelegten Szenengröße sehr groß.

Außerdem kann durch den flachen Verlauf der Aufwandfunktion ein starker Leistungsgewinn auch dann erzielt werden, wenn durch Einfügen oder Löschen von Geo-Objekten die durchschnittliche Szenengröße während der Laufzeit schwankt.

6 Zusammenfassung und Ausblick

Wir haben eine *Speicher- und Zugriffsarchitektur für geographische Datenbanksysteme* vorgeschlagen. Dazu wurden eine Reihe von prinzipiellen Konzepten und Techniken zur effizienten Anfragebearbeitung in Geo-Datenbanken in eine Gesamtarchitektur eingebettet.

Der *R*-Baum* bildet die Basis-Komponente unserer Geo-Architektur. Er organisiert die Daten auf dem Sekundärspeicher und ermöglicht eine effiziente räumliche Indizierung. So kann der Suchbereich von räumlichen Anfragen rasch eingeschränkt werden. Die nächste Stufe in der Architektur bilden die *Objektapproximationen*. Sie unterstützen eine einfache Vorauswahl, ob ein Geo-Objekt eine Anfrage erfüllt oder nicht. Gegenüber dem üblicherweise verwendeten minimal umgebenden Rechteck hat das Fünfeck eine sehr gute Approximationsgüte. Die exakte Geometrierepräsentation eines Objektes wird durch den *TR*-Baum* verwaltet. Er strukturiert das Geo-Objekt in *Zerlegungskomponenten* und organisiert diese räumlich. Damit kann die Lokalität von Anfragen ausgenutzt und auf die entscheidenden Teilkomponenten direkt zugegriffen werden. Aufgrund der einfachen geometrischen Teilobjekte entfallen aufwendige Tests mit dem Gesamtobjekt. Thematische Anfragen werden durch entsprechende *Sekundärindizes für thematische Attribute* unterstützt, die über eine Link-Tabelle mit dem räumlichen Primärindex verbunden sind.

Die beschriebene Architektur hat insbesondere den räumlich-selektiven Objektzugriff und kleinräumige Bereichsanfragen unterstützt. Für einen effizienten mengenorientierten Zugriff großräumiger Bereichsanfragen haben wir die *Szenen-Organisation* in die Geo-Architektur integriert. Hierbei werden größere Teile der Daten in physisch zusammenhängenden, aber nur objektweise geordneten Speicherbereichen zusammengefaßt. Diese Szenen werden über den primären R*-Baum organisiert. Das Leistungsverhalten der Szenen-Organisation haben wir näher untersucht. Für großräumige Bereichanfragen konnten massive Leistungssteigerungen um einen Faktor bis zu 150 gegenüber anderen Speicherungsansätzen erzielt werden.

Für unsere zukünftige Arbeit planen wir die Integration unserer Geo-Architektur in existierende erweiterbare Datenbanksysteme für geometrische Anwendungen. Vielversprechende Kandidaten für diese Idee sind DASDBS, GRAL und POSTGRES. Weiterhin ist die Entwicklung einer *parallelen Geo-Architektur* eine herausfordernde Aufgabe für zukünftige Foschungsaktivitäten. Diese zielt in zwei Richtungen. Durch Nutzung von Multiprozessor-Systemen besteht die Möglichkeit, die Anfragebearbeitung zu parallelisieren. Insbesondere der Zerlegungsansatz dürfte hier entscheidende Leistungssteigerungen erlauben. Das große Datenvolumen andererseits macht den Einsatz von Multidisk-Systemen sinnvoll. Eine zentrale Frage dabei ist die Bestimmung einer geeigneten Verteilung der Geo-Daten auf die verschiedenen Platteneinheiten.

Die Übertragung der vorgestellten Konzepte auf *dreidimensionale Geo-Objekte* ist ein weiteres künftiges Arbeitsfeld. Eine Anwendungsmöglichkeit liegt beispielsweise im Bereich der Bioinformatik. Erster Schritt in diese Richtung ist die Entwicklung und Implementierung dreidimensionaler Approximations- und Zerlegungsverfahren.

Literatur

[Arn 90] Arnold F.: *'GIS Geo-Informations Systeme'*, Technischer Bericht, Bundesforschungsanstalt für Naturschutz und Landschaftsökologie, 1990

[Bar 88] Bartelme N.: *'GIS Technologie: Geoinformationssysteme, Landinformationssysteme und ihre Grundlagen'*, Springer, 1988

[BKS 93a] Brinkhoff T., Kriegel H.-P., Schneider R.: *'Comparison of Approximations of Complex Objects used for Approximation-based Query Processing in Spatial Database Systems'*, Proc. 9th Int. Conf. on Data Engineering, Vienna, Austria, 1993.

[BKS 93b] Brinkhoff T., Kriegel H.-P., Schneider R.: *'A New Technique to Support Large Window Queries in Spatial Database Systems'*, 1993, in Vorbereitung.

[BKS 93c] Brinkhoff T., Kriegel H.-P., Seeger B.: *'Efficient Processing of Spatial Joins Using R-trees'*, 1993, eingereicht zur Veröffentlichung.

[BKSS 90] Beckmann N., Kriegel H.-P., Schneider R., Seeger B.: *'The R*-tree: An Efficient and Robust Access Method for Points and Rectangles'*, Proc. ACM SIGMOD Int. Conf. on Management of Data, Atlantic City, NJ., 1990, pp. 322-331.

[Bur 86] Burrough P.A.: *'Principles of Geographical Information Systems for Land Resources Assessment'*, Oxford University Press, 1986.

[Bur 89] Bureau of the Census: *'TIGER/Line Percensus Files, 1990 Technical Documentation'*, Washington, DC., 1989.

[CDRS 86] Carey M. J., DeWitt D. J., Richardson J. E., Shekita E. J.: *'Object and File Management in the EXODUS Extensible Database System'*, Proc. 12th Int. Conf. on Very Large Data Bases, Kyoto, Japan, 1986, pp. 91-100.

[Cra 90] Crain I.K.: *'Extremely Large Spatial Information Systems - A Quantitative Perspective'*, Proc. 4th Int. Symp. on Spatial Data Handling, Zurich, Switzerland, 1990, pp. 632-641.

[Fra 91] Frank, A.U.: *'Properties of Geographic Data'*, Proc. 2nd Symp. on Large Spatial Databases, Zurich, Switzerland, 1991, in: Lecture Notes in Computer Science, Vol. 525, Springer, 1991, pp. 225-234.

[GC 87] Gorny A.J., Carter R.: *'World Data Bank II: General Users Guide'*, Technical report, U.S. Central Intelligence Agency, Washington, 1987.

[Gue 89] Güting R. H.: *'Gral: an extensible relational database system for geografic applications'*, Proc. 15th Int. Conf. on Very Large Data Bases, Amsterdam, Netherland, 1989, pp. 33-44.

[Gut 84] Guttman A.: *'R-trees: A Dynamic Index Structure for Spatial Searching'*, Proc. ACM SIGMOD Int. Conf. on Management of Data, Boston, MA., 1984, pp. 47-57.

[HS 92] Hoel E.G., Samet H.: *'A Qualitative Comparison Study of Data Structures for Large Line Segment Databases'*, Proc. SIGMOD Conf., San Diego, CA., 1992, pp 205-214.

[HSW 88] Hutflesz A., Six H.-W., Widmayer P.: *'Globally Order Preserving Multidimensional Linear Hashing'*, Proc. 4th Int. Conf. on Data Engineering, Los Angeles, CA., 1988, pp. 572-579.

[HWZ 91] Hutflesz A., Widmayer P., Zimmermann C.: *'Global Order Makes Spatial Access Faster'*, Int. Workshop on Database Management Systems for Geographical Applications, Capri, Italy, 1991, in: Geographic Database Management Systems, Springer, 1992, pp. 161-176.

[KBS 91] Kriegel H.-P., Brinkhoff T., Schneider R.: *'An Efficient Map Overlay Algorithm based on Spatial Access Methods and Computational Geometry'*, Int. Workshop on Database Management Systems for Geographical Applications, Capri, Italy, 1991, in: Geographic Database Management Systems, Springer, 1992, pp. 194-211.

[KHS 91] Kriegel H.-P., Horn H., Schiwietz M.: *'The Performance of Object Decomposition Techniques for Spatial Query Processing'*, Proc. 2nd Symp. on Large Spatial Databases, Zurich, Switzerland, 1991, in: Lecture Notes in Computer Science, Vol. 525, Springer, 1991, pp. 257-276.

[Kri 91a] Kriegel H.-P., Heep P., Heep S., Schiwietz M., Schneider R.: *'An Access Method Based Query Processor for Spatial Database Systems'*, Int. Workshop on Database Management Systems for Geographical Applications, Capri, Italy, 1991, in: Geographic Database Management Systems, Springer, 1992, pp. 273-292.

[Kri 91b] Kriegel H.-P., Heep P., Heep S., Schiwietz M., Schneider R.: *'A Flexible and Extensible Index Manager for Spatial Database Systems'*, Proc. 2nd Int. Conf. on Database and Expert Systems Applications, Berlin, Germany, 1991, pp. 179-184.

[Ore 89] Orenstein J. A.: *'Redundancy in Spatial Databases'*, Proc. ACM SIGMOD Int. Conf. on Management of Data, Portland, USA, 1989, pp. 294-305.

[PH 90] Paterson D., Hennessy J.: *'Computer Architecture: A Quantitative Approach'*, Morgan Kaufman, 1990.

[PS 88] Preparata F.P., Shamos M.I.: *'Computational Geometry'*, Springer, 1988.

[Sam 90] Samet H.: *'The Design and Analysis of Spatial Data Structures'*, Addison Wesley, 1990.

[Sch 92] Schneider R.: *'Eine Speicher- und Zugriffsarchitektur für Geo-Datenbanken'*, Dissertation, Institut für Informatik, Universität München, 1992, in Vorbereitung.

[SK 91] Schneider R., Kriegel H.-P.: *'The TR*-tree: A New Representation of Polygonal Objects Supporting Spatial Queries and Operations'*, Proc. 7th Workshop on Computational Geometry, Bern, Switzerland, 1991, in: Lecture Notes in Computer Science, Vol. 553, Springer, 1991, pp. 249-264.

[SV 89] Scholl M., Voisard A.: *'Thematic Map Modelling'*, Proc. 1st Symp. on the Design and Implementation of Large Spatial Databases, Santa Barbara, CA., 1989, in: Lecture Notes in Computer Science, Vol. 409, Springer, 1990, pp. 167-190.

[SR 86] Stonebraker M., Rowe L.: *'The Design of POSTGRES'*, Proc. ACM SIGMOD Conf. on Management of Data, Washinton D.C., 1986.

[SW 86] Schek H.-J., Waterfeld W.: *'A Database Kernel System for Geoscientific Applications'*, Proc. 2nd Int. Symp. on Spatial Data Handling, Seattle, Washington, 1986, pp. 273-288.

[Wei 89] Weikum G.: *'Set-Oriented Disk Access to Large Complex Objects'*, Proc. 5th Int. Conf. on Data Engineering, Los Angeles, CA., 1989, pp. 426-433.

[Wid 91] Widmayer P.: *'Datenstrukturen für Geodatenbanken'*, Entwicklungstendenzen bei Datenbanksystemen, Oldenbourg Verlag, 1991, pp. 317-361.

Aufwandsabschätzung für die Prozessierung vager Anfragen auf der Basis des Datenstrom-Ansatzes

Ulrich Pfeifer, Norbert Fuhr[1]

ZUSAMMENFASSUNG Wir betrachten vage Anfragen, die als Kombination mehrerer vager Kriterien formuliert werden. Ein einzelnes Datenbank-Objekt kann dabei ein vages Kriterium graduell erfüllen. Hier beschränken wir uns auf solche Anfragen, bei denen die Berechnung der Antwort effizient auf die (evtl. wiederholte) Kombination von Rangordnungen zu neuen Rangordnungen zurückgeführt werden kann. Da der Benutzer i.a. nur einige der besten Antwortobjekte inspizieren wird, müssen auch die jeweiligen Rangordnungen nur soweit berechnet werden, daß ihm diese angeboten werden können. In diesem Beitrag zeigen wir Ansätze auf, wie abgeschätzt werden kann, wieviele Elemente von Rangordnungen zu einem einzelnen Kriterium benötigt werden, um eine festgelegte Anzahl von Ausgabeelementen zu erzeugen. Experimente an einer großen Textdatenbasis belegen die Anwendbarkeit unseres Ansatzes.

1 Motivation

Mit der Verbreitung von Datenbanksystemen in immer weiteren Bereichen des täglichen Lebens wird es dringlicher, Konzepte wie Vagheit und Unsicherheit in diese Systeme zu integrieren. Betrachten wir zum Beispiel eine Gebrauchtwagendatenbank. Ein Kunde könnte seinen Wunsch vielleicht wie folgt angeben: „Ich suche einen PKW-Kombi mit höchstens 30 000 km für weniger als 20 000 DM". Würde nun der Händler diese Kriterien strikt interpretieren, so würde er wahrscheinlich wenige Wagen verkaufen. Aufgrund der Situation ist aber beiden Partnern klar, daß manche Einzelkriterien vage aufzufassen sind, daß der Kunde z.B. wahrscheinlich auch einen Wagen mit einem Kilometerstand von 35 000 km kaufen wird, wenn der Preis stimmt.
Läßt sich eine solche Anfrage mit teilweise sich wiedersprechenden Kriterien (möglichst neu – möglichst billig) mit einem konventionellen System bearbeiten? Entweder müßte der Verkäufer die Anfrage (Abbildung 1) durch Variation des Kilometerstandes und des Preises solange reformulieren, bis er eine Antwortmenge vernünftiger Größe erhielte, oder er müßte die Anfrage so weit fassen, daß alle in Frage kommenden Wagen in der Antwortmenge sind und diese dann geeignet sortieren. Das Problem bei der zweiten Lösung ist aber, daß eines der vagen Ein-

---

[1] Anschrift der Autoren: Universität Dortmund, Lehrstuhl Informatik VI, W-4600 Dortmund 50, E-mail: [pfeifer|fuhr]@ls6.informatik.uni-dortmund.de

```
select *
       from   Wagen
       where  Typ   =  Kombi
       and    Preis ≤  20 000
       and    km    ≤  30 000
```

ABBILDUNG 1. Übersetzung der Anfrage in SQL

zelkriterien bei dem optimalen Wagen möglicherweise nicht erfüllt ist. In einem konventionellen System enthielte also die Antwort auf jede der vagen Teilanfrage alle Objekte der Datenbank. Die Verarbeitung solcher Teilergebnisse ist wohl nur bei sehr kleinen Datenbanken möglich. Das Informationsbedürfnis das Verkäufers könnte natürlicher wie in Abbildung 2 formuliert werden, da er von der Rangliste nur die obersten Elemente untersuchen will.

```
select top  10
       from   Wagen
       where  Typ   =  Kombi
       rank by
              Preis ≤  20 000
              km    ≤  30 000
```

ABBILDUNG 2. Formulierung als vage Anfrage

In der Vergangenheit wurde schon verschiedene Versuche unternommen, das Konzept der Vagheit in DBMS zu integrieren. Wir betrachten hier nur Vagheit auf Seiten der Anfrage. Unter vagen Anfragen verstehen wir dabei solche, bei denen für Datenbankobjekte (mit präzisen Attributwerten) nicht eindeutig entschieden werden kann, ob sie eine Antwort darstellen oder nicht.
Bei älteren best-match-Verfahren (siehe [Shasha & Wang 90] für einen Überblick) wurden meist eigene Zugriffsverfahren für spezielle Typen von Anfragen implementiert. Das in [Motro 88] beschriebene System VAGUE wendet das aus dem Information Retrieval bekannte Vektorraum-Modell auf die Prozessierung vager Anfragen in Faktendatenbanken an. Das System ist als Frontend zu einem relationalen Datenbanksystem realisiert. Einen ähnlichen Ansatz verfolgt das System FRDB ([Zemankova & Kandel 85]), das auf Fuzzy Logik basiert. Jedem der Objekte der Antwortmenge wird eine reelle Zahl (Gewicht) zugeteilt, die den Grad seiner Zugehörigkeit zu der Antwortmenge angibt. Bei der booleschen Verknüpfung mehrerer Kriterien werden die zugehörigen Gewichte mit den üblichen *min*- und *max*-Operatoren verknüpft. Die Implementierung arbeitet mit Schwellenwerten, um die (Teil-) Antwortmengen klein (und damit berechenbar) zu halten. Wir wollen dieses Konzept auf verschiedene Arten erweitern.

- Zunächst können die Gewichte bezüglich einzelner Kriterien meist nicht isoliert gesehen werden. Für unseren Käufer im Gebrauchtwagenbeispiel besteht zwischen Preis und km-Stand sicher ein Zusammenhang, der nicht mit *min*- und *max*-Operatoren auszudrücken ist. Wir lassen daher beliebige Funktionen zur Kombination von Gewichten zu. Z.B. könnten das Produkt oder eine gewichtete Summe der Einzelgewichte verwendet werden. Auch in der Fuzzy Logik werden inzwischen weitere Operatoren diskutiert ([Zimmermann & Altrock 91]).
- Durch die Schwellenwerte im System FRDB wird nicht in jedem Fall die optimale Antwort gefunden. Wie oben schon bemerkt, kann es im Extremfall sein, daß ein Kriterium beim optimalen Ergebnis nur zu einem sehr geringen Grade erfüllt ist. Der Benutzer muß sich hier zwischen kurzen Antwortzeiten und guten Ergebnissen entscheiden.
- Bei den meisten Anwendungen läßt sich die Menge der den Benutzer interessierenden Objekte am ehesten durch deren Umfang charakterisieren. Die Vorgabe eines Mindestgewichts für Antwortobjekte ist hingegen aus Benutzersicht unnatürlich. In jedem Fall sollte das System eventuelle Nachforderungen des Benutzers effizient beantworten können.

In [Fuhr 90] wird ein Modell vorgestellt, das die empirische Bestimmung probabilistischer Gewichte bezüglich vager Kriterien erlaubt. Eine Erweiterung des vorgeschlagenen Schemas, das auch textuelle Anfragen einschließt, wird in [Fuhr 92] vorgestellt.
In diesem Beitrag wollen wir Konzepte für die Implementierung eines auf diesem Modell basierenden Systems diskutieren, wobei wir hauptsächlich die Aufwandsabschätzung für die Zwecke der Anfrageoptimierung untersuchen. Wir stellen einen generellen Ansatz für die Verknüpfung mehrerer Rangordnungen zu einer einzigen Rangordnung vor. Dieser Ansatz wird dann am Beispiel der probabilistischen UND-Verknüpfung illustriert und experimentell untersucht.
In Abschnitt 2 stellen wir die wesentlichen Architekturkonzepte unseres Systems vor. Dann (Abschnitt 3) entwickeln wir die theoretischen Grundlagen der Aufwandsabschätzung und vertiefen sie an einem einfachen Beispiel (Abschnitt 4). In Abschnitt 5 wenden wir unser Modell auf eine Textdatenbasis an und fassen schließlich in Abschnitt 6 unsere Ergebnisse zusammen.

2 Prozessierung mit Datenströmen

Typisch für vage Anfragen ist, daß den Nutzer meist nur die ersten Elemente der Rangordnungen interessieren. Die genaue Anzahl der gewünschten Objekte läßt sich zudem nur schlecht im voraus festlegen, weswegen eine iterative Berechnung der Rangfolge wünschenswert wäre. Das System sollte somit nur die obersten m Elemente der Rangordnung berechnen, wobei m vorgegeben wird. Bei Bedarf sollte es möglich sein, weitere Elemente zu liefern. Antwort des Systems ist

also eine nur teilweise berechnete Rangordnung der Objekte in der Datenbank. Wir beschränken uns hier auf den wichtigen Fall, daß diese durch Kombination von Rangordnungen, die die Antworten auf Teilanfragen sind, effizient erstellt werden kann. Da die resultierende Rangordnung nicht vollständig benötigt wird, muß auch die Prozessierung der Teilanfragen nicht vollständig erfolgen, sondern es muß jeweils nur der Beginn dieser Rangfolgen bestimmt werden. Wie wir sehen werden, müssen i.a. deutlich mehr Elemente für jede Rangordnung zu den Teilanfragen berechnet werden, als für die Rangordnung der gesamten Anfrage. Weiter können wir ausnutzen, daß mithilfe von Zugriffspfaden solche Rangordnungen effizient zu erstellen sind. Liegt z.B. für den Kilometerstand in unserer Gebrauchtwagendatenbank ein eigener Zugriffspfad – etwa ein B*-Baum – vor, können wir über einen Indexscan effizient die Rangordnung bezüglich des Kriteriums „km $\leq$ 30 000" erzeugen, indem wir den Index beginnend mit dem kleinsten Kilometerstand durchlaufen.
Wir verfolgen daher den Ansatz, Anfragen in einem solchen System durch Kombination von Rangordnungen schon in tieferen Systemschichten zu prozessieren. Dies kann iterativ erfolgen: Ein Modul, das zwei oder mehrere Rangordnungen kombiniert, kann jeweils soviele Elemente der Teilrangordnungen anfordern, wie benötigt werden, um die Anforderung an das Modul zu befriedigen.
Wir können solche Rangordnungen als Ströme von Elementen auffassen, die jeweils mindestens aus Objektidentifikator (OID) und ihrem Gewicht bezüglich der entsprechenden Teilanfrage bestehen. Auf diesen Strömen können auch zusätzliche Attribute – z.B. der Kilometerstand – transportiert werden. Etwas verallgemeinert können solche Ströme auch nach anderen Elementattributen als ihrem Gewicht, also z.B. ihrer OID, sortiert sein. Man kann so die Ergebnisse verschiedener Zugriffsverfahren als Ströme auffassen. Diese werden in Verarbeitungsstationen (Knoten) zu neuen Strömen kombiniert. Eine Anfrage kann folglich auf einen gerichteten azyklischen Graphen aus solchen Strömen und Knoten abgebildet werden. Auch Zugriffspfade und das Ausgabemodul können als Knoten in einem solchen Graphen modelliert werden.
Für unsere Beispielanfrage wären die Alternativen in den Abbildungen 3 und 4 möglich. Beide gehen davon aus, daß Zugriffspfade existieren, die zu den Kriterien „Preis $\leq$ 20 000", „km $\leq$ 30 000" und „Typ = Kombi" die OIDs mit Gewichten bezüglich des Kriteriums, nach fallenden Gewichten geordnet, liefern. Für das strikte Kriterium „Typ = Kombi" seien nur binäre Gewichte (1 und 0) zugelassen. Bei Variante 1 wird durch den Rank-Knoten zunächst mithilfe einer Bewertungsfunktion f die Rangordnung bezüglich der beiden vagen Kriterien gebildet. Diese wird in einem $\wedge$-Knoten mit der Liste der Kombis geschnitten. In Variante 2 werden zuerst die beiden Rangordnungen mit diese Liste geschnitten und die resultierenden Rangordnungen anschließend im Rank-Knoten zur Ergebnisrangordnung kombiniert.
Es stellt sich nun die Frage, welcher der beiden Anfragegraphen der günstigere ist. Diese führt uns auf das grundlegende Problem der Anfrageoptimierung. Voraussetzung zur Anwendung der verschiedenen Ansätze zur Anfrageoptimierung sind Verfahren zur Aufwandsabschätzung für die einzelnen Operationen der Anfrage.

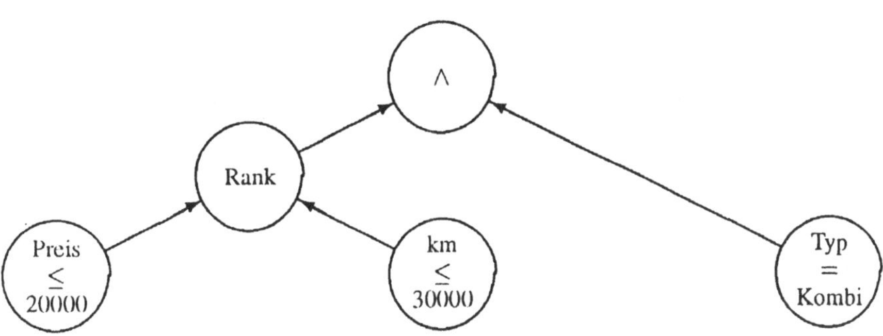

ABBILDUNG 3. Anfragegraph Variante 1

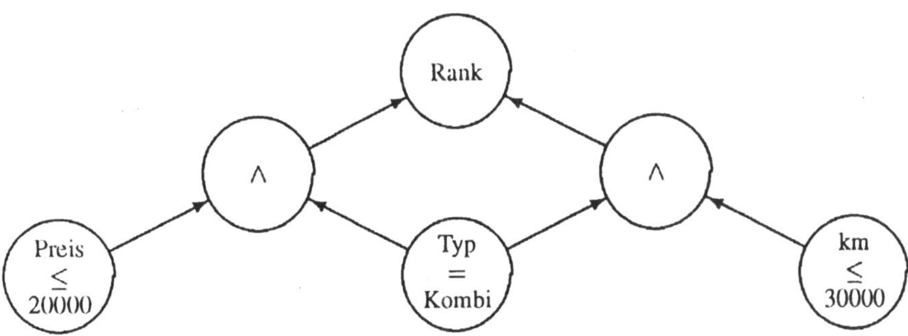

ABBILDUNG 4. Anfragegraph Variante 2

Da für boolesche Operatoren solche Verfahren bekannt sind, wollen wir hier den Rank-Knoten untersuchen.

3 Aufwandsabschätzung

Wir benötigen Mittel, um abzuschätzen, wieviele Elemente wir von eingehenden Strömen lesen (bzw. generieren) müssen, um eine vorgegebene Anzahl von Ausgabeelementen zu erzeugen. Diese Anzahl hängt ab von

- der Verteilung der Gewichte in den Strömen,
- der Korrelation zwischen den Strömen,
- und der Bewertungsfunktion in den Knoten, die die Gewichte kombiniert.

Wir beschränken uns hier aus Gründen der Anschaulichkeit auf Knoten, die zwei Eingabeströme kombinieren. Die Verallgemeinerung auf mehrere Eingabeströme ist offensichtlich. Die Gewichte seien reelle Zahlen aus dem Einheitsintervall und mögen die Wahrscheinlichkeit approximieren, daß ein Benutzer das Objekt als

Antwort auf die korrespondierende Teilanfrage akzeptieren würde. Die Elemente in den Strömen seien nach fallenden Gewichten x bzw. y geordnet. Aufgabe des Knotens sei es, einen Ausgabestrom zu erzeugen, dessen Elemente das Gewicht $f(x,y)$ erhalten und fallend nach diesem sortiert sind. Die Funktion $f(x,y)$ sei monoton zunehmend in x und y. Wir erhalten eine graphische Interpretation des Problems, wenn wir die Objekte als Punkte (x,y) in ein Diagramm eintragen. Beim

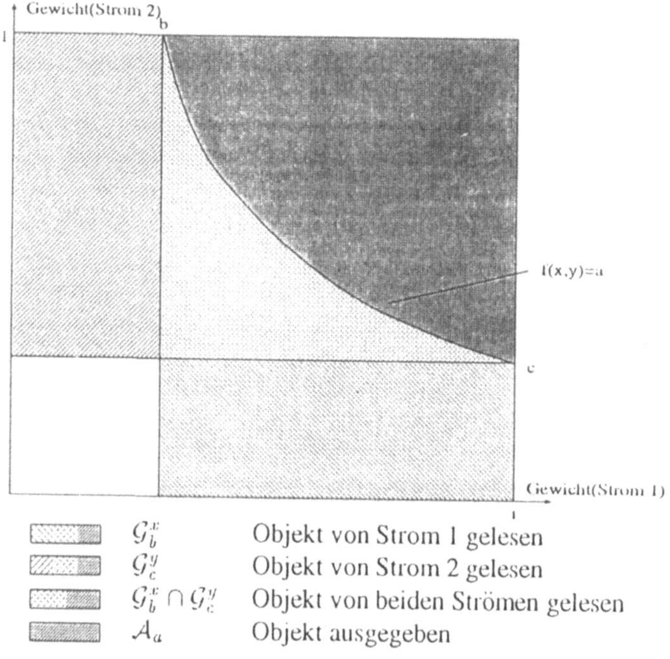

ABBILDUNG 5. Geometrische Interpretation

Lesen von Strom 1 überstreichen wir das Einheitsquadrat von rechts nach links, beim Lesen von Strom 2 von oben nach unten. Abbildung 5 zeigt den Zustand des Systems zu einem Zeitpunkt, wo die Objekte von Strom 1 bis zum Gewicht b und die Objekte von Strom 2 bis zum Gewicht c gelesen wurden. Bezeichne $\mathcal{G}_b^x$ den Bereich $\{(x,y)|x \geq b\}$ und entsprechend $\mathcal{G}_c^y$ den Bereich $\{(x,y)|x \geq c\}$; dann können wir die Gewichte der Objekte, die von beiden Strömen gelesen wurden, also im Bereich $\mathcal{G}_{bc} = \mathcal{G}_b^x \cap \mathcal{G}_c^y$ liegen, vollständig bestimmen. Darunter befinden sich auch Objekte, deren Gewicht von dem solcher Objekte übertroffen werden kann, die noch nicht von beiden Strömen gelesen wurden, die also in den Bereichen $\mathcal{G}_b^x \backslash \mathcal{G}_c^y$ bzw. $\mathcal{G}_c^y \backslash \mathcal{G}_b^x$ liegen. Bezeichnen $\mathcal{A}_z$ den Bereich der Objekte mit einem Mindestgewicht z also $\mathcal{A}_z = \{(x,y)|f(x,y) \geq z\}$. Dann bestimmen wir zu dem von beiden Strömen gelesenen Bereich $\mathcal{G}_{bc}$ den maximalen Schwellenwert z für den gilt $\mathcal{A}_z \subseteq \mathcal{G}_{bc}$ und nennen diesen a. Die Elemente das zugehörigen Bereiches $\mathcal{A}_a$ können wir sortiert ausgeben.

Man wählt also sinnvollerweise die Einlesestrategie so, daß der von beiden Strömen gelesene Teil gerade einen solchen Bereich überdeckt. Wegen der Monotonieeigenschaft von $f(x,y)$ ist das der Fall, wenn die Kurve $f(x,y) = a$ durch die Ecken des vollständig gelesenen Bereiches geht[2]. Kennt man die Dichtefunktion $g(x,y)$ der Gewichte, kann man die Erwartungswerte $G_x(a)$ und $G_y(a)$ der Anteile der in den Gebieten $\mathcal{G}_b^x$ und $\mathcal{G}_c^y$ liegenden Objekte, also der zu einem bestimmten Zeitpunkt gelesenen Objekte, berechnen.

$$G_x(a) = \int_0^1 \int_b^1 g(x,y)\, dx\, dy \tag{1}$$

$$G_y(a) = \int_0^1 \int_c^1 g(x,y)\, dy\, dx \tag{2}$$

Dabei sind b und c gegeben durch die Bedingungen:

$$\begin{aligned} f(b,1) &= a \\ f(1,c) &= a \end{aligned}$$

Der Anteil der im Gebiet $\mathcal{A}_a$ liegenden, also zu diesem Zeitpunkt ausgegebenen, Objekte kann bestimmt werden durch:

$$A(a) = \oint_{f(x,y)\geq a} g(x,y)\, dx\, dy \tag{3}$$

Im nächsten Abschnitt wollen wir diese Überlegungen an einem Beispiel vertiefen.

4 Beispiel: Der probabilistische UND-Knoten

Wir untersuchen ein einfaches Beispiel, den Rank-Knoten mit der Bewertungsfunktion $f(x,y) = x\,y$. Die Punkte gleichen Gewichts $f(x,y) = a$ liegen auf den Hyperbeln $y = a/x$. Lesen wir also beide Ströme bis zum Gewicht a, können wir alle Objekte über der Hyperbel $f(x,y) = a$ sortiert ausgeben. Sei $g(x,y)$ die Dichtefunktion, nach der die Gewichte in den Strömen verteilt sind. Dann ist der Anteil der gelesenen Objekte G_x bzw. G_y und der Anteil der ausgegebenen Objekte A bestimmt durch:

$$G_x(a) = \int_0^1 \int_a^1 g(x,y)\, dx\, dy$$

$$G_y(a) = \int_0^1 \int_a^1 g(x,y)\, dy\, dx$$

[2] Der *min*-Operator kann nach dem gleichen Schema behandelt werden, wobei hier $\mathcal{A}_a = \mathcal{G}_a^x \cap \mathcal{G}_a^y$ ist. Beim *max*-Operator kann auf die Bedingung, daß beide Gewichte bekannt sein müssen, verzichtet werden; hier ist $\mathcal{A}_a = \mathcal{G}_a^x \cup \mathcal{G}_a^y$

$$A(a) = \int_a^1 \int_{\frac{a}{x}}^1 g(x,y)\, dy\, dx$$

Sind beispielsweise die Gewichte unabhängig und gleichverteilt ($g(x,y) = g_x(x) \cdot g_y(y) = 1$), so erhalten wir:

$$G_x(a) = G_y(a) = 1 - a$$
$$A(a) = 1 - a + a \log a$$

Enthielte also unsere Gebrauchtwagendatenbank 1 000 Wagen, deren Gewichte bezüglich der Kriterien „Kilometerstand“ und „Preis“ unabhängig gleichverteilt sind (eine zugegebenermaßen unrealistische Annahme), so müßten, um die besten 10 Wagen zu bestimmen, im Durchschnitt nur die ersten 138 Elemente der Ströme berechnet werden. Ein konventionelles DBMS müßte beide Teilfolgen berechnen, die Gewichte über einen Join zusammenführen oder einen Relationenscan durchführen; in jedem Fall müßte anschließend des Ergebnis nach fallendem Gesamtgewicht sortiert werden. Der Aufwand wäre also mindestens $O(n \log n)$. Wäre die Anzahl der Elemente m der Rangordnung, die bestimmt werden müssen, bekannt, könnte schon während des Joins/Scans die Liste der zum jeweiligen Zeitpunkt m besten Elemente mitgeführt werden. So könnte kann der Aufwand auf $O(n \log m)$ reduziert werden. Eine Nachforderung des Benutzers könnte dann aber nur durch erneutes Starten der Anfrage bearbeitet werden.
Es ist klar, daß die Vorteile der verzögerten Berechnung bei unserer Vorgehensweise mit wachsender Größe der Datenbank zunehmen.

5 Experimentelle Überprüfung

Wie in [Fuhr 92] gezeigt wurde, besteht kein prinzipieller Unterschied zwischen vagen Anfragen an Faktendatenbanken und solchen an Textdatenbanken. Daher können wir die experimentelle Validierung des vorstehend beschriebenen Ansatzes an einer Textdatenbank durchführen, wobei wir aber auch Kombinationen mit vagen Faktenanfragen betrachten. Als Datenbasis dient uns die TREC Kollektion ([Harman 93]). TREC (Text REtrieval Conference) ist eine US-amerikanische Initiative zur Evaluierung von Retrievalverfahren auf großen Textdatenbanken. Im Rahmen dieser Initiative wird eine Datenbasis mit rund 2 GB Text aufgebaut. Für eine vorgegebene Menge von 50 Anfragen werden die Retrievalantworten der verschiedenen Systeme miteinander verglichen. Für unsere Experimente verwenden wir den „ap“-Teil dieser Datenbasis, der 84 930 Meldungen mit 266 MB Text des AP Newswire von 1989 umfaßt.
Für unsere Experimente erstellen wir die Rangordnungen der Meldungen zu jeweils 10 Teilanfragen für drei Anfrageklassen:

g_l^i seien die Gewichte bezüglich natürlichsprachiger Anfragen.[3] Die Gewichte

[3] Es handelt sich um durch einen Fragebogen strukturierte Anfragen mit durchschnittlich

wurden mit dem Smart-System erzeugt, wobei für die Dokumente das *nnc*-, für die Fragen das *ntc*-Verfahren gewählt wurde (siehe dazu [Salton & Buckley 88]).

g_d^i seien die Gewichte bezüglich des Datums. Dazu wird für jede Meldung der Abstand d in Tagen vom Anfragedatum berechnet und das Gewicht g_d wie folgt bestimmt:

$$g_d = \frac{1+p}{p(1+p-p(365-d)/365)} - \frac{1}{p} \qquad p > 0 \qquad (4)$$

Dabei wurde $p = 200$ gewählt. Mit „31.12.89"als Anfragedatum erhielten Meldungen vom gleichen Tag das Gewicht 1, vom 1.1.1989 das Gewicht 0.000 014 und vom 30.11.89 das Gewicht 0.050 876.

g_s^i seien die Gewichte bezüglich einer Ähnlichkeitsfunktion für Zeichen in der Schlagzeile der Meldung (z.B. für die Suche nach Eigennamen). Zur Bestimmung des Gewichts erzeugten wir die Menge aller Trigrams (Teilzeichenketten der Länge 3) für die Anfrage und die jeweilige Schlagzeile und ermittelten den Anteil der Trigrams der Anfrage, die in der Meldung auftraten. Dadurch sollten Schreibfehler kompensiert werden. Bei einer Anfrage „Czechoslovakia" erhielte etwa eine Meldung mit „Czecholsovakia" in der Schlagzeile das Gewicht 0.692 308.

5.1 Die Verteilungsfunktion

Die Gewichte bezüglich dieser drei Kriterien sind in der Datenbasis nicht gleichverteilt. Wenn Gewichte sich aus der Kombination von unabhängigen Texteigenschaften ableiten, unterliegen sie oft einer verallgemeinerten Zipf-Verteilung ([Sichel 75]) mit Dichtefunktionen $g(x) = 1/(x+1)^\alpha$ mit $\alpha > 1$. Da wir uns hier auf Gewichte aus dem Einheitsintervall beschränken wollen, benötigen wir eine Dichte, die nur für Werte aus einem beschränken Bereich (dem Einheitsintervall) von 0 verschieden ist. Wir definieren also eine leicht modifizierte Dichte $g(x)$ mit einem Parameter $p > 0$.

$$g(x) = \frac{1+p}{(1+px)^\alpha} \quad \text{für} \quad x \in [0,1) \quad \text{und} \quad g(x) = 0 \quad \text{sonst} \qquad (5)$$

Mit dieser Klasse von Dichtefunktionen wollen wir die Verteilung sowohl der von Smart als auch der bezüglich der Trigrams berechneten Gewichte approximieren. Wir beschränken uns hier auf $\alpha = 2$.
Die Funktion g_d (Gleichung 4) ist so gewählt, daß bei Annahme einer Gleichverteilung bezüglich des Datums die Verteilung der zugehörigen Gewichte durch die Gleichung 5 beschrieben wird (es sind natürlich nur 365 diskrete Werte möglich!).

150 verschiedenen sinntragenden Worten pro Frage.

Nehmen wir die Unabhängigkeit der Gewichte an, erhalten wir für die zweidimensionale Dichte $g(x, y)$:

$$g(x,y) = \begin{cases} \frac{1+p}{(1+p\,x)^2}\frac{1+q}{(1+q\,y)^2} & x, y \in [0,1) \\ 0 & \text{sonst} \end{cases}$$

Die Gleichungen 1, 2 und 3 werden dann mit $f(x, y) = xy$ zu:

$$G_x(a) = \frac{1-a}{1+p\,a} \tag{6}$$

$$G_y(a) = \frac{1-a}{1+q\,a} \tag{7}$$

$$A(a) = \begin{cases} \frac{(p\,q-1)^2}{2(1+p)(1+q)\,p\,q} & a = \frac{1}{p\,q} \\ \frac{a-1}{p\,q\,a-1}\frac{a\,(1+p)(1+q)}{(p\,q\,a-1)^2}\log\frac{a\,(1+p)(1+q)}{(1+p\,a)(1+q\,a)} & a \neq \frac{1}{p\,q} \end{cases} \tag{8}$$

Wollen wir nun bestimmen, wieviel Elemente wir von den Strömen lesen müssen um etwa 1% der resultierenden Rangordnung zu berechnen, müssen wir zunächst den Wert a bestimmen, für den $A(a) = 0.01$ ist. Sind p und q bekannt, können wir die Gleichung 8 numerisch lösen. Dabei können wir uns auf den Fall $a \neq 1/(p\,q)$ beschränken, da sich die Funktion im Punkt $a = 1/(p\,q)$ stetig fortsetzen läßt. Ist a bestimmt, können wir den Anteil der von den Teilrangordnungen zu erzeugenden Elemente durch Einsetzen in Gleichung 6 bzw. 7 bestimmen.

5.2 Der Verteilungsparameter p

Es bleibt das Problem, den Parameter p der Dichtefunktion zu schätzen. Ein Optimierer könnte dazu Statistiken über die Datenbasis verwenden. Nachdem die Anfrageprozessierung angelaufen ist, können diese Schätzungen anhand bereits gelesener Teile der Rangordnungen verbessert werden. Da uns entsprechende Statistiken noch nicht vorliegen, haben wir die Parameter anhand der obersten n Elemente der Rangordnungen geschätzt. Hat das letzte gelesene Element das Gewicht x, kann man, wenn die Datenbasis N Objekte enthält, bei einer Verteilung mit Dichte nach Gleichung 5 und $\alpha = 2$ schließen:

$$\frac{n}{N} \approx \int_x^1 g(t)\,dt = \frac{1-x}{1+p\,x}$$

Somit erhält man für p_n:

$$p \approx p_n = \frac{1-x-A}{A\,x} \text{ mit } A = \frac{n}{N}$$

Eine andere Möglichkeit ist, den Mittelwert der Gewichte in die Gleichung für den Erwartungswert (9) einzusetzen und diese Gleichung numerisch zu lösen. Das ist nur möglich, wenn alle Gewichte bezüglich der Teilanfrage bekannt sind, was in einer Anwendungssituation nicht der Fall ist. Dieser Schätzwert p_E kann aber zur Validierung der p_n dienen.

$$\begin{aligned} E(X) &= \int_0^1 \frac{x\,(1+p)}{(1+p\,x)^2}\,dx \quad = \quad \frac{1+p}{p^2}\log(1+p) - \frac{1}{p} \qquad (9) \\ \overline{X} &= \frac{1+p_E}{p_E^2}\log(1+p_E) - \frac{1}{p_E} \end{aligned}$$

5.3 Simulation

Um Abweichungen von der angenommenen Verteilung und Fehler bei der Parameterschätzung auszuschließen, untersuchen wir zunächst eine synthetische Stichprobe. Für 10 Teilanfrage wurde eine Gewichtung mit einer Dichte nach Gleichung 5 erzeugt, wobei $\alpha = 2$ und p gleich einem nach Gleichung 9 geschätzten Werte p_E einer echten Teilanfrage gewählt wurde.
Für diese testen wir im ersten Schritt die Aufwandsabschätzung mit den bei der Generierung verwendeten Parametern p. Im zweiten Schritt schätzen wir den Parameter p nach den beschriebenen Verfahren und überprüfen wieder die sich ergebenden Voraussagen für den Aufwand.
Ausgehend von k Teilanfragen können wir $k\,(k-1)/2$ Paare bilden. Für jedes dieser Paare werden die Schätzungen der Anzahl der benötigten Elemente $G_x \cdot N$ und $G_y \cdot N$ mit der Anzahl der tatsächlich gelesenen Elemente n_x und n_y verglichen. Tabelle 1 gibt den Median q_{50} und die 10%- und 90%-Quantile q_{10} und q_{90} der Beträge der relativen Abweichungen der Schätzungen von den im Experiment auftretenden Werten für die Fälle an, daß $m = 10$, 100 und 1 000 Elemente der Ergebnisrangordnung erzeugt werden.

TABELLE 1. Simulation

m	q_{10}	q_{50}	q_{90}
10	0.022458	0.073743	0.406812
100	0.014303	0.055608	0.151072
1 000	0.003689	0.011432	0.032939

Tabelle 1 zeigt, daß bei bekannter Verteilungsfunktion sehr genaue Abschätzungen des Aufwands möglich sind. Die im Experiment auftretenden Werte weichen bei der Berechnung von nur wenigen Elementen der Ergebnisrangordnung naturgemäß am weitesten von den Voraussagen ab.
Der zweite interessante Punkt ist der mittlere Gesamtaufwand, der zur Berechnung nötig ist. Um die 10 obersten Elemente der Rangordnung zu berechnen, müssen im Mittel nur 2.3% der Teilrangordnungen generiert werden. Das sind nur 3 975 von zweimal 84 930 Elementen! Für die ersten 100 bzw. 1 000 Elemente werden 10% bzw. 43% der Teilrangordnungen benötigt.

Nun verwenden wir die synthetischen Stichproben, um unsere Schätzverfahren zu testen. Wir setzen also nicht die Kenntnis des Verteilungsparameters p voraus, sondern schätzen ihn nach den oben beschriebenen Verfahren.
Um bewerten zu können, wie sich die Abweichung der Schätzung vom tatsächlichen Verteilungsparameter auf die Qualität der Aufwandsabschätzung auswirkt, haben wir für jeden Satz von Schätzungen analog zu Tabelle 1 die Abweichung der Aufwandsabschätzung von den im Experiment auftretenden Werten berechnet. Tabelle 2 zeigt, daß alle Schätzverfahren Parameter liefern, die es ermöglichen, den Aufwand für die Berechnung eines bestimmten Teils der Rangordnung mit vernünftiger Genauigkeit abzuschätzen. Am schlechtesten schneidet die Schätzung p_E für die kürzeste Rangliste ab, ist aber trotzdem noch erfreulich genau. Abbildung 6 gibt die Werte graphisch wieder. Die senkrechten Balken

TABELLE 2. Simulation mit Parameterschätzung

p_x	m	q_{10}	q_{50}	q_{90}
p_{100}	10	0.024 843	0.099 837	0.362 673
	100	0.028 685	0.074 581	0.138 423
	1 000	0.018 997	0.051 044	0.090 745
p_{200}	10	0.028 615	0.086 753	0.359 626
	100	0.018 482	0.060 277	0.114 372
	1 000	0.008 529	0.033 913	0.051 856
p_{1000}	10	0.025 617	0.070 906	0.398 026
	100	0.019 483	0.052 087	0.156 927
	1 000	0.007 094	0.014 185	0.034 064
p_E	10	0.022 917	0.076 610	0.404 180
	100	0.013 323	0.053 752	0.148 136
	1 000	0.004 760	0.011 025	0.032 000

geben den Bereich zwischen q_{10} und q_{90} an, die Mediane werden durch die Ebene angedeutet. Die Abbildung zeigt, daß die Fehler bei der Aufwandsabschätzung bei diesen Stichproben mit idealer Verteilung weniger von der Anzahl der zur Parameterschätzung verwendeten als von der Anzahl der auszugebenden Elemente abhängt.
Die Versuchsreihe ergibt, daß schon aus den ersten 100 Elementen zweier Teilrangordnungen bei bekannter Verteilung die Verteilungsparameter so genau geschätzt werden können, daß der Aufwand bei der Kombination, abhängig von der gewünschten Anzahl, mit einer Abweichung von weniger als 100% geschätzt werden kann.

5.4 Experimente mit den echten Daten

Nun wenden wir uns den realen Daten der Textdatenbasis zu. Aus den drei Gruppen von Teilanfragen können die in Tabelle 3 angegebenen 5 Klassen von Teilanfragen gebildet werden. Eine Kombination zweier Datumsanfragen wäre ja wenig

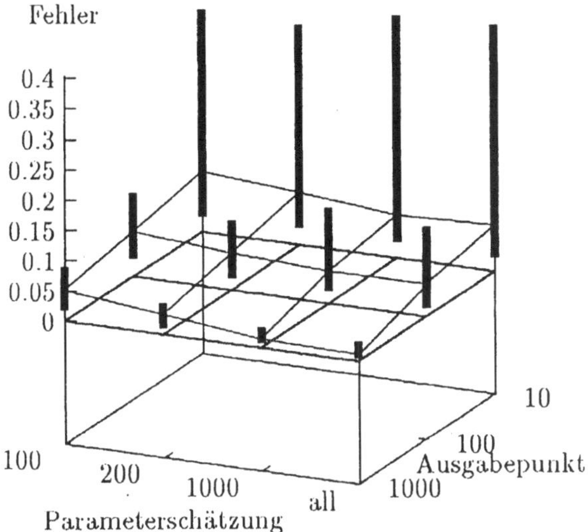

ABBILDUNG 6. Simulation mit Parameterschätzung

sinnvoll. Dabei enthalten die Klassen A und E je 45 die Klassen B, C und D

TABELLE 3. Klassen von Teilanfragen

	y_t	y_d	y_s
y_t	A	B	C
y_d			D
y_s			E

je 100 Paare. Insgesamt ergeben sich so 390 Tests. Die gesamte Testreihe liefert die in Tabelle 4 und Abbildung 7 angegebenen Abweichungen. Wir erkennen, daß hier die Fehler weniger von der Anzahl auszugebender Elemente als von der zur Schätzung der Parameter verwendeten Datenmenge abhängt. Es treten bei den 90% Quantilen Abweichungen von mehr als 350% auf.
Ursache für die großen Abweichungen kann nach unseren Voruntersuchungen nur sein, daß die Gewichte nicht unserer postulierten Verteilung unterworfen sind. Einerseits könnte schon die Funktionsklasse falsch gewählt sein. Zum anderen könnte unsere Schätzmethode für den Parameter p gegenüber leichten Abweichungen von der idealen Verteilung zu empfindlich sein. Untersuchungen der einzelnen Klassen von Paaren (Tabelle 3) unterstützen beide Vermutungen. Wenden wir uns zunächst der Klasse A zu, wo natürlichsprachige Anfragen miteinander verknüpft werden. Hier mußten wir die größten Abweichungen (Tabelle 5, Abbildung 8) feststellen. Es liegen große Abweichungen (mehr als 900%) bei den

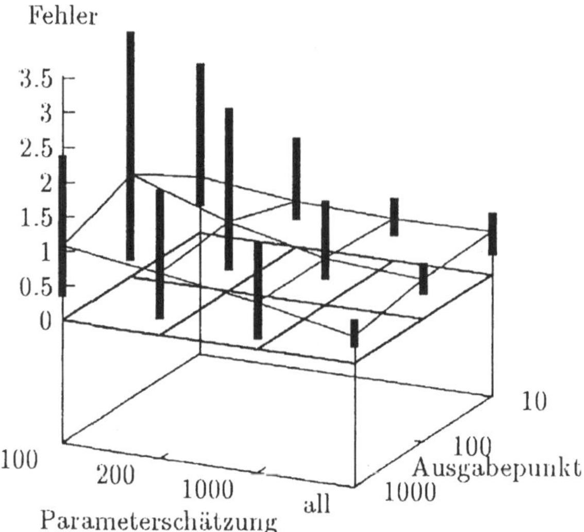

ABBILDUNG 7. Echte Daten: gesamt

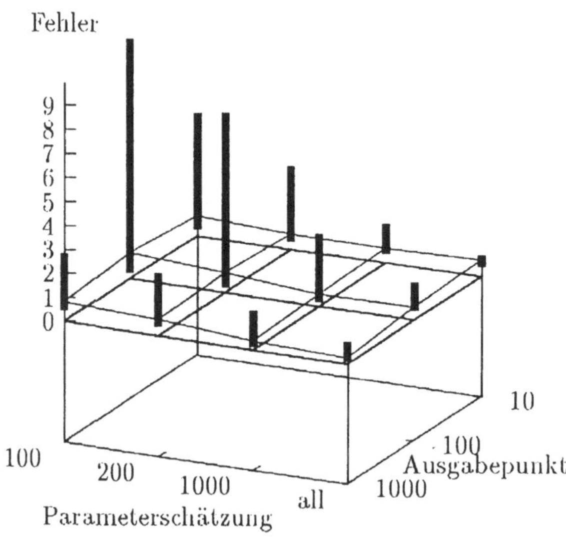

ABBILDUNG 8. Kombination natürlichsprachiger Anfragen

TABELLE 4. Echte Daten: gesamt

p_x	m	q_{10}	q_{50}	q_{90}
p_{100}	10	0.397660	0.811360	2.431985
	100	0.235734	1.488473	3.534468
	1000	0.336085	1.084368	2.379080
p_{200}	10	0.380701	0.658236	1.574180
	100	0.295906	1.002968	2.636005
	1000	0.229361	0.900385	2.116940
p_{1000}	10	0.353345	0.606358	0.910303
	100	0.366265	0.673302	1.507632
	1000	0.137425	0.675209	1.539503
p_E	10	0.277360	0.627851	0.907932
	100	0.340139	0.573631	0.813665
	1000	0.220040	0.384071	0.637371

TABELLE 5. Kombination natürlichsprachiger Anfragen

p_x	m	q_{10}	q_{50}	q_{90}
p_{100}	10	0.280779	0.841580	5.061363
	100	0.239581	1.080809	9.970574
	1000	0.453749	0.812066	2.827986
p_{200}	10	0.309171	0.655276	3.460825
	100	0.204337	0.816961	7.476904
	1000	0.363244	0.676765	2.584869
p_{1000}	10	0.353345	0.608282	1.658173
	100	0.139062	0.506766	3.061570
	1000	0.135935	0.368993	1.655135
p_E	10	0.398148	0.679148	0.896354
	100	0.353479	0.528628	1.556468
	1000	0.094246	0.243656	0.914217

Schätzungen vor, bei denen p aus nur 100 Elementen bestimmt wurde. Untersucht man die geschätzten Parameter, sieht man, daß die Schätzungen von im Mittel 2964 bei 100 über 1862 bei 200 auf 733 bei 100 Elementen korrigiert werden, wärend p_E im Mittel bei 227 liegt. Um eine bessere Schätzmethode zu erhalten sollte man nicht nur die Daten aus dem aktuellen Eingabestrom betrachten sondern auch globale Statistiken über die Datenbank berücksichtigen. Ein Ansatz der dies ermöglicht ist die Bayes'sche Schätzmethode, die die globalen Statistiken als a-priori-Verteilungen verwendet und durch Kombination mit den aktuellen Daten eine a-posteriori-Verteilung des zu schätzenden Parameters ableitet. Als ersten Schritt zur Wahl einer besseren Verteilungsfunktion könnte man in Gleichung 5 für α beliebige Werte (statt des angenommenen festen Wertes von 2) zulassen. Da die p-Schätzungen für wachsendes n immer weiter nach unten korrigiert werden, sind jeweiligen α_i der vorliegenden Verteilungen größer als 2.

Weiter unterliegen nur die von 0 verschiedenen Gewichte dieser Verteilung. Bisher hatten wir implizit angenommen, daß keine solchen Elemente auftreten. Beispielsweise treten im Mittel bei den natürlichsprachigen Anfragen nur 74 540 positive Gewichte auf. Dadurch wird unsere Schätzung von p natürlich beeinträchtigt.
Ein Blick (Tabelle 6, Abbildung 9) auf die Klasse C zeigt, daß auch sehr gute Aufwandsabschätzungen möglich sind, obwohl auch sich hier die Fehler bei der Parameterschätzung für die natürlichsprachigen Anfragen niederschlagen.

TABELLE 6. Natürlichsprachige Anfragen mit Trigram-Anfragen

p_x	m	q_{10}	q_{50}	q_{90}
	10	0.330533	0.519429	0.694890
p_{100}	100	0.148148	0.360116	0.843268
	1 000	0.190047	0.475643	0.957969
	10	0.372867	0.595659	0.756529
p_{200}	100	0.195115	0.371921	0.561995
	1 000	0.116058	0.352274	0.751740
	10	0.558996	0.743894	0.858984
p_{1000}	100	0.406571	0.562403	0.701033
	1 000	0.088426	0.162377	0.363709
	10	0.682555	0.823246	0.908337
p_E	100	0.641655	0.749905	0.825925
	1 000	0.323665	0.427514	0.523864

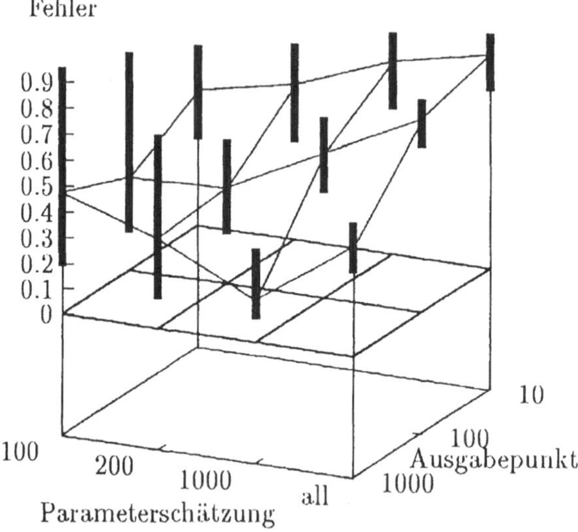

ABBILDUNG 9. Natürlichsprachige Anfragen mit Trigram-Anfragen

Auch bei den echten Daten zeigt sich, daß die nur teilweise Berechnung von Rangordnungen sehr effizient ist. Für die Bestimmung der obersten 10, 100 und 1 000 Elemente der kombinierten Rangordnung wurden im Mittel nur 9%, 23% und 49% der Teilrangordnungen benötigt.

6 Zusammenfassung und Ausblick

Wir haben in diesem Beitrag gezeigt, daß die Bearbeitung von vagen Anfragen mithilfe des Datenstromparadigmas effizient möglich ist. Unser Vorschlag nutzt dabei aus, daß ein Benutzer nur Teile der letztlich resultierenden Rangordnung inspizieren wird, also auch nur Teile berechnet werden müssen, und daß Ausgangsrangordnungen mithilfe von Zugriffspfaden effizient erstellt werden können. Dabei ist die Schätzung des Aufwands zur teilweisen Berechnung der Kombination von Rangordnungen mit dem in Abschnitt 3 beschriebenen Modell möglich. Dies wurde am Beispiel einer Textdatenbasis exemplarisch gezeigt.
Die konkrete Anwendung setzt zum einen die Wahl geeigneter Verteilungsfunktionen voraus, wobei entweder theoretische Verteilungen herangezogen werden können – wie sie insbesondere für Textmerkmale von vielen Autoren diskutiert wurden – oder rein mit den empirischen Daten gearbeitet werden kann. Zum anderen können durch die zusätzliche Berücksichtigung der Korrelation die Schätzungen verbessert werden. Alternativ zu der hier gewählten symbolischen Integration sind auch numerische Integrationsmehoden zu berücksichtigen, insbesondere bei empirischen Verteilungsfunktionen.
Gegenwärtig implementieren wir an der Universität Dortmund den Prototyp eines Datenbanksystems, das die Prozessierung von Anfragegraphen wie in Abbildung 3 und 4 erlaubt. Hierfür wird eine Klassenhierarchie von Knoten (von denen hier nur ein einfaches Beispiel vorgestellt wurde) implementiert. Der Datenstrom-Ansatz erlaubt außerdem die parallele Bearbeitung des Anfragegraphen, indem die Knoten auf verschiedene Rechner verteilt werden. Ein ähnliches Konzept wird in [DeWitt & Gray 92] vorgeschlagen.
Die in diesem Beitrag beschriebene Vorgehensweise ist Teil der Optimierung von Anfragegraphen. Da vage Anfragen vornehmlich in interaktiven Informationssystemen auftreten, sind kurze Antwortzeiten und damit eine effiziente Prozessierung dieser Anfragen besonders wichtig

7 Literatur

DeWitt, D.; Gray, J. (1992). Parallel Database Systems: The Future of High Performance Database Systems. *Communications of the ACM 35(6)*, S. 85–98.

Fuhr, N. (1990). A Probabilistic Framework for Vague Queries and Imprecise Information in Databases. In: McLeod, D.; Sacks-Davis, R.; Schek, H. (Hrsg.): *Proceedings of the 16th International Conference on Very Large Databases*, S. 696–707. Morgan Kaufman, Los Altos, Cal.

Fuhr, N. (1992). Integration of Probabilistic Fact and Text Retrieval. In: Belkin, N.; Ingwersen, P.; Pejtersen, M. (Hrsg.): *Proceedings of the Fifteenth Annual International ACM SIGIR Conference on Research and Development in Information Retrieval*, S. 211–222. ACM, New York.

Harman, D. (1993). Overview of the First Text REtrieval Conference. In: Harman, D. (Hrsg.): *The First Text REtrieval Conference (TREC1)*. National Institute of Standards and Technology Special Publication 500-207, Gaithersburg, Md. 20899.

Motro, A. (1988). VAGUE: A User Interface to Relational Databases that Permits Vague Queries. *ACM Transactions on Office Information Systems 6(3)*, S. 187–214.

Salton, G.; Buckley, C. (1988). Term Weighting Approaches in Automatic Text Retrieval. *Information Processing and Management 24(5)*, S. 513–523.

Shasha, D.; Wang, T.-L. (1990). New Techniques for Best-Match Retrieval. *ACM Transactions on Information Systems 8(2)*, S. 140–158.

Sichel, H. (1975). On a Distribution Law for Word Frequencies. *Journal of the American Statistical Association 70*, S. 542–547.

Zemankova, M.; Kandel, A. (1985). Implementing Imprecision in Information Systems. *Information Sciences 37*, S. 107–141.

Zimmermann, H.-J.; von Altrock, C. (1991). Prinzipien und Anwendungspotential der Fuzzy Mengentheorie. *KI 5*, S. 6–12.

Building an Hypermedia Metamodel for the PORTINARI Project

Marisa Marques *Rosana S.G. Lanzelotte*

PUC-Rio - Depto. Informática

Rio de Janeiro - Brazil

Email: marisa, rosana@inf.puc-rio.br

ABSTRACT

Databases constitute a natural repository for storing information dealt with by hypermedia applications. Many works have investigated how to design the database model to support an hypermedia application. Another viewpoint consists in starting from an existing database and designing hypermedia front-ends to it. In this paper, we propose an approach to design hypermedia applications using the data stored in an existing database. The approach is based on a *metamodel*, that integrates the two environments through their respective models, thus enabling the hypermodel application evolve with the database. We apply the proposed approach to the PORTINARI Project, concerning the most famous Brazilian painter. The approach is generic and can be used to build hypermedia interfaces to any existing database.

1 - INTRODUCTION

Hypermedia and database systems are both concerned with the storage and retrieval of data. Hypermedia systems are concerned in providing an easy way to browse data through associative links. On the other hand, database systems (DBMS) provide efficient storage and retrieval of data. The integration of the two technologies is strongly stressed in many recent works , the hypermedia application regarded as a front-end to the database.

Two approaches are possible to integrate hypermedia and database applications. The first one, adopted in previous works [ZDON87], focus mainly on the hypermedia component and considers the database only as a support for it. Another viewpoint, adopted in this work, is to start from an existing relational database application and to develop hypermedia front-ends to it. In this latter case, the database is accessed independently of the hypermedia interfaces, the data stored in the database being retrieved either through the usual DBMS interfaces or through the hypermedia ones.

Integrating the two paradigms and preserving the autonomy of the DBMS applications poses some problems. Consistency must be enforced: changes in the database must be automatically perceived in both environments. Another difficulty is due to the fact that hypermedia systems work on graph structures, composed of nodes and links, as opposed to relational databases.

The main goal of this work is to propose an approach to integrate hypermedia and database applications avoiding the previously mentioned difficulties. We start from an existing relational DB model and from a conceptual model of the hypermedia application. Then, we propose a *metamodel*, which integrates the two models and supports the development of hypermedia front-ends over the data stored in the database. The metamodel provides for the consistency of data and preserves, at the same time, the independence of the DB applications.

We apply our approach to the PORTINARI Project, concerning the most famous Brazilian painter.

The rest of this work is as follows. The history of the Portinari Project and the related DB model we developed are described in Section 2. In Section 3, we model the hypermedia application using a generic conceptual framework, the Hypermodel Design Model [GARZ91]. The metamodel approach to integrate both models is discussed in Section 4. Section 5 compares ours with related works and concludes.

2 - THE DATA MODEL FOR THE PORTINARI PROJECT

The Portinari Project provides an ideal background for hypermedia applications. It deals with multimedia information, such as photographs of the paintings, related documents and recorded interviews. Part of this data is currently stored in a relational DBMS, which will serve as the basis fot the hypermedia applications. This section presents a brief history of the Project itself, as well as the existing conceptual and logical DB models.

2.1. The History of the Portinari Project

The Portinari Project ("Projeto Portinari", in portuguese) has been engaged, since 1979, in research and other activities related to the work of the Brazilian painter Candido Portinari (1903-1962).

The Project has been able to locate, document and catalog 5.000 works and 25.000 documents.The works have all been photographed, include paintings, drawings and prints. Among the documents, there are many letters exchanged with the main writers, poets, musicians, architects, artists, journalists, educators and politicians of Portinari's generation. This material is a true synthesis of all aspects of Brazilian life of that period and will constitute a large multimedia database of the main aesthetical, artistic, cultural, social and political concerns of one of the most creative and important periods in the history of our country.

The project may be divided into two sub-projects. The first, which is considered in this paper refers to the information related to the artist's works. It may be seen as the essence of the Catalogue Raisonné, which constitutes the unique instrument that allows a global analysis of the artist's trajectory. The other, which is much more vast, deals with the information related to the personal life of the artist and his contemporaries, and is a true initiative in the sense of preserving the richest period of the Brazilian cultural life. In the rest of this section, we describe the DB model concerning the first sub-project only.

2.2. The Conceptual DB Model

To develop the conceptual DB model, we adopted the Inside-outside strategy [CERI92], where the main concepts are established at a first moment (works, techniques, themes, for instance) and, moving from inside to outside, we gradually concentrate on new concepts (friends of the painter, Brazilian cultural events in a specific period of time and so on).

The starting point for the full understanding and further modelling of the artist's work was the Work Description Card (Ficha de Cadastro de Obra - F.C.O. - in portuguese). All the paintings had been previously identified and described through the F.C.O.'s and this is the starting point to design the conceptual DB model. Each F.C.O. is associated to one and only one work of the artist and contains all the relevant data about that specific work.

As usual, we chose an extension of the Entity-Relationship Model (ER) [CHEN76] to design the conceptual DB model. The ER diagram for the Portinari Project is shown in Figure 1.

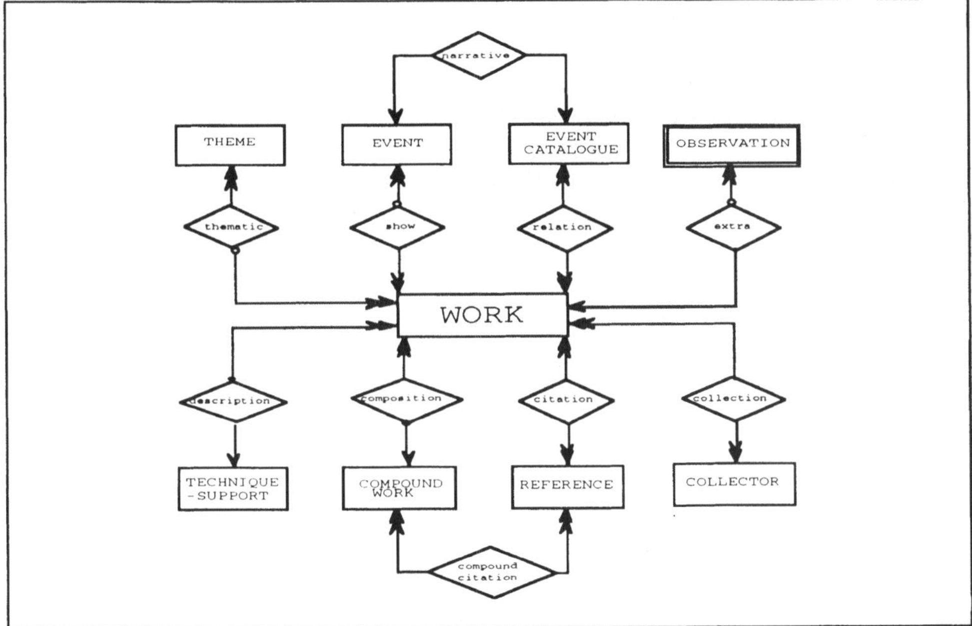

FIGURE 1 - The Entity-Relationship Diagram of the Portinari Project database

As expected,the main entity in the diagram is **WORK** and almost all the other entities relate with it..

The integrity constraints are also specified as part of the conceptual model. For example, one constraint concerns the trajectory of a work. When a work is acquired, inherited, given, the database must be updated and the present owner becomes the previous one.

A detailed description of all the attributes, entities and relationships of the conceptual DB model may be found in [MARQ92].

2.3. The Logical DB Model

When designing the logical DB model, we build an implementable model of the reality, considering the users' requirements found in the conceptual DB model. The output of this step of the DB design is a schema to be implemented by the DBMS. So, the logical DB model depends on the DBMS kind (network, object-oriented, semantic, relational, and so on).

The relational model was adopted because of its universality (The Portinari Project database is implemented using Oracle on Macintosh computers). Another important point is that the database will be accessed by users from different platforms, through computer networks, in the future.

The logical DB model is obtained by mapping the ER diagram to the relational model, according to the following steps :

1) mapping the regular entities, generating the WORK, THEME, EVENT, EVENT-CATALOGUE, TECHNIQUE-SUPPORT, REFERENCE, COMPOUND-WORK and COLLECTOR relations;

2)mapping the weak entities, generating the OBSERVATION relations;

3)mapping the functional binary relationships (1:1) e (1:n) (no relations generated);

4)mapping the non-functional binary relationships (m:n), implying the generation of the Thematic, Show, Relation, Citation, Collection, Compound-citation relations.

Integrity constraints were considered in the logical DB model. Triggers were specified in order to mantain the database integrity. A complete description of the logical DB model may be found in [MARQ92].

3 - THE HYPERMEDIA MODEL FOR THE PORTINARI PROJECT

The retrieval of information in a more natural way than in text form is a pressing need nowadays. The Portinari Project bears a strong multimedia characteristic. Some entities, like filmed or recorded documents or historic mails, are dealt with by the Project and will be available to different kinds of users. For this reason, there is a clear need for the utilization of hypermedia front-ends, which allow information to be retrieved in several ways. This section describes the hypermedia model proposed to support the hypermedia applications to be developped for the Portinari Project. It is specified using a generic modelling framework, the Hypertext Design Model (HDM) [GARZ91].

3.1. - Hypermedia Browsing and Authoring

Hypermedia applications involve the managing of data under the form of graphs, composed of nodes and links between them. Two different needs arise in these systems. The first one refers to the navigation and information retrieval, also known as *browsing*. Browsing allows the navigation through paths previously established in a step called *authoring*. The ease of use of an hypermedia application strongly depends on its author ability to capture the semantics of an application and to adequately organize the structure of the hypermedia graphs.

The clear and rational organization of hypermedia applications is thus much more critical as the more complex is the application. The complexity of an application is measured by the ammount of data to be managed or by the intrinsical complexity of the data itself.

Just like the database project is divided into distinct phases, the authoring or hypermedia applications project is composed by distinct aspects:

•*authoring-in-the-large* refers to the design of the structural and global aspects of the applications;

•*authoring-in-the-small* refers to the development of the contents of the nodes; it is largely dependent on the media to be used; for example, loading a *text* node requires completely different techniques than dealing with a node which is *animated.*

3.2 - The HDM Approach

Some design methodologies have been proposed to model hypermedia applications. One such methodology is the Hypertext Design Model - HDM [GARZ91], which supports authoring-in-the-large. It provides a framework that allows the author to describe the hypertext application clearly and concisely, in a more formal way prior to thinking of the contents of the nodes.

An HDM model consists of a *schema,* composed of some components, such as, **ENTITY,** that means a conceptual or concrete object within the application domain; **COMPONENT**, that is a feature of an entity (an entity is described by the set of its components); **PERSPECTIVE,** that represents the way of presenting the information of an entity or component and is related not only to the used media (text, voice, image) but also to the rethoric style (discursive, schematic, formal) or to the language (english, portuguese); **UNIT**, that is the contents of a component with respect to a given perspective; and, finally, the **LINK** that establishes the relationships between the previous concepts. The links, however, may be classified into Application Links, that connect an entity to another entity and are defined by the author taking into account the semantics of the hypermedia application; Structural Links, that connect an entity to its components, providing the navigation through the structure of the entity; and Perspective Links, which connect a component to its perspectives, allowing the presentation of a component.

A particular hypermedia application in a given domain is specified by instantiating the schema, i.e., by instantiating its entities and links.

We have so far dealt only with the structural aspects of hypermedia application. The application behavior must also be specified, i.e., how the application objects are shown to the user, how he can activate a link and which is the feedback he gets when a link is activated. These aspects constitute what is called *browsing semantics*, and is mainly related to the user interface with the hypermedia application.

Links are activated through *buttons* or *anchors*, which are represented by icons or screen areas. When a link is activated, the user moves from the current node to one or more *destination* nodes.The activation of links is perceived by the user through some kind of feedback. For example, the current node may stay visible or not, after a link is activated, and the destination node is presented. Specifying the interface with the user, concerning anchors and feedbacks, is part of the authoring-in-the-small step of the hypermedia application. It is not the focus of the present work.

3.3. The HDM model for the Portinari Project

We present part of the HDM model for the Portinari Project, depicting its main entities and links. Figure 2 shows the screen corresponding to the starting node of the application. After selecting the WORK anchor, the user begins to navigate through the application, either watching the compound-works or the Catalogue Raisonné or merely the painter's works.

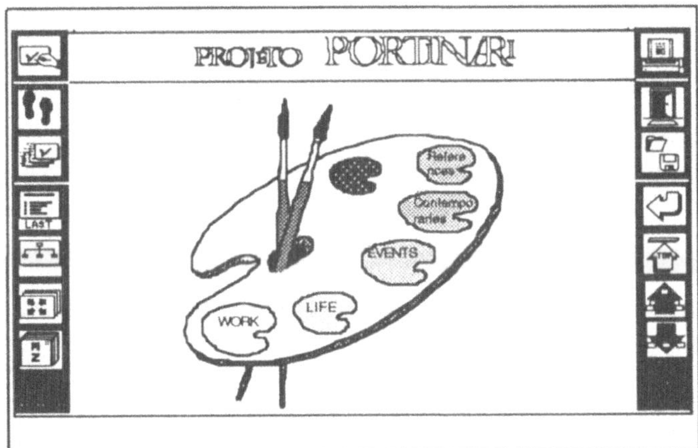

FIGURE 2. The starting screen of the hypermedia application of the Portinari Project

This is an example of how a node is presented, a task which is intrinsically related to authoring-in-the-small. Our focus is to define the authoring-in-the-large model, based on the model described in Section 2.

The application links and the entities of the schema are shown in Figure 3. In the diagram, the oval elements represent the HDM entities. The links are denoted by the arcs connecting the entities and the labels on the arcs denote the semantics of the links. All the links are bidirectional (WORK *is shown* in EVENT, as well as EVENT *shows* WORK, for example), although they are drawn only once.The Hypertext Design Model also provides the notion of path. A path is a data element related to a link. It is denoted in the HDM schema by an oval connected to an arc. For example, the path between WORK and CATALOGUE is the *page number*, between WORK and EVENT is *work number*, and so on.

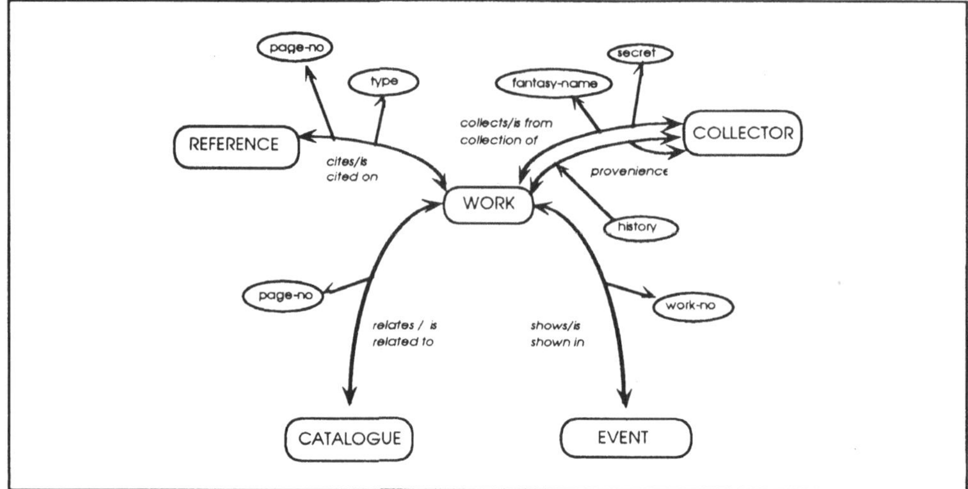

FIGURE 3 - HDM Schema of the Portinari Project's hypermedia application

Refering to the DB model, we notice that THEME, TECNIQUE and OBSERVATION are not present in the HDM model, because they do not provide any kind of navigation. For this reason, they are included as components of the WORK entity.

The COMPOUND-WORK entity is defined as a HDM *derived* entity. It has no components of its own (its components are sub-trees of the WORK entity).

After the definition of the schema and further instantiation, it is possible to implement the model using any hypermedia system. When implementating, the authoring-in-the-small aspects of the application are specified, for example the presentation screen for nodes, the buttons, feedbacks, etc.

4 - A METAMODEL TO INTEGRATE HYPERMEDIA AND DBs

Several hypermedia systems use DBMS as a back-end. The hypermedia application use the DBMS functionalities, as storaging the nodes and links, access and lock control, query processing and optimization. Typically, the database stands only for supporting the hypermedia application. In our approach, we start from an existing database model and from an HDM schema and integrate them throughout a *metamodel*, as described in this section.

4.1 Mapping HDM Concepts to the DB model

Let us investigate how the concepts of the HDM model are implemented using those of the DB model. This is the starting point for building the integrating metamodel.

From the structural viewpoint, the common basic element in the various hypermedia systems is the *node*, which represents the basic information unit. Typically, hypermedia applications store the contents of nodes in a database managed by the hypermedia system itself. As in the Portinari Project the relational DB already exists, the contents of a node are specified as *views* . Suppose, for example, the node that presents the catalographic data of a specific Portinari work. The instances of this node are composed of some columns of WORK and TECHNIQUE-SUPPORT tables. Note that in the WORK table there is no description of the technique used in the work, but the code corresponding to the adopted technique. Thus, the need to bring from the TECHNIQUE-SUPPORT table the description associated with the code (the Where clause in the view provides the join of the two tables, considering the common column Tech-code).

Concerning links, some of them correspond to the relationships of the ER model and others don't. An example of the first is the relationaship between WORK and EXPOSITION. It exists in the DB model *and* in the HDM model. If, in a given moment, while observing a specific work node, the user wishes to "see" the expositions at which that work was presented, he will activate the link between WORK and EXPOSITION. On the other hand, browsing the nodes sequentially one after the other, which is possible way to navigate does not correspond to any relationship in the DB model.

The links are not implemented explicitly on the DB model, contrary to the nodes, which are implemented by views. They will be represented in the *metamodel* for the integration of the database and the hypermedia model which will be discussed further.

4.2 The Portinari Project Metamodel

One of the main goals of the present work, diiscussed in this section, is to combine the DB and hypermedia paradigms, at the same time preserving the autonomy of the DB applications. Integrating the two models does not modify the functionnalities of anyone but corresponds to interpreting "hypertextually" the elements of the DB model.

To implement the hypermedia concepts, we build a *metamodel*, which is a complementary data model to the Portinari Project DB model itself and to the HDM model. The metamodel provides a layer that implements the HDM concepts using those of the DB model.

4.2.1 Conceptual metamodel

To develop the conceptual metamodel, we take the elements of the conceptual DB model (i.e., entities, relationahips) and consider them as *data*. This is the reason why we call it *meta*, in the sense that it is "data which describe data". The graphic representation of the metamodel is shown in Figure 4. The fundamental entities in the metamodel are exactly the basic elements in the relational data model, that is **TABLE** and **DATA ITEM** and, in the hypermedia model, **NODE** and **LINK.**

With respect to the TABLE entity, a *generalization* concept arises, as needed to the TABLE entity (in this case a superentity) into the subentities REAL and VIEW. The specializations of TABLE have some attributes of their own and others that are common to the superentity. The generalization is needed because some relationships only occur with respect to one of them. It is the case, for example, of the relationship Instantiation between NODE and VIEW. One table by itself does not instantiate a node. A view, as we have already seen, is the one that will do it.

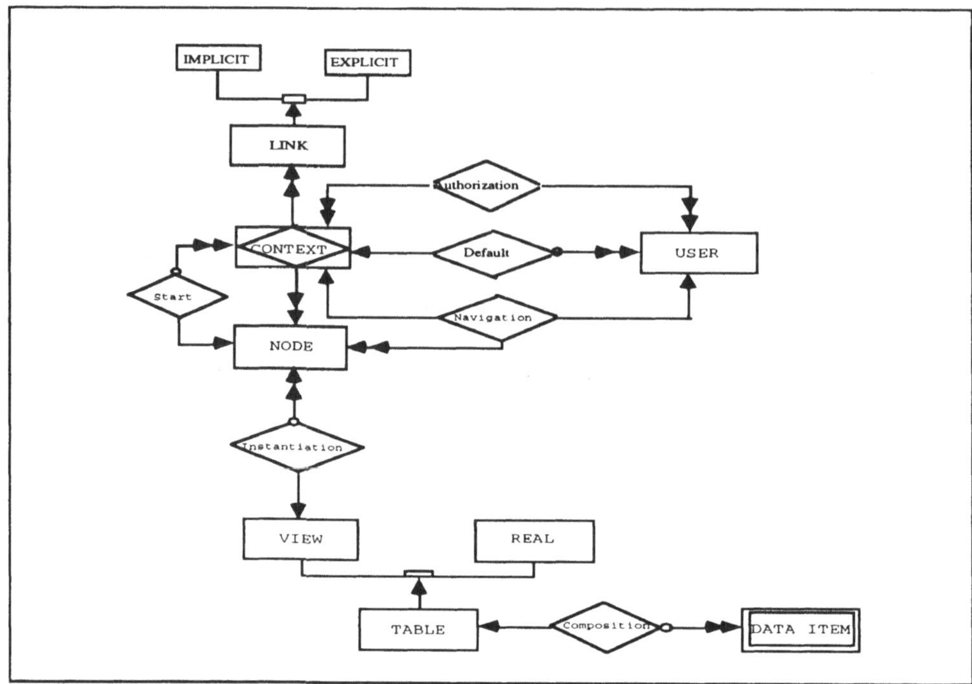

FIGURE 4. Portinari Project Metamodel Entity-Relationship Diagram

By defining the entities TABLE, DATA ITEM, NODE and LINK we build the *metamodel*, taking into account only the hypermedia application authoring requirements. In addition to these, the metamodel must also encompass the browsing and navigation requirements. For that purpose, we included in the model the USER and CONTEXT entities, whose function is to record the path followed by a user in any application context to which he is enabled. Important to notice that the CONTEXT entity embodies the *aggregation* entity-relationship concept, that didn't appear in the data model itself. Aggregation is an abstraction mechanism through which a new class of objects is defined from others component classes. In the metamodel, the NODE and LINK entities are the components that build the CONTEXT entity. Suppose, for instance, that a casual user wishes to know who are Portinari works collectors. We think it is not ethical to let him know their personal data, such as telephone number or home address. So, the nodes that contain the collectors' personal data will not be included into the context allowed to common users. However, those nodes will exist in the context viewed by the Project researchers, who will be able to handle all data in the DBMS.

Besides this security question, another issue arises related to the user's lack of orientation when navigating. It often happens that hypermedia applications readers walk through a same node many times, coming from different paths. With this in mind, we thought it is interesting to assist the user in his "walk". There are many ways to achieve this goal, that we intend to implement as a future extension of the metamodel.

The last point we wish to emphasize is that the nodes and links build a graph that represents the hyperdocument. An integrity constraint to be observed is that this graph must be connex, for this is the only way to assure that the complete navigation within the context willl be sucessful.

4.2.2 Logical Metamodel

Within the metamodel logical design, we map the ER meta-entities to relations, considering the requirements surveyed during the conceptual design stage.

The basic rules for the mapping were adopted in building the metamodel:

1)Generation of USER, CONTEXT, NODE, TABLE and LINK tables from the mapping of regular entities.

2)Generation of REAL and VIEW and EXPLICIT and IMPLICIT tables, taking into account the mapping of those regular entities which are part of the generalization hierarchies.

3)Generation of the DATA-ITEM table, from the mapping of weak entities (this table will not be implemented because it belongs to the data dictionary of the DBMS that will be adopted).

4)Generation of the Navigation and Authorization tables, from the mapping of the relationships (m:n).

One interesting aspect of the metamodel is to implement the concepts of *explicit* and *implicit* links. Explicit links are the usual application links, whose instances are defined by the authoring-in-small. For example, a explicit link may be established between two paintings that have the same stilistic features. An explicit link is implemented as a tuple in the meta-table EXPLICIT_LINK. This is recognized by an expert and cannot be deduced from the data stored in the database. Implicit links are those which could be deduced from the DB data, e.g., the link connecting all the paintings that use the same technique. The existence of this link allows the user to navigate from one work to any other painted using the same technique. Contrary to explicit links, instances of implicit links are not implemented one at a time. Each instance of the IMPLICIT_LINK table is a *query* leading to the destination nodes, given a current node. Supposing that Current is the current node, the implicit link for the same technique is implemented as the query

```
SELECT * FROM FCONode WHERE Tech-descript = Current.Tech-descript
```

The definition of some triggers implement the metadatabase integrity constraints. When a node is deleted from the database it is necessary, for example, to scan for which contexts have the initial node pointing to the presently deleted node, and then to update the context, electing the new initial node. The same happens in the deletion of a context. It is necessary to survey which users had it as default and update their new context. Another trigger is be created to shoot at the moment that the user ends up his navigation. By this time, the navigation entity must be updated, being deleted all the instances which do not have annotation nodes.

It is important to remark that the last visited node must be saved, for it will be the starting point for the user's next navigation within that context.

5 - CONCLUSION

Throughout this work we investigated how the relational data model supports hypermedia applications, using the Portinari Project as the research platform because of its great "multimediality". In this sense, the data model was built to contemplate the Project main application, which reflects solely on the works of the painter Candido Portinari. The hypermedia model for that application was also built, using the HDM aproach .

The main contribution of this work consists in the specification of the metamodel, which responds to the integration of the hypermedia and data models of any application. We also developped the data model that supports the Catalogue Raisonné, as well as the hypermedia application essence that will be used to access the information surveyed by the Project.

Our work relates to two other integrating databases and hypermedia applications. One of the most well known is Intermedia [ZDON87], a "large, object-oriented hypermedia system". It uses a relational DBMS on the background, though it was developed with an object-oriented approach. The objects (blocks, links, keywords and so on) are defined as classes and stored in the relational tables. Contrary to our approach, the database is not autonomous and stands only for supporting the hypermedia application. The DBMS is used solely to implement the structures that the hypermedia application handles. In "The Dual Approach" [DURR91], the hypermedia is regarded as a navigation functionality on existing object structures (either nodes or links). The objects themselves are part of the application domain and, through an interpretation mechanism, can be hypertextually manipulated. In this case, as in our approach, hypermedia is not considered an isolated data model but a "new look" on the existing data.

A drawback arises as the hypermedia application lays over an existing database: browsing may require building very complex queries. Therefore, the hypermedia interface must provide assistance to build the query . So, it is our further intention to expand the metamodel in order to include those entities required for the creation of the assisted interface.

Finally, we hope that this work may be an example of methodology to be adopted in retrieving the work of any artist in any country.

ACKNOLEDGEMENTS

We would like to thank Daniel Schwabe for his help and valuable contributions to this work.

We are extremely grateful to the Portinari Project team, specially to João Candido Portinari, who contributed so much to the early discussions on the design of the data model.

REFERENCES

[CERI92] CERI, S. & BATINI,C. & NAVATHE,S.; Conceptual Database Design; The Benjamin/Cummings Publishing Company,Inc.; 1992.

[CHEN76] CHEN, P.P; The Entity-Relationship Model: Towards a Unified View of Data; ACM Transactions on Database Systems - March 1976.

[DURR91] DURR,M. & LANG,S.; Hypertext and Object-Orientation: The Dual Approach; Datenbanksysteme in Buro, Germany - March 1991.

[GARZ91] GARZOTTO, F.; PAOLINI, P.; SCHWABE, D. - "HDM, a model for the design of hypertext applications", Proc. Hypertex'91, San Antonio, USA, Dec. 1991.

[MARQ92] MARQUES, M.P.; Banco de Dados e Hipermídia: Contruindo um meta-modelo para o Projeto Portinari; Relatório Interno - PUC Rio; Julho 1992.

[ZDON87] ZDONIK,S. & SMITH,K.; Intermedia: A Case Study of the Differences Between Relational and Object-Oriented Database Systems; OOPSLA 87 Proceedings - October 1987.

Grammatiken und Syntaxbäume in Datenbanken

Volker Linnemann
Institut für Informatik
Universität Würzburg
Am Hubland
W-8700 Würzburg
email: linneman@informatik.uni-wuerzburg.de

Zusammenfassung

Grammatiken und Syntaxbäume spielen bei der Definition und Übersetzung von Programmiersprachen eine sehr große Rolle. Dies liegt daran, daß Grammatiken eine elegante Möglichkeit darstellen, unendliche Mengen von Zeichenketten endlich darzustellen. Ein Syntaxbaum ist eine baumartige syntaktische Beschreibung einer Zeichenkette. Trotz der großen Bedeutung von Grammatiken und Syntaxbäumen bei der Definition und Übersetzung von Programmiersprachen spielen diese für Anwender nur eine untergeordnete Rolle, weil in der Regel keine benutzerfreundliche Unterstützung für die Verwendung von Grammatiken und Syntaxbäumen geboten wird. Es gibt zwar einige isolierte Lösungen zur Integration von Grammatiken und Syntaxbäumen in Datenbanksysteme, es fehlt jedoch an einer allgemeingültigen Lösung, welche für möglichst viele Anwendungsbereiche verwendet werden kann. In dieser Arbeit wird gezeigt, wie Grammatiken und Syntaxbäume in Datenbanken universell verwendet werden können. Dies geschieht dadurch, daß jedes Nonterminal einer kontextfreien Grammatik einen Datentyp definiert, dessen Wertebereich sämtliche Syntaxbäume bezüglich der zugrundeliegenden Grammatik sind. Syntaxbäume können in andere Syntaxbäume eingesetzt werden, wenn das entsprechende Nonterminal an der Einsetzungsstelle syntaktisch erlaubt ist. Hierdurch wird gewährleistet, daß stets nur syntaktisch korrekte Syntaxbäume entstehen können. Derart definierte Datentypen lassen sich beispielsweise sinnvoll zur Modellierung von Formeln oder zur Speicherung von Softwarebausteinen in Datenbanken verwenden. Darüberhinaus können durch Grammatiken definierte Datentypen zur allgemeinen Beschreibung von Sichten verwendet werden.

1. Einleitung

Grammatiken und Syntaxbäume sind grundlegende Strukturen der Informatik. Definition und Übersetzung von Programmiersprachen ist ohne sie undenkbar. Bereits in den 70er und frühen 80er Jahren wurde ihre Anwendbarkeit auch in der Anwendungsprogrammierung erkannt [16, 10, 11]. In die Programmiersprache PROLOG [2] wurden Grammatikregeln für den Programmierer fest integriert. Darüberhinaus haben Maluszynski und Nilsson [15] die Verwendbarkeit von Grammatiken beim syntaxorientierten Unifikationsprozeß in PROLOG erkannt. Umso erstaunlicher ist es, daß Grammatiken und Syntaxbäume in Datenbanken eher eine untergeordnete Rolle spielen. Dies liegt nicht an der Unbrauchbarkeit dieser grundlegenden Konzepte, sondern eher daran, daß keine adäquate sprachliche Unterstützung bereitgestellt wird. Der Anwendungsbereich von Grammatiken und Syntaxbäumen in Datenbanken ist sehr groß: Einerseits können Grammatiken und Syntaxbäume zur Modellierung von Dokumenten Verwendung finden, wie Barbic und Rabitti [1] beschreiben, andererseits können sie nach Gonnet und Tompa [5] zur Modellierung von Texten verwendet werden. Die Benutzung von Grammatiken zur Beschreibung von Integritätsbedingungen beschreiben Ridjanovic und Brodie [18]. Darüberhinaus können Grammatiken in Hypertextsystemen Verwendung finden. Einen anderen wichtigen Bereich stellt die Modellierung von mathematischen Formeln dar. Als Anwendung kann man sich eine Datenbank vorstellen, in der Formeln, z.B. Integrationsregeln etc. mit zusätzlichen Informationen gespeichert sind. Zusätzlich zum Speichern und Wiederfinden der Formeln möchte man die formale Ableitung zu einer Formel bilden oder Formeln aus einfacheren Teilformeln zusammensetzen u.s.w. Formeln können als Text dargestellt werden, eine Darstellung als Baumstruktur ist jedoch im allgemeinen wegen der einfacheren Handhabung bei der Formelmanipulation günstiger. Will man Formeln mit konventionellen relationalen Datenbanksystemen mit flachen Relationsstrukturen modellieren, so ergeben sich sehr unübersichtliche Strukturen. Die Umsetzung in Baumstrukturen muß manuell explizit in einem Anwendungsprogramm programmiert werden. Sprachen wie SQL bieten hier keine Unterstützung. NF^2 Strukturen [19] oder rekursive Datenstrukturen [8, 9] oder Klassenhierarchien in objektorientierten Systemen sind zwar besser zur Modellierung geeignet, das Problem der expliziten Integration und Implementierung der Umsetzung von Texten in Baumstrukturen bleibt jedoch auch hier. Zur Beschreibung der Baumstrukturen bieten sich eigentlich Grammatiken geradezu an. Die Umsetzung einer Formel von einem Text in eine Baumstruktur könnte von einem Parsersystem automatisch vorgenommen werden, wenn die Grammatik vorliegt. Wenn es also eine Möglichkeit gibt, Grammatiken und Syntaxbäume direkt in einem Datenbanksystem zu verwenden, so ist die Darstellung von Formeln erheblich vereinfacht und übersichtlicher. Ein weiteres Gebiet, wo Grammatiken und Syntaxbäume in Datenbanksystemen eine große Rolle spielen können, ist das Gebiet der Datenbankunterstützung für CASE Systeme [7]. Programmbausteine in einer CASE Datenbank können direkt als Syntaxbäume gespeichert werden. Auch im Gebiet der interoperablen Informationssysteme können Grammatiken und Syntaxbäume sinnvoll verwendet werden, z.B. zur Beschreibung von Sichten.

Die soeben zitierten sprachlichen Lösungen für die skizzierten Anwendungsbeispiele für Grammatiken und Syntaxbäume beschreiben nur isolierte Einzellösungen. Es gibt zwar inzwischen von Gyssens, Paredaens und Van Gucht [6] einen ersten Ansatz, eine Algebra für Grammatiken und Baumstrukturen in Datenbanken zu definieren, die beschriebene Algebra ist jedoch ähnlich wie die relationale Algebra für Anwender weniger geeignet. Das Ziel dieser Arbeit ist es, allgemeine Sprachkonstrukte aufzuzeigen, welche in möglichst vielen Anwendungsbereichen zum Tragen kommen können. Die grundlegende Idee hierbei ist es, Nonterminalsymbole einer Grammatik als Datentyp aufzufassen, deren Wertebereich jeweils die aus dem Nonterminal ableitbaren Syntaxbäume sind. Syntaxbäume können in andere Syntaxbäume eingesetzt werden, wenn das entsprechende Nonterminal an der Einsetzungsstelle syntaktisch erlaubt ist. Hierdurch wird gewährleistet, daß stets nur syntaktisch korrekte Syntaxbäume entstehen können.

Diese Arbeit ist wie folgt gegliedert: In einem zweiten Abschnitt werden die Sprachkonstrukte für

Grammatiken und Syntaxbäumen zunächst in einem ersten Unterabschnitt anhand von Beispielen allgemein unabhängig von einem speziellen Datenmodell eingeführt. Ein zweiter Unterabschnitt wird als ein Beispiel die Integration in das Non-Standard-Datenbanksystem AIM-P zeigen. Ein dritter Abschnitt wird verschiedene Anwendungsbeispiele bringen. Ein vierter Abschnitt wird einige Schlußbemerkungen und einen Ausblick beinhalten.

2. Sprachliche Konstrukte für Grammatiken und Syntaxbäume

Dieser Abschnitt ist in zwei Unterabschnitte gegliedert. Im ersten Abschnitt sollen die grundlegenden sprachlichen Konstrukte definiert werden, welche ein übersichtliches Arbeiten mit Grammatiken und Syntaxbäumen erlauben. Diese Sprachkonstrukte werden unabhängig von einem konkreten Datenbanksystem und auch unabhängig von einem Datenmodell definiert. Die einzige Voraussetzung, die gemacht werden muß, ist, daß das Datenmodell Datentypen kennt, welche der Anwender explizit definieren kann. Diese Voraussetzung ist beispielsweise in objektorientierten Datenmodellen und Datenbanksystemen erfüllt.

Der zweite Unterabschnitt behandelt als ein Beispiel die Verwendung der im ersten Unterabschnitt beschriebenen Konzepte im Non-Standard-Datenbanksystem AIM-P.

2.1. Allgemeine Sprachdefinition

Wie bereits in der Einleitung erwähnt, ist die grundlegende Idee, Datentypen durch eine Grammatik in der Weise zu definieren, daß jedem Nonterminal ein Datentyp zugeordnet wird. Ein Beispiel:

```
DECLARE GRAMMARTYPES
    <expr>       ::= <expr> + <term> | <term>
    <term>       ::= <term> * <factor> | <factor>
    <factor>     ::= <integer> | <identifier> | ( <expr> )
    <identifier> ::= <identifier> <letter> | <identifier> <digit> | <letter>
END
```

Hierdurch werden die Datentypen expr, term, factor und identifier definiert. Die Datentypen integer, letter und digit werden als Standarddatentypen aufgefaßt mit den offensichtlichen Bedeutungen. Es wird hierbei angenommen, daß für diese Standarddatentypen entsprechende Syntaxregeln existieren. Der Wertebereich für einen durch Grammatikregeln definierten Datentyp ist die Menge aller aus dem entsprechenden Nonterminal ableitbaren Syntaxbäume.

Es muß nun definiert werden, wie durch Syntaxregeln definierte Werte generiert und manipuliert werden.

Zur Generierung von Werten gibt es **Generierungsausdrücke**, welche u.a. in **Generierungsfunktionen** Verwendung finden können. Ein **Generierungsausdruck**, welcher einen Wert vom Typ expr liefert, kann beispielsweise wie folgt aussehen:

```
expr( a+b+c+d )
```

Dieser Ausdruck liefert einen Syntaxbaum für die Zeichenkette a+b+c+d. Es verbirgt sich also in einem Generierungsausdruck der implizite Aufruf eines Parsers. Falls der Ausdruck syntaktisch falsch ist, liegt ein Laufzeitfehler vor. In Generierungsausdrücke können andere durch die Grammatik definierte Werte eingesetzt werden, allerdings nur dort, wo diese Werte aufgrund der Syntax zulässig sind. Ein Beispiel:

```
expr( <e>+<t> )
```

Hierbei muß e einen Wert vom Typ expr bezeichnen, t muß einen Wert vom Typ term bezeichnen. Falls e einen Baum für den Ausdruck a+b und t einen Baum für den Ausdruck x*y enthält, so liefert dieser Generierungsausdruck einen Baum für den Ausdruck a+b+x*y.

Eine **Generierungsfunktion**, welche einen Wert vom Typ expr liefert, kann beispielsweise wie folgt aussehen:

```
GENERATE FUNCTION f(e:expr, t:term): expr( <e>+<t> )
```

Die Funktion f kann angewandt werden auf aktuelle Werte und liefert einen entsprechenden expr - Wert.

Zur Zerlegung von Bäumen gibt es **Traversierungsfunktionen**. Diese Funktionen bestehen im wesentlichen aus einer CASE-Anweisung, welche die Wurzel inspiziert und die Unterbäume an entsprechende Namen bindet. Diese Traversierungsfunktionen können rekursiv aufgerufen werden. Traversierungsfunktionen zur Berechnung der formalen Ableitung einer Formel können beispielsweise wie folgt definiert werden:

```
TRAVERSE FUNCTIONS
   TRAVERSE FUNCTION ediff(e:expr): expr;
   CASE e OF
     <e1:expr> + <t1:term>: expr( <ediff(e1)> + <tdiff(t1)> )  |
     <t2:term>            : expr( <tdiff(t2)> )
   END
   TRAVERSE FUNCTION tdiff(t:term ): term;
   CASE t OF
     <t1:term> * <f1:factor>: term( (<tdiff(t1)>*<f1>+<fdiff(f1)>*(<t1>)) )  |
     <f2:factor>            : term( <fdiff(f2)> )
   END
   TRAVERSE FUNCTION fdiff(f:factor ): factor;
   CASE f OF
     <i1:integer>     : factor( 0 )  |
     <id1:identifier>: IF string(id1) = ''x''
                        THEN factor( 1 ) ELSE factor( 0 )  |
     ( <e1:expr> )    : factor( ( <ediff(e1)> ) )
   END
END
```

Dies ist wie folgt zu verstehen: Die CASE - Anweisung untersucht einen Baumwert und stellt fest, welche Alternative der Grammatik zur Generierung des Wurzelknotens und seiner direkten Unterbäume verwendet wurde. Die Unterbäume, welche keine Blattknoten darstellen, sind dann jeweils über die angegebenen Namen ansprechbar. Zur Illustration ein Beispiel: Betrachten wir den Ausdruck a+b*c. Dieser Ausdruck werde mit e bezeichnet. Der entsprechende Syntaxbaum sieht wie folgt aus:

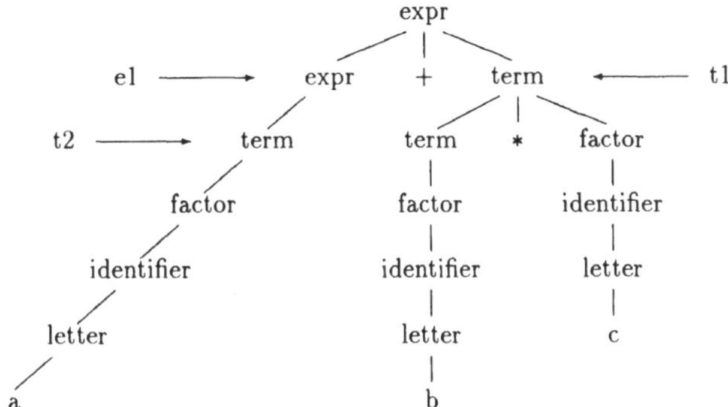

ediff(e) bindet e1 und t1 an die im Baum entsprechend markierten Unterbäume. ediff(e1) bindet t2 an den entsprechenden Unterbaum. Der Generierungsausdruck

```
expr( <ediff(e1)> + <tdiff(t1)> )
```

berechnet damit rekursiv die formale Ableitung.

Man sieht, wie Traversierungsfunktionen und Generierungsausdrücke sinnvoll zur Analyse von Bäumen und zur Generierung von neuen Bäumen kombiniert werden können. Die Terminierung der Traversierungsfunktionen ist garantiert, da stets nur endliche Bäume betrachtet werden.

Die soeben beschriebenen Sprachkonstrukte sind unabhängig von einem konkreten Datenbanksystem und einem konkreten Datenmodell. Zum Einfügen von Syntaxbäumen in eine Datenbanktabelle etc. sind die Standardanweisungen des konkreten Datenbanksystems zu verwenden. Als ein Beispiel wird im nächsten Unterabschnitt die Einbettung von Grammatiken und Syntaxbäumen in AIM-P betrachtet.

2.2. Einbettung in AIM-P

In diesem Unterabschnitt soll beispielhaft gezeigt werden, wie die im vorigen Abschnitt beschriebenen sprachlichen Konstrukte in das Non-Standard-Datenbanksystem AIM-P integriert werden können.

Das Datenbankssystem AIM-P (**A**dvanced **I**nformation **M**anagement **P**rototype) ist ein vom Wissenschaftlichen Zentrum der IBM in Heidelberg entwickeltes Prototypdatenbanksystem zur Unterstützung erweiterter geschachtelter Tabellen, das sind geschachtelte Tabellen (sog. NF^2 Tabellen), welche nicht nur ungeordnete Mengen enthalten können, sondern auch Listen mit einer definierten Ordnung. Die Anfragesprache für AIM-P, genannt HDBL (**H**eidelberg **D**ata **B**ase **L**anguage), ist eine SQL-ähnliche Anfragesprache. Die wesentliche Eigenschaft ist, daß SELECT - FROM - WHERE - Ausdrücke entsprechend der Schachtelung des entsprechenden Datenwertes geschachtelt werden können. Darüberhinaus bietet AIM-P dem Benutzer die Möglichkeit, eigene Datentypen zu definieren mit entsprechenden benutzerdefinierten Funktionen. Nähere Einzelheiten zu AIM-P und HDBL können in [3, 13, 17, 14] nachgelesen werden.

Unter Zugrundelegung der Grammatikdatentypen aus Abschnitt 2.1 können wir beispielsweise eine Tabelle mit Formeln wie folgt anlegen:

```
CREATE formeltabelle
  { [ id: string(5), beschreibung: string(20), formel: expr ] }
END
```

{ ... } bezeichnet hierbei eine Menge, [...] bezeichnet ein Tupel. Wir können diese Tabelle beispielsweise mit der folgenden INSERT - Anweisung füllen:

```
INSERT
    { [ id: 'f1', beschreibung: 'konstante Formel', formel: expr( a+b+c ) ],
      [ id: 'f2', beschreibung: 'lineare Formel', formel: expr( a*x+b )   ] }
INTO formeltabelle
```

Wir wollen jetzt eine Tabelle, welche zusätzlich zu jeder Formel die Ableitung nach x enthält, anlegen und füllen. Wir verwenden die Traversierungsfunktionen aus Abschnitt 2.1:

```
CREATE ableitungstabelle
    { [ id: string(5), beschreibung: string(20),
        formel: expr, ableitung: expr          ] }
END
INSERT
    { [ id: f.id, beschreibung: f.beschreibung,
        formel: f.formel, ableitung: ediff(f.formel) ] }
INTO ableitungstabelle
FROM f IN formeltabelle
```

Wenn wir jetzt beispielsweise alle einfachen Formeln zusammen mit der jeweiligen Ableitung suchen wollen, so können wir das mit der folgenden SELECT Anweisung tun:

```
SELECT a FROM a IN ableitungstabelle
WHERE a.beschreibung CONTAINS 'einfach'
```

Häufig ist es sinnvoll, keine vollständigen Syntaxbäume zu speichern, sondern nur Schablonen, d.h. Bäume, welche erst durch späteres Einsetzen von anderen Bäumen entsprechender Typen zu vollständigen Bäumen werden. Dies kann erreicht werden, indem Generierungsfunktionen als Datentypen verwendet werden können, d.h. Generierungsfunktionen können als Komponenten in Tabellen verwendet werden. Eine Tabelle mit Polynomen, deren Unbestimmte nicht vorher festgelegt werden soll, kann beispielsweise wie folgt angelegt werden:

```
CREATE polynomtabelle
    { [ id: string(5), beschreibung: string(20),
        formel: GENERATE FUNCTION (identifier): expr ] }
END
```

Die formel-Komponente ist hierbei in offensichtlicher Weise eine Generierungsfunktion, welche einen identifier als Parameter hat und welche einen Wert vom Typ expr liefert. Wir können die Tabelle beispielsweise wie folgt füllen:

```
INSERT
    { [ id: 'p1', beschreibung: 'lineares Polynom',
        formel: GENERATE FUNCTION (name: identifier):
                          expr( a*<name>+b )              ],
      [ id: 'p2', beschreibung: 'quadratisches Polynom',
        formel: GENERATE FUNCTION (name: identifier):
                          expr( (a*<name>+b)*<name>+c )   ] }
INTO polynomtabelle
```

Die folgende INSERT Anweisung fügt die Polynome aus polynomtabelle in formeltabelle ein, wobei als Unbestimmte y gewählt wird:

```
INSERT
    { [ id: p.id, beschreibung: p.beschreibung,
        formel: p.formel(identifier(y))        ] }
INTO formeltabelle
FROM p IN polynomtabelle
```

Die Verwendung von Generierungsfunktionen ist ähnlich der Benutzung von Funktionen als Attributwerte in POSTGRES [20]. Generierungsfunktionen sind jedoch spezieller, daher ist eine größere Sicherheit gegeben. Darüberhinaus ist eine Terminierung garantiert.

Im Rahmen eines Projektpraktikums "Datenbanksysteme" wurden im Sommersemester 1992 Grammatiken und Syntaxbäume mit Hilfe des Datenbanksystems AIM-P in einer ersten Prototyprealisierung implementiert. Dies geschah durch die Abbildung von Syntaxregeln und Syntaxbäumen auf geschachtelte Datentypen des AIM-P Systems und die Implementierung von Funktionen zum Einlesen einer Grammatik und zum Erzeugen und zum Traversieren von Bäumen. Ein kurzer Überblick über das Praktikum findet sich in [12].

3. Beispiele

Wir wollen in diesem Abschnitt einige weitere Anwendungsgebiete behandeln, in denen sich die skizzierten Sprachkonstrukte sehr sinnvoll verwenden lassen.

3.1. Programmbausteine in Datenbanken

In CASE Anwendungen ist es häufig sinnvoll, Programmbausteine in einer Datenbank abzulegen, damit diese später wiederverwendet werden können [4]. Es ist beispielsweise sehr unökonomisch, wenn Programmierer immer wieder die verschiedenen Alternativen für die Implementierung eines Stack neu programmieren müssen. Sinnvoller ist es, Stack-Programmbausteine in einer Datenbank abzulegen, so daß jeder Programmierer den gewünschten Baustein bei Bedarf abrufen kann. Wir können die in Abschnitt 2 eingeführten Sprachelemente verwenden, um Programmbausteine so abzulegen, daß die syntaktische Korrektheit der Programmbausteine garantiert ist. Wir nehmen in unserem Beispiel an, daß die Programmiersprache durch eine Syntax definiert ist, in der ein Nonterminal statementlist existiert, welches für eine Folge von Anweisungen steht. Eine Tabelle mit Programmbausteinen können wir nun wie folgt definieren:

```
CREATE bausteine
    { [ id: string(5), beschreibung: string(20), baustein: statementlist ] }
END
```

Wir können eine Stack-Implementierung wie folgt in die Tabelle einfügen

```
INSERT
    { [ id: 'p1', beschreibung: 'pop für verketteten Stack',
        baustein:
          statementlist( IF anker = NIL THEN error('Stack leer');
                         ergebnis := anker§.inhalt; anker := anker§.next )  ],
      [ id: 'p2', beschreibung: 'push für verketteten Stack',
        baustein:
          statementlist( h := anker; new(anker);
                         anker§.inhalt := element; anker§.next := h )       ] }
INTO bausteine
```

In ähnlicher Form könnte man Programmbausteine für eine Array-Realisierung eines Stacks oder für eine Listenverwaltung (einfach verkettet, doppelt verkettet, Array-Realisierung) u.s.w. ablegen. Ein Programmierer kann nun mit entsprechenden SELECT - Anweisungen seine gewünschten Programmteile selektieren und in sein Programm einfügen. Wenn ein syntaxorientierter Editor verwendet wird, können die Bäume aus der Datenbank direkt verwendet werden, eine Umsetzung in Textform ist dann nicht notwendig.

3.2. Beschreibung von Sichten durch Syntaxbäume

In diesem Abschnitt soll gezeigt werden, wie Syntaxbäume zur allgemeinen Beschreibung von Sichten verwendet werden können. Als Beispiel betrachten wir den Fall, mit Hilfe einer Sicht zwei flache Tabellen, beispielsweise departments(depno,depname) und projects(depno,prono,proname), zu einer geschachtelten Tabelle zusammenzufassen. Wir verwenden die in [14] beschriebene Syntax von HDBL. Dort gibt es ein Nonterminal select_expr, welches alle SELECT-Anweisungen beschreibt und ein Nonterminal expr, welches u.a. boolesche Ausdrücke beschreibt. Darüberhinaus gibt es ein Nonterminal field_list für die Komponenten eines Tupels. Wir können damit eine Generierungsfunktion für die geforderte Sicht definieren:

```
GENERATE FUNCTION nest
   (tab1,tab2: expr, name: identifier, list1,list2: field_list, e: expr):
     select_expr( SELECT [ <list1>,
                           <name>: ( SELECT [ <list2> ] FROM r2 IN <tab2>
                                     WHERE <e>                          ) ]
                  FROM r1 IN <tab1>                                       )
```

Die Anwendung

```
nest( expr(departments), expr(projects),.name(projects),
      field_list(r1.depno, r1.depname), field_list(r2.prono, r2.proname),
      expr(r1.depno = r2.depno)                                           )
```

liefert die folgende SELECT Anweisung:

```
SELECT
   [ r1.depno, r1.depname,
     projects: ( SELECT [ r2.prono, r2.proname ] FROM r2 IN projects
                 WHERE r1.depno = r2.depno                          ) ]
FROM r1 IN departments
```

In sehr einfacher Weise ist eine tiefere Schachtelung möglich, zum Beispiel wenn zusätzlich Angestellte für die Projekte hinzukommen. Die Speicherung von Nest-Anweisungen in einer eigenen Tabelle kann völlig analog zur Speicherung von Programmbausteinen gemäß Abschnitt 3.1 durchgeführt werden. Aus Platzgründen soll hier darauf verzichtet werden.

Anwendungen hierfür finden sich in interoperablen Informationssystemen, d.h. Informationssysteme, welche die Verwendung verschiedener Datenmodelle und Datenbanksysteme in einem integrierten System erlauben. In solchen Systemen benötigt man i.a. eine Metadatenbank, in welcher Informationen über die beteiligten Datenbanksysteme und über Abbildungsvorschriften festgehalten werden. Das obige Beispiel könnte Teil einer solchen Metadatenbank sein, nämlich ein Ausschnitt aus der Beschreibung der Abbildung von flachen Tabellen in geschachtelte Tabellen.

4. Schlußbemerkungen und Ausblick

In dieser Arbeit wurde gezeigt, daß Grammatiken und Syntaxbäume sinnvoll universell in Datenbanksystemen verwendet werden können, wenn geeignete Sprachhilfsmittel zur Verfügung gestellt werden. Die hier definierten Ausdrucksmittel sind ebenso einfach wie universell: Jedem Nonterminal einer Grammatik wird ein Datentyp zugeordnet. Hierdurch wird gewährleistet, daß nur syntaktisch korrekte Syntaxbäume entstehen können, d.h. die den Bäumen entsprechenden Zeichenketten sind syntaktisch korrekt. Es wurde die Verwendung der Sprachelemente für verschiedene Anwendungsbereiche anhand von Beispielen erläutert, nämlich für das Gebiet der Formelmanipulation, für das Gebiet der Software-Wiederverwendung und für das Gebiet der interoperablen Informationssysteme. Viele andere Anwendungsgebiete sind denkbar, aus Platzgründen konnten in dieser Arbeit keine anderen Gebiete behandelt werden.

Im Rahmen eines Projektpraktikums "Datenbanksysteme" wurden im Sommersemester 1992 Grammatiken und Syntaxbäume mit Hilfe des Datenbanksystems AIM-P in einer ersten Prototyprealisierung implementiert.

Die Arbeit hat hoffentlich gezeigt, daß es sehr sinnvoll ist, Datentypen, welche durch Grammatikregeln definiert sind, standardmäßig in Datenbanksystemen zur Verfügung zu haben.

Selbstverständlich ist mit der Bereitstellung von Grammatik-Datentypen nur ein erster Schritt in Richtung auf eine komfortable Unterstützung für CASE-Systeme und für allgemeine interoperable Informationssysteme getan.

In der Zukunft ist geplant, zu untersuchen, wie sich die skizzierten Ideen mit objektorientierten Systemen verbinden lassen. Insbesondere ist hier an die objektorientierte Programmiersprache EIFFEL gedacht. In diesem Zusammenhang ist es auch wichtig, zu untersuchen, ob die Generierungsfunktionen und die Traversierungsfunktionen zu allgemeinen berechnungsuniversellen Funktionen verallgemeinert werden sollten.

Literatur

[1] F. Barbic, F. Rabitti. The Type Concept in Office Document Retrieval. In *Proc. 11th Int. Conf. on Very Large Data Bases, Stockholm*, pages 34–48, 1985.

[2] W.F. Clocksin, C.S. Mellish. *Programming in PROLOG*. Springer-Verlag, 1981.

[3] P. Dadam, V. Linnemann. Advanced Information Management (AIM): Advanced Database Technology for Integrated Applications. *IBM Systems Journal*, 28(4):661–681, 1989.

[4] A. Endres. Software-Wiederverwendung: Ziele, Wege und Erfahrungen. *Informatik-Spektrum*, 11(2):85–95, 1988.

[5] H. Gonnet, F.W. Tompa. Mind Your Grammar: A New Approach to Modelling Text. In *Proc. 13th Int. Conf. on Very Large Data Bases, Brighton*, pages 339–346, 1987.

[6] M. Gyssens, J. Paredaens, D. Van Gucht. A Grammar-Based Approach Towards Unifying Hierarchical Data Models. In *Proc. Int. Conf. on Management of Data, Portland, Oregon, ACM SIGMOD RECORD 18(2)*, pages 263–272, 1989.

[7] S.E. Hudson, R. King. Object-Oriented Database Support for Software Environments. In *Proc. Int. Conf. on Management of Data, San Francisco, ACM SIGMOD RECORD 16(3)*, pages 491–503, 1987.

[8] W. Lamersdorf. Recursive Data Models for Non-Conventional Database Applications. In *Proc. First Int. IEEE Conf. on Data Engineering, Los Angeles*, 1984.

[9] W. Lamersdorf, G. Müller, J.W. Schmidt. Language Support for Office Modelling. In *Proc. 10th Int. Conf. on Very Large Data Bases, Singapore*, pages 280–290, 1984.

[10] V. Linnemann. Sprachelemente zur Generierung und Umformung syntaktischer Strukturen auf der Basis von ALGOL-68 und deren theoretische Untersuchung. *Dissertation Naturwissenschaftliche Fakultät der Technischen Universität Braunschweig*, 1979.

[11] V. Linnemann. Kontextfreie Grammatiken und Ableitungsbäume als Hilfsmittel bei der Programmierung. *Angewandte Informatik*, 1980(2):60–66, 1980.

[12] V. Linnemann. Einsatz von AIM-P in einem Projektpraktikum "Datenbanksysteme", Vortrag Workshop "Objektorientierte Datenbanksysteme - Forschungsergebnisse, Produkte, Einsatzerfahrungen" der GI-Fachgruppe "Datenbanksysteme", Universität Frankfurt, September 1992. In *Datenbank-Rundbrief der Fachgruppe Datenbanken der Gesellschaft für Informatik, Ausgabe 10, November 1992*, pages 33–34, 1992.

[13] V. Linnemann, K. Küspert, P. Dadam, P. Pistor et al. Design and implementation of an extensible database management system supporting user defined functions. In *Proc. 14th Int. Conf. on Very Large Data Bases, Los Angeles, USA*, pages 294–305, 1988.

[14] V. Linnemann, P. Pistor, N. Südkamp. User Manual of the AIM-P Online Interface. *IBM Wissenschaftliches Zentrum Heidelberg Technical Note 91.08*, 1991.

[15] J. Maluszynski, J.F. Nilsson. Grammatical Unification. *Information Processing Letters*, 15(4):150–158, 1982.

[16] H. Maurer, W. Stucky. Ein Vorschlag für die Verwendung syntaxorientierter Methoden in höheren Programmiersprachen. *Angewandte Informatik*, 1976(5):189–195, 1976.

[17] P. Pistor, F. Andersen. Principles for designing a generalized NF^2 data model with an SQL-type language interface. In *Proc. 12th Int. Conf. on Very Large Data Bases, Kyoto, Japan*, pages 278–285, 1986.

[18] D. Ridjanovic, M.L. Brodie. Defining Database Dynamics with Attribute Grammars. *Information Processing Letters*, 14(3):132–138, 1982.

[19] H.-J. Schek, P. Pistor. Data Structures for an Integrated Data Base Management and Information Retrieval System. In *Proc. 8th Int. Conf. on Very Large Data Bases, Mexico City*, pages 197–207, 1982.

[20] M. Stonebraker, L.A. Rowe. The Design of POSTGRES. In *Proc. Int. Conf. on Management of Data, Washington, D.C., ACM SIGMOD RECORD 15(2)*, pages 340–355, 1986.